SYDNEY E. AHLSTROM

A
RELIGIOUS
HISTORY
OF THE
AMERICAN
PEOPLE

VOLUME I

A DIVISION OF DOUBLEDAY & COMPANY, INC.

IMAGE BOOKS

GARDEN CITY, NEW YORK

1975

Image Books edition published by special arrangement
with Yale University Press
Image Books edition published November 1975

ISBN 0-385-11164-9
Library of Congress Catalog Card Number 75–22362
Preface Copyright © 1975 by Sydney E. Ahlstrom
Text Copyright © 1972 by Yale University
All Rights Reserved
Printed in the United States of America

A RELIGIOUS HISTORY OF THE AMERICAN PEOPLE
*has received widespread reviews and critical acclaim seldom
accorded any book in this century. Here are just a few samples:*

"No previous religious history of America has achieved [such] fine balance of scope and proportion. . . . It is so massive, thorough and comprehensive that it is a fitting conclusion to an honorable tradition. Historians, present and future, will have to come to grips with it, but from its perspective it will be difficult to improve upon."
—Church History

". . . this monumental history of American religion [is] a labor of love which was ten years in the making and will undoubtedly have the field to itself for the indefinite future. There is really nothing like it on the market. It's a model of historical scholarship and also makes for delightful reading. Enthusiastically recommended." *—Commonweal*

"The work is massive in scope. . . . The fact that [it] took a full decade to write is no surprise. It is a monumental feat of scholarship which places religious history in the larger framework of world history."
—John Barkham, Saturday Review Syndicate

"Sydney E. Ahlstrom's huge but readable *A Religious History of the American People* has already become a standard."
—Time

"[Ahlstrom's work] is the fruition or fulfillment of the accepted religious history, the longest, most detailed, most polished of the works in its tradition." *—The New York Times*

". . . a first, full-scale, comprehensive history of religion in American society. The craftsmanship of his research, teaching and writing skill stand forth on a distinctive plateau. Ahlstrom has succeeded to an eminent degree in giving a panoramic view of the full religious dimension in American life. . . . This volume is a must for any basic library on American life. It has not been attempted before and will remain not only a 'first' but unique in its creative and stimulating approach to a fascinating subject."
—Religious Education

FOR
MY MOTHER

CONTENTS

VOLUME 1

8 *Contents*

PART III: THE CENTURY OF AWAKENING AND REVOLUTION

PART IV: THE GOLDEN DAY OF DEMOCRATIC EVANGELICALISM

PART V: COUNTERVAILING RELIGION

CHAPTERS TO BE FOUND IN VOLUME 2

PART VI: SLAVERY AND EXPIATION

PART VII: THE ORDEALS OF TRANSITION

PART VIII: THE AGE OF FALTERING CRUSADES

PART IX: TOWARD POST-PURITAN AMERICA

ILLUSTRATIONS

by Michael Graham

Page 43: The mission church San Luis Rey de Francia, near Oceanside, California, built under the supervision of Padre Antonio Peyri between 1811 and 1815. The mission had been founded in 1798 by Padre-Presidente Fermin de Lasuén.

Page 165: The second meetinghouse of the church in Plymouth, Massachusetts, built in 1683. A conjectural rendering based on early specifications and sketches.

Page 325: Independence Hall, Philadelphia, Pennsylvania, originally the Pennsylvania State House, designed by Andrew Hamilton and Edmund Wooley and constructed between 1732 and 1748. The wooden steeple depicted here was taken down in 1781 but restored along more elaborate lines in 1828.

Page 467: An evangelical camp meeting. A conjectural rendering based in part on a drawing (c. 1820) by the French artist and naturalist J. G. Milbert and on George Caleb Bingham's painting *Stump Speaking* (1853–54).

Page 615: Temple B'nai Yehurun, Cincinnati, Ohio, the first Neo-Moorish synagogue in America. Designed by James Keys Wilson and constructed in 1864–65, when Rabbi Isaac Mayer Wise was spiritual leader of the congregation.

PREFACE TO THE IMAGE BOOK EDITION

As this preface to the Image Edition is being written, the American people are in the midst of a vast and disconcerting crisis which is rearranging many national and personal priorities. With varying attitudes and degrees of awareness they are also entering what is officially referred to as a Bicentennial Era. This somewhat ambiguous term refers back to that period of nation-making between Paul Revere's ride in 1775 and George Washington's inauguration in 1789. People are being asked to remember and ponder the American Revolution. Many institutions, however, have announced observances that look forward to a *new* era in American history. They are concentrating on the future in the hope that the country's third centennium may see a rebirth of freedom and justice.

For either kind of reflection, and no doubt still others, the country's moral and religious history should have considerable relevance. A nation that is unaware of its past bears an alarming similarity to a person suffering from amnesia: a crucial element of its being is lacking. Nor is the situation much different for non-Americans who are trying to understand the behavior of the United States. The present, after all, is but a thin film on the past, an imaginary figment; while the future exists only as a possibility—or a negation. In a certain sense, therefore, we all live and have our being in the past.

For these and other less abstruse reasons, I will be pleased if this edition reaches a larger and perhaps different range of readers. And I still extend the invitation given in the concluding paragraph of the text proper and repeated at the end of my bibliographical essay: that each reader become an interpreter of contemporary history and accept the challenge of actuating the profounder elements of our national hope.*

This invitation, naturally enough, raises the question: Would I now revise those final reflections, which some readers have considered too austere and bleak? To that question a strictly honest answer would have to be yes. No person and no society remains the same through time. The shocks and outrageous fortunes that have beset this nation since I wrote the last sentence of this book are now part of the world's collective consciousness—and my own. We have all changed. Yet it does not seem to me that my basic orientation needs revision. The rise of the "unmeltable ethnics" along with countless other developments, both material and spiritual, have underlined the fact that we live in a post-Protestant, post-Puritan culture. The energy problem and the larger question of world resources dramatize even more vividly than one could have done a few years ago that a great epoch of economic individualism and bourgeois optimism has ended or gone underground. Even young people who were born in the Eisenhower years now look back on the Fifties as a carefree halcyon age. So I would still contend that during the last decade we have experienced a very significant break in the continuity of this nation's moral and religious history.

One of the interesting, even ironic, aspects of these discussions of a possible turning point in American history has been the suggestion, made by several reviewers, that this work of mine marks the end of one era in the historiography of American religion and the inauguration of another. This is a flattering notion; but I think it rests upon a failure to recognize that not even the most extravagantly successful attempt to give a post-Protestant account of America's religious experience could reach into the future for its vantage point. Historians, like other mortals, must stand and wait for time's surprising disclosures. On the other hand, I see no grounds for expecting drastic changes in the Western historiographical tradition, to which this work is a small contribution. This tradition began to free itself from ecclesiastical surveillance and providential interpretations during the Renaissance; and ever since then, despite the pride and petulance of historians and interference from both church and state, the overall accuracy, coherence, and plausibility of its explanations have improved. Historiography may be an ideal construction in

* See Volume 2, pp. 617–18 and pp. 619–20.

constant need of revision; but it is not a trick or a fable. So the work goes on. Fads and fashions come and go. The ideas of even the most magisterial thinkers, like Marx and Freud, are only very slowly assimilated. Yet week by week, in seminars, classrooms, and scholars' studies the effort is sustained. And it is against this background that my aim can be simply stated. It was to advance this cause by linking religion and the national experience in a broad and comprehensive historical account which would, in turn, relate the American experience to its larger Western background. If this effort should have the effect of marking out some new lines of departure, I shall be very pleased. If it heightens the general interest in religious history, I shall be overjoyed. But my expectations are modest. Turning points in the historical tradition are almost imperceptible.

In this light my emphasis on the continuing influence of Puritanism, or on the long and oppressive dominance of the Protestant Establishment, or on the wearing and tearing of doctrinal controversy and denominational competition does not identify this work with the so-called "Protestant synthesis," which often made church history an adjunct of theology and apologetics, or even evangelism. My concern, rather, is simply to delineate the rise, heyday, and decline of certain major elements of the American experience. Pluralism, to be sure, is my primary theme, but that does not justify a retributive slighting of Protestantism. Yet new interests will constantly move historians toward new areas. Appropriate to our technocratic times a machine, the computer, is facilitating the study of those people who leave almost no written record of their convictions, aspirations, and accomplishments. Quantified study of political behavior, for example, has pointed to the importance of ethnicity and religion in American voting patterns. Other valuable and novel historical efforts will also take their place in a constantly changing pattern of historical activity.

This brief discussion of theoretical issues suggests certain other considerations that are appropriate to a preface. First of all I would like to make it known that the present edition is in no sense a revision, though I have, naturally, used the occasion of a new printing to make a number of small typographical, stylistic, and factual corrections. More important is it to express my indebtedness to the many, many scholars who in letters and reviews have made me the beneficiary of their most serious thoughts about the history of religion in America. In this broad land there are authorities on the subject-matter of virtually every paragraph in this book, and I am very grateful not only for the details on which they have corrected me, but also for their thoughts on larger matters of interpretation and scope. Academic duties have prevented me from responding to many of these contributions with the thoroughness they deserve; but my gratitude for the criticism as well as the warm encouragement they have offered is boundless.

This leads in turn to the matter of revision, which large task I do plan to undertake as soon as time allows. Even now I clearly recognize the need to expand the account in several areas: institutional history and ethnic differentiation in the Roman Catholic Church, post-colonial Quaker developments, religious and theological education, the missionary enterprise, worship, the religious bearings of literature, art, and architecture, certain religious thinkers such as Bushnell, Royce, and William James, the trans-Mississippi region, and divers matters on women in religous history. The size of this agenda should make clear that a revised edition will not be published soon and that it will be a larger work than the present one.

On the other hand the basic guidelines which I marked out in the original preface of this book will no doubt continue to inform my efforts, especially since my convictions as to the explanatory value of historical exposition have, if anything, grown stronger. Ever since the summer day after my second year in college, when I decided to exchange professional plans in medicine for those of history, my enthusiasm and love for this discipline have steadily grown. I have come increasingly to appreciate Ernst Troeltsch's dictum that all things human are historical without remainder. The claims of the nomothetic disciplines—from hypotheses on the birth and death of stars to the latest general theory on the transmission of myths—come more and more to be seen as auxiliary to a comprehensive historical view of reality.

Another characteristic of this work, often emphasized by reviewers and likely to become more prominent, is an attitude often associated with J. R. Green's *History of the English People,* a title whose similarity to my own is by no means accidental. Green saw his life work as a protest "against the tendency to a merely external political view of human affairs." He sought always "to get at men's lives and thoughts and feelings."* Even more than Green would I stress the importance of human intentionality, both personal and collective, to an understanding of historical change. Aside from human feelings and intentions, social conditions would be not only mute but static, whereas human history, perhaps especially religious history, is kinetic, propulsive, and alive.

Finally, for help in many very important ways and for seeing my corrections through the press, I wish now to express my thanks to Susan Hartt and Nancy Paxton.

S.E.A.

Yale University
New Haven, Connecticut
31 March 1975

* Leslie Stephen, ed., *Letters of John Richard Green* (London: The Macmillan Company, 1901), pp. 425–27.

PREFACE

Postmodern man proclaims himself to be also posthistoric—or at least he often exhibits himself as present-minded. Eschewing tradition, fearing the grip of the past, pessimistic about the future, he lives—or tries to live—within the narrow confines of today. The life of one-dimensional man is thus temporally flat; he avoids the mysteries of time and process; he does not take his own historicity seriously. Even when he is radically critical of society, he often ignores both the social circumstances of his protest and the historical sources of his critique.

Yet no work of history can be written from such a standpoint, regardless of its purpose or the sources of its inspiration. And this particular book was written in the firm conviction that the moral and spiritual development of the American people is one of the most intensely relevant subjects on the face of the earth. The United States—its nature and its actions—presents one of the world's most difficult challenges to the understanding, and a comprehensive account of its religious history holds promise of bringing light where light is sorely needed. Unlike Philip Schaff and many of my predecessors in this field, however, I do not believe that the necessary illumination can be provided by "church history" in its classic forms. Only a minority of Americans have ever believed that Christianity holds the central ruling position in history, or considered themselves to be part of what Schaff called the objective, organized, visible Kingdom of Christ on earth.[1] Christianity is by no means the only cur-

[1] Schaff elaborates his profound conception of Christian church history in section 4 of the general introduction to his *History of*

rent in American religious history, although it has been the major one. Even this current consists of many quite discrete substreams, and from one or another of these separate confessional positions much of America's religious history has been interpreted in terms of heresy. So a broader stance, a wider conception of the "rule of charity," is essential, and this sympathy must be extended far beyond the explicitly Judaeo-Christian traditions. Not least it must include the propensity of Americans to view the state itself in a religious light. All of the country's varied religious movements, however, can be brought within a reasonably comprehensive and coherent account if four conditions are observed. Since these have been guidelines for me, they should be enumerated.

First, religious history as a field of study must be placed not only spatially but theoretically within the larger frame of world history. It enjoys no rights of sanctuary, no immunity from the demands for evidence and plausibility that are made on historians generally. The historian cannot claim divinely inspired sources of insight, nor can he place one body of holy scripture above another. "Orthodoxy" and "heresy" may not be used as dogmatic judgments, but only as historically conditioned designations. This prescription, it may be added, even disqualifies the kind of *theologia gloria* that has informed many supposedly secular accounts of this Redeemer Nation.

Second, the concept of religion must be extended to include "secular" movements and convictions, some of which opposed or sought to supplant the churches. Agnosticism does not preclude religiosity and moral seriousness. In 1970 the courts were taking this step by broadening the acceptable grounds for conscientious objection to war, and religious historians must similarly widen their scope.

Third, constant attention must be given to the radical diversity of American religious movements. This means that holistic interpretations of a single, unified "American tradition" must be cautiously employed. The national experience has, to be sure, put its mark on all of the country's disparate

---

the Apostolic Church (first German ed., 1851; first English ed., 1853). His multivolume *History of the Christian Church* is surely one of the greatest works of history by an American. Yet Schaff's doctrinal stand severely limits the scope of his prodigious labors (see chap. 38, n. 3).

religious impulses, and white Anglo-Saxon Protestantism enjoyed a long hegemony. Yet one must constantly observe both the diverse denominational forces that flowed within this "mainstream" and the varying responses of groups outside the "quasi-establishment."

Fourth, the social context—including its demographic, economic, political, and psychological dimensions—must ever be borne in mind. Churches, sects, cults, and denominations exist as human communities, despite the unique sanctions and commitments that distinguish them from many other human groups and institutions. Their search for a transcendent reference above and beyond mundane considerations undoubtedly gives them a special character; indeed, it is this persistent search for absolute grounds for faith and action that makes them so fundamental—and so revealing. Yet the religious historian must remember that for this very reason his responsibility for rigorous analysis is intensified rather than reduced.

That I have fallen short of these exacting demands goes without saying. I exist in the middle of things and inherit the limitations of my situation. Not only the inadequacy of my knowledge, but also my hidden presuppositions and my unexamined major premises will in due course be exposed. I encourage my readers to call attention to these shortcomings with all possible speed and thoroughness.

In the meantime let me suggest the extent of my indebtedness, first of all to the innumerable band of historians who have worked in this field before me. Let no man say that he can in one lifetime write an American religious history "from the sources." If my obligations to the work of other scholars had been fully expressed in footnotes, this book would have been barnacled to the sinking point. In general, therefore, I have usually cited only those works which I directly quote at some length, though my annotation does increase slightly as I approach the contemporary period. For the same reason my bibliography has been limited largely to relatively recent works which themselves contain valuable bibliographical data on the subjects they treat. Works cited without publication data in the footnotes are listed in the bibliography. For similar reasons of space and efficiency the index is intended to take the place of innumerable footnote cross-references.

My most ardent thanks are, of course, conveyed to my wife, Nancy, who did not type a single word of the manuscript, but who bore with me. Her constant demands for clarity should benefit many readers. I must also make amends to my children, Alexander, Promise, Constance, and Sydney, who remember few times in their lives when one chapter or another was not denying them various imagined pleasures, but who have been, withal, remarkably considerate of the task that kept me so many hours in library and study.

Then how should I acknowledge my teachers and colleagues? The debt runs back to Carl G. Tideman in my Cokato, Minnesota, high school and Conrad Peterson in Gustavus Adolphus College. With deepening specificity it includes my professors and many fellow graduate students at Harvard and my colleagues at Yale. To mention names is impractical, despite the vividness of my remembered indebtedness. I hope they know—or knew—the depth of my gratitude. To Clarence C. Goen, Robert L. Ferm, Robert Stuart, Sanford Wylie, Vera Houghtlin, and several other research assistants, and to many exceedingly considerate typists—especially Helen Kent, Florence Sherman, Rose Stone, and Ascencion Day—I am grateful in ways beyond telling. In a special category are the Bollingen Foundation, which provided a generous grant, and the staff of the Yale University Press, who have transformed a huge pile of manuscript into a book. I would like to thank especially Cynthia Brodhead, whose careful editing of every page redounds to the benefit of every reader including myself, and Constance Sargent, who made the index. A word of special gratitude is owed to Michael Graham, whose illustrations grace the book.

For both the routine and the extraordinary solicitude shown by librarians and curators of special collections in dozens of institutions I feel a special sense of indebtedness. To the Yale University Library I am most of all beholden, and particularly to Raymond P. Morris and the Yale Divinity School library staff.

Then there are the dozens of scholarly readers of individual chapters, groups of chapters, or the entire manuscript, who have made me the beneficiary of their knowledge and wisdom. In a similar category are the many undergraduate, graduate, and divinity students at Yale University who in lecture courses and seminars have disputed and corrected my views and brought fresh insights to the subject through their research papers and discussion. That I have not and could not acknowledge the contributions made by these many concerned and talented people is sadly obvious, but I cherish the interest they manifested, thank them for the many ways in which they have saved me from error, and exonerate them absolutely from the flaws that still testify to my ignorance and perversity.

Yet my final thought is of another sort entirely. It springs from an intense awareness of the numberless communities of faith and moral conviction with which I have dealt inadequately or not at all. Faced with the inescapable limitations of space, and also of time, I think of Bishop Joseph Hall's Elizabethan lament: "This field is so spacious that it were easy for a man to lose himself in it; and if I should spend all my pilgrimage in this walk, my time would sooner end than my way." Remembering the many written pages that had to be abandoned or rudely abridged and countless cases where my interest had to be restrained, I can now only hope that these pages do succeed in presenting something of the vitality and diversity of the religious commitments that over the years have brought the American people to their present engagement with the future.

S.E.A.

Yale University
New Haven, Connecticut
16 December 1971

1

AMERICAN RELIGIOUS HISTORY IN THE POST-PROTESTANT ERA

History in its earliest and primal form celebrates the deeds of men and of gods, often of god-like men and man-like gods. And many of these very elements are wonderfully exhibited in what is possibly the oldest document of American history, the Icelandic *Saga of Eric the Red*.

> Eric was married to a woman named Thorhild, and had two sons; one named Thorstein and the other Leif. . . . Thorstein lived at home with his father in Greenland [while] Leif had sailed to Norway where he was at the court of King Olaf Tryggvason. . . . Upon one occasion the king came to speak with Leif, and asked him, "Is it thy purpose to sail to Greenland in the summer?" "It is my purpose," said Leif, "if it be your will." "I believe it will be well," answered the king, "and thither thou shalt go upon my errand to proclaim Christianity there." . . . Leif put to sea when his ship was ready for the voyage. For a long time he was tossed upon the ocean, and came upon lands of which he had previously no knowledge. There were self-sown wheat fields and vines growing there. . . . Leif found men upon a wreck, and took them home with him [to Greenland], and procured quarters for them all during the winter. In this wise he showed his nobleness and goodness, since he introduced Christianity into the country, and saved the men from the wreck; and he was called Leif the Lucky ever after.[1]

[1] Julius E. Olson, ed., "The Voyages of the Northmen," in *The Northmen, Columbus, and Cabot, 985–1503* (New York: Charles Scribner's Sons, 1906), pp. 23–26. Of the two major Icelandic

Already present in this medieval account are the major themes of the American saga: a religiously oriented sense of mission, an abundant land, a noble hero, and a favoring Providence. Even the vital ingredient of luck was there. And as soon as English settlers in the New World began sending reports back to the Old, the same themes recur. Overcoming strong contradictory evidence, the Reverend Alexander Whitaker's *Good Newes from Virginia* began the celebrationist tradition in 1613. Edward Johnson extended it to New England in 1654 with his *Wonder-Working Providence of Sions Saviour*. A half-century later Cotton Mather in his *Magnalia Christi Americana* provided copious documentation of "Christ's Great Deeds in America." Even Jonathan Edwards took up the refrain as he pondered the Great Awakening in 1740:

> 'Tis not unlikely that this work of God's Spirit, that is so extraordinary and wonderful, is the dawning, or at least a prelude, of that glorious work of God so often foretold in Scripture, which in the progress and issue of it shall renew the world of mankind. . . . And there are many things that make it probable that this work will begin in America.[2]

Following the lead of Johnson, Mather, and Edwards, American historians have continued without hesitation to see God Almighty and the Lord Jesus Christ as day-by-day participants in the country's struggles. "It is the object of the present work," wrote George Bancroft in the 1876 edition of his vast American history, "to explain how the change in the condition of our land has been brought about; and, as the fortunes of a nation are not under the control of blind destiny, to follow the steps by which a favoring Providence, calling our institutions into being, has conducted the country to its present happiness and glory."[3]

---

narratives of Leif Ericson's discoveries, this one is regarded as the more reliable and older (ca. 1310–20). The passage quoted is, of course, a very minute portion of the evidence for Norse visits to the North American continent.

[2] Jonathan Edwards, *Thoughts on the Revival in New England*, in *The Works of President Edwards*, 4 vols. (New York: Robert Carter & Brothers, 1879), 3:313.

[3] George Bancroft, *History of the United States*, 1:3. In this revised edition Bancroft let these words of his introduction stand

In the later twentieth century the mythic quality of the American saga has evaporated. The historian of the American religious experience who draws his work to a close as the nation's bicentennial observance draws near must speak in terms more somber than those which Bancroft used. The air seems less salubrious, the future more ominous. Institutionalized urban ghettoes and the "warfare state" make it possible to see America's "present happiness and glory" as proof of a "favoring Providence." Indeed, if one forswear "blind destiny" as a guiding principle, the categories of divine judgment and wrath seem more appropriate. Yet the present day gives us no vantage point for making Olympian judgments. The historian of one age, as Leopold von Ranke insisted, stands no closer to God than those of other times—not even when the churches of God are his special subject matter, we might add. Each generation can only say that a different portion of the past is open for its examination, that its angle of vision is altered, and that new standards of explanation and relevance prevail. A new present requires a new past; and the historian's responsibility for creating a meaningful and usable past depends more on his interpretation of accepted historical knowledge than on his additions to the world's overflowing treasury of fact.

The latter chapters of this book describe the conditions under which this first chapter and all those that follow had to be written. There is no human escape from that enclosing circle. One experiences very vividly the truth of Max Lerner's retrospective comment on the ten years he spent in writing *America as a Civilization* (1957): "I found when I came to the end of the decade that a number of things I had written about America were no longer valid. The American civilization had been changing drastically right under my fingertips as I was writing about it."[4] The present-day historian's predicament is, if anything, more difficult than Lerner's, in that social and intellectual developments of the last decade have profoundly altered our interpretation of the entire course of American history. The terrible moral dilemmas that began to intensify during the sixties have had an especially

---

substantially as first written in 1834, when Andrew Jackson was in the White House.

[4] Thomas R. Ford, ed., *The Revolutionary Theme in Contemporary America* (Lexington, Ky.: University of Kentucky Press, 1965), p. 1.

rude impact on long-accepted views of the country's religious development.

In addition to this revolutionary situation, the sheer brevity of American history makes it particularly susceptible to revisionism. The United States offers the first major instance in the modern world of "the birth of a nation." Not only was it discovered and colonized in the clear light of recorded history, but it constituted itself as an independent republic as the Atlantic community entered its late modern phase. John Ruskin declared that he could not "even for a couple months, live in a country so miserable as to possess no castles."[5] As late as 1789 the "American" barely existed. Having almost no past of his own and lacking the confident selfhood of older nations, he lived for the future. In 1909 Israel Zangwill in his celebrated play *The Melting-Pot* still spoke in the present progressive tense: "[Here] all the races of Europe are melting and re-forming. . . . God is making the American."[6] The historian of America, even when he speaks in the present tense, is dealing with national parturition.

The religious history of the American people—like the political and social history of which it is the spiritual corollary —is, nevertheless, one of the grandest epics in the history of mankind. The stage is continental in size, and the cast is produced by the largest transoceanic migration and the most rapid transcontinental dispersion of people the world has ever seen. More difficult for the historian than the newness of America, therefore, is the unequaled complexity of its makeup. The compounding of the country's ethnic and confessional diversity has continued almost unabated since Spain founded Saint Augustine in 1565. In the radical antinomian tradition alone the accretions have been continuous, from Mistress Anne Hutchinson in the 1630s to Timothy Leary in the 1960s—both of whom, incidentally, confronted the upholders of public order in the neighborhood of Boston before carrying their message to more remote regions. As these instances suggest, moreover, many strong religious impulses have not been neatly housed in churches. The sheer multifariousness of the American religious heritage is the central problem of any historian who would undertake the general synoptic task.

---

[5] John Ruskin, *Fors Clavigera*, Letter 10 (7 September 1871).
[6] Israel Zangwill, *The Melting-Pot* (New York: Macmillan Co., 1909), p. 37. See also pp. 157, 193.

A traveler in 1700 making his way from Boston to the Carolinas would encounter Congregationalists of varying intensity, Baptists of several varieties, Presbyterians, Quakers, and several other forms of Puritan radicalism; Dutch, German, and French Reformed; Swedish, Finnish, and German Lutherans; Mennonites and radical pietists, Anglicans, Roman Catholics; here and there a Jewish congregation, a few Rosicrucians; and, of course, a vast number of the unchurched—some of them powerfully alienated from any form of institutional religion. With the passing years the variety would increase, and in the year of the nation's officially recognized independence (1783) Ezra Stiles in his famous sermon "The United States Elevated to Glory and Honor" prophesied that in due course the country would "embosom all the religious sects and denominations in Christendom"— and allow freedom to them all.[7]

As the great tide of immigration poured in, Stiles's prophecy began to be fulfilled. Is 1854 Philip Schaff, somewhat less ecstatically, observed that the United States offered "a motley sampler of all church history,"[8] though the sample was then far from complete. But by the 1920s the Monophysite Church of Armenia—the oldest established church in Christendom—had put down American roots, as had each of the three main branches of the Syrian church—Jacobite, Nestorian, and Orthodox. Virtually every surviving heresy and schism in Christian history had its representatives in America. Small wonder that in the 1930s Dietrich Bonhoeffer would comment that "it had been granted to the Americans less than any other nation on earth to realize the visible unity of the Church of God."[9]

For many decades this plenitude of religious variation was little more than a cause of scorn, an occasion for bitter polemics, or a source of fascinated bewilderment. Among those with more scholarly interests, however, another response came to be manifested. It took the form of handbooks dealing with these diverse "religious bodies" according to one

[7] Ezra Stiles, *The United States Elevated to Glory and Honor: A Sermon* (New Haven, 1783).

[8] Philip Schaff, *America: A Sketch of Its Political, Social, and Religious Character*, p. 80.

[9] Dietrich Bonhoeffer, *No Rusty Swords: Letters, Lectures, and Notes, 1928–1936, from the Collected Works of Dietrich Bonhoeffer*, vol. 1, ed. Edwin H. Robinson (New York: Harper & Row, 1965), p. 94.

or another scheme of classification. Hannah Adams, a Unitarian school teacher, set high standards for this genre in 1784 with her *Alphabetical Compendium of the Various Sects*, which through several editions also pioneered in the field of world religions. She has been followed by a long line of authors who adopted the same method, from Samuel Goodrich later in the nineteenth century to Frank Mead and Frederick E. Mayer in the twentieth. Some of these efforts have been extremely useful, even profound; the genre should by no means be deprecated. But it is not history except in a very limited sense.

Another venerable solution was candidly adopted by Samuel D. McConnell in the 1880s, when he set out to write a history of American Christianity—and I single him out from among many only because his rationale was better stated:

It has been frequently noticed that the Christianity of America possesses characteristics of its own. It is not only different in many regards from that which subsisted in Europe at the time of settlement of the colonies; but it is different from that which subsists in any other portion of Christendom now. Christianity here wears a garment of American weaving and American adornment. The religious history of the country is quite as striking as its political; it has had as many and as marked epochs; the influences which have shaped it have to be sought for in more numerous and more diverse sources; and those influences are more actively at work now than are those which produce political changes.

With this fact in view I thought to trace the stream of religious life in the United States to its many various sources, to estimate the relative size and importance of the affluents which have colored it, and maybe to forecast its future course.

McConnell, one notes, had laudable objectives. He was proposing a genuinely cultural interpretation. He goes on, however, to announce a decision that many another historian has envied: "I found the project to be so difficult that I abandoned it. . . . The coherence of the facts in the religious history of our land cannot yet be seen. The facts themselves are abundant to embarrassment; but they cannot yet be strung upon any single thread which I have been able to discover." Noting that the unity of the church in America had lagged far behind the political development of the country, he insisted that "while this condition of things remains there cannot be written a history of the American Church." He then announced an anticlimactic decision: "I have undertaken therefore the more modest task to set out the history of the Protestant Episcopal Church in the United States."[10]

McConnell, of course, was not the first who chose to concentrate on a single denomination. Indeed, some of the greatest achievements in American religious historiography have been made in this realm, with Governor Bradford and Cotton Mather producing classics in the early colonial period. Even as McConnell went about his task, Philip Schaff was projecting the American Church History Series, in which some of our finest ecclesiastical history was published. But both of these alternatives (i.e. handbooks and denominational histories) are evasions of a responsibility that could not be escaped; and long before McConnell took the easy way out, more temerarious souls had forged a strong American tradition of synoptic interpretation.

In retrospect one can see that the decisive preparation for the emergence of general histories was provided by the colonial Great Awakening. Only through that convulsive outburst of piety did "American Evangelical Protestantism" become aware of itself as a national reality and alive to its culture-shaping power. The Revolution, moreover, as we have already heard Ezra Stiles testify, was to add another vital ingredient to the American's sense of religious solidarity. The Puritans had long thought of England as an Elect Nation, and Jonathan Edwards spoke of it with complete assurance as "the principal kingdom of the Reformation." By a remarkable process of transfer this notion was now attached to the raggle-taggle republic being created in America. Even in 1777, when the military issue was still unclear, Timothy Dwight would pen his incredibly confident lines:

> Columbia, Columbia, to glory arise,
> The queen of the world, and the child of the skies;
> Thy genius commands thee; with rapture behold,
> While ages on ages thy splendors unfold.[11]

[10] *History of the American Episcopal Church, 1600–1915*, pp. xvii–xix.

[11] See Kenneth Silverman, *Timothy Dwight*, pp. 40–41, 139–40.

The realistic view of man's sinfulness that tempered Dwight's optimism gradually disappeared in later forms of patriotic piety, and after the Loyalists had departed, only an occasional very eccentric American ever doubted that the Star-Spangled Banner waved over the Lord's Chosen Nation. In many minds the American was conceived as a new Adam in a new Eden, and the American nation as mankind's great second chance. Nothing better illustrates the continuity of this tradition than the patriotic hymns that were entered in the national book of psalms—from *America*, struck off in an inspired moment by an Andover seminarian for a Fourth of July observance in 1832, to *The Battle Hymn of the Republic*, written by Julia Ward Howe as if by the hand of God in 1861, to *America the Beautiful*, published in the *Congregationalist* in 1893. This mythic theme of America as a beacon on a hill and an exemplar for the world became a constituent element in historical interpretations of the nation's religious life.

Equally powerful as an integrating idea was the metaphor of the melting pot, the conception of the United States as a crucible in which the diverse base metals of the world would be marvelously transformed into pure Anglo-Saxon Protestant gold. A former French soldier who temporarily underwent that transformation described the process in his *Letters from an American Farmer*, published in 1782:

> Here individuals of all nations are melted into a new race of men. . . . The Americans were once scattered all over Europe; here they are incorporated into one of the finest systems of population which has ever appeared. . . . Here religion demands but little of him: a small voluntary salary to the minister and gratitude to God; can he refuse these? The American is a new man, who acts upon new principles; he must therefore entertain new ideas and form new opinions. . . . This is an American.[12]

Crèvecoeur would have been disappointed and surprised by the Second Awakening, which would soon transform the slumbering churches and make the "evangelical united front" a potent force in the land. But he would probably have been

[12] J. Hector St. John de Crèvecoeur, *Letters from an American Farmer, and Sketches of Eighteenth-Century America*, ed. Albert E. Stone (New York: Signet Classics, 1963), p. 64.

assuaged by the degree to which his melting pot metaphor
became a working principle of Protestant historical interpretations during the entire course of the century which followed. Anti-Catholicism and nativism would flame up recur-
rently; then as the great revivals followed one after the other,
a quasi-establishment of evangelical Protestantism emerged.
Not even the great antebellum sectional controversy inter-
fered with its progress, because evangelicalism deepened its
hold in both the North and the South. The Civil War, indeed,
became a kind of double holy war. In 1893 the general secretary of the American branch of the Evangelical Alliance,
Josiah Strong, looking beyond the shining seas, depicted the
American nation as the new Rome whose destiny it was to
"Anglo-Saxonize" the entire world.[13] During the Gilded Age
this spiritual hegemony was threatened by factories, immigrants, and disconcerting modern ideas, but the united
evangelical front closed ranks for the temperance crusade,
the Little War of 1898, and the Great War of 1914–18. Protestant America, consequently, did not really face its first
great moment of truth until it marched onto the moral and
religious battlefields of the twenties, the tumultuous decade
of prohibition, immigration, evolution, jazz, the KKK, short
skirts, the movies, Al Smith, and the Crash. Here, indeed,
was the antipodes of the Great Awakening. Yet a general
awareness of the painful fact that evangelicalism was no
longer a culture-shaping power was almost miraculously delayed for another thirty years. Only in the 1960s would it
become apparent that the Great Puritan Epoch in American
history had come to an end.

Perhaps inevitably it was during the last century of this
epoch that the twin motifs of the elect nation and the
melting pot gained their fullest historiographical expression.
A new synthesis of American church history emerged—
proud, nationalistic, and stridently Protestant. Most decisive
in shaping its major lineaments was Robert Baird, an American Presbyterian missionary to Roman Catholics in Europe
who published his famous *Religion in America* (1843) first in
England, then in other languages and in several widely read
American editions. This was not simply the first important
panoramic history of American religion: it was a manifesto
for a worldwide reformation of Christianity that took Ameri-

[13] Josiah Strong, *The New Era; or, the Coming Kingdom* (New
York, 1893), pp. 41–80, esp. p. 80.

can Protestant voluntaryism as its model. To Baird the religion of America simply *was* revivalistic evangelicalism—though he did include a brief, condescending section on the unevangelical bodies. His basic value judgment is suggested by the mere two pages he allotted to the Roman Catholic church, which was in 1850 the largest denomination in the United States.[14]

The next historian-laureate of note was the Methodist Daniel Dorchester, a prominent temperance leader and sometime national superintendent of Indian schools. He described himself as an admiring disciple of Baird, but he worked on a far vaster scale and with much greater attention to factual and statistical detail. His eight-hundred-page account *Christianity in the United States* (1887) is probably the finest work of its kind ever published. It is far more balanced and open-minded than Baird's book in its treatment of "unevangelical" movements, relatively generous in the amount of space allotted to Catholicism, and uncensorious on intra-Protestant doctrinal issues. Yet Baird's heavy evangelical and outspokenly nativist bias remains. Both in its distributions of praise and in its thematic structure Dorchester's book belongs in the "great tradition" of the American Protestant historiography.

At the century's end, Leonard Woolsey Bacon was chosen to provide the capstone volume for the American Church History Series. And his *History of American Christianity* (1897) deserves remembrance. It is a masterpiece of organization, with a steady kind of eloquence that sweeps the reader from triumph to triumph. Its judgments show the moderating force of theological liberalism; yet at bottom, Bacon presents still another version of the Protestant American's *theologia gloria*, in which patriotism and religion are inextricably entwined. "By a prodigy of divine providence," he begins, "the secret of the ages [that a new world lay beyond the Western Sea] had been kept from premature

---

[14] See the critical abridgment of Baird's *Religion in America*, edited by Henry W. Bowden. Because of Baird's great zeal for facts, Schaff and many other historians relied heavily on him. Though not an influential interpreter of the American religious tradition, Schaff probably did more than any other church historian to establish the "historical standpoint" in the American mind (see James H. Nichols, *Romanticism in American Theology: Nevin and Schaff at Mercersburg*).

disclosure. . . . If the discovery of America had been achieved . . . even a single century earlier, the Christianity to be transplanted to the western world would have been that of the church of Europe in its lowest stage of decadence." He ends with his heart still strangely warmed by "those seventeen wonderful September days of 1893" when the World Parliament of Religions had met in Chicago as part of the four hundredth anniversary celebration of Columbus's discovery. With the memory of that truly ecumenical gathering in mind (representatives of other world religions had also attended), Bacon closes his work with thoughts of "great providential preparations as for some 'divine event' still hidden behind the curtain that is about to rise on the new century." Incapable of pessimism as he seems to have been, one suspects that his vision included the Melting Pot, perhaps in the shape of the Holy Grail, containing all of America's churches, Catholic and Protestant, amalgamated somehow, but in such a way that Protestants would have no problems in adjusting to the new reality.[15]

The Protestant synthesis by no means culminated in the work of Bacon, however. That honor unquestionably belongs to William Warren Sweet (b. 1881), whose *Story of Religions in America* first appeared in 1930, and who from 1927 to 1946 was extremely influential as professor of the history of American Christianity at the University of Chicago. Deeply and permanently impressed by Frederick Jackson Turner, Sweet's thought was dominated by the shaping force of the frontier. Even more important in the long run was the way in which his accent on cultural factors in church history eclipsed the pious providentialism of his predecessors. Yet we should not overstate the case, for Sweet emphatically did not betray the great Protestant tradition of historiography. He translated it into the idiom of the "scientific history" and accented the role of the Baptists and Methodists; but the uncritical celebrationism of Baird remains an aspect of his many books.[16] The older forms of nativism disappear, yet Catholics, Eastern Orthodox, Jews, Negroes, immigrants, and the city

[15] *History of American Christianity*, pp. 2, 419. Bacon, who had Yale degrees in both theology and medicine, was a widely traveled Congregational minister.

[16] In addition to general accounts, Sweet turned his American church-historical attention to the Civil War, revivalism, and his own Methodist denomination.

are on the periphery of his scholarly interest. Anti-intellectualism and the idea of progress consistently undermine his treatment of Puritanism, systematic theology, doctrinal developments, and the rise of humanistic modernism.

Due in part to Sweet's example, an active new generation of American church historians arose. Among them were many who stemmed from the "Chicago School," as the mere mention of Brauer, W. E. Garrison, Handy, Hudson, Marty, Nichols, and above all, Sidney E. Mead makes apparent. Few of these Chicago men, furthermore, were subservient to Sweet, and some were explicitly critical. Yet the revival of interest in the American field was by no means limited to Chicago. Indeed the surge of scholarship became too vast to be considered here, except insofar as this book as a whole is a tribute to it.[17] Even in the new generation, however, the major concern continued to be the rise and development of the Protestant tradition. Until fairly recently, moreover, seminary professors have provided the great bulk of the published work; and these men have been understandably concerned with problems of diagnosis and prescription for the white Protestant churches. Very few of them have been fundamentally critical of the mainstream trend, or of its relation to American culture as a whole, or of that culture itself. Their tendency, with vital exceptions, has been to contribute to the "concensus tradition" in American historiography.[18]

Certain powerful countervailing tendencies did appear, however; and some of these dissents from the received interpretation have been of great personal significance to me. One trend of this sort, showing some Marxist influence, is marked out by Vernon L. Parrington's famous *Main Currents of American Thought* (1927–1930) and by H. Richard Niebuhr's *Social Sources of Denominationalism* (1929). Another is the remarkable rediscovery of Puritanism pioneered by Samuel Eliot Morison, Kenneth B. Murdock, and William Haller. This tradition culminates in the massive works of Perry Miller—who, coincidentally or not, also had a link to Chicago that preceded his long identification with Harvard.

[17] One or more works by each of the historians who are mentioned by name only in this chapter are included in the bibliography of this volume.

[18] Perhaps the man whose work best incorporates this Protestant consensus into a full-scale interpretation of the American mind is Ralph Henry Gabriel in *The Course of American Democratic Thought.*

In this context one must also include the powerful Neo-orthodox impulse, represented best, perhaps, by H. Richard Niebuhr's *Kingdom of God in America* (1937) with its thoroughgoing reconsideration of judgments rendered by the previous generation of liberals. The combined impact of these dissents brought a serious challenge to the optimistic progressivism that had heretofore dominated the historiographical mainstream.

To complete the picture one must add the name of the elder Arthur Meier Schlesinger, whose pivotal essays "The Significance of the City in American History" and "The Critical Period in American Religion," along with countless other works which he wrote, edited, or inspired, made him a major figure in America's rediscovery of the city as a vital factor in its religious history.[19] Nor is this tribute sufficient, for Schlesinger also played a major role in the revival of concern for the history of immigration and ethnic minorities. In this effort he by no means labored alone, in part because many immigrant groups inspired their own historians to impressive accomplishments. Due to the importance of religion to the cultural cohesion of these groups, many eminent works on specific religious traditions have been published. To mention individual achievements would be impossible, but Monsignor John Tracy Ellis and Oscar Handlin stand out—both for their own works and for the innumerable students they have guided and inspired.

Against this background of vigorous activity, Henry F. May in 1964 could describe a veritable thirty-year "renaissance" in the writing of American church history; and with this revived and renovated situation before them, later authors of general American religious histories have done their work. So valuable have the works of these scholars been to me that I must acknowledge my indebtedness: to Clifton E. Olmstead's *History of Religion in the United States* (1960) for the first major presentation of the whole story since that of Sweet; to the impressive two volumes of expertly interpreted documents of *American Christianity* (1960) edited by H. Shelton Smith, Robert T. Handy, and Lefferts A. Loetscher; to the survey accounts of Winthrop S. Hudson (*Religion in America*, 1965) and Edwin Scott Gaustad (*A*

---

[19] Among many other titles in my bibliography, those of A. I. Abell, T. L. Smith, Ira Brown, W. R. Cross, and H. F. May testify to Schlesinger's strong influence.

Religious History of America, 1966); and finally, to the editors and authors of *Religion in American Life* (4 vols., 1961), which provided the first comprehensive overview of the American religious experience since that given in the American Church History Series of the 1890s. Especially memorable in this composite work was the learned two-volume bibliography prepared by Nelson R. Burr.[20] It is this last-mentioned work more than any other which justifies the decision to limit the extent of my own bibliography.

As the foregoing survey very inadequately suggests, and as Burr's bibliography incontestably shows, anyone in the 1970s who would again venture a general history of American religion is the legatee of an awesome body of scholarship. It behooves him not only to profess his profound gratitude, but to say why he has deemed it worthwhile to devote a decade of his life to the task. Such an apologia does not come easily, but the simplest answer is that the "renaissance" described by Professor May calls for a new, synthetic effort on a fairly large scale. Closer to the heart of the matter is the conviction, declared early in this chapter, that events have so radically transformed the American situation that our whole view of what is relevant in the past must be revised. A new set of circumstances now stands in need of historical explanation. We are driven to an awareness of historiographical crisis by the mere mention of John XXIII and John Kennedy, of Martin Luther King, Malcolm X, and the Beatles, or if we think of the student movement, the environmental awakening, the alleged death of God, and the new mood in which American priorities at home and abroad are being reevaluated. Post-Protestant America requires an account of its spiritual past that seeks to clarify its spiritual present. And such an account should above all do justice to the fundamentally pluralistic situation which has been struggling to be born ever since this country was formally dedicated to the proposition that all men are created equal.

The basic paradigm for a renovation of American church history is the black religious experience, which has been virtually closed out of all synoptic histories written so far— closed out despite the obvious fact that any history of America that ignores the full consequences of slavery and

[20] James W. Smith and A. Leland Jamison, eds., *Religion in American Life.* Volume 4 consists of the two book-length parts of Burr's bibliography. Volume 3 has not yet been published.

nonemancipation is a fairy tale, and that the black churches have been the chief bearers of the Afro-American heritage from early nineteenth-century revivals to the present day. This paradigm of restoration must then be applied to the other traditions that the Protestant synthesis left to one side, such as the Catholic, Jewish, and Eastern Orthodox, as well as such large nonecclesiastical religious movements as New Thought, Theosophy, and Rosicrucianism. In the same spirit one is led to emphasize more strongly than has been usual two seemingly contradictory aspects of American church history: the degree to which denominational traditions even in the Protestant mainstream modify the behavior of individual churches, and the way in which the long development of modern religious ideas undermines these confessional commitments and thus prepares the ground for the emergence of radical theology in the 1960s.

Basic to the effective fulfillment of all these aims is the recognition of the degree to which American civilization is a New World extension of Christendom. Unique it certainly becomes, but its distinctiveness springs almost as much from the continuing impact of diverse and sometimes contradictory European influences as from the fact that it occupied a vast and rich wilderness. An account of its religious development thus requires a constant concern for men, movements, and ideas whose origins are very remote in both time and space. One must, of course, forswear the temptation to make American religious history a pretext for writing the history of Western civilization; yet it has seemed imperative, for example, to deal with such immensely significant developments as the rise of East European Jewish Orthodoxy or the shaping of the Greek Orthodox Christianity, even though the full impact of these religious impulses was not felt in the United States until early in the twentieth century. It is for such reasons that this history does not begin with the traditional American sequence running from the Reformation on the Continent through that in Great Britain and on to the planting of the American colonies, but opens instead with chapters on Western Catholicism, New Spain, and New France. In this way one can better understand the ways in which medieval Christianity was still very much alive even in the catechisms and sermons of Puritan New England.

I

European Prologue

For the Lord had said vnto Abram, Get thee out of thy Countrey, and from thy kindred, and from thy fathers house, vnto the land that I will shew thee. And I will make of thee a great nation, and will blesse thee, and make thy name great, and thou shalt be a blessing. I will blesse them also that blesse thee, and curse them that curse thee, and in thee shall all the families of the earth be blessed. [Genesis 12:1–3]

Being the text used by the Reverend William Symonds, preacher at Saint Savior's, Southwark, in A Sermon Preached At White Chappel, In The Presence of . . . the Aduenturers and Planters of Virginia, . . . Published For The Benefit And Vse Of The Colony, Planted, And to bee Planted there, and for the Aduancement of their Christian Purpose. (25 April 1609)

America became the Great Frontier of Western Christendom in 1492, and five centuries after Columbus opened the sea trails to this New World the people of the United States in overwhelming numbers still recognize Europe as the source not only of the languages they speak, but of much that animates their most dearly held convictions. Even those with ties to Africa or Asia or those most ancient of migrants from Asia who are called Indians spend most of their lives in contexts and institutions that were shaped by the Western tradition. The American who listens to news of Marxism in China on a Japanese transistor radio may well wonder if Europe is not the chief source of an emerging global civilization.

The imperial designs awakened in European capitals by the discovery of America and the process by which those designs became an actuality were closely related to the religious turmoil which featured European history during the age of discovery and colonization. It is the purpose of Part I to consider this background. It begins with a chapter on Roman Catholic Christendom before the Reformation, which is followed by accounts of New Spain and New France, the two Catholic empires that long encircled the English colonies. These are followed by a chapter on the Continental Reformation, followed by two others that deal with religious developments in Great Britain. It closes with a chapter that surveys the belated and sporadic—yet remarkably successful —enterprises by which England and, in passing, the Netherlands and Sweden, carried out their imperial intentions along the North Atlantic mainland during the seventeenth century. As a result of these efforts Protestantism, predominantly in its Puritan form, became a major factor in the spiritual shaping of a "great nation."

2

WESTERN CATHOLICISM

On Saint George's Eve, 22 April 1418, the forty-fifth and last general session of the Council of Constance was dissolved, and the departing prelates were granted full absolution by the new pope, Martin V. The most splendid assembly that Western Christendom had ever seen, after lasting three years and six months, came to an end without any tumult (though Europe's peace was broken elsewhere), without any rise in the prices of provisions (though the city was crowded with visitors), and without any extraordinary sickness (though a plague broke out soon after). This council, said one of its eminent participants, "was more difficult than any other general council that preceded it, more strange, surprising, and hazardous in its course, and lasted a longer time."[1]

The Great Schism of the papacy was no more: this was the leading fact. In November 1417 the considerably reconstituted College of Cardinals had elected as Christ's new vicar Oddo Colonna, one of their number who had come to Constance with Pope John XXIII. Rival claimants were safely out of the way: John was now a prisoner in Heidelberg Castle, Gregory XII had abdicated, and Benedict XIII was a shadow pope soon to be isolated till he died on Peñíscola, a miniature Gibraltar rising out of the sea near Tortosa, Spain.[2]

[1] Cardinal Guillaume Fillastre's Diary, in John Hine Mundy et al., eds., *The Council of Constance: The Unification of the Church*, Records of Civilization no. 63 (New York: Columbia University Press, 1961), p. 446.

[2] When Cardinal Angelo Giuseppe Roncalli was crowned pope in 1958 he became John XXIII, thus using a name which had lapsed since the John XXIII known to historians was deposed at Constance. Number XXIII was used again because the church

Martin V began his return to Rome in May 1418, traveling with great pomp as the only head of a united church; and although he was unable to enter the Eternal City until 1420, he was able eventually to swing all factions in the church to his support. In June the Emperor Sigismund quietly left Constance, knowing that his determination to reunite the Church had at least made possible the council's chief accomplishment.

One can hardly conclude, however, that the Council of Constance reformed the Roman church "in head and members," as many had hoped it would. It had convened with three ostensible purposes: to heal the disastrous schism, to deal with heresy, and to reform the church. Its spectacular achievement of the first two goals blunted the desire for reform; and the new pope, once his election was confirmed, was anxious for the council to adjourn before it meddled too much in the internal affairs of the papacy.

But Constance, as an event, does provide most remarkable testimony to the complex character of the church in late medieval times. There at the Christmas Mass in 1414 had stood Emperor Sigismund, wearing the stole and dalmatic of a deacon, taking part in the holy office as lector for the day—but symbolizing nevertheless the authority of the secular power which was to be so decisive in the council's result. In the same cathedral three days later preached Cardinal Pierre d'Ailly, chancellor of the University of Paris and indefatigable champion of reform. He upheld the supremacy of a general council with a persuasiveness that made his words the manifesto of the conciliar party, and personified a different principle of authority. Also in the cathedral on 6

recognizes Gregory XII as the true pope up to the time of Martin V's election at the Council of Constance. Gregory XII was in the line of popes who had stayed at Rome after Gregory XI had returned from Avignon in 1377. Benedict XIII, also deposed at Constance, belonged to the line that returned to Avignon, and along with his single predecessor he is designated an "antipope." At the Council of Pisa (1409), which sought to remedy the Great Schism, Alexander V was elected, and John XXIII became his successor in 1410; but these popes of the "Pisan line" are also regarded as antipopes. In the fifteenth century, of course, these determinations had not been agreed upon. Perhaps there is some significance to the fact that the modern Pope John XXIII was a church historian.

July 1415, John Huss, the patriot reformer of Bohemia, whose spiritual descendants three centuries later would be evangelizing the Indians in Pennsylvania, was condemned as a heretic and led out of the city to be burned for the manner of his invoking still another principle of authority, that of the Bible. There, almost a year later, on 30 May 1416, having recanted his recantation, Jerome of Prague, philosopher, hu manist, orator, and superb Latinist, met the same fate, prais- ing Huss as the smoke filled his lungs and leading the cul- tured Poggio Bracciolini of Florence to lament that the world had lost its most remarkable humanist scholar. At Constance, the learned Poggio, symbol of the new love for antiquity, would set aside his nominal duties as a papal secretary to forage in nearby monastic libraries for lost manuscripts of his beloved Latin classics, and would rejoice to find what still remains our best manuscript of Quintilian. His quest symbol- ized the rising interest in classical antiquity as still another principle of authority. On 1 February 1415, Constance had witnessed a contrasting ceremony in which Pope John XXIII proclaimed the canonization of Saint Brigitta of Sweden— mystic, seer, reformer, pilgrim, doer of many charitable works—a fitting tribute to ancient ideals not otherwise much in evidence.

All these tendencies converged in the old imperial free city on the Bodensee, giving rise to the conflicts between secular and churchly power, the problems of religious authority, the clamor over corruption and abuse, the reassertion of medi- eval mystic piety, the flowing tide of Renaissance enthusiasm, and much more. The fifteenth is an exciting century: it is the quattrocento of Italian art and humanism; it marks the criti- cal stage in the struggle between curialism and conciliarism; it unfolds many portents of the upheaval we call the Refor- mation. It is also an open-ended age that reveals the chang- ing texture of European culture.

THE ETHOS OF THE AGE

These hundred years are frequently viewed as a one-way street from Constance to Wittenberg, or from Constance to Trent, depending on whether the viewer is Protestant or Catholic. Historians with humanistic inclinations have taken a less specifically religious route and charted the literary and artistic wonders of the Renaissance to their flowering in Medicean Florence and Rome. Those whose concern is primarily economic have mapped the fifteenth century as a time of expanding trade culminating in a "commercial revolution" and the discovery of new worlds. And there are other categories by which to describe the period.

Each of these modes of interpretation captures an essential aspect of fifteenth-century life and therefore can claim a measure of validity. But our understanding of church history can be enriched, perhaps, if we pause for a moment and regard the period as a self-contained epoch in which to observe the manifold interests, the depths and wonders, the spirit and zest of Western Christendom before the tumultuous events of the Reformation harden party lines between Roman Catholics and various reforming groups. Protestants sometimes forget that this culture produced other religious phenomena besides Tetzel and Pope Leo X—for example, Luther and Calvin, not to mention Loyola and many other Catholic reformers. The vast reservoir of popular piety, the widespread acceptance of mystical devotion, the intermingling of world and church—these are all factors that help to explicate the religious resurgence of an age which is also prologue to the whole American adventure.

Popular Piety

Historians, in their concentration upon leaders of thought and action, tend to neglect the common people whose belief and devotion necessarily undergird and nourish the Church's institutional life in every period. Johan Huizinga has reminded us of this danger in his sensitive discussion of the forms of life, thought, and art in the late Middle Ages. He puts his finger on an elemental factor in the fervor of the age.

To the world when it was half a thousand years younger, the outlines of all things seemed more clearly marked than to us. The contrast between suffering and joy, between adversity and happiness, appeared more striking. . . . Calamities and indigence were more afflicting than at present; it was more difficult to guard against them, and to find solace. . . . Honours and riches were relished with greater avidity and contrasted more vividly with surrounding misery. We, at the present day, can hardly understand the keenness with which a fur coat, a good fire on the hearth, a soft bed, a glass of wine, were formerly enjoyed.[3]

Modern man has almost lost the sense of darkness; he can hardly imagine a dark village, a dark city street, a dark monastery. By the same token, alas, he has lost the full sense of light and of day. He has made silence almost unknown; hence he can hardly comprehend the greatest of late medieval sounds, the ringing of church bells. Modern man's mobility, moreover, has robbed him of that sense of place and station, of both isolation and rootedness, which were familiar facts in the Western nations until the last century or two. We can scarcely conceive a time when each district, even each town, spoke the vernacular language with a dialect or accent of its own. And because of these cultural changes we are hindered in understanding the piety of premodern ages. A considerable imaginative effort is required.

The first step in any such effort to reenter this late medieval atmosphere is an obliteration of the sharp distinction moderns make between the sacred and the secular.[4] Because we separate the churchly from the worldly more decisively than Geoffrey Chaucer or Martin Luther would or could, we tend to consider Luther's *Table-Talk* as vulgar and Chaucer's *Canterbury Tales* as anticlerical. But the fact is that the tension between the Christian and the world, which was real enough to first-century Christians in their hostile and religiously heterogeneous world, had almost disappeared, and Christianity (in the West, at least) was not only politically

[3] *The Waning of the Middle Ages,* trans. F. Hopman (London: E. Arnold & Co., 1927), pp. 1–2.

[4] No distinction essential to a discussion of religion and the church offers greater obstacles to clarity than that suggested by the two sets of terms *sacred, religious, churchly,* etc., on the one hand, and *secular, profane, worldly,* etc., on the other. The 1960s, in particular, were deluged by a literature which has significantly altered the traditional value judgments. Theologians, both Christian and Jewish, have sought "nonreligious" categories and stressed the excellencies of "secularity." Historians have emphasized the profane contributions of the churches. Regardless of these trends, however, the objective function of the distinction remains, and without praise or blame intended, it is used as needed throughout this book (see Michael J. Taylor, ed., *The Sacred and the Secular* [New York: Prentice-Hall, 1968] and William A. Clebsch, *From Sacred to Profane America*).

established but so socially domesticated that the sense of an alien "world" over against the church was almost unknown. For one thing, the Church—with its institutions, its clergy, its confraternities and lay-brotherhoods—had become omnipresent. Its rites surrounded not only the great life events of birth, marriage, and death, but also the organizations of crafts and professions, the acts and offices of government, and international relations. Theology and science were also interpenetrated. In the fifteenth century, indeed, the Church was enjoying its last years as the relatively unchallenged custodian and interpreter of the cosmos.

What we call superstition was ever-present in all of its many forms. "The sky hung low," says Shirley Jackson Case in describing the thought-world of the early Church; and after the passage of a millennium it had not lifted noticeably. It may even have lowered. Demons, fairies, sprites, and the mysterious workings of unknown and largely unpredictable powers had a firm hold on the imagination. It follows that the interpenetration of the sacred and the secular became characteristic of this realm as well. Worship, theology, and biblical exegesis often incorporated fanciful and magical elements. Even the sneeze had theological overtones, which our "bless you" still commemorates. By a reserve process, folklore and mythology were sublimated or partially reshaped to Christian purposes. Thomas Malory's *Le Morte d'Arthur*, printed by William Caxton in England in 1485, provides an excellent example of this process, and latter-day scholarly battles over the origins of this masterpiece emphasize the way in which sacred tradition had been woven into five centuries' accumulation of historical fact, heroic legend, courtly romance, and chivalric aspiration. Here incontinent desire, ideal love, and the Holy Grail coexist, but the range and tone of the narrative as well as the unselfconscious blending of earthiness, chivalry, barbarity, adultery, and other-worldly piety have made the work an open door to the late medieval mind just as surely as Tennyson's eminently respectable *Idylls of the King* is to the Victorian.

If the piety of the common people lacked depth, it certainly did not lack outward expression. Measured in terms of church buildings, attendance at worship, endowment bequests, charitable deeds, religious pilgrimages, and a thousand other modes of pious expression, there is no evidence that popular devotion flagged. Especially in northern Europe it flourished with great zeal and sincerity. As Gerhard Ritter has remarked, "Even the most passionate and most embittered German criticism of the church could still be called the anger of disillusioned love."[5]

Devotional Life

The spirit which characterized the piety of the common people came to classical expression in the devotional writings and sermons of the Rhineland mystics. The roots of this impulse go deep into the preceding centuries. Behind the Rhenish "Friends of God" stands the commanding figure of the Dominican mystic, Meister Eckhart (1260–1328?), in whose train come that distinguished group, Heinrich Suso (1295–1366), Johannes Tauler (1300–1361), and the author of the *Theologia Germanica* (ca. 1350). Each of these made a permanent contribution to the Church's devotional life which was to be studied and republished by Dominicans and Jesuits no less than by Martin Luther and John Wesley. Their widespread appeal, then and since, has probably stemmed as much from their practical piety as from their speculative theology. To read them is to be stirred into a personal search for the meaning of love, which Tauler called the "beginning, middle, and end of virtue," and which he taught could be found only by losing oneself in the love of God as a drop of water is lost in the ocean.

The *devotio moderna* of the Brethren of the Common Life and the Windesheim Congregation of monasteries in the Netherlands endeared itself even more strongly to later generations. *The Imitation of Christ* by Thomas a Kempis (1380–1471), a canon of Saint Augustine at Windesheim, has become the most treasured work to issue from this spiritual movement. It is an extended gloss on the dominical message, "He who follows me shall not walk in darkness." The exceedingly human tendency apparent at every stage of history, to convert the Christian life into a well-defined and legalistic regimen, was much in evidence in the world that Thomas contemplated. So were many grosser corruptions. But Thomas summoned professing Christians to a higher life of discipleship. Then as in all succeeding centuries great numbers responded; the dedicated Christian life which these

[5] Gerhard Ritter, "Why the Reformation in Germany," *Church History* 23 (June 1958): 103.

men and movements exemplified, and the ageless way in which they sought to bring persons directly to a deeper understanding of the mercy and holiness of God and the nature of Christian discipline, are intrinsic aspects of the age.

The Secularization of the Church

If the church was not an alien in the world, neither was the world a stranger to the church. The distinction between what we are pleased to call the sacred and the secular was further blurred by what, for lack of a better term, may be styled the secularization of the church. In saying this, however, one can transcend the harsh debates of G. G. Coulton, Cardinal F. A. Gasquet, and G. K. Chesterton concerning the religiosity of cultures such as Chaucer's "merrie England." The point is that with so large a portion of Europe's resources under the church's jurisdiction, and with so large a percentage of the population numbered among the "religious," secular interests and "worldly" ways of life and thought entered cloister and chapter house. Abbots and archbishops became rulers, priests became secretaries of state or administrators, monks became wandering men of letters (like Erasmus), other clerics became physicians and scientists (like Copernicus), papal secretaries were humanistic dilettantes (like Poggio), and a pope (Julius II) even served as a field general. Gentleladies like Chaucer's winsome pilgrim became nuns without ceasing to be gentleladies—which may remind us that pilgrimages, too, became something more than simple works of penance or piety. All of this could be established by quoting only the great reformers of the religious life: Saint Odo of Cluny, Saint Bernard of Clairvaux, or Thomas a Kempis—not to mention the writings of Erasmus or countless other less friendly observers.

Though an isolated, unchallenged, and basically agrarian culture, medieval Europe was the most completely realized "Christian society" the world has yet seen. Its fabric was even then rent by urbanism, capitalism, nationalism, and science—making "neomedievalism" impossible—but one can hardly deny its beauty, profundity, or overall achievement. As for its faults, none pointed to them more relentlessly than churchmen themselves: Pierre d'Ailly's reform sermon at Constance was on a theme to which many of Christendom's greatest and most dedicated men devoted themselves. They held Pope

Martin V to his promise to call another general council in five years, but the proceedings at Pavia and Siena in 1423 came to an indecisive conclusion. When Martin died in 1431, they bound his successor, Eugenius IV, to convene another general council immediately. How the Council of Basel got out of hand, defied the papal decree of dismissal and elected a counterpope, only to see the official proceedings transferred to Italy, is a complex series of events which cannot be surveyed here. The outcome was that papal power and "curialism" triumphed, and that a general pacification was achieved in time for the jubilee celebrations of 1450.

Pacification was not reform, however; and although the main lines of the superficial settlement made by Pope Nicholas V (1447–55) were held intact until the Reformation, discontent and frustration continued to build up. Neither the popes nor the dominant leaders of the papal Curia during the next half-century were able to apprehend the explosive power that ecclesiastical malpractice was generating throughout the length and breadth of Europe. Even if Nicholas V, or Alexander VI (1492–1503), or Julius II (1503–13) had been aware of the depth of concern that was stirring men everywhere, it is doubtful that they could have channeled it into a genuine reformation without the kind of cataclysmic disruption that broke into the pleasant and cultured world of Leo X (1513–21).

Even the word "cataclysm" scarcely suggests the magnitude of the forces then at work. In many ways they were greater than either the reformers, the pope, or the emperor. The old order for the Western nations and for the sprawling Roman church was crumbling. This was true in all realms— social and political, intellectual and spiritual. The Reformation as a whole is an event of the magnitude of the Fall of Rome, and one does not pinpoint some single occurrence or circumstance as the "cause" of it except as a form of amusement. For the Holy Roman emperors as for their Roman predecessors, the whole material and spiritual world was subjected to such pressures that its institutional structures, no longer amenable to modification, gradually cracked and fell to pieces. And the forces active in this process would not only promote the formation of new ideologies and structures in Europe, but almost inevitably they would bring American history—and American church history—into actuality. It is important to see that the impulses which led Luther to the Wittenberg church door were integrally related to those which sent Spanish caravels out across the Western Sea.

SOME FACTORS OF CHANGE

The New Learning

One factor altering the situation was that complex of attitudes and enthusiasms which are associated with the Renaissance: the so-called rebirth of learning, the revival of antiquity, the passionate reassertion of individuality, and with these, the search for standards of beauty, truth, and relevance independent of the Church and its dogmas. Philosophy, theology, ethics, and art—not to mention political and economic theory—were taken out of the Church's domain and patronized by princes, merchants, and bankers; and they were now often practiced by laymen, as well as priests who regarded holy orders very casually. The vast scholastic enterprise was often jettisoned as a preoccupation of the "dark ages." For some, Latinity almost replaced theology as the "queen of the sciences." Castiglione's *Life of the Courtier* replaced the *Golden Legend* of the saints as a guide to personal behavior, and Machiavelli's *Prince* would in due course replace the medieval "mirrors for kings" as a guide for rulers.

Machiavelli also suggests another aspect of the intellectual trend of the century: the growing concern for reality as against ideality. Just as Machiavelli was to describe the way a successful prince *did* rule rather than the way he *ought* to rule, so an increasing number of men were becoming concerned with *how* events in the physical universe occur rather than *why* things are as they are. Observation and induction began to displace speculation and deduction. In artistic expression as well, realism came to the fore: compare, for example, a Madonna by Duccio to one by Raphael. In philosophy, nominalism as taught by William of Ockham began to prevail. At the University of Padua, where the most signal scientific advances were to be made, there was a more direct continuity with Aristotle and the scholastics than with the antiquarian effusions of the humanists; but the results were entirely new, and they fired new aspirations by inspiring a new confidence in the power of human reason. At this point at least, the scientific movement joined hands with the humanistic.

But by no means all of the ancient concerns of the Church were abandoned, for the new learning was also opening up the "strange world of the Bible." In France, the Low Countries, England, and Germany, many men turned with renewed vigor to the Scriptures—encouraged in theory at least by the nominalists, with their emphasis on the supreme will of God and the limitations of reason in matters of faith. At Oxford John Colet (1467–1519) was lecturing on Romans, and his enthusiasm seems to have aroused Erasmus to more serious religious concerns. In France the biblical studies of Jacques Lefevre d'Étaples (1450–1537) directed the humanistic group of Meaux into more evangelical interests, and ultimately influenced both Luther and Calvin. Erasmus's Greek text of the New Testament, published by Froben of Basel in 1516, was not only the first work of its kind (Ximénes's Complutensian Polyglot was prepared earlier though not published until 1517), but a major milestone in the textual study of the Bible. Together with a parallel emergence of Hebrew and Old Testament studies, it became the basis of most of the scientific exegesis of the entire Reformation period. This renascence of biblical study on the part of men who, for the most part, were inclined less to speculate than to investigate, is an important confluence of scientific and humanistic interests in the service of theological inquiry and religious concern.

Economic Factors

The chief economic reality that underlay the profound dislocations and anxieties of the pre-Reformation century are summed up in the statement that Europe, first in Italy and then farther north, was making a transition from an "economy of status" to an "economy of money." This "commercial revolution" was enjoyed by almost no one but the great merchants and bankers, and even they were constantly attacked by rulers and populace as scapegoats in a process which few understood. The dynamic instabilities of early capitalism appeared: men of lowly origin grew rich and powerful enough to put even kings and popes in their debt, the old guilds became moribund, knights and squires went begging, peasant debt reached intolerable proportions. The entire social and economic equilibrium of medieval society was upset. In an effort to stem the tide, governments passed laws and the church invoked traditional moral sanctions; but in the last analysis there were usually more who preferred the monetary advantage of trade, rent, and interest to the security of status. In their distress men reaffirmed the ideals they were abandoning, but the change went on.

The result was that the institutions of capitalism prospered. Above all, the cities grew into great centers of industry, trade, and banking: Florence, Milan, Venice, Antwerp, London, Augsburg, Basel, Cadiz, Lisbon, and many others. As trade increased, the possibilities for extending it were enlarged. Africa, India, and the Spice Islands beckoned, and it was Portugal under the leadership of Prince Henry which made the first bold response. After a few tentative thrusts down the west coast of Africa, Bartolomeu Dias in 1488 rounded the Cape of Good Hope, and ten years later Vasco da Gama made his way around to India and back. These early efforts encouraged explorers from other nations to brave uncharted seas in search of new routes to riches, a development which has obvious implications for the history of Christianity.

National Feeling

To mention Portugal is to draw attention to another factor in the late-medieval upheaval, the rise of national states and the emergence of national feeling. "Nationalism" is too strong a word to describe the phenomenon in this early period; but both of its chief psychic and organizational elements, patriotism and the nation-state, were clearly taking shape. In England geography cooperated with the trend of the times; and after the house of Tudor secured the throne in 1485, national feeling grew apace. In France, too, a self-conscious spirit was developing, and not even the diplomacy of Pope Nicholas V could resist the demands of Gallican churchmen for more liberties. In Germany and Italy the "national reality" was obscured by petty rivalries among tiny states and independent cities which existed in a heterogeneous pattern at once more parochial and more cosmopolitan than in other countries. Yet Luther would lay bare a German national consciousness not dissimilar to that called forth in Bohemia by John Huss a century earlier; and Machiavelli would join others in the vision of a peninsular unity transcending Italy's continual intercommunal strife.

Just as the interests of the new learning converged on the biblical text to usher in a new era in the study of the Scriptures, so the new forces of economic concern and national feeling combined to inaugurate a new period in Western imperialism. 1492 was particularly fateful. In this year Pope Alexander VI undertook to send out a venerable Benedictine monk to supervise the long-neglected diocese of Gardar in Greenland, an interesting commentary on the dissolution of what had once been a promising link to new and distant worlds.[6] As if to document the rapidly developing activities in warmer waters, the same pope two years later arranged between Spain and Portugal the famous Line of Demarcation defining their respective areas of exploitation and evangelism. More significant to Spain than a treaty (which would be often flouted) was the hard fact that in 1492 Queen Isabella, "the Last Crusader," finally achieved the definitive expulsion of the Moors from Iberian soil, thus ending the long Islamic occupation that had begun under the Ommiad caliphs in 711.

When Columbus on 12 October 1492 dropped anchor at San Salvador in the Bahama Islands, his feat symbolized as nothing else could the way in which the lure of trade and the emergence of a strong united nation would combine to kindle anew the missionary zeal of the Church. Francisco Garcia Cardinal Ximénes (1436–1517) was then archbishop of Toledo, primate of Spain, chancellor of Castile, and chief adviser to Isabella. Ascetic Franciscan, zealous reformer, and energetic promoter of learning, he would do much to make Columbus's discovery the beginning of a new era in Spanish and world church history. And from Spain would come many other heroes of the faith, for there the Catholic Reformation was earliest and most completely realized.

Interrupting or culminating these many forces of transition came that convulsive series of events which constitute the Reformation proper, the decisive rupture of Western Christendom, and the emergence of evangelical territorial churches in most of Northern Europe as well as large Protestant movements in several Roman Catholic countries. The

[6] Excavations made during 1963 on the northernmost peninsula of Newfoundland strengthened already existing evidence that the Vikings actually did reach and live in "Vinland," the lands west of Greenland of which their sagas frequently speak.

significance of these events can hardly be exaggerated; far more than the so-called Renaissance they brought an end to the old order in Europe and inaugurated the modern age. Through several accidents of history the American colonies, out of which grew the United States, were molded by the Reformation with a directness and intensity unequaled in any other country. For this reason the history of these colonies must begin with the emergence and development of Protestantism on the Continent and in Great Britain (see chaps. 5 and 6, below). The general course of Roman Catholic history, however, though also profoundly altered by the Reformation, was not changed in so fundamental a manner. In Spain and Italy where Protestant inroads were slight, as in France and Germany where religious conflicts were long and severe, Roman Catholicism was in the long run powerfully challenged and aroused by the Reformation. Everywhere, however, its response was ordered and informed by ancient heritage and medieval tradition. The character and advancement of the great Roman Catholic empires in the New World, therefore, are best understood without prior preoccupation with the details of Protestant church history.

ROMAN CATHOLIC REFORM MOVEMENTS

Individual Efforts

In March 1517, a half-year before the Ninety-five Theses would be posted in Wittenberg, the Fifth Lateran Council—ecumenical in theory, Italian in fact—concluded five years of fitful sessions during which the perennial problem of reforming the Church terminated in the same impasse which had frustrated so many similar proceedings. Gilles of Vitterbo, general of Luther's own order of Augustinians and a participant in the revival of interest in their great patron saint's theology, had opened the meetings with a ringing summons to renewal. He voiced the universal complaints against the corruption of the clergy and the cupidity of the Curia. Yet a great Roman Catholic historian summarizes the result in negative terms:

The times were not ripe for a profound transformation of manners in the Italy of the Renaissance. The corruptions of the Curia were not corrected. Pope Leo X, sunk in the utterly profane luxuries of his court and worship of the arts, remained inert in the face of the church's needs.[7]

To say that "the times were not ripe," however, or that early efforts toward ecclesiastical reform lacked papal leadership, is not to say that reformers were nonexistent. A deeply rooted concern for purifying the Church was manifest in several sectors of European Christendom; and the most important of these many impulses maintained their characteristic spirit despite the events of 1517 and after.

One prominent example is the fiery Dominican preacher, Girolamo Savonarola (1452–98), who became the virtual ruler of Florence in 1496–97 and almost succeeded in turning that center of Renaissance culture into a penitential city. (He is best remembered by Protestants for his great hymn, "Jesus, Refuge of the Weary.") In quite another and far less sensational way this reforming spirit was also revealed by the austere Dutchman, Florensz Dedal, who for the last twenty months of his life succeeded Leo X as Pope Adrian VI (d. 1523). Rising from humble origins to become tutor of Charles V, cardinal-bishop of Tortosa, and a papal legate in Spain, he had shown his moral rigor as a reformer, especially of the monastic life. His pontificate was too short to be influential, but he personified a religious type that would finally awaken the Roman church from its complacency and impotence.

In theological realms diverse movements of correction were also found. A long line of scholars, often in the nominalist tradition of William of Ockham, had been stressing the need for study of the Bible in its central literal sense, often supporting such claims by an emphasis upon the unknowableness of God and his will by any other means. These tendencies had doctrinal corollaries in men who were emphasizing again Saint Augustine's and Saint Bernard's concern for justification by faith. Perhaps most outstanding of these efforts were those fostered by Guillaume Briçonnet in France. As abbot of Saint Germain-des-Prés and later (1516 ff.) as bishop of Meaux he encouraged and then applied the pronouncedly evangelical biblical labors of Lefevre d'Étaples and his circle—a circle in which John Calvin himself for a time was numbered.

7 L. Christiani, *L'Eglise à l'Époque du Concile de Trente*, ed. A. Fliche and V. Martin (Paris, 1948), p. 247. My translation.

Even among the humanists a deep strain of piety often fused with outspoken enthusiasm for the new learning, leading them from an exclusive passion for classical scholarship to a concern for church reform. And of these men none was more accomplished and famous than Erasmus of Rotterdam (1466?–1536), whose work ranged from the blistering ridicule of church and clergy in his *Praise of Folly* (1509) to his epoch-making Greek edition of the New Testament. He also edited many works of the early church fathers and wrote a simple, earnest, and widely read *Handbook of the Christian Soldier*.

More directly important for the Catholic Reformation, however, were those movements which were more consciously rooted in medieval piety and motivated by a concern for reinvigorating ascetic ideals and practices. The reforming impulse of the order of Augustinian Hermits indicates the degree to which, in Germany especially, sensitive souls reacted against the prevailing laxity. The Franciscans also evolved a new and stricter branch, the Observants, in 1517, and yet another ultra observant branch, the Capuchins, in 1525. It is unquestionably true that in Europe as a whole the monastic orders were so deeply enmeshed in social and economic affairs that total root-and-branch reformation was impossible, but the instances cited were more than isolated examples. Everywhere during the fifteenth century, as during most preceding ages, important movements of monastic reform were set in motion.

Of the individual champions of spiritual renewal perhaps none was more profound or influential than Saint Theresa of Avila (1515–82) who, despite the dates of her lifespan, represents a long-developing Spanish tradition; and Saint John of the Cross (1542–91), who was virtually her spiritual son. Both were of aristocratic birth, both entered the ranks of the Carmelites, and both became fervent exponents of rigorous asceticism, mystical devotion, and the contemplative life. For years they labored together to found and foster the Reformed, or discalced, order of Carmelites, in which the monastic rule was observed with all possible austerity. Like so many others who were equally highborn and elitist in their strategy, they sought to reform the Church not by wide-sweeping legislation or popular appeals, but by the spiritual renewal of individuals, especially the clergy and religious orders. Their central concerns were the knowledge of "the dark night of the soul," the subjugation of self, and the attainment of "the spiritual and secret kingdom of God." Yet such efforts were not "sectarian" in spirit even when they were pronouncedly individualistic, nor were they at first "counterreformatory" in temper. This quest for mystical union with God through withdrawal from the world and stringent self-discipline sprang from within the ancient life of the Church. Nowhere more than in Spain was the ascetic ideal combined with ecclesiastical discipline to enforce a program that would elevate morals, educate priests, and coerce heretics. Given the long tradition of the crusade against the Moors, it was perhaps natural enough that the land of Ximénes and Isabella would produce a Loyola while Germany was producing a Luther.

New Monastic Orders

Such efforts at reform had several parallels in Rome itself, a fact which gave them an obvious special significance. Here the most influential line of development was represented by the Society of Divine Love, a confraternity of secular priests whose activities centered in the Church of Saints Sylvester and Dorothea. Officially recognized by Leo X in 1514—three years before Luther's Ninety-five Theses—it was led by Saint Cajetan of Thiene (1480–1547), an almost archetypical representative of sixteenth-century Catholic reformation. He sought systematically to arouse intense ardor for the sacraments, along with a program of rigorous asceticism, moral earnestness, and charitable sacrifice. Though never numbering more than sixty, the society was able to attract to its ranks many able and zealous men, who were often very influential members of the papal court. Both in Rome and as emulated elsewhere this type of movement became a powerful instrument for reform. Similar in some respects were the later efforts of Saint Philip Neri (1515–95). His oratory in Rome, with its authorized congregation (1575), directed its efforts to the devotional life, sacramental practice, and theological commitment of the laity. The oratory not only attained important influence in the Curia, but won acceptance as a model in other countries, notably in France.

Saint Cajetan, however, went further in harnessing this kind of zeal, and in 1524 he gained papal approval for an order of clerks regular, the Theatines, which he hoped would provide a disciplined and elite model for reforming the clergy and redirecting its concern for the whole parish ministry. Pietro Caraffa (1476–1559), formerly associated with the Society of Divine Love, became the first superior of the Theatines. He was a Neapolitan nobleman who began his active career as a reformer in 1504 after becoming bishop of Chieti. In later years while serving as a papal legate in several countries, his determination deepened, largely due to the influence of the Spanish reformers like Ximénes and Dedal. He became archbishop of Brindisi as well, but renounced these offices to enter the new order. Later as Pope Paul IV (1555–59) he would personify the Counter-Reformation in its most strenuous, authoritarian, and uncompromising form. In post-Reformation years still other prelates, like Bishop Gian Matteo Giberti of Verona (1495–1543) and Archbishop Carlo Borromeo of Milan (1538–84), both of them closely affiliated with Saint Cajetan, continued and broadened this type of reform, concerning themselves with all aspects of diocesan life, piety, and worship.

By far the most momentous aspect of these reforms was the new way in which the monastic life was conceived. Out of such efforts emerged a new kind of religious order, a creative contribution equal in importance to the mendicant idea embodied in the Dominican and Franciscan orders. Its newness lay in adapting the ascetic ideal to the needs of the time by organizing priests under a strict rule or into an order, but for the purpose of intensifying their priestly and pastoral labors "in the world." This objective often required the substitution of new disciplinary measures for the old cloistered life and corporate participation in the daily offices of worship. Inwardly the priests were dedicated to the renewal of Christian piety, charity, and instruction, and they submitted themselves obediently to such demands as this task would impose. Following the example and impetus afforded by the Oratory of Divine Love and the Theatines, several such orders were formed in Italy during the sixteenth century, but not all of them adopted Cajetan's rigorous demands that even the order as such remain poor and without endowments.

The order founded upon these general principles which played by far the most revolutionary role and whose activity marks most decisively the transition to Counter-Reformation objectives was the Society of Jesus, founded by Saint Ignatius of Loyola (1491–1556). His army career cut short by a crippling wound, Loyola resolved in August 1521 to live a life of self-denial in the service of Christ. In 1522 he placed his sword and dagger on the altar of Our Lady Montserrat, and exchanged his fine clothes for the sackcloth gown and pilgrim staff of a knight of God. He then walked on to Manresa, where for almost a year he practiced the most rigorous asceticism, deepening his devotional life and continuing his meditation on the life of Christ. Finally, in a vision received nearby on the river Cardona, he felt the climactic "enlightening of the understanding" that was to make him both a great spiritual teacher and the founder of a militia that would put itself in the service of Jesus. Hereafter he would be a soldier of the Virgin.

During this stay at Manresa, Loyola also wrought out a series of remarkable Christ-centered spiritual exercises by which to discipline himself and others whom he persuaded to adopt his rigorous program. As fully articulated over the years, the *Spiritual Exercises* provide in twenty-eight general divisions a specific and detailed routine for every hour of every day; they include intense contemplation of some biblical event, invocation of the presence of Christ, examination of the sinful self, and meditation on the glories of redemption. Loyola was so severe in his piety and so zealous in recruiting converts to his system of spiritual discipline, not only at Manresa, but on his pilgrimage to the Holy Land, and later at Barcelona, Alcala, and Salamanca, that he incurred the suspicion of the officers of the Inquisition and suffered considerable persecution.

In Paris in 1528 Loyola devoted himself to arduous study in order to overcome his educational deficiencies; but he remained alert for young men whom he could overpower with his enthusiasm for self-sacrificial labors on behalf of the Church. Among the able youths mastered by his indomitable energy were Peter Faber, Francis Xavier, Alfonso Salmeron, Jacob Lainez and Nicholas Bobadilla—all Spaniards or (like himself) Basques. On 15 August 1534 (the anniversary of the Assumption of the Virgin), in Saint Mary's Church at Montmartre, these men took upon themselves a most solemn vow to enter upon missionary work in Jerusalem, or, if this were impossible, to go without questioning wherever the pope might send them. They received formal recognition from Paul III as the Company or Society of Jesus on 27 September 1540, and from that time forward they increased rapidly in

numbers and influence. The Jesuits, as they were called, soon
moved into many diverse positions of influence, and after a
very few years they were able to shape the policy of the entire church. With their avowed aim "the greater glory of
God," they became the most effective agents for reclaiming
many vast segments of Protestantism for the Roman Catholic
church, for evangelizing large portions of the newly opened
lands of the East and West, for founding and maintaining
great educational institutions, and for strengthening the authority of the pope within the church. Their flexibility, adap-
tiveness, and perennial interest in innovation would be constantly evident in these undertakings. Just as the *Spiritual
Exercises* were the soul of the constitution which Loyola
provided for his order, so did the Society of Jesus institutionalize some of the deepest themes of the Catholic Reformation.

Culmination

From 1534 to 1549 the chair of Peter was occupied by
Paul III, under whom reform decisively reached the papacy.
He not only brought to the office a measure of discipline—
although his successors were by no means agreed in their estimates of his austerity and zeal—but he granted formal recognition to the Jesuits and cooperated with the forces that
had long sought a definitive council to deal with corruption
and to formulate doctrine in answer to the charges of the Protestants. The Council of Trent is both the culmination and the
documentation of the entire process of Roman Catholic Reformation. Like the Jesuits, who had so much to do with its
outcome, it represents the double aspect which all Roman
Catholic activity showed after 1541, when the failure of the
Conference of Regensburg revealed the hopelessness of reconciliation with the Protestants. On the one hand, it was intensely loyal to the medieval heritage of the Church. On the
other, it took calculating cognizance of the Protestant revolt,
anathmatizing its distinctive tenets and formulating Catholic
dogma in an unprecedentedly thorough way.

The Council of Trent met in three main sessions from 1545
to 1563, one adjournment lasting nearly a decade while Pope
Julius III provided a brief Indian summer for the Renaissance. Between its beginning and end there were frequent
changes in personnel, and consequently, in opinion. On many
issues opposing views clashed sharply, and mediating posi-

tions were adopted—making the council far less reactionary than most Protestants and many Roman Catholics have supposed. But its final results constitute an ecclesiastical landmark as important as the rupture between the Eastern and Western churches. In this sense Trent is the birthplace of modern Roman Catholicism and "post-Tridentine" becomes one of the most meaningful adjectives in church history. In its decrees the council defined the authority of Scripture and holy tradition, the nature of Original Sin, and the doctrines of the sacraments; it devoted a long section to justification by faith as a specific answer to Protestants, and closed by asserting that the authority of the pope was "to be preserved." Thus the door to rapprochement with Protestants was shut, and it would remain closed for almost exactly four centuries. Within Catholicism itself large areas of doctrine previously open to discussion were narrowed to more precisely defined limits. As interpreted by those charged with carrying out the work of Counter-Reformation, Trent's decrees became a standard of inflexible conservatism.

The council's importance will be appreciated more fully when, in a later chapter, the Reformation is considered. Before describing anti-Roman movements, however, it is worthwhile to follow out the colonial and missionary endeavors of the two Roman Catholic powers whose imperial designs became involved in American religious history. We must, of course, remember that after 1517 Europe was shaken to its roots by the Reformation. Yet it remains true that in the vast Roman Catholic empires pre-Reformation piety and Counter-Reformation zeal were dominant influences. For this reason the imperial ventures of Spain and France are recounted before we consider the religious background which had the heaviest early influence on the future United States.

3

THE CHURCH IN NEW SPAIN

American church history begins on Thursday, 11 October
1492, and the circumstances are set down tersely in the journal of Christopher Columbus, "Admiral of the Ocean Sea,
Viceroy and Governor of whatever territory he might discover."

> The course was W.S.W. and there was more sea than there
> had been during the whole of the voyage. They saw sand-
> pipers, and a green reed near the ship. . . . Everyone
> breathed afresh and rejoiced at these signs. . . . After sun-
> set the Admiral returned to his original west course, and
> they went along at the rate of 12 miles per hour. As the
> caravel *Pinta* was a better sailer, and went ahead of the
> Admiral, she found the land, and made the signals ordered
> by the Admiral. The land was first seen by a sailor named
> Rodrigo de Triana. But the Admiral, at ten o'clock, being
> on the castle of the poop, saw a light, though it was so un-
> certain that he could not affirm it was land. . . . At two
> hours after midnight the land was sighted at a distance of
> two leagues.[1]

On the following day Columbus landed, took possession of
this island in the name of King Ferdinand and Queen Isabella, and named it San Salvador (Holy Savior). To the assembled natives he gave "red caps, and glass beads to put
around their necks, and many other things of little value,

[1] Edward G. Bourne, ed., "The Voyages of Columbus and of
John Cabot," in *The Northmen, Columbus, and Cabot, 985–1530*
(New York: Charles Scribner's Sons, 1906), pp. 108–10.

which gave them great pleasure, and made them so much our friends that it was a marvel to see." He surmised that they would be "more easily freed and converted to our holy faith by love than by force." With an optimism that the Anglo-American experience of succeeding centuries would hardly justify, he also declared, "I believe that they would easily be made Christians, as it appeared to me that they had no religion."

After returning to Spain, Columbus made a final entry in his journal (15 March 1493) voicing the same confidence:

> I know respecting this voyage that God has miraculously shown his will, as may be seen from this journal, setting forth the numerous miracles that have been displayed in the voyage, and in me who was so long at the court of your Highnesses, working in opposition to and against the opinions of so many chief persons of your household, who were all against me, looking upon this enterprise as folly. But I hope, in our Lord, that it will be a great benefit to Christianity, for so it has ever appeared.[2]

Thus, in the very year that Granada's fall terminated "the Last Crusade," the vista for another vast campaign opened before the Catholic rulers of Spain.

SPAIN'S EARLY ACTIVITIES IN THE NEW WORLD

Exploration and Conquest

Unlike England, which in 1497 remunerated the intrepid John Cabot with "ten pounds for him that found the isle" and followed this generous act with nearly a century of exploratory and colonial neglect, Spain responded with vigor. At the insistence of Ferdinand and Isabella, Pope Alexander VI issued two bulls, *Inter Caetera I* and *II*, which granted to Spain all lands not under Christian rule and set a line at one hundred leagues (263 miles) west of the Azores and Cape Verde Islands, beyond which all future discoveries not held by a Christian ruler on 25 December 1492 would belong to Spain. This was in May 1493. In September Columbus set sail again, not with three ships and ninety reluctant men, but

[2] Ibid., pp. 257–58.

with an imposing armada of seventeen ships bearing over twelve hundred men (but no women), at least five priests, livestock, seeds, and building materials. On Hispaniola (Haiti), where the colony was planted, very little was to flourish besides discontent and disease, but Spain had made a serious colonizing effort which would be followed by countless others before the revolutions of the nineteenth century collapsed her American empire.

After his third voyage in 1500, Columbus and his two brothers were accused by the colonists of maladministration and sent home in chains. Although he managed to clear himself in time to make a fourth and last voyage in 1504, his authority over his discoveries were transferred permanently to the crown. By this time, other adventurers—many of them his former captains—had added three thousand miles of South American coastline to the gradually growing knowledge of the cartographers. Alonso de Ojeda and Juan de la Cosa, Vincente Yāñez Pinzón, Peralonso Niño, Diego de Lepe, and others had coasted and traded from the Isthmus to far down the Brazilian shore. In 1513 Vasco Núñez de Balboa pushed across Panama to discover the Pacific Ocean; and scarcely fifteen years later Lucas Vasquez de Ayllón and Esteban Gómez were bringing in sketchy reports of the North American coast to Nova Scotia.

Added to the thrilling feats of the navigators were the exploits of the *conquistadores*. By 1515 Puerto Rico and Cuba were conquered and San Juan and Havana founded. Cortes toppled the Aztec empire in 1521, establishing Spanish control of central Mexico and launching the earliest probes of the Pacific coast. Guzmán made savage forays into north-central Mexico. Pizarro began the sorties that were to culminate in his victories over the Incas and the founding in 1535 of Lima, City of the Kings and future capital of all South America.

Government of the Settlements

To consolidate these gains and regulate the new empire, a House of Trade (1503) and a governing council of the Indies (1524) were organized in Spain. Furthermore, all the conquered territories from Florida to Honduras, the patrimony of Isabella of Castile, were in 1527 put under the supervision of the *audiencia* of New Spain, with headquarters in Mexico

City. After 1535 the chief administrative officer was the viceroy. A similar office was established for South America five years later. Beneath the viceroy were governors appointed in more settled areas, or captains-general in areas requiring military defense. Beneath these in the administrative hierarchy were the *alcaldes, mayores,* and *corregidores,* who represented royal authority in towns and metropolitan districts. At the lowest level were the various municipal offices which, though elective at first, soon became appointive. Colonial administration was held accountable to the crown: short terms, the requirement of detailed reports, and a constant flow of royal inspectors strove to maintain strict control. In this way the absolutism of the Spanish monarch reached out into the New World. But because of the enormous difficulties of supervision, the fruits of autocratic paternalism—graft, venality, and the decay of civic concern—were evident from first to last.

The Participation of the Church

Churchmen were important at every level of the social and political structure in New Spain. The spirit of Spanish Catholicism, forged in the long campaign against Jews and Moors, was transplanted with little attenuation of either its fierce orthodoxy or its ardent piety. Perhaps most decisive for the future was the fact that, by embarking on the course of empire a full century before her northern competitors, Spain transmitted to the New World a culture that had been little affected by the Renaissance, the Reformation, or the commercial revolution. "Thus a medieval civilization, revering intellectual and spiritual as well as political authority, acquired a new lease on life and became the heritage of modern Hispanic America."[3]

From the first, conquest and conversion were assumed to go together, and every ship that brought soldiers and settlers brought also its share of priests. The representatives of the church were backed by the same royal power that dispatched the captains and the viceroys. A series of papal concessions to the Spanish monarchs, known as the *Real Patronato,* had granted to the Spanish king ecclesiastical powers which were

[3] Irving A. Leonard in his foreword to Mariano Picón-Salas, *A Cultural History of Spanish America, from Conquest to Independence,* p. x.

extraordinarily large even for the home country but which for lands across the sea made him virtually a vice-pope. He had authority to collect all tithes and to present the candidates for all churchly offices from the lowliest curate up to an archbishop; he had arrogated to himself the right to review the decrees of all councils and synods held in the Indies; and he demanded the privilege of approving papal decrees, bulls, and ordinations affecting Spanish interests before they were allowed to become official.

With this vast grant of authority it was, of course, Spain's responsibility to promote the church throughout her growing empire—a duty that she did not shirk. Especially after the Protestant Reformation gave increased emphasis to the missionary motive, evangelism was prosecuted with determination, though not always with charity. In Spain as nowhere else, church and state partook of the same spirit, sought the same goals, and to a large extent employed the same methods. The religious zeal of rulers like Isabella, Charles V, and Philip II (whose combined reigns covered more than a century), no less than the administrative ability of ecclesiastics like Ximénes and his successors, made certain that the Great Commission to baptize all nations was taken seriously. Especially notable were the procedures and policies established by the archdeacon of Seville, Juan de Fonseca, who served as virtual colonial minister during the entire reign of Ferdinand and Isabella and Father García de Loaísa (ca. 1479–1546), general of the Dominican Order and later cardinal-archbishop of Seville, who served as president of the Council of the Indies.

In 1523 Charles V granted to Vásquez de Ayllón the right to plant settlements on the North American coast "eight hundred leagues up" from San Domingo. The *cedula* by which this ill-fated colonial enterprise was authorized was explicit and typical in its exhibition of the emperor's religious interest:

> Our principal intent in the discovery of new lands is that the inhabitants and natives thereof who are without the light of the knowledge of faith may be brought to understand the truths of our holy Catholic faith, and that they may come to the knowledge thereof and become Christians and be saved, and this is the chief motive you are to bear and hold in this affair, and to this end it is proper that

religious persons should accompany you . . . and I command that whatever you shall thus expend in transporting the said religious, as well as in maintaining them and giving them what is needful, . . . and for the vestments and other articles required for the divine worship, shall be paid entirely from the rents and profits which in any manner shall belong to us in the said land.[4]

In 1526 this colony of San Miguel was founded near where Jamestown would rise nearly a century later. The colony benefited from the ministrations of Antonio de Montesinos, the Dominican friar who had already become an outspoken champion of Indian rights, but the problems of survival precluded active evangelism. Ayllón himself died; and after a cold winter marked by mutiny, a slave revolt, and Indian attacks, the 150 men who remained of the initial 600 returned to Hispaniola. But a chapel had been built, and the Mass celebrated.

After a half-dozen failures the first permanent colony in what would become the United States was finally established at Saint Augustine in 1565 by Pedro Menéndez de Avilés in order to protect the sea route of treasure ships. Here all of the characteristics of the sixteenth-century church were evident. Intolerance was savagely manifested at the massacre of the French Huguenots who had settled at the mouth of the Saint Johns River to the north. (Spain at that time was exceedingly jealous of exclusive rights in her newly discovered domains, and would make no concessions to any other group, least of all to Protestants.)[5] As in Spain, church and state were closely identified; indeed, the entire life of the citadel-town revolved around the *plaza mayore* facing the harbor, the chapel on one side, and the governor's palace on the other. Later two hospitals and a convent were added, and missions to the Indians were begun. The first efforts by Jesuits under Menéndez proved abortive, but permanent labors were resumed in 1568 and expanded in 1595 with the arrival of eleven Franciscans. Among several ambitious Jesuit ventures was another unsuccessful attempt to found a

[4] Quoted in John G. Shea, *The Catholic Church in Colonial Days,* 1:104–107.

[5] This short-lived colony was founded at a time when Huguenot influence in French government was strong. Subsequently, New France was closed to Protestants (see chap. 4).

mission colony in the Chesapeake area (1570–71). By 1634
some thirty-five Franciscans were maintaining forty-four missions and ministering to twenty-five or thirty thousand Indian
converts. Catechisms were translated and some elementary
schooling attempted.

Although church life in Florida was under the jurisdiction
of the bishop of Santiago de Cuba, the whole system suffered
from inadequate supervision. The British were expanding in
the north; and when the War of the Spanish Succession
broke out in 1701, the whole fragile structure of Spanish life
in Florida began to crumble. The consecration of a resident
bishop for Saint Augustine in 1709 did not halt the decay.
When the third bishop, Ponce y Carasco, arrived in 1751,
there were in the immediate vicinity of Saint Augustine only
four Indian missions, with 136 souls; in other words, there
was no Catholic presence in Florida outside of the Spanish
population of the city. It was only out in the west, far from
the British and French, where imperial wars were but rumors
and where a more settled type of Indian civilization prevailed, that the characteristic institutions of the Church of
New Spain were to reveal their genius—in sharp contrast
with the Anglo-Saxon mode of expansion.

THE EXPANSION OF NEW SPAIN

Florida never became a vital part of Spain's empire. The
dangers and difficulties were many; the attractions few. In
the Caribbean Islands (notably Hispaniola and Cuba), in the
viceroyalties of South America, and especially in "New
Spain" (which extended from Panama City to Monterey),
her empire flourished. From this last area came a series of
northern thrusts which constitute one of the most colorful
chapters in North American history. Drawing men into these
unknown lands were the tales of wanderers like Cabeza de
Vaca, that amazing survivor of the Narváez expedition to
Tampa Bay (1528), who finally emerged from his wanderings on the Rio Fuerte in Mexico in 1536. In 1540, enticed
by reports of the fabulous Seven Cities of Cibola, the viceroy
commissioned Francisco Vásquez de Coronado to lead a major
expedition; this resulted in the discovery of the Grand Can-
yon, Kansas, Oklahoma, the Texas panhandle, and some
pueblo villages of the Zuñi in western New Mexico—a vast

mission field, but no silver or gold. For sixty years interest in the northern country languished. It was left for Don Juan de Oñate to enter the northern lands in 1598, claim them for Spain, and found at San Juan de Caballeros the first colony in what is now New Mexico.

New Mexico

Oñate's initial company included over a hundred soldiers, four hundred settlers, seven Franciscan fathers and two lay brothers under Father Martinez, many slaves, eighty-three wagons, and seven thousand head of stock. It came to stay, and despite many difficulties it did stay. In 1609 Oñate was replaced as governor by Pedro de Peralta. He moved the capital to Santa Fe, which became the permanent center of Spanish dominion in New Mexico. *Encomiendas* were granted to soldiers and settlers; other towns were founded, and a new agricultural commonwealth began to flourish. As missionaries the friars made rapid if somewhat superficial headway, in 1630 reporting fifty priests at work in twenty-five missions embracing sixty thousand converts in ninety pueblos.

A fierce revolt by the Indians in 1680 resulted in a terrible massacre, and the remaining Spaniards were forced back to El Paso for over twenty years. But near the centenary of Oñate's entry, the territory was reconquered and the old Spanish pattern of life restored for another century and a quarter. The Indians, sullen but subdued, were the basic source of labor in the fields, the mills, and the mines. With the passing years their burden was increased by heavy debts to Spanish and *mestizo* merchants and lenders. Nor was this system of virtual vassalage obnoxious to the friars, who were generally content to work within the existing framework of colonial rule, though they were in almost constant conflict with the civil authorities over control of the Indians.

By 1744 the slowly growing non-Indian population had risen to about ten thousand, with two-thirds of the people living in the four principal cities, Santa Fe, Santa Cruz, Albuquerque, and El Paso. At that time the Franciscans were still administering about twenty-five missions and about 17,500 Indians. Yet the missionary work was seriously retarded by the failures of the friars to learn the Indian languages and by jurisdictional conflicts with the bishop of Durango. By 1800

the number of Indians in the missions had fallen to about ten
thousand. The Apaches, moreover, remained a constant
threat throughout the eighteenth century. Mercantilistic trade
regulations also limited the area's economic growth. The
great event of the year was the annual caravan down to
Chihuahua when the agricultural produce of New Mexico
could be exchanged for needed goods from abroad. There
was naturally some illicit trading with the French in Louisiana, the British, and later the Americans; but these outside
avenues of trade became important only after Mexico's independence and the opening of the Santa Fe Trail to Saint
Louis, both of which occurred in 1821. Amid the anticlericalism and political disorder of the early decades of
Mexican rule the state of the church deteriorated still further.
When the province of New Mexico (including Colorado,
Utah, Nevada, and most of Arizona) became part of the
United States in 1848, it had a population of about sixty
thousand, perhaps half of which was Spanish or *mestizo*.
Twenty or more priests were serving the area, but the missions were in nearly total disorganization. Two years later the
vicariate of New Mexico was erected to order the church's
affairs in the region. Chosen to direct the task was a French-
born priest then serving in Kentucky, Jean-Baptiste Lamy.
When he resigned as archbishop in 1875, he reported fifty-six
priests and 203 places of worship in his vast province.

Arizona

Except for the area south of the Gila Valley, much of modern Arizona—or Piméria Alta, as it was called—had a character and history of its own. Unlike New Mexico, it experienced
little white occupation and few extended missionary efforts,
remaining for the most part a forbidding, dangerous and
half-explored challenge to a relatively small number of intrepid Jesuits and their Franciscan successors. Even in the
south, missionary efforts were not begun until the
1680s—and with few enduring results. Yet much dedication
was displayed by the Black Robes who did seek the conversion of the hostile tribes in this area, and one of their number
has become almost the archetypical hero of the Spanish borderlands. Eusebio Kino (1644–1711), born in the Tyrol and
educated at Ingolstadt, came to Mexico in 1681 and entered
upon his life work in the north in 1687. Before his death
twenty-four years later he had baptized four thousand Indi-

ans, covered thousands of miles in over forty expeditions, explored and mapped the area, introduced stock raising in five or six valleys, and assisted in the founding of several missions. These missions, however, remained precarious due to Indian hostility, the shortage of priests, and quarrels with civil authorities. And even the small gains made were decimated after 1783 when the decree of Charles III expelling the Jesuits was carried out.[6] Here as elsewhere the Franciscans strove to maintain the work, but aside from the beautiful new church erected at San Xavier del Bac (1797), little remained of the Arizona mission in 1821, and still less when the United States acquired the territory.

Texas

Spanish concern for the Texas territory was aroused by the arrival of LaSalle and the French in the lower Mississippi Valley between 1682 and 1689, though a few missionaries had ventured east and north from El Paso during the preceding decades. Under Alonso de Léon, governor of Coahuila, a series of expeditions was sent out, and in 1690 he claimed the area for Spain. San Francisco de los Tejas (Texas) was founded as a Spanish mission in that year by the Franciscan Father Damian Massanet, but it was abandoned three years later. In 1718 renewed efforts produced more permanent results, of which the San Antonio, or Alamo, mission is the most famous. By 1722 there were ten missions, four *presidios*, and four centers of settlement in the Texas territory; and a governor resided at Los Adaes (now Robeline, Louisiana).

The overall Spanish influence in Texas was very weak, however, because of the unavailability of settlers and the intractability of the Comanches and Apaches. From 1762 to 1800 even the military occupants were withdrawn from Texas, for France had ceded to Spain the entire Louisiana territory. In 1810 the Spanish population of Texas probably did not exceed 3,000—and only 432 Indians were left in the six missions that remained. The United States purchased Louisiana in 1803, Mexico broke away from Spain in 1821, and Texas won independence from Mexico in 1836, at which time only two priests of Mexican origin remained, and they were a source of scandal. The religious history of old Texas contains a record of fifty missions and much heroism, but the

6 See pp. 103–04, 412, 636, and 641–42 below.

end result in so vast and unsettled a region was barely discernible. Subsequent immigration, however, has again given Texas a considerable population of Spanish Catholic heritage.

California

In the Far West the early story is very similar to that in Texas. During the great period of Spain's expansion in the New World, California was largely ignored. In the 1540s Juan Rodríguez Cabrillo, Bartolomé Ferrelo, and others had pushed up the western coast, and in 1602 Juan Vizcaino bestowed names on many of the bays and islands he discovered along the coasts of California and Oregon. But not until 1702 did Father Eusebio Kino, as he pressed out from inland settlements, determine after extensive labors in Arizona that Lower California was a peninsula and not an island. Attention was focused on Texas; and while Father Salvatierra and other Jesuits were advancing an important work in Lower California, the upper part of that region was forgotten or ignored.

All this was changed by the Russian advance down the coast from Alaska. In 1728 the Russian captain Vitus Bering had sailed through the straits that now bear his name, and in 1741 he reached Alaska, whereupon he claimed for Russia a slice of America as large as western Europe. As with Texas, the presence of an alien power spurred Spain to action. José de Gálvez, the vigorous visitor-general of Spain's new and energetic King Charles III, organized an expedition in 1769, putting Don Gasper de Portola in charge. Because of the expulsion of the Jesuits from the Spanish Empire, six Franciscans were assigned the spiritual tasks, with Father Junípero Serra (1713–84), a university-trained native of Majorca, as their leader. In July 1769 the mission of San Diego de Alcala was founded, and nearby, the *presidio*. The expedition then struggled northward over rugged terrain in search of Monterey, which they missed; but in November they became the first white men to view the Golden Gate and the magnificent bay that lies behind it. A year later they found Monterey and established the San Carlos (Borromeo) mission, and by 1772 three others. Then, after an heroic search for an overland route, Juan Batista de Anza, commander of Tubac (Arizona), with Father Francisco Garcés as guide, led out the company of soldiers and friars—thirty families in all—that were to constitute the first Spanish post on San Francisco Bay. While he was seeking a suitable site for a settlement in the bay area, far away in Philadelphia a group of American patriots were signing their names to a Declaration of Independence. A few years later, after Spain had joined France in an anti-British alliance, Father Serra would enjoin his brothers to pray for the success of the Revolution.

In the next decade Santa Barbara, San Jose, Los Angeles, and others were added to the thin line of missions around which was to be gathered the romantic history of old California. There were also four military *presidios* and three small towns along the coast, but even as late as 1800 a Spanish population of only twelve hundred lived there. In California the mission system prospered as nowhere else, chiefly because the Indians were not warlike, olive trees flourished, grain grew bountifully, and sheep and cattle multiplied so rapidly that whole herds had to be slaughtered for lack of an adequate market. Equally important was the fact that white settlers did not swarm in to disrupt the situation. In the later eigheenth century, Spanish settlers were not swarming anywhere, and in any event there were vast tracts awaiting potential claim seekers in the more accessible southern areas. The gold for which Coronado and others had searched so tirelessly was not discovered until after the American flag flew over the *cabildo* in Monterey—a fact which Methodist Bishop Matthew Simpson would interpret as a sure sign of God's special role for the United States. The *presidios* were there, of course, and with them came the perennial conflicts between secular and ecclesiastical authority that were the ugliest feature of the church's work in New Spain. But in California the Franciscans had less interference than elsewhere, and the full scope of the mission idea could be expressed, not least because their work was led for fifteen years by a friar who to an unusual degree combined an intense ascetic piety with great administrative ability. By every external standard, indeed, Father Serra seems to have embodied the Spanish ideal of the missionary as saint.

Each of California's twenty-one missions was adjacent to a village where from one to three thousand Indians lived. Between 1769 and 1845 perhaps a hundred thousand of them were baptized through the labors of 146 Franciscans, of whom 45 were at work in 1805—their year of maximum strength. After they had been won from their wilderness ways, they were given the rudiments of Christian nurture, then fitted to the demands of a hundred Western tasks. In the Spanish sense of the terms, they were Christianized and civilized. They tilled the land, herded stock, tanned cowhides, built roads and bridges, and in order to raise a mission chapel, they quarried stone, hewed beams, and molded bricks. At the period of greatest prosperity there were in the twenty-one missions over 230,000 head of cattle, 268,000 sheep, 8,300 goats, 3,400 swine, 3,500 mules, and 34,000 horses, with the farms yielding 125,000 bushels of grain.

The missions were thus the most important institutions of Old California, undergirding both its social and economic life. Aside from them life was meager. Towns were small, soldiers had few duties, and Indians did the work. Government was at a minimum, the viceroy was far away, the king farther still. Life was slow, graceful, and easy.

LIFE IN THE BORDERLANDS

The Spanish domains which became parts of the United States were all borderlands. Advances into these areas were always chiefly defensive; and in every case except Arizona and New Mexico the initial threat was imperial—British, French, or Russian. This was a frontier civilization: vastly different from the peculiarly Anglo-American frontier about which Frederick Jackson Turner launched his bold thesis, yet a frontier nevertheless. To interpret the life of the area, this fact must always be kept in mind, for none of these border provinces attained the complex cultural development of the Spanish lands to the south. Although a score of Spanish-American universities conferred 150,000 degrees before 1821, formal educational institutions were virtually nonexistent in the borderlands. Books were exceedingly rare. The Far Southwest did not have its first printing press until after Mexican independence. The chief artistic achievements were architectural, for the Spanish mission occupies an honored place in the procession of great occidental architectural styles. Its unique loveliness is not owed merely to borrowings from the Moorish, baroque, or classical, or even the American Indian, but rather to a creative, harmonious, and profound response to the demands of the spirit, the land, and the times. Nowhere else have frontiers led to the creation of such timeless beauty.

The most important institutions peculiar to the borderlands were the *presidio* and the mission. The former was the military outpost, consisting usually of an unruly company of soldiers which the padres wanted to keep as far from the Indians as possible, and a commander whose efforts to aggrandize his power and profit often precipitated a clash with the clerics. The mission, on the other hand, represented the religious and educational—and thus the civilizing—forces on this remote frontier. In addition to these major institutions, there were many private ranches, or *encomiendas,* often originating with generous grants and almost invariably dependent on Indian labor. Finally, there were the widely scattered towns which grew up around military or governmental centers and became by a natural process the centers of trade and of whatever social life existed. There were, properly speaking, no cities in the borderlands except perhaps New Orleans, but it was Spanish only from 1763 to 1800.

The fundamental feature of the borderlands was the Spanish way of life itself, which not even the rude demands of the frontier could deprive of grace and color. An English gentleman who visited Saint Augustine just two years before Florida was purchased by the United States in 1819 caught something of its character:

> I had arrived at the season of general relaxation, on the eve of the Carnival, which is celebrated with much gayety in all Catholic countries. Masks, dominoes, harlequins, punchinellos, and a great variety of grotesque disguises, on horseback, in cars, gigs, and on foot, paraded the streets with guitars, violins, and other instruments; and in the evenings, the houses were open to receive masks, and balls were given in every direction. . . .
>
> Dancing formed one of their most common amusements. . . . These assemblies were always informal, and frequented by all classes, all meeting on a level; but were conducted with the utmost polite decorum, for which the Spanish character is so distinguished.[7]

[7] G. R. Fairbanks, *The History and Antiquities of the City of Saint Augustine* (1858), quoted by Herbert Ingram Priestly, *The Coming of the White Man, 1492–1848,* History of American Life Series, vol. 1 (New York: Macmillan Co., 1929), pp. 80–81.

The same impression is provided by the picture of California
towns during the late 1830s painted by Richard Henry Dana
in his *Two Years before the Mast* (1840). It is worth quoting
at length.

It was a fine Saturday afternoon that we came to anchor at
Monterey; the sun was about an hour high, and everything
looked pleasant. The Mexican flag was flying from the little
square presidio, and the drums and trumpets of the soldiers, who were out on parade, sounded over the water,
and gave great life to the scene. There is no working class
(the Indians being practically serfs, and doing all the hard
work) and every rich man looks like a grandee, and every
poor scamp like a broken-down gentleman. I have seen a
man, with a fine figure and courteous manners, dressed in
broadcloth and velvet, with a noble horse completely covered with trappings, without a *real* in his pockets, and absolutely suffering for something to eat.

The women wore gowns of various texture—silks, crape,
calicoes, etc.—made after the European style. . . . They
wore shoes of kid or satin, sashes or belts of bright colours,
and almost always a necklace and earrings. . . . If their
husbands do not dress them well enough, they will soon receive presents from others. . . . Next to love of dress, I
was most struck with the fineness of the voices and the
beauty of the intonation of both sexes.

The houses here as everywhere else in California, are of
one story, built of adobe. . . . Some of the more wealthy
inhabitants have glass to their windows, and board floors;
and in Monterey nearly all the houses are white-washed on
the outside. . . . The Indians . . . do all the hard work,
two or three being attached to the better houses, and the
poorest persons are able to keep one at least; for they have
only to feed them, and give them a small piece of coarse
cloth and a belt for the men, and a coarse gown, without
shoes or stockings, for the women. . . .

Nothing but the character of the people prevents Monterey from becoming a large town. The soil is as rich as
man could wish, climate as good as any in the world, water
abundant and the situation extremely beautiful. The har-
bour, too, is a good one. . . . There are a number of English and Americans . . . who have married Californians,
become united to the Roman church, and acquired consid-

erable property. Having more industry, frugality, and enterprise than the natives, they soon get nearly all the trade into their own hands.[8]

Are such descriptions within the proper realm of religious history? It would seem so. They form an authentic picture of a way of life nurtured by centuries of Roman Catholicism as it prevailed in the Latin civilizations of Europe. These modes of living are as important as the missions and the padres. They are as rooted in church history as Puritan severity; and as Dana's final paragraph suggests, the lineaments of each culture were to have a crucial bearing on the growth and conflict of empires in the New World. The prevalence of this "un-American" way of life helped perpetuate the colonial status of New Mexico and Arizona—and during the so-called Progressive Era even delayed their admission to statehood for a decade.

THE SPANISH HERITAGE

The nineteenth century brought rude shocks to the vast Spanish Empire. In the home country the impact of the French Revolution and Napoleon's invasion was in many respects annulled by the Congress of Vienna and the reestablished monarchy. But in the New World, where the United States now stood for another type of revolution, the old imperial order sustained heavy blows. Led by Miranda, Bolívar, San Martín and others, independence was won in country after country. In Mexico it came in 1821—just three hundred years after Cortez's victory over Montezuma. But the initial royalist conservatism under Augustín de Iturbide soon yielded to three decades of political chaos during which Texas won its independence. In 1819, meanwhile, Spain had sold Florida to the United States lest it be lost without remuneration. By 1854 all of New Spain that was ever to become part of the continental United States had been obtained through revolution, annexation, conquest, or purchase. We very naturally ask, therefore, what was the religious significance of these vast acquisitions?

[8] Richard Henry Dana, *Two Years before the Mast* (New York: Penguin Books, 1948), pp. 73–86.

In evaluating the American legacy from New Spain, one's first temptation is to accept Father O'Gorman's summation:

> In time the work of the Spanish Church in the territory of the United States extended from 1520 to 1840. . . . In space it extended from the Atlantic to the Pacific. . . . It was a glorious work, and the recital of it impresses us by the vastness and success of the toil. Yet, as we look around us today, we can find nothing of it that remains. Names of saints in melodious Spanish stand out from maps in all that section where the Spanish monk trod, toiled, and died. A few thousand Christian Indians, descendants of those they converted and civilized, still survive in New Mexico and Arizona, and that is all.[9]

Yet this minimal statement will not do. The marks of Spanish Catholicism on American religious and cultural life were more deeply etched. Aside from the large Spanish-speaking ethnic minority in the United States, much of which has come from Puerto Rico and Cuba as well as from Mexico, considerable weight must be given to the place that old imperial Spain occupies in the consciousness of all Americans, though especially of Roman Catholics. Because the federal Union came to include most of the Spanish borderlands, many Americans can draw sustenance from the fact that the country's oldest heritage is not Puritan but Catholic. Other Americans are usefully reminded of Spain's larger cultural achievement, a work that Herbert Eugene Bolton has eloquently described:

> One of the marvels in the history of the modern world is the way in which that little Iberian nation, Spain, when most of her blood and treasure were absorbed in European wars, with a handful of men took possession of the Caribbean archipelago, and by rapid yet steady advance spread her culture, her religion, her law, and her language over more than half of the two American continents, where they still are dominant and still are secure.[10]

[9] Thomas O'Gorman, *History of the Roman Catholic Church in the United States*, ACHS, vol. 9 (New York, 1895), pp. 111–12.

[10] Herbert E. Bolton, *The Mission as a Frontier Institution in the Spanish-American Colonies*, pp. 1–2.

Within this larger memory, moreover, the Spanish mission has lived on as symbol and inspiration—through crumbling ruins in New Mexico, the haunting beauty of Santa Barbara, or at the Alamo, now a shrine overlaid with still other kinds of memory. The mission represents a concern for Christian conversion and a humane regard for primitive peoples despite the background of governmental corruption, ecclesiastical cynicism, and ruthless subjugation. The missions, of course, were instruments of imperial politics, and their immense economic involvement inevitably affected their inner life. They also encouraged a kind of serfdom which, early and late, led to violent uprisings. In the northern borderlands which became part of the United States the end effect was worse than elsewhere. Due to the small Spanish population and the attenuated cultural context, the Indian was left in a state of disorientation, uprooted from his old ways, yet unwesternized. But from beginning to end the missions did bear witness to an ideal that was far removed from the savagery of the *conquistadores* and the exploitative social order that prevailed in succeeding centuries.

These developments north of the Rio Grande naturally invite attention to the work of missionaries in New Spain generally, and to the long record of holiness and zeal written by the Dominicans, Jesuits, Carmelites, Augustinians, Mercedarians, and, above all, Franciscans, who together accomplished one of the most epoch-making expansions in the history of the church. In 1521 Pope Leo X gave extravagant authority to the Franciscans in this new mission field; and after 1524—when their first company arrived—they swiftly won a reputation for piety, zeal, and effectiveness. By the time Don Juan Zumarraga became the first archbishop of Mexico in 1533, he reported that they alone had baptized one and a half million Indians. Other orders were soon engaged with equal vigor, and within a century Mexico south of the Rio Grande was at least superficially a Christian country. Certain characteristics of the indigenous culture and its religions made their work easier, as the utter failure to Christianize or subdue the Apaches and Comanches serves to indicate. A willingness to adapt to the religious tendencies of the Indians was equally important. But a passion for saving souls was the prime necessity—and this passion the spirituality of the Spanish church provided in abundant measure.

An excellent indication of the success as well as the

methods of Spanish evangelism is the great shrine of Our Lady of Guadalupe, one of the richest and most lavishly decorated of Mexican churches, which was erected on "the very place sacred to the goddess Teotenantzin, 'mother of gods' who among all the figures in the Mexican pantheon, most closely resembles the Holy Virgin."[11] The Mary beheld in the miraculous portrait which is the central object of veneration for the throngs who visit the church is in every feature an Indian.

From the legal standpoint the Indian was from the first a subject of the crown. For the Spanish ruling class in Mexico, the Indian was an underling, not a caste apart (given the shortage of Spanish women), but above all a source of labor, a peon; and in the long run he was to respond with resentment, revolution, and anticlericalism. The church, though inescapably part of this cloven society, unequivocally regarded the Indian as a child of God and sought to bring him within her embrace. The Dominican Antonio Montesinos (ca. 1486–ca. 1530) inaugurated a campaign to prevent the rise of Indian slavery, and Bishop Las Casas (1474–1566) was successful in gaining its formal prohibition. It was the friars, however, traveling on foot, living amid the Indians without wealth or display and learning their languages, who came to understand the Indian: "In contrast to the chronicles of the great military leaders or aristocratic observers of the Conquest," writes Mariano Picón-Salas, "the friar-historians, who

[11] Charles S. Braden, *Religious Aspects of the Conquest of Mexico*, pp. 302–07. Our Lady of Guadalupe is the name of a picture, transferred to a church, and thence to a town. The events connected with its origins are among the most remarkable in the church history of sixteenth-century New Spain. On 9 December 1531, just a century before the settlement of Boston, a fifty-five-year-old Indian, a Franciscan neophyte, beheld a vision of the Virgin, who bade him ask the bishop to build a church at that spot. On the next day, fulfilling the demand for a sign, she instructed him to pick roses in a certain place, though they were out of season. He did, and brought them to the bishop. As the Indian opened his tilma to exhibit the roses, however, he discovered upon it the now famous picture of the Virgin. The church was built and, upon becoming New Spain's most popular shrine, has been repeatedly enlarged. In 1754 Pope Benedict XIV decreed Our Lady of Guadalupe to be the national patron of Mexico and made 12 December a holy day of obligation.

were almost always at odds with these overlords, touched what might be called the inner life of the aborigines."[12] Because of facts such as these the achievements of the missionaries are a meaningful challenge to Anglo-Saxon Protestant solutions of similar problems. It is by no means an accident that Helen Hunt Jackson's *Ramona* (1884), which was part of a campaign to reform American Indian policy, portrayed Spanish California in idyllic tones.

On the other hand, Spain participated actively in Western Christendom's rape of Africa and soon instituted Negro slavery in its empire on a vast scale, though far less in Mexico than in the islands, and almost not at all in the northern borderlands. Spanish church leaders, moreover, did not extend their solicitude for American Indians to African blacks with equal zeal, and the antislavery efforts of the Jesuit Alphonso Sandoval and others came to naught. Both canon and civil law did provide a measure of protection to slaves, but enforcement was often lax. It thus becomes apparent that comparative judgments in the complex area of slavery and race relations cannot be made until scholarship on these matters gives detailed attention to the full historical and cultural experience of each New World country.

Effect on Other Nations

The final and most enduring consequence of Spanish exploration and settlement for American religious history was that it spurred France and England to increasingly vigorous imperial activity. Quite aside from its internal qualities, the mere existence of the Spanish empire became a vital stimulus to nations which were profoundly affected by the Reformation. French Catholics, once their domestic religious wars were over, saw an opportunity to regain in the New World what they had lost in the Old; while England saw on distant shores a new Canaan that must be made safe from the encroachments of popery.

The account of English exploits must follow a discussion of the Reformation, but the establishment of New France should be viewed in conjunction with Spain. Both empires were pervaded by the influence of Roman Catholicism, and after 1701 the Bourbon kings on both Spanish and French

[12] Picón-Salas, *Cultural History of Spanish America*, p. 59.

thrones frequently collaborated in their colonial enterprises. Moreover, both of these empires stood as massive challenges to the main thrust of Anglo-American advances in the New World. Especially in the seventeenth and eighteenth centuries this "Popish menace" would condition the attitudes and loyalties of the American colonists. The anti-Catholicism thus engendered would be strengthened and further stimulated by various domestic and international factors down at least to the Spanish-American War of 1898. Well into the twentieth century it was a vital component of Protestant patriotism and a spur to expansionist ambitions.

American religious history is strangely incomplete if Europe's competition for American empire is ignored. We proceed, therefore, to a survey of the empire which the French tardily launched, and in which pre-Reformation piety and counter-Reformation zeal were far more pervasively evident than in France itself.

4

THE CHURCH IN NEW FRANCE

During the fierce winter of 1604–05 the entire American empire of France consisted of one miserable colony which lay freezing and half-dead with scurvy on the little island of Saint Croix in Passamaquoddy Bay. Yet this winter of suffering was the prologue to a continuous process of French expansion which would end only with the fall of Montcalm on the Plains of Abraham a century and a half later. In sharp contrast, the Lions of Castile had already in the sixteenth century been borne to the heartlands of two continents, and a new Spanish colonial civilization had taken root. By 1604 Mexico City had a cathedral, a university, and two theological seminaries. Indians were kneeling at the shrine of Our Lady of Guadalupe. Saint Augustine was an established citadel-town, and New Mexico had been subdued.

Why, one may ask, was France so dilatory in pushing her colonial enterprises when for many reasons she might have been first? Cousin, it is claimed, sailed to Newfoundland in the 1480s; and fishing fleets from Saint-Malo and other Breton and Norman ports made repeated voyages to the Grand Banks during the fifteenth century. Cardinal Richelieu, moreover, was essentially right in declaring that "No realm is so well situated as France to be mistress of the seas, or so rich in all things needful." Why then were not these early expeditions followed by many more? The answer is not easily given.

It is true that under Francis I (1515–47) the potential prosperity of the French people began to be realized. But the very force of this fact brought France into the fierce dynastic struggles of the period, causing her to dissipate her energies on the battlefields of Italy and Spain. For a time the king

himself was a hostage of his bitter rival the Emperor Charles
V. An uneasy truce followed the Peace of Cambrai (1529),
but soon another shadow fell across the realm. The Protestant
Reformation shattered the unity of Roman Christendom—
and with it the unity of France. In 1534, the year that
Jacques Cartier first sailed into the Saint Lawrence Gulf, a
brilliant young lawyer from Noyon was converted to evangelical views and forced to flee the land. And in 1536, the year
Cartier returned from his second voyage, this lawyer—John
Calvin—dedicated his *Institutes of the Christian Religion* to
the French king in an immortal preface which assured that
monarch he had nothing to fear from a revival of evangelical
Christianity.

With the Concordat of Bologna (1516), Francis I had
gained a drastic subordination of the church to the state. Yet
he vacillated for a time in his attitude toward the reformers
—for political reasons and because a strain of piety and
humanistic concern ran strong in his own family. Then after
1533 he adopted a policy of vigorous suppression which was
continued by his successors, but the strength of the Protestant party nevertheless continued to grow. Between 1562 and
1594 France was ravaged by the Wars of Religion. It had
become a nation divided against itself.

At several points the balance of power was such that the
Huguenot Admiral Coligny was able to send out small colonies to the New World. In 1564 one such group went to the
Saint Johns River in "Florida," where it was viewed as a
threat to the interests of Spain and annihilated by Menéndez,
the founder of Saint Augustine. Coligny himself was struck
down in the massacre of Saint Bartholomew's Eve (1572);
and another period of bloody fighting began. The assassination of Henry III in 1589 left Henry of Navarre, the Huguenot hero, as the only surviving heir to the throne. But
because not even a victorious Protestant could hope to rule
France peacefully, he renounced his "heresies" and was received into the Roman Catholic church. (As cynics have put
it, he decided "Paris was worth a Mass.") He became Henry
IV, founder of the Bourbon dynasty. Protestant liberties were
secured by the Edict of Nantes promulgated at Henry's insistence in 1598. Thus peace came to the distracted kingdom,
which then entered upon another era of prosperity and
power.

The interest in overseas empire, however, was still small.

Henry and Sully, his great minister of state, shared the immemorial view of Frenchmen that there is no place like France, and so did little more than yield grudging permission to adventurers of various types. First, they undertook a series of mere trading voyages. The De Monts colony, already mentioned, set forth in 1604. It, too, would have been only another dismal episode, had not one of its survivors been Samuel Champlain, the royal geographer and a man of extraordinary vision and determination. Champlain aroused renewed interest in the colonial venture, and in 1608—on the third of his eleven voyages to Canada—he founded Quebec. All but eight men perished in that first Canadian winter; but by the time of his death in 1635 Champlain could believe that a permanent foothold had been gained. Meanwhile other Frenchmen returned to the Bay of Fundy and began to make Port Royal a center of French influence.

French outposts in North America rested on an exceedingly tenuous footing, remaining little more than fur trading posts until Richelieu's rise to power in 1627. Richelieu was far more interested in aggrandizing royal prerogatives and advancing the French cause in European power struggles than he was in colonies, but he gave New France at least a semblance of support. He organized the Company of One Hundred Associates to control and sustain the colonists in Canada, and encouraged positive measures for settlement. These steps, however, were more impressive in theory than in substance.

COLONIAL POLICY AFTER 1663

After the death of Cardinal Mazarin, who had continued the policies of Richelieu, Louis XIV assumed personal responsibility for foreign policy, including the work of colonization. This was in 1661. Two years later Canada was made a royal domain. The old Company was upbraided for its pitiful performance and dissolved; supervision was transferred to the intendant (a new royal office), and a Sovereign Council composed of the governor, the bishop of Quebec (after 1674), and five councilors appointed by the king. In addition, the new minister of finance, Jean Baptiste Colbert, promoted a thoroughgoing mercantilist policy whereby the mother country was to enjoy a trade monopoly in its colonial empire. Under Colbert, France became a serious competitor of her European rivals in the race for empire.

The condition of Canada was nevertheless still deplorable, chiefly because of her widely scattered population. About twenty-five hundred traders, officials, and priests were clustered in small, isolated settlements which were totally defenseless against the ever menacing Iroquois. The new form of government also failed to inaugurate an era of peace and prosperity, for the governor was often arrayed against the royal intendant on one hand and the bishop on the other. Brushes with the British frequently led to bloody battles along the disputed border line. And after the passing of Colbert and Louis XIV, military and economic support from the homeland became sporadic and undependable. Yet in spite of these difficulties, New France continued its immense territorial expansion.

In a sense, the source of both the expansion and its difficulties was that dreamer, adventurer, and explorer, René Robert Cavalier, Sieur de la Salle (1643–87). It was he who first conceived the highly contagious idea of a greater New France. After a series of incredibly long and difficult expeditions, he convinced the royal court that the fleur-de-lis should fly over a fortified area extending from Quebec to the mouth of the Mississippi, and from the headwaters of the Ohio to the Rocky Mountain springs of the Missouri. This would make New France a vast inland empire covering the entire Great Lakes basin and the heart of the North American continent. La Salle's own colonizing venture at the mouth of the Mississippi ended in tragedy, but the grandiose idea had been sown.

The next years saw a series of ventures in expansion. Pierre le Moyne, Sieur d'Iberville, established Fort Maurepas on Biloxi Bay in 1699, while his brother, Jean Baptiste le Moyne, Sieur de Bienville, planted New Orleans in 1718. Fortresses were built at crucial points in the north: Louisbourg on Cape Breton (1720), Niagara on Lake Ontario (1720), Vincennes on the lower Wabash (1724), and several others, including Fort Duquesne (Pittsburgh) in 1753. In the west Pierre Gaultier de Varennes, Sieur de la Verendrye, prepared to defend the Saskatchewan and the Missouri valleys (1734, 1738).

The area thus fortified was both thinly populated and

badly governed. John Law's infamous Company of the Indies had backed the founding of New Orleans in hope of speedy profits, but maladministration threatened the very existence of the settlement. In 1731 "Louisiana" was rescued from total pandemonium by being placed under royal control as Canada had been, with a governor and an intendant. But by this time the end of French domination was near.

In 1713 at the Treaty of Utrecht the Hudson's Bay area was signed away to England. Even more vitally, so was Nova Scotia. Around Port Royal the old French inhabitants were at first permitted to remain, but later (during King George's War) they were suspected of anti-British activities. In 1755 Colonel Charles Lawrence, governor of Nova Scotia, drove six thousand Acadians into exile. Their tragic fate entered the American consciousness belatedly with the publication of Longfellow's *Evangeline* in 1847. In 1762 the entire Louisiana territory was ceded to the Bourbons of Spain to keep it out of English hands, and so it remained almost until the Louisiana Purchase of 1803. By that time Canada, too, would be gone. It was ceded to Great Britain in 1763, but General Wolf's capture of Quebec in 1759 was the decisive military event.[1]

France may have been late in entering the competition for empire in America; her efforts may have often miscarried; her colonial government may have been haphazard or unwieldy; even her greatest successes may have been impermanent. But taken as a whole, New France was an astonishing achievement, and its church-historical dimension both in the mother country and in the vast reaches of North America merits our concern.

---

[1] France's "race for empire" was a peripheral but inseparable part of a great European power struggle which dated at least to the Reformation era and included, later still, the devastating Thirty Years War (1618–48). Usually included among the "French and Indian Wars" on the North American continent are the following:

Date	In Europe	In America	Major American Results
1688–97	War of the League of Augsburg	King William's War	Treaty of Ryswick. Port Royal, though

Date	In Europe	In America	Major American Results
			captured by English, returned to France.
1701–13	War of the Spanish Succession	Queen Anne's War	Treaty of Utrecht. Hudson's Bay area and Nova Scotia (Port Royal) ceded to England.
1740–48	War of the Austrian Succession	King George's War	Treaty of Aix-la-Chapelle. Louisbourg on Cape Breton Island though captured by English and colonials, returned to France.
1756–63	Seven Years War	The French and Indian War	Treaty of Paris. All of continental New France in Canada and east of Mississippi ceded to England. Spanish Florida to England; Louisiana territory, west of Mississippi, ceded to Spain.

In America all of these wars involved intermittent but often cruel and bloody border fighting, burnings of towns, massacres, and continuous feelings of suspicion and hostility. Each war also featured one or more military efforts on a larger scale. After the "World War of the American Revolution" England returned Florida to Spain, who sold it to the United States in 1819. Napoleon recovered the Louisiana territory from Spain in 1800, but sold it to the United States in 1803.

THE ECCLESIASTICAL BACKGROUND IN SEVENTEETH-CENTURY
FRANCE

Royal Absolutism and the Church

In France as in Spain, church and state were closely inter-
woven, and both institutions had been powerfully affected by
the rise of national feeling. Though France had no *Real Patronato* granting her rulers nearly papal powers in governing
the ecclesiastical establishment, both king and clergy were
exceedingly jealous of "ancient Gallican liberties." Philip IV
had defied Rome by disputing papal claims to supremacy and
cutting off papal revenues, and had forestalled excommunication by imprisoning Pope Boniface VIII in 1303. The
"Pragmatic Sanction" of 1438 and the Concordat of Bologna
(1516) had further reduced papal authority in France. The
quondam Protestant Henry IV showed scant solicitude for
papal desires; and as his Bourbon successors accelerated the
trend toward royal absolutism, the papal voice in French
affairs became increasingly weak. Louis XIV, with the concurrence of Bishop Bossuet, declared in 1682 that the temporal sovereignty of kings was independent of the pope, that
a general council was above the pope, that the usages of the
French church limited papal interference, and that the pope
was not infallible. Louis also successfully appropriated the income from all vacant bishoprics.

One must not conclude, however, the Gallicanism loos-
ened the ties between church and state within the nation;
actually it strengthened them. Churchmen could and did
serve as statesmen to advance the national interest—as did
Cardinal Richelieu under Louis XIII, the Italian-born Cardinal Mazarin during the regency of Louis XIV, and Cardinal
Fleury during the regency of Louis XV. Men like these, as
much as the kings themselves, were architects of a foreign
policy of which the chief goal was dynastic and territorial
gain. During the religious wars that wracked the continent
in the wake of the Reformation, they supported the Protestant cause (or even the Turks) against the pope and the
Hapsburgs whenever this would advance the interests of
France. And within France, king and clergy worked together,

though only so long as the latter conceded that their traditional prerogatives were a dead letter and that a new absolutistic order prevailed.

New Movements in French Catholicism

During the century in which France's colonial aspirations awakened, there also occurred a remarkable resurgence of Catholic piety. Reform in the French Catholic church had been delayed by the Wars of Religion, but a revival beginning with the coming of peace reached its peak under Louis XIV. The Society of Jesus spread rapidly and widely, opposition by the Sorbonne notwithstanding. Capuchins, Recollects, reformed Cistercians, and Benedictines were joined by newer orders in stimulating the return to purified religion.

One of the most influential of these reformist impulses was the new order of secular priests constituting the French Oratory, founded by the pioneer of modern French mysticism, Pierre de Bérulle (1575–1629). Under his successor, Charles de Condren, the oratory's interest in revitalizing the clergy continued, but Condren also became a strong champion of the devotion to the Sacred Heart of Jesus, a form of piety which before long gained a most remarkable popular appeal due to the support of the Jesuits and the testimonies of Saint Margaret Mary Alacoque.[2]

Bérulle and Condren had a decisive influence on Jean-Jacques Olier (1608–57), who founded several seminaries and through them the Society of Saint Sulpice (named for his church located in a Paris slum, where he carried on a vigorous program of reform), and on Saint Vincent de Paul (1576–1660), who formed in 1625 the Congregation of the Priests of the Mission and in 1633 the Sisters (or Daughters) of Charity. Other reformers were Saint Francis de Sales, who left a treasure of writings on the life of the spirit; Saint Jean Eudes, who established the Congregation of the Good Shepherd (the Eudists) to care for fallen women and inaugurated the liturgical worship of the Sacred Hearts of Mary and

[2] The devotion to the Sacred Heart, which experienced so strong a revival in seventeenth-century France, is an important clue to the intense and often sentimental ardor that pervaded the period. On the history and controversies related to this devotion, see Josef Stierli, ed., *Heart of the Saviour* (New York: Herder and Herder, 1957).

Jesus; and Saint Jean de la Salle, whose work in founding
schools earned him recognition as one of the fathers of modern pedagogy in France.

The Catholic Reformation in France was free from neither
theological controversy nor political interference. A revival of
Augustinianism, emphasizing divine predestination, personal
religious experience through conscious conversion, and direct
relationship of the believer with God, was promoted by
Cornelius Jansen (1588–1638), bishop of Ypres. He was
followed by Antoine Arnauld, author of *Frequent Communion;* Pasquier Quesnel, author of *Moral Reflections of the
New Testament;* Blaise Pascal, famous for his *Pensées* and a
fierce attack on the Jesuits in his *Provincial Letters;* and by a
large group of "Jansenists" centered at the abbey of Port
Royal, near Paris. Because the Jansenists were openly critical
of the Jesuits' alleged Pelagian tendencies and utilitarian
ethics, they incurred the bitter opposition of the Jesuits, who
badgered both king and pope until they secured the condemnation of Jansenism in the bull *Unigenitus* (1713).

Of a different nature was the controversy over the Neoplatonic and "quietistic" mysticism of Madame Guyon and
François Fénelon. They were opposed by Bishop Bossuet,
who persuaded the pope to condemn their views and the king
to proscribe their activities. Finally and most unfortunately
for France, the Jesuits pressured Louis XIV into revoking the
Edict of Nantes in 1685, marking the culmination of a long
process by which Protestant privileges had been gradually
withdrawn. Very soon large numbers of Huguenots, among
them some of the country's wealthiest, most industrious citizens, emigrated to Germany, Holland, England, and
America, thus dealing a severe and permanent blow to the
vitality of the French nation and strengthening the economic
and political life of France's chief Protestant rivals. For her
colonial empire, however, the revival of Catholic fervor in
France itself had a direct and powerful significance. To a
most remarkable degree the New World beyond the sea and
its heathen population became the object of pious zeal.

FRENCH MISSIONS IN AMERICA

In New France the faith and institutions of the Roman
church gained a centrality and importance that was equaled

in no other empire, not even New Spain. The statement can be narrowed further: it was not simply transplanted French Catholicism, but preeminently the Society of Jesus, which shaped the spirit of New France. George Bancroft's assertion is not significantly overdrawn: "The history of missionary labors is connected with the origin of every celebrated town in the annals of French Canada; not a cape was turned nor a river entered but a Jesuit led the way."[3]

Early Labors in the East

Before the first Jesuit team, consisting of Pierre Biard and Ennemond Massé, arrived at Port Royal (Nova Scotia) in 1611, two secular priests had been there and had baptized more than a hundred Indians. In 1615 the Recollects, a semicontemplative reform branch of the Franciscan order, began their mission out of Quebec with four priests; and that summer Fathers Le Caron and Jamet set off up the Saint Lawrence River for the country of the Hurons. But after only slight success and many difficulties with the trading company, the Recollects themselves requested aid from the Society of Jesus, not least because this would provide more leverage at the centers of power. In 1625 the first five Jesuits arrived at Quebec, and for a time the Society was assigned the sole responsibility for French missions out of Quebec. They faced a disappointing prospect. There were only fifty-one winter residents in all of New France; and the first news they received was that the Recollect Father Viel had just been drowned or murdered while returning from his mission to the Hurons. Then Champlain died in 1635. But under the leadership of Paul LeJeune the Jesuits began to write a magnificent chapter in the history of Christian missions and the expansion of New France. By 1649 eight of them had won the martyr's crown.

The story of almost any one of these early missionaries would illustrate how fervent piety combined with a passionate desire to Christianize Canada's Indians could draw men and women out of the familiar institutional life of France and impel them to sacrificial labors in the wilderness. That of Jean de Brébeuf serves as well as any. Born in 1593 to a prosperous manorial family living near Saint Lô in Nor-

---

[3] George Bancroft, *History of the United States*, 2:300.

mandy, he entered the Society of Jesus in 1617. He was serving as a college administrator when his plea to join the first Jesuit mission to Quebec was accepted. For the rest of his life —except for a brief return to academic work during the British occupation—the conversion of the Hurons was virtually his sole earthly preoccupation. Living with this harassed and plague-ridden tribe, learning its ways, preparing a grammar and lexicon of its language, trying tirelessly (for a time as superior of the mission) to win converts and to allay suspicions that the missionaries were the source of tribal woe, baptizing the dying and the newborn, he personifies the concept of total commitment. At the same time his notebooks record a personal religious life of unabated self-discipline and ecstasy: "On the 9th of May, [1640] when I was in the village of Saint Joseph, I was, as it were, carried out of myself and to God by powerful acts of love, and I was transported to God, as if to embrace Him." This union, he goes on to say, was disturbed by the appearance of an old woman whom he supposed to be the devil in disguise. In a later entry (27 May) he speaks of his experience while at prayer before the Blessed Sacrament on the feast of the Pentecost: "I saw myself in a moment invested in a great fire which burned everything which was there around me, without consuming aught. While these flames lasted, I felt myself inwardly on fire with the love of God, more ardently than I had ever been."

Nine years later the flames would be real. Just as some signs of large scale conversions were being detected, the Hurons were set upon even more furiously than before by the western Iroquois. Amid the carnage Brébeuf was captured, and after brutal preparatory punishment he was scalded and burned to death on 16 March 1649 at a village then named for Saint Ignace on the Sturgeon River, near the easternmost bay of Lake Huron. "At his death," writes the most thorough historian of these exploits, "began the irreparable ruin of the Huron nation."[4] Soon the whole Huron tribe, on whom such great labors had been expended, was uprooted and driven west to Wisconsin by the Iroquois, who were backed by the

[4] Francis X. Talbot, *Saint among the Hurons: The Life of Jean de Brébeuf*, pp. 213, 214, 300, 310. Already at his burial Brébeuf was regarded as a martyr and saint. Pope Pius XI proclaimed his canonization along with seven other Jesuit martyrs in 1930.

Dutch and English in an effort to limit French expansion and control of the fur trade. Yet the Jesuits continued their efforts undaunted, following the Hurons westward.

After 1680 the Society of Jesus also worked strenuously among the Abenakis of Maine. Among these Indians the Capuchins had conducted a mission between 1632 and 1655, but even with Jesuit aid during the subsequent years, their efforts had resulted in only a few feeble villages of transplanted converts. The arrival of Father Sebastian Râle in 1694 led to a revival of the mission and they finally gained the whole tribe's lasting commitment to the Christian faith. Unfortunately, this story is so intertwined with Anglo-French hostilities, Indian intrigue, and frontier fighting that the Abenaki mission is very difficult to evaluate. Despite his effectiveness as a missionary, events conspired against Râle, beginning in 1704, when the Indian allies of the French perpetrated the famous massacre at Deerfield, Massachusetts. In 1713 the Treaty of Utrecht conveyed Hudson's Bay, Newfoundland, and Nova Scotia (Acadia) to England. Border disputes and intermittent raiding followed, and finally, in 1722, the English declared war. Two years later Râle was shot and scalped. During the last years of New France missionary activity declined, and the work in Maine languished. Yet the Abenaki remnant was true to its new faith, and after the American Revolution they were allowed to receive the ministrations of a Roman Catholic priest.

Though not alone in their efforts, the Jesuits were also particularly successful in arousing interest in France for their projects in the New World. They recruited supporters from other orders as well as among laymen. Of greatest importance was a Sulpician group including Jean Jacques Olier himself, which obtained a grant on the island of Montreal and convinced a pious military officer, Paul Chomedy, Sieur de Maisonneuve, to lead a colony to the place. In 1641 he sailed with a small company that included one Jesuit priest and Mademoiselle Jeanne Mance, who was to found Montreal's Hospital of Saint Joseph. In the following spring, Maisonneuve began his twenty-four year stay at that dangerous outpost. Further reinforcements arrived in 1653, including four Sulpician priests and Sister Marguerite Bourgeoys, who soon carried out her intention of founding the Congregation de Notre Dame and its school for girls. After a trip to France in 1659, the two women returned with further helpers for the work—six nuns and two Sulpician priests. In time, an enclave of Sulpician influence and piety developed here, never powerful, but testimony nonetheless to a deep measure of missionary concern.

In Quebec French piety flowered similarly among courageous women. Madame de la Peltrie, of Normandy's *haute noblesse*, was a leading spirit: fired by Jesuit appeals, she devoted herself and her fortune to the Indian women of Canada, first enlisting the help of the Ursulines, a teaching order closely related in its founding to the Jesuits, then coming herself to Quebec in 1639. Under their Mother Superior, Marie de l'Incarnation, the Ursulines began a school for Indian girls. At the same time, a hospital was begun under the patronage of the Duchess d'Aiguillon by a group of nuns who arrived on the same ship with the Ursulines.

Evangelism and Exploration

In eastern Canada, missionary efforts were rendered impractical not only by the hostility of the Indians but by determined English and Dutch resistance to France and to Catholicism. Jesuit attention consequently was shifted farther west and north, far beyond Iroquois and foreign influence, until Sault Sainte Marie and the western Great Lakes region became the final scene of their labor. In this new locale their concern began to shift from evangelism to exploration. Missionary interest remained, of course, but the charting of unknown territory and careful reporting on the land and its savage people took on increased importance. The missionaries lost their early optimism.

The exemplar of these later endeavors is Father Jacques Marquette (1637–75), whose exploits have become an enduring part of American folklore. Born in Laon, he entered the Society of Jesus at the age of seventeen, came to New France in 1666, and for four years labored on the upper Great Lakes. Devout and intrepid, he was in every sense a true counterpart of the early Jesuit martyrs. In 1673 he joined the trader and explorer Louis Joliet in a search for the Mississippi River, an expedition which took them more than twenty-five hundred miles by birchbark canoe. After paddling from the Mackinac Straits through Green Bay and up the Fox River, they went overland to the Wisconsin River and down it to the Mississippi, which they followed as far as the mouth of the Arkansas River. Convinced now that the

great river emptied into the Gulf of Mexico rather than the
Pacific Ocean, and fearing to go farther lest they fall into the
hands of the Spanish, they returned by way of the Illinois
River. Here Marquette conceived his final venture, the
founding of a mission in the Illinois country. This was
fulfilled in 1674 with the establishment of the mission of the
Immaculate Conception of the Blessed Virgin at Kaskaskia
(near present-day Utica, Illinois); but Marquette contracted
dysentery on the trip and died the following spring on the
eastern shore of Lake Michigan.

Decline of Jesuit Influence

Despite their energetic efforts, the Jesuits with the passing
years gradually lost their missionary monopoly. The Sulpicians at Montreal were one small encroachment. Far more
significant, indeed, one of the most important events in the
church history of New France, was the appointment of a
bishop for Quebec. François Xavier de Laval-Montmorency
(1623–1708) was the Jesuits' own choice. Descended from
one of the great families of France, he had early been caught
up by the Catholic revival. Educated by the Jesuits at La
Flèche and the Collège de Clermont in Paris, ordained priest
in 1647 and appointed archdeacon of Evreux, he was leading
a semi-cloistered life of contemplation when he was consecrated bishop of Petraea *in partibus infidelium* and sent as
apostolic vicar to Quebec in 1659. Yet jurisdictional disputes
continued. His education notwithstanding, Laval soon intruded on Jesuit prerogatives. The archbishop of Rouen,
moreover, objected that this papal appointment violated Gallican rights.

Despite such resistance, Laval was installed in 1674 as
bishop of the newly erected see of Quebec; and in this role
he was a powerful alternate ecclesiastical force in New
France until his resignation in 1688. Enormously jealous of
episcopal authority, he made clear from the beginning to
governors, intendants, and clergy that he would be bishop in
very fact. Laval led the long, bitter fight against trading
brandy to the Indians. He founded his own diocesan seminary and obtained for it the right of transferring and recall-
ing the parish clergy of the diocese. In short, he laid foundations and established precedents that go far to explain the
resolutely church-oriented culture which ultimately flourished
in the region whose spiritual center was Quebec.

Another event fraught with great significance for Jesuit missions was the appointment of Louis de Buade, Comte de Frontenac (1620–98), as governor of New France in 1672, just as Louis XIV was becoming involved in another exhausting war. The "Iron Governor" was a capable leader, and he would demonstrate that fact even more clearly during his second term (1689–98) than during his first (1672–82). He distrusted the Jesuits because of their ultramontane sympathies and removed them on every possible occasion, replacing them with Recollects and Sulpicians wherever he could. La Salle, his great lieutenant, was in complete agreement with this view; indeed, three of the Recollects who accompanied La Salle are among the most memorable heroes of their order: the adventurous Father Louis Hennepin, explorer of the upper Mississippi and teller of tales; Gabriel Ribourde, murdered in Illinois by a band of Kickapoos; and Zenobe Membré, "the Franciscan Father Marquette," whose martyr death came in the wilds of Texas when Indians slaughtered the last remnant of La Salle's ill-fated expedition (1689).

La Salle himself never saw the consequences of his prodigious efforts, but the Cross was carried to the vast lands his enterprises opened. In addition to the overwhelming scope of the task, however, three major factors impeded missionary progress: a succession of governmental arrangements that kept civil affairs on the verge of anarchy, bitter jurisdictional conflicts between the bishop of Quebec and the missionary orders on the one hand and between the Jesuits and Capuchins or Recollects on the other, and finally, the unmistakable waning of religious fervor both among the supporters of missions in France and in the missionaries themselves. Dedicated men did give their lives to the missionary cause: at his death in 1689, after indefatigable work throughout the inland area, Father Allouez was said to have baptized ten thousand Indians. Yet in 1750 Father Vivier reported only a handful of converts and great irreligion in the scattered French villages.

In the later years of New France the Jesuits finally suffered the penalty for their aggressive advances. They came to be hated as masters of intrigue in both Catholic and Protestant countries. When Louis XIV died (1715), the archbishop of Paris forbade them to preach or hear confession in his diocese. By 1750 they were in disrepute everywhere. Portugal expelled the order from all its lands in 1759, and

France followed suit between 1761 and 1764, just when particularly evil times had befallen Canada. Spain did likewise in 1767. Harshly criticized by several earlier popes, the society was suppressed by Clement XIV in the bull *Dominus ac redemptor noster* (21 July 1773). In New France they were deported and their properties sold at public auction; and despite its recent cession to Spain, this was done in Louisiana as well.

THE LASTING EFFECTS OF NEW FRANCE

The century and a half during which France carried out its bold design for a North American empire was rarely free from conflict. The clash of two civilizations underlies the entire story of the rise and fall of New France. Every European struggle had its American counterpart in colonial retaliations and Indian wars. But from the earliest times, the blows struck by the English, whether from the mother country or the colonies, were the most decisive. There might be momentary reversals when European treaties would forfeit American conquests, but ineluctably New France yielded—at Port Royal, Newfoundland and Cape Breton, in the Hudson Bay area, and finally at Quebec and New Orleans.

This was more than mere "competition for empire," however. It was also a conflict of cultures beneath which lay two contrasting interpretations of the Christian faith. Precisely because fiercely contended religious issues underlay the constant warfare, the most enduring effect of New France on the British colonies was to intensify an already vehement hatred of "popery." The antipathy, moreover, long outlasted the political peace treaties. American Protestantism would sustain itself on memories of "the Old French Wars" until nineteenth-century immigration provided new grounds for nativist persecutions. The continued loyalty of French-Canadians to the Roman Catholic church, on the other hand, was strengthened by their determination to preserve their cultural integrity against the politically dominant British.

The third culture involved in the struggle for North America, the Indian, played a special role. Every power with an interest in America sought to use the Indians, both as protective buffers and as allies in offensive campaigns. The Dutch and later the British generally maintained an alliance with the Five Nations of the Iroquois, while the French remained friendly with the Abenakis, the Hurons, and the Algonquins. French missionary activity thus became more and more politically motivated, and Indian treachery was often charged to priestly intrigue. The way in which missionaries were regarded as a military necessity is shown by a letter of 1726 from the ecclesiastical director of the Company of the Indies in Louisiana to the French minister of the navy:

> Allow me, Sir, to detail in the present conjuncture my own remarks:
>
> 1) It is necessary to establish missionaries among the savages. We have dared to diminish our troops on the supposition they will be granted. They are, therefore, essential.
>
> 2) The first missionaries must be placed around *the savages who separate us from the English,* and since the latter try incessantly to gain them in order to stir them up against us, it is absolutely necessary that the missionaries sent to them be men of spirit, active, alert.
>
> 3) Among the religious bodies of the whole world *the Jesuits alone are such;* therefore, we need them.[5]

The Indian's strategic importance for the success or failure of individual white settlements as well as of large imperial designs ruled out benign and altruistic Indian policies on all sides. And with the passage of time not even the elimination of French competition for empire would alleviate the problem. In areas not yet open to settlement, as in the trans-Mississippi West during the days of the "mountain men," the American would prove to be quite as capable of "embracing" the Indian as anyone else. With the gradual westward movement of the American population, however, neither the French nor the Spanish "solution" to the probelm was a live alternative. Perhaps the surest fact is that only one misfortune to befall the Indian was greater than his being caught up in the crosscurrents of imperialism; his greatest tragedy was to be overrun and enveloped by the "Atlantic Migration," the centuries-long movement of Europeans into the British dominions of North America.[6]

Apart from these legacies of intolerance and misfortune,

---

[5] Claude L. Vogel, *The Capuchins in French Louisiana, 1722–1766* (New York: Joseph F. Wagner, 1928), p. 87.

[6] On the nature and extent of this continuing migration to the United States see Volume 1, chaps. 7, 31, 33; and Volume 2, chaps. 45, 57, and 59, esp. pp. 208–09.

there was a record of saintliness and heroism written by the French missionaries that challenges even the rhetoric of professional hagiographers, and in modern times it has come to be widely appreciated. Protestant Americans no longer consider Sebastian Râle as the type of the sinister Jesuit, but modify the image of the wilderness conspirator with that of the martyr dying at the foot of a cross in the village square of the tribe with the largest Christian population north of New Mexico. At the same time, the early record of holy exploits has provided Roman Catholics in America with an heroic colonial tradition.

The lasting impact of New France on American religious life has been slight. In that part of La Salle's imagined empire which became United States territory, very little that was French or Roman Catholic endured except, as in New Spain, a treasure of melodious but soon hopelessly mispronounced place-names. A few small communities remained along the Mississippi and its tributaries, but these were soon enveloped by America's westward expansion. Only in New Orleans and the Louisiana bayou country, where the transplanted Acadians settled, did anything like French culture leave a lasting deposit; and even here three decades of Spanish rule left traces of yet another culture. In this area, however, religious affairs were radically different from those in Quebec. Disorder and laxity were the rule; and not until 1785, under Spanish rule, did New Orleans receive a resident bishop. Only after the purchase of Louisiana by the United States was ecclesiastical anarchy gradually ended and a reunion of church and people attempted.

The reasons for the evanescent character of French Catholicism in the region between the Saint Lawrence River and New Orleans are readily apparent. The French were disinclined to emigrate, and as the wars of Louis XIV continued, his ministers discouraged what little migratory impulse there was. The one group that did leave in such large numbers as to affect the vitality of the nation—the Huguenots—were not allowed to settle in New France. Those who came to America contributed their wealth and acumen to the British colonies instead.[7]

[7] In 1763 the population of lower Louisiana numbered about five thousand, plus half again as many slaves; the Saint Lawrence region, about sixty thousand. The population of the English colonies, by contrast, exceeded one and a quarter million at this time.

One might expect that a lasting contribution of the French in America would have resulted from their Indian missions. Yet even here the verdict must be negative. The priests mollified the Indians, interpreted them, and probably understood them. To some degree they may have influenced tribal attitudes and politics. They also baptized innumerable infants and dying adults—yet genuine conversions were extraordinarily rare. The North American Indians were very resistant to Christian conversion. It seems likely that, even against these odds, and despite growing population pressures on the frontiers, the Indian missions in the various British colonies were more successful, though they have been far less heralded by historians.

Yet New France did not die, even though Great Britain won the French and Indian Wars. The integrity of French Canada was respected in the Treaty of Paris of 1763, and even honored (to the exasperation of English colonials) by Parliament's Quebec Act of 1774, which extended Canada's boundaries south to the Ohio River and granted the Roman Catholic church a privileged position in a highly centralized colonial government. The French Canadians continued to be a powerful faction in Canada long after it became British, doing much to keep it loyal to the crown during the American Revolution. The province of Quebec would perpetuate the spirit of the *ancien régime* long after it had died in France. Successfully resisting assimilation, this proudly French province would in the later twentieth century become the catalyst of a much larger Canadian resistance to the Americanization of the country. French-Canadians would nevertheless move in growing numbers into the New England commonwealths that had once mounted campaigns against Quebec and Louisbourg. But this is rather a chapter in the history of American industrialism, immigration, and politics.

The church of New France, meanwhile, would become a confusing element in the average American's badly focused picture of Canadian history: on the one hand, dark complicity in colonial wars, Indian massacres, and a reactionary social order; on the other, a colorful saga of intrepid explorers and supremely dedicated missionaries.

5

THE REFORMATION

The Spanish conquest of the New World had taken large strides before the great events of the Reformation shook the structures of Europe. This blow to the universality of the Roman church did provide Spain with a powerful external stimulus to missionary zeal, religious rigor, and intolerance; but the spirit and purpose of the Reformers had no other positive effect on her empire in America. When New France came into existence more than a century later, France itself had been racked by decades of controversy and religious war. But again, the work of the church in the colonial empire was inspired and conducted chiefly by those who were most determined to rejuvenate the ancient Catholic faith and to counteract Reformed influences. In both Spain and France imperial rivalries were heightened and intensified by a Counter-Reformation spirit. Except in this indirect way, however, the Reformation failed to put its mark on the colonial culture and institutions of either New Spain or New France.

On the other hand, the primarily British "intermediate empire" which in time forced its way between these two Roman Catholic giants was molded by the Reformation in ways that are almost beyond the possibility of exaggeration. Here, too, economic and imperial rivalry was a factor at once fierce and enthusiastic; but far more importantly, the spirit of the colonies that took shape along the Atlantic coast was with few exceptions informed and shaped by the spiritual resurgence which broke the unity of Roman Christendom in the sixteenth century. The Reformation, of course, was closely related to innumerable other secular developments that, taken together, constitute a decisive abrogation of the medieval tradition. The effects of this vast revolution are also visible in Britain's New World empire. But just as no true or adequate comprehension of the Reformation is possible without a vision of its setting in the late Middle Ages, so an understanding of American colonial foundations must rest on a comprehension of that evangelical unleashing which constitutes the heart of the Reformation.

The great Reformation events have roots that twine their way back into virtually every crevice of Europe's medieval experience. Interpreters of the Reformation have traditionally stressed certain historical factors. In the immediate ecclesiastical realm they point to the decay of papal prestige and the increase of corruption, which accelerated national feeling in both the secular and religious realms, aroused the advocates of conciliarism, and provoked widespread demands for reform. In the closely related area of popular piety, the growing dissatisfaction with worldly church leadership and overly institutionalized forms of religious expression, together with official unresponsiveness to the religious needs of individual Christians, spawned in virtually every part of Europe a steady succession of movements for spiritual, devotional, mystical, and evangelical renewal. The importance of underlying economic transformations is generally acknowledged, with particular stress given to the increase of commercial activity, the growth of towns and cities, important shifts in the bases of economic power, and the emergence of new social groups with increasingly secular sources of patronage.

Almost inseparable from economic transitions are political changes, both general and specific: above all, the steady rise of something that may with caution be termed the "national state," and within such states, the advent of rulers determined to overcome the splintering effects of feudal tradition, papal power, and the church's independence. The widening of certain intellectual horizons and the narrowing of others in the "Renaissance" is perhaps the most complex influence of all, for this phenomenon includes not only the rebirth of interest in the literature, art, and philosophy of antiquity, but also a renewal of interest in scholarship of all kinds and an advance in man's knowledge of both nature and mankind based on scientific observation, experimentation, and exploration. All of these modern forces tended to cast medieval formulations into disfavor.[1] Quite independent of these devel-

[1] In his important psychoanalytic study *Young Man Luther* (New York: W. W. Norton & Co., 1962), Erik Erikson speaks of

opments were others equally disturbing: the rising Turkish menace on the eastern frontier, and at least one circumstance for which not even the most zealous Marxist has been able to give an economic explanation—the appearance of Halley's comet in 1531 and other celestial visitations during the years 1554, 1556, and 1558. Religious life, theology, and the functioning of the church were profoundly affected. Specifically religious interests, in turn, conditioned the course of these secular developments.[2]

The interplay of so many convergent forces makes it impossible to designate any one person, event, or set of conditions as the *cause* of the Reformation. Nothing so demonstrates the pervasive spontaneity of the Reformation or shows to what a remarkable degree this vast uprising was the response of Europe's soul to Europe's condition as does the wide range of religious reform, redefinition, and revitalization which was manifested during its central decades. That the Reformation was in one fundamental sense a great time of Christian revival is best indicated by considering the several major forms of the impulse for renewal.

These many reform movements may with small injustice be grouped under the traditional headings: Lutheran, Anglican, Reformed, and Radical (as well as the Roman Catholic renewal already considered in chaps. 2, 3, and 4). A history of religion in America obviously cannot treat these separate movements in all the details of their entanglement with Europe's social, political, and diplomatic history. But because of their crucial importance for American Christianity, the dominant forms require brief exposition. This résumé, however, will give special emphasis to the character of the

the "grim willingness" of both Luther and Freud "to do the dirty work of their respective ages: for each kept human conscience in focus in an era of material and scientific expansion" (p. 9). He also sees "Luther's emancipation from medieval dogma [as] one of the indispensable precursors both of modern philosophy and psychology."

[2] On the terminological hornet's nest that the decade of the 1960s has built around the distinction between the secular and the religious or sacred, see p. 51, n. 4 above. I think the distinction is necessary, though the referent of the concepts keeps changing. The Reformation itself had a massive impact on this whole discussion, especially Luther, with his emphasis on the goodness of the Creation and all that is therein.

Reformed tradition (or as it is so often misnamed, the "Calvinistic" tradition). Because this phase of the Continental Reformation struck Great Britain with far greater transforming power than either the Lutheran or Radical movements, special attention must be given to its driving concerns and central ideas. In a later chapter we will consider the ferment which "Reformed" theology aroused in England, and how, quite independently of Continental Radicalism, it ultimately generated its own Anglo-American type of radical "Puritanism," which would in turn become one of the most vital elements in the foundations of American thought and culture.

THE LUTHERAN REFORMATION

When Martin Luther celebrated Mass in Rome during his visit there in 1510, he was appalled that the Italian priest at the adjacent altar had said his last amen before Luther had gone farther in the order of service than reading the gospel lesson. At San Sebastiano he saw seven masses completed in an hour; and he encountered priests who did not know how to hear confession. Only at the "German Church" on the Piazza Navona did he find liturgical practice passably reverent. Both provincialism and Germanic pride may have conditioned his judgment; yet in the years ahead Saints Cajetan of Thiene and Philip Neri would inveigh against the same liturgical abuses; and many an Italian traveler in Germany, both earlier and later, would remark on the greater religious earnestness of northern Catholicism. Catholic and Protestant historians have agreed that it was this earnestness that made the German situation critical, with Catholics lamenting that so promising a circumstance should have been disrupted, and Protestants seeing the "disruption" as a proper flowering of evangelical truth. There is widespread agreement that the prevalence of ecclesiastical abuse, clerical ignorance, and theological decadence made this vast reservoir of popular religious concern highly explosive. So long as reformist demands were merely legalistic or institutional, and so long as criticism was chiefly the game of Renaissance humanists, large-scale effects were unlikely. Only if these various types of unrest were aroused by a thorough and profound protest would the existing structure be broken. And this, as Gerhard

Ritter has eloquently stated it, was precisely what came to pass with the publication of the Ninety-five Theses and the emergence of Martin Luther (1483–1546).

> He is the man of the people, an agitator in the grandest style, and the most popular speaker and writer that Germany has ever produced. . . . He shares the moral indignation of his contemporaries over the outward corruption of the church; he uses all the slogans of anticlerical and antipapal opposition of the preceding hundred years and still outdoes them—but at the same time he is the most brilliant and profound theological thinker, the most powerful and strong-willed prophet-figure of his people, and a religious genius whose experience of faith is of unprecedented inwardness and intimacy.[3]

In this light it is not difficult to explain why, when Luther was summoned before Charles V and the Imperial Diet in 1521, the populace of Worms greeted him in the streets as a liberating hero.

Yet that aspect of the Reformation to which Luther's name is attached was not radical. The old and often used phrase, "Evangelical principle, Catholic substance," very aptly describes both Luther's intention and the Lutheran church which gradually came into existence. Though his doctrine of Christian freedom was fundamentally radical, the reformation he sought was conservative. Luther's thought had been profoundly affected by Saint Augustine, the hero if not the founder of his order; and "justification by faith," so often designated the "material principle" of Lutheranism, was preached to his satisfaction by saints and doctors of the Church in all centuries. *Sola gratia,* defended so doggedly by Augustine, recurs in Aquinas, and had been affirmed by the Council of Trent. There is considerable truth in the contention of some Roman Catholic scholars that efforts for the reunion of Christendom must be channeled toward a thoroughgoing reevaluation of Luther. There is also much truth in the Roman Catholic claim that if Luther had possessed a profound knowledge of Saint Thomas or even of the full tradition of medieval exegesis of Saint Paul, he would have been spared much anguish. But these points are at best academic, for the assault on Thomism had begun even before

[3] Gerhard Ritter, "Why the Reformation in Germany," p. 106.

the Angelic Doctor's death, and it had continued unabated. In succeeding centuries the influence of Duns Scotus, William of Ockham, Pierre d'Ailly, and John Gerson was far more pervasive than that of Saint Thomas, and new nominalistic methods of biblical interpretation were widespread. The tradition in which Luther was schooled was the *Via Moderna*, stemming from Ockham and maturing in Gabriel Biel. And this tradition probably deserved the evangelical antischolastic strictures which Luther delivered against it, as well as the emphasis on justification by faith which he championed. Moreover, his cry of "grace alone" did run counter to the prevailing emphasis of the *Via Moderna* and, above all, to the practical working of the Church's sacramental system as the average lay Christian experienced it in 1500.

The "evangelical principle" in Luther's thinking is probably most forcefully expressed through his *theologia crucis* (theology of the Cross), in which he elucidated the righteousness of God and God's gift to man.

> All good things [he said in 1518] are hidden in the Cross and under the Cross. Therefore they must not be sought and cannot be understood except under the Cross. Thus I, poor little creature, do not find anything in the Scriptures but Jesus Christ and Him crucified. For Jesus Christ is every benefit which is attributed to the righteous men in the Scriptures, such as joy, hope, glory, strength, wisdom. But He is a crucified Christ. Therefore only such people can rejoice in Him as trust and love Him, while they despair of themselves and hate their own name.[4]

Luther was to repeat again and again that only the Word in preaching and sacrament was the vehicle of God's grace; but he always returned to his insistence that there must be a death of self and a new birth in Christ. His famous emphasis on Holy Scripture was also rooted in the *theologia crucis:* he insisted that the substance of the Bible was the central divine act—God's judgment and forgiveness in and through the incarnate, crucified, and risen Jesus Christ. This is "the Gospel" and this message shaped Luther's understanding of both Old and New Testaments, freeing him from literalism and the

4 From a lecture on the Psalms, 1518. Quoted by Regin Prenter, "Luther on Word and Sacrament," in *More about Luther* (Decorah, Iowa: Luther College Press, 1958), pp. 65–66.

trammels of traditional interpretation. Probably never in the history of the Church has any one person shown such rich theological insight in biblical interpretation, or made the Scriptures speak to people with such power and relevance. Basic to this timeliness and ethical relevance were three other persistent themes.

One was the conception of Christian freedom expounded in his classic treatise *On Christian Liberty* (1520). It left no ground for legalism (or salvation by the law), but rooted man's faith, love, and hope in God's unbounded mercy, and defined the Christian life as a free response to God's self-giving love. Here one also perceives his opposition to a *theologia gloria* according to which the visible Church was a safe ark of salvation if only one climbed aboard and obeyed the captain's rules. A second theme was his understanding of man as "at once justified and sinner" (*simul justus et peccator*) which stood squarely across the tempting road to perfectionism and spiritual arrogance, at the same time that it turned man to acts of love in this world. Finally, Luther's thought was suffused by a deep emphasis on God the Creator. All the orders of Creation—that is, the institutional structures of the secular world: family, government, marketplace, etc.—were seen as divinely ordained means of serving one's neighbor in one's vocation. Every just human calling was an opportunity for "faith active in love." Man's proper response to God's love-engendering deed in Christ lay in the callings of this world, not in withdrawal from them or in ascetic denials of man's essential nature. If we remember the enormous degree to which the Church had, for a thousand years, been directing Europe's most talented and pious people into the clergy and the monastic establishment, the full force of this Reformation demand becomes more apparent.

That there is much "Catholic substance" in these insistences goes without saying; but the most explicit witness to Luther's basic conservatism, and the most momentous for the subsequent development of the Reformation churches, is his stand on the sacraments, especially the Eucharist. He made his position explicit at the Colloquy at Marburg in 1529—possibly a watershed in Reformation history—where Luther and Melanchthon met the reformers of Strasbourg and Zurich, Martin Butzer and Huldreich Zwingli. "Hoc est corpus meum: this is my body," Luther wrote on the table; and no amount of discussion could shake his insistence on

Christ's Real Presence in the sacrament. Better the Roman Mass, he would declare, than to understand the Lord's Supper in memorial, symbolic, or spiritual terms. *Vos habetis alium Spiritum quam nos,* "You are of another spirit," was his famous summation; and because Luther also had grave doubts about advancing the evangelical cause by force of arms, the great alliance projected by Zwingli and Landgrave Philip of Hesse was unachieved. Zwingli seems to have been moved from a purely memorial to a more spiritual view of the sacrament by these and other discussions; and Calvin would later teach a noncorporeal presence which was still closer to the Lutheran position. Yet the cleavage remained a basic point at issue between the Lutheran and nearly all other phases of the Protestant Reformation.

Luther and his successors would face "the floodgates of Protestantism" in Germany as well; but these experiences with radicalism only strengthened Lutherans in their conservatism. Their protest was not against the time-honored government, vestments, and liturgy of the Church; it was a reform within traditional channels, which entirely justifies the term "magisterial reformation." In Sweden even the apostolic episcopal succession remained unbroken, and in Scandinavia generally the externals of worship and church government were continued. Luther all his life denied that there was any "Lutheran" church; and the Augsburg Confession of 1530, which became the great manifesto of his evangelical cause, was one of the most remarkably irenic documents of a polemical century.

The writings of Luther and the news of his deeds soon reached far beyond the borders of Saxony, arousing intellectual and spiritual ferment in Germany, England, the Netherlands, France, Switzerland, Austria, Bohemia, and Scandinavia. In countless places unquenchable evangelical movements of reform arose, and often extremist elements carried the movement far beyond Luther's intention or desire. In other areas traditional views and powers quickly asserted themselves. Within a decade or two of the Peace of Augsburg (1555), however, churches acknowledging the Augsburg Confession had been formed in most of the provinces of Northern Germany, along the Baltic, and in Scandinavia. By 1580, when the Formula of Concord was agreed upon by many of these churches, Lutheranism had achieved something like its "classic" positions on the main disputed issues, and had established itself for the most part in the areas where it would continue to prevail for centuries despite wars of religion and continuing controversy.

THE REFORMED TRADITION

Before the pope or the emperor or even Luther had fully realized the significance of the events in Wittenberg, an almost completely independent series of Reformation events took place in Switzerland. There, as elsewhere, discontent was rife. A scandalous incident of indulgence selling, parallel to Luther's encounter with Tetzel, had occurred, and in some respects conditions were particularly acute because the Confederation itself and especially the cities within it had attained an independence which the church's diocesan arrangements did not recognize. The bishops were not only corrupt symbols of an older feudal order; they were also foreigners. Other nationalistic motives included widespread resentment against the use of Swiss mercenaries. By 1523, the magistrates of Zurich, led by their great preacher-theologian Huldreich Zwingli (1484–1531), had instituted a full-fledged purge and reform of the church. On some points Zwingli voiced the central demands of Luther, as in his denunciation of works-piety and the proclamation of justification by faith. But he went much farther: the Mass was abolished, its liturgy denounced, and frequent celebration of Holy Communion discouraged. The traditional government of the church was disallowed; and very soon, as the Zurich example took effect in the other German cantons of Switzerland and then in many parts of Germany along the Rhine, this movement assumed a characteristic theological spirit and religious temper. As it advanced into the French cantons and into France itself, it merged with other reformist impulses of humanistic spirit, and gained some of its most influential apostles. William Farel, for example, left the evangelical group at Meaux and helped to prosecute the reform in French Switzerland. The movement began to take on the main features that mark it as a distinct phase of the Reformation. In fact, the Reformed tradition was an established reality by the time John Calvin (1509–64), another French humanist, was converted to evangelical views in 1534, the year after King Francis I embarked on a positive policy of repression. Calvin became a major prophet with the publication of the first edition of his mighty *Institutes of the Christian Religion* in 1536, and he continued to imbue the Reformed movement with confidence and theological rigor. Although in many ways he sought (though largely without avail) to make that movement less radical, basically he became a part of it. For this reason it is more accurate to speak of the tradition with which he is so inseparably associated as "Reformed" rather than as "Calvinistic." The power of his words and the influence of his work is incalculable. After Geneva became his permanent home in 1541, he stands out as the chief source of energy and inspiration during the "second phase" of the Reformed tradition's development. Especially important among the new areas won during this period were Scotland and the Netherlands.

Calvin very directly influenced John Knox (c. 1513–72), the man who came almost to personify the Scottish Reformation. Knox was an admiring participant in Geneva's reformation during his exile, and upon his return in 1558 he brought his native land decisively into the Reformed tradition, laying the groundwork for a system of presbyterian government which would in later years have vast influence on American church order.

In the Netherlands, the early seeds of Reformation were sown by many Augustinian canons regular who perpetuated the devotional emphasis of Gerhard Groote and Thomas a Kempis, by Lutheran writings and converts, and by considerable Anabaptist activity. Gradually, however, Reformed ideas (with much help from Calvin) came to dominate the Protestant movement. In 1571, strongly influenced by the French Reformed, the Dutch adopted the Belgic Confession prepared ten years earlier by Guy de Bres. The conversion of William the Silent in 1571 was a vital turning point for these provinces, and by 1609 they had thrown off Spanish domination and become an independent Dutch republic.

In France, too, as we have seen (chap. 4), Reformed views made considerable headway. In 1559 a synod met in Paris and took its stand upon the Gallic Confession which, like its sister confession in the Netherlands, owed much to Calvin and the Reformed tradition. The movement's growth led to fierce wars of religion and an ambiguous sort of Huguenot "victory" under Henry of Navarre, though he abjured his Protestantism in order to occupy the throne in 1589. Henry soon flouted papal desires, however, by promulgating an edict of toleration in 1598 which remained in effect until revoked by Louis XIV in 1685. There were also significant Reformed advances in Bohemia, Hungary, Austria, Poland, in the German Rhineland and, as will be indicated later, in England.

The lineaments of the Reformed outlook on God, man, society, and history have become very familiar; but both familiarity and controversy have obscured the genius and power of the movement with which Calvin's name is inseparably associated. The best clues to the animating spirit of this movement are the confessions which its leaders formulated, defended, and died for: the Heidelberg Catechism in Germany, several Helvetic confessions, the Belgic, Gallic, and old Scottish confessions, and most detailed of all, the formularies issued by the Westminster Assembly in Great Britain (1643–45). The themes that run so consistently through these great confessions and the writings of their chief expositors deserve reiteration; for they are ideas which had an enormous impact on subsequent history. For the United States they were to become a powerful culture-forming influence.

First of all, one must underline a truism and designate the notion of God's awful and absolute sovereignty as a central precept. One historian argued that this emphasis on God's eternal decrees gave theological grounds for the Puritan's disinclination even to celebrate the Festival of the Incarnation, Christmas. This goes too far, but not in the wrong direction. The majesty, power, "otherness," utter transcendence, and unknowableness of God were themes upon which Reformed thinking and meditation constantly dwelled. Early and late this austere Hebraic legacy led men away from sentimentalism, triviality, and all efforts to cajole the Almighty.

If God is sovereign, man is not. The doctrine of human depravity also stood to the fore in Reformed preaching, and with it, in all of its sharp clarity, a doctrine of "double predestination," that God in his almighty wisdom had elected some men to eternal salvation and reprobated others. Within the Reformed churches organized dissent from this strict logic did appear—notably in the School of Saumur (France), among the Arminian "Remonstrants" of the Netherlands, and, as will appear later, in Great Britain and America. In their early stages, however, even these deviationists did not move far from the central tradition. For both the strict and moderate parties, however, the doctrine of assurance—how to know if one is among the Elect—became increasingly important. In this way the doctrine of predestination portended much, both in theory and in practice, for the future history of religious "enthusiasm." Men could not help speculating on the signs of election, nor could they help being tempted to conceive of the church as constituted by those who bore those signs. The experience of regeneration or of "God's effectual call" necessarily took on earthshaking significance. In many ways the various national or territorial "Reformed" churches were as "magisterial" as those of the Lutherans; but in their aroused concern for designating the Saints, or Elect of God, they share a vital trait with many of the "Radical" reformers soon to be discussed.

The third characteristic or theme also flows from the doctrines of divine sovereignty and human depravity, namely, the intense concern of Reformed theology for God's revealed Law. First and most obviously, this concern was applied to churchly matters. It was rarely if ever doubted that the Scriptures provide authoritative direction for the church with respect to doctrine, discipline, and worship. The visible Church, in other words, was literally "re-formed" or reconstituted according to biblical prescription, the *jus divinum*. All the rites, offices, and ceremonies that were not explicitly provided for in the Bible were prohibited, including "profane" hymnody and instrumental or polyphonic music and even great festivals like Christmas. The Sabbath, on the other hand, came to be observed with almost Judaic austerity and legalistic rigor. As in so many other cases, Calvin himself counseled moderation in the application of such reasoning; but he was by no means successful in preventing the rise of extreme legalism in the Reformed tradition.

God's Law also regulated personal behavior. Reformed theologians dissented vigorously from Lutherans and insisted that the Law was an explicit guide to human morality. They held (in the famous phrase) to the *tertius usus legis*, the third use of the Law: that it was a teacher. In this traditional formulation the first use of the Law was to proclaim God as the Creator of the universe; in this context the law in all its forms, but especially as enforced by governments, keeps the sinful proclivities of men in check. The second use was to judge man by laying bare the deficiencies of his faith and conduct, and to bring him to repentance and humility.

This emphasis on the Law led to a fourth feature of

Reformed theology, one which Puritanism would make highly consequential in America. Reformed theologians—like most Christian thinkers of the time—felt that the Church and the world, Christ and culture, existed in a tension-filled relationship. Church and world were not at odds, but neither was to be dominated by the other. Yet within this consensus Reformed thinkers to a remarkable degree regarded the world as amenable to Christian control and discipline. Even though culture was understood to be fallen, perverted, and opposed to Christ, it could be shaped and regulated—or "converted," to use the term H. Richard Niebuhr has employed in his profound analysis *Christ and Culture* (1951). Reformed leaders were thus exceedingly optimistic in their plans for reorganizing society and institutions according to their understanding of God's law. Indeed, they were made strong in their purposes by the belief that they were but instruments in God's plan for reordering human society. When coupled with the insistence that monasticism had no legitimate place in the world, and that every Christian had a calling (*vocatio*) to service and work in the world rather than to withdraw from it, this doctrine provided a sure basis for that austere "this-worldly asceticism" which devoted Reformed communities have demonstrated the world over.

A final and inclusive way in which the Law assumed a distinctive place in the Reformed tradition was through its enlivening of an Old Testament world view. The most tangible evidence of this tendency is the frequency with which Reformed adherents named their children after Israel's heroes. But of all the aspects of this Old Testament attitude, none would have more momentous consequences (for America especially) than the Puritan determination to make God's revealed Law and the historical example of Israel an explicit basis for ordering the affairs of men in this world, and their conviction that this could be done to God's glory by specific colonial commonwealths or even by an entire nation.

THE RADICAL REFORMATION

Christian radicalism, of course, is as old as the Church. The gospel is a radical message. Saint Paul was already dealing with "radical" tendencies in his letters to the Corinthians. And a long succession of often very strong heretical movements testify to the continuing tension between the world and the faith of the Christian Church. Radicalism is premodern even if we define it so as to include only those protests against compromise, acculturation, and institutionalization which become "sectarian" in form. During its first three centuries, the Church often heard demands that it be purged of all but the visible saints, that it eschew all that is formal and objective in worship, or that it establish itself as a perfectionist community withdrawn from the world. In the Middle Ages much of this potential radicalism was channeled into the monastic and mendicant orders and the lay brotherhoods associated with or similar to them. There were also signs of it among the Waldensians, the Lollards of England, and the Hussites. But in the age of the Reformation there was a mighty and immensely diversified resurgence of such radicalism. So mighty was the popular resurgence, in fact, that both rulers and spiritual leaders of the "magisterial reformation" (whether Lutheran or Reformed) feared that the "left wing" would take over. Luther rushed back to Wittenberg from his hiding place in the Wartburg to deal with the excesses of Carlstadt. And as other radical movements arose, Zwingli and Calvin showed similar fears about the Swiss Anabaptists. In Austria, the Lowlands, and around Strasbourg apprehension and controversy rose to a higher pitch. At times this radicalism in religion was accompanied by revolutionary violence, as in the Peasants' Revolt (1524) and in the seizure of the city of Münster (1534). Such actions provoked both secular repression and churchly anathemas.

In spite of persecution and polemics, however, several enduring radical movements emerged, at least three of which are perpetuated in America. One of these, the least organized, consisted of "spiritual reformers," the free spirits in every land, but especially in Spain, France, and Germany, who together constituted an almost subterranean mystical tradition. Rejecting the world and its demands, recoiling from the objectivity of formal worship, forsaking objective scriptural interpretation, living in the tradition of earlier mystics, they emphasized the primacy of spirit and the Christlike life. Kaspar Schwenkfeld (1489–1561) was one of these persecuted wanderers; and some of his followers, the "confessors of the Glory of Christ," were one day to seek refuge in Pennsylvania. Erasmus himself has been placed in this category, and there were many others, some of them highly sophisticated expositors of spiritual religion, others simpler advocates of inner peace and moral self-discipline.

More rationalistic in character were the antitrinitarians, best organized in the Socinian movements of Poland and Transylvania, but probably best remembered through the adventurous thought, and martyrdom in Calvin's Geneva, of Michel Servetus. The connection between these movements and the latter-day Unitarians of Boston would be largely sentimental, but the rationalistic tendency which they represent was to be of continuing significance during the intervening centuries.

The most widespread form of radicalism was the composite movement which included the true "Anabaptists"—those widely separated yet interrelated efforts to restore or revive the primitive Church according to the biblical pattern. Their profoundest wish was to gather a visible church of true Christians; yet their search for an adequate understanding of what form this "true Church" might take was almost as tortuous as efforts of later historians to penetrate the polemical histories of their enemies. Gradually, however, certain more or less distinct movements defined themselves despite strong centrifugal tendencies: the Swiss Brethren on whose development Conrad Grebel and Balthasar Hübmaier had much influence; the harried and wandering Hutterites whom Jacob Hutter molded into an enduring community that was at once church and *societas economica;* and the Mennonites, the largest body to survive, comprising the followers of Menno Simons of the Netherlands, whose preaching led to the foundation of many small congregations in his homeland, in northern Germany, Alsace, and elsewhere.

Unity was something that these Anabaptist groups never achieved, and it is doubtful that even the absence of persecution would have improved matters in this regard. They are nevertheless united by certain persistent convictions; above all, by the desire to reconstitute the Church as a community of earnest believers whose conversion had been sealed by adult baptism (they rebaptized, hence Anabaptist). Behind this lay their protest against state churches and their insistence that the Church as a whole had "fallen" when it entered into cooperation with rulers, identifying itself with whole peoples regardless of their personal dedication. Almost universally these Anabaptists were pacifists; personal uprightness and charitableness were the constant conditions of good standing in their churches. Their frequent refusal to deal with governments meant that invariably they experienced an enormous tension with the world of magistrates and economics. These traits drove them toward a communitarianism which was at times almost tantamount to a new noncelibate monasticism. They are best known in contemporary America as devout and sequestered communities, archaic, simple, and prosperous.

Many of the principles for which Anabaptists struggled and testified would be realized in America, above all the separation of church and state. This American tradition, however, probably owes far more to the simple fact of religious pluralism than to these harried underground churches. What the sixteenth-century radicals most relevantly manifested was the dynamic fertility of the European religious consciousness during Reformation times. They reveal with special clarity the kind of internal logic that seemed to press the reforming spirit into all social classes and out across the whole possible spectrum of theological and ecclesiastical solution.

In due season, virtually every aspect of the Continental Reformation which has here been touched upon, and many variations that have not even been mentioned, would find their place on American soil. In later chapters these events will be dealt with to such lengths as space will allow. For the present, however, it is imperative to consider more directly the way in which the Reformation was being carried out in Great Britain. From this realm would come the colonial impulses—imperial, commercial, and evangelistic—which would form the chief foundations—political, economic, and religious—of the American tradition.

6

THE REFORMATION IN GREAT BRITAIN AND THE
AGE OF PURITANISM

With Richard III dead on Bosworth Field and the army of the house of York in flight, the victorious Henry Tudor, earl of Richmond, had England's royal crown set upon his head. This was 21 August 1485. All England hoped that the long turbulence of the War of the Roses was over, and Parliament authenticated the universal desire for peace, stability, and orderly government by validating the victor's claim to reign. In November he was officially crowned as Henry VII, and four months later, as if to concede the arrival of a new day, the archbishop of Canterbury died. Ecclesiastical affairs continued in their normal course for a while, but a turning point in the history of the English church had been passed. During the next half-century, England would become capable of a world-historical role that one could hardly have expected in 1485.

THE REFORMATION IN GREAT BRITAIN

The Reign of Henry VIII, 1509–47

When Henry VII died in 1509, his energetic and brilliant son inherited a remarkably consolidated nation. Of serious rivals for the crown there were none; the feuds of Lancaster and York were past, domestic peace was sure, prosperity beckoned. Of great moment for the future of the church, governmental authority had been centralized to a remarkable degree. What his father had begun, Henry VIII continued, aided by the incomparable Thomas Cardinal Wolsey, lord chancellor, archbishop of York, and papal legate with authority over the whole English clergy. Wolsey's ability and zeal were equal to the authority given him by the king, and his pride matched his power. On the other hand, his diplomatic failures and military involvements on the Continent caused fiscal difficulties and aroused popular animosity which were ultimately his undoing. Yet his self-assertiveness had one far-reaching result: he taught his monarch how to manipulate the church. This lesson proved helpful in 1527 when Henry determined to seek a divorce from Catherine of Aragon, his brother's widow, whom he had married after receiving a papal dispensation. Even the cardinal was forced to bow to the royal will. Wolsey, failing to obtain papal sanction for the divorce after two years of negotiations, was stripped of power, accused of treason, and summoned for trial. He died while en route to London, but his enormous unpopularity was turned to the king's advantage.

Pope Clement VII at the time was a virtual prisoner of Charles V, Holy Roman emperor and nephew of Catherine; thus he had neither the inclination nor the ability to grant Henry's wish. The king decided to take matters into his own hands, and in a swift series of royal and parliamentary acts, England's ties with the papacy were cut, one by one. By 1531 the clergy had been cowed into accepting the king as "Singular Protector, only Supreme Lord, and, as far as the law of Christ allows, even Supreme Head" of the church in England. This was followed, without the qualifying reservation, by the famous Act of Supremacy in 1534. "Thus in the course of a few years Henry had carried through a major revolution . . . [in which] the Church of England had played little part. . . . It is, therefore, no exaggeration to say that the English Reformation, at any rate in its earlier stages, was 'a parliamentary transaction,' or an 'act of state.'"[1]

The same could be said for the king's next series of moves. By 1539 England's entire monastic establishment was liquidated, its vast lands transferred to lay owners, its inmates scattered, and its buildings left to moulder. This was done for money or favor, without reforming fervor or theological justification; yet so thoroughly had the institution decayed or

[1] John R. H. Moorman, *A History of the Church in England*, pp. 168–69. He in turn quotes F. M. Powicke, *The Reformation in England*, pp. 1, 38.

outlived its usefulness that not even the monks and friars offered serious resistance or manifested much concern for their vows, though at least three abbots were hanged for resisting the crown's action. People and Parliament seemed, in general, to have accepted the deed without protest.

When Henry died in 1547, the English church presented the most anomalous state of affairs in the Christian world. An enormous revolution had been accomplished; nearly nine hundred years of undisputed papal authority had been overthrown and the entire edifice of medieval monasticism spoliated. Yet doctrine was for the most part unchanged, popular piety was relatively undisturbed, and parish life went on much as before. Despite earlier signs of opportunism and vacillation, the traditional faith and order of medieval Catholicism were perpetuated by the Six Articles of 1539 and the King's Book of 1543.

But England had not been insulated from the Continental Reformation. At Cambridge Luther's writings were already stirring Thomas Cranmer and the circle of future bishops who had counseled Henry on his marital problems in 1529. Henry VIII himself had won a papal title as Defender of the Faith for an anti-Lutheran polemic. In later years, however, the king contemplated a league with the Protestant princes of Germany, and with this end in mind he and his theological counselors came close to signing the Wittenberg Articles in 1538. The Ten Articles of 1536 also exhibit definite Reformation influences. Vernacular translations of the Bible, certain to be a potent force in the nation's religious life, were beginning to circulate: and although the version of Tyndale was suppressed, the Coverdale and Rogers versions were licensed and the "Great Bible," a somewhat more tradition-minded version of "Matthew's Bible," was published by royal order in 1539.[2] Cranmer, who had become archbishop of Canterbury in 1533, was advocating plans for liturgical reform, and he succeeded in translating a great litany into English before Henry's death. The king had also put his son under Protestant tutelage.

The Reign of Edward VI, 1547–53

The son of Henry VIII and Jane Seymour was a frail lad of nine years when he came to the throne. Having received a

[2] On English versions of the Bible see n. 9 below.

Protestant education, he was hailed by some as a new Josiah to purify the Temple of its idolatries. In view of his minority, however, the real responsibility of ruling devolved upon two successive regents, both of whom were chiefly motivated by political and economic considerations. The king's uncle, Edward Seymour, duke of Somerset, was protector from 1547 to 1549 and permitted moderate reforms; he was displaced by John Dudley, earl of Warwick and duke of Northumberland, who encouraged far more radical religious policies. Thus during the brief reign of Edward VI, the nation moved many long strides down the road to reformation—though often by legislative fiat no more popular or churchly than Henry's enactments.

Gradually, however, Protestant influence began to deepen and become more pervasive. Lutheran refugees from the Augsburg Interim (1548) were welcomed, while brilliant and forceful Reformed theologians became professors in Oxford and Cambridge. Among the latter were Peter Martyr Vermigli, a former Capuchin, now a distinguished Reformed theologian, Martin Butzer, the reformer of Strasbourg, and John à Lasco, an influential Polish Protestant. Moreover, an energetic and capable group of "Henrician exiles" were back at work in the English church after instructive sojourns in Reformed centers during the previous king's final reactionary period. Under these several influences and with the hearty cooperation of the archbishop, the protectors, and Parliament, new and far more drastic reforming acts were passed. In 1549 and 1552 new prayer books were prepared and enforced by Acts of Uniformity. In 1553 the Forty-two Articles of Religion were issued; and they, like the latter prayer book, revealed a decided influence from the Reformed tradition. Although subscribing to the common Reformation doctrines, Cranmer tended toward Reformed formulations, most notably perhaps with regard to predestination and on the crucial Eucharistic issue which divided Lutherans and Reformed. He moved steadily in the direction of those views of the Eucharist advocated by Tyndale, Rogers, Hooper, and many other English reformers of the time.

Edward died three weeks after signing the Forty-two Articles, but by that time the form and spirit of the English church, as well as a whole range of externals, had been massively altered. While early Lutheran influences remained visible and important in the prayer book and English Bibles in general, Lutheran conservatism and Luther's distinctive theological emphases—especially on law and gospel—yielded to the more radical attitudes of the Reformed tradition, particularly to the evangelical reformulation expounded by Zwingli and Bullinger in Zurich, Oecolampadius in Basel, and other Rhineland reformers. To a surprising degree the theological groundwork for later English Puritanism, including its emphasis on the covenant, was laid during these years. In the same spirit, action was taken to forbid many traditional practices and ceremonies and to destroy "popish" vestments, ornamentation, and church furnishings. Indeed, John Hooper, bishop of Gloucester during these years, has been justifiably named the "father" of Puritanism. The transformation wrought under these auspices, however, was accompanied by surprisingly little overt resistance—evidence that the reforms were still lacking in depth or popular appropriation.

The Reign of Mary, 1553–58

Nothing indicates the superficiality of the Edwardian reforms as well as the astonishing enthusiasm with which the fervently Roman Catholic Mary Tudor, half sister of Edward, was welcomed to the throne, and the ease with which she persuaded Parliament to repeal nearly all of the church legislation of the previous two regimes. The only surviving child of Catherine of Aragon by Henry VIII, she felt compelled to reverse insofar as possible the national apostasy which had begun with the illegal and unholy divorce of her parents. Had Mary sought only to return to the compromise which Henry VIII tried to achieve, she might have been successful; but nothing less than a complete purge of Protestants and a full return to Rome would suit her.

In 1554–55 the Protestant bishops Hugh Latimer, Nicholas Ridley, and John Hooper were burned at the stake. The next year Archbishop Cranmer suffered a similar fate, while Cardinal Reginald Pole (who as papal legate had absolved the nation and readmitted it to the Catholic fold) was consecrated as his successor on the very next day. Three hundred others, immortalized in John Foxe's *Book of Martyrs,* "made their sad way out to face the fires of Smithfield," led by the protomartyr John Rogers, editor of the pseudonymous "Matthew's Bible" of 1537.

Popular displeasure mounted. Yet even the reconciliation

with Rome (1555) might possibly have been accepted had not Mary already sealed her doom by marrying Philip II of Spain (12 January 1554), and then by becoming deeply involved in Continental military ventures that brought defeat and humiliation to the nation. The almost simultaneous death of the harassed queen and her archbishop in November 1558 seemed like a decisive stroke of providence.

The Reign of Elizabeth, 1558–1603

The daughter of Henry and Anne Boleyn—untested but surely Protestant—succeeded to the throne. English Protestants who had been nursing their sorrow in exile on the Continent or in quiet seclusion at home waited hopefully to see what the new sovereign would do. Her decision, however, was gauged to give unqualified satisfaction to no one.

> Her father may be said to have seized the church. Her brother and sister before her had in contrary ways and with unhappy results tried to reform it. She perceived that she must govern it or be ruined. . . . What she chiefly wanted, after all, was to be queen of England and live. She had the common sense to know that her people would permit her to do this provided they also were permitted to live and go about their accustomed affairs with as little interference as might be. So, without troubling to be either logical or zealous, she made herself safe. . . . The only religious test she unfailingly insisted upon was willingness to swear allegiance to herself as the church's governor.[3]

The queen's determination to ensure the institutional continuity of the Church of England was indicated by her provision for an apostolic episcopacy. She appointed Matthew Parker, who had been ordained to the priesthood before the break with Rome (1527), as archbishop of Canterbury in 1559.[4] The principles which underlay Elizabeth's policy of

[3] William Haller, *The Rise of Puritanism*, pp. 6–7.

[4] The Roman Catholic historian Philip Hughes would refer to the English bishops as a "self-consecrated hierarchy of heretics" (*A Popular History of the Catholic Church* [New York: Macmillan Co., 1951], p. 251), and Pope Leo XIII declared Anglican orders null and void in 1896; but Queen Elizabeth was excommunicated in 1570 by Pope Pius V. Matthew Parker, her first archbishop of

comprehension and accommodation were documented in two acts of Parliament passed the same year. The Act of Supremacy designated her as the "supreme governor" of England's church and provided an oath to be subscribed by the clergy. The Act of Uniformity reinstituted a significantly moderated version of the second Edwardian prayer book (1552). The publication of a full doctrinal statement was delayed until 1563, and not until after she had been excommunicated by the pope was subscription to it made compulsory for all the clergy (1571). The Thirty-nine Articles of Religion as then promulgated were based on the Forty-two Articles of 1553, and they have never been substantially revised.

The spirit and meaning of the Elizabethan Settlement is apparent when one examines the Book of Common Prayer and the Articles of Religion. Both are clearly aimed at maximum inclusiveness within the limits of uniformity and loyalty, yet both show the continuing appeal of the influences which had been operating at the time of their formulation during the closing years of Edward's reign. The Thirty-nine Articles naturally show more doctrinal precision than the prayer book, and they indicate the immense degree to which the Reformed tradition had made its mark on the leading English divines of the Edwardian and Elizabethan periods. They are moderate, to be sure; considerable evidence of Lutheran influence remains, and at important points they are purposely vague. But it is not accidental that precise Puritan theologians like Increase Mather would at a later day find them "substantially consonant" with the rigorous doctrines of the Westminster Confession. In Elizabeth's day, however, and far more explicitly since, they were understood as an historical document rather than as a church confession, as something not to be contradicted rather than as an exposition of the church's faith.

The Book of Common Prayer, both under Elizabeth and throughout the subsequent history of the Anglican communion, has been infinitely more powerful in its influence. Quite appropriately it served as the virtual standard of doctrine in the decade preceding the promulgation of the Articles of Religion in 1571. It is by far the greatest and most lashing monument of the early Tudor phase of the English Reforma-

Canterbury, had been consecrated by four bishops, two of whom had been consecrated in the reign of Henry VIII under the old order.

tion. It garners an immense wealth of the church's liturgical treasures from English medieval, Eastern, and Lutheran traditions and renders it in an English that only the strictest Puritans could resist. The rich stamp of Cranmer's ecumenical genius remains on every page. At the same time, his sacramental doctrine is retained, along with many of the sharply Reformed features of the 1552 version, with the result that in some ways it is far more Protestant than Henry VIII would have expected, more so than many of the contemporary Lutheran liturgies. Stately in language, scriptural in quality and in much of its substance, it endeared itself to generation after generation, becoming in time the quintessential expression of Anglicanism.

Undoubtedly the Reformed spirit of the Elizabethan Settlement would have been less marked if the Queen and her immediate advisers had prevailed. But in 1559 a vigorous and numerous reforming party was already in existence, whose demands not only could not be ignored, but whose loyalty was urgently needed on account of the European political situation. At the convocation of 1562–63 these "Puritans" very nearly gained control. But even when frustrated in their more extreme efforts, they were grateful to have defender of the Protestant cause as queen, and they tempered their demands accordingly. With Continental Protestantism in confusion, Good Queen Bess was, after all, the very palladium of the Reformation's stand against the resurgent Roman host. She gave purpose, focus, and even glamor "to the fresh ideology of that age—Protestantism."[5] During the reigns of her Stuart successors her accession on 17 November was remembered as a "birthday of the gospel," and for Puritans and other opposition elements its anniversaries became a rally day.

THE AGE OF PURITANISM

The great "second phase" of the English Reformation, stretching from the accession of Elizabeth to the Restoration of Charles II (or perhaps to the Glorious Revolution), may be justly designated the "Puritan Century." From the stand-

[5] Sir John E. Neale, "England's Elizabeth" (Paper delivered on the Fourth Centenary of the Accession of Queen Elizabeth I, Folger Shakespeare Library, Washington, D.C., 17 November 1958), pp. 2–8.

point of America, the reforming movement which sharpened the religious issues of the age is so important that its nature and aims will receive more extended discussion in a later chapter (chap. 8). For the present its place in England's church history can be only briefly suggested.

Characteristics of Puritanism

Puritanism in its very vital negative aspect has been defined by Professor G. M. Trevelyan as "the religion of those who wished either to 'purify' the usage of the Established Church from the taint of Papacy, or to worship separately by forms so 'purified.'"[6] Its affirmations are inevitably more important, however, though more easily ignored. Puritans, like devoted Christians in every age, were first of all determined to conform the Church Militant to their understanding of the fact that man's redemption is of God in Christ. With remarkable intensity they focused their reformatory zeal in Alan Simpson's excellent phrases, on what they deemed to be two kinds of wickedness, that of people who appeared to be "living without any benefit of religion" and those "who had embraced the wrong religion."[7] They sought not only to "purify" England's religion, but to revive it. The peculiar power and distinctive witness of the Puritans are explained by their adherence to Reformed theology in the midst of a situation where centuries of spiritual decline and decades of political and ecclesiastical upheaval had left both clergy and laity alike, in almost every sense of the term, unreformed, and where the established institutional and liturgical forms impeded their program for renewal of the church.

The negative as well as the positive convictions which they held had been brought to England first by fugitive tracts and books, then by living emissaries like Martin Butzer and Peter Martyr; these influences in turn were constantly reinforced by a stream of letters and other writings from the Continental reformers—most prominent of which were Heinrich Bullinger's *Decades* and, later, John Calvin's masterful *Institutes of the Christian Religion*. In this way those who came to be known as Puritans drew upon a firm tradition of English Protestantism that had been established during the reigns of Henry and Edward. The returning Marian exiles, most of

[6] George M. Trevelyan, *England under the Stuarts,* 16th ed. (London: Methuen and Co., 1933), pp. 60–71.

[7] Alan Simpson, *Puritanism in Old and New England,* p. 7.

whom had taken refuge in Reformed strongholds on the Continent, added their passionate testimony to the chorus.[8] To encourage still others there was the example of Scotland, where John Knox—come straight from Geneva—had so successfully challenged the "monstrous regiment of women" and by 1560 made over the Kirk of Scotland along presbyterial lines.

The growing influence of the Bible served to increase popular dissatisfaction with England's religious situation. In fact, Holy Scripture was both the practical and the theoretical fountainhead of the movement. Among the clergy scriptural study completely renovated the role and method of theological inquiry, while among the people it created a vast hunger for evangelical preaching. Puritanism was a "movement of the Book" among an increasingly literate people, and an essential accompaniment of its expansion was the publishing of popular versions of the Bible. The earliest of these was the Geneva Version of 1560, with its highly provocative yet immensely instructive marginal notes.[9]

[8] Miles Coverdale (1488–1568), famed as a translator of the Bible but also a strenuous Puritan, was back from his third exile. He fled first in the days before the Act of Supremacy, next during Henry's period of reaction, and finally under Mary. Between 1551 and 1553 he was bishop of Exeter.

[9] The first English effort to render the Scriptures in the vernacular was that of John Wycliffe (1380), a translation of the Latin Vulgate. William Tyndale's translation from Erasmus's Greek text was printed surreptitiously in Antwerp and distributed in England after 1526. The first complete Bible in English was done by Miles Coverdale in 1535 with considerable indebtedness to Tyndale and Luther; it included the intertestamentary "apocryphal" books. John Rogers issued in 1537 a translation based on the work of Tyndale and Coverdale which was printed under the pseudonym "Matthew," and hence called "Matthew's Bible." A recension of this by Richard Tavener appeared in 1539. The "Great Bible" of 1539 was the first Bible to be specifically prescribed for use in the churches of England. It, too, was virtually a reissue of Matthew's Bible, edited by Coverdale. The second and later editions bore a preface by Archbishop Cranmer commending its use. This is the version quoted in the Book of Common Prayer.

The Geneva Bible (1560) was the work of several Marian exiles, including Coverdale. Its numbered verses, lucid prose, improved scholarship, extensive prologues, and marginal notes gave it wide popularity. It was authorized for use in Scotland, and until superseded by the King James Version, it was the most

The Growth of Puritanism

The first solid impact of the Puritan movement was felt during the days when the Elizabethan Settlement was being hammered out. Its theological leader at that time was Thomas Cartwright, a professor at Cambridge for whom presbyterianism was the only lawful, scriptural church polity, and who saw in Geneva or Scotland the proper model of a Christian establishment. Among all but the most zealous of these early reformers, however, there was little inclination to become "separatistic" or openly disloyal; most Puritans were willing to "tarry for the magistrate." They would even follow Calvin's counsel to accept the traditional episcopate when it did not hinder truth. Only later in Elizabeth's reign were there any sizable groups advocating "reformation without tarrying for anie"—in Robert Browne's famous phrase (1582).

During the reign of James I (1603–25), who as King James VI of Scotland had developed a jaundiced view of presbyterianism, royal opposition to Puritanism became increasingly overt. Among Puritans, therefore, the grounds for hope and the willingness to tarry became appreciably less. One indication of the declining optimism about national reformation was the gradual rise of increasingly congregational ways of thinking. This trend was evident even among the great theologians and preachers who had made Cambridge University, and especially Emmanuel College, a nursery of

---

widely distributed English Bible. The "Bishop's Bible," a revision of the Great Bible supervised by Archbishop Parker and carried out by him, his fellow bishops, and a few other scholars who later became bishops, appeared in 1568, but it was never widely accepted in either churches or households. The Douai-Rheims Bible (N. T., 1582; O. T., 1609–10) was translated by exiled Roman Catholics for use in England; as revised from time to time it has remained a standard Roman Catholic Bible in England.

The version which captured the hearts and minds of English speaking non-Catholics for three centuries is, of course, the one authorized by King James in 1604—his sole positive response to the many complaints brought by churchmen and theologians to the Hampton Court Conference of that year. The king himself paid close attention to the work, and the translation was accomplished by forty-seven men drawn from the best scholars of the day. It was first issued in 1611. See F. F. Bruce, *The English Bible, A History of Translations* (New York: Oxford University Press, 1961).

Puritanism. The sense of estrangement deepened as James's political behavior became more autocratic and as he showed increasingly solicitude for religious spokesmen and leaders of the Arminian, less strictly Reformed, more ritualistic type. Even then, however, the majority resisted separatism. John Foxe and others had imbued them with the conviction that England was an "Elect Nation" destined to save the Reformation; and they still hoped for some circumstance by which church and state could be bound together in a single polity and a single confession of faith. Despite the unfavorable shift of ecclesiastical power, those who yearned for a more complete purification could sustain their hope so long as the see of Canterbury was occupied by men such as Parker, Grindal, Whitgift, Bancroft, and Abbot—these men were all Calvinists, and to a degree Puritans also.

In 1625, however, Charles I took the throne, and also took to himself a Roman Catholic queen; worse still, he showed marked favoritism to a new party in the church which was both "Armininian" and dogmatically "prelatical." Charles made the leader of that party, Bishop William Laud of London, one of his most trusted advisers, and in 1633 appointed him archbishop of Canterbury. Coupled with the king's high-handed dealings with Parliament and his weak foreign policy in the face of the growing power of Roman Catholic France, these policies began to dim Puritan hopes for England's future. As a consequence the more dogmatic and especially the more congregationally inclined among them began in ever larger numbers to despair of root and branch reform. Singly or in groups some fled to Holland. Then, during the decade of the 1630s, the great Puritan migration to America took place.

When the "swarming of the Puritans" ceased, it was largely due to the fact that in 1640, after the failure of Charles and Laud's schemes for subjugating Scotland, the Long Parliament met with the antiprelatical party in the ascendancy. Episcopacy was abolished and plans for a Puritan reformation of the Church of England were carried forward with vigor. An assembly of divines was summoned to prepare a blueprint for the new establishment. To gain Scottish support the antiprelatic Solemn League and Covenant was pressed upon the English nation, and Scottish commissioners were added to the assembly. A strictly Reformed *Directory of Worship* was prepared and enacted by Parliament; a presbyterian form of church government was prescribed and partially enacted. Archbishop Laud having been executed, the assembly proceeded to formulate its famous confession, and then the larger and shorter catechisms which were adopted by the General Assembly of the Church of Scotland and, in slightly modified form, by Parliament, with the subscription of over two-thirds of England's beneficed clergy.

Taken together, these Westminster standards constitute one of the classic formulations of Reformed theology. That so many learned and contentious men in an age of so much theological hair-splitting could with so little coercion establish so resounding a consensus on so detailed a doctrinal statement is one of the marvels of the century. Nor were these formulations forgotten amid wars and violence; they remain normative in Scotland and their immense influence on the thought and practice of American Congregationalists, Presbyterians, and Baptists makes them by far the most important confessional witness in American colonial history. Insusceptible to easy or brief summary, they and the derivative confessions deserve close attention from any student of early American Protestantism. Westminster is the pinnacle confession of Reformed scholasticism of the strict predestinarian covenant school.

Westminster notwithstanding, more radical tendencies in religion soon emerged, especially in the Parliamentary army. After the execution of the king in 1649 and Oliver Cromwell's assumption of political authority, congregational "Independency" and other far more extreme groups flourished. Baptists grew in number, and left-wing sectarian movements proliferated. Toleration was soon seen as the only viable solution. To mark off their position in this turbulent scene, the Independent divines met at the Savoy Palace in 1658 to formulate the Savoy Declaration, affirming congregational principles of church order but otherwise following Westminster very closely. But by then the lord protector was dead; and in the chaos that followed, it was less than two years before Presbyterians cooperated with the episcopal party to restore Charles II and the traditional church order. The Puritans in their time of triumph had proved unable to provide peace, order, and stability, or to gain popular support and sympathy.

The restored church was Laudian without apology or mercy; compromise and accommodation were forsworn.

Successive acts of uniformity and restoration were enacted. For Puritans of all types, the Great Persecution began on Saint Bartholomew's Day 1662, when two thousand nonconforming clergymen were deprived of their livings. For Presbyterians, Congregationalists, Baptists, and Quakers—not to mention Roman Catholics and Unitarians—social inequality, imprisonment, and legal harassment became the order of the day.

Puritan nonconformity had become dissent, and the tradition continued to show considerable vitality in several ways quite apart from American developments. An immense spiritual treasure was conveyed to the whole Christian world through an entire library of devotional literature. John Bunyan's *Pilgrim's Progress*, the most widely read of Puritan classics, was produced during the Baptist author's twelve-year stint in Bedford jail. Other popular works included Richard Baxter's *Saint's Everlasting Rest* (1650), then Philip Doddridge's *Rise and Progress of Religion in the Soul* (1745) and the hymns of Isaac Watts. Even later, when Puritanism as an integrated theology, way of life, and intellectual movement had passed out of existence, Puritan morality would make a deep mark on both the established church and the wider ranges of English life. One historian has designated the decades before and after 1700 as a time of "moral revolution."[10] Puritanism's legacy figured strongly in the organized activities of that period and in eighteenth-century political thought.

The New Anglicanism

No less certainly forged on the anvil of the Puritan century, however, was "normative Anglicanism," which came properly into its own and took its distinctive and enduring shape during the period between 1660 and 1690. Between Henry's Act of Supremacy and the Restoration the religious travail of England had turned upon one many-faceted problem: What should Anglicanism be? What form should the church of the English nation be given? With the coming of the Stuarts to England's throne, the further question of Scotland's church was added. The Restoration settled the basic issue. Scotland was allowed to go its way with a Presby-

10 Dudley Bahlman, *The Moral Revolution* (New Haven: Yale University Press, 1957).

terian church, though "Anglicanism" survived there as a form
of recognized dissent. In England, however, episcopacy won
the day, due to the determined efforts of a fairly small group
of Cromwellian exiles led by Edward Hyde (Lord Clarendon), who until 1667 at least did more than any other statesman to steer the course of England's restored monarchy and
restored church. The Glorious Revolution of 1688–89
modified the harsher lineaments of this settlement, but the
Anglicanism which emerged from these struggles became
normative during the centuries which followed.

Several elements or tendencies vied for centrality in this
"new" Anglicanism. One was the idea of continuity with
England's Catholic past, the determination to retain traditional forms of the ministry and the ancient diocesan government of the church. Another was a preference for the liturgical forms enshrined in the Book of Common Prayer
substantially according to its Elizabethan revision, though
some six hundred minor changes were made. Both of these
factors ensured a strong link between church and state. Since
the Thirty-nine Articles were also retained, the Reformation
heritage of the church with its strong biblical or evangelical
emphasis was preserved. Most decisively, however, the idea
of a comprehensive church as it had been affirmed by King
Henry, Archbishop Laud, *and* the Westminster Assembly was
abandoned. The existence of other Christian communions in
the United Kingdom was recognized. Indeed, the expulsion
of Nonconformists created "Dissenting churches" which after
1689 were given a measure of toleration. The idea of Christian "denominationalism" as it had been formulated by a few
of the congregational "dissenting brethren" at Westminster
was thus given a kind of official recognition.

In theology "Anglicanism," though still defiantly anti-
Roman and much influenced by Puritan moral attitudes,
became pronouncedly anti-Calvinistic, Arminian, and rationalistic. In this way certain not always entirely compatible
elements of England's long Reformation experience were ret-
rospectively appropriated as "Anglican," while others were
extruded. Especially appreciated were Cranmer's liturgical
reforms, the King James Version of the Bible, Richard
Hooker's views on polity, law, reason, and tradition, the
irenic rationalism of the Cambridge Platonists, and the
preaching tradition and forms of piety associated with
George Herbert, Lancelot Andrewes, Jeremy Taylor, and

other kindred spirits. Within strict institutional limits "normative Anglicanism" was by nature broad, undogmatic, and, as time would shortly reveal, extremely open to the new currents of "reasonableness" associated with John Locke and the Enlightenment.

The reign of Charles II (1660–85) was religiously ambiguous, in that "Anglicanism" was firmly established and enforced despite the prevailing laxity in public morals. For Puritans and Roman Catholics it was a time of persecution, as the king's solicitude for the latter was harshly countered by Parliament. Charles II was received into the Roman Catholic church in his last hours, and his brother and successor, James II (1685–88), was avowedly a Catholic. He remained "governor" of the Church of England, and like his brother, he sought unsuccessfully to win toleration for both Dissenters and Roman Catholics. Unpopular in any event, he was forced in the brief Glorious Revolution to flee the realm and thus make way for Parliament's settlement of the crown on his Protestant daughter, Mary, and her Dutch Reformed consort, William of Orange. Nonjuring Anglicans who refused to swear a new oath of loyalty, including four hundred clergy, six bishops, and the archbishop of Canterbury, were deprived, and in due course they were replaced by men more agreeable to the "revolution." The Bill of Rights as well as a toleration act was passed in 1689. Non-Anglicans continued to suffer many humiliating disabilities and inequities, but England moved into a new and clearly postreformation phase of its history with Parliament greatly enhanced in its authority and as an officially Protestant country.

In retrospect, the impact of the Puritan century on English civilization is incalculable. R. H. Tawney's judgment on this point is not exaggerated:

> The growth, triumph and transformation of the Puritan spirit was the most fundamental movement of the seventeenth century. Puritanism, not the Tudor secession from Rome, was the true English Reformation, and it is from its struggle against the old order that an England which is unmistakably modern emerges. But, immense as were its accomplishments on the higher stage of public affairs, its achievements in that inner world, of which politics are but the squalid scaffolding, were mightier still. . . . The revolution which Puritanism wrought in Church and State was

less than that which it worked in men's souls, and the watchwords which it thundered, amid the hum of Parliaments and the roar of battles, had been learned in the lonely nights, when Jacob wrestled with the angel of the Lord to wring a blessing before he fled.[11]

What is true for England applies equally to America. By the most remarkable happenstance, almost the entire spectrum into which Christian life and thought were refracted by the tumultuous English Reformation was recapitulated in the American colonies. Sometimes the circumstances were strangely reversed, with Quakers dominant in Pennsylvania, Roman Catholics in Maryland, and Congregationalists in New England—while Anglicans often found themselves an unprivileged minority. In the colonies, moreover, private and public life could respond to all of the vital forces unleashed by the Reformation. In one colony or another each major reformatory tradition would gain full expression; and because of the principle of toleration, other non-English traditions would in due course make their contribution. Persecution and harassment of minority groups would also erupt in the New World, but ultimately all churches would flourish in a degree of freedom unknown elsewhere. Puritanism, above all, would leave a legacy in America no less significant than the impact of Luther upon the German nation.

[11] R. H. Tawney, *Religion and the Rise of Capitalism*, p. 165.

7

EMPIRE, COMMERCE, AND RELIGION: A SURVEY
OF EARLY COLONIZATION

Just how merry "merrie England" was in the late fourteenth century when Geoffrey Chaucer told his tales has been a subject of violent dispute. There is little doubt, however, that England's economy was stagnant, that her people were poor, and that immediate prospects for improvement were dimmed by the large role of agriculture, serfdom, and the manorial system in her national life. But by the time of Shakespeare, this state of affairs had changed no less drastically than the language itself. The two intervening centuries had witnessed steady but in the long run drastic social change. Continental demands for wool had disrupted the old methods of farming, so that herds of sheep now grazed where serfs had toiled. With the increase of available manpower, textile manufacturing had grown in importance; new markets were being sought and found. Towns grew, trade guilds were formed, and the rising merchant class gained increasing economic and political power. During the years 1575–1620 these several trends culminated in a minor industrial revolution.

As money circulated more freely, economic localism was less pronounced and dependence on foreign shipping declined. Merchants and rulers alike became convinced that a favorable balance of trade, and hence the inward flow of more money, was necessary for national prosperity. With the centralization of government under the Tudors came acceptance of the mercantile system, which in turn meant redoubled efforts in the search for advantageous markets and a growing desire for a colonial empire. The chief purpose of this chapter, however, is not to follow these internal developments but to survey the process by which England reached out across the Atlantic. First to be considered are the new land itself and the fate of its native Indians. Then will follow an account of colony-founding on the North American mainland and an examination of the way in which the economic, imperial, and religious aspects of this complex sequence were interrelated. In subsequent chapters each of these colonies or groups of colonies will be discussed separately with special attention to its religious significance.

THE NEW LAND AND THE FIRST AMERICANS

The land which England was now poised to occupy was vaster and richer than anyone then knew; but the English would discover only very slowly that its wealth was not like that which had dazzled Cortez and Pizarro. The material abundance, so decisive in shaping the character of future Americans, was not there for the taking; it would have to be produced by an industrious people—and their slaves. Between the dream and the achievement of a flourishing colonial empire, however, was the Indian.

The British knew, of course, that the terrain of the future United States was already inhabited. In fact, the conversion of heathen tribes would figure prominently among the stated objectives of imperial expansion in the New World, and long-lasting stereotypes of the Indians, as well as of the newly discovered Africans, were already taking shape. Yet nobody knew or could have guessed how diverse these indigenous people were, or how resistant to conversion and incorporation they would be. As for the Indians—who have so often been depicted standing on the shore in friendly expectation as a sailing ship hove into view—they even less could have imagined that the ships would not stop coming until the greatest folk migration since the Germanic invasions of Europe had brought over forty-five million rapidly multiplying people to America.

The Indians living north of present-day Mexico in 1600 probably numbered around a million. More conservative estimates run toward 750,000, which is not far from the size of the Indian population of the United States and Canada in 1970. Their presence in America was the result of a long process that had begun possibly thirty thousand years ago during the last glacial age and continued for perhaps twenty centuries. Asian peoples of widely differing physical types and speaking diverse tongues seem to have made their way across Bering Strait (and possibly by sea to points other than Alaska) and then slowly spread out over the two continents, moving in various directions for a variety of reasons, adapting to the land in such ways as the topography and other tribes allowed. (A three-mile move per week could bring a nomadic group from California to southern Argentina in seventy years—though no one has suggested that such a journey was ever undertaken.)

By the time European settlement began, Indian civilization had achieved a degree of stability, though intertribal conflict continued, and a war between the Iroquois and Hurons was in progress when the French arrived on the St. Lawrence. All of the habitable areas were occupied, albeit very thinly, by more or less Mongoloid peoples who had no more in common than the varied Caucasian peoples of Europe. The Indians north of Mexico were divided into more than two hundred linguistic groups which spoke mutually incomprehensible languages and many dialects, about half of which survive. Beneath these groupings were many civil or tribal organizations, some very small, others large and, as with the Iroquois, politically complex. Despite many enclaves and anomalies, the Indian population was also divided into widely variant cultural groups according to the distinctive means of existence prevailing in various physiographic regions of the country. All across the far north from the Aleutians to Greenland were the Eskimos, the most linguistically unified group and probably the latest to arrive. In almost all of the other areas the confusion of tribes and tongues was more pronounced: the vast Athabascan region west of Hudson's Bay, the great plains, the northeastern and southeastern woodland areas, the north Pacific, the northwest mountain-plateau area, California, and the far southwest. The major differences in ways of life among these regions (and many subregions) had much to do with geography and climate, and most present-day Americans know or can imagine something of the variety that prevailed.

Likely to be forgotten, however, are the vast changes in the Indian way of life that would reach all the way to the Pacific even before Americans began scouting the trans-Appalachian region. "The hunting economy of the red man," writes one sympathetic and experienced scholar, "was doomed from the moment that prancing Arab chargers were taken off the Spanish caravels; from the moment that the crude cannon and muskets of Champlain sounded out across the waters of the lake that bears his name. It was a doom slow in progress, but as inevitable as the procession of day and night."[1] Whether doom was that inexorable can be questioned, but there is no doubt that even by 1750 the horse had altered the lifeways of almost every tribe from the Mississippi to the mountains—while guns, traps, and the fur trade were extending their effects far out beyond the Great Lakes and into the upper Missouri. Spanish Christian culture, meanwhile, was moving northward from Mexico and after 1769 into California. Defensive needs were already leading to intertribal cooperation and confederation.

With regard to the Indian's religion, the modern American imagination falters. The Christian has considerable difficulty understanding the piety of the Jew (and vice versa), but the spiritual life of the pre-Columbian Indian is removed at another order of magnitude. Beyond this fact is the sheer diversity of cultures. Ruth Benedict, for example, tells how one type of supernatural vision experienced in many North American tribes functions differently in each of them.[2] Anthropological and archaeological data on fertility rites, harvest festivals, war and sun dances, death and birth ceremonies, or chants and prayers for rain and the healing of disease are phenomenologically empty unless described in a precise cultural context. But with distinguished anthropologists disagreeing on the interpretation of individual tribes, generalizations about *all* of the tribes must be of the simplest sort. It is almost futile to speak of "Indian religion" in general. One can say perhaps that the American Indian, like other peoples, stood in awe and relative helplessness in the face of the mysteries of nature and life. His religion was a response to this circumstance and a means of conditioning the forces of nature. His beliefs were animistic—the world of multifarious forces and things was animated or controlled by a hierarchy of spirits whose acts and intentions could in some degree be interpreted or conditioned through shamans and

[1] Gustavus E. E. Lindquist, *The Indian in American Life* (New York: Friendship Press, 1944), p. 7.
[2] Ruth Benedict, *Patterns of Culture*, pp. 35–40.

by appropriate ceremonies and rituals. Genesis myths often told (in diverse ways) how the world in ages past had been transformed by a culture hero whose messianic return was expected. For these and other reasons most tribes tended to regard the earth and its powers with greater veneration and respect than the Europeans who would cut down the trees and plough up the prairies. It seems clear, too, that the Indian's way of life contrasted sharply with the Puritan view of work and individual advancement. Western acquisitive society with its notions of fee simple land tenure mystified and outraged him. Though he sought the new trading wares, he did not envy or imitate the ways of the newcomers, and with surprising tenacity he maintained his own culture despite deprivation and mistreatment. For this reason prophecies of cultural "doom" and predictions of assimilation have been only very slowly borne out. Indians of the Taos Reservation who in 1970 had 48,000 acres of land returned to them made their plea on religious grounds—this land was sacred to them, nature is their church, Blue Lake their *sanctum sanctorum*. Essential to our understanding, however, is the fact that the religion of each of the many tribes and nations upon which the white man intruded was a functional element of its culture. The sanctions and consolations of religion were and are intricately related to a whole way of life. The gun, the horse, and the trap, therefore, were as powerful instruments of religious change as the missionaries; and the subsequent encroachments of modern technology, individual wage earning, private property, and American politics would have an even heavier impact. From the earliest days, however, the most massive and irresistible instrument of change was the arrival, year after year, of more immigrants whose livelihoods in Europe had been disrupted by strange unbidden social forces not totally unlike those which may have led the Indians to leave the Asian continent long before. As these new Americans occupied the land and moved westward frontier after frontier, the United States became a theater of more direct contact between Indian and European peoples than was the case in New Spain.

As actors in this great continental drama Junípero Serra, Jacques Marquette, Johan Campanius, and John Eliot (to name four dedicated missionaries, Spanish, French, Swedish, and English Puritan) committed their lives to very similar evangelistic aims; they all sought to Christianize the Indian. Yet the differences between these mission enterprises were enormous, and they sprang from the large imperial situation. New Spain, with vast lands and few immigrants, would seek to integrate the Indian into a New World form of Western Catholic culture. New France during the brief and harried existence of its great forest empire would seek (with very modest success) to convert Indians to Christianity within the old tribal context. The Anglo-American empire, with equally vast lands, but with immigration accelerating at a rapid rate, would for more than two centuries treat the Indians as independent nations or wards of the government who had a right to a share of the land; most Christian missions were conducted within that assumption and on reservations. Yet as settlement moved westward countless battles and wars were fought, an American epic was written, and as Teddy Roosevelt would say, the West was "won." Yet the principle of the Indian's right to land, despite centuries of perfidy, would not be abandoned, as 55,340,000 acres in his possession in 1971 still attest. Yet most of the land (almost all of the good land) was cleared of its earlier inhabitants in the name of progress and the greatest good, and the Indian was pushed into various pockets and corners. During the late decades of the twentieth century, when the idea of inevitable progress seemed less convincing than in its nineteenth-century heyday, the Indian's inexorable absorption and disappearance is neither advocated nor predicted with the old confidence. When every aspect of America's racial dilemma was being reconsidered and when an environmental crisis had awakened a nationwide need for the Indian's respect for nature, the questions of cultural encounter and Indian policy were receiving renewed attention. But this by no means meant that a consensus on policy was any nearer than it had been a century before. Both white and red Americans were still about evenly divided between "romantic" and "realistic" views, with the more forceful Indian militants moving toward their more numerous Mexican-American brethren in demanding greater equality and participation in American society rather than a return to tribal life on reservations. To say this is, of course, to get far ahead of the story—but at least a glimpse of the tragedies that lay ahead is essential to a consideration of the beginning.

ENGLAND'S COLONIAL ENTERPRISE IN AMERICA

Early Efforts

During the first century after Columbus's momentous discoveries, England's response was anything but vigorous or concerted. Authorized by Henry VII, John Cabot sailed from Bristol in 1497 and returned with enough information on the northern regions of Newfoundland, Nova Scotia, or Labrador to stimulate interest and backing for a second expedition, which carried him down the North American coast possibly as far as the Chesapeake Bay. Cabot thus by the law of prior discovery established the basis for England's claim to the northern American landmass. English interest in western lands and waters then languished for a half-century, but sprang to life upon the accession of Queen Elizabeth, for whom the papal demarcation line was more a challenge than a hindrance. John Hawkins and Francis Drake made their famous inroads on Spain's American empire in the 1560s and 1570s, while in 1576–78 Martin Frobisher led three voyages to northern waters in search of gold and a northwest passage to the Orient. Between 1585 and 1587 John Davis made three more such excursions, while Humphrey Gilbert and his half-brother, Walter Raleigh, made abortive efforts to plant colonies in the New World, on the Newfoundland and North Carolina coasts respectively.

Only after 1588, when Spain's "Invincible Armada" was swept from the seas, did England begin to attain that maritime mastery which would make possible the entertainment of imperial dreams. Again there were a series of failures; but finally on 2 May 1607, three ships brought to the mouth of the James River a company of 105 colonists, with whom the history of continuous Anglo-American settlement begins. This first planting resulted from an effort by a group of London and Plymouth merchants to establish a trading outpost in the New World. Having organized a joint-stock company, they obtained in 1606 a charter which designated two tracts of land along the Virginia coast, each one hundred miles square, for colonization. As revised in 1609 and again in 1612, the charter allowed the Virginia Company all powers "fit and necessary" for the government of the colony; and in 1619 the company saw fit to establish popular government. Exasperated by the violent factionalism among the company's leaders and dismayed by their meager accomplishments, King James finally annulled the charter in 1624 and made Virginia a royal colony.

The cost of the experiment was high. The company lost over £200,000 in the enterprise, and finally collapsed in bankruptcy. By 1616 some 1,600 colonists had been sent from England; but only 350 were still alive. By 1618 the population had grown to about 1,000, yet in 1623, despite the immigration of 4,000 more, the population still numbered only 1,200. Ravaged by Indian massacres, pestilence, misgovernment, sloth, avarice, disorderliness, and neglect, the Jamestown settlement all but expired. But Virginia survived, and the colony's unbroken church history begins immediately after the first landing, with the celebration of Holy Communion by the Reverend Robert Hunt, pastor of the struggling outpost of English civilization.

The Settlement of New England

After Virginia, the next permanent English plantations were in New England. The first of these, organized by the "Pilgrim Fathers" whom America has taken so close to her heart, was intended to be within the grant of the Virginia Company. In an epoch-making royal decision, James I had promised freedom from molestation to this radical dissenting group.[3] But they landed, apparently by accident, far to the north, within the vast grant of the Council for New England, a loosely organized venture headed by Sir Ferdinando Gorges, the mayor of Plymouth, England. Dominated by men of strong "prelatical" and royalist inclinations, the council had already begun one permanent settlement in Newfoundland; but when its other efforts came to naught, it surrendered its charter (1635), leaving the Pilgrims at Plymouth without royal title to their lands. The Plymouth colony, however, was permitted to conduct its own affairs until it was incorporated in the reconstituted royal colony of Massachusetts by the charter of 1691.

The next decade saw only desultory colonial activity in

---

[3] Concessions by the king were made, however, only after the "Pilgrims" themselves had made extremely sweeping concessions as to royal authority, even in ecclesiastical affairs.

New England. After its first agonizing winter, the Plymouth colony grew very slowly, numbering scarcely three hundred by 1630. A dozen or so other tiny outposts also maintained a bare existence at various points along the coast. The decade's end, however, was marked by the arrival of a colonial enterprise of much grander dimensions. Its beginnings lay in a fishing post established in 1623 at Cape Ann on the Massachusetts coast by a group of Dorchester businessmen. In 1626 the colonists, led by Roger Conant, moved to Salem. Meanwhile John White, a Dorchester clergyman of moderate Puritan sympathies and great missionary zeal, persuaded various Puritans of means to form a new company. This enterprising group first obtained a grant from the Council for New England; but when it was contested, they applied directly to the king and achieved one of the most surprising coups in colonial history. In March 1629 Charles I chartered the Massachusetts Bay Company with a land grant that carved the heart out of the council's vast though substantially unsettled tract. It extended from three miles north of the Merrimac River to three miles south of the Charles River, and, with the prodigality born of imperial optimism and geographical ignorance, "from sea to sea."

As the prospect for Puritans darkened in Laud's England, the leaders of the company voted to transfer its charter and government to a group which was planning a large scale migration under John Winthrop. In 1630 nearly a thousand of these congregationally inclined Puritans set sail from Southampton in eleven ships. Bearing their charter with them, they crossed to Massachusetts Bay, founded a cluster of towns and established a virtually independent self-governing colony. As the prospect for church reform grew even dimmer in England and the plight of earnest Puritans proportionally more dire, New England attracted an increasingly large number of immigrants. By 1641, when the power of the king and his archbishop was finally broken, at least another twenty thousand had migrated, though not all of these were of one mind in theological matters, and a fair number had no more than a passing interest in church affairs. Yet the Bible Commonwealth which they founded and settled endured as such until its charter was revoked in 1684.

Although the Bay Colony held the dominant place in New England, neighboring colonies soon were founded. In 1632 Massachusetts men began exploring the Connecticut Valley where the Dutch and later Plymouth had set up outposts. Within four years practically the entire congregation from Newtown had migrated with their pastor, Thomas Hooker, to found a new colony. As others joined the trek, settlements grew at Windsor, Hartford, and Wethersfield; and by 1662, just before it was joined with New Haven, Connecticut included fifteen towns. Though often remembered for its more liberal franchise, this colony was a Bible Commonwealth pervaded by much the same spirit and ideals as its parent colony—a fact made very clear in the Fundamental Orders adopted in 1639, and even more clear by its subsequent history.

By this time Theophilus Eaton, a London merchant, and his pastor, John Davenport, had founded another independent jurisdiction at New Haven, with affiliated settlements at nearby points. These towns formalized their relations in 1643, when they adopted a frame of government. The New Haven colony enforced stricter principles of church membership and took the example of ancient Israel more seriously than any other of the Bible Commonwealths. It lacked a formal charter, however, and much to Davenport's chagrin, New Haven was annexed to Connecticut in 1662.

Down the coast from New Haven still another Puritan outpost was founded in 1635 on a grant which two ambitious Puritan noblemen, Lord Saye-and-Sele and Lord Brooke, had obtained from the Council for New England three years previously. John Winthrop, Jr., son of the Massachusetts governor, was the first head of this small settlement at the mouth of the Connecticut River; but he enlarged the field for his administrative talents by engineering in 1644 the sale of Saye-Brooke to the colony of Connecticut—of which he became governor in 1657. In 1662 he succeeded in obtaining from Charles II a royal charter for Connecticut, whose sole title up to this point had been possession of its land and an arrangement with the Bay colony. At this time it was incorporated with New Haven, which had incurred the royal wrath by harboring three of the regicides of 1649. The younger Winthrop thus brought Connecticut to approximately its present size.

The New England colonies mentioned so far, in addition to a fair number of tributary communities in Maine, New Hampshire, and Long Island, were all in substantial agreement on matters pertaining to Christian doctrine and the ordering of God's church. So much could not be said of Rhode Island, which was founded by nonconformists expelled from the Bay Colony. By far the most important of these exiles was Roger Williams, whose irreconcilable differences with the established colonies led him to found Providence on Narragansett Bay in 1636. In the next few years, various neighboring settlements were begun by other outcasts and bold spirits: Pocasset (Portsmouth) by Anne Hutchinson and her friends in 1638, Newport by William Coddington in 1639, and Shawomet (Warwick) by Samuel Gorton in 1643. (Portsmouth and Newport united in 1640.) For this entire group Roger Williams was able to obtain from Parliament in 1644 a land patent and permission to form a government. None was established until 1647, however, probably because of the hesitancy of these freedom-loving radicals to form a central government of even the loosest kind. The first charter had no legality after the Stuart Restoration, but John Clarke, the colony's patient emissary, was able to secure from Charles II in 1663 a royal charter confirming the land grant, approving the government, and guaranteeing religious liberty. From the beginning the colony had separated church and state and offered freedom of conscience to all, with the result that it became a sanctuary for Baptists, Quakers, and other independent spirits, including those who wished freedom from *any* kind of religious obligation. Rhode Island was thus unique in New England, though its history was hardly less informed by the Puritan spirit than was that of its imperious and more authoritarian neighbors.

The Middle and Southern Colonies

The decades of the twenties and thirties, so eventful in New England, were also a time for diverse kinds of colonizing activity further south. First to arrive were the Dutch, for whom Henry Hudson had explored in 1609 the great river which bears his name. By 1624, when the first permanent settlers arrived at Manhattan Island, Dutch traders had already set up posts at widely scattered points on Long Island Sound and on the Hudson and Connecticut rivers. When Spain finally recognized the long-declared Dutch independence in the Peace of Westphalia in 1648, a major cause for emigration was removed, and New Amsterdam was only very slowly peopled by a small multinational group of settlers. In

1655, when the shifting European situation made it propitious, Peter Stuyvesant (who governed New Netherland from 1647 to 1664) conquered and annexed the small Swedish settlement that had been planted on the lower Delaware River in 1638.

The Dutch West India Company was a trading concern, never interested in a thriving agricultural community overseas, and the government it provided was harsh, dictatorial, and generally unattractive. The patroon system of vast baronial estates on the Hudson never flourished because of widespread discontent with the company's land policies, arbitrary rule, and religious intolerance. When England took possession of the little colony in 1664, therefore, there was little internal resistance and much relief in the neighboring colonies. With the duke of York (later James II) as the sole proprietor of this vast, ill-defined tract, New York became a thriving and much more religiously tolerant colony. He and his governors ruled with a strong hand, but in 1683 the need for a more adequate taxation system led to the establishment of a representative colonial assembly. The chief legacy of the colony's founders was a self-conscious minority of Dutch people and the Dutch Reformed church, which maintained a continuous and lively existence, especially in New York and New Jersey. The Swedish colony in the meantime disappeared almost without a trace. Its small population of four hundred soon lost its identity, while the Swedish Lutheran church gradually and by a natural affinity merged with colonial Anglicanism.[4]

Immediately to the south of the Swedish settlement on the

[4] The legal situation of "Delaware" (as we now call it) became uncertain after the Dutch collapse and remained so until the American Revolution. The duke of York "leased" it to William Penn in 1682; but his title to lands west of the Delaware River was very uncertain (as Penn, the duke, and most others continued to recognize). With these leases, however, Penn asserted effective rule over the "three counties" (a subdivision of the area instituted by Governor Andros of New York in 1680). The people in the "lower counties" remained restive, however, and finally gained the right to secede in the Pennsylvania charter of liberties of 1701. Their separation was authorized by the Privy Council in 1703 and exercised in 1704. Its governor was appointed by the proprietor of Pennsylvania, but otherwise the territory was a royal colony, though it was never closely regulated, nor were the laws of its assembly reviewed in England.

Delaware arose another almost contemporary colony. Maryland, though English, was in some respects even more alien to the emerging pattern of settlement than the Dutch and Swedish colonies. It was conceived by George Calvert, Lord Baltimore, secretary of state under James I, a former stockholder in the Virginia Company, and founder of an unsuccessful Newfoundland colony. After becoming a Roman Catholic, Calvert obtained in 1632 an extremely liberal proprietary grant from Charles I. By no means a simple charter for a trading company, this grant resembled a feudal fief that awarded the proprietor the independence and authority of a "Count Palatine." When carried into actuality by his son Cecilius, the colony purported to be chiefly a refuge for harassed Roman Catholics; but to achieve this end it became necessary (or at least highly expedient) to establish the principle of toleration. Maryland has the distinction of being the first colony to announce this principle, though in other respects an anachronistic semifeudal social order was planned. In the first two shiploads of colonists arriving on 3 March 1634, Roman Catholics were dominant, but from the first Protestants were a numerical majority.

The two decades between the ending of Charles I's personal rule (1640) and the Restoration of Charles II (1660) was a period of salutary neglect for the American colonies and a time of internal growth and consolidation. Political and commercial regulation was at a minimum, and only Maryland was seriously torn by civil strife—a Puritan revolution which overturned Roman Catholic rule between 1655 and 1658. A second rebellion in 1689 led two years later to the assertion of royal authority, which continued to be exercised even after the proprietary was returned in 1716 to the next Lord Baltimore, now become an Anglican. No new colonies were founded on the mainland during the Interregnum, though Cromwell's "Western Design" did involve activity in the Caribbean and resulted in the acquisition of Jamaica.

The return of the monarchy brought varied sorts of enterprises, including the formulation of more definite governmental and commercial policies. In New England, Connecticut was consolidated and chartered, Rhode Island was chartered, and the scattered settlements of New Hampshire organized as a royal colony. Several new colonies also were formed. New Netherland yielded to New York in 1664; then three and a half months later the duke of York made over a large part of his domain—Nova Caesaria, or New Jersey—to John Lord Berkeley and Sir George Carteret, who were already proprietors of an undeveloped Carolina grant. They regarded themselves as "true and absolute Lords" of this sparsely settled and disorganized tract, but their hopes for prosperity were lost in a welter of confused land grants and governmental concessions. In 1670 Berkeley finally sold his rights to two Quakers, and in 1684 the Carteret interests were sold to a group of twenty-four oddly assorted men, most of whom were Quakers. With complications thus compounded, the crisis deepened, until finally in 1702, at the recommendation of the Board of Trade, all of the proprietors were required to surrender their governmental authority, and New Jersey became a royal colony of the usual type. So ended thirty-eight years of conflict and litigation that nearly destroyed the colony.[5]

Carolina, too, originated in the immediate post-Restoration period, when in 1663 a vast tract of land south of Virginia was made over to a group of proprietors on terms similar to those for Maryland. With feudal visions even more grandiose than the Calverts', these men faced many hindrances, not least of which was their own inexperience. After several false starts, they inaugurated their enterprise in 1670 with a plantation at Charles Town, vaunting an absurd neofeudal constitution in which John Locke allegedly had a hand. Farther north around Albemarle Sound, meanwhile, other groups had settled. This "North Carolina" district received its own governor in 1712, though proprietary ineptitude and poor transportation long kept formal governance to a minimum.

The final seventeenth-century colony to be founded was the great proprietary province of Pennsylvania, whose early history is inseparable from the life and ideals of its founder, William Penn (1644–1718). Son of the great Admiral Penn, he was eminently a man of the world: sometime student at Christ Church (Oxford), Saumur, and Lincoln's Inn, friend of the duke of York, manager of his father's Irish estate, widely traveled and deeply involved in the affairs of his time. Yet he was also a man of the spirit: youthful convert to Quaker principles and their lifelong defender, friend of

[5] The governor of New York served as its governor until 1738. Reflecting the colony's dual origins, its assembly alternated its place of meeting between Perth Amboy (East Jersey) and Burlington (West Jersey).

George Fox, John Locke, and Algernon Sidney, compassionate humanitarian, mystic, theologian, and profound political theorist. No man was better fitted to undertake a colonial venture whose express purpose was to provide a sanctuary for the persecuted people of Europe. Particularly disturbed by the disabilities imposed on his fellow Quakers, he began after 1679 to lose his confidence in England; and like John Winthrop a half-century before, he set his eyes and hopes on the New World. From his involvement in the miserable tangle of New Jersey, he also knew at least one way *not* to proceed. On 1 June 1681 his charter received the great seal. There were discordant notes in that charter—its extensive grant of authority to the proprietor and his heirs, for example, in addition to its insistence on obedience to royal authority and English trade laws—but it gave the great idealist an opportunity to carry out his "Holy Experiment." For his vast, rich, inland domain, Penn provided a full set of laws, "a code of Quaker principles applied to actual government." The Frame of Government called for a resident governor, a small elective council, and a large elective assembly with very limited powers. The franchise was restricted to men with land and property. Preferential treatment for Anglicans was nominally exacted by the charter, but freedom of worship and toleration were assured for all who believed in God.

When Penn arrived in 1682, the population had already reached four thousand, and a year later people were reported to be "coming in fast." As Penn's brochures and advertisements circulated throughout the British Isles and northern Europe, the tide of immigrants swelled. Germantown was founded in 1683. Welshmen and Englishmen came too; and after the Glorious Revolution the people demanded and ultimately obtained greater political rights.

The widely divergent backgrounds and outlooks of the people brought together in Pennsylvania created many tensions and problems. In 1705 Penn himself was discouraged: "I am a crucified man between Injustice and Ingratitude there [in America] and Extortion and Oppression here [in England]." Yet as Charles M. Andrews says,

> Two circumstances favored him: his charter was less proprietary than had been the earlier ones; and he himself was an idealist. On the other hand, two things were against him: first, aristocratic by instinct, he was certain to be

influenced by the power he exercised; secondly, neither practical nor sagacious, he had to learn by bitter experience that ideals are difficult of application.[6]

Though troubles and dissensions naturally came, for the most part they were transcended. The colony grew strong and prospered despite its boundary disputes, governmental clashes, and personal dissensions. By 1709, when the British Parliament provided for the naturalization of foreign (i.e. American) Protestants, Pennsylvania flourished as a model state where people of diverse ethnic and religious backgrounds could live together under equitable laws in a single commonwealth. Despite the heavy predominance of Quakers in managing the affairs of the colony, and despite the large vestiges of proprietary privilege, its solutions to these manifold problems made it more nearly a paradigm of latter-day American democracy than any other colony.

The "Empire" in Retrospect

In 1714 Queen Anne died and the Stuart line of English monarchs passed into history. Her death marks the end of an era, making this a convenient point to cast a retrospective eye over the farflung empire created during the rule of her predecessors.

By one way of reckoning, England's seventeenth-century empire building on the North American coast would hardly be called a "burst of colonial activity." A score or so of feeble "plantings" plus two others gained by conquest constituted a few islets of Western civilization along a thousand-mile stretch of coastal plain. Such a result from a century's labor calls for moderate language. Yet compared with the colonial accomplishments of her two chief competitors (Spain and France), England's achievement assumes dramatic proportions. Pennsylvania, for example, had more European colonists in 1710—thirty years after its founding—than the whole vast expanse of New France from Quebec to New Orleans had attracted in a century. And France not only had begun her North American empire almost simultaneously with England, but had given to Quebec alone more royal subsidies than all the Anglo-American colonies had received

[6] Charles M. Andrews, *The Colonial Period in American History*, 3:303–04.

together. At the same time, the white population of Mexico also outnumbered that of New France; but the population of New England alone, containing just over a third of those in the English colonies, outnumbered the entire white population of Spain's enormous holdings in the New World—and this despite Spain's head start of an entire century. In view of these facts, the energy and vitality of the English nation arrest attention and require explanation. And in a religious history such as this one, religious factors in relation to commercial and imperial concerns must be especially probed.

RELIGION AND THE NEW AGE

The connection of the religious upheaval of the sixteenth century to England's imperial expansiveness is both undeniable and extremely difficult to describe. If even the economic effects of an objective event like the dissolution of the monasteries are nearly impossible to establish, the larger fact of the abandonment of the monastic *idea* involves long-term ramifications that overwhelm the imagination. Other problems are still more baffling. Difficulty has not stopped speculation, however, and some of the most challenging theories of historical action have been focused on these intriguing issues. Oldest and most continuously asked are questions of causation and explanation that almost any historical narrative (including this one) must confront and seek to answer.

A traditional but very superficial approach to the problem of relating religion to English colonization is the classification of colonies as "religious" or "nonreligious." In this manner, the Puritan commonwealths, Maryland, and Pennsylvania are often put in the first category, and the others in the latter. But such a procedure takes much too simple a view of the motives of both founders and settlers: in the first place, men simply do not act single-mindedly for patriotic, or commercial, or religious reasons, any more than they go to the beach single-mindedly to swim, or sun, or watch other people. Even if the founders had such a singleness of purpose, they would have been unable to exclude less purely motivated settlers from their colonies. The situation is complicated by the presence of settlements of intensely dedicated religious groups in colonies such as New Jersey or Carolina, whose proprietors were chiefly interested in profits. Another anomaly was the Puritan population of Roman Catholic Maryland, which had already become a majority when this colony's famous Act of Toleration was passed in 1649.

A much more useful mode of analysis is that which stresses the remarkable degree to which religious and missionary motives functioned in the thought of the entire age, even for Elizabethan sea dogs like William and John Hawkins. "Serve God dayly, love one another, preserve your victuals, beware of fire, and keep good companie"—thus Sir John admonished his crew when he led a slaving expedition to Guinea and thence to the West Indies in 1564–65. Later, when he quoted the Bible to excuse his failure to intercept the Spanish treasure fleet, the Virgin Queen replied, "This fool went out a soldier and is come home a divine."

The seventeenth century was an age of faith, a time when few Englishmen would take lightly any precept clearly set forth in Scripture, and when God's providence was seen behind every occurrence. Scoffers and skeptics were the exception. To forget this fact is to imperil our understanding of these undertakings. In the early colonial period the United States has its one historical contact with a civilization that was still recognizably medieval. It is thus as dangerous to attribute purely secular motives to anyone as it is to regard pious phraseology as proof of any exceptional degree of religious concern. We must also concede that no instruments are at hand for gauging the depth and seriousness of statements made or acts performed. When was a chaplain taken along merely as a talisman, and when did his presence show genuine desire to maintain Christian worship? And who can get behind the rationalizations?

More important relationships of religion, commerce, and colonization may be seen in the immense stress placed by the clergy upon the New World as a challenge to Christian evangelism. Here we face a vital chapter in the development of the British Empire, for in England the clergy played a leading role in awakening kings, ministers, merchants, and people to their obligation to carry the gospel to all parts of the earth, and especially to the New World, a Western Canaan for the claiming and evangelizing of which the English were a chosen people. There was a strong anti-Roman Catholic animus to their pleading, as well as a fervent hope that the "errors of popery" would not be sown in areas still unclaimed; and in fact, a fierce tradition of anti-Catholicism, both visceral and dogmatic, is one of Puritanism's most active legacies to Anglo-American civilization. Yet John Donne, when dean of Saint Paul's, transcended such acrimony in his lofty summons to the stockholders of the Virginia Company in 1622:

> You shall haue made this Iland, which is but as the Suburbs of the old world, a Bridge, a Gallery to the new; to ioyne all to that world that shall never grow old, the Kingdome of Heauen. You shall add persons to this Kingdome, and to the Kingdome of heauen, and adde names to the Bookes of our Chronicles, and to the Booke of Life.[7]

Few could express the ultimate vision so well as Donne; yet hundreds of others stated the same case, putting before patriots, merchants, and churchmen the challenge of a divinely appointed destiny. In the process, they took it upon themselves to prove that colonial expansion would also cure England's other ills, whether moral, social, economic, or political. On no other set of issues were all of the preachers, Conformist and Puritan, so nearly in agreement. All this took place, moreover, when the pulpit had an importance in English life that it has enjoyed in no other period.

But not even in the widespread proclamation of missionary duty do we reach the principal nexus of religion and England's expansion. The most basic aspects of the relationship are far more subtle, far less explicitly rationalized. True it may be that England was spurred to large-scale Protestant colonial expansion in North America by the challenge of Spain and France. But why, we must ask, *why* did the English respond with such energy and power? What dynamic motive underlies the swarming of the English in the New World? What is the secret not only of England's expansion but of her expansiveness? Few partial answers to these exciting questions lead into some of the most heated controversies of recent historiography. The appearance of historical interpretations based on economic materialism in its Marxian form did most to intensify these debates. Later in the nine-

---

[7] *A Sermon Vpon the VIII. Verse of the I. Chapter of the Acts of the Apostles* (1622), quoted in Louis B. Wright, *Religion and Empire: The Alliance between Piety and Commerce in English Expansion, 1558–1625,* p. 111. This valuable book has also been used and quoted in other parts of this chapter.

teenth century positivists contributed their deterministic emphasis on environmental factors. Romantics and idealists kept the controversy well heated. Concern with such issues may, to be sure, carry one beyond the traditional boundaries of church history, yet it is difficult to see how they can be avoided.

Most insistently these controversies have had to do with the relation of the great Reformation events and ideas to the growth of modern institutions, attitudes, and ideals. What effect, it is asked, did the Reformation—particularly the Protestant Reformation—have upon the rise of democracy, of individualism, and of capitalism? Each of these questions looms large in a discussion of England's energetic role in international affairs in the Elizabethan and subsequent periods. In answering, one must first insist upon the inadequacy of any simple "economic interpretation." It will never do to explain historical events, religious or otherwise, solely as functions of the social environment. Ralph Barton Perry's words are to the point:

> Men act when they decide; men act together when they agree. Having gone so far, there is no just ground for denying the potency, the unique social potency of those interrelations, reciprocities, and identities of emotion and expectation which constitute collective ideals. . . . If a factor such as an ideal makes any difference, then there may be situations in which it makes all the difference.[8]

The ideas which shape ideals have a life of their own; and, almost like meteors from outer space, many great ideas come into the world on the wings of individuated human genius—by means of a Luther, a Newton, a Rousseau, or an Adam Smith. Believed, propagated, and subtly altered by many devotees, these ideas become operative forces in history, hindering or encouraging the course of events of which they become a part.

Reformation ideas or events, of course, did not cause the commercial revolution that transformed England, any more than the economic upheaval caused the Reformation. Yet the spirit of capitalism latent in so much of England's expansion was intensified by the way in which the Reformation accentuated certain motifs of the Judaeo-Christian tradition, motifs

[8] Ralph Barton Perry, *Puritanism and Democracy*, pp. 22–23.

which for centuries had a dynamic effect on Western civilization. The Reformation, in the British Isles as elsewhere, was essentially a Christian revival in which the biblical understanding of man and history was forcefully proclaimed. This meant a renewal of concern for *this* life, *this* world, and all their impinging problems, moral and social. Other religions may be otherworldly; but the Jew, the Christian, and even the Moslem are all impressed by the prophetic demands of the Bible and its peculiar concern for the irreversible course of history, in which men participate in this world as morally responsible persons.

Beyond being simply Christian, the English Reformation was a vast and variegated evangelical revival which felt the impact of each major phase of the Continental Reformation. Most important of all was the influence of the Reformed tradition on English life; the total outlook involved in this rigorous and radical reconception of Christianity implied a whole new social order. In certain small areas and for a short time this "new social order" would be made explicit; in this fact lies the fascination (and possibly the wider importance) of New England's Bible Commonwealths. But the implicit order was equally important. This is the vital truth behind R. H. Tawney's previously quoted pronouncement that "the growth, triumph and transformation of the Puritan spirit was the most fundamental movement of the seventeenth century. Puritanism . . . was the true English Reformation, and it is from its struggle against the old order that the England which is unmistakably modern emerges."[9] In the social and political order, in other words, the expansion of Reformed and Puritan convictions had revolutionary implications; it was a threat to arbitrary and despotic governance. The English "revolution" of 1640–90 is unimaginable and inexplicable if the concomitant "Puritan reformation" is not borne in mind.[10]

[9] R. H. Tawney, *Religion and the Rise of Capitalism*, p. 165.

[10] Stuart E. Prall states that modern scholarship on the role of Puritanism in England's great upheaval of 1640–60, "has really done nothing to undermine the essential accuracy" of his title, though he also wishes to make clear that he is not dealing with the "Glorious Revolution" of 1688–89 (*The Puritan Revolution: A Documentary History*, p. x). Actually the latter revolution documented what the earlier one had wrought—and what Charles II and James II had tried to ignore. Taken together they constitute the "English Revolution."

Yet "struggle" and revolution should not be overemphasized. Richard Hakluyt, who had as great an influence on English expansion as any other single Englishman of the sixteenth century, provides an excellent case in point, for his lifelong effort to awaken England to her colonial destiny was not a "struggle against the old order" in the political or institutional sense. He had been converted to geography as a schoolboy, and he simply wanted to awaken Englishmen to their world mission. Throughout his life (1552–1616) he was a favorite of the Elizabethan court and the object of much preferment. The same could be said of many of those churchmen whom he influenced most, Samuel Purchas, for example, or George Abbot, who became archbishop of Canterbury. These men were unaware of accomplishing a revolution; yet what happened in their lifetimes was the transformation of character implicit in Reformed Christianity as a whole—not just its "Protestant ethic," or its repudiation of monasticism, or its emphasis on the "priesthood of all believers," or its advocacy of congregational or presbyterian polity. The essence of it was expressed in the archepiscopal pronouncements of every English primate under Elizabeth and James; there is more of it even in Archbishop Laud than he knew, and it reappears in more secularized form under Charles III, in the sermons of his appointee to the see of London, John Tillotson.

Elemental to this transforming power was the knowledge that God rules the world which he made, that the earth is the Lord's, that all the orders and stations thereof are good, and that man's highest worldly duty is to glorify God. Sloth and idleness dishonor the Creator. Typical abhorrence for such dishonor was shown by the Reverend Richard Eburne, when he pleaded with King James I for more royal support for the colonies. "Our so long continued rest and peace . . . our unspeakable idleness and dissolute life, have so corrupted and in manner effeminated our people generally . . . that they cannot endure the hearing, much lesse the doing of any laborious attempts, of any thing that shall be troublous or any whit dangerous unto them."[11] In other contexts the same insistence was echoed up and down the land and throughout

[11] *A Plain Path-Way to Plantations* (1624); quoted by Wright, *Religion and Empire*, p. 149.

the realm, decade after decade. Long after its overarching theology had crumbled, men spoke of the "gospel of work" in semireligious accents.

Most influential was the new emphasis on serving the Lord in one's vocation—as a tradesman, as a merchant, as an artisan, or as a magistrate or "citizen." Formerly it was thought necessary to withdraw from the tainted world in order to develop the highest spirituality; monasticism was the surest way to perfection. Now it was the life of withdrawal which was regarded as tainted and opposed to God's will. In the Reformed tradition especially, an additional premium was put on austerity, frugality, and sober living. The effect of such zeal—such "this-worldly asceticism," to use Max Weber's famous phrase—on commercial life and attitudes is apparent.[12]

There were other more subtle influences. One of these was the inevitable concern aroused in human hearts by the transcendence of God, a major emphasis of Reformed theology. This was acted out in an abhorrence of all the ways by which the Church had previously sought to make God's nature and works near and almost palpable in painting, sculpture, architecture, and liturgical ceremony. To speak in the Reformed and Puritan manner of the transcendence of God is basically to witness to his power and to the inscrutability of his ways; and in no way were these doctrines more firmly underlined than by that much-discussed doctrine of election, of God's absolute predestinating decrees unto salvation or unto damnation. This was awesome doctrine; and in a sermon-dominated age when it was preached from every pulpit—by no one more firmly than by that arch-Conformist, Archbishop Whitgift—only very blithe or very hardened souls would regard lightly the burning question of assurance: "Am I of the chosen?" And again, rare would be the person who, taking the question seriously, would proclaim his unfavored status by profligacy, dishonesty, or laziness. Reformed theology unquestionably encouraged rectitude, probity, and industry; and it did so even among those who in no way entertained

12 Max Weber, *The Protestant Ethic and the Spirit of Capitalism.* The vast ensuing literature is sampled and bibliography given in Robert W. Green, *Protestantism and Capitalism: The Weber Thesis and Its Critics.* My general inclination to Weber and kindred thinkers is apparent.

the "bourgeois heresy" that worldly success is a sure sign of election, or worse still, a means of earning redemption.[13]

Individual responsibility in religious matters was made even more explicit by the doctrine of the priesthood of all believers which the Reformers affirmed so emphatically. Most obviously, this doctrine led to the increased importance of the laity in Protestant church life. It also put a new emphasis upon personal confrontation with the great issues of the faith, thus giving still another whirl to the "inner gyroscope" which a contemporary sociologist has used to symbolize a classic but now disappearing type of personal moral responsibility. Indeed the rise of moralism was an inescapable consequence of the blows to sacramental and sacerdotal religion struck during the Puritan century. In this sense Puritanism won a resounding, long-term victory. By the time of Queen Anne "the active religious life of the whole of England, as of most of Scotland and Wales, had become Puritan."[14] In the Evangelical Revival of the eighteenth century and the Victorianism of the nineteenth, it would continue to be a dynamic factor in British life. By the affinity of its assumptions and claims, Reformed and Puritan theology also smoothed the way for the progress of social-compact notions of government, as well as for other scientific and philosophical departures from tradition.

Britain's transformation was wrought by many other forces besides religion. The New World itself, to which preachers and church leaders pointed with such eagerness, became a great frontier for all of Europe and a leaven to European life in a hundred ways. It would disrupt monetary systems as well as cosmologies. Yet in a religious age, one indeed given over to churchly contentions and rivalries that none could ignore, Christian concern was a shaping force of such strength as to be almost unfathomable to the modern mind.

[13] It may be doubted that any responsible Christian ever entertained this so-called "bourgeois heresy" in either of its forms —except perhaps as a desperate effort of self-justification.

[14] Maurice Ashley, *England in the Seventeenth Century, 1603–1714* (London: Penguin Books, 1958), p. 238.

II

The Protestant Empire Founded

Government seems to me a part of religion itself, a thing sacred in its institution and end. For if it does not directly remove the cause, it crushes the effects of evil and is as such (though a lower yet) an emanation of the same divine power that is both author and object of pure religion. . . . But that is only to evil doers, government itself being otherwise as capable of kindness, goodness, and charity as a more private society. They weakly err that think there is no other use of government than correction which is the coarsest part of it. Daily experience tells us that the care and regulation of many other affairs, more soft and daily necessary, make up much of the greatest part of government and [this] must have followed the peopling of the world had Adam never fell and [it] will continue among men, on earth, under the highest attainments they may arrive at by the coming of the blessed Second Adam, the Lord from Heaven.

William Penn, Preface to the Frame
of Government of Pennsylvania (1682)

For no country was the travail of Reformation more protracted than for Great Britain: nowhere was it more tumultuous, and nowhere were the consequences so revolutionary. It is no figment of Whiggish pride or British insularity that the Glorious Revolution (whether misnamed or not) marked the advent of modern democratic individualism and put the *ancien régime* on borrowed time. It was only in a series of almost accidental colonial commonwealths strung along the North American seaboard, however, that the distilled essence of this Puritan Revolution could manifest its full historical significance.

In the "howling wilderness" between Maine and Georgia, plans for medieval baronies were cancelled by physical circumstance. Old World commercial ventures fell into disarray. Yet of far greater importance to the gradual emergence of this strange piecemeal empire was the English government's willingness to encourage the founding of almost any kind of colony and to welcome into them almost any interested person or group, however radical or eccentric. Equally significant is the fact that nearly all who did come to America were disposed in one way or another to make the most of the liberties made available by England's revolution and America's "free air."

The most influential colony founders were those with clear, firmly held ideals and a determination to institutionalize the distinctive results of the British Reformation. Because people who shared these views were dominant in several colonies and numerous almost everywhere, the society which gradually emerged did embody many of these intentions. There were, of course, countercurrents: leaders with aristocratic ideals, and many settlers who opposed Puritan radicalism. Migrants from the European continent often had their own aspirations. Far more fateful were the importation of Africans and the steady extension of chattel slavery. Yet the coexistence of so much diversity—religious, ideological, and ethnic—tended to foster a libertarian consensus and advance the practice of religious freedom. The foundations of the

American religious tradition, therefore, are best understood through the separate consideration of the various colonial commonwealths that took shape along the Atlantic coast during the seventeenth century.

8

THE RISE AND FLOWERING OF THE PURITAN SPIRIT

Under Henry VIII England had gained a national church without reformation, but the power of Protestantism proved irresistible. In due course it visited upon Great Britain the longest and most turbulent Reformation experience in Christendom. By the time of the Glorious Revolution in 1689, the country's settlement of religious and civil affairs had gone through at least a dozen major stages, two kings had been deprived of rule, and a civil war had been fought. By this time Britain had also become a major Atlantic power, and its rapidly growing empire was becoming a prosperous extension of English civilization. Great Britain, in short, had experienced an economic, political, imperial, and religious transformation. In comparison with the changes wrought in the mother country, moreover, the colonial civilization taking shape on the North American continent represented an even more drastic break with the old order in Europe. Because unrest at home had prevented regulation of the very emigration which it had stimulated, the American colonies were developing in unexpected and unprecedented ways. Among other things, they had become the most thoroughly Protestant, Reformed, and Puritan commonwealths in the world. Indeed, Puritanism provided the moral and religious background of fully 75 percent of the people who declared their independence in 1776.[1] In order to understand the new civilization that was arising in the wilderness, therefore, a sym-

[1] If one were to compute such a percentage on the basis of all the German, Swiss, French, Dutch, and Scottish people whose forebears bore the "stamp of Geneva" in some broader sense, 85 or 90 percent would not be an extravagant estimate.

pathetic effort to comprehend the Puritan impulse is peculiarly important.

The term Puritanism in its broadest sense refers to a widely ramified movement of religious renovation that gradually took shape in Great Britain under the leadership of men who were committed to the Continental Reformed tradition. The movement began to gain a special kind of self-consciousness under the reign of Queen Elizabeth (1558–1603). During the next century its votaries increased greatly in both numbers and variety, achieving political dominance in England for a time after the Civil War, and moral dominance for a still longer period after the Glorious Revolution. From the outset these reformers were determined to achieve a threefold program for purifying the visible church: through a purging of popish remnants and the establishment of "apostolic" principles of worship and church order, through the implantation and teaching of Reformed doctrine, and through a revival of discipline and evangelical piety in clergy and laity alike. The first of these objectives was the most disruptive, because convictions as to church polity naturally took such clear and objective institutional forms. Yet the movement as a whole embraced a wide range of ecclesiastical arrangements. Many Puritans—with Calvin's word to support them—were content to accomplish their reforms within an episcopal church under the crown's governance. A growing number of others began to conceive of "purification" in increasingly radical terms, and gradually institutional changes of a more drastic nature were proposed. Voltaire in the eighteenth century was commenting on the divisive effect of this ferment of the left when he observed that the English, alas, have a hundred religions but only one sauce.

The appearance of multitudinous sects does not alter the fact that some "Anglican" archbishops as well as some itinerant Ranters can properly be referred to as Puritans. The latter group simply carried their program for England's church to an individualistic extreme. This great diversity of expression has led some scholars to regard England's ferment as totally amorphous:

Before the Revolution the term was almost invariably pejorative, and if one knows the circumstances surrounding its use, one may easily enough understand why the word is used and what is communicated by that use. But the conclusion arising from detailed knowledge of the prerevolutionary uses of the term is that "puritan" is the "x" of a cultural and social equation: it has no meaning beyond that given it by the particular manipulator of an algebra of abuse.[2]

Such a statement, unfortunately, overlooks both the common origins and the shared objectives of Puritan reformers. A primary purpose of this chapter, therefore, is to consider England's great contribution to the family of Reformed traditions. If special concern is shown for the groups which came to dominate the Holy Commonwealths of Massachusetts and Connecticut, it is only because those particular groups provide especially vivid instances of a broad impulse which was of great consequence to the entire American colonial scene.

THE PURITAN SPIRIT

A Revival of Experiential Piety

In some ways the Puritan spirit is ageless. One senses a fundamental aspect of its temper in the prophetic demands of Amos:

Seek good, and not evil,
    that you may live;
And so the Lord, the God of hosts, will be with you,
    as you have said.
Hate evil, and love good,
    and establish justice in the gate;
it may be that the Lord, the God of hosts,
    will be gracious to the remnant of Joseph.
   . . . .
Woe to those who are at ease in Zion,
    and to those who feel secure on the mountain of Samaria. . . .
Woe to those who lie upon beds of ivory,
    and stretch themselves upon their couches,

[2] Charles and Katherine George, *The Protestant Mind of the English Reformation: 1570–1640*, p. 6.

and eat lambs from the flock,
> and calves from the midst of the stall;
who sing idle songs to the sound of the harp,
> and like David invent for themselves instruments of
> music;
who drink wine in bowls,
> and anoint themselves with finest oils,
> but are not grieved over the ruin of Joseph!

> [Amos 5:14–15; 6:1–6]

In 1115 the same moral passion led Saint Bernard out into the wilderness of the Aube valley to reconstruct Benedictine life within the somber, unadorned walls of Clairvaux, and to begin there the Cistercian movement of monastic reform. Hugh Latimer also heard this ancient call in the early days of England's reformation. His grief over "the ruin of Joseph" spurred him to attack "unpreaching prelates" with sharply drawn contrasts between apostolic simplicity and episcopal magnificence; it nerved him to dramatize this theme even on that day in 1525 when the bishop of Ely entered Cambridge's Great Saint Mary's while Latimer was preaching, and it strengthened him as he was led to the fires by Queen Mary's executioners a quarter-century later. John Milton's *Lycidas* (1645) would express the same outrage. Gradually this demand for purity came to inform a popular movement.

No less was the Puritan spirit infused with what Perry Miller calls "the Augustinian strain of piety":

I venture to call this piety Augustinian . . . simply because Augustine is the arch-exemplar of a religious frame of mind of which Puritanism is only one instance out of many in fifteen hundred years of religious history. . . . There survive hundreds of Puritan diaries and thousands of Puritan sermons, but we can read the inward meaning of them all in the *Confessions* [of Saint Augustine].

Puritan theology was an effort to externalize and systematize this subjective mood. Piety was the inspiration for Puritan heroism and the impetus in the charge of Puritan Ironsides. . . . It was foolishness and fanaticism to their opponents, but to themselves it was life eternal. . . . It blazed most clearly and most fiercely in the person of Jonathan Edwards, but Emerson was illuminated, though from afar, by its rays, and it smoldered in the recesses of Hawthorne's intuitions.[3]

At times one can even find among professed Puritans the sort of mystical piety which transported Augustine from the window in Ostia into other realms of being and led him to discover that there was no peace outside of rest in God. Thomas Hooker in Connecticut shared this spirit: "The soul was made for an end, and good, and therefore for a better than itself, therefore to enjoy union with him, and communion with those blessed excellencies of his. . . ." The recurrence of these mystical flights reminds us that the Puritans were heirs not only of the Reformation but of the medieval tradition out of which it grew, and that they also communed with those Platonic ideas which so often offered the Renaissance humanist a way of rejecting scholastic theology.

Yet there was an element in Puritan inwardness more basic, more decisive, and far more fraught with historical consequences than Platonic mysticism: it was the inescapable example of Saint Paul on the road to Damascus. The Puritans were spiritual brethren with a practical mission. They called England, and later America, to a spiritual awakening; and nearly every one of those who uttered the call had had his own road to Damascus. For Henry Burton, who had his ears lopped off as Laud's prisoner but who returned to work with a Puritan following during Parliament's power, the great personal awakening came at Cambridge University. He describes the impact of sermons by Laurence Chaderton, master of Emmanuel College, and William Perkins, also of Emmanuel and the "angelical doctor" of the movement: "From my first entrance in the College, it pleased God to open mine eyes by their ministry, so as to put a difference between their sound teaching, and the University Sermons, which savoured more of humane wit, than of Gods word." Thomas Goodwin, perhaps the most influential of the Independent "dissenting brethren" at the Westminster Assembly, states in his autobiography that the change occurred "Monday the second of Octob. 1620 in the Afternoon," when he casually attended a Cambridge funeral service being conducted by Thomas Bainbridge. The experience was a water-

[3] Perry Miller, *The New England Mind: The Seventeenth Century*, pp. 3–5.

shed between a life in Adam's bondage, when "God was to me as a wayfaring Man," and one of assured implantation into Christ.

Yet assurance that the transition had truly been made was often the result of prolonged—even continual—self-analysis. In Perry Miller's words, the Puritans "liberated men from the treadmill of indulgences and penances, but cast them on the iron couch of introspection." Whether or not the Puritan made conversion experiences normative, he always regarded the Christian faith as a decisive, renovating commitment. Anglo-American Puritanism is in fact the fountainhead of a new conception of evangelical inwardness, a type of piety in which the unmerited and purely gracious work of divine mercy in the human soul becomes a cardinal fact of Christian existence. In due course this experiential tradition would inspire a rich body of hymnody and a devotional literature that stands in marked contrast to the older mystical tradition.[4]

Emphasis on Law and Discipline

Puritanism at its core, however, was something more than an austere exodus from the fleshpots of Egypt or a resurgence of experimental piety. It was a vigorous effort to bring God's discipline to this world, its people, and, preeminently, to God's Church. If the Puritan's Bible reading led him to Amos and Saint Paul, it also led him to Moses. The Law was dear to his heart, and through the centuries he and his Reformed kindred have dwelt unremittingly on the value of the Law as teacher and moral guide for the Christian. Detesting those who were "at ease in Zion," determined to have a church whose holiness was visible, the Puritan turned to Holy Scriptures, where he found a witness to the Creator that inspired him to be a fruitful part of God's order as a citizen and in his vocation. He recognized that governments, constitutions, and laws were instituted to restrain man's sin and hence were truly of God. So long as conscience allowed, therefore, he was law-abiding and loyal. He also found much specific guidance in the Scriptures, very often in the Old Testament, for

4 Puritanism is thus a major source of the religious outlook which animated the great evangelical revivals of the eighteenth century and the rise of pietism on the Continent. See F. Ernest Stoeffler, *The Rise of Evangelical Pietism.*

the ordering of personal life, the regulation of society, and the structuring of the Church.

With regard to personal life, the Puritan demanded of himself—and of others—a reformation of character, the rejection of idle recreations and vain display, and sober, obedient godliness. Meditation on God's Law revealed in Holy Writ brought him to contrite awareness of his sinful condition. If he were favored with an experience of the Holy Spirit's regenerating work, he would, as a "visible saint" nevertheless continue to live out his life in a "covenant of evangelical obedience." The Puritan preachers sought nothing less than a new kind of Englishman. Their aims, to use a modern expression, were countercultural; their straightforward, earnest, plain-style sermons were meant to accomplish "a revolution of the saints."

In the public realm the Puritan sought, in Governor John Winthrop's words, "a due form of government both civil and ecclesiastical." In civil affairs this demanded respect for England's legal tradition, system of government, and social traditions. Because of his concern for dutiful living, the Puritan was usually more orderly than disruptive so long as governments did not obstruct or harass those who sought to obey God's Law. When free to speculate or encouraged to innovate, however, the more thorough-going Puritans moved toward modern democratic ideas. The practical advocacy of Governor Winthrop, Thomas Hooker, Roger Williams, or William Penn is of a piece with the theoretical writings of Puritanism's greatest political philosopher, Algernon Sidney.

The Scriptures—even passages like the one from Amos quoted above—provided explicit directives regarding church order, and the Puritan was determined to follow these directives. Collision with established practice thus became almost inevitable, for liturgies, ceremonies, vestments, church furnishings, and ecclesiastical institutions were both public and visible, on the one hand, and regulated by canon or civil law, on the other. The Puritan's characteristic "precisianism" nearly always exhibited itself first in such matters. Often Puritan wrath was directed at seemingly trivial externals, such as the giving of a ring in marriage or the wearing of the surplice. At other times, however, such massive social realities as the bishop's office or a state-established church were called in question. Perhaps most characteristic and revealing was the creation of the "Puritan Sabbath" as a meticulously observed tribute to the glory of God and the authority of his Law. Matters of this sort, both little and large, offered almost infinite occasion for controversy, schism, and violence. Even separated congregations in exile would be disrupted by conflicts over such issues; and the New World, as we shall see, was by no means exempt.

Calvinistic Theology and the Covenant

However deeply the Puritan was convinced of his call from God, however inflamed with prophetic fire, however moved by a conversion experience, his response was very rarely one of unstructured enthusiasm. Even left-wing movements like the Quakers did not defend religion without doctrinal ordering, careful biblical exegesis, and theological responsibility. Mainstream Puritans shared a strong systematic propensity. Their leaders were usually university graduates and often academicians who were also bent on making the universities more fit instruments of reform. "Dumme Doggs" in the pulpit were anathema, a learned ministry and an informed, literate laity were prime necessities. Though looking back with thanksgiving to the great confessions of the Reformation era, the Puritans also entered into the making of new confessions with thoroughness and vigor. In Britain, as it happened, their thinking seemed to lead almost inexorably to the doctrinal views so carefully articulated in the Westminster standards and their derivative symbols. Doctrine, moreover, was almost always felt to stand in need of support from both philosophical reason and common experience. Puritanism, in short, is generally marked by careful thought; it is an intellectual tradition of great profundity.

One of the most characteristic tendencies of Puritan theology was to adapt Reformed dogma to the needs of public and personal religion by means of the idea of covenant. Federal theology, as it is called (*foedus,* covenant), has, of course, a long pre-Puritan history. Some of its roots are to be found in certain writings of Calvin, and they achieve special clarity and emphasis in the extremely influential writings of Heinrich Bullinger, Zwingli's successor in Zurich. Prominent in the Heidelberg Catechism (1563), covenant ideas were developed in more detail by a succession of theologians in the Rhineland and the Netherlands. In England they were elaborated by several great Puritan divines at Cambridge University: William Perkins (1558–1602), John Preston (1587–1628), Richard Sibbes (1577–1635), and above all, William Ames (1576–1633). Ames had to give up his university appointments in 1610 because of his refusal to wear the surplice. Later he fled to Holland, serving as professor of theology at the University of Franeker from 1622 to 1632. His pupil, Johannes Cocceius (1603–1669), carried federal theology to its fullest and most systematic expression and became the leader of an extremely influential school of thought. Ames himself was the chief theological mentor of the New England Puritans. His *Medulla Theologiae* (Amsterdam, 1623; translated in 1642 as *The Marrow of Sacred Divinity*) was their prime theological text; his *De Conscientia* (*Cases of Conscience*, 1632, translated 1639) their chief guide to moral theology.

In Scotland, meanwhile, the particular adversities of the Reformed cause gave special strength to the covenanting idea by making individually sworn convenants the means of formalizing opposition to prelacy of all types, whether Roman or Anglican. Scottish Presbyterians became literally a people of the covenant. These various influences converged in the Westminster Assembly and made its historic declarations the most definitive covenantal confession in post-Reformation history. As followed or adapted by later groups and churches, the Westminster Confession would become by far the most influential doctrinal symbol in American Protestant history.[5]

The heart of covenant theology was the insistence that God's predestinating decrees were not part of a vast impersonal and mechanical scheme, but that, under the Gospel dispensation, God had established a covenant of grace with the seed of Abraham. This was to be appropriated in faith,

[5] Adherence to the doctrines of the Westminster Assembly was attested at the Cambridge Synod of the New England Puritans in 1648. In 1680 the Massachusetts "Reforming Synod" and in 1708 the Connecticut Saybrook Synod adopted explicitly that version of Westminster formulated by the English Independents in 1658 and published as the Savoy Declaration. Westminster was also adapted by the English Baptists in 1677, and in 1707 this London Confession was adopted by the immensely influential Philadelphia Association of Baptists in America. The unaltered Westminster Confession (and Catechism) were made normative for the Church of Scotland in 1689, and in due course for American Presbyterians as well.

and hence was irreducibly personal. Puritans disagreed as to how much was God's work, and how much preparation for grace the natural man could do; but they tended to agree that the effectual call of each elect saint of God would always come as an individuated personal encounter with God's promises. One would then make a covenant with God, as had Abraham of old (Gen. 17). Of course, the encounter was at the divine initiative, and therefore a gift of grace; by the Covenant of Redemption, indeed, God the Father had covenanted with his Son to accomplish man's salvation. But more was demanded of man than mere intellectual acknowledgment of divine mercy. True faith involved inward, overt, and obedient preparation, appropriation, humility, dedication, gratitude—and a commitment to walk in God's way according to his Law. A specific conversion experience was at first rarely regarded as normative or necessary, though for many it was by this means that assurance of election was received. Gradually, as Puritan pastors and theologians examined themselves and counseled their more earnest and troubled parishioners, a consensus as to the morphology of true Christian experience began to be formulated. In due course —and with important consequences for America—these Nonconforming Puritans in the Church of England came increasingly to regard a specific experience of regeneration as an essential sign of election. In New England and elsewhere "conversion" would become a requirement for church membership. After Cromwell's ascendancy these notions would also become widespread in England.

THE PURITAN SPECTRUM

The proper manner of organizing particular churches, the relation of these congregations one with another, and the question as to whether established national churches were sanctioned by Scripture occasioned constant and inevitable controversy. Those who believed that a formal church covenant was required of local congregations, or even that a national covenant was the responsibility of a committed commonwealth, raised other problems, as did underlying doctrines of the ministry and the sacraments. As thoughtful men addressed these diverse issues and sought to develop self-consistent views, patterns gradually emerged which make it useful for the historian to describe a broad spectrum of Puritan reformism. At the right was the Prelatical party, which accepted the ancient structures of England's church and at least the basic notion of a Book of Common Prayer, but which doubted the values of strict conformity, stressed the need for a renewal of preaching and pastoral care, for greater ceremonial austerity, and for an increase of Christian discipline at all levels. Carrying these ideas somewhat further were the Presbyterians, who took the established church of Geneva or Scotland as their model. Like the Episcopalians, they accepted the notion that the church should be nationally organized, but prelacy was to be replaced by a system of ascending judicatories or church courts: local sessions, presbyteries, synods, and a general assembly, with the clergy and laity of the presbytery serving as a kind of elective, representative, and composite "bishop." It would still be the church of the entire nation, and infant baptism would prevail everywhere. Such advocacy was strong in Elizabeth's time; and later, under the Long Parliament, Presbyterians had their way for a time in England. Many Puritans of this general persuasion also emigrated to America, but only much later, when joined by thousands of Presbyterians of Scottish background, would their church principles be fully institutionalized.

Puritans of congregational tendency became more numerous as covenantal notions gained deeper hold and as Stuart intransigence made national reform seem unlikely. They conceived of the church as ideally a congregation of "visible saints" who had covenanted with God and with one another. A church so formed they regarded as utterly complete in itself: it could determine who were the saints, discipline and excommunicate its members, and ordain its duly called ministers, who would administer the ordinances (sacraments) only to those in the covenant. Congregationalists, however, were not of one mind as to how separate a particular church should be, nor were they agreed in their judgments of the "unreformed" Church of England. Some "Separatists" viewed the established church as no better than Romanism and hence not a church of Christ at all. With Robert Browne they would refuse to "tarry for the magistrate" and go their own way. Still others, the Baptists, would press the covenant logic even farther, abandon the idea of infant baptism, redefine this sacrament as simply the external seal of the Spirit's work, and insist upon complete separation of church and state. They would also diminish the significance of ordination and the Lord's Supper. Such Separatists, whether Baptist or not, often put themselves in a position where exile or persecution was their lot. Radical separatism, however, was rare in the period before the Civil War, though various kinds and degrees of "Independency" flourished during the Interregnum.

The great majority of congregational thinkers and covenant theologians remained with the establishment in the hope that they could reform it according to their views. With varying degrees of recalcitrance these nonseparating Congregationalists discharged their religious obligations within the Church of England. They did not deny that it was a true church and they hoped for a national settlement on their terms, but in the meantime they carried Nonconformity as far as conscience demanded or as bishops allowed. The repressive measures of Charles I and Archbishop Laud finally convinced many of this persuasion that their hopes for reform were in vain, thus providing the impetus for the great Puritan migration to America. Even then they were conspicuously *not* separating from the Church of England, but simply providing an example for the world to see. After 1640, when Parliament made it possible for Puritans to reorganize the national church in England, the Presbyterians were dominant, and Congregational delegates were again forced into dissent. Under the Commonwealth, however, more radical tendencies flourished: Baptists became numerous, and to their left still other groups took shape. Most notable of these was the Society of Friends, among whom a Spirit-filled fellowship took the place of an ordained ministry and objective sacraments. Other groups were more radical still: some completely individualistic, some consumed with millennialist doctrines, some with social revolution in mind. Yet even in these extremes there remained a common interest in reform, revival, and personal faith that made at least some of the radicals recognizable spiritual companions of at least some bishops at the other extreme of the Puritan movement.

Nearly every component of this wide spectrum, and still other components as well, would enter into the religious life of colonial America. An "Anglicanism" deeply colored by Puritan convictions would shape the early religious life of Virginia—as long as possible, to the legal exclusion of other

churches. In due course similar but less homogeneous Anglican establishments would be erected in Maryland, the Carolinas, New York, and Georgia. Quakers would be prominent
among both founders and settlers of New Jersey and Pennsylvania, and would also find their way in significant numbers to
Rhode Island and the Carolinas. In virtually all of the colonies Baptists would found churches—first in Rhode Island,
most influentially in eastern Pennsylvania, but also in the
South. Presbyterians were widely scattered, but in the Middle Colonies they were able to organize a farflung presbytery
in 1706. This group also won many neighboring Congregationalists to their persuasion, and shared important aspects of
their tradition with the Dutch, German, and French Reformed who gathered in the same colonies. Plymouth is
remembered as the colony of more or less separatistic Congregationalists. Among the early founders of Rhode Island
were extremist Puritans of various sorts, many of them exiles.
Finally, in the Holy Commonwealths of Massachusetts, Connecticut, and New Haven, a "magisterial" nonseparating Congregationalism would be so fully institutionalized that the
very term Puritan has often been reserved for them alone.
Because they are in a sense archetypical, and because for
almost two centuries it was their fortune to be spared both
encroachment or molestation, logic if not chronology makes
them the proper starting point for an account of religious
developments in the American colonies.

9

THE HOLY COMMONWEALTHS OF NEW ENGLAND

All over the world New England is known as the place where Puritanism achieved its fullest, least inhibited flowering. And for well over two centuries after its founding, this region self-consciously understood its own vocation in these terms. These colonies, to be sure, were not the only ones to have some special sense of purpose. William Penn, Lord Baltimore, and Roger Williams also launched their plantations as holy experiments of one sort or another. But the four chief New England colonies were instilled with a peculiarly corporate spirit. In each of them, covenantal ideas, though no magic bar to schism or fragmentation, put a curb on purely individualistic endeavors, while an underlying conception of government by social compact gave further strength to the feeling of solidarity. The idea of a "national covenant" also bound together the people of each commonwealth, as well as the visible saints, in a common task. In the early years, this sense of a common calling was strengthened by the widely held conviction that the reformation being carried out in these commonwealths was actually a decisive phase in the final chapter of God's plan for his Church in this world. England in these latter times was conceived as truly an "Elect Nation," and the Puritans of New England were now corporately performing its ultimate task.

THE PLANTING OF PLYMOUTH

There is no better place to begin an account of New England church life than with Governor William Bradford's *History of Plimoth Plantation,* for none can match his description of the Pilgrims' arrival in Cape Cod Bay in November 1620.

Being thus arived in 'a good harbor and brought safe to land, they fell upon their knees & blessed ye God of heaven, who had brought them over ye vast & furio'us ocean, and delivered them from all ye periles & miseries thereof, againe to set their feete on ye firme and stable earth, their proper elemente. . . .

But hear I cannot but stay and make a pause, and stand half amased at this poore peoples presente condition; and so I thinke will the reader too, when he well considers ye same. . . . They had now no friends to wellcome them, no inns to entertaine or refresh their weatherbeaten bodys, no houses or much less townes to repaire too, to seeke for succoure. . . . And for ye season it was winter, and they that know ye winters of ye cuntrie know them to be sharp & violent, & subjects to cruell & feirce stormes, deangerous to travill to known places, much more to serch an unknown coast. Besids, what could they see but a hidious & desolate wildernes, full of wild beasts & willd men? and what multituds ther might be of them they knew not. Nether could they, as it were, goe up to ye tope of Pisgah, to vew from this wildernes a more godly cuntrie. . . . For sumer being done, all things stand upon them with a wetherbeaten face; and ye whole countrie, full of woods & thickets, represented a wild & savage heiw.[1]

A month of anxious searching for a harbor and town site followed, until finally on Christmas Day they asserted their freedom from "popish festivals" by beginning work on their common stores building. But before landing they had formed a "combination" as "ye first foundation of their governmente in this place; occasioned partly by ye discontented & mutinous speeches that some of the strangers amongst them had let fall." The famous Mayflower Compact reads as follows:

In ye name of God, Amen. We whose names are underwriten, the loyall subjects of our dread soveraigne Lord, King James, by ye grace of God, of Great Britaine, France & Ireland king, defender of ye faith, &c., having under-

[1] William Bradford, *Of Plimoth Plantation* (Boston, 1901), pp. 94–95.

taken, for ye glorie of God, and advancemente of ye Christian faith, and honour of our king & countrie, a voyage to plant ye first colonie in ye Northerne parts of Virginia, doe by these presents solemnly & mutualy in ye presence of God, and one of another, covenant and combine our selves togeather into a civill body politick, for our better ordering & preservation, & furtherance of ye ends aforesaid; and by vertue hereof to enacte constitute, and frame such just & equall lawes, ordinances, acts, constitutions, & offices, from time to time, as shall be thought most meete & convenient for ye generall good of ye Colonie, unto which we promise all due submission and obedience. In witness whereof we have hereunder subscribed our names at Cap-Codd ye 11. of November, in ye year of ye raigne of our soveraigne lord, King James, of England, France, & Ireland ye eighteenth, and of Scotland ye fiftie fourth. Ano. Dom. 1620.[2]

The social compact thus accomplished accords with Puritan political theory and stands in close relationship to an event sixteen years before, when some of these very persons in the manorhouse at Scrooby had, "as ye Lords free people, joyned them selves (by a covenant of the Lord) into a church estate." They had consciously separated from the Church of England, and were therefore "hunted & persecuted on every side." Their afflictions were made no easier by the epithet "schismatic" visited upon them by nonseparating Puritans no less than by the strictest Conformists. Realizing the impossibility of their predicament, the Scrooby congregation had decided in 1607 to flee to the Netherlands. After many misadventures the congregation was gradually assembled in Leyden, "yet it was not longe before they saw the grime & grisly face of povertie coming upon them like an armed man, with whom they must bukle & incounter . . . and though they were sometimes foyled, yet by Gods assistance they prevailed and got ye victorie." Due to their "hard and continuall labor" they prospered. Under the able ministry of John Robinson and Elder William Brewster "they grew in knowledge & other gifts & graces of ye spirite of God . . . and many came unto them from diverse parts of England, so as they grew a great congregation." Influenced doubtless by the large-spirited Robinson, their temper moderated to a much more charitable form of Separatism than many had previously shown.

Yet a comfortable life in Holland was not their goal, and inquietude over this prospect eventually led them to contact the Virginia Company in London. In this they were favored by both the company's desperate need and the deeply sympathetic efforts of Edwin Sandys, but even these advantages did not preclude an enormously complex series of negotiations. After the most vexatious delays, the little Leyden group set sail from Delfshaven on 22 July 1620 in the *Speedwell*. Joined by others of their group in England, the whole company finally took passage on the *Mayflower*, which left Plymouth harbor on 16 September, an overcrowded and underprovisioned ship, bearing, in addition to its crew of forty-eight, one hundred and one passengers. Of the latter, fifty-six were adults, fourteen were servants and hired artisans (not Separatists), and thirty-one were children, of whom at least seven belonged neither to the passengers nor to any English Separatist, but were probably waifs and idlers. The figures include thirty-five from Leyden and sixty-six from London and Southampton who were recruited for the venture. On the voyage itself, though it took sixty-five days, only one passenger died, while two were born. But the first winter compensated horribly for that good fortune: by spring half of the company had died of scurvy, general debility, and other unascertainable causes.

The heroic beginnings and unostentatious life of the Plymouth colony have won for it a secure place in American hearts. From the viewpoint of church history, moreover, its symbolic significance is great, for it remains the classic instance in America of congregational Separatism. From humble or lower middle class backgrounds, the "Pilgrim Fathers" had few intellectual or academic pretensions or aspirations. Less than twenty university men came to the colony during its first three decades, and only three of them, all ministers, remained. For fifty years the colony lacked a public school and sent no one away to a university. Perhaps as a consequence of these facts, but also because the colony as a whole attracted few immigrants, its churches were frequently without ministers. Until 1629 there were none in the whole colony; indeed, it is something of an anomaly that for almost a decade these pious Pilgrims scarcely had a church even by their own definition. A Dutch visitor in 1627 saw them marching in solemn procession and by drumbeat to Sabbath meeting, where Elder Brewster, a layman, "taught twise every Saboth, and yt both powerfully and profitably, to ye great contemment of ye hearers, and their comfortable edification; yea, many were brought to God by his ministrie." But Brewster, on advice from his Amsterdam pastor, did not administer the sacraments; and until the Reverend Ralph Smith came from Salem, Plymouth had no regular minister. The company had sent the Reverend John Lyford, an Anglican of sorts, in 1624; but when he proved unworthy, Bradford ran him out of Plymouth.

Only a few men—notably Elder William Brewster, Deacon Samuel Fuller, Edward Winslow, and possibly the fabled Myles Standish—are remembered as significant champions of the colony's "way." As to literary achievements, Governor Bradford's simple yet eloquent history stands almost alone as its great religious epic. John Robinson, their most powerful advocate, remained in the Netherlands, where he died in 1625 before he could join his congregation. The American representatives of Separatism at Plymouth were not theologically minded, nor were they aggressive or self-conscious in their churchmanship. It is unlikely that they influenced the church views of the Bay Colony, and in later years they probably adopted the Massachusetts demand for a converted church membership. They sought and found freedom to create a "body politick" and a thoroughly congregational church way, and this is the chief significance of their courageous venture.

There are reasons for the failure of the Pilgrim Fathers to achieve greatness—which they never aspired to in the first place. For one thing, "the howling wildernesse" to which they came was something less than lush. Having landed outside of the Virginia grant, moreover, they were involved in financial and legal difficulties which were not resolved until the "Old Colony" became duly chartered in 1691 as part of Massachusetts. The government nevertheless was orderly. All freemen voted for the governor and seem to have elected John Carver even before they left England. When he died, Bradford took his place and through thirty annual terms of office came virtually to personify the mind of the colony. In 1636 the *Great Fundamentals*, a legal code, was enacted; and in 1643 a representative form of government was established for the ten towns then existing. Their delegates met annually in Plymouth with the governor and his assistants as a unicameral general court. Despite the absence of a religious test, the franchise became no broader than it was in the Bay Colony—limited in practice to propertied men of stable orthodox views.

For reasons not entirely clear, the colony grew only very slowly. It took two years to replenish the losses of the first year's decimation. After a decade there were only three hundred, and by 1643 there were about twenty-five hundred people widely scattered among ten towns. As the attraction of remoter lands increased, Bradford reported that Plymouth town itself became "thin and bare." In 1691 the colony's population was estimated at seventy-five hundred. By that time its mode of life, its problems, and its churches had lost most of their distinctiveness. The nature of this transformation, as well as of the colony's most besetting problem, is better highlighted in the history of Plymouth's large and overbearing neighbor to the north.

THE COLONY AT MASSACHUSETTS BAY

Preliminary Activities

To suggest that New England waters and harbors were seething with activity between 1620 and 1630 would be misleading, but it would be still more inaccurate to imagine a time of empty silence broken only by the prayers of the Pilgrims. Actually a great deal happened. Through the efforts of Ferdinando Gorges the Plymouth Company (a branch of the old Virginia Company) was reorganized in 1620 as the Council for New England. The group of aristocrats who accomplished this feat was then incorporated as a land company, with a grant to all the territory between 40° N and 48° N.

Though unauthorized within the council's grants, Thomas and Andrew Weston founded an unruly and short-lived colony at Wessagusset (Weymouth) in 1622. Captain Wollaston led a similar venture to Mount Wollaston (Quincy) about the same time. When it failed, Thomas Morton, a London lawyer of dubious virtue, regrouped the colony in accordance with his plans for traffic with the Indians in liquor and firearms; but by 1628 Myles Standish of Plymouth had driven him out. Gorges and the council also encouraged sporadic activity in Maine, where fishing and furs were the primary attractions. In 1623–24 Robert Gorges (son of Ferdinando), now invested with formal authority and the high-sounding title of governor general, had hopes of a vast proprietary principality at Wessagusset; but after a miserable winter he decamped, leaving several of his men behind. One of these, the Reverend William Blaxton, established himself in self-sufficient isolation on Beacon Hill. Other settlements or trading posts at Nantasket and several other points were set up, some of them by fishermen, including those from Plymouth. In 1623 there were at least forty authorized sailings to areas held by the Council for New England; and in 1625 at least fifty ships were fishing in New England waters. By that time there must have been several hundred permanent or semipermanent "settlers" at various points along the coast besides those at Plymouth.

Only one of these scattered efforts has any place in church history, except insofar as they all made the area better known. This single important exception begins with the colony at Cape Ann (Gloucester) founded by a company organized in the Wessex seaport of Dorchester by John White, the minister of Holy Trinity Church there. White was a man of Puritan sympathies who had a deep pastoral concern for the fishermen and crewmen in New England. Since there seemed to be promising commercial advantages as well, the Dorchester Company was organized. Fourteen men were sent out in 1623, and thirty-two more in the year following. When after three years they had turned no profit and provided little pastoral care to wandering mariners, the company called on Roger Conant, a merchant who had spent one year in the Plymouth colony and had recently visited Nantasket, to take over the company's New England affairs. By the time he accomplished his mission, however, the company had collapsed, having discovered that "no sure fishing place in the Land is fit for planting, nor any good place for planting found fit for fishing, at least neere the Shoare, And secondly, rarely any Fisher-men will worke at Land, neither are Husband-men fit Fisher-men but with long use and experience."[3] Conant was left in America as a kind of caretaker "governor" to pick up the debris, a task which he accomplished well by

[3] Clifford K. Shipton, *Roger Conant, A Founder of Massachusetts* (Cambridge, Mass.: Harvard University Press, 1945), p. 55.

moving the colony's twenty souls to Naumkeag (Salem), where a viable agricultural colony could be maintained. On observing the situation there, he wrote back to White that this new site "might prove a receptacle for such as upon account of religion would be willing to begin a foreign plantation," and received assurances in turn that appropriate measures would be taken.

In England meanwhile the efforts of White and some of his Dorchester associates converged with the interests of "some Gentlemen of London" and the colonial desires of an earnest group of Puritans in East Anglia. Ninety of these interested persons ultimately gained legal status and were chartered in 1628 as the New England Company, with a title (such as it was) to lands "from the Atlantic Ocean to the South Sea" between a point three miles north of the Merrimac River to a point three miles south of the Charles. Under these auspices and with John Endecott as "chief in-command," a party of about forty sailed from Weymouth on the *Abigail* on 20 June 1628, reaching Naumkeag on 6 September. Here, with little solicitude for the "Old Planters" under Conant, Endecott ruled with a hard hand until 1629, when word was received that the New England Company had been reconstituted on a radically different basis as the Massachusetts Bay Company.

The Salem Settlement

When the imperious Endecott began to exercise his authority, the old settlers of Naumkeag rose up in resentment. A peace of sorts was worked out, and the settlement was renamed "Salem," meaning "peace." The colony began to prepare for winter, and since their preparations seem to have been adequate, perhaps we may infer that Edward Johnson's idyllic picture of the first winter applied to that which was soon upon them.

> They made shift to rub out the Wintern cold by the Fireside, having fuell enough growing at their very doores, turning down many a drop of the Bottell, and burning Tobacco with all the ease they could, discoursing betweene one while and another, of the great progresse they would make after the Summers-Sun had changed the Earths white furr'd Gowne into a greene Mantell.[4]

[4] Ibid., p. 62.

If these men talked about their homeland, as undoubtedly they did, it was no doubt frequently about the declining state of affairs there and the likelihood that many would soon be seeking refuge in New England. With the summer of 1629, the situation of the settlement was drastically altered. The Massachusetts Bay Company gave instructions for the appointment of Endecott as governor, and the formation of a council of twelve. The Old Planters were placated by receiving two representatives on the council, a generous grant of fine land, and the right to grow tobacco, though sale of the latter to company settlers was forbidden "unless upon urgent occasion, for the benefit of health." Later instructions permitted it "to be taken privately by ancient men, and none others," a restriction which was more than a Puritan foible, for King James himself had written *A Counterblast on Tobacco* in 1604. As it turned out, something more substantial than tobacco was to become necessary, for during June and July four ships bearing nearly three hundred settlers arrived —the largest and best equipped expedition which had been sent to New England up to this point.

Since the new arrivals included three ministers of pronounced Puritan persuasion, John Higginson, Samuel Skelton, and Francis Bright, the governor set aside 20 June 1629 as a special day for investing them with authority. The morning was given over to prayer and teaching, the afternoon to the solemnities of election. The candidates spoke on the subject of the ministry, and were found to be thoroughly congregational in conviction. Ballots were cast by "every fit member."

> So Mr. Skelton was chosen pastor and Mr. Higginson to be teacher; and they accepting ye choyce, Mr. Higginson with 3. or 4. of ye gravest members of ye church, laid their hands on Mr. Skelton, using prayers therwith. This being done, there was impossission of hands [on] Mr. Higginson also.[5]

Another "day of Humiliation" was set for 6 August, when deacons and elders were to be elected. But before that time it was decided that the church in Salem must itself be more properly constituted, and thirty persons, including Roger

[5] Charles Gott to William Bradford, 30 July 1629, in Bradford, *Of Plimoth Plantation*, p. 317.

Conant and probably some others of the Old Planters, were by some means selected for the task. What criteria they used is not known, but there is no evidence that accounts of saving experience were required. The now famous Salem church covenant was then prepared and signed:

> We Covenant with the Lord and one with an other; and doe bynd our selves in the presence of God, to walke together in all his waies, according as he is pleased to reveale himself unto us in his blessed word of truth.[6]

Since a body with proper ecclesiastical powers now existed, not only to rule upon the admission of new members and to discipline themselves, but also to call a ministry, in due course Skelton and Higginson were again "ordained to their several offices." In this way the Massachusetts Bay Colony had a ministry ordained in New England even before Plymouth did, for it was late in 1629 before Ralph Smith, a Separatist minister who had come out on the ship with Higginson, having "exercised his gifts" among the Pilgrims, was duly called and ordained there.

Considerable controversy has arisen over both the "facts" and the significance of these events. Most agitated has been the argument over the "Deacon Fuller myth"—the theory that during the winter and spring Plymouth's good but rather eccentric physician, while attending the ailing settlers at Salem, persuaded the Massachusetts men that in Congregationalism as practiced at Plymouth was the true Scripture doctrine of the church. By this chance occurrence, it is claimed, the whole ecclesiastical drift of the Bay Colony was so altered that its leaders, lay and clerical, intoxicated by the "free aire" of the New World and torn from the old ways by the persuasions of Deacon Fuller, changed their minds about the Church of England and became Separatistic Congregationalists. Following this line of reasoning, even the learned Leonard Bacon found the "germ of New England" in the church founded at the house of William Brewster in Scrooby. Far more plausible, however, is the view that Higginson, already silenced and on the verge of arrest in England, insisted that a covenanted church be formed in Salem in order to val-

---

[6] Williston Walker, *The Creeds and Platforms of Congregationalism*, p. 116.

idate his ministry there. This view conforms with the words he allegedly uttered as his ship left England: "We will not say, as the separatists were wont to say at their leaving of England, 'Farewell, Babylon' . . . but . . . 'farewel, the Church of God in England.'" Men who for years had been pondering and debating these matters of doctrine and polity, and who were ready to risk exile rather than violate their convictions, were not likely to be deflected from their course by hearsay accounts of a Separatist church in Plymouth. Deacon Fuller's visit probably did convince Endecott that the facts were "farr from ye commone reporte that hath been spread of you." In other words, Endecott perceived that his people could be in communion with the church at Plymouth. Considering the reputation that Separatists had in the eyes of many nonseparating Puritans, and that acknowledged fellowship with extremists could hardly please the Massachusetts stockholders in England, this was no small accomplishment on Deacon Fuller's part. It proved permanent, too, for in churchly matters moderately good relations between New Plymouth and the Bay Colony continued.[7]

Removal of the Massachusetts Bay Company to New England

What neither Governor Endecott nor Deacon Fuller could have known or even imagined had meanwhile been accomplished by the Bay Colony's leaders in England. Meeting on 28 July at Sempringham, the stockholders in East Anglia conceived the bold idea of transferring the entire company to New England, and of taking with them the charter with its surprisingly large grant of governmental authority. On 26 August twelve of these Puritans met in Cambridge and signed an agreement "to inhabite and continue in New England. Provided, always that . . . the whole government together with the Patent for the said plantacion, bee first by an order of Court legally transferred and established to remayne with us and others which shall inhabite upon the said plantacion." Two days later the proposal was presented to the

[7] Plymouth sent fraternal messengers to the Cambridge Synod in 1647, and its church institutions came gradually to resemble those in the Bay Colony, even to include the requirement that a candidate for membership give account of his experience of God's effectual call.

General Court by the company, and on 29 August the way was officially cleared for the colony to displace the company.

With the election of John Winthrop (1588–1649) as governor in October, emigration plans were pressed vigorously. By spring a fleet of eleven ships had been assembled at Southampton, and vast amounts of stores had been purchased. England's largest colonial migration was under way. The first four ships with four hundred passengers set sail on 29 March 1630, with Governor Winthrop in the *Arbella*. Before the year was out six hundred more would follow; and by 1643, when the reins of government passed from Charles I to the Puritan-dominated Long Parliament, opening new opportunities for reform in England itself, more than twenty thousand people had made their way to Massachusetts. But before discussing this "swarming of the Puritans" in New England, it would be well to inquire into the convictions, hopes, and ideals of those who projected and guided this Holy Commonwealth.

They were, of course, Puritans in the broad sense in which that movement has been defined in foregoing pages. They shared its Reformed and reforming spirit and its convictions about the need for the magistrate and the church to cooperate in establishing a civil and ecclesiastical order. More specifically, they were a self-conscious, tightly knit group within the larger movement. They had gone beyond presbyterian conceptions of a national church to one that was categorically congregational. They no longer accepted the pure preaching of the gospel and correct administration of the sacraments as sufficient marks of a true church. And they believed that the church should consist only of "visible saints" and their children, with a knowledgeable profession of faith and consistent God-fearing behavior as the tests of visibility. In the darkening fourth decade of the seventeenth century, they had finally abandoned hope that such a church way could be established in England. They could "tarry for the magistrate" no longer, lest they be extinguished altogether. As a saving remnant they left England behind, to become a kind of Church of Christ in Exile, a "citty on a hill" for all the world to see, or even the final purification of church and state before the Last Days.

Yet they were not separating themselves from England's church any more than Higginson had when at Land's End he saw England slipping from view. This conviction was expressed in the *Humble Request* which Winthrop and the other leaders had written just before they departed.

> We . . . esteem it our honor to call the *Church of England* from whence we rise, our dear mother . . . ever acknowledging that such hope and part as we have obtained in the common salvation we have received in her bosom and sucked it from her breasts. We leave it not, therefore, as loathing that milk wherewith we were nourished there; but blessing God for the parentage and education, as members of the same body, shall always rejoice in her good.[8]

Congregationalism was not synonymous with Separatism, nor was the distinction a labyrinthine sophistry. Though convinced of grave defects in England's church, these Puritans did not consider it the Whore of Babylon or an engine of Antichrist. They sometimes emigrated as groups from English parishes, as did those from Chelmsford who were reunited with their former preacher, Thomas Hooker, in Newton, Massachusetts; but they simply could not unchurch the relatives, friends and fellow-Christians they left behind. Their willingness to see implicitly—and hence authentically—covenanted churches and truly "called" ministers in Old England was a realistic and charitable refusal to yield to fanaticism.

The one crucial characteristic of "classic" New England Puritan thought that is not revealed by the famous Salem events was the conviction that particular churches should be formed only by men and women who could give credible evidence that they had inwardly experienced God's effectual call. On this point they had not arrived at consensus by 1630, though years of private introspection and collective searching of hearts led in that direction. By 1635, however, with John Cotton probably leading the way, the leaders of the Bay Colony reached this significant corporate decision. They made a narration of the experience of regenerating grace a requirement of adult church membership. Seen in full perspective, this was a radical demand. For the first time in Christendom, a state church with vigorous conceptions of enforced uniformity in belief and practice was requiring an internal, experiential test of church membership. Many future

[8] Quoted in a very important account of the matter by Perry Miller, *Orthodoxy in Massachusetts*, p. 139.

problems of the New England churches stemmed from this decision. It would appear, moreover, that its influence beyond New England was proportionate to its revolutionary character.

Building the Bay Colony

Formation of the Holy Commonwealth began immediately, for the simple act of joining the enterprise was taken to mean involvement in and responsibility for its corporate tasks in the world. Even aboard the *Arbella* Governor Winthrop had drawn out some of these implications:

> It is of the nature and essence of every society to be knit together by some covenant, either expressed or implied. . . .
> For the work we have in hand, it is by mutual consent, through a special over-ruling providence and a more than ordinary approbation of the churches of Christ, to seek out a place of cohabitation and consortship, under a due form of government both civil and ecclesiastical. . . .
> Therefore we must not content ourselves with usual ordinary means. Whatsoever we did or ought to have done when we lived in England, the same must we do, and more also where we go. . . .
> Neither must we think that the Lord will bear with such failings at our hands as He doth from those among whom we have lived. . . .
> Thus stands the cause between God and us: we are entered into covenant with Him for this work; we have taken out a commission, the Lord hath given us leave to draw our own articles. . . .
> We shall find that the God of Israel is among us. . . . For we must consider that we shall be as a city upon a hill, the eyes of all people are upon us.[9]

On 12 June the *Arbella* arrived at Salem and put ashore its weary, weakened passengers. As other ships arrived, Winthrop shifted the colony's center to the fine landlocked harbor at the mouth of the Charles River. Soon Boston, on its easily protected peninsula, became the seat of government. Before the year was out, eleven ships had come, and the colo-

[9] Perry Miller, ed., *The American Puritans*, p. 82.

nists they brought had made the beginnings of a famous cluster of towns in the Bay area.

Prompt measures were taken to establish the civil government on the foundation provided in the royal charter they had brought with them. On 23 August 1630 Governor Winthrop, Deputy Governor Thomas Dudley, and seven "assistants" of the company began their governmental tasks. But on 29 October, at a meeting thrown open to "the whole body of settlers," they carried out a minor political revolution: it was decided "by the generall vote of the people, and ereccion of hands" that the freemen of the colony, not the stockholders of the company, "should have the power of chuseing Assistants . . . and the Assistants from amongst themselves to chuse a Governor and Deputy Governor, whoe with the Assistants should have the power of makeing lawes and chuseing officers to execute the same." At the next meeting of the General Court 116 newcomers were added to the original group of twelve "freemen"; this probably included most of the adult males. In 1632 the freemen were empowered to elect the governor and deputy governor directly.

The trading company thus became a commonwealth, though it was far from being a "democracy" in the modern sense. The governor and assistants were still to enact such laws as God's Word and passing exigencies might require; and only church members had the franchise. In 1634 the freemen asked and received still larger concessions, according to which the representatives of the several towns gained legislative powers. The Bay Colony governed itself by the resultant bicameral system without essential modification for over sixty years. To call it a "theocracy" is therefore absurd. Its franchise was wider than England's, and "of all the governments in the Western world at the time, that of early Massachusetts gave the clergy least authority."[10] The clergy's influence was large, to be sure; but it was both informal, depending on the Puritan's reluctance to ignore ministerial counsel, and indirect, resting largely on the minister's important role in determining church membership.

Towns in the Bay Colony were laid out more or less after the pattern of an English manor. Population growth meant new towns; but in order to guard against the dispersion and

[10] Edmund S. Morgan, *The Puritan Dilemma, The Story of John Winthrop*, p. 96.

isolation of families that an unlimited land supply made possible, each new town was incorporated with responsible proprietors in charge. At its center were the meetinghouse, the common pasture, and the village. In 1642 and 1647 laws requiring a common school were passed. Radiating from the center of town were the fields and farmlands. The church was not only the geographical and social focus of town life, but its spiritual center as well, formed at the earliest possible time by the covenanting of the town's visible saints. Thereupon the lay officers were elected and a minister called, who in due course would be ordained, in all probability for a lifetime ministry in the same town, possibly dividing his duties with a colleague (or "teacher") if the town were able to obtain full clerical "equipment." With a church formed, a meetinghouse would be erected for worship and civic assembly, a plain and usually small building, with a centered pulpit, no holy altar (only a serviceable table), and no "popish" tower until a much later day. On the Sabbath there were morning and afternoon services—each with its lengthy free prayers, discordantly sung psalms, and a very long sermon. The sermons, delivered in plain style on a wide range of subjects, offered solid biblical exposition, stated the doctrine explicitly, and gave particular attention to its practical "use." The congregation was concerned above all with the way of salvation and its moral implications.

Town meetings were at first both civil and ecclesiastical in their scope, electing hogreeves and selectmen, attending to the repair of roads, and arranging for the maintenance of minister and meetinghouse. In some instances they retained this dual character on into the nineteenth century. Since an increasingly large number of townsmen failed to meet the experiential demands of church membership, strictly ecclesiastical elections and discipline came to be reserved for the church itself, while more general matters of supporting public worship fell to the town or "parish." The General Court in turn made such support obligatory and in many ways sought to uphold the churches and protect them from their enemies. The civil government also enforced the "first table" of the Decalogue, punishing blasphemy, heresy, and vain swearing, and requiring that the Sabbath be kept. Urian Oakes (1631?–81), minister in Cambridge and sometime president of Harvard, stated the theory behind this close cooperation of church and state with admirable precision and typical Puritan confidence:

> According to the design of our founders and the frame of things laid by them the interest of righteousness in the commonwealth and holiness in the Churches are inseparable. . . . To divide what God hath conjoyned . . . is folly in its exaltation. I look upon this as a little model of the glorious kingdom of Christ on earth. Christ reigns among us in the commonwealth as well as in the Church and hath his glorious interest involved and wrapt up in the good of both societies respectively.[11]

The New England Way as exemplified in the Bay Colony rested on the conviction that the entire commonwealth was intended to be as faithfully "under God" as it could possibly be.

The general welfare thus required the maintenance of a learned ministry. *New England's First Fruits* (1643) stated that need in memorable words:

> After God had carried us safe to *New England,* and wee had builded our houses, provided necessaries for our livelihood, rear'd convenient places for Gods worship, and settled the Civill Government; One of the next things we longed for, and looked after was to advance *Learning* and perpetuate it to Posterity; dreading to leave an illiterate Ministry to the Churches, when our present Ministers shall lie in the Dust.[12]

To this end in 1636 the General Court voted "to give 400 [pounds] towards a schoale or colledge." A year later, they chose a plot in Newtown (later Cambridge), where Thomas Shepard was minister, and appointed as master Nathaniel Eaton, brother of Theophilus Eaton, the London merchant and cofounder of New Haven. The first classes were held in 1638, and in that year, too, John Harvard, a young minister and Cambridge graduate, died and left his property and library to the infant nursery of learning. Although Eaton proved unsatisfactory, the next president, Henry Dunster,

[11] Urian Oakes, *New England Pleaded With* (1673), p. 49.
[12] Samuel Eliot Morison, *The Founding of Harvard College,* p. 432. Appendix D gives the document in its entirety.

brought many improvements. Before Dunster's conversion to Baptist views required his resignation in 1654, the college had received a new charter (1650—and still in effect at present), was granting degrees, and had self-consciously committed itself to liberal education in the old university tradition. In 1674 President Hoar could publish the names of two hundred Harvard graduates.

The first printing press in the American colonies was set up at Cambridge in 1639, and from it in 1640 issued the first book, *THE VVHOLE BOOKE OF PSALMES Faithfully TRANSLATED into ENGLISH Metre, Whereunto is prefixed a discourse declaring not only the lawfullnes, but also the necessity of the heavenly Ordinance of singing Scripture Psalmes in the Churches of God.* It is not clear why a new metrical version and so large a printing venture was undertaken; but the desire to indicate the Bay Colony's ecclesiastical self-sufficiency was probably paramount. Whatever the reason, the accomplishment was impressive. It suggests the degree to which a miniature Puritan version of English civilization had taken shape in a corner of the vast American wilderness.

Of all the achievements of Puritanism, however, none was more important than that which the Puritan himself would have insisted to be a work of God: its capacity to shape a type of person. It could take a brilliant young Cambridge graduate like John Cotton, who might easily have been led by vanity and his own rhetorical gifts into the very kind of hireling ministry that Milton excoriated in *Lycidas,* and turn him down the hard path to exile. Or it could take a young country gentleman and graduate of Trinity College, Cambridge, like John Winthrop, and so utterly reshape his life's purpose that he would sacrifice all the security of England to lead the Bay Colony's venture. Only through biographical study of such men as these—clerical or lay—can the movement's central achievement be grasped. And it is no small feat that the colony itself would similarly shape a new generation of men and women—even a long posterity.

10

TENSIONS IN THE NEW ENGLAND WAY

The New England Zion was never an untroubled Christian utopia. Settlement brought unsettlement. Indian wars, political crises, and problems of diplomacy were added to the serious difficulties of economic depression which ensued after the victories of Cromwell brought an end to the great Puritan emigration from England. In due course, the Restoration created other issues. Intrinsic religious tensions also emerged, at least five of which raised major problems. The first involved the fundamental theological question as to the place of law and "legal obedience" under the gospel order, a matter with which the American churches were still wrestling in the later twentieth century and which in one form or another has aroused heated controversies during most of the intervening decades. The second and third had to do with ordering the church, with settling ecclesiological questions that stand very near to the center of the Puritan idea of reformation. The fourth was peculiarly American in that it involved the matter of how properly to regard the indigenous Indian population. The fifth was the comprehensive problem of sustaining the fervor of the Holy Commonwealths—more specifically, how to halt or roll back the seemingly inexorable process of routinization and declining fervor.

NATURE AND GRACE

Early and late one central question recurs in Christian history: What is man's role and what is God's in the work of redemption? And if the Reformation opened the question anew, it certainly did not close it. For the Puritans as for

Augustine the issue was serious and inescapable. The builders of the Bay Colony had barely addressed the problems of physical survival before they encountered the question—and dealt with it in their characteristic way.

First of all, like all Reformed theologians, they allowed neither the doctrine of predestination nor that of human depravity to undermine their conception of man as a responsible moral being, living under God's law and obliged to glorify his Creator by obedience regardless of his state of grace. Their firmness did not make them "Arminians" or "Pelagians," since they did not attribute saving merit to such obedience. But their violent disagreements as to whether or not external amendment of life was a sign of election made the "Antinomian Controversy" the opening chapter in American intellectual history.

Closely related to this conflict was the question of preparation for grace which had agitated theologians since the earliest days of the Reformation. Could the natural man, or one who was merely in the "external covenant" by virtue of baptism, respond to God's promises? Could he (or must he) prepare his heart for the moment of the Spirit's regenerating work, for his "effectual call"? Most of the early Puritan leaders said yes. Such great founding fathers of the New England Way as Thomas Hooker of Hartford, Thomas Shepard of Cambridge, and Peter Bulkley of Concord, each in his own way, developed elaborate doctrines of preparation for grace until the process came to be regarded as an essential stage in the order of salvation. John Cotton of the Boston church, on the other hand, stressed the unconditional nature of election and understood regeneration as a more arbitrary work of grace; his powerful emphasis on the inner experience of regeneration, moreover, went far toward making a credible account of the Spirit's internal work a requirement of church membership in Massachusetts. Yet strongly felt disagreements on these issues doubtlessly contributed to the founding of New England's second Bible Commonwealth.

In 1634 Thomas Hooker and most of his congregation moved far westward, out of the Bay Colony's grant, to plant Hartford and a cluster of towns in the lower Connecticut Valley. Although desire for more land was a major cause of their exodus, Hooker also had a larger conception of the work of the Law in conversion and hence a broader conception of his ministry and a less restrictive conception of church mem-

bership. The need for greater freedom, a wider franchise, and
more restricted exercise of the magistrate's authority seems
also to have figured in the decision. In any event, Hooker and
Cotton probably were too forceful and too much at odds for
one small colony. Once established, the Connecticut colony
did not categorically require freemen to be church members.
Hooker, too, was less stringent in applying the experiential
test of true sainthood. Yet the conception of church and state
underlying the Fundamental Orders of Connecticut (1639)
was in actual practice no more "liberal" than the constitution
of the Bay Colony. Hooker, in fact, remained an honored exponent of the New England Way, opposed those who would
alter its basic principles, and, in his great posthumously
published treatise, *Survey of the Summe of Church-Dis-
cipline*, provided an officially approved defense of New England Congregationalism. In the long run his colony became
the most impregnable bastion of those principles in the entire
region.

The founding of Connecticut was not the only "event" to
issue from the nature and grace problem, however, for in
John Cotton's Boston congregation there appeared that
remarkable woman, lay theologian, and prophetess, Anne
Hutchinson. An admirer of Cotton from his days in Old England's Boston, she not only praised him for his insisting on
inward signs of saving grace but criticized those who stressed
sanctification as a sign and taught a mere Covenant of
Works. The so-called Antinomian Crisis resulted—one of the
most basic and revealing controversies of the early years. In
1637 even Hooker came back to moderate a ministerial synod
which condemned eighty-two Hutchinsonesque propositions.
Lest both the peace and reputation of the colony be shattered, the General Court then took very decisive action, ex-
iling Mrs. Hutchinson's brother-in-law, the Reverend John
Wheelwright (who thereafter founded a dissident congregation in Exeter, New Hampshire). The unfortunate prophetess
rendered her already difficult case impossible by invoking
special revelations that had purportedly come to her. She was
banished by the General Court in November 1637 and in
exile exerted a small influence in the development of Rhode
Island. Cotton was slow to recognize error in his admiring
parishioner, but ultimately he made an ambiguous peace with
his ministerial brethren.

"Preparation" thenceforward became a recognized feature

of the New England Way, occupying a large place in the works of its most influential early expositors. They by no means defended Arminianism, for they did not believe that God's sovereign will could be coerced by human effort; but they demanded a law-abiding response to God's gracious promise, recognized the role of God's Law in bringing sinners to humble contrition, and emphasized the need for godly obedience in all who chose to live in the commonwealth. It is hard to see how they could have done otherwise without relinquishing their conviction that their commonwealth as a whole was in a "national covenant" with God. A steady drift toward Arminianism was to become visible in the decades that followed, but only in the eighteenth century, under very different conditions, would an emphasis on man's cooperation in his redemption be frankly preached. In that day Jonathan Edwards would oppose these liberal tendencies with a stricter predestinarianism than New England's great founding divines had been able to accept.

THE PROBLEM OF SEPARATISM

A second difficulty sprang from the psychology and practice of Separatism, which in various manifestations was a serious threat to the very existence of a holy commonwealth. The most thoroughgoing and troublesome exemplar of this tendency was Roger Williams (1603?–83) who reached the Bay Colony in 1631. Called to minister to the Boston church, he refused on the ground that it had not formally separated itself from the Church of England and would not expressly repent its past connection. He further antagonized the leadership of the colony by denying the right of the magistrate to enforce the "first table of the Law" (i.e. that part of the Decalogue having to do with man's direct responsibility to God), by objecting to the practice of having unregenerate persons take an oath (i.e. swear) in God's name, and by denouncing the charter as an unlawful expropriation of lands rightfully belonging to the Indians. Made unwelcome in the Bay Colony, he then spent a controversy-ridden two years in Plymouth. The General Court of Massachusetts finally moved against him in 1635 when, after returning as the newly elected minister of Salem, he threatened the order and uniformity of the colony by asking that church to separate from the other churches of Massachusetts. In October he was ordered to leave the colony. To escape deportation, he fled in January 1636, journeying through the wilderness first to Plymouth and then on again farther, where he founded Providence and began what in time would become the charter colony of Rhode Island. Since Anne Hutchinson, whose views also savored of Separatism, and many other extremists took refuge in Rhode Island, orthodox Puritans began to regard that colony as a veritable "sewer of New England."

Epithets, however, could not solve the problem. In Rhode Island it would receive a historic solution through the legal separation of church and state. The Quakers would work toward the same end in New Jersey and Pennsylvania. Yet the problem was undoubtedly intrinsic to the Puritan idea of a truly purified church of regenerate Christians. The state could always be suspected of bringing impure influences to bear on ecclesiastical affairs and of making unacceptable demands on "visible saints." Quite aside from the state, moreover, a given church's fellowship with other allegedly impure churches might at any time come to be regarded as intolerable in God's sight. Hence separatism would remain a latent source of turmoil in churches of the strict Puritan tradition. During the Great Awakening and in all subsequent periods of revived piety, even in the twentieth century, the old issue was repeatedly to provoke rancor and division.

QUESTIONS OF CONNECTIONALISM

A third besetting problem of New England's leaders was the indefinite state of theory with regard to the proper relation of one particular church to all the others. On this matter the position of New England's churches had never been precisely settled. When civil war erupted in England with the Presbyterian party predominant, radical movements of many sorts all increased their agitation, making questions of polity crucial. In Massachusetts the Williams and Hutchinson incidents had also created serious problems of interchurch authority; the latter difficulty, indeed, provoked the call of a ministerial "synod." Then in 1645 Robert Child and others raised a formidable threat by petitioning for "presbyterian" church order, vowing to appeal their case to Parliament if it were rejected. In September 1646, therefore, at the behest of certain ministers, the General Court called a synod, and, after reluctant compliance by the Boston and Salem churches, the Cambridge Synod began its historic sessions.

The sessions were attended by delegates from all of the twenty-nine Massachusetts churches except Concord as well as two delegates from New Hampshire and a few goodwill observers from Plymouth, New Haven, and Connecticut. The synod reconvened on 8 June 1647, after a long adjournment during which the Independent cause triumphed in England, and then, at a final session in August 1648, announced its result:

A PLATFORM OF CHURCH DISCIPLINE GATHERED OUT OF THE WORD OF GOD AND AGREED UPON BY THE ELDERS AND MESSENGERS OF THE CHURCHES ASSEMBLED IN THE SYNOD AT CAMBRIDGE IN NEW ENGLAND. TO BE PRESENTED TO THE CHURCHES AND GENERALL COURT FOR THEIR CONSIDERATION AND ACCEPTANCE IN THE LORD.

This document became the seventeenth-century platform of the New England churches, marking them off as clearly Congregational at a time when British Puritanism was dividing between a strict Presbyterian party and a kind of "Independency" which would tolerate all sects and allow each particular group to revel in whatever "heresy" it might prefer.

Against the Presbyterians the Cambridge Platform defined the polity of Congregationalism in great detail, documenting the New England Way as history had already exhibited it yet making explicit "the communion of churches one with another" and giving to councils and synods strong advisory and admonitory powers but not legal coercive authority. Opposing the principle of toleration, it committed the churches to the doctrinal position of the Westminster Assembly. The delegates also declared that uniformity was to be maintained by the power of the magistrates, "the nursing fathers" of the church; heresy, disobedience, and schism were "to be restrayned, & punished by civil authority."

Almost simultaneously with the publication of the Result of the Cambridge Synod there also appeared a number of apologetical works answering various attacks on the New England Way. Among them were John Cotton's *The Way of the Congregational Churches Cleared, in Two Treatises,* Thomas

Hooker's *Survey of the Summe of Church Discipline,* and John Norton's *Responsio,* as well as other works by John Davenport and Thomas Shepard. Taken together, these works constitute an illustrious definition of one of the major ecclesiastical traditions in modern Protestantism, and they set New England's Holy Commonwealths on their course. Many critical problems were left unresolved, but a crucial foundation had been laid. So supported, the Cambridge Platform long held a central place in the confessional history of American Congregationalism.

EVANGELISM AND THE INDIANS

It may seem odd to move from problems of church order to Indian relations, but the Indian has always been tragically odd in American history, and the Puritans had their share of difficulty. Their conviction that England was an elect nation tended to minimize other peoples, and it may be that the theology of the covenant had a similar effect. Yet the Bay Colony's charter did contain a clear pledge to "wynn and incite the Natives of the Country to the knowledge and obedience of the onlie true God and Savior of Mankinde, and the Christian fayth." Further incentive to evangelism was provided by theories that the Indians were descendants of the Lost Tribes whose conversion would betoken the prophesied return of Christ, an event which the early Puritans longed for —and expected. Nevertheless, the extension of settled areas into Connecticut and the failure of most of the colonies to respect Indian rights led to the Pequot War (1637) and, as a defensive measure, the New England Confederation (1643).

War notwithstanding, the latter year also saw the beginning of Thomas Mayhew's mission to the Indians on Martha's Vineyard, a work which ministers in his family sustained for a century with permanent results. The first Puritan to become famous in England for his knowledge of the American Indian was Roger Williams. He had from the first shown extreme solicitude for their land rights, and in 1643 he published *A Key into the Language . . . of the Natives in that part of America, called New England.* He expressed his hope that God "in His holy season" would bring this race sprung "from Adam and Noah" away from their idols; but later, as Williams became more radical, his interest in evangelism waned.

He is properly remembered for an understanding and respect for the Indian that was most unusual for his age—or later ages.

In the field of Indian missions the labors of John Eliot are most memorable. As a minister in Roxbury, near Boston, he began a lifetime's dedication to this work in 1646, and within thirty years he had inspired a mission that claimed the conversion of about four thousand Indians, who were gathered in twenty-four congregations, some of them with ordained Indian ministers. He published an Indian-language catechism for his converts in 1653, and in 1661–63 the Old and New Testaments, the first Bible printed in America. Eliot and his colleagues also publicized the American missionary challenge and contributed to the interest that led Parliament in 1649 to incorporate the Society for the Propagation of the Gospel in New England—an organization that was still able to support Jonathan Edwards in his work among the Indians over a century later.[1]

The years 1675–76 brought a tragic interruption to this promising work in the form of King Philip's War, in which the Wampanoags and Narragansets devastated the outlying white settlements, pressed back the frontier, and but for the coordinated offensive of the New England Confederation might have carried the day. In the end, southern New England was permanently cleared of Indian danger, but in the north the Abenaki tribe turned to France for aid. And in a very few years the terrible French and Indian Wars would begin, holding New England at bay and restricting its northward and westward expansion until the fall of Quebec in 1759. With massacre and treachery an actuality or an imminent possibility, missions were necessarily restricted, but they by no means came to a halt, despite suspicions of French intrigue and the near disappearance of an accessible Indian population. Yet a decline in Indian evangelism tended to accompany the same general decline of zeal in the Bible Commonwealths that led many to interpret King Philip's War as a divine punishment. Considering the total seventeenth-century predicament of the New England colonies, however, one may claim for them a degree of concern for and success in Indian

[1] This "New England Company," as it came to be called, is not to be confused with the Society for the Propagation of the Gospel in Foreign Parts, founded by the Church of England a half-century later (see chap. 14, especially pp. 278–80).

missions which equals the far more heralded efforts of New Spain and New France. Unlike these great Catholic empires, moreover, New England and her American neighbors were already beginning to experience the surge of European migration which would continue for three centuries in ever increasing volume. In the face of this steady movement of peoples all "solutions" of the Indian problem would crumble.

DECLENSION AND THE QUESTION OF CHURCH MEMBERSHIP

The most troublesome spiritual problem for the Puritan commonwealths was the decline of "experimental" piety that was almost inevitable in communities organized at so high a pitch of fervency. Very significant for this trend was a series of disputes over the qualifications for church membership and the rights of children to baptism. On these issues the founders of New England's "church-way" had been from the first between two fires. Presbyterians applauded them for not yielding to the doctrine of believer's baptism but denounced them for seeming to render baptism almost nugatory by their radical demand for a personal religious experience as a prerequisite to communicant status in the church. Baptists, on the other hand, commended their demand for congregations of regenerate saints but lamented their continuation of infant baptism. The New England Puritans for the most part compromised by limiting infant baptism to the children of parents who had owned the covenant. Yet this situation was highly unstable and confusing. Some churches, more "presbyterian" or simply more lax than others, either did not "quibble too much" over evidences of a conversion experience or defined the family in broad terms. More radical individuals, like Roger Williams or Henry Dunster of Harvard College, became openly Baptist.

More distressing than theological uncertainty was a circumstance which normal biological processes laid bare. Among the second and later generations of Puritans (as well as among the immigrants who continued to arrive) there were many duly baptized members to whom the experience of saving grace never came. Though these unconverted persons were usually professing Christians and leading morally respectable lives, they were still only in "external covenant" and therefore could not present their children for baptism.

This problem was already looming large in the controversies leading to the Cambridge Synod of 1648, but that body ignored its instructions and evaded the matter. The issue continued to be a cause for concern, however, in part because various social and psychological factors gave it political and economic overtones, but chiefly because it posed a critical ecclesiastical problem. The colonial establishment was being plagued by the very forces that had made the Church of England's parish system odious. Their people, including many baptized children of saints, were becoming a mere cross-section of English types, the pious and impious, the fervent and the stolid.[2] Of professing Christians there was no lack, but many were not qualifying for full membership even though it brought both access to the Lord's Table and the right to bring children to baptism. The churches, despite their wide responsibilities for the spiritual welfare of individual lives and the body politic, simply were not being nourished by a sufficient influx of "visible saints." Fears arose that the saving remnant would become too small to save. Baptists, in the meantime, kept alive the doctrinal conflict on the meaning of baptism, while many others raised theological objections to the prevailing restrictions on the sacraments.

The clamor increased during the 1650s. In 1657 a Connecticut-Massachusetts ministerial council met and approved certain "half-way" measures; but the Massachusetts General Court went further and summoned a formal Synod in 1662. According to its historic deliberations, baptism was declared to be sufficiently constitutive of church membership to allow

[2] As with the *Mayflower*'s company in 1620, the great migration to New England and to other parts of America was very much a mixed multitude. Early and late the ministers lamented that most of the population was chiefly interested in making money and getting ahead. In enlarging on this point the scholarship of Darrett Rutman and others (see bibliography) has done much to improve our understanding of New England society. It is important to remember, however, that what made New England a distinctive social order and what accounts for its spiritual influence was the winnowed Puritan minority and its leaders, including not only the clergy, but such lay persons as Theophilus Eaton, Governor Winthrop, and Anne Hutchinson. Demands for increased rigor and discipline—as among the Baptists —were often lay movements even late in the century, though the trend for a time was in the other direction. Yet a great revival lay in the not too distant future.

its recipients to bring their children also within the baptismal covenant, although an experience of regeneration was still required of full communicant members. This so-called Half-Way Covenant gained wide acceptance throughout New England, making its way even into the strict New Haven jurisdiction after that colony was merged with Connecticut in 1662. This is not to say that the Half-Way Covenant met no opposition, however. Just as some churches had practiced "half-way" measures long before 1662, many resisted it after. In Connecticut several churches were split in a dispute over its adoption, including those at Hartford, Windsor, and Stratford. The Reverend Abraham Pierson of Branford led a majority of his congregation to New Jersey, where they perpetuated the old New Haven constitution in New Ark. Here, ironically, they were gradually absorbed into the Presbyterianism of the Middle Colonies, though not without injecting some New England leaven into the Scottish tradition. John Davenport, the venerable pastor of the First Church in New Haven who bitterly opposed both the half-way measures and New Haven's absorption by Connecticut, was called by a majority of the First Church in Boston to oppose the innovation there, whereupon the minority withdrew to form the Third, or "Old South," Church of that city.

Widespread adoption of the Half-Way Covenant solved some important doctrinal uncertainties, but it could hardly be expected to relieve New England's religious ills. "Declension" continued uninterruptedly, the lamentations of the clergy intensified, and their sermonic jeremiads came to constitute a major literary genre. To the generalized woes of declining piety were added the very material facts of royal Restoration, which brought England's reassertion of governmental authority and the regulation of trade. On top of these developments came other tragedies: an increase of shipwrecks and pestilence, enormous losses of life and property in King Philip's War, and the devastating Boston fires of 1676 and 1679. In desperation the General Court finally called for a synod to make "full inquiry . . . into the Causes & State of Gods Controversy with us." On 10 September 1679 the "Reforming Synod" was convened and after ten days had readied its result on *The Necessity of Reformation,* in effect a summary of all past jeremiads. "That God hath a Controversy with his New England people is undeniable," the delegates declared, "the Lord having written his displeasure in dismal Characters against us." They went on to prescribe the cures, calling for a "solemn and explicit Renewal of the Covenant," and, as a further antidote to waywardness, they devoted a second session in May 1680 to the adoption of a Confession of Faith, the first to be formally published in New England.[3]

The Synod's Confession was virtually a verbatim edition of the Declaration issued by the English Congregationalists at Savoy in 1658. This Savoy Declaration, in turn, was based very closely on Parliament's slight revision of the Westminster Confession. The essential doctrines are the same, except that Congregational polity is substituted for Presbyterian and the authority of the magistrates to interfere with the free exercise of conscientious religious convictions is denied. This same confession would also be adopted by the Connecticut churches in 1708, and it stood as the official symbol of American Congregationalism for nearly two hundred years.

Yet God's controversy only grew more intense. In 1684 the Bay Colony's charter was annulled, and a year later the Roman Catholic James II became king. A consolidated "Dominion of New England," including also New York and New Jersey, was created, with the imperious Edmund Andros as royal governor. These plans, of course, went awry: King James fled, Andros was deposed, a Protestant monarch was settled on the English throne, and Connecticut and Rhode Island regained their former status. But the Bay Colony was rechartered in 1691 on vastly different terms; thereafter it had a royal governor and a franchise based on property rather than church membership. Toleration was imposed, and Anglicanism was provided a foothold in Boston. By this time the mantle of churchly leadership had fallen on the willing shoulders of Increase Mather (1639–1723), since 1664 the minister of Boston's Second Church and since 1685 president of Harvard College. He was aided by his brilliant son, Cotton (1663–1728), who in 1683 had become his ministerial colleague.

Before the Mathers were fully launched on their many-pronged campaign for renewing the churches and asserting

3 See Williston Walker, *Creeds and Platforms of Congregationalism,* pp. 367–439. Walker's careful editing and scholarly commentary make this work indispensable for the study of New England's major ecclesiastical deliverances from the Cambridge Synod of 1648 to the Saybrook Synod of 1708.

the "rule of the saints," the entire clerical cause was embarrassed by the infamous witchcraft hysteria, particularly in Salem during 1692. This episode as a whole, despite its notoriety, does little to elucidate the Puritan mind of the age; but it did lead to chagrin and public remorse, which in turn reduced respect for the colony's religious leadership, especially in the eyes of the merchant class whose social and political importance were notably increased under the new charter.

Already in the 1630s the merchants had expressed doubt that the Bible as interpreted by the clergy made adequate allowance for the exigencies of a healthy commerce. In the Anne Hutchinson affair, oddly enough, the merchants had aligned themselves against the clerical party. With the need to expand foreign trade after the drying up of the Great Migration, old restrictions derived from the Pentateuch became increasingly burdensome. By 1691, as a self-conscious element in society, the merchants would welcome both the limitations of ecclesiastical power in the new charter and the improved mercantile relations with England. Against this background the two decades between 1690 and 1710 may be designated as a most critical period, a turning point in New England's intellectual and religious history.

Some of the events of this crisis period have already been suggested, notably the new charter. But others followed swiftly. In 1699 a group of Boston merchants led by John Leverett and William and Thomas Brattle issued their "manifesto" justifying the formation of a new church along "broad and catholick" lines. In this new and innovative Brattle Street Church, professors of Christian belief were to be given full communicant, not merely "half-way," status; all who helped support the minister were to have a voice in his call; the Lord's Prayer was to be used ritually in worship; and, as a final assault on the cherished Boston tradition, Benjamin Colman—a Harvard graduate with Presbyterian ordination obtained in England—was called to be pastor. As if to document the ascendancy of this new group in the colony's affairs, Increase Mather was removed from the presidency of Harvard in 1701, being replaced in 1707 by John Leverett himself (though a layman), with the two Brattle brothers also in important positions to influence the college's affairs. The clerical party suffered another rebuff in 1705 when the Mather-

sponsored "Proposals" for a more effective connectional relation among the churches were rejected.

While these various events were signalizing the emergence
of a distinguishable social ethos and intellectual tendency in
the seaboard area, still other portents were appearing in the
west. Out at Northampton, Solomon Stoddard (1643–1729)
had also been attempting to heal the woes of a declining
church by startling innovations of theory and practice. Neither "broad" nor "catholick" and in many ways more Calvinistic in spirit than most New Englanders, he called for the
abandonment of church covenants, demanded more effective
preaching, redefined the Lord's Supper as a "converting ordinance" which was open to all morally responsible "professors," and advocated a "presbyterial" organization to prevent
local churches from wandering into doctrinal errors. In his
eschatology he also accented the individualism of his approach by deemphasizing the holy commonwealth's role in
God's plan for the church. He instead concentrated his revival preaching on each person's concern for the final judgment. He defended himself against Cotton Mather and other
critics in two powerful volumes, *The Doctrine of the Instituted Churches* (1700) and *An Appeal to the Learned*
(1709). By the time of his death his policies had won wide
acceptance in western Massachusetts and Connecticut, five
"seasons of harvest" had given practical vindication to his
measures, and the place of Northampton in the annals of
American Christianity had been secured by the ordination of
his grandson, Jonathan Edwards, as his colleague and successor. Even before that ordination Stoddard had in effect
begun New England's Great Awakening, thus proving that
declension need not be permanent.

In Connecticut still other developments exhibited a parting
of the ways between eastern Massachusetts and the rest of
New England. Disturbed by the declining state of the colony's church life and its inadequate educational opportunities, three ministers in the old New Haven jurisdiction
revived John Davenport's dream of a collegiate institution.
After broadening their group to include other ministers of the
colony and ripening their plans in consultation with the
Mathers, they presented their proposed charter to the Connecticut General Court. Their petition was favorably received,
and on 9 October 1701 the Collegiate School was duly char-

tered, with ten ministers as its trustees. After fifteen years of great instability, the infant institution finally ceased its peregrinations among various Connecticut parsonages and came to rest permanently in New Haven. As Yale University, the institution's influence would ultimately be measured in national and even world-wide terms; but its most important first fruits were strictly ecclesiastical and limited largely to the colony of Connecticut and its spiritual dependencies in the upper Connecticut Valley.

The College trustees at once became the most important ministerial gathering in Connecticut, and they soon busied themselves with the problem of the colony's deplorable religious condition. Most of the ministers shared the conviction of the Mathers that the answer to its ills lay in a stricter ecclesiastical constitution. Unlike the men of Massachusetts, they were able to carry their designs to fruition because of the absence of a strong merchant class to thwart them and because they were not only unhindered by a royal appointee as governor but had one of their own number, the Reverend Gurdon Saltonstall of New London, elected to that office in 1707. A year later the General Court ordered the churches of each county to send lay and clerical delegates to a synod for religious reformation, and in September of 1708 the men so appointed—including eight of the college trustees—met at Saybrook. A month later the result of their deliberations, the Saybrook Platform, was enacted into law.

The platform dealt decisively with two fundamental problems in ways that would have far-reaching consequences. In the realm of doctrine it adopted, almost verbatim, the Savoy Declaration, just as the Reforming Synod of Massachusetts had done in 1680; this placed the colony firmly in the Westminster theological tradition, a move which had already been indicated in the college regulations. In the realm of polity, on the other hand, it deviated from the old Cambridge Platform by instituting a semipresbyterian structure which provided for county consociations to enforce discipline and doctrine in the churches, ministerial associations to regularize ordinations and other matters, and a General Association of ministers to oversee the commonwealth's church affairs. For a century and a half the Saybrook Platform exercised a determinative influence in Connecticut affairs, making this commonwealth a stronghold of orthodox Puritanism, with Yale College as its intellectual center. The Platform's stand on polity also led to ever closer ties between the Connecticut churches and the Presbyterians of the Middle Colonies, who had organized their first presbytery in 1706. Probably no legal instrument in Connecticut's history was to have wider religious and cultural consequences. From it one may date the definitive emergence of two New Englands: a "maritime province," with Boston and Harvard College at its center, and a "Connecticut valley province," with Yale the chief institutional bulwark of its farflung parishes.

As New England stood at the threshold of the eighteenth century, the religious situation as a whole exhibited a static quality which another outbreak of the French and Indian wars only intensified. For Massachusetts especially the situation is perhaps best summarized by an old aphorism which Cotton Mather had quoted in his survey of the Plymouth colony: "*Religio peperit Divitias, Filia devoravit Matrem; Religion* brought forth *prosperity,* and the *daughter* destroyed the *mother.*"[4] In Connecticut order had replaced chaos but with no apparent revivification of spirit. In Rhode Island, where the fires of religious enthusiasm once had burned so brightly, a pluralistic status quo had won acceptance and, except for various controversies among the Baptists, the drift to quiescence was equally noticeable.

Such references to declension and a static situation, however, can easily be misleading; one must not regard the value judgments of contemporary Puritans or even less of the Great Awakening's champions as the last and only word. Even the unsympathetic report of the Anglican Society for the Propagation of the Gospel in Foreign Parts stated that New England in 1710 was the only well-churched area in the American colonies. A faithful, learned, and numerous clergy—now being trained at Harvard and Yale—was steadfastly if unsensationally serving its many territorial parishes. A large, prosperous, and remarkably well-educated population was organized in towns, governing itself without disorder and loyally supporting the churches. These were not insignificant accomplishments.

The dramatic flowerings of New England in Edwardsean theology, revolutionary activity, and Unitarian culture were

----

[4] *Magnalia Christi Americana,* 2 vols. (Hartford Edition, 1820), 1:59. "There is danger," he went on to say, "lest the *enchantments* of this world make them to forget *their errand into the wilderness.*"

as yet in the future, though the foundations were laid and intimations of things to come were already visible. Also on the horizon was the Great Awakening—and a new age of American revivalism. As for the "worldly Puritans" who were becoming more numerous and more outspoken, they, too, had been enriched by an important Puritan legacy. The commitment to useful labor, the sense of civic responsibility, the concern for lawful government, the passion for learning—these and many corollaries in the New England character had been central elements of puritan preaching since the beginning. By 1700 this moral and practical message was becoming still more prominent. If zeal was now flagging, there were still many signs of vitality and promise. At least this could be said of the Bible Commonwealths. As for Rhode Island, it had been a world by itself from the earliest days and therefore deserves a chapter to itself.

11

RELIGIOUS DIVERSITY IN RHODE ISLAND

The commonwealth of Rhode Island and Providence Plantations has the longest name and the smallest area of any state in the American union, hence its name rather than its size is the better symbol of its vexed, often turbulent history. Conceived in Puritan "heresy" and maturing as a remarkable seat of religious pluralism, it provides both an invaluable insight into the "left wing" of the Puritan movement and in important anticipation of later American problems and solutions. After Roger Williams and Anne Hutchinson established settlements, Baptists and Quakers flourished in the area and used it as a base point for evangelism. Anglicans and Congregationalists also founded significant churches. Still later its tolerance made it a colonial center of Judaism, and eventually it would come to have more Roman Catholics, in proportion to its population, than any other state in the Union. All but these latter two developments are best considered in the context of Rhode Island's early history.

ROGER WILLIAMS AND THE FOUNDING

In the middle of January 1636 Roger Williams fled from Salem in the Bay Colony, made his way southward, and after grueling exposure to "winter miseries in a howling wilderness," finally found refuge among Indians whom he knew from his earlier ministry at Plymouth and with whom he would retain friendly relations all his life. Purchasing land from them, he and five other refugees settled at Sekonk, but when warned by Governor Winslow that this was Plymouth territory, they moved to the head of Narragansett Bay. Here they again purchased land from the Indians and planted a straggling settlement on the Great Salt River.

Late in 1638 Williams and twelve "loving friends and neighbors" joined together in a social compact whereby all promised to submit themselves "in active or passive obedience, to all such orders or agreements as shall be made for the public good of the body, in an orderly way, by the major consent of the present inhabitants, masters of families, incorporated together into a township, and such others who they shall admit into the same, *only in civil things.*" (The italicized phrase appears in the second, but not the first draft of the instrument.) Naming the place Providence, Williams later wrote: "I desired it might be for a shelter for persons distressed for conscience." Equal shares of land were accordingly allotted to newcomers, though with special concern for refugees. Rhode Island, therefore, is justly remembered as a sanctuary of freedom, though in the seventeenth century Williams's community was only one of the several which caused men in the Holy Commonwealths to regard Rhode Island as a catch-basin for heresy and eccentricity, not even worthy of membership in the New England Confederation.

In the spring of 1638 another band of exiles had purchased, with the help of Williams, the island of Aquidneck in Narragansett Bay. This group was under the dominant religious influence of Anne Hutchinson (who had been expelled from the Bay Colony two years after Williams) and the astute political leadership of William Coddington, who would later become a Quaker. Nineteen persons joined in the following agreement: "We whose names are underwritten do here solemnly, in the presence of JEHOVAH, incorporate ourselves into a body politic, and as he shall help, will submit our persons, lives, and estates, unto our Lord Jesus Christ, the King of kings and Lord of lords, and to all those perfect and most absolute laws of his, given us in his holy work of truth to be guided and judged thereby." They laid out Portsmouth at the northern end of the island and chose William Coddington as "judge" of the colony. Dr. John Clarke served as physician and preacher to the settlement.

For a few months affairs proceeded smoothly in the new community. But the peacefulness ended with the coming of Samuel Gorton (1593?–1677), an extreme individualist whose religious radicalism went far beyond that of Mrs. Hutchinson. He had since 1637 worn out his welcome first in

Boston, then in Plymouth, and before founding his own settlement at Shawomet (Warwick) in 1642 he would also spend some time in Providence and Pawtuxet. At this stage in his stormy career, however, he precipitated a revolt which put Coddington out of his judgeship and elected William Hutchinson (Anne's husband) in his place. Coddington and his followers, prominent among whom was John Clarke, withdrew to the south end of the island, where they established Newport on 1 May 1639. As governor of the new plantation, Coddington began immediate negotiations with his sympathizers at Portsmouth looking to a union of the two towns, which were consolidated under a common administration in March 1640. The next year Coddington tried to secure for Aquidneck a patent which would legalize his proprietary control of the island and make it an entirely independent jurisdiction. In this he was unsuccessful, but his ambitions were checked only when Roger Williams was able to draw the towns of the whole Narragansett area into a federation for mutual cooperation and support.

In 1643 Williams became convinced that if his colony were to resist successfully the encroachment of its enemies, it must have a stronger legal claim than was afforded by the uncertain title of an Indian deed. He went to England therefore and in 1644 published his classic defense of religious freedom, one of the greatest of Puritan books, *The Bloudy Tenent of Persecution for the Cause of Conscience Discussed*. With the assistance of Sir Harry Vane, he also obtained from Parliament in that year a patent authorizing the union of Providence, Portsmouth, and Newport under the name of "Providence Plantations." This patent fully empowered the inhabitants "to govern and rule themselves and such others as shall hereafter inhabit within any part of the said tract of land, by such a form of civil government as by voluntary consent of all or the greatest part of them, shall be found most serviceable in their estates and condition."[1]

An assembly composed of freemen from the four towns met at Portsmouth in 1647 and laid plans for a federal commonwealth. The preamble of their instrument of government declared that "the form of government established in Providence Plantations is DEMOCRATICAL, that is to say, a government held by the free and voluntary consent of all, or the

---

[1] Rhode Island Historical Society, *Collections*, 4 (1838): 221–25.

greater part of the free inhabitants." The document closes
with a ringing manifesto that reveals how Rhode Island too
deemed itself a holy commonwealth.

> These are the laws that concern all men, and these are the
> penalties for the transgressions thereof, which, by common
> consent, are ratified and established throughout the whole
> Colony. And otherwise than thus, what is herein forbidden,
> all men may walk as their consciences persuade them,
> every one in the name of his God. And let the saints of the
> Most High walk in this Colony without molestation, in the
> name of Jehovah their God, for ever and ever.[2]

The governing body possessed legislative as well as judicial
functions. It was at first a primary assembly of freemen, but
after 1650 it became a representative body with strictly
delimited powers. The doctrines of religious liberty and the
separation of church and state were jealously guarded.

In 1651 John Clarke and Roger Williams went to England
again to counteract further efforts of Coddington, and this
time Williams followed up his earlier tract on religious liberty, with a sequel, *The Bloudy Tenent Yet More Bloudy*. It
was a reply to John Cotton's *The Bloudy Tenent Washed and
Made White in the Bloud of the Lambe* (1647). Clarke also
did his part for the cause, writing *Ill Newes from New
England*, the story of how he and two other Baptists had
been tried, fined, whipped, and imprisoned in Massachusetts
for expounding their views there. When Williams arrived
home in 1654, internal and external difficulties required his
urgent attention, and he accepted the presidency of the
colony even though he was tired and broken in health. A letter from Oliver Cromwell in 1655 urging him to take whatever measures were necessary to insure the peace and safety
of the plantation had a salutary effect, and the next year Coddington himself freely submitted to the authority of the
colony "with all my heart." When Williams retired from the
presidency in 1657, the worst of the internal dangers were
past.

It is well that they were, for the colony soon had to face
threats from without. A land speculation company led by
John Winthrop, Jr., of Connecticut and including members
from Massachusetts and even Rhode Island itself, purchased

[2] Ibid., pp. 228–30.

in 1659 a tract of land in northern Narragansett and began to press vigorous claims to ownership. When this struggle was at its height, the Rhode Island patent was further imperiled by the restoration of Charles II to the throne in England. Rhode Island immediately recognized Charles as king and commissioned Dr. John Clarke, still in England, to act as its agent in securing royal confirmation of its patent. Despite Winthrop's efforts, Clarke succeeded in keeping the boundary between Rhode Island and Connecticut at the Pawcatuck River, where it had always been, and in gaining a royal charter (8 July 1663). Freedom of conscience had been included prominently in all of Clarke's presentations, in which the colony's historic stand on religion was reiterated:

> no person within the said Colony, at any time hereafter, shall be in any wise molested, punished, disquieted or called in question, for any differences in opinions in matters of religion, and do not actually disturb the civil peace of our said Colony; but that all . . . may from time to time, and at all times hereafter, freely and fully have and enjoy his and their own judgments and consciences, in matters of religious concernments . . . not using this liberty to licentiousness and profaneness, nor to the civil injury or outward disturbance of others.[3]

The charter was received in the colony with appropriate rejoicing and gratitude. Rhode Island no longer needed to fear the calumnies and encroachments of its haughty neighbors; it could become, on the contrary, an important nursery of several important Protestant traditions.

THE BAPTISTS

The church at Providence which was formed by Roger Williams and his fellow refugees is generally called the first Baptist church in America. In March 1639 Ezekiel Holliman, who had been a member of Williams's church at Salem, baptized Williams, probably by immersion, who in turn baptized Holliman and ten others. Williams seems to have accepted this method, because, like so many other radical Puritans both in England and America, he placed great emphasis on

[3] Ibid., pp. 243–44.

the conversion experience and on the strong New Testament testimony concerning believers' immersion. Regardless of the source of his views, however, they were not held long. Richard Scott, who later became a Quaker, wrote to George Fox of the next stage in Williams's spiritual pilgrimage:

> I walked with him [Williams] in the Baptists' way about three or four months, in which time he brake from the society, and declared at large the ground and reasons of it; that their baptism could not be right because it was not administered by an apostle. After that he set upon a way of seeking (with two or three of them that had dissented with him) by way of preaching and praying; and there he continued a year or two, till two of the three left him.[4]

Going even further, Williams left the ministry and denied the legitimacy of instituted churches altogether. In the corruption of the Middle Ages, he said, the church had lost its authority. "God's people are now in the Gospel brought into a spiritual land of Canaan. . . . Therefore, an enforced settled maintenance is not suitable to the Gospel as it was to the ministry of priests and levites under the law." Restoration could come only by a mighty interposition of God—and to Williams the day of its coming was not far off.

From Williams's conviction that the church in his time lacked clear authority stemmed his further denial that governments had any legitimate right to regulate "the spiritual Israel" or to restrict anyone's freedom of conscience. Insisting that Old Israel was done and gone, Williams made his most extreme departure from the mainstream covenantal Puritanism of the Holy Commonwealths. He, like them, interpreted the Old Testament typologically; but to him "the former types of the land, of the people, of their worships, were types and figures of Spiritual land, spiritual people, and spiritual worship under Christ." After the coming of Christ, therefore, Old Israel was no longer a model for church *and* state, but only for the church.

In these respects he was more radical than the Quakers, with their increasingly well-ordered meetings and well-

---

[4] Quoted in Isaac Backus, *A History of New England, with Particular Reference to the Denomination of Christians Called Baptists,* ed. David Weston (Newton, Mass.: Backus Historical Society, 1871), 1:189.

defined membership. As his later debates with the Quakers would reveal, however, Williams's thought retained the conservative and orthodox cast of his earlier years on many vital doctrines, especially that which held Scripture to be the only source of saving knowledge. His rationale for religious freedom, one may say in conclusion, was worlds removed from that of John Locke or Thomas Jefferson; and the same could be said for the various Protestant movements that gave Rhode Island its distinctive history. Of these perhaps none was to play a larger role in the colony and in the nation than the Baptists. Their complex story, moreover, provides an invaluable example of how controversy, schism, and evangelism became intrinsic elements in the long history of Baptist growth in America.

Rise of the Baptists in England

Historians generally concede that modern Baptists bear little direct relation to the Continental Anabaptists who arose as part of the "Radical Reformation" of the sixteenth century. They emerged rather from the left wing of the Puritan movement in England during the early years of the seventeenth century in what were actually two strands of development: an Arminian group called General Baptists because of their belief in a general provision of redemption, or unlimited atonement, and a more Calvinistic group called Particular Baptists because of their belief in particular election and limited atonement.

The origins of the General Baptists are associated with the name of John Smyth, a graduate of Cambridge who was serving as City Preacher in Lincoln when he became a convinced Separatist and assumed the leadership of a Separatist congregation at Gainsborough. To escape persecution they fled in 1607 (or 1608) to Amsterdam. Soon they were reasoning that if the Church of England were a false church, its baptism must also be invalid, and that only those who professed personal faith in Christ were the proper subjects of baptism. In 1609 they dissolved their previous covenant relationship to make a new start. Smyth baptized himself (by affusion) and then baptized all the rest. When Smyth showed inclinations to merge with the Dutch Mennonites, however, part of his congregation, led by Thomas Helwys, broke away. Becoming convinced that they had erred in flee-

ing persecution, they returned to England in 1612 and
founded at Spitalfields (outside London) the first known
Baptist church on English soil.

These Baptists continued to hold the Arminian theology
they had espoused in Holland and, in spite of severe persecution, showed surprising growth. The General Baptist fellowship included five churches by 1626 and forty-seven by 1644.
During the days of the Cromwellian Commonwealth they
multiplied rapidly, and not even the repressive measures of
the Stuart Restoration were able to prevent them from developing a corporate denominational life. A General Assembly
was formed in 1671, an elaborate creed promulgated in 1678,
and a program of church extension pushed in the western
counties. Many Baptists of this persuasion migrated to
America, mainly to Rhode Island, Virginia, and North Carolina.

The roots of the Particular Baptists, on the other hand, lie
in nonseparatist Puritan Independency. In 1616 a congregation of this sort was formed in Southwark, near London, by
Henry Jacob, who designated himself one of "the rigidest sort
of those that are called Puritanes." In 1622 Jacob removed to
Jamestown, in Virginia, and was replaced by John Lathrop.
Because of severe persecution Lathrop and some thirty
members of the church emigrated in 1634 to Scituate, in
Plymouth Colony, and later planted themselves at Barnstable,
on Cape Cod. The Southwark congregation meanwhile continued to grow—and divide. In 1633 one group withdrew
because they were dissatisfied with the noncommittal attitude
of the church toward the issue of separating from the Church
of England. After another group of seceders had joined with
these in 1638, they all came to the conclusion that baptism
was not for infants, and two years later they adopted the
view that baptism ought to be "by diping ye Body ino ye
Water, resembling Burial & riseing again." In 1641 they were
all immersed—thus culminating a three-step process by which
the administrator, then the subject, and finally the mode of
baptism were successively investigated.

The independent Puritan congregation of Henry Jacob
eventually spawned six other churches, five of which became
Baptist. These all retained the Calvinistic theology of their
forebears and remained more or less in fellowship with their
Congregational cousins. In 1644 seven Particular Baptist
churches of London joined in publishing their first Confession

of Faith, which was replaced in 1677 by a longer confession modeled closely after the Westminster Confession. In 1689 a second edition was subscribed by 107 churches. The area of their strength outside London was Wales, and from here many Particular Baptists came to America. The first Baptist church in Wales, forced to emigrate after the Restoration of Charles II, became also the first Baptist church to establish permanent rootage in Massachusetts; it came with pastor John Myles to Swansea, in the territory of Plymouth Colony, in 1663. Welsh Baptists were most numerous in the Middle Colonies, and early placed their characteristic stamp on the churches of the Philadelphia Association, formed in 1707. Thus, while some Baptist congregations emigrated bodily to the New World, many individuals brought their sentiments with them or adopted them soon after arriving. Roger Williams was doubtless of the last category, but many who flocked to his Rhode Island haven were already convinced Baptists, mainly of the Arminian type.

Baptists in Rhode Island

After the withdrawal of Williams, the leadership of the Baptist church in Providence fell to Thomas Olney, who had been censured for "great error" at Salem in 1639. He was one of the original freeholders of Providence Plantations and a convinced Calvinist, though his leading laymen were General Baptists. The Arminians in this church followed the English General Baptists in believing that the laying on of hands was an apostolic practice requisite to the reception of the Holy Spirit and necessary to interchurch fellowship. Those who held to this controversial doctrine (and Roger Williams was among them) drew support from Hebrews 6:1–2, which lists it as one of the six "foundation principles" of Christianity: repentance, faith, baptism, laying on of hands, resurrection of the dead, and eternal judgment. Hence, the term "Six Principle Baptists."

The controversy over this point at Providence came to a head in 1652, when the church divided over the issue. The five-principle, Calvinistic faction was headed by Thomas Olney, who ministered to the group until his death in 1682. They represented the minority party, and since their losses were not replenished by new converts or immigration, they passed out of existence about 1720. The Six Principle, Arminian faction continued as the original church but accomplished little that is memorable either in the way of evangelism or wider social influence. They did not even have a meetinghouse until 1700. When Rhode Island College (founded in Warren, 1764) was moved to Providence in 1770, President James Manning became pastor of this church and brought it back to Calvinistic sentiments. The future history of the Providence church merged with that of the other churches of the Warren Association, which was formed through Manning's influence in 1767.

In Newport, Dr. John Clarke became the spiritual leader. Born in England in 1609, he had practiced medicine in London before coming to Boston in 1637 as a convinced Separatist. The time of his conversion to Baptist views is unknown, but a Particular Baptist church seems to have been formed in Newport in 1644, and he was its pastor until his death in 1676. Thereafter the church often languished under less able pastors, though it remained one of the few Particular Baptist churches in New England and kept contact with its counterparts in England. The Baptists of Newport, however, were even more contentious than those of Providence. In 1656 a Six-Principle church was formed out of adherents won by "missionaries" from Providence. A decade later an English Sabbatarian collected a large enough following to form a Seventh-Day Baptist church there.[5]

Baptist Expansion

There had been isolated opposition to infant baptism in Massachusetts since the days of Roger Williams at Salem. The first place where definite efforts were made to form a church, however, was at Rehoboth, where several withdrew from the Congregational church and were immersed in 1649 by John Clarke. After citation by the court in Plymouth the

[5] For Christians bent on ordering their lives, worship, and churches according to God's express will, the Old Testament's Sabbath laws were not easily ignored. The Emperor Constantine had set aside Sunday as a day of rest in 321; but the fully developed idea of a strictly observed Christian Sabbath is a creation of English Puritanism, with Lancelot Andrewes, Nicholas Bownde, and Thomas Greenham as major early theorists. More literal and legalistic thinkers, such as John Trask (ca. 1573–163?), demanded a Seventh Day observance, and this view continued to find favor among some radically antitraditional Puritans.

next year, they removed to Newport. In 1651, when Clarke and two other men from the Newport church accepted an invitation to Lynn, Massachusetts, they were arrested for holding an unauthorized religious meeting.

The net result of this incident was to publicize further the sentiments of the Baptists and win for them more sympathizers in the Bay Colony. In 1653 Henry Dunster, the first president of Harvard College, withheld his fourth child from baptism and had to resign from his post the next year. Before moving to the more tolerant town of Scituate, he associated himself with Thomas Gould, who soon became the recognized leader of the Boston Baptists and the pastor of the church formed there in 1665. Being arraigned before the courts and sentenced to banishment, this little group withdrew to Noddle's Island for a time, but then returned in 1680 to erect a meetinghouse in the heart of Boston. By this time other Baptist churches had been formed in Newbury and Kittery, two Indian Baptist churches were in process of being gathered on Nantucket and Martha's Vineyard, John Myles's Welsh church was well established at Swansea, and there was a growing cluster of Baptist churches along the Plymouth–Rhode Island border. In 1717 both Increase and Cotton Mather indicated a degree of rapprochement by participating at a Baptist ordination in Boston.

Baptist beginnings in Connecticut stemmed from the influence of Rhode Island. Before 1705 there were only temporary preaching missions in Connecticut, but in that year a church was planted in Groton by the Reverend Valentine Wightman of Rhode Island. He remained pastor of that church till his death in 1741, and was succeeded by his son and grandson until 1841, so that the Wightmans became literally the patriarchs of Connecticut Baptists. A second church was formed in 1726 at New London by Stephen Gorton, also from Rhode Island, and from these two centers Baptist principles spread slowly into other areas of Connecticut.

It is often said that the first association of American Baptists (referring to the Particular tradition) was formed at Philadelphia in 1707. The Rhode Island Yearly Meeting of General, or Six Principle, Baptists, however, seems to have been in existence several years earlier. Including churches from Providence, Newport, and North Kingston, this association functioned in a purely advisory capacity and disclaimed any authority over the internal affairs of the churches. Growth was slow because all the churches were poor and feeble and travel was difficult; but in 1729 this association held what the youthful John Comer called "ye largest Convention yt ever hath been." Thirty-two messengers (eight ministers, three deacons, and twenty-one laymen) from thirteen churches (eight in Rhode Island, two in Massachusetts, two in Connecticut, and one in New York City) met at Newport on 21 June. In its early years the Rhode Island Yearly Meeting included nearly all the Baptist churches of New England except the Calvinistic churches of Newport, Swansea, and Boston. Although the body began to decline after the Great Awakening had revitalized Particular attitudes, it remained fairly strong throughout the eighteenth century and counted seventeen churches in 1764. Having changed its name to the Rhode Island Association, it has continued to eke out a meager existence. In 1955 the Association embraced five churches with 324 members; by 1965 the numbers had decreased to three churches with 96 members.

When the Great Awakening burst upon the scene in 1740, there were perhaps two dozen Baptist churches in New England—eleven in Rhode Island, eight in Massachusetts, and four in Connecticut—and an unknown number of small Baptist groups. None of them at that time were particularly strong or vigorous, and as a group they would not have a strong or sustained organic relation to the vast expansion of Baptist churches (in that sense the Philadelphia Association was to be far more important); yet, as we shall see in later chapters, a characteristic impulse from New England Puritanism would play a vital role in the development of Baptist strength in the southern states.

THE QUAKERS

Rhode Island was extremely important not only for Baptist history but for the early expansion of the Society of Friends in America. Before the opening of Pennsylvania to settlement, it was second only to the island of Barbados as a base of operations for Quaker missions in the New World. Within its safety they established a beachhead from which to carry their witness into the neighboring colonies. Conversely, the Quakers were important to Rhode Island, contributing to the political development of the colony perhaps more than any other group. Among the earliest converts were William Coddington, who served as governor successively of Portsmouth, Newport, Aquidneck Island, and Providence Plantations; Nicholas Easton, who served several times both as deputy governor and governor of the whole colony; and other leading citizens such as John Easton, Joshua Coggleshall, Walter Clarke, and Caleb Carr. A fruitful field for Quaker growth was also prepared by Anne Hutchinson, whose thought in several ways qualifies her as a proto-Quaker.

The Society of Friends arose in England out of left-wing Puritanism. As a movement, it exhibits the relentless movement of the Puritan-Reformed impulse away from the hierarchical, sacramental, and objective Christianity of the Middle Ages toward various radical extremes in which intensely individualistic and spiritual motifs become predominant. There were, to be sure, many evanescent sects and movements to the "left" of the Quakers—indeed, they often forced Quakers to define themselves more conservatively and to tighten the discipline of their societies. But the movement which looks to George Fox as its founder is overwhelmingly the most important and enduring manifestation of Puritan radicalism in either England or America.

George Fox (1624–91) was a weaver's son, born in Leicestershire and apprenticed as a shoemaker. He early evidenced a serious religious disposition, but as his spiritual anguish deepened, he could find no solace in the existing churches. He began to despair: "And when all my hopes in them and in all men were gone, so that I had nothing outwardly to help me, nor could tell what to do, then, oh then, I heard a voice which said, 'There is one, even Christ Jesus, that can speak to thy condition.' "[6] This experience offered him direct access to God, apart from all human mediation, through the gracious activity of the Holy Spirit.

In 1648 Fox began to witness to an inward spiritual faith in various public places, and sometimes in the parish churches ("steeple-houses") after the minister was finished with the service. Despite imprisonment, beatings, and the scoffing of mobs, he persevered, and his powerful witness, homely eloquence, and wonderful tenderness began to win followers to his way. The traditional date for the origin of the Society of Friends is 1652, when Fox brought "convince-

6 *The Journal of George Fox*, p. 11.

ment" to a group of seekers in the household of Judge Fell
and his wife Margaret of Swarthmore Hall in Lancashire.

The distinctive Quaker testimony is to the direct revelation of Christ to the soul, although this is not understood to
be contradictory to or even apart from the revelation in
Scripture. It does mean, however, that true revelation is an
experienced reality. As the great Quaker theologian Robert
Barclay (1648–90) put it in his *Apology for the True Christian Divinity*, "the stamp of God's spirit must be known by
inward acquaintance." Fox made the same point:

> Now I was sent to turn people from darkness to the light,
> that they might receive Christ Jesus, for to as many as
> should receive him in his light, I saw that he would give
> power to become the sons of God, which I had obtained by
> receiving Christ. And I was to direct people to the Spirit
> that gave forth the Scriptures, by which they might be led
> into all truth, and so up to Christ and God, as they had
> been who gave them forth. . . . I saw that the grace of
> God, which brings salvation, had appeared to all men, and
> that the manifestation of the Spirit of God was given to
> every man to profit withal.[7]

Such a statement reveals the remarkable degree to which
the early Quaker message belongs not only within a broadly
defined Christian tradition but even within the narrower Puritan tradition, with its intensely Christocentric experientialism, its total reliance on the grace of God, and its emphasis on salvation. Mysticism and moralism were extremely
peripheral or absent altogether. This message was nevertheless regarded as dangerous in a century when the conception of the Bible as a closed and static body of doctrine
reached its zenith and predestination was a tenet of popular
orthodoxy. It must be said, too, that Quaker teaching was
feared because it undermined the establishment by minimiz-
ing the liturgical and teaching function of an ordained
ministry, abandoning the idea of objective sacraments, and
inspiring conduct which was attributed to the promptings of
an inner voice. Most ominous of all to the authorities was the
phenomenal missionary zeal which flowed from the Quaker
conviction of the universality of the Holy Spirit's work.

In July 1656 the ship *Swallow* anchored in Boston Harbor.

[7] Ibid., p. 34.

It became known quickly that on board were two Quaker women, Mary Fisher and Ann Austin, who had shipped from Barbados. The authorities moved swiftly. The women were kept on the ship while their belongings were searched and more than one hundred books confiscated. Although there was as yet no law against Quakers in Massachusetts, the two were hurried off to jail, stripped of all their clothing, and inspected for tokens of witchcraft. After five weeks, the captain of the *Swallow* was placed under a £100 bond to carry them back to Barbados. Two days after the ship left, another carrying eight Quakers docked in its place. The prison was ready—and for eleven weeks it was their home. But before they were shipped back to England, they had made at least one convert, Nicholas Upsall, who fled to Rhode Island. The Bay Colony then enacted a law providing that any shipmaster bringing a Quaker into the colony would be fined £100, that any colonist possessing a Quaker book would be fined £5, and that any Quaker coming into the jurisdiction would be arrested, whipped, and transported out of the colony without conversing with any person.

Thus barred from boarding any boat bound for Boston, the Quakers built their own. Robert Fowler of Bridlington, at the bidding of the Lord, built a small craft (the *Woodhouse*), loaded it with Quakers who felt impelled to missionary service in America, and (disclaiming any navigational skill) followed the guidance of God to New England. They landed at Newport on 3 August 1657. This so aroused the commissioners of the united Puritan colonies that they requested the officials at Providence to prevent the arrival and settlement of Quakers. But to this demand Governor Benedict Arnold returned a crisp negative. Rhode Island, he said, does not meddle with matters of conscience, and regards the reception of Quakers as less dangerous than "the course taken by you to send them away out of the country."

It was not peace, however, for which the Quakers had come to Rhode Island. They rejoiced in their freedom to "publish" in the Narragansett region, of course, but they also felt a mandate to tell their tidings in Massachusetts. Within a few weeks Mary Clark was in Boston to test the new law, and before long "twenty stripes of a three-corded whip, 'laid on with fury,'" and twelve weeks of prison silence testified that the statute as not a dead letter. Plymouth Colony was also "invaded," with the result that meetings were established at

Sandwich and Falmouth, and by 1660 "the whole southern part of Massachusetts was . . . honeycombed with Quakerism," the Plymouth laws notwithstanding.

The Friends' dogged persistence in returning to preach in the very stronghold of Puritan orthodoxy prompted stronger repressive measures. In October 1658 Massachusetts took the final step, and under this law William Robinson, Marmaduke Stephenson, Mary Dyer, and William Leddra died on the gallows between 1659 and 1661. In the latter year a published notice of these atrocities came to the attention of King Charles II, who—unwilling to lose an opportunity to discommode the Puritans—ordered that all Quakers were to be sent to England for trial. No Quakers were sent to England, lest their testimony endanger Massachusetts' already precarious charter, but neither were any more hung, though punishment and deportation continued.

A new phase of Quaker expansion in New England as well as in other colonies opened with the visit of George Fox in 1672. Arriving at Newport on 30 May, he was entertained most cordially by Governor Nicholas Easton. He was accompanied by some of the most eminent Quakers of England, and the meetings which they conducted in Rhode Island gave a new lease on life to Friends all over New England. Fox describes one of the more momentous of his meetings:

> We went to Narragansett (North Kingston), about twenty miles from Rhode Island, and the Governor, Nicholas Easton, went with us. We had a meeting at a Justice's house, where Friends had never had any before. It was very large, for the country generally came in; and people came also from Connecticut and other parts round about, among whom were four Justices of the Peace. Most of the people had never heard Friends before; but they were mightily affected with the meeting, and there is a great desire amongst them after the Truth.[8]

Another result of Fox's visit was the arousing of Roger Williams to one of his last controversies. The old Seeker had never wasted any affection on Quaker "heresies," and now drew up fourteen propositions for debate with the founding

[8] Quoted in Rufus Jones, *The Quakers in the American Colonies,* p. 114. Cf. Fox's *Journal*, pp. 623–24.

father himself. Though some seventy years old, he rowed alone the thirty miles to Newport, only to find that Fox had departed before the challenge reached him. Williams was obliged to debate instead with three other Quaker ministers who had remained behind. He published the result in *George Fox Digg'd Out of His Burrowes* (1676), in which he stood fast for strict biblical authority and condemned illuminism, pantheism, and the spiritualization of Christ. He was answered by Fox and John Burnyeat in *A New England Firebrand Quenched, Being Something in Answer unto a Lying, Slanderous Book, Entitled George Fox Digged Out of His Burrowes, Etc.* (1678). As usual in such disputes, both sides claimed to have the better part; but the practical result was to give wider dissemination to Quaker doctrines.

While Friends were taking increasingly larger part in the affairs of Rhode Island, they did not neglect the further publishing of the truth in New England. They ranged from Nantucket to New York, and as far north as New Hampshire. "Meetings" (the name used to designate a local group) were formed in many of these places, and their members were bound together in a remarkably homogeneous fellowship. As in England, so across the Atlantic traveling Quakers became "the bearers of ideas and ideals which formed a common stock of thought and aspiration, and without knowing it the native ministers shaped their message and formed their manner of delivering it under the unconscious suggestions supplied by their visitors, so that the Quaker in Dover and the Quaker in Sandwich were almost as alike in inward tissue as they were outwardly in cut of coat!"[9] In America the same unifying process was soon in evidence. Formal organizational structure began to take shape with the organization of Monthly Meetings in 1658, Quarterly Meetings about 1680, and a nascent Yearly Meeting at Newport in 1661.[10]

Quaker occupation of political office created many problems in Rhode Island, as it would later in Pennsylvania during the Indian and Dutch wars, because of the Friends' pacifism and aversion to oath-taking. In Rhode Island far more than in a heavily settled Quaker area like Pennsylvania, however, they compromised their principles so as to provide

[9] Jones, *The Quakers in the American Colonies*, p. 140.
[10] For Quaker activity as it moved into other areas, see pp. 246–47, 253, 263–70.

for armed defense, though they exempted conscientious objectors from military duties. During the eighteenth century, in fact, the Rhode Island Quakers were to lose much of their distinctive spirit and zeal, though their libertarian convictions stood the colony in good stead. It was the Quaker Stephen Hopkins, five times governor, who led the little colony in its prompt rejection of the Stamp Act, its call for a Continental Congress, and its acceptance of the Declaration of Independence, which he signed.

CONGREGATIONALISTS AND ANGLICANS

The first Congregational ministry in Rhode Island was carried on as a mission from the established churches of Massachusetts and seems to have begun around 1695 in Newport as a mission "to some who had desired it." In 1720 a church was gathered with Nathanael Clap as pastor. In 1728 a second church was formed. These two influential Congregational churches were served in distinguished fashion later in the century by Ezra Stiles, later president of Yale, and Samuel Hopkins, the disciple of Jonathan Edwards. In 1722 the Congregationalists also formed a church in Providence, erecting a meetinghouse a year later, and in 1728 ordaining Josiah Cotton, a descendant of John, as its minister. There was also a Congregational missionary to the Pequot Indians after 1733.

The beginnings of Anglican worship in Rhode Island were due to the Society for the Propagation of the Gospel in Foreign Parts, whose missionary assembled a small group in Newport in 1698. His successor, the Reverend James Honeyman, developed this field further, founded another church in North Kingston, and helped to obtain a minister for an Anglican group that had gathered itself in Providence. The society was also supporting a minister in Bristol after 1719. All four of these churches—the only permanent ones in the early period—were greatly encouraged between 1729 and 1731 by the lengthy visit to Newport of Dean George Berkeley, who on returning to England would earn world renown as a philosopher. In later years Anglicanism would flourish in Rhode Island, becoming proportionately stronger there than in any other state.

THE RELIGIOUS SIGNIFICANCE OF RHODE ISLAND

In the full retrospect of history the place of Rhode Island in the development of American religion is anomalous in the extreme. An important chapter was undoubtedly written there, and the many historians who have dwelt at length on its tiny details are not simply lusting after eccentricity. Yet the influence of its many extreme and atypical modes of church life has been very small. Indeed, most of its supposed importance has been based on the most egregious kinds of misunderstanding. Rhode Island's chief religious significance arises from the fact that through geographical accident it became a place of refuge for Separatists, Baptists, Quakers, and other radicals whose controversial actions serve wonderfully to reveal the nature and full range of the Puritan religious impulse. By providing a very sharply defined reverse image of convictions dominant in Massachusetts and Connecticut, which were immensely influential, Rhode Island illuminates the intensely held and violently disputed religious issues of early New England. Yet in the colony itself these passionate little movements soon lost their intensity and frittered away. Roger Williams adopted an extreme theological position which made discipleship almost impossible; Anne Hutchinson moved on to an isolated death in New York; the propulsive power behind Baptist growth in America, or even its revival in Rhode Island, came from elsewhere; the Quakers accommodated to Yankee ways. The colony became a kind of composite dead-end street for its founding churches.

The other reason for dealing with early Rhode Island is essentially ideological and commemorative. It is the first commonwealth in modern history to make religious liberty (not simply a degree of toleration) a cardinal principle of its corporate existence and to maintain the separation of church and state on these grounds. This honor cannot be withheld. Maryland was formally chartered though not settled and organized at an earlier date, but the liberties it granted were not so clearly grounded in libertarian conviction and theory. On the other hand, Roger Williams's separatistic and radical route to a notion of "soul liberty" had almost nothing in common with the rationale by which the idea of religious liberty became operative in United States history. Williams's views were conceived in an "orthodox" Puritan context, based on an unusual form of scriptural interpretation, and clothed in an extreme doctrine of the Church. The Puritan mentality of Rhode Island's founding fathers, moreover, stands in an almost polar relation to the Enlightened conceptions of the "rights of man" which prevailed among the nation's Founding Fathers. The ground of Rhode Island's early liberties was neither practicality nor natural law philosophy; nor can it be interpreted simply as religious indifference.

Rhode Island's influence was limited by still other factors. Long after its early religious fires had cooled to the point of offering no offense to anyone, the state won a reputation for intractability and monetary irresponsibility which made it anything but exemplary or influential. It was the stormy petrel of the Confederation period (1783–87), it boycotted the Constitutional Convention, and it was brought into the Union by coercion after the basic American pattern of religious liberty and church-and-state had been formally established. Roger Williams and his confreres did, to be sure, express their convictions in both charter and statute. The history of the colony's early years is thus a welcome relief from seventeenth-century intolerance and a foretaste of latter-day American freedoms. Yet in view of the pragmatic way in which Americans have in fact resolved the problems of democracy, liberty, and order, Rhode Island seems to illustrate in an almost tragic way the political corollary of a dictum often voiced by historians of science, that premature discoveries are uninfluential.

12

EARLY PROTESTANTISM IN THE SOUTHERN COLONIES

VIRGINIA

Virginia was named for Elizabeth, the Virgin Queen, and it was an appropriate memorial to an immensely capable champion of England's cause in an age of religious and imperial conflict. During her reign the prayer book was carried by Martin Frobisher's expedition to the shore of Hudson's Bay and by Francis Drake's to the California coast. Then on 24 May 1607, four years after Elizabeth's death, the *Susan Constant*, the *Godspeed*, and the *Discovery* disembarked their motley cargo of 105 men on the low-lying shore of the James River, and an English colony finally took permanent root. What also had its American origin under these inauspicious circumstances was not the mere "germ of a church," as Leonard Bacon declared, but the established Church of England. And it was present not just because a chaplain had been put aboard, but because the leaders of the Virginia Company were convinced that Englishmen needed the church's ministrations and were dedicated to propagating the gospel in the New World.

Religious motives were hardly primary for the London merchants who supported this venture. Like most of the first settlers, they sought commercial profits; if possible, such treasure as Spain had been hauling out of Mexico and South America for nearly a century. In all seriousness they told Captain Newport of the *Susan Constant* that he must find a way to the South Sea, or a lump of gold, or one of White's lost colonists—or else not come back and show his face in England. As proud Englishmen they wanted to check the expansion of England's major rival, and as fervent Protestants

they wanted to halt the advance of popery. But closely
related to all these aims was a desire to evangelize the Indians, an obligation formally recognized in their own, and
nearly every subsequent, colonial charter. The sealed instructions that went out with the colony, now carved on the
monument at the site of the first settlement, point to still
profounder convictions:

> Lastly and chiefly, the way to prosper and achieve good
> success is to make yourselves all of one mind for the good
> of your country and your own, and to serve and fear God,
> the Giver of all goodness, for every plantation which our
> Heavenly Father hath not planted shall be rooted out.

Another vital glimpse into the mind and will that underlay
the Virginia Company's enterprise is provided by Sir Edwin
Sandys (1561–1629), who more than any other exemplified
its highest aims. The son of a Puritan-minded archbishop of
York, and a student of Richard Hooker at Corpus Christi
College, Oxford, Sandys had given much serious thought to
the nature of the faith as well as the mission of the church. A
long-time member of Parliament, he had angered James I by
an attack on royal authority in 1614. Five years later he
became treasurer of the Virginia Company and began to
implement his ideals through a committee that was set up to
codify the regulations for the colony, institute a form of government, appoint colonial officers, and define their duties.

Initially charged with the supervision of Jamestown's
church affairs was Robert Hunt, sometime vicar of Reculver
in Kent, selected by the colony's president, Edward-Marie
Wingfield, and approved by Archbishop Bancroft as a man
"not anywaie to be touched with the rebellious humors of a
popish spirit, nor blemished with the least suspition of a fac-
tius scismatick," and described by Captain John Smith as "an
honest, religious, and courageous Divine." Soon after landing,
on the Third Sunday after Trinity, Hunt celebrated the
colony's first Holy Communion, and thus began a ministry in
Virginia to which the rest of his life was devoted. He survived the "starving time" which ran through the winter of
1609–10, and seems to have been a stabilizing influence during those early years when acrimonious dissension wracked
the colony. He was among the ragged and sickly remnant

who were stayed from abandoning the colony by the arrival of Governor De La Warr in 1610.

This new governor's first act was to lead them all to a service in the dilapidated chapel, where they heard from the clergyman he had brought with him a sermon on vanity and idleness. De La Warr also brought more substantial things: much-needed supplies and absolute powers of government authorized by a new charter and vested in him by the company. His compassionate nature and good judgment made his power a blessing to the distraught colony; but within a year, after seeing most of his people go down before the pestilence, and almost carried away by disease himself, he returned to England. The staggering colony was bolstered again in 1611 by the arrival of large and well-provisioned groups under Thomas Dale and Thomas Gates, who between them were to govern the colony until 1616. With Dale came still another clergyman, Alexander Whitaker, whose contribution to Virginia's spiritual welfare would be rich and manifold.

From Commonwealth to Royal Colony

Governor Dale figures strongly in the ecclesiastical history of Virginia because of his strict concern for *The Lawes Divine, Morall and Martiall* which Gates and William Strachey, secretary of the company, had drawn up. Here, in effect, was "divine" law for civil conduct and "martiall" law for the church—virtually the outline for a Holy Commonwealth. As put into effect by a tough-minded veteran of the Dutch wars like Dale (and later Samuel Argall), the parallel with Cromwell's Commonwealth in Old England becomes striking. Army officers were commanded to see "that the Almightie God bee duly and daily served" and that those who absented themselves from morning and evening prayers were punished. It was further ordered that "everie man and woman duly twice a day, upon the first towling of the Bell, shall upon the working daies repaire unto the Church to hear divine service," and that the Lord's day be given over even more to public and private religious exercises. Ministers were enjoined to discipline their flocks as well as to perform diligently a wide range of church duties. That these laws contemplated a far more settled community and a more numerous army than then existed is painfully obvious. But the fact remains that a period of Puritanic strenuousness was entered upon, and the colony for the first time began to show signs of stability. To the writer of *The New Life in Virginia* (1612), prospects were "good."

Complementary benefits flowed from Dale's founding of a second settlement at Henrico, a less ague-ridden and more easily protected tract fifty miles up the James River. The intervening lands were opened and the colony's economy began to shift from a communal to a more individualistic basis. The population increased slowly but steadily. As a result of this expansion a second parish was formed at Henrico and a "fair-framed Parsonage impaled for Master Whitaker." From this point the first and foremost "Apostle of Virginia" extended his influence. Most familiar of his many achievements are the conversion and baptism of Pocahontas.

After Governor Dale returned to England, the colony again fell on evil times, due most of all to the incompetent administration of Deputy Governor Samuel Argall (1617–18). In London opposing factions struggled for control of the company. These difficulties were finally resolved in favor of Sir Edwin Sandys, who then ordered the formation of a representative House of Burgesses in the colony (1619) and the repeal of "Dale's Lawes." Though it is certain that no Virginia governor was ever able to enforce such defiantly cross-grained legislation as William Strachey had conceived, it is highly significant that the men who took the oath of office and met in the choir loft of the Jamestown church as America's first elective assembly did not wish for more than slight modification of the "morall lawes." According to their enactments, idleness and gaming were still punishable offenses; immoderate dress was prohibited; and ministers were to reprove the intemperate, publicly if need be. There were fines for swearing, and excommunication and arrest for persistent sinning. Morning and afternoon services were required on Sunday, and neglectful persons were subject to censure. The governor set apart "glebes," or lands to support the church and ministers in each of the four parishes into which the colony had been divided. To promote evangelism among the Indians, each town was to educate "a certain number" of natives and prepare them for college. There was even talk of founding a missionary "university" at Henrico, and Sandys obtained company approval to set aside ten thousand acres for its maintenance. The project was premature, both from the standpoint of the company's condition and the Indians' readiness, and it was soon abandoned.

Disturbances within the home company, aggravated by general political difficulties in England, became even more serious after 1619. King James denounced the company as the "seminary of a seditious Parliament," and accused Sandys of contriving to erect in America a republican and Puritan state. In June 1621 James confined Sandys to the Tower (though he found it politic to release him the next month) and quashed the company's plans to present a still more liberal charter to Parliament. To make matters worse, the colony was ravaged in 1622 by a frightful Indian massacre which brought death to 347 colonists, reducing the population to 1,800 and the number of tobacco plantations from eighty to a bare dozen. In 1623 the king set about to destroy the company entirely. He appointed an investigating commission which reported on its woeful state, cited evidence of gross mismanagement, and recommended a larger measure of royal control. The company protested in vain, and on 26 June 1624 Virginia became a royal province. It probably would have lost its representative assembly as well had not James died the next year. His son and successor, Charles I, had less specific grievances, and therefore allowed it to continue. The next two decades were nevertheless marked by constant strife between the royal governor, the council, and the assembly. The most violent resentment was aroused when Charles permitted Maryland to be carved out of the Virginia grant and turned over to a Roman Catholic proprietor. Only with the appointment in 1642 of William Berkeley as governor did the colony affairs begin to settle down.

Yet "settled" is not the word for anything English in the mid-seventeenth century. In 1644 a second Indian massacre occurred, in which over five hundred people in outlying communities were killed. (This tragedy was followed by a treaty which lasted until 1676.) More serious were the distant rumblings of civil war in England. Governor Berkeley was, of course, a Royalist and a champion of the established church, and he took stringent measures to halt Nonconformist inroads on his colony. He was supported in these attitudes by the more wealthy and powerful planters. Strangely enough, Parliamentary sympathizers in the colony remained relatively quiescent, even after Charles I was beheaded in 1649. Berkeley was forced to resign in 1652, while a fleet of the English

Commonwealth stood off the coast, but even then he remained in Virginia. In 1659, while the future of the government was still in doubt in England, the House of Burgesses *elected* him governor, a proceeding which in due course Charles II authenticated by appointment. During the turbulent years of the interregnum, therefore, Virginia experienced little of the mother country's violence.

The Anglican Establishment

The Stuart Restoration meant a return to royal control in Virginia. This provides a convenient occasion to survey the situation of the Church of England in the colony, especially since the relationships then in effect were to prevail without substantial modification until the Revolutionary War. A church settlement had been reached through three successive stages. From 1607 to 1619 the colony's religious affairs were guided by the Virginia Company, which framed its laws and sent out ministers in the capacity of chaplains. The rudiments of parochial government were present in this period, being modeled on traditional English practice. The establishment of the House of Burgesses in 1619 marks another stage, for then a representative body included ecclesiastical legislation among its responsibilities. The third stage begins in 1624, with the appointment of a royal governor who ruled with an appointive council and an elective assembly. Only during this last stage could Anglicanism be said to be established in Virginia; and even then, as elsewhere in America, it enjoyed only a partial establishment. A resident bishop—or even clear ecclesiastical jurisdiction—was lacking; organization of the clergy was informal; canon law was unenforced; and Nonconformity was widespread. On the other hand, the ecclesiastical laws of England defined the religion of the colony; its support was guaranteed by law; parishes were created and divided by the assembly; and the governor exercised formal jurisdiction over many phases of church life, including the authority "to induct (a minister) into any parish that shall make presentation of him."

The fortunes—and misfortunes—of the church rested most directly on the vestry of the individual parish. In operation from the earliest times and officially recognized by 1643, these small trustee groups were elected in each parish to manage parochial affairs, most important of which were supervising the property and arranging for a ministry. By 1662, when they were made self-perpetuating, they had fairly established their practical rights to "present" a living to the rector, or (as was frequently done) to withhold this final action and keep the priest on a temporary basis. This gave the vestry a far larger control over local church affairs than a strict application of English law would have allowed Such powers rendered almost nugatory the tradition and law which made the ministers responsible for discipline, because their tenure and livelihood were in nine out of ten cases dependent on the pleasure of a religiously tepid constituency. Since financial niggardliness often added to the minister's difficulties, such a situation almost guaranteed an equally tepid ministry. Except in a few more closely settled areas, priestly and pastoral labors were often sacrificed to the sullen performance of minimal duties, or to bickering for more regular payment of the meager support the vestry had promised. It may be that the unattractiveness of clerical livings in Virginia kept away the more indolent types, but it also failed to draw many selfless servants of the church. The seeds of many eigheenth-century difficulties were being sown.

No one was more concerned about the low tenor of religion in Virginia than James Blair (1656–1743). Arriving in Virginia in 1685, Blair served as minister at Henrico until 1694, at Jamestown until 1710, and at Williamsburg until his death. In 1689 he was appointed by the bishop of London as commissary for Virginia, the first such authorized representative in any of the colonies. As the highest ecclesiastical officer in Virginia, Blair's nominal powers were practically those of a resident bishop, and he exercised them rigorously, though tactlessly, in a futile effort to elevate the character of the colonial clergy. The interlocking interests of the assembly and the vestries, however, precluded any substantial result. He did not so much amend the existing state of affairs as point out its seriousness. His most lasting memorial is the college for which he secured a charter in 1693, naming it in honor of England's sovereigns, William and Mary. Located at Williamsburg, and eventually an institution of great usefulness, its early years under Blair's presidency were little more than a struggle for existence. It rarely had more than twenty students at one time, and was described by a contemporary as "a college without a chapel, without a scholarship, without a statute; having a library without books, a president without a fixed salary, a burgess (this right was included in the charter) without certainty of electors."[1]

The magnitude and liveliness of operations at William and Mary were but a reflection of Virginian Anglicanism at large. The first accurate knowledge of the church's extent comes from the year 1720. At that time there were forty-four parishes in Virginia's twenty-nine counties, each with a church and some of the larger ones with auxiliary chapels, so that the total number of places of worship was about seventy. Every parish had a parsonage, some including glebes of more than 250 acres; but only about half the churches were supplied with ministers, while lay readers performed services in the vacant parishes. Taken altogether, the state of religion in Virginia was low; and so it would remain until the Great Awakening began to shift the ecclesiastical center of gravity.

In the realm of theology and on the issues of church order so fiercely contended in England and New England, the Virginia clergy were not very vocal. Yet the colony's errand, in Perry Miller's important words, "was fulfilled within the same frame of universal references as the Puritans assumed. . . . In fact, professions of Virginia adventurers sound much like Massachusetts Puritans."[2] The leaders in England revealed this temper, so did the early governors, so did the first elected assembly, and, as it seems, so did the people, though for obvious reasons they had not been "winnowed" as were the early New England settlers. The clergy, of course, did not flout England's ecclesiastical laws, but in the early seventeenth century at least their theology was not contrary to "Dale's Lawes." Alexander Whitaker, Virginia's greatest early divine, was the son of William Whitaker, master of Saint John's and Regius Professor of Divinity at Cambridge, and one of the university's most outspoken predestinarians. The judgments made by the son in 1613 reveal that he followed his father in theology. His *Good Newes from Virginia* declared that some of the company's leaders were "miserable covetous men," while the settlers they sent out were often drawn from the dregs of society. Too many, he said, "had not been reconciled to God nor approved of Him." Yet men like Whitaker were unable to change colonial policy; and in later

[1] Quoted in Charles C. Tiffany, *A History of the Protestant Episcopal Church in the United States of America*, ACHS, vol. 7 (New York, 1895), pp. 38–39.

[2] Perry Miller, *Errand into the Wilderness*, pp. 99–101.

years both the royal governor and the parish system precluded the recruitment and support of a rigorous ministry.
Thus Virginia never felt the shaping power of institutional
Puritan nurture, even in the early days. Accordingly, there
are profound religious sources of the "Southern ethic" which
gradually came to pervade an entire region.[3]

Religious history has a vital place in any explanation of the
characteristic Southern attitudes toward work and leisure.
Neither idleness nor the propensity to live by the sweat of
another man's brow was ever encouraged by the Puritan doctrine of vocation. On the other hand, it is equally obvious
that church life—or the lack of it—in early Virginia was
decisively affected by the dramatic rise of tobacco culture
after its introduction in 1619, and by the increasing dependence on African labor, which began in the same fateful year.
The servitude of blacks was soon made involuntary, and slavery became a fundamental feature of Virginian culture, as it
would in the other southern colonies wherever agricultural
needs made the institution profitable. In 1667 Virginia lawmakers accelerated this development by making clear that
"Baptisme doth not alter the condition of the person as to his
bondage or freedom." Gradually, the colony's social structure
and every major feature of its life began to be conditioned by
the presence of a rapidly growing slave population. Commissary James Blair would report the fully developed fact in
1743: "From being an instrument of wealth, [slavery] had
become a molding power, leaving it a vexed question which
controlled society most, the African slave or his master." And
by that time the same could be said of the neighboring colonies. For over a century, moreover, extreme unconcern for
the religious nurture of the slaves was a feature of this social
order, despite the professed aims of the society for the Propagation of the Gospel in Foreign Parts. In 1731 George
Berkeley complained that American slaveholders held the
blacks in "an irrational contempt . . . as creatures of another
species who had no right to be instructed or admitted to the
sacraments."[4] Thus by a complex process that has challenged

3 See David Bertelson, *The Lazy South*, p. 21; C. Vann Wood-
ward, "The Southern Ethic in a Puritan World," *William and
Mary Quarterly*, 3d ser., 25 (July 1968): 343–70. See also pp.
385–86 below, and pp. 150–54 in Volume 2.

4 See Winthrop D. Jordan, *White over Black: American Attitudes toward the Negro, 1550–1812*, chap. 5, "The Souls of
Men."

historians ever since did political, economic, and ecclesiastical policy, plus slavery, immigration, soil, and sun, conspire to bring the "first South" into existence.

In addition to the emergence of a remarkably rural culture, topography accounted for still another feature of Virginia church life. Many long and wide river estuaries made the tidewater region a series of peninsulas, and with the rise of immense waterfront plantations, the parish as it had been understood for centuries in western Christendom simply ceased to exist. A Virginia "parish" was sometimes sixty miles long: a vast, thinly populated territory which had some logical reality on a map, but little actuality for the hapless priest charged with the spiritual care of its scattered population. These economic and geographic factors also accelerated the process of class stratification. With tax-exempt councilors and the royal governor possessing wide authority over church and land policy, with self-perpetuating vestries controlling the local churches and dominating the House of Burgesses, and with slaves performing much of the colony's productive labor, the church became inescapably associated with social privilege. To be sure, there was a large degree of social mobility, and for whites the transition from plebeian to patrician status was sometimes accomplished in a single generation. But by and large, prevailing patterns of caste and class account for the church's declining popular influence.

Dissent in Virginia

Virginia's charter specified that her religious life was to be governed by the "ecclesiastical laws of England," and during the entire colonial period this policy was officially maintained. In 1629 Virginia was able to secure the ejection of Lord Baltimore and his Roman Catholic followers by demanding that they take the Oath of Supremacy. A law of 1643 required Nonconformists to depart the province "with all convenience." In that year three New England ministers were prohibited from responding to calls from Independent congregations in Virginia, and by 1649 several hundred Puritans had migrated to Maryland where milder laws prevailed. In March 1661/62 Virginia passed very stringent laws against Baptists and Quakers, and a year later John Porter was expelled from the assembly for being "loving to Quakers." In regard to the Baptists, this legislation seems to have accomplished its ends: not even their most aggressive anti-quarians have found evidence of seventeenth-century congregations, or anything more substantial than occasional North Carolinian Baptists who said they had left Virginia.

Presbyterian ideas found some advocates among the Anglican clergy with whom vestments and ceremony carried little weight, but not to the extent of formal dissent. Before 1710 a few men with Presbyterian ordination even occupied Anglican parishes. Two definitely Presbyterian ministers, Josias Mackie and Francis Makemie, registered preaching points in Virginia (in 1692 and 1698 respectively), but their efforts were sporadic and no presbytery was organized.

Quakers seem to have been far more successful than any other Dissenters in resisting restrictive legislation. Friends were active on the Virginia coast after 1650, and a meeting was in existence there by 1662. When George Fox visited the colony in 1672, he addressed many large gatherings. His Journal reveals a whole network of Quaker relationships, and he is noticeably proud that many people of "quality" and authority were sympathetic. In October 1672 he wrote:

> So we passed all the day through the woods and bogs, and sometimes in to the knees, and at the night we made us a fire to lie by, and dried us. And the next day we passed through the woods and bogs and were sorely wet. . . . And the next day we had a precious meeting, for the people of that country (Somerton) had heard of me and us and had a great desire to hear me. . . . The 25th day we passed by water six miles, to a Friend's house called Thomas Goode where we had service. And on the 28th day we came about four miles where we had a meeting pretty large. . . . And there in this county they said the high Sheriff had an order to take me; but I met him by chance, and he took me by the hand and was very civil and courteous. And we passed about six miles by land and water to take in Friends for Maryland.[5]

Fox's account of his travels suggests the obstacles to evangelism everywhere in the South, and explains why Anglican and Nonconformist churches alike tended to be small, poorly supported, and isolated.

[5] *The Journal of George Fox*, pp. 645–47.

MARYLAND

The proprietary colony founded by Lord Baltimore in 1634 is remembered chiefly for the prominent place of Roman Catholicism in its founding and early growth (see chap. 21). After the Glorious Revolution, however, the colony underwent a gradual but fundamental transformation of its ecclesiastical makeup. In the later colonial period it was to become, with Virginia, one of the two places where Anglicanism was most thoroughly instituted. Seventeenth-century developments, however, made only a very small contribution to this result.

The Church of England

Compared to its strong position under state support in Virginia, the Church of England in Maryland maintained only a feeble existence during the entire Stuart period. An ordained Anglican minister served on the Isle of Kent under the Virginian William Claiborne, but when that island passed to Lord Baltimore, his ministry came to an end. There were also some loyal Anglicans among the first settlers; led by a lay reader, they held services in Saint Mary's during the early years, possibly using the same building as the Roman Catholics. Although a chapel was built in 1642, there is no record of an ordained Anglican clergyman in Maryland until 1650, and even then he had no settled relation to a church, making his living rather by trade. In 1676, when John Yeo sent to the archbishop of Canterbury a plaintive petition for an establishment of the Church of England, he reported that he had only two ministerial colleagues in the whole colony of over twenty thousand souls, and that "many Dayly fall away either to Popery, Quakerism or Phanaticisme."[6]

Despite this Macedonian call the situation remained unamended until King William III bore off the fruit of Goode's Rebellion and made Maryland a royal colony in March 1691. Soon after Governor Copley arrived, an "Act for the Service of Almighty God and the Establishment of the Protestant

[6] Quoted from Maryland Archives, 5:129, 133, in Percy G. Skirven, *The First Parishes of the Province of Maryland* (Baltimore: Norman, Remington, 1923), pp. 30, 33.

Religion" was passed. This act, like three others passed with the same intent in 1694, 1696, and 1700, was disallowed by the Board of Trade in London because it violated the English Act of Toleration. Finally, in March 1702, when the assembly accepted legislation written in England, the establishment of the Anglican church became a legal fact. But in the meantime many important actions had been taken. Close restrictions were placed on both Roman Catholics and Protestant dissenters, although the act of 1702 removed those which applied to the latter group. Thirty parishes were mapped out despite the small number of "conforming" Christians among the colony's twenty-five thousand people; vestries were organized in twenty-two of these parishes, and the number of ministers was increased to nine. An annual church tax of forty pounds of tobacco was levied.

Governor Francis Nicholson, who arrived in the summer of 1694, was far more energetic in his aid to the church, partly because he and subsequent governors were unhindered by local vestries of the Virginia type. He personally subsidized the building of churches and petitioned the authorities to send priests and a commissary. Both these pleas were answered: in 1697 there were eighteen clergymen in the colony, and in March 1700 Commissary Thomas Bray arrived for a brief but significant stay.

Bray had been appointed in 1696 as commissary of the bishop of London, and he immediately busied himself with the needs of the church in the New World by gathering libraries for use there. The most important results of his zeal are the two societies which he founded: the Society for the Promotion of Christian Knowledge (SPCK), and the Society for the Propagation of the Gospel in Foreign Parts (SPG). Because their impact was felt throughout the colonies, especially where colonial governments offered little or no aid to the church, both of these agencies are discussed in the next chapter.

Of hardly less moment for the church in Maryland was the restoration of the proprietary charter to the Calvert family. Benedict Leonard Calvert became a member of the Church of England in 1713; when he died two years later, his son and heir, Charles, the fourth Lord Baltimore, received a charter substantially the same as that of 1632. These later Calverts provided very unimpressive governance, but the new arrangements did accent the social benefits accruing to conformity, and an Anglican constituency gradually arose among the landowning classes. This transition was facilitated by the steady waning of Puritan fervor among the Dissenters. Maryland's chief distinction derived from the fact that its laws and its prosperity provided better clerical livings than any other colony, and hence drew to itself a more dissipated and ease-loving ministry. During the eighteenth century, nevertheless, its church life would blend increasingly with the establishments in Virginia, the Carolinas, and Georgia, to create a unique tradition of southern Anglicanism.

Dissent in Maryland

Dissenters were from the first very numerous in the Calvert colony. When answering official queries regarding his conduct, the second Lord Proprietor stated in 1675 that "the greatest part of the Inhabitants of that Province (three of four at least) doe consist of Presbiterians, Independents, Anabaptists and Quakers, those of the Church of England as well as those of the Romish being fewest." In explaining how this situation came to be, he reported that he had found "very few who were inclyned to goe and seat themselves in those parts but such as for some Reason or other could not live with ease in other places. And of these a great part were such as could not conforme in all particulars to the several Lawes of England relating to Religion."[7] The same state of affairs was repeatedly lamented by Anglican ministers and missionaries in the colony, by none more eloquently than by Thomas Bray.

The strength of Maryland's Puritan population was demonstrated in several outcroppings of rebellion during the seventeenth century. The primitive state of the colony seems to have prevented any very effective or lasting organization among these groups, however. On the other hand, the presence of Roman Catholics neutralized or at least tended to moderate the opposition of Dissenters to the Anglican establishment, with the result that after 1690 Maryland lacked the intra-Protestant contentions which were so prominent in Carolina and Virginia. This relative peacefulness was also reflected in the failure of non-Anglican Protestants to organize and maintain their church life until well into the eighteenth century.

[7] *Maryland Archives*, 5:267–68.

THE CAROLINAS

Early Settlements

Unlike the men who combined to form the Massachusetts Bay Company or even the Virginia Company, the men who set their eyes on the vast territory south of Virginia showed scant interest in church affairs. Tangential to church history are the complicated proceedings by which a group of London adventurers and a coterie of court favorites became proprietors of this vast feudal barony in 1663. Although most of the eight original proprietors were Anglican in sympathy, they granted liberty of conscience to all who settled within their grant. Yet even this inducement was insufficient to overcome the unattractiveness of the area. A group of New England Puritans migrated to Cape Fear in 1663, but soon abandoned the site. Another group from Barbados made a similar attempt in the same area two years later, but they also withdrew. In 1669 a larger expedition of about 140 people under Joseph West left England in three ships, the *Carolina*, the *Port Royal*, and the *Albemarle*. After stopping at Barbados and Bermuda, they landed at Port Royal Sound, whence they moved north to the Ashley River and established Charles Town in 1670. Some commerce, largely in tobacco, was conducted quite apart from regulations by Puritan captains from New England, and by 1700 this district had a population in the neighborhood of four thousand.

The incompetence of the proprietary government became increasingly apparent. In the south the French and Spanish menace, together with the terrible Yamassee War, precipitated a crisis in the colonial administration that provoked the king to establish royal control in 1721. In the north the Tuscarora War, combined with many other signs of disorder and incompetence, led to the gradual assertion of royal control until proprietary rights were extinguished completely in 1729.

The Fortunes of the Church of England

For reasons not difficult to imagine, the church in any form had a very slender hold in the wild, sparsely settled and ill-governed expanses of early Carolina. In the scattered settlements of the northern district there were no organized parishes with a settled ministry until well into the eighteenth century, though Saint Paul's in the Chowan precinct traces its origins to 1701. Before that date even missionary visitations were few and irregular.

John Blair toured the colony on behalf of the SPG in 1701, baptizing children and appointing a lay reader at three places where he was able to organize vestries. Since the people did not permit him to settle in one place, however, he returned to England when his funds were exhausted. The society was unable to send more missionaries until 1708, when two men were dispatched; these were replaced in a few years by John Urmiston and Giles Rainsford. Urmiston was suspended from the ministry for immorality and died in a drunken fit, but Rainsford later went to Maryland where he had a useful ministry.

The North Carolina Assembly passed an act establishing the church in 1701, but it was vigorously protested and speedily disallowed by the proprietors. In 1705, after Quaker members of the assembly had been expelled, a Vestry Act was passed. It too was nullified (by Cary's Rebellion), and not even half-effectively restored until 1741. By that time life in North Carolina had become more settled, and the royal government was as firmly in power as it could expect to be in that land of many uprisings.

In South Carolina the Anglican situation was somewhat better. The first church in Charleston, Saint Philip's, was built in 1681 of black cypress on a brick foundation. It was served by Atkin Williamson until 1696, when he was replaced as rector by Samuel Marshall. By 1723 there were thirteen parishes; and those in the more populous areas were fairly prosperous, boasting substantial buildings, comfortable parsonages, glebes of several hundred acres, and governmental guarantees of support. In more remote areas, the work sometimes languished for lack of a settled minister, though the society endeavored to supply missionaries for these parishes. The office of Commissary of the Bishop of London was established in 1707, and was usually occupied by men of energy and sagacity.

In 1704 the assembly passed two acts concerning religion, one requiring conformity to the Church of England, and the other a full-blown act of establishment. The latter, in addition to setting up parishes and providing for vestries and ecclesiastical taxes, authorized a lay commission to supervise clerical activities. This was a source of great discomfiture to the clergy. Samuel Thomas, who had come in 1702 as the first missionary of the SPG, returned to England in 1705 and called it to the society's attention, whereupon they pressured the bishop of London to send no more ministers to the colony until the obnoxious law should be repealed. The House of Lords and the queen were also led to condemn the act, and it was repealed by the assembly in 1706. The supply of ministers and missionaries was resumed, and many men of ability came to labor fruitfully in the colony. The Anglican clergy of early South Carolina was above average; even John Wesley, visiting Charleston during the Annual Visitation of 1737, found their religious life above reproach.

Dissent in the Carolinas

One result of Virginia's fairly stringent laws against Nonconformity was a gradual exodus of Dissenters to neighboring areas, including the Albemarle Sound region which ultimately became North Carolina. In this wild and unregulated area, Anglicans were a very small minority. Quakers seem to have been the most numerous; and when they were not temporarily outmaneuvered or disqualified, they played a significant role in the assembly. George Fox was the first missionary of any denomination in North Carolina. He spent a month among these people in 1672, healing the wife of a former governor, holding a disputation in another governor's house, visiting many Friends, and conducting several meetings. There were also Baptists and people of Presbyterian persuasion in the area, and no doubt even a number of New England Puritans; but for the most part these various groups were not organized into churches, and only resistance to acts for establishing the Church of England brought them to any kind of concerted activity.

In South Carolina, where life was somewhat more settled, Dissenters were also in the majority. William Sayle, the first governor, was a Puritan, and some in the party of ninety-three who came out with him seem to have been of Baptist persuasion. In 1683 Lord Cardross founded a settlement of Scotsmen, some of whom had Baptist leanings, while the Baptist tincture of another group led out of Somersetshire by Humphrey Blake in 1682–83 was even more pronounced.

About this time a group of Baptists from Kittery, Maine, may also have arrived, although their minister, William Screven, seems not to have come until 1696. In any event, by 1700 there was a Baptist congregation in Charleston. A group of Huguenots formed a congregation in 1680. Quakers were fairly numerous here also, and one of their number, John Archdale, served as governor in 1694–95. Numerical preponderance notwithstanding, the strength of these scattered and disorganized groups in southern Carolina as elsewhere in the South, was potential rather than real. Their future would be heavily conditioned by immigration, revivals, and external organizational impulses.

In the South generally churches were weak and poorly organized. Except among the Roman Catholics of Maryland and in a few other places, the absence of a trained and dedicated ministry was paralleled by the lack of a religiously concerned laity. The sparseness of the population, the growth of the plantation system, the difficulty of travel, and the scarcity of towns or cities created other obstacles, while the diversity of religious views impeded those who desired to found churches. Help from across the seas was sporadic and meager until very late in the century, when certain governors and a few determined individuals began to awaken interest in England. The SPG repeatedly expressed its inadequacy for the awesome challenge. Often the effectiveness of such aid as came was vitiated by uncooperative vestries or the hostility of Dissenters. All told, it is remarkable that anything was done. There is no doubt, moreover, that the patterns of the seventeenth century go far toward explaining southern religious developments during the remainder of the colonial period.

Southern Anglicanism became a dominant tradition not by force of popular vitality, but because of governmental support and the social prominence of its membership. The prevailing theology in these churches drifted steadily away from the earlier Puritanism toward a mild, rationalistic Arminianism, while remaining firmly Protestant and strongly anti-Roman in spirit. For many, church membership came to be increasingly nominal.

By 1700 the enlightened ideas and attitudes marked out by John Locke and Archbishop John Tillotson were gaining ground, though this trend was, of course, by no means limited to southern Anglicans. The whole Atlantic community was involved. By the nature of the case, however, such views were ordinarily the concomitant of advanced education, cosmopolitan intellectual contacts, and therefore, to a certain degree, of social privilege. Because social privilege was not usual among Dissenters in the southern colonies, theological distinctions tended to enforce social distinctions. Since Anglican evangelism was weak and the dissenting churches were both poor and very feebly organized, one of the primary characteristics of the growing southern population was that it was unchurched. At the dawn of the eighteenth century, therefore, the religious situation in the South provided many reasons for the pious to hope that a Great Awakening would come.

13

THE MIDDLE COLONIES: DUTCH, PURITANS, AND
QUAKERS

The "Middle Colonies" were fated to bear a bland and un-dignified name, one that would develop none of the loyalties of "the South" and connote nothing of New England's re-gional homogeneity. These in-between colonies are distin-guished by neither a unifying social-political-economic out-look, nor a common religious tradition. Yet they do have a distinctive character, deriving from a cultural and religious pluralism which in some ways anticipated the experience of the future American nation. This multiplicity of heritages ap-peared early: in 1644 Governor Kiefft of New Amsterdam told Father Isaac Jogues that eighteen different languages could be heard on the island of Manhattan and its environs. The Dutch conquest of New Sweden added still another—indeed two more, for many settlers in that area were Finns. Then came the English conquest, followed by the parceling out of New Jersey with its congeries of diverse settlements, and finally the opening of Pennsylvania to immigrants from all parts of Europe. George Bancroft, who saw God's hand so clearly in American history, could well point to the Middle Colonies as a providential training ground where colonial settlers might rehearse the destiny of the United States as a sanctuary for peoples of all lands.

NEW NETHERLAND AND NEW YORK

Political Background

John Fiske found "something romantic in the fact that in the summer of 1609 the first founders of the Dutch, the

French, and the English powers in America were pursuing their adventurous work but a few hundred miles from each other." In July of that year Champlain in a forest battle by the lake that bears his name was making the Iroquois the implacable enemy of France and the ally of the Dutch and English. A few months later, John Smith in a friendly parley was buying the tract of land on which Richmond now stands. And in September Henry Hudson, an Englishman in the employ of the Dutch East India Company, was steering his eighty-ton *Half Moon* up the majestic river that is named for him. His imagination, says Bancroft, "peopled the region with towns." Hudson's imagination—and perhaps even that of the romantic Bancroft—would eventually be outrun by reality, though not under a Dutch ensign.

The year 1609, in which Spain began to recognize the futility of further attempts to subjugate the Dutch, marks the beginning of the amazing commercial and imperial expansion of the Netherlands. All around the world its merchants, bankers, and seamen gained fame. It was appropriate, therefore, that they recognized Manhattan and the valleys of the Delaware, Hudson, and Connecticut as lands of promise. By 1613 they had a few trading houses on Manhattan, while a fort erected about this time on Castle Island (Fort Nassau, later Orange) was transferred in 1617 to the present site of Albany. After 1621 colonial affairs in America became the monopoly of the new Dutch West India Company. Two years later the first party of permanent settlers arrived at New Amsterdam and Fort Nassau, and established still other settlements on Long Island (Brooklyn), on the Delaware (across from the future Philadelphia), and on the Connecticut (near the site of later Hartford). With the appointment of Peter Minuit as director in 1626, New Netherland became a full-fledged colonial enterprise.

In contrast to the well-executed maneuvers of these early years, however, the subsequent history of New Netherland is a tale of misgovernment, internal dissension, and exceedingly slow growth. Perhaps the chief factor in its mismanagement was the unchecked authority of the governors, who in addition were not temperamentally or morally equipped to wield such extensive power. An equally great blunder was the adoption of decadent feudal methods, ostensibly to stimulate colonization. The large grants to "patroons" actually discouraged prospective settlers, while at the same time creating another divisive element in the colony. Large-scale immigration was also hindered by the West India Company's close restrictions on the fur trade, which was the chief source of wealth, by the inadequacy of the land and climate for producing the necessary agricultural staples, and by the relative prosperity of the mother country which made most Dutchmen satisfied to remain at home, despite vigorous efforts by all concerned to increase the flow of immigrants. Several charming Dutch communities and farms grew up in New Netherland, but only on the lower tip of Manhattan did anything like a real town come into being. In 1650, when New England's population had grown to thirty thousand, the Dutch colony numbered only about two thousand—and half of these were of British origin. In 1667 a glowing description of the colony (part of a futile plea that New Netherland be recovered from the English) could say no more than that it consisted of "two tolerably well built inclosed towns, one open town and fifteen villages, besides divers extensive Colonies, bouweries and plantations." It had a population at that time of about eight thousand souls, composing about fifteen hundred families.

England had never conceded the Dutch claims in North America, and after the Stuart Restoration (as part of a larger reorganization of her "empire") she determined to challenge her commercial rival. To this end a vast proprietary grant of the land between the Delaware River and the Connecticut, including also part of Long Island, Nantucket, and Martha's Vineyard, and even part of Maine, was deeded to James, duke of York, the brother of Charles II. The duke then sponsored the naval operation which secured New Amsterdam's peaceful surrender in 1664. Thereupon the Dutch holdings were divided, the duke of York retaining control only of New York, which he governed through a series of appointed deputies. Compared to Dutch rule the new government was liberal and humane, since by this time the economic advantages of religious liberty were generally conceded by colonial entrepreneurs; moreover, the conversion of James to Roman Catholicism in 1672 led him to seek toleration for his coreligionists. Compared with other colonies, however, the New York government was restrictive and arbitrary. The "Duke's Laws," approved by the Dutch deputies in 1665, perpetuated the feudalistic paternalism and class structure of the patroon era. The English were ousted by the Dutch temporarily in

1673–74; and when the duke of York regained control he appointed as governor Sir Edmund Andros, who reinstated the "Duke's Laws" and resisted appeals for representative local government.

New York hardly prospered under Stuart rule. In 1678 there were probably not over three thousand people in Manhattan, nor over twenty thousand in the whole colony. The great estates remained practically empty, with what settlers there were hugging the Hudson and eking out a meager agricultural livelihood. Wealth was concentrated in the hands of a few landed gentlemen, merchants, and fur traders. The heterogeneity of the population heightened the problems of government. The Dutch were not particularly good subjects of the English crown, and the Puritans on Long Island regarded the Catholic James and his deputies with grave suspicion. Due to constantly shifting boundaries, there was little provincial loyalty or chance for a sense of community to develop. Only a tenth of the population was enfranchised; and although the townsmen succeeded in setting up an elective assembly in 1683, what progress it might have made was upset by Leisler's Rebellion and the Glorious Revolution in 1688. The feeble and disordered church life of New York, therefore, stood as the product of turmoil and discontinuity which did not abate until well into the eighteenth century.

Religious Developments

The religious factor in seventeenth-century New York was singularly weak, though in later years it came to be highly significant. This is basically explained by the ethos of New Netherland and not by the nature of the Dutch Reformed church, which was as noble and profound as any current of Christianity the age produced. It had manifested unity and unambiguous adherence to the Reformed tradition at the Synod of Emden in 1571. The ravages inflicted by Philip II of Spain had only deepened and strengthened its faith, and its universities and theologians had made the country a major center of Protestant influence. The Synod of Dort, convoked in 1618 to deal with the Arminian controversy, became a virtual ecumenical council of Reformed churches, and was the chief event in Reformed confessional history between the death of Calvin (1564) and the Westminster Assembly

(1643). Even the Dutch princes were devoted champions of the Reformed cause.

The religious ferment of the mother country, however, is notably absent in New Netherland. In the first place, conditions in the homeland forced very few to emigrate for religious reasons; Holland was already the chief sanctuary for the persecuted in Europe. In the second place, the colony attracted those least likely to have burning religious motivations; it was only "a by-venture in a great scheme of combined money-making and state-craft." The Dutch West India Company did "establish" the Dutch Reformed church, but it was anything but conscientious in carrying out its commitments. Two lay *Kranken-besoeckers* (comforters of the sick) were sent out in 1626, but only in 1628—five years after the first settlers came—did an ordained minister finally arrive.

This was Jonas Michaelius. He found the 270 souls then at Manhattan to be "free, somewhat rough, and loose." Nonetheless, he organized a congregation and had fifty communicants at his first administration of the Lord's Supper. In addition, he held separate services for the French-speaking Walloons. His report on the situation is an invaluable historical source, but he had already left the colony in 1633 when Domine Everardus Bogardus arrived. This second minister presided over the colony's religious life during its best years. He saw the old meeting place in a mill loft replaced by a wooden church, and it in turn by a stone church (1642). He quarreled constantly with Governor Kiefft, however; and when Peter Stuyvesant arrived in 1647, both men sailed for home to appeal their cases. Their appeal reached a higher court than they planned, however, for their ship was lost at sea. In 1642 a third domine, Jan van Mekelenburg, better known as Megapolensis, arrived to serve the manor of Patroon van Rensselaer, thus becoming the first Dutch minister on the upper Hudson. Here he also pioneered as a missionary among the Indians and helped the Jesuit Father Jogues to escape from the Mohawks.

The annals of the Dutch Reformed church in this province could be continued down to the time of the English conquest, but such a narrative would include only a dozen struggling congregations formed by some fifteen ministers whom the company sent out. Six of these men were in service when the English assumed control in 1664, but only three remained when the Dutch reconquered the region briefly in 1673. One had arrived from Holland during this period. At the request of the English governor the newly organized classes (or synod) in 1679 ordained Peter Tesschenmaeker, who lost his life when the French and Indians burned Schenectady in 1690. In the decade before the Glorious Revolution, there was much discussion of religious affairs, grandiose instructions from the king for the provision of churches and ministry, much popular clamor against official efforts to discredit the Dutch church and establish the English—but there was very little congregational activity. When the conservative Dutch clergy almost unanimously opposed Leisler's Rebellion, their relation to the people became even more distant.

With William III, the Dutch stadtholder, on England's throne, attempts to establish the Church of England were intensified. Such efforts were forestalled until 1692, when an ambiguous act was passed providing for the public support of religion in four of the province's ten counties (see pp. 273–74 below). Yet even this had little effect; though the first church officially incorporated under the new act was a Dutch church in New York City in 1696. By 1705 there were thirty-four Dutch congregations in the province, but most of them held only a few services a year, with seven ministers remaining in service of some twenty-three who had served since the English occupation. Perhaps the most promising circumstance in the situation was the important beginning that had been made among the Dutch migrants to New Jersey, where ultimately the "garden of the Dutch church in America" would come to flower in the next century.

PURITANS AND QUAKERS IN NEW JERSEY

Like several other American colonies, New Jersey began as an ill-fated County Palatine, with (in the imagination of Sir Edmund Plowden at least) all the feudal trappings of a medieval barony. In 1648 there appeared "A Description of the province of New Albion" dedicated to the "mighty Lord Edmund" and others. But nothing more permanent: the reality of New Sweden on the Delaware and of New Netherland to the east was substantial; yet so far as "New Jersey" is concerned, the lands between the Delaware and Hudson remained a wilderness. Peter Stuyvesant's conquest of New Sweden in 1655 did little to establish Dutch influence in the intervening territory. The patroonship of Pavonia (including Hoboken) was stillborn in 1630; and most of what few advances the Dutch made around Jersey City were lost in the Indian wars of 1643. When it came within the power of the duke of York to grant "Nova Caesaria" to Lord John Berkeley and Sir George Carteret (1664), he could give them an almost virgin land. Their *Concessions and Agreements* accepted the idea of religious freedom and provided for an appointive governor and council and an elective assembly.

Scattered settlements were made during the first decade, but the only one of much consequence for church history was the planting of "New Ark" in 1666 by the strictest of the strict Puritans from the New Haven jurisdiction. This marks the beginning of developments that eventually made New Jersey a major religious sanctuary. The trend took a decisive turn between 1674 and 1676, when a group of Quakers led by William Penn gained possession of Berkeley's share, "West Jersey." With its generous *Concessions and Agreements*, this colony became an attractive haven for both economic adventurers and spiritual pilgrims. After 1682 East Jersey came under similar proprietorship. The crowning of James II, the abortive formation of a vast Dominion of New England under Governor Andros, and the accession of William III made events in the Jerseys far more complex than a religious history can pause to unravel; but the development of two distinctive subprovinces nevertheless went forward. The patterns thus established existed long after 1702 when Queen Anne, at the request of the Jersey proprietors, unified the province as a royal colony.

East Jersey

Following the lead of Newark, East Jersey became predominantly Puritan. These were days when some men were in flight from the "great persecution" visited upon Puritans in Restoration England, when Baptists and Quakers were kept on the move by legal and corporeal harassment, and when considerable numbers of New Englanders emigrated to new frontiers to found more strictly regulated Puritan communities. As ever, the lust for new land drew men on. One after another towns were founded: Shrewsbury, Perth Amboy, Middletown, Elizabethtown, Woodbridge—each of them conceived as a New Zion and enacting laws appropriate to that conception. Town and church were integrated; in each village the church was at the center, while homestead lands and outlying fields were drawn by lot. The East Jersey Assembly worked with the same ideals as the towns, though their diversity mitigated the rigor of their laws; nor could they often bend the royal or proprietary governments to their will.

Yet a new "New England" it remained until well into the eighteenth century. Thereafter, the encroachment of non-Puritan settlers, the inevitable decline of fervor in subsequent generations, and the antipathy of royal governors all served to turn these people from their original ways. In one sense, however, these threats to their ecclesiastical traditions brought them toward their most enduring contribution. Unfriendly circumstances impressed upon them the advantages of Presbyterian forms of church government, and as Presbyterians who retained their New England loyalties, during the Great Awakening of the eighteenth century they would give a second birth to Puritan influence in the Middle Colonies.

West Jersey

West Jersey was from the first a predominantly Quaker colony. George Fox, after his travels in New Jersey, had interested certain of his English followers in its possibilities, and William Penn took a prominent part in stimulating its settlement after the territory passed into Quaker hands. In 1675 the ship *Griffin* brought the first group under John Fenwick to Salem. Two years later another ship brought two hundred more who founded the town of Burlington. Still other ships followed, and within eighteen months fully eight hundred Quakers had arrived. By the time Penn received his Pennsylvania grant in 1681, there had come fourteen hundred, "many of them persons of large property and wide influence." Because most of the proprietors of New Jersey were Quaker, they also controlled the governorship, and awarded it in 1682 to Robert Barclay, the Scottish apologist and systematic theologian, though he remained at home and governed by deputy until New Jersey became a royal colony.

"Meetings" were organized at each new point of Quaker settlement, the first apparently started by Quakers from New England at Shrewsbury by 1670, followed by one at Salem in 1675. Burlington became the center of Quaker organizational life; here a Monthly Meeting was set up in 1678, a Quarterly Meeting in 1680, and a Yearly Meeting in 1681. After 1686, the Yearly Meeting alternated between Burlington and Philadelphia, and only in 1760 was it removed permanently to Philadelphia.

West Jersey developed a way of life quite different from that of its Puritan neighbor and more nearly approximating that of Maryland, in part because of its fertile plains and river frontage. The retention of primogeniture and the Quaker insistence on marriage "within meeting" also conduced to the emergence of a strong class of large landholders, as well as extensive reliance on slave labor. With these influences came a conservative, aristocratic social structure to which family interrelationships and county government, rather than the town meeting, were basic. On the other hand, it was a society pervaded by Quaker piety and sobriety, from which emerged during the eighteenth century two of America's greatest Quaker leaders: John Woolman, the mystic and reformer, and Stephen Grellet, the preacher. Both of these men left memorable journals that witness to the enduring nature of the West Jersey tradition.

At the end of the century the proprietors yielded to a recommendation of the Board of Trade that a unified government under the crown be established. This was achieved by Queen Anne in 1702; and Lord Cornbury became the first royal governor a year later, serving jointly New Jersey and New York. The Instructions prepared for him and his successors took cognizance of New Jersey's religious traditions, which included liberty of conscience for all but "papists." Drastic property restrictions, however, made political life highly undemocratic, and this led Quaker landholders to support royal authority, while the townsmen and farmers of East Jersey became an increasingly vocal opposition. Fed by old Puritan convictions and strengthened by the immigration of large numbers of sturdy and devout Scotch-Irish, East Jersey became the seedbed of an aroused Presbyterianism before it rose up against royal authority. But this is an eighteenth-century story.

THE QUAKERS IN PENNSYLVANIA

William Penn and the Holy Experiment

The most exciting adventure in the settlement of the Middle Colonies was unquestionably the Holy Experiment of

William Penn, which marks the convergence of religious, social, political, and imperial history in a particularly interesting way. Expressly formed as a Quaker venture in statecraft, it became something of a laboratory for testing the viability of those views. Because of Penn's methods of opening the land to settlement, it also became a populous antecedent of America's pluralistic society. Finally, the testing of both Quakerism and pluralism was made especially acute by Pennsylvania's extraordinarily strategic location between the Atlantic seaboard and the wilderness empire of the French and the Indians.

The nature of the Society of Friends lies at the heart of the experiment. This radical phase of Puritanism has been mentioned before, and its votaries have been observed in virtually every American colony. Often they were resisted or suspected; in some cases they sought (and found) the martyr's crown. The Quakers would have played a significant role in American history with only their New England or southern roots to sustain them, and they would have made a major contribution if they had been halted at the Delaware River in New Jersey. But with the founding of Pennsylvania their ideas and institutions assume decisive importance. To speak of Pennsylvania is to speak of the man who put upon it the stamp of his own genius to an extent that no other colony's founder was able to do.

William Penn (1644–1718) was the son of Admiral Penn (1620–70), conqueror of Jamaica under Cromwell and friend of Charles II and the duke of York, whom he also served. The younger Penn inherited and made the most of these advantages, but no capsule biography can indicate the depths and anomalies of his mind and spirit or the extraordinary range of his activities. For he was almost "all things": the pacifist son of a naval hero; the favorite of kings (Charles II and James II) who was also the friend of the philosophers John Locke and Algernon Sidney; the sometime student of Christ Church (Oxford), Saumur, and Lincoln's Inn who was also a Quaker convert, friend of George Fox, and author of a minor devotional classic, *No Cross, No Crown;* the devout adherent of a radical Protestant sect, democratic theorist, and champion of religious freedom who was yet an aristocrat, accused of Jesuitry and suspected of Jacobitism; the visionary idealist who was also the founder and longtime proprietor of the most successful colony in the British Empire. A practical man of affairs, yet truly a man of the spirit. His long life charts an important path across the terrain between the age of Puritanism and the dawning Age of Reason.

The modest success of colonization in New Jersey seems to have stimulated Penn's larger plans for a colony where religious freedom, representative government, cheap land, and strictly feudal proprietary arrangements would furnish a haven for poor and oppressed peoples, an example of enlightened government for the world, and a continuous source of income for the Penn family. His plans were carried out with amazing dispatch. In 1681 he persuaded Charles II to discharge a £16,000 obligation by making him owner and governor of a tract of land west of Delaware between 40° N. and 43° N. The ambiguity of the description left the status of the lower Delaware in doubt, but the next year the duke of York (although he himself lacked clear title to the area) deeded the western shore of Delaware Bay to Penn. By July 1681 his deputy governor had taken possession, and in the fall of 1682, after a harrowing passage during which a third of the passengers died of smallpox, Penn himself arrived at New Castle in the ship *Welcome*. Before the year was out, the Assembly had been called and Penn's Frame of Government adopted.

In the first year Philadelphia was laid out in the geometric criss-cross which was to be copied all across America. Nine months after Penn's arrival the town had 80 houses surrounded by 300 farms; when he returned to England in 1684 it had 357 homes. Many difficulties attended the development of political institutions, but the colony grew apace—as did its Quaker population. In 1699, as if to mark the end of the century, Penn himself returned. Quitrents had amounted to little more than a trickle, and his debts were vast; but his colony was thriving. Philadelphia was a "city" and the Society of Friends had become probably the most potent religious movement in the colonies outside Puritan New England. Before leaving Pennsylvania for a second time, Penn saw it invested with a constitution largely of its own making. There was now little to cloud its future but the incompetence of deputy governors, the constant harassment of royal officials, the decline of Quaker piety, and the threat of the French and Indians on the frontier.

Problems of Growth

During these early decades, the growth of Pennsylvania meant expansion of the Society of Friends, for the immigration was overwhelmingly Quaker. By 1700 there were over forty meetings, some of them very large and flourishing. They were organized as Fox would have desired into a Yearly Meeting and radiating groups of Quarterly Meetings, all under the "Canons and Institutions" issued by the London Yearly Meeting in 1668. In doctrine they agreed with George Fox's letter to the Assembly of Barbados (1671).

There were four developments, however, which darkened the prospect for unimpeded growth and prosperity. Two of these were external and implied serious threats for the future, while two were internal and more immediately troublesome. The first and most rudimentary to describe is the growth of a vigorous non-Quaker element. Immigration brought a steady stream of Scotch-Irish and various German groups to Pennsylvania, and while these did not become really formidable until later in the eighteenth century, they were a sizable minority before 1710. A second and perhaps more critical factor was the European War of the League of Augsburg, which broke out in 1688 when Louis XIV of France arrayed himself against a large coalition including England under William and Mary. The long series of conflicts thus generated gave impetus to German immigration, and more importantly, became part of the international struggle for empire which, as the years went by, brought French military pressures to bear on the Pennsylvania frontier in ways which would finally drive the pacifistic Quakers from their place of prestige and power.

Of a far different sort was the crisis brought on by the Keithian schism, a harsh jarring within the society itself. George Keith (1639–1716) was a brilliant Scotch Presbyterian who converted to Quakerism around 1663. He became a close friend and associate of Penn, and the headmaster of the school at Philadelphia (now the William Penn Charter School). Possibly he aspired to leadership of the entire Quaker movement upon the deaths of George Fox (1691) and Robert Barclay (1690). At all events, in the year of Fox's death he began a series of public attacks on the society, deploring lax discipline and doctrinal heresy. Since many of the objects of his broadsides were also magistrates, he was found guilty of sedition. In 1692 the Yearly Meeting found him guilty of "a mischievous and hurtful separation," and disowned him. After carrying his case to various other Quaker bodies, including the London Yearly Meeting, and being disowned by them also, he led the formation of a separate body of "Christian Quakers and Friends." These actions may have contributed to Penn's temporary loss of his proprietorship (1691–94), and the Keithians remained an active and long-lived element in the resistance to Penn's policies in the province. But Keith's sect as such fell to pieces very quickly, with Baptists probably drawing off its more strictly Puritan adherents. Keith himself entered the Church of England in 1700, took orders, and worked off his grudge against the Quakers by serving as the first traveling missionary of the SPG in America. After two years in America he returned to a living in Sussex, where he served until his death.

Keith's charges of disciplinary laxity and doctrinal deviation doubtless contained some truth. Formalism was creeping up on Quaker religious life, and many historic traditions were being compromised. Magistrates were resorting to force, the Scriptures were being neglected, the redemptive work of the historic Christ was being underemphasized, and increased reliance was being placed on immediate spiritual revelation. Had Keith proceeded with more charity and less vituperation, he might have been remembered as an important reformer. But his actions and attitude were a repudiation of the Quaker heritage; both the offensiveness of his manner and the crudity of his language bespeak highly compulsive behavior.

The final and by far the most critical development among the Pennsylvania Friends was the gradual and subtle transformation of the Quaker spirit, a change which has been designated as a shift in concern from the meetinghouse to the countinghouse. This can be noted in Penn himself, in both his actions and his theology; and there is little doubt that an awareness of this transition underlay the Keithian protest. But what was premonitory in 1700 became fully apparent during the next few decades, as Quaker merchant princes and political leaders continued to dominate the life of the city and the province despite the rapid growth of the non-Quaker population. In the midst of economic and political preoccupations they tended to lose hold of George Fox's early counsel: "My friends, that are gone, and are going over to plant, and make outward plantations in America, keep your own plantations in your hearts, with the spirit and power of God, that your own vines and lilies be not hurt."[1] One may see the trend illustrated in the return to Anglicanism by William Penn's own sons, or the tendency in Philadelphia for Quaker membership to become a birthright. The entire development reveals how the Quakers' rigorous ethical discipline conduced to commercial success. It also indicates the great difficulty of transmitting sectarian enthusiasm to the second generation. Finally, it shows the virtual impossibility of applying a perfectionist moral code to the whole gamut of human activity from personal behavior to international policy.

Despite difficulties and compromises the Pennsylvania Quaker community persisted for seventy-five years in its effort to guide and transform the world. Unlike the Mennonites, the Friends were too filled with Reformed optimism to forego the challenge. Only in the deepening crisis of the French and Indian Wars did they find it necessary to withdraw from public life and return to the vines and lilies of the inward plantation, thus bringing to a close the Holy Experiment. In 1756 the Quaker Samuel Fothergill reflected on the spiritual cost:

Their fathers came into the country, and bought large tracts of land for a trifle: their sons found large estates come into their possession, and a profession of religion that was partly national, which descended like a patrimony from their fathers, and cost as little. They settled in ease and affluence, and whilst they made the barren wilderness as a fruitful field, suffered the plantation of God to be as a field uncultivated, and a desert. . . . A people who had thus beat their swords into plough-shares, with the bent of their spirits to this world, could not instruct their offspring in those statutes they had themselves forgotten.[2]

When in the 1750s the Philadelphia Friends relinquished the "world" and resumed their role as a "peculiar people," a

[1] Quoted in Frederick B. Tolles, *Meeting House and Counting House, The Quaker Merchants of Colonial Philadelphia, 1682–1763*, p. 3.
[2] Ibid., p. 4.

new spirit of "Quaker tribalism" settled down over the life of the society. This new quiestistic temper, even when it took a strongly humanitarian turn as it did in the life and thought of John Woolman, was almost as far removed from George Fox's Puritan enthusiasm as the worldly concerns of Quaker politicians had been.

Yet William Penn's Holy Experiment, the last great flowering of Puritan political innovation, with the City of Brotherly Love at its heart, was truly to become the "Keystone State" of American religious history. Facing Europe through Philadelphia's teeming harbor, with Pittsburgh at the gateway to the Ohio Valley and the great West, and astride the valleys leading into the southern back country, Pennsylvania was to become a crossroads of the nation. It would remain a world center of Quaker influence. The country's first presbytery would be organized in Philadelphia and a later influx of Scotch-Irish would keep the state a Presbyterian stronghold. For more than a century after its founding in 1707, the Philadelphia Association was a dominant force in the organization and expansion of the Baptists, and the national headquarters of the American Baptist Convention is still located there. The Protestant Episcopal church in the United States would be constituted in Philadelphia with that city's Bishop White playing a major role. Its toleration would allow the Roman Catholic church to lay deep foundations on which later immigration would build. For similar reasons the Pennsylvania Ministerium would become a key force in American Lutheranism. The German Reformed church also had its chief strength in this state, and its theologians at Mercersburg Seminary would write a brilliant chapter in the church's intellectual history. Moravians, Mennonites, Amish, Schwenkfelders, Dunkers, and other German groups, including Rosicrucians, would flourish there. During the early decades of the nineteenth century followers of Otterbein, Albright, and Winebrenner would first be marshaled in Pennsylvania; and from its western edge the Restorationist movement of Thomas and Alexander Campbell would be launched. In Philadelphia, too, the African Methodist Episcopal church—the first independent Negro denomination—had its origins. As the chief residence of Benjamin Franklin, the seat of the American Philosophical Society, and the birthplace of both the Declaration of Independence and the Constitution, Philadelphia also served as a symbol of the Enlightenment's vast contribution to American religion. Finally, it was in this province that all of these groups experienced the difficulties and discovered the possibilities for fruitful coexistence that American democracy was to offer. Within the borders of no other state was so much American church history anticipated or enacted.

14

THE EXTENSION OF ANGLICANISM

Outside of Virginia, Maryland, and the Carolinas, the Church of England during most of the seventeenth century was only a flickering and uncertain reality in the American colonies. In hardly a dozen localities was there a self-sufficient parish or a sustained ministry before 1700. Yet some of these little focal points of Anglican loyalty were in time to become important centers of influence.

The first place in New England where the flame burned for a while before it sputtered out was at Sabino Beach at the mouth of the Sagadohoc River in Maine. Here George Popham of the Plymouth-Virginia Company erected Fort Saint George in the fall of 1607; a church was built and Chaplain Richard Seymour conducted a ministry marked by many funerals. Calamity followed calamity, the weather proved "unseasonably cold," and the colony returned to England in the following year. For the next eight decades the history of Anglicanism in New England is a story of wandering ministers, occasional lay protests against Puritan claims, and a few abortive efforts to colonize Maine and New Hampshire: the Reverend William Blaxton "discovered" by Winthrop's party living alone with his books and his herb garden on Beacon Hill; Thomas Morton with his maypole and Indian maidens, his whiskey, gun, and fur trade, twice routed from Merrymount by Puritans; the Reverend John Lyford, of uncertain reputation, ejected after a brief, uneasy time at Plymouth who, after faring little better at Cape Ann, finally moved south to less hostile environs; the brothers John and

Samuel Brown, packed off to England by Governor Endecott for refusing to approve the congregational church order instituted at Salem in 1629. These incidents remain, and others like them—but not much more.

There were of course many other persons, perhaps hundreds of others, who, like the Brown brothers, would have welcomed the prayer book and an Anglican ministry. Such people grudgingly conformed to the New England Way while maintaining traditional usages in their private religious life, or else they drifted outside the influence of the church altogether. Since church party lines were indistinct in this early period, a large number of settlers no doubt tipped their loyalties the other way, and like many episcopally ordained ministers entered wholeheartedly into the churches of Massachusetts and Connecticut, whose nonseparation made them, in effect, "purified" extensions of England's church.

Only after the Stuart Restoration was the Church of England securely planted in New England. The first premonition of the change came in 1686, when Robert Ratcliffe brought the surplice and prayer book to Boston on the same ship which served notice on Massachusetts that her charter had been revoked. Ratcliffe began his ministry under the enormously unpopular Edward Randolph, secretary of Governor Andros's council, and his efforts were roundly condemned from every Puritan pulpit. When Andros arrived, he pressed plans for the erection of King's Chapel, commandeered Second Church for part-time Anglican use, and by other high-handed measures provoked a crisis which eventually erupted as the Massachusetts phase of the Glorious Revolution. The little congregation survived the ordeal, however, and entered upon nearly a century of modest growth. But because of its dependence upon the royal governor's retinue and the social prestige associated therewith, King's Chapel did not have a secure future. During the Revolution, when the rector and most other Tories had fled, it passed over into Unitarianism. As the "Old Stone Church" of present-day Boston, King's Chapel remains the oldest Unitarian congregation in America.

BEGINNINGS IN NEW YORK

Virtually the only seventeenth-century breach made by the Church of England between Boston and Chesapeake Bay occurred in the New York area. Anglican rites came with the English conquerors in 1664, but for thirty years this foothold consisted of no more than services conducted by the governor's chaplain in the old Dutch church within the fort on Manhattan. Since British immigration was exceedingly slight during these years, little more was needed. Even as late as 1695, 700 of New York City's 865 families were Dutch or French Reformed. There was also a scattered congregation of Lutherans, and a sprinkling of English Dissenters. These facts notwithstanding, Governor Benjamin Fletcher in September 1693 extorted from the reluctant assembly an act of establishment calling for six "good sufficient Protestant Minister[s]" to serve in New York City, Westchester and Queens counties, and on Staten Island. The studied ambiguity of the act's provisions was a deliberate flouting of the governor's wishes, and led to an endless series of conflicts in the colony.

The act received royal confirmation in 1696, and produced its first fruit in the same year, when a Dutch church was chartered in Manhattan. (At this time there were five Dutch ministers in service: at New York, Albany, Kingston, Long Island, and New Jersey.) This was followed in the next year by the chartering of Trinity parish, the first Anglican church in New York City. William Vesey (Harvard College, 1693), an Independent minister on Long Island, was elected by the vestry on condition that he procure episcopal ordination in England. The governor's grant of the "king's farm" in lower Manhattan was highly significant, for it eventually made Trinity the wealthiest parish in America. With the expansion of royal officialdom and of a closely related merchant class, this parish and its offshoots came to enjoy the status of establishment and social dominance during the remaining years of English rule. Outside Manhattan, varying degrees of indifference and dissent prevailed, though several Anglican churches in Westchester County and on Long Island survived.

BEGINNINGS IN PENNSYLVANIA AND DELAWARE

Although the original charter of Pennsylvania specified that Anglican worship might be set up in any community where twenty or more people desired it, no effort was made to introduce such worship until 1694. The first building for Christ Church, Philadelphia, was erected a year later; but services were held only occasionally until Thomas Clayton came three years later as the first regular incumbent. Shortly before his death in the plague of 1700, he wrote that "in less than four years' space from a very small number her community consists of more than five hundred sober and devout souls in and about this city." During these years the preponderance of Quakers in the colony was turned in a peculiar way to the advantage of the Church of England by the Keithian controversy which began in 1691 (see pp. 267–68 and 280–83).

Delaware was until 1701 a part of Pennsylvania. The first churches in the territory had been built by the Swedish Lutherans as early as 1638, when a log chapel was erected in Wilmington. In 1677 the Reverend John Yeo, who had pleaded so eloquently for an established ministry in Maryland, came from that colony to New Castle and with the governor's approval was appointed minister in the Delaware region. Because of cultural differences, the people here were not receptive to Anglican forms at first, but gradually as these circumstances changed they passed into the Anglican fold. The Old Swedes' (Trinity) Church in Wilmington, erected in 1698, abandoned the Swedish language in the next century and, along with the Old Swedes' (Gloria Dei) Church of Philadelphia and a few other Swedish congregations, gradually became Anglican.

THE MISSIONARY SOCIETIES

By the end of the seventeenth century it was fairly clear to any acute observer that lay initiative could not guarantee the future of Anglicanism in America, not even when dedicated laymen were royal governors and not even when the church was supported by official acts of establishment. In the midst of this growing awareness emerged a number of farsighted and energetic churchmen whose actions and organizational work greatly altered the colonial prospect for the Church of England.

The American Situation

Some idea of the strength of the English church in the American colonies at the close of the seventeenth century may be gained from the estimate of the Society for the Propagation of the Gospel that in 1701 there were forty-three thousand Anglican church members in all the colonies, of which twenty thousand were in Virginia, twenty thousand in Maryland, and one thousand in New York. Clergymen numbered in this year about fifty; twenty-five were in Virginia, seventeen in Maryland, and two or less in each of the other colonies. The description of the situation in the society's charter was not an exaggeration: "in many of our Plantacons, Colonies, and Factories beyond the Seas . . . the provision for Ministers [is] very mean," many places were "wholly destitute, and unprovided of a Mainteynance for Ministers, and the Publick Worshipp of God; and for Lack of Support and Mainteynance for such," and many English subjects were "abandoned to Atheism and Infidelity."[1]

Around the turn of the century a series of developments significantly altered the attitude of the Church of England toward the American colonies. The first of these was England's overall "imperial awakening," the dawning awareness on the part of statesmen and merchants that England's overseas possessions were not a meaningless string of feeble outposts but an empire—sadly in need of organization and consolidation—but an empire nevertheless. This awareness begins to be noticeable during the Interregnum, deepens under Charles II and James II, comes more fully to consciousness under William III and Queen Anne, and finally overreaches itself under George III. The church, too, slowly became aware of the "empire."

During these years one may also observe the gradual realization of another important fact: that a comprehensive national church for all English Christians was an impossibility. This fact had been recognized officially well before the Act of Toleration in 1689, above all by the mass deprivation of Nonconforming clergy on that fateful Saint Bartholomew's Day in 1662 and the harsh, uncompromising administration of the Clarendon Code which followed. The flight of James II awakened interest in reconciliation for a time, with Archbishop Tillotson and Bishop Compton of London taking prominent roles. Basically, however, it was the Restoration policy which prevailed, and under Queen Anne, the High

[1] C. F. Pascoe, *Two Hundred Years of the SPG*, 2 vols. (London: SPG, 1901), 1:86–87. Cf. H. P. Thompson, *Thomas Bray*, p. 64.

Church party was again in the ascendancy (1704–14). Its aims are apparent in the instructions to royal governors in America to seek acts of establishment wherever possible. The effects are visible in the efforts of Andros in Massachusetts and Fletcher in New York, as well as in the partially successful enactments in Maryland and the Carolinas. There may even be some connection between the designs of Governor Fletcher in New York and the organization of Christ Church in Philadelphia during a brief (1692–94) suspension of Penn's proprietorship.

Yet all of these measures were futile attempts to turn back the clock, and despite their desire for uniformity, more sensitive churchmen were beginning to see that the church must win its way not through coercive legislation, but by an appeal for personal commitment on the basis of a convincing presentation of Christian truth. In 1711 Colonel Lewis Morris, though a fervent Anglican who believed New England's population to be "the scum of the old," testified eloquently to this view. He was then in New York, but from 1738 to 1746 he was governor of New Jersey.

> If by force the salary is taken from [the people] and paid to the ministers of The Church, it may be a means of subsisting those Ministers, but they wont make many converts among a people who think themselves very much injured. . . . Whereas, let this matter be once regularly determined . . . and then the Church will in all probability flourish, and I believe had at this day been in a much better position, had there been no Act in her favor; for in the Jerseys and Pensilvania, where there is no act, there are four times the number of church men than there are in this province of N. York; and they are soe, most of them, upon principle, whereas nine parts in ten, of ours, will add no great credit to whatever church they are of; nor can it well be expected otherwise.[2]

Whether expressed in the terms of Colonel Morris or not, a vital feature of the times was the awakening of the missionary spirit, a closely related resurgence of moral concern, and the formation of various societies for the reformation of

[2] Letter to John Chamberlayne, secretary of the SPG, in *Documents Relative to the Colonial History of New York,* ed. E. B. O'Callaghan, 15 vols. (Albany, 1853–87), 5:321.

manners. No aspect of these movements is more important to Anglican history in America than that which created the "Venerable Society" to which frequent reference has already been made.

Thomas Bray and the SPG

English interest in North American missions was articulated early. The Society for the Propagation of the Gospel in New England had been founded in London and chartered by Parliament in 1649, in response to the labors of John Eliot (1604–90) among the Indians in Massachusetts. This work was severely curtailed after King Philip's War, and the responsibility for sponsoring Christian missions in the English colonies devolved on individual colonies, churches, and persons, or, rather haphazardly, upon the bishop of London. Henry Compton was the incumbent of this strategic post from 1675 until his death in 1713, except during the period of his rupture with James II (1686–89), and it was he who sent James Blair to Virginia in 1685 and appointed him four years later as the first commissary of the bishop in any American colony. In 1696, in an act fraught with significance for the future of Anglicanism in America, he appointed as commissary for Maryland the Reverend Thomas Bray, to whose energy and foresight both the Society for Promoting Christian Knowledge (SPCK) and the Society for the Propagation of the Gospel in Foreign Parts (SPG) may be attributed.

Thomas Bray (1656–1730) was born on a farm near the Welsh border. Attending All Souls' College, Oxford, as "puer pauper," he took his B.A. in 1678 and entered orders the same year. In his first pastorate at Sheldon, Warwickshire, Bray planned *A Course Of Lectures Upon the Church Catechism, in Four Volumes,* completing only the first volume (consisting of twenty-six lectures), which was published at Oxford in 1696. It secured for him not only considerable profit with which to finance his later ventures, but also the recognition of the bishop of London. Bray's interest in the teaching role of the church and his concern for the adequate equipping of the clergy made him a natural choice for the task in Maryland. His first project was to organize a voluntary society to provide libraries at home and abroad; its first meeting in March 1699 marks the beginning of the SPCK.

Although it was an unchartered organization, Bray's exertions resulted in the foundation of nearly forty libraries in the American colonies from Boston to Charleston. The largest, at Annapolis, Maryland, was one of the first semipublic lending libraries in the New World.

By December 1699 Bray was ready to sail for Maryland. Arriving in March 1700, he soon became convinced that he could promote the religious interests of the colony better in England; and less than six months later he was home again. Bray secured a royal charter for a second society, the Society for the Propagation of the Gospel in Foreign Parts, in June 1701, a date which became a watershed in the American history of Anglicanism, for the society from the first had powerful royal, political, and episcopal support. Archbishop Tenison himself officiated at the first meeting. The society became the chief means of extending the Church of England beyond the seas, and for the next eighty years, America was its almost exclusive concern. Its primary task lay in securing suitable men to serve as missionaries, thus preventing the dissolute dregs of the English clergy from gravitating to the unregulated colonial parishes. It helped support ministers in existing colonial parishes and sent itinerant missionaries to organize congregations where possible in colonies which showed little or no solicitude for Anglicanism. It also professed a concern for evangelizing the Indians and slaves. Finally, it sought to coordinate this farflung enterprise so as to make maximum use of the funds it could raise. Its records, and the reports of its missionaries, then as now, were an invaluable source of information on the fields, the sowers, and the harvest.

The impetus thus given was desperately needed even in the most favored colonies. Commissary James Blair reported in 1700 that more than half the parishes of Virginia lacked a ministry; yet through his efforts and with SPG aid all but two of these were staffed in the year of Blair's death (1743). In Maryland too the need was great, since the governors who followed Francis Nicholson lacked his churchly zeal. Governor Hart in 1714 secured approval for two commissaries, one on the eastern shore, another on the western, but neither the legislature nor the clergy wished to acknowledge the ecclesiastical jurisdiction of the bishop of London. Men and aid from the SPG made a great difference. The importance of SPG missionaries in the Carolinas has already been indicated.

In the northern colonies this new source of support had a still more decisive effect, as Anglican history literally began in some cases with the arrival of the first SPG missionary. The man to whom this honor fell first was the petulant ex-Quaker, George Keith, whose earlier accomplishments have already been noted. Keith's *Greater and Lesser Catechism* was published by the SPCK shortly after he entered the Anglican ministry, and in 1702 he was sent on an exploratory tour of the colonies, joined by John Talbot, chaplain of the ship on which he crossed. They traveled eight hundred miles from Maine to North Carolina, and accounted for the first formal Anglican "presence" in several colonies. In their wake came hundreds of others, 309 altogether, before the Revolution ended the enterprise. Since no detailed account can be given here of all their multifarious labors, some typical accomplishments and a few especially significant ones must suffice.

THE MIDDLE COLONIES

In New Jersey the visit of Keith and Talbot came almost simultaneously with the union of East and West Jersey as a single crown colony (1702). Talbot remained in Burlington, founding Saint Mary's Church and staying on as its rector. His High Church views and suspected sympathy with the deposed house of Stuart aroused much criticism, however, and during a three-year period he was kept from his church. His interest in missions nevertheless took him all over the province, and only a lack of ministers and money prevented him from establishing many permanent places of worship. Talbot was also prominent among those who urged the appointment of a bishop for America; he was even suspected of performing episcopal acts himself. In 1705 John Brooke arrived as missionary of the SPG and laid the foundations for Saint John's Church in Elizabethtown; by the time of his death two years later he was ministering at seven other stations across the fifty miles of his "parish." Thomas B. Chandler, a Yale graduate who was later put in charge of this cure, continued to organize the movement to obtain an American bishop. (He himself was later designated the first bishop of Nova Scotia.) During the three quarters of a century before the Revolution, New Jersey was served by forty-four SPG missionaries.

In Pennsylvania the unusually fruitful ministry of Thomas Clayton was continued with equal success by the Reverend Evan Evans, a Welshman sent out by the bishop of London. His ability to preach in Welsh helped to cement the ties of the many Welsh settlers in the Philadelphia area, and his sincere concern for spiritual matters allayed the suspicions of the many Quakers who still distrusted the institution which had caused them so much suffering in England. In Pennsylvania, as elsewhere, many "Keithian Quakers" proved most ready to conform to the Church of England. Evans remained in charge of Christ Church in Philadelphia for eighteen years, nurturing a strong, well-organized parish. He also introduced Anglican worship in seven other communities in the vicinity, baptized several hundred former Quakers, and helped to found churches at Oxford, Chester, and New Castle (Delaware), which were functioning permanently by the time of his retirement in 1718 to an easier living in Maryland. From the time of Keith and Talbot's visit until the Revolution, nearly fifty missionaries of the SPG served the Anglicans of Pennsylvania, though regular services were held in scarcely half a dozen places outside Philadelphia.

In New York the society was able to lend a similar kind of support, especially to outlying parishes in Westchester County and on Long Island. Fifty-eight missionaries were sent during the years before the Revolution. In addition, more Indian missions were attempted here than elsewhere, but due to weak official support they had very little success. Only after the fall of New France, with aid provided by Sir William Johnson, the northern superintendent of Indian affairs, was a small apostolate to the Mohawks carried out.

Higher Education in Pennsylvania and New York

Until the middle of the eighteenth century one of the chief hindrances to the prosperity of the Anglican churches in America was the inadequacy of its educational institutions. William and Mary existed to alleviate this situation, but for many reasons (not least of which was the tactlessness of its first president, James Blair) this college grew very slowly. In the Middle Colonies the needs were especially acute, and Anglicans were to figure importantly in two of the most promising responses to these needs, one in New York, the other in Philadelphia. By an interesting coincidence some constructive advice was provided to both of these efforts by the distinguished philosopher, George Berkeley, who between 1729 and 1731 took up residence near Newport, Rhode Island, while waiting for financial support to implement his own plans for an Indian college in Bermuda. After returning to England he became a generous benefactor of both the Harvard and Yale libraries, and through his most fervent American disciple, Samuel Johnson, the Anglican minister in Stratford, Connecticut, he made his own educational ideas felt. When Benjamin Franklin on behalf of the Philadelphia trustees requested Johnson to become president of their nascent institution, Berkeley's plans were forwarded, though Johnson himself declined the position. After receiving aid from various sources, the Philadelphia College and Academy finally gained a firm footing in 1754. The Reverend William Smith, an Anglican minister and educational theorist, was appointed provost, and under his leadership a new charter was obtained in 1755. In 1757 the first bachelor's degrees were awarded. What was to become the University of Pennsylvania was in existence.

By this time similar plans had been carried forward in New York, and here too Anglicans led the effort. Trinity Church was a kind of godfather of the project, though this very fact blighted the early years of the institution, on account of the opposition it aroused among non-Anglicans. The assembly approved a fund-raising lottery in 1753, and then in 1754 a royal charter was issued. In that year Samuel Johnson reluctantly left his Connecticut parish and assumed the presidency of King's College (later renamed Columbia). Now by another more direct channel Bishop Berkeley's educational ideas were instituted, and in 1758 King's College awarded its first bachelor's degrees.

Neither of these schools were church-related in the forthright way in which Harvard, Yale, William and Mary, and Princeton were, and such Anglican connections as existed at the outset soon became fairly tenuous. Yet in both places Anglicans were most prominent among the institutions' early supporters and in their faculties, and both institutions received modest royal patronage partly on that account. From both of them many prominent leaders of the Episcopal church would be graduated.

NEW ENGLAND

In the Puritan sanctuaries of New England the SPG made more impressive gains than in the other colonies, and it figured in one sensational triumph, though here as elsewhere the proportion of its efforts was modest. Congregations were widely scattered and usually so small that extensive support from the SPG was required everywhere except in the Boston area. Boston was the starting point for the missionary journey of Keith and Talbot, but the presence of King's Chapel there made their visit less significant than elsewhere. Some years later, the role of Puritan gadfly was filled in the unlikely person of a young Massachusetts-born, Harvard-educated layman of Jacobite tendencies and polemical disposition, John Checkley. Beginning around 1719 he wrote or edited a series of works that opened issues of theology and church order. In 1723–24 he even became the object of legal proceedings for libel. Naturally a spate of controversial publication followed, but Checkley remained steadfast in his views. Many years later he was ordained in England at the age of fifty-nine, whereupon he began a fourteen-year Anglican ministry in Providence, Rhode Island.

In the meantime the Anglican constituency of Boston was growing. In 1723 Christ Church was opened for worship, the historic "North Church" associated in American memory with Paul Revere's ride. Trinity Church was built in 1735 on a still larger scale, and all three Anglican churches as well as several in surrounding towns, notably Christ Church in Cambridge, showed considerable vitality until they were disrupted by the Revolution and the exodus of Loyalists. The dominant Anglican spokesman during these years was Dr. Timothy Cutler, rector of North Church during forty-two eventful years (1723–65). Cutler's forthright pronouncements suggest the degree to which Anglican growth in these years profited, first from the declining vitality and assurance of the older Puritan spirit, and then from widespread revulsion for the excesses of the new forms of fervency promoted by the Great Awakening. The growing prosperity and widening intellectual horizons of the Boston area also increased the attractiveness of the broad and liberal rationalism, the dignified worship, and the freedom from strict conceptions of church discipline which characterized eighteenth-century Anglicanism. In Rhode Island a similar process could be observed, though in that seat of sectarian dissension the Church of England became an even more attractive haven, especially in the areas where commercial growth was most marked.

In Connecticut the pattern of Anglican growth was very different, for in this "land of steady habits" the disparities of country and city were much less marked, the government was in colonial hands, and the Standing Order had been much more firmly knit together in accordance with the Saybrook Platform. Except for occasional individual representations, the colony's first public manifestation of Anglicanism was the services of Keith and Talbot in New London (1702). For the next twenty years the SPG made very small advances. Only one weak "parish" was in existence, at Stratford, founded in 1707 by a New York missionary but still without a building and usually without clergy. 1722 became memorable, however, as the year of the "great apostasy" in the New Haven area. The leader of this defection was Timothy Cutler, sometime Congregational minister in Stratford but since 1719 rector of Yale College, who seems to have been somewhat influenced by Checkley's polemics in Massachusetts. In close contact with him was a group of Yale graduates including Daniel Brown, the college's one tutor, Samuel Johnson, a former tutor now minister in West Haven, James Wetmore, minister in North Haven, and three somewhat less avid ministers in nearby towns. These men during a period of several years had been reading and discussing many works of Anglican divinity and recent philosophy that had been given to the Yale library by various English donors. They were fascinated by these broader, more urbane attitudes, and became correspondingly less committed to the stricter doctrines of New England theology. They also began to have serious doubts as to the validity of "presbyterial" (i.e. nonepiscopal) ordination. Finally, after stating their doubts to the college trustees, they were asked by the Reverend Gurdon Saltonstall, a trustee who was then also governor of Connecticut, to discuss their problems with a group of Congregational ministers. On the day after commencement (13 September 1722) this historic colloquy was held in the college library, but to no effect other than to strengthen the resolve of the incipient Anglicans, who very soon thereafter proceeded to England for ordination.

They returned within a year to New England. Cutler, now with an honorary doctorate from Oxford, began his long ministry in Boston; Johnson went to Stratford, where he completed the first Anglican church building in Connecticut and for two decades acted as "dean" of the small but slowly growing group of SPG missionaries serving congregations in Connecticut; Wetmore was sent to Rye (New York). By 1742 there were fourteen churches and seven clergymen in the colony; by 1760, thirty churches and fourteen ministers.[3] By 1775 there were twenty ministers and perhaps twice as many parishes or missions, but by this time the revolutionary spirit and the rising anti-British sentiment was gravely hindering Anglican growth.

The Anglican constituency in Connecticut, laity and clergy alike, was in several ways unique. More than any other in America it stood without official or governmental support, gained no social prestige or favor due to its religious affiliation, and suffered considerable harassment by the authorities of church and state, despite the colony's toleration law of 1708. Many of the clergy were native-born, Yale-educated "converts," firm in their convictions and generally committed to High Church attitudes on the church and sacraments, and to Tory views on governmental and colonial issues. They tended to be more conservative politically, and after the Stamp Act crisis of 1765, their Loyalism began to bring another kind of odium upon them. Had they not been reasonably inured to obloquy, the war would probably have eliminated their advances. As it was, they persevered, and during the difficult postwar years they were able to contribute very significantly to the formation of the Protestant Episcopal church in the United States.[4]

[3] Included among this Connecticut group was also the minister to a small flock in Great Barrington, Massachusetts.

[4] Among the missionary rectors of Connecticut was Samuel Seabury, a former Congregational minister of North Groton who after his ordination in England served as an SPG missionary in New London before moving to an extended ministry on Long Island. His son, Samuel, Jr., after attending Yale, also became an SPG missionary in New York, and after many vicissitudes was elected by the Connecticut clergy to seek consecration in England or Scotland. Successful in this effort, he returned in 1784 as the first Anglican bishop in the United States, thus gaining an old objective of Dr. Bray and a persistent goal of the SPG (see chap. 23).

GEORGIA

The last of the old southern colonies, Georgia was founded because of England's need to protect her other possessions from Spanish and French depredations. Also decisive, however, was a genuine philanthropic concern for the victims of poverty then being thrown into filthy debtors prisons. The event thus figured in the great European competition for American empire as well as in the moral and humanitarian movements arising in England after 1690. By an interesting series of interconnections, Georgia is also an important theater of activity for the SPG, the realization of a life-long interest of Thomas Bray, and a direct product of his organizing activity. A recent biographer even asserts that "Bray may perhaps claim to have originated [Georgia]."[5]

Bray's active association with the SPG lasted only a few years beyond its founding, but in later years, as rector of Saint Botolph, Aldgate, in London, he carried on diverse works in education, composed a vast "martyrology" on the "encroachments and invasions of Popery," and became increasingly interested in moral and humanitarian movements. In this latter connection he came in contact with James Oglethorpe, a military hero of the War of the Spanish Succession who, as a member of Parliament, had instigated an investigation of prisons in which Lord Percival, a friend of Bray's, was also involved. In 1723 Bray had formed a group of Associates to administer a fund for the evangelizing of Negroes in America, and shortly before his death twenty-four new Associates were added with a view to combining and broadening their objectives. These Associates of the late Dr. Bray then worked in concert with other interested parties, including Thomas Coram, founder of London's Foundling Hospital, to obtain royal and parliamentary support for a colony between South Carolina and Florida, the highly touted earthly paradise of "Azilia."

King George II granted the Georgia charter in 1732, giving to a group of twenty-one trustees full proprietary rights to the vast pine-forested area between the Savannah and Altamaha rivers—and from their headwaters west to "the Great South Sea." Parliament also granted generous financial aid.

[5] Thompson, *Thomas Bray*, p. 100.

With Oglethorpe in charge, the first company landed early in 1733. Savannah was founded, land was purchased from the Creek Indians, and in the first year over five hundred objects of charity entered the colony, to be followed during the next twenty years by a thousand more. As in Pennsylvania, moreover, the offer of haven to distressed Europeans was often accepted. In 1735 Moravians from Saxony arrived at Savannah, taking up lands which had earlier been offered to the harassed Schwenkfelders. The first of four contingents of the persecuted Salzburg Lutherans also came in that year, founding Ebenezer twenty-five miles up the Savannah, and later a New Ebenezer. Supported by the pietists of Halle and supplied by a remarkable series of pastors, Ebenezer became one of the few prosperous settlements in early Georgia, while also remaining a center of intense pietistic spirituality.

But Georgia as a whole did not prosper. The trustees ruled without a duly constituted governor or popular assembly; discontent was increased by the prohibition of hard liquor, slaves, and fee-simple land ownership, unrealistic regulations for the planting of mulberry trees, and general administrative ineptitude. Oglethorpe's two unsuccessful campaigns against Saint Augustine occasioned further hardship and wrangling, though his ambush of a Spanish attack on Saint Simon's Island seems to have vindicated the colony's worth as a buffer. In 1742 rum was legalized, in 1749 slavery was permitted, in 1750 fee-simple land ownership was provided; but to no avail. The trustees yielded up their charter in 1752, a year before it expired, and three years later John Reynolds, a naval captain, became the first royal governor. Georgia's population, which then consisted of two thousand whites and one thousand slaves, continued to grow very slowly, reaching eighty-two thousand by 1790. It remained the least populous and least prosperous of the colonies.

The religious history of Georgia is desultory and rather sad. Anglicanism was nominally favored and the trustees provided a chaplain. When their first appointee died, they sought and received a replacement from the SPG. He promptly returned to England, complaining bitterly about lack of cooperation from the authorities, yet the trustees were unable to amend the situation. Nor did things improve after the institution of crown colony government, despite the passage of an act of establishment in 1758. Of the long series of ministers who came and went, the predominant traits seem to have been extreme susceptibility to fatal disease, marked eccentricity, strong desires to serve elsewhere, or unusual faults of character. Aside from the Moravian and Salzburger settlements, Savannah, Frederica, and Augusta were the only three places of settled worship, and rarely were all three fitly supplied. Only Bartholomew Zouberbuhler, a Swiss-American ordained in England, conducted a long and fruitful Anglican ministry in Georgia in the years before the Revolution. Most notorious was the Reverend Thomas Bosomworth, who left his station at Frederica to marry an already twice-wed Indian "princess" and later instigated an Indian outbreak. For extended periods the colony was without benefit of any Anglican clergy.

Yet Georgia has withal an illustrious colonial church history; great names abound. It was in this remote outpost that the famous Wesley brothers began their ministry in 1736 with such magnificent lack of success. Coming at Oglethorpe's urging, John began his ministry at Savannah, Charles at Frederica; and both of these men, still in the extreme High Church phase of their careers, at once instituted a legalistic, rubrically punctilious ministry to rapidly shrinking congregations who soon denounced them as papistic and unreasonable. Most objectionable were their insistence on baptism by immersion, and John Wesley's rigorous restriction of admission to the Lord's Supper. After four months Charles gave up and returned to England, but John endured a year and five months longer, his departure at that time being precipitated by a severe altercation involving a woman he seems to have loved and sought, the man she married, and her uncle who was the colony bailiff and "chief magistrate." What these troubles meant for the Wesleys' spiritual development is difficult to say, but there is much evidence that at least John Wesley's contacts with the Moravians and the Salzburgers both on shipboard and later in the colony were decisive for the spiritual quickening which was soon to set him upon his remarkable career (see pp. 304, 396 below). The Moravian Bishop Spangenberg almost deserves rank as a patriarch of Methodism.

The ship that bore the future founder of Methodism back to England crossed that which brought his friend and associate, George Whitefield, to Georgia. With Whitefield's arrival the church at Savannah experienced a new problem: it could no longer contain the multitudes who thronged to hear one of the greatest preachers ever born. But after a half-year he, too, returned to England to seek ordination and to raise funds for an orphanage he planned in the colony. After returning to America a year later and making a sensational preaching tour in the Middle Colonies (see pp. 335–36 below), he returned to Georgia to prosecute plans for his beloved orphan house, now named Bethesda and located nine miles from Savannah. During the next thirty years he gave $16,000 of his own money to the institution and raised over four times that amount. By 1770 plans to make it into a "university" were firmly afoot; but in that year Whitefield died, conveying Bethesda to his pious patroness, the Countess Huntingdon. The chaplain she dispatched failed to prevent the institution's breakup during the Revolutionary War; its inmates were dispersed and the buildings destroyed.

Dissent in Georgia during this period was even less organized than Anglicanism, except insofar as it be identified with the broad ministry of Whitefield himself, who after 1740 was replaced as minister of Christ Church in Savannah and gradually thereafter became estranged from the Church of England both in America and in the mother country. Before he died, this "Grand Itinerant" would put a more permanent mark on the Great Awakening and on American evangelical religion in general than any other single colonial figure. In filling this great role, however, he had to defy the Anglican establishments in virtually every colony; he was excoriated by the SPG missionaries who carried on the chief work of the Church of England in America. Both sought to win souls, rekindle piety, and plant churches, but they worked at opposite ends of the British religious spectrum. Perhaps the greatest irony lies in the fact that, whereas Whitefield's zeal led most of all to the strengthening of Congregational, Baptist, and Presbyterian churches, the SPG developed a clergy and constituency so fervently Anglican that its work was decimated by the Revolution and the exodus of the Loyalists.

15

THE GERMAN SECTS AND THE RISE OF PIETISM

Unfavorable connotations have accrued to the term "sect" until it is often understood as condescending and abusive. Nothing of the sort is intended here—or anywhere in this book. The word derives from *sequi* (to follow) not from *secare* (to cut); it thus emphasizes a group's response to a leader and not the group's existence as a tiny fraction or section of the whole. More important than etymology for the historian's usage of the word is Ernst Troeltsch's conception of a "sect" as a religious group which is gathered or called out of some natural organic group or state church on positively anticonformist grounds, sometimes by a charismatic leader, but as often by some principle of greater strictness, more single-minded dedication, or more intense abnegation of the world and its attractions. Often, even usually, the sect has as its main principle some aspect of the orthodox faith which is being lost or neglected. In this sense left-wing Puritan groups often showed "sectarian" tendencies even though circumstances, especially in America, sometimes made them comprehensive, inclusive and "churchly" in their stance, rather than exclusive.

One index of the fertility and fervor of the Reformation's underlying religious motivation was the luxuriant growth of sectarianism which accompanied it. Early colonial arrivals especially are worth close attention, because they illustrate a long-term process that was to be repeated over and over again on the American scene.[1] And none played a more prominent role than the various German groups who from early times made Pennsylvania famous. Among the emigrants

[1] More extensive consideration is given to the characteristically American features of sect formation in chap. 29.

from Germany were also many Lutherans or Reformed people from inclusive state-church traditions, but they will be dealt with in the succeeding chapter. Our present concern is with those who came frankly and by intention as sectarians, some tracing their heritage back to the earliest Reformation years or even earlier, others moving in the more extreme vanguard of German pietism which was already taking shape in the closing decades of the seventeenth century. If they are treated here with brief reference to their future fate and not discussed in later chapters, it is only because space limitations make continuous references impossible.

Many types and degrees of radicalism flowered during the sixteenth-century Reformation, some rationalistic and antitrinitarian, some intensely biblical, some predominantly "spiritual." These radicals tended to agree on a number of points: (1) that the Christianity of the first century was ideal and that the institutional church had "fallen" from the pristine purity of that primitive age; (2) that the Roman Catholic church as well as the "magisterial reformation" placed too much emphasis on the sacraments, the priesthood, and dogma; (3) that the true Church is a visible community of disciplined saints, whereas the inclusive attitude of the Middle Ages had unwisely equated the church with the total society; (4) that the use of force and civil authority in religion were unchristian, and that all regulation of the church by the state was illegitimate; and (5) that the Christian should withdraw so far as possible from the "world," i.e. civil and social concerns. They were, in other words, more or less subversive of established conceptions of law and order in church and state alike. They were "revolutionary" in several senses of that word; at times their revolutionary subversion took the form of chiliastic judgment upon all existing society, while at other times their principles and leaders became allied with social rebellion (as in the Peasant War). In one historic case —at Münster in 1534—the sectaries established themselves in power with bloodshed and violence.

Within and throughout this larger left-wing movement there were certain groups which deserve and proudly claim the name Anabaptist (re-baptizer), though the major groups of Baptists in America are properly traced not to these Continental movements but, as we have seen, to the left-wing Puritanism of the English Reformation. Very prominent among the Anabaptists were two interrelated and enduring groups, one in Switzerland and southern Germany, where Zwingli's revolt from Rome had inspired an extremely persistent left wing; the other, in or near the Netherlands, rising some dozen years later from the work of Menno Simons (1496–1561). Menno strove to disengage this movement from violent forms of action and gradually had a great deal to do with molding a quiet and pacifistic type of evangelical Anabaptist movement.

THE MENNONITES AND AMISH

From the sixteenth to the late seventeenth century, regardless of who was in power, these groups led a harried existence, sometimes (as in Holland) enjoying intermittent toleration, though usually forced into semiseclusion. When offers of a haven in Pennsylvania began to be circulated, the combination of intolerance, wars, and economic uncertainty led a group of Mennonites from Crefeld (near the Dutch border) to migrate to America. Penn granted eighteen thousand acres to a group of six men, all Mennonites, on the condition that they plant a colony. The first group of thirteen families arrived in Germantown in 1683. Whether all were Mennonites is doubtful; probably many were Dutch Quakers.

In Germantown they met a remarkable attorney, scholar, mystic, and Lutheran pietist, Francis Daniel Pastorius (1651–1720). Pastorius was agent for the Frankfurt Land Company, an originally utopian group of pietists in Frankfurt-am-Main who had been granted twenty-five thousand acres, and he became agent for the Mennonite group as well. Until his death in 1720 he was one of the most fascinating and profound figures in Pennsylvania. As chief citizen of the town, Pastorius was mayor, clerk, schoolmaster, and assembly representative. In 1688 he joined three Friends in sending to the Monthly Meeting a protest against slaveholding, the first such action in the American colonies. The document was transmitted to the Yearly Meeting at Burlington, which quietly suppressed it.

Under Pastorius's leadership Germantown became a flourishing village. Because the location was ideal, the soil good, and the settlers industrious and peaceable, no special difficulties were encountered. In 1686 a common meeting-house was built for Quakers and Mennonites, although by

1690 it proved more expedient for each group to hold separate services, and the former built their own place of worship in 1705, the latter in 1708. At first the Mennonites took an active part in governmental affairs, but as complexities increased they withdrew, leaving such matters to the Quakers and later the Scotch-Irish and Anglicans. They also virtually ceased to exert any missionary efforts despite their unusual freedom to do so. Under the pressure of an expanding population and attracted by the rich farm lands, especially after the arrival of brethren emigrating from Swiss communities, the Mennonites began their occupation of the rural areas of what is now Lancaster County. Gradually other Mennonites joined the movement westward, their churches marking the westward flow of population along the way. After 1760 there was for half a century very little new immigration of Mennonites to America.

Toward the latter part of this colonial immigration period the Amish began to arrive in significant numbers. They were a more conservative group founded by Jacob Amman (1644?–1730?), a Mennonite preacher of Berne, Switzerland, who around 1693 urged stricter observance of earlier practices, especially that of shunning excommunicated members. After gaining a few additional adherents in Alsace-Lorraine and the Palatinate, the Amish began to emigrate to America in 1727, then in larger numbers during the 1740s. They settled first in Berks and Lancaster counties, but gradually they drifted by "colonies" farther west, always continuing to be more conservative in their religious life, manners, dress, and language than other Mennonites. Opposing the use of church buildings as the first step to ritualism, they used barns or dwellings instead. They also refused to form any general church organization, or to found any colleges. In the twentieth century their descendants still use hooks and eyes rather than buttons, eschew motorized farm machinery, and insist on educating their own children.

Later Mennonite Migrations

The successive seventeenth-century movements of Mennonites to the colonies and their gradual migration south into Virginia and Carolina, west into Ohio, Indiana, and even beyond into Ontario (Canada) by no means constitute all of Anabaptist history in America. Though it will not be possible to refer to later events in their proper place in this book, some indication of their nature is needed.

Between 1810 and 1830 large numbers of Mennonites came from Berne (Switzerland) to Ohio and Indiana, organizing many congregations there which were at first unaffiliated with the Pennsylvania groups. During the pre-Civil War period these and similar groups also migrated into other western states, frequently torn by schisms caused by the appearance among them of advocates of greater or lesser adherence to American Protestant practices. They took the revolutionary step of founding a college at Goshen, Indiana, in 1902. By force of numbers, and perhaps aided by a greater willingness to meet the demands of the American environment, these descendants of the Swiss Brethren of Zwingli's day gradually became the dominant element among American Mennonites.

In the midst of this process came a dramatic migration from southern Russia. Mennonites had been moving from Germany to unoccupied lands in southern Russia since 1786, when Catherine the Great, herself once an impoverished princess in Anhalt-Zerbst, welcomed German immigrants to the wasteplaces of her vast, undeveloped realm. The migration soon became a tide, and by 1870 there were two or three million Germans prospering in the Sea of Azov and lower Dnieper areas and enjoying a measure of protection from the Prussian government. Due in part to increasing difficulties under German laws, and to exemption from military service and other advantages granted in Russia, Mennonites joined this migration in considerable numbers. But by 1870, when the Russian Mennonites numbered from twenty to thirty thousand, the prospect that their special status would be discontinued led a large minority to another exodus. During the next decade many moved to Manitoba, while others chose the United States, especially Kansas. They soon founded another college and an important church publishing house. This immigration brought an important invigorating impulse to the older Mennonite community with which it became closely interrelated.

Even in the twentieth century Mennonites are withdrawn and largely rural. Their church discipline continues to be sectarian in practice: intergroup relations and many "modern" customs and fashions are still prohibited, plain attire prevails, and insurance, television, public athletic contests, and bathing beaches are often frowned upon. Ethnic ties are close, and old Mennonite families continue to people the church. From earliest times, to be sure, other Protestant groups and American culture generally have wielded a covert influence not only on their quaint customs and anachronistic regulations, but also in the areas of evangelism and Christian education. Later still, Fundamentalist and Holiness doctrines gained entrance. Yet the movement flourishes best where these influences are restrained. Indeed, the most conservative among the score of different Anabaptist church bodies in North America (usually those who are least interested in "new blood") are the very ones which show the greatest growth rate, with the Hutterites leading the list.

The Hutterian Brethren

The Mennonites were by no means the only branch of the early Anabaptist movement, though they are the largest group, both in America and elsewhere. In the great exodus of "Russian Germans" during the 1870s still another remnant made its way to the United States and Canada. This group was composed of the spiritual followers of Jacob Hutter, who was burned at the stake in Innsbruck in 1536, the same year in which Menno Simons renounced the Roman church. These "Hutterites" were chiefly Swiss who had fled to Moravia after 1526 to escape persecution. Here the Swiss Anabaptists prospered under the leadership of Balthasar Hübmaier. From this larger group Hutter led a secession of those who felt compelled to obey the apostolic practice of community of goods, and at Austerlitz in 1533 they organized themselves as a thoroughly communistic or communal society. By 1548 there were twenty-six such colonies in Moravia, and here their tradition became firmly rooted.

When their survival was endangered by the outbreak of the Austro-Turkish wars in 1593, the Thirty Years War, and Counter-Reformation activities, many of them made their way separately and in groups into Hungary. Within a century Austrian intervention had made their continued stay there impossible; and they moved again—this time into Wallachia (Romania), then under Turkish rule, where they were joined by Lutherans from Carinthia who had also been expelled by the Hapsburgs. When Russian armies invaded this territory in 1777, the Hutterites accepted an invitation to Russia.

Their next move was in the early nineteenth century, after Czar Alexander I granted them crown lands on terms like those offered to the Mennonites. Under these circumstances they prospered materially, but their communal practices deteriorated until revived by certain leaders in the 1840s and 1850s. By 1879 the czar had withdrawn their special privileges. The entire reconstituted group, numbering less than 500, together with as many other noncommunal Hutterites (who organized themselves separately or affiliated themselves with the Mennonites) migrated to southeastern South Dakota. By World War I there were nineteen communities; by 1931, thirty-three; by 1950 they numbered 8,542 persons distributed in about ninety communities in the Dakotas, Montana, Manitoba, and Alberta. Showing the highest net reproduction rate of any modern population, and losses by apostasy of a mere 2.5 percent, they seemed likely to double their numbers in sixteen years.

The Hutterites have undertaken no significant evangelism since earliest days, and the family names that constitute the group now go back chiefly to the Lutherans who joined them in Transylvania. Three of these family names now embrace nearly half the present-day membership. Their growth indicates the degree to which they have prospered in the New World; but their unusual pattern of life and their isolation have also aroused bitterness and discriminatory legislation. Their chief impact has probably come through their testing of American ideals of religious freedom—a test in which America has been found wanting. It should be added, however, that they have greatly enriched our understanding of Anabaptist history by preserving through all their harrowing experiences a most remarkable *Chronicle,* which provides not only an illuminating account of this unique group, but a great deal of information on the Anabaptist impulse itself. Their quiet tenacity through the centuries is one of the marvels of church history.

The Mennonites, Amish, and Hutterites as a people are thrifty, industrious, and predominantly rural. The places they settled in Germany, Russia, and America have become garden spots. Yet because they lived together in groups, seldom moving into new areas as isolated individuals or families, they have perpetuated themselves and their faith despite their unpopular pacifism. "Perpetuation," in fact, is the word to describe their history. Well before they began leaving

Europe they had lost their aggressiveness; they were the *Stillen am Lande*. Even in the mid-twentieth century one cannot but marvel at the degree to which the Mennonites have preserved their tradition. But it has been accomplished so quietly, so inoffensively, in a manner so withdrawn, that until fairly recently they have existed on the American scene more as a picturesque souvenir of Anabaptism than as an influence on the nation's religious life.

THE PIETISTIC SECTS

Sectarian groups similar in some respects to the Mennonites arose from later developments in Europe. Pietism as a distinct religious movement began to take recognizable shape in the later decades of the seventeenth century. It is an exceedingly difficult movement to define, however, despite the fact that few Protestant impulses have been fraught with larger or more enduring consequences. Described most simply, it was an effort to intensify Christian piety and purity of life. At the outset it also involved a protest against intellectualism, churchly formalism, and ethical passivity. With the passing decades this protest broadened; pietists also began to inveigh against the new forms of rationalism and the spiritual coldness of the Enlightenment. Pietism was thus a movement of revival, aimed at making man's relation to God experientially and morally meaningful as well as socially relevant. It stressed the feelings of the heart. It emphasized the royal priesthood and sought to revive the laity. It called always for a return to the Bible.

The Thirty Years War (1618–48) and the decades of political and military turmoil which followed created an immense need for reconstruction and church renewal. Against the background of war and dynastic conflict, pietism may be seen as a reaction from the scholastic period of Protestant Orthodoxy, during which the doctrinal implications of the Reformation were being carefully—some would say too carefully —worked out. This "Orthodox" movement was from the first highly rationalistic, showing great dependence on Aristotelian concepts and methods of theological argumentation, a tendency that was accentuated by the prominence of the continuing controversy with Rome, and between Reformed and Lutheran theologians. There is also a connection between the

rationalistic confidence of Orthodoxy and the later emergence
of intellectual trends associated with the Enlightenment,
since both scholasticism and rationalism tended toward intel-
lectualistic formalism and religious complacency.

Another important provocation of pietistic attitudes was
Reformed doctrine itself, with its powerful emphasis on the
remoteness and inscrutability of God and the awfulness of his
predestinating decrees. In the face of this awesome teaching,
questions of assurance were inescapable, and the practical
solution was often to regard a conversion experience as a sign
of election. This was the Puritan answer, and in this sense
Puritans like William Ames were important forerunners of
pietism. Ames's great Dutch pupil, Johannes Cocceius, was
even more influential on the Continent. Similarly motivated
were a whole group of German and Dutch theologians, such
as Witsius and Vitringa. A less orthodox tradition stems from
Jean de Labadie, leader of a quietist movement within the
Dutch Reformed church, and some would see Theodore Un-
tereyk, a Dutch disciple of Labadie, as the founder of the
pietist movement. Thus there is much truth to the claim that
the Dutch Reformed church was the "cradle of pietism."

Philip Jacob Spener (1635–1705) is usually cited as the father of pietism, however; and a brief glance at his career is
instructive. Spener was in background and by explicit commitment a Lutheran, and he found in Luther a powerful
witness to the kind of existentially relevant faith which he
sought for himself and others. Yet as with so many other
pietists, Christian experience concerned him more than doctrinal precision. He drew much inspiration from the mys-
tically inclined Johann Arndt, who has been called the "second Luther" because his devotional classic, *Wahre
Christenthum (True Christianity,* 1605–09), for three centuries almost rivaled Luther's Catechism in its influence. But
Spener was indebted most immediately to his personal contacts and reading among the Puritan, Dutch, and German
Reformed champions of a more "spiritual" Christianity. He
had studied in Geneva and Strasbourg, and been a pastor in
Strasbourg before coming to Frankfurt-am-Main in 1666.
Here he sought to renew the life of his congregation not only
by preaching and Bible study but by organizing *collegia pie-
tatis* (spiritual societies) within it. In 1675 he published the
first edition of his famous *Pia Desideria,* in which he explained his methods, defended his strict "pietistic" moral de-

mands, and gave theological and biblical substance to his program of renewal.

A few short passages cannot expose the theological grounds of Spener's "Heartfelt Desires" for the church, but they can indicate the spirit and aims of his classic work:

> Nobody can read Luther's writings with some care without observing how earnestly the sainted man advocated this spiritual priesthood, according to which not only ministers but all Christians are made priests by their Savior, are anointed by the Holy Spirit, and are dedicated to perform spiritual-priestly acts. Peter was not addressing preachers alone when he wrote, "You are a chosen race, a royal priesthood, a holy nation, God's own people, that you may declare the wonderful deeds of him who called you out of darkness into his marvelous light." [1 Peter 2:9]
>
> Every Christian is bound not only to offer himself and what he has, his prayer, thanksgiving, good works, alms, etc., but also industriously to study in the Word of the Lord, with the grace that is given him to teach others, especially those under his own roof, to chastise, exhort, convert, and edify them, to observe their life, pray for all, and insofar as possible be concerned about their salvation. If this is first pointed out to the people, they will take better care of themselves and apply themselves to whatever pertains to their own edification and that of their fellow men.
>
> As for me, I am very confident that if several persons in each congregation can be won for these two activities (a diligent use of the Word of God and a practice of priestly duties), together with such other things as, especially, fraternal admonition and chastisement (which have all but disappeared among us but ought to be earnestly prosecuted, and those preachers who are made to suffer in consequence should be protected as much as possible), a great deal would be gained and accomplished. Afterwards more and more would be achieved, and finally the church would be visibly reformed.[2]

Spener was later called to Dresden, and later still, in 1691, he accepted an invitation to Berlin from the Reformed

[2] Philip Jacob Spener, *Pia Desideria*, ed. and trans. Theodore G. Tappert (Philadelphia: Fortress Press, 1964), pp. 92–95.

prince, Frederick of Brandenburg (and later Prussia). Here
Spener achieved the peak of his influence, inducing King
Frederick to found the University of Halle and to appoint
August Hermann Francke as pastor and professor there.
Francke, and his son after him, made Halle the mecca of
pietism and a worldwide evangelical influence. Under the
leadership of Johann Albrecht Bengel, another influential
school of pietism flourished in Württemberg.

With the passing decades pietist concern for the "experience" of regeneration, or the "new birth" steadily intensified.
Constantly pietists raised the urgent question, "How do I
know I am saved?" And they answered their question with an
increasing tendency toward subjectivism. Their moral emphasis directed men to charitable concerns, and led to a great
flowering of Christian philanthropy, the founding of schools,
orphanages, and hospitals. They gave immense impetus to
the Protestant missionary spirit. Less gloriously, pietism also
tended to formalize its own legalistic code of "Christian behavior" in terms of a wide range of prohibitions on such practices as dancing, card playing, and even play or recreation in
general. Within the church it sought to transform the minister's office, making him a shepherd of souls and a preacher
of salvation, not simply an administrator of sacraments and a
protector of pure doctrine. In developing the pious life the
Lutheran pietists put great emphasis on the catechetical instruction of the young and the rite of confirmation. They encouraged Bible study and sought to organize *ecclesiolae*
within the churches as means for Christians to deepen their
piety and minister to one another. These "little churches"
were not intended to be gatherings of the "saved" in con-
tradistinction to the "worldly" church, but the separatistic
tendency was always present, and under certain conditions it
manifested itself.

Taken as a whole, pietism performed an immense revivify-
ing role in all Protestant churches during the eighteenth century, not only on the Continent but in England and America
as well. More controversial were the blows that it struck at liturgical worship, its depreciation of philosophical and doctrinal concerns, and its encouragement of legalistic moralism.
In addition, its accent on the religious feelings combined with
its denigration of theological rigor opened the doors to rationalism, even at the University of Halle. The charge that its
stress on personal piety undermined the church's sense of

community is ill-founded, but there can be no doubt that it unleashed centrifugal forces that soon resulted in separatistic movements. Some of these new groups, moreover, would enter the stream of American religious history. Methodism, which arose in the Anglican communion, is obviously the most important of these groups, but it is dealt with in a later context. Among the German pietists who emigrated to America in early colonial times, the most significant and revealing were the Dunkers and the Moravian Brethren.

The Dunkers

Earliest of the organized pietist groups in America was the Church of the Brethren, also known as Dunkers, Tunkers, or Taufers. Their founder was Alexander Mack (1679–1735), a radical Pietist who withdrew from the Reformed church of the Palatinate and in 1700 took refuge in Schwarzenau, a village in the county of Wittgenstein (Westphalia). Here eight years later he and seven others of like mind recapitulated a process familiar in Puritan history: they "covenanted and united together as brethren and sisters into the covenant of the cross of Jesus Christ to form a church of Christian believers." One of the seven, selected by lot, baptized Mack in the river Eder, after which he baptized the others in the same fashion. In many respects this group revived the ideas of the early Anabaptists, and for a time at Schwarzenau they advocated both celibacy and community of goods. They also practiced many primitive rites with biblical precedent: footwashing, the holy kiss after Communion, and the love feast. But their most distinctive practice was derived not from the Bible but from the work of the pietistic historian Gottfried Arnold, whose account of early Christian customs led the Brethren to insist on trine (i.e. thrice repeated) immersion, face forward, in a flowing stream.

The community at Schwarzenau grew with some rapidity during these years, as did another at Marienborn in the Palatinate, but later increasing intolerance caused the two communities to move, one to West Friesland, the other to Crefeld. In 1719 Peter Becker led the first of these to Germantown, and Mack followed with the other group a decade later. With these migrations the European history of the sect came to an end.

Becker did not reassemble his congregation in America

until 1722, but within a year from this time two more congregations were formed at Coventry and Conestoga. Several others were formed during the next decade, but growth was slow and sporadic. Meetings were usually held in the homes of members. Later the Brethren moved west with the other Germans, and consequently suffered not only the normal adversities of a small group on a thinly settled frontier, but from the proselyting efforts of other sectarian prophets as well. By the time of the Revolution the Brethren seem not to have numbered over a thousand members divided among twenty congregations in eastern Pennsylvania, New Jersey, and Maryland, and in 1825 their number had only doubled. By 1882 they counted some fifty-eight thousand members in congregations strung all the way to the Pacific coast, but by this time the character of the sect had changed considerably.

The most famous Dunker in American history is probably the elder Christopher Sauer (or Sower, 1693–1758). Born in Germany and educated at the University of Halle, Sauer came to America in 1724. After farming for a while in Lancaster County, he moved in 1731 to Germantown where he practiced medicine. He established a printing press and began in 1739 to publish the *Hoch-Deutsch pensylvanische Geschichts-Schreiber*. In 1743 he issued a large quarto edition of Luther's Bible complete with the Apocrypha, the first Bible in a Western language printed in America. (The type was brought from Frankfurt.) He also established a papermill, an ink factory, and a type foundry (the first in America); and helped to found a high school in Germantown. The Sunday school cards which he printed for the Dunkers appeared many years before Robert Raikes introduced Sunday school work into England.

Of all the pied pipers of Pennsylvania, none was more colorful and disruptive than Conrad Beissel (1691–1768), who had been converted in the Palatinate and had joined the Dunkers at Schwarzenau, Crefeld, and finally in Germantown, where he was baptized by Becker. An ascetic at heart, Beissel soon withdrew to the wilderness and gathered around him a congregation which, after various vicissitudes, became the Ephrata Community. In this "Order of the Solitary" a seventh-day Sabbath was observed, the sexes separated, and a communal semimonastic economy inaugurated. Beissel was a gifted leader with a flare for the dramatic, and his venture soon became a widely publicized success. For a time, after the conversion of the gifted Reformed minister and theologian John Peter Miller (1710–96), the Ephrata Brethren posed a serious threat to Pennsylvania's German Reformed population; from the first it had drawn heavily from the Brethren and other groups of strong pietistic persuasion. But after 1768, when Miller succeeded Beissel as superintendent, the community began to fall on evil days; and after Miller's death it was disbanded. At its height the community was in its way a cultural center for all the Pennsylvania Germans.

The Moravian Brethren

The most important of the pietistic sects in America was the Renewed Church of the United Brethren. The *Unitas Fratrum* was an evangelical branch of the old Hussite movement which had flourished in Moravia and Bohemia in the fifteenth century. Virtually stamped out by the Counter-Reformation, it had maintained a tenuous clandestine existence until the early eighteenth century. By the time Christian David gathered together a few of the "hidden seed" and led them to a promised refuge on the estate of Count Nicholaus Ludwig Zinzendorf (1700–60) in Saxony, the *Unitas Fratrum* had retained its succession of apostolic bishops but lost almost everything else.

Gradually the settlement at Herrnhut (as they called it) grew. In the meantime, the count became increasingly interested in the Moravians and gradually identified himself with them, though seeking at the same time to convert them to the unique form of Lutheran pietism which he had developed after being trained in his youth at Halle. Zinzendorf considered their semimonastic, semicommunal brotherhood as an *ecclesiola* within the *ecclesia Augustana* (Lutheran church) even after he was consecrated their "bishop" in 1737. He also broke away from the almost scholastic legalism of Francke's latter-day pietism, with its negative moralism and its highly ritualized conception of the order of salvation. Zinzendorf's emphasis on God's love for man as revealed in Christ was recognizably Lutheran, but his intense concentration on the passion of Christ tended to alienate him from the stricter sort of Lutherans, as did his insistence that his type of community could be affiliated to virtually any Christian church. Evangelism was a major Moravian concern from the first, as it was for nearly all pietists, and it was this that brought them to

America—to minister to the American Indians—very soon after they had been reorganized in Saxony.

The first party of Moravians destined for America sailed for Georgia in 1735 under the leadership of Augustus Gottlieb Spangenberg (1704–92). Their plans were to occupy lands made available by that colony's philanthropic trustees, and to evangelize the Creek and Cherokee Indians. Their second voyage to the same place is even more memorable, since it was then that Spangenberg met a brilliant English High Churchman who was also bound for Georgia to minister to the colonists and to convert the Indians—John Wesley. The passages in Wesley's Journal which describe the character of the Moravians are justly famous. By a succession of Moravian contacts Wesley would be brought to his notable "conversion." Spangenberg's party, meanwhile, was led from Georgia to Philadelphia by George Whitefield, in whose employ they settled at Nazareth, where the great revivalist hoped to found a school for Negroes. The Moravians were to construct the buildings; but as their theology clashed with Whitefield's increasingly firm Calvinism, the friendship turned to enmity, and the Moravians moved on to the lovely site which Zinzendorf himself—newly arrived in the colonies—named Bethlehem on Christmas Eve 1741. Nazareth was also purchased from Whitefield two years later.

The count had been banished from Saxony. Impelled by reports of the religious destitution of the Pennsylvania Germans, he had arrived there with hopes of founding for the Germans one communion that would transcend or avoid the confessional divisions of the Continent. Seven meetings of representatives from the various Pennsylvania German groups were convened to this end, and during the 1740s a few ministers fitfully remained committed to his Congregation of God in the Spirit. For a time Zinzendorf served the Lutheran church in Philadelphia; later, when dissensions arose, he founded the First Moravian Church there. He also helped organize the Moravian congregations at Nazareth, Bethlehem, and a half-dozen other places. He made long trips into the Indian country, laid plans for extensive missions, and then went off for a long stay in London to organize the English province of his "church." In 1749 the English parliament formally granted the *Unitas Fratrum* special rights as an ancient Protestant Episcopal church.

By 1748 the impossibility of Zinzendorf's ecumenical idea

was apparent, and the American Moravians began to steer a self-consciously independent course. There were then congregations in thirty-one localities; and about fifty Indian missionaries and itinerant preachers, with circuits ranging from Maine to the Carolinas, were being supported. At the heart of this whole American enterprise were the thriving semicommunistic settlements at Nazareth and Bethlehem, where over thirty industries and several farms were in operation. Between 1753 and 1763 a similar colony was begun at Salem, North Carolina, with southern responsibilities. These communities were by no means simply self-centered utopias. All of their surplus was contributed to the support of Moravian work in Europe and to their large missionary program among the American Indians. After the French and Indian Wars, however, the communal aspect of the Moravian settlements was gradually abandoned.

The Moravians never succeeded in entering American life as an influential church movement, despite the unique way in which they blended churchly and sectarian traditions. They were hindered at the outset by Zinzendorf's grandiose ecumenical projects, and then for a century they were cramped by the supervision of authorities in Germany. The border wars in the West from the 1750s through the War of 1812, and still later, President Jackson's removal of the Cherokees, brought tragedy and disruption to their Indian missions. They remained a relatively static movement, numbering about 3,000 in 1775, 8,275 in 1858, about 20,000 in 1895, and over 60,000 in 1965, scattered widely across the country, but still concentrated in Pennsylvania. Their largest influence in America probably came through the Wesleys, but more intrinsic to the *Unitas Fratrum* has been its characteristic form of pietism, its devotional literature, and a tradition of hymnody and church music that would make its mark on many churches in Europe and America.

The Schwenckfelders

Closely associated with the Moravians but by no means similar were the Schwenckfelders. Like the Moravians they claimed an old but attenuated tradition that linked them to Reformation times. Furthermore, the generosity of Zinzendorf provided an occasion for a reconstitution of both groups. But beyond this, the similarities cease. Where the *Unitas Fra-*

trum was hierarchical, highly organized, and rigorously doctrinal despite constant disclaimers, the Schwenckfelders continued to manifest their founder's quiet concern for inner spirituality.

Kaspar Schwenckfeld von Ossig (1489–1561), traditionally grouped among the "spiritual reformers," taught an inward, somewhat mystical faith. Unlike the "magisterial reformers" he emphasized the spirit rather than the letter, and spoke of a living word beneath and beyond the Scriptures. Unlike the Anabaptists, with whom he is sometimes linked, he was concerned not to restore the apostolic church, but to build the invisible church. Men of this type simply do not become organizers of tightly knit churchly institutions, or founders of sectarian communities. "The devotees of such a church," says Professor Bainton, "are bound to be rejected of men, and their only recourse is to make a cloister of their own hearts."[3] So it was with Schwenckfeld and his followers.

By the eighteenth century Schwenckfelders survived as scattered and unorganized spiritual communities in only a few areas of Germany. In the face of Roman Catholic pressure they drifted to Saxony and other Protestant states, and for eight years some of them gathered on Count Zinzendorf's estates. In 1734 this group was to take up a land grant in Georgia, but at Zinzendorf's behest they went to Pennsylvania instead. Here they were joined by other small groups who came via Denmark and the Netherlands; and in Bucks, Montgomery, and Berks counties they maintained an unostentatious but continuous existence. They did not consider themselves a church or denomination, nor did they attempt to erect any church buildings until the time of the American Revolution. At first they had recognized religious leaders—George Weiss to 1741, Balzer Hoffman to 1749—but the response was slight and almost no evangelism was carried on. In terms of impact or influence on American religious life the Schwenckfelders were not important. In 1895 they reported a total of six church edifices, all in Pennsylvania, with 306 communicants; in 1950, five churches with 2,400 members. They stand as representatives of a quiet phase of the Reformation, filling out the wide spectrum of early Pennsylvania's highly diversified church life.

[3] Roland H. Bainton, *The Reformation of the Sixteenth Century*, p. 129.

16

THE GERMAN REFORMED AND LUTHERAN CHURCHES

The political history of the German-speaking regions of Europe in the centuries following the Reformation is an incredibly complex tangle, involving over two hundred independent or semi-autonomous states, episcopal principalities, and free cities, most of which bore some relationship to the Holy Roman emperor. Ecclesiastical division compounded these complications, not only because confessional loyalties deepened interstate hostilities, but also because doctrinal issues were fiercely debated. Lutheranism probably reached its greatest territorial advance by 1566. Some conquests came still later, but at that point the Roman Catholic powers began to make important recoveries. After 1560, moreover, Germany experienced a powerful surge of Reformed strength, with the Elector Frederick III of the Palatinate becoming the great standard bearer of this cause. Convinced that Reformed theology offered a more decisive alternative to Catholicism, he put his powerful duchy where it would remain for a century: squarely athwart the Roman Counter-Reformation. In 1562 he made the Heidelberg Catechism the confessional basis of his realm, and in due course other Rhineland provinces (Anhalt, Hesse, Nassau) followed the Palatine example. Bremen and the Hohenzollerns of Brandenburg responded to the same influences A powerful "third force" emerged in Germany.

THE GERMAN REFORMED CHURCH

The distinct German Reformed tradition which came into existence both as a theology and as a political force naturally owed much to the Reformation in German Switzerland, above all to Zwingli and Bullinger of Zurich. Yet in the family of Reformed communions it has a character of its own, expressed most compellingly by the pious, irenic, and experiential tone which Kaspar Olevianus and Zacharias Ursinus gave to the Heidelberg Catechism. In this confession one may also perceive the mediating influences of Luther's great associate, Philip Melanchthon. In German Reformed churches, moreover, the Lutheran liturgical tradition was never completely replaced by the thoroughgoing reforms of Zwingli, nor did the doctrinaire spirit, rigorous discipline, and dogmatic concern for ecclesiastical polity of "ultra-Calvinism" condition its church life as they did the Reformed churches of Holland, Switzerland, or France. Perhaps due to its proximity to Lutheran churches and universities, perhaps too because of the pre-Reformation German tradition, it also nourished an extremely fertile tradition of devotional writing and theological inquiry, a tradition, incidentally, that was of immense importance to Puritan divines in England and which, in turn, would be much indebted to reciprocal Puritan influences during the formative period of German pietism.

Between 1618 and the Peace of Westphalia (1648), when the Thirty Years War raged in Germany, these states—and especially the Palatinate—were terribly ravaged. Later in the seventeenth century dynastic conflict continued, leading among other things to French invasions of the Rhineland under Louis XIV, whose victories resulted in the temporary establishment of Roman Catholicism in the Palatinate, and the overturning of Protestant rule in Strasbourg. During the eighteenth century the competition of the great European powers led to four more devastating wars, which had as their counterparts the French and Indian Wars fought by American colonists. In this unsettled state of affairs serious economic dislocations and continual outbreaks of religious persecution led great numbers of harassed peoples of every religious affiliation to seek haven in America. Anabaptist and other sectarian groups had come earlier—they had been persecuted by everybody—but now they were joined by others: Reformed, Lutheran, and in much smaller numbers, Roman Catholics.

THE GERMAN REFORMED CHURCH IN AMERICA

The planting of the German Reformed church in Pennsylvania was one result of these upheavals. By 1730 it was estimated that the German Reformed church had fifteen thousand potential adherents in Pennsylvania. The bulk of the immigration came from the provinces of the Rhineland; indeed, so many Palatines came to America that the word became almost a synonym for "German." Many came as "redemptioners," indentured as servants for a stipulated length of time in repayment for their passage. Because very few of them moved as organized religious groups, they lacked a ministry. Like many others who came to America out of state churches in Europe, moreover, they were habituated to having ecclesiastical matters ordered by the authorities, and were ill prepared to take them into their own hands.

The primitive state of the country and the dispersion of the people were also obstacles to organized church life and the support of a regular ministry. These conditions at the same time provided a fine opportunity for various religious freebooters to impose themselves on the ill-informed and isolated settlements. Especially disruptive of the Reformed church were the various sectarian groups which abounded in Pennsylvania, notably Conrad Beissel's semimonastic community at Ephrata. When John Peter Miller, the highly gifted young minister at Tulpehocken, joined that colony in the 1730s, he took a good number of his parishioners with him into ascetic retirement. On the other hand, they could not be absorbed by Dutch Reformed congregations, as had happened in New Amsterdam, because most of these Germans were scattered far away from the Dutch in an unchurched wilderness. A "founder" of a German Reformed congregation, therefore, would be faced with a difficult task. At the outset, nevertheless, churches were formed, sometimes by devout laymen and at other times by ministers. The earlist congregation was gathered at Germantown in 1719, though it had no minister. John Frederick Hager and John Jacob Oehl ministered in succession among Palatines in the Hudson-Mohawk region. Henry Hoeger gathered a church at New Berne, North Carolina, Samuel Guldin in Berks County, and the Dutch minister, Paulus van Vlecq, at Neshaminy in Montgomery County, Pennsylvania.

John Philip Boehm (d. 1749) undertook his important work on foundations laid by van Vlecq. Coming to America as a schoolteacher and lacking ordination, he yielded to the insistent demands of the people he had been serving informally and accepted the pastoral office over three related congregations formed at Falckner's Swamp, Skippack, and White Marsh. Two years later his status was challenged by George Michael Weiss (ca. 1700–ca. 1770), the founder of the Reformed Church in Philadelphia (1727), who had been ordained in Heidelberg and sent out by the Church of the Palatinate. On the advice of the Amsterdam classis, Boehm was ordained by the Dutch ministers in New York in 1729, and thus reconciled to Weiss. These two continued to serve the Philadelphia area, while others carried the work beyond the Schuylkill out to Lancaster County and beyond. One important result of the Boehm-Weiss controversy, and of the latter's subsequent visit to Europe, was the Amsterdam classis's assumption of responsibility for the increasing number of Germans in Pennsylvania. In sending Michael Schlatter to work among the Germans of America, the Synods of North and South Holland performed one of the most important acts in the colonial history of the German Reformed church. But the decisive importance of this event can be comprehended only against a background of the more specific troubles that beset the church after the early years.

The arrival of Zinzendorf in America in November 1741 created a crisis for the Reformed church even as it would for the Lutherans. The count's ruling passion, as we have seen, was to form a "Congregation of God in the Spirit," among the hundred thousand Germans then resident in Pennsylvania. Each of the German churches, while retaining its individuality, would be lifted up to a higher unity in the new "Congregation." To a distracted and scattered church, it was a tempting prospect; and during the 1740s Reformed leaders participated in the count's "Pennsylvania synods," with John Bechtel, Reformed pastor in Germantown, and the layman Henry Antes playing prominent roles. Had the scheme succeeded, it is highly doubtful that the scattered Reformed peoples could have withstood the distinctive doctrinal tendencies of so strong-willed a man as Zinzendorf, or so tightly knit an organization as that of the *Unitas Fratrum*. But the plan collapsed after the seventh conference, by which time only the Moravians, Lutherans, and Reformed were participating.

It was into a church situation fraught with these actual and potential difficulties that Michael Schlatter (1716–90) came in August 1746. Born and educated in Saint Gall, Switzerland, he had worked as a teacher in the Netherlands, where he was ordained. After serving briefly in Switzerland, he offered himself to the Dutch synods as a missionary to the destitute German Reformed churches in Pennsylvania. Within three weeks of his arrival he had demonstrated not only his amazing energy, but his gifts as a conciliator as well, restoring harmony in a number of distracted congregations and inspiring renewed zeal in some of the more lethargic ones. He was installed as pastor of the united churches of Germantown and Philadelphia on 1 January 1747, and in this position he soon won enthusiastic commitments from the other ministers to cooperate in forming a coetus (or synod) the next year.

On 29 September 1747 four ministers and twenty-seven elders representing twelve churches convened in Philadelphia, the first organizational gathering of the German Reformed church in America. They adopted the Heidelberg Catechism and the Canons of Dort, and determined to meet annually for general oversight of the work. The coetus was somewhat handicapped in that it was not an autonomous judicatory in a fully presbyterian sense; the Dutch synods acting though the classis of Amsterdam retained a veto power over all its acts and did not grant it the authority to ordain ministers. Its organization was nevertheless a historic milestone.

Schlatter proved a tireless overseer of Reformed churches from northern New Jersey to the Great Valley of Virginia. In four years he traveled eight thousand miles and preached 635 times. In 1751 he estimated that in Pennsylvania there were thirty thousand German Reformed people gathered into fifty-three churches, yet among these churches there were only four settled ministers. So Schlatter embarked on a trip to Europe to solidify ecclesiastical arrangements in Holland, to plead for money, and to recruit ministers. He was highly successful, returning in 1752 with considerable missionary funds, the guarantee of a stipendium from Amsterdam in return for its supervisory rights, and six able young ministers. This closed the period of his greatest work.

Schlatter's subsequent usefulness was severely curtailed by his unfortunate involvement in the work of the [English] Society for the Promotion of the Knowledge of God among the Germans. He had prepared an appeal in Dutch and German to aid him in presenting the cause of the Germans in Europe; this was translated into English by the Reverend David Thomson of Philadelphia who then worked for the formation of the society. Schlatter, because of his passionate interest in education, allowed himself to be made superintendent of the society's "charity schools" in 1755. But the society's propaganda drew such an insulting caricature of Pennsylvania Germans and was so widely (and perhaps justly) suspected of having Anglicanization as its ultimate end, that the whole program became exceedingly unpopular. Schlatter resigned in disillusionment after two years, spent two ensuing years as a military chaplain, and in 1759 retired to private life.

Another critical aspect of the Reformed situation was the growing strength of an extreme pietist wing, the "new lights," who were encouraged by similar developments among the increasing numbers of Presbyterians in the area and by the ferment of the Great Awakening. For many so disposed, the attractiveness of Zinzendorf's proposals was heightened, as was that of various sectarian appeals. The rise of radical pietism also fostered a tendency to simplify the content of the traditional Christian teaching, to minimize Reformed doctrine, to disparage a regularly constituted ministry, to discourage concern with church order, and to make the conversion experience the essence of Christianity. Ironically, the leader of this movement, Philip William Otterbein (1726–1813), came to America in 1752 as one of Schlatter's most promising new ministerial recruits. He had been educated and ordained in Nassau under strong pietistic influence, and in his ministry there he had already become known for his strenuous views of Christian life and experience. After serving several parishes in Pennsylvania and Maryland with considerable distinction, he was called in 1774 to the Second Reformed Church in Baltimore. This was formed by a group which had seceded from the First Church out of loyalty to an enthusiastic lay revivalist. After long deliberation, Otterbein accepted. In Baltimore his strong pietistic tendencies, his convictions about the value of *ecclesiolae* in the church, and his growing doubts regarding Reformed dogmatics led him into close connection with the Methodist societies; and in 1784 he participated in the ordination of Francis Asbury as bishop of the Methodist Church in America. After two more decades he would finally become the founder of a "New Reformed Church," the United Brethren in Christ. This event belongs to a later phase of American church history, but it demonstrates the force and significance of the more extreme sort of pietism which was at work in the eighteenth century.

The tensions revealed by Otterbein's career were to be continuous problems for the German Reformed church throughout the eighteenth and nineteenth centuries, but they did not prevent the coetus from carrying on its work even after Schlatter's retirement. After 1772 this body began to ordain its own ministers, and in 1791, a year after Schlatter's death, it declared itself, though in a friendly way, to be independent from the Dutch synods. Two years later at a meeting in Lancaster attended by thirteen ministers, the first fully self-sufficient synod of the German Reformed Church in America was formed. The church at that time consisted of about thirteen thousand communicants, perhaps as many as forty thousand adherents, gathered in 178 congregations scattered between New York City and northern New Jersey, through Pennsylvania and Maryland, and on into the valley of Virginia, with a few congregations (but only one pastor) beyond the Alleghenies. The shortage of pastors and the lack of a seminary were the church's most critical handicaps. With little help now coming from either Holland or Germany, many members and whole congregations were lost to other churches, especially to the Lutherans, Presbyterians, and later still, to several more pietistic churches. In the nineteenth century, however, these institutional deficiencies would be amended.

THE LUTHERAN CHURCH IN AMERICA

In 1703 the Swedish Lutheran Provost Andrew Rudman, with two Swedish associates, proceeded by authority of the Archbishop of Uppsala to ordain a German graduate of Halle, Justus Falckner, and to commission him for service in the Dutch Lutheran church of New York. The incident illustrates the interweaving of the three main strands of Lutheran life in the early colonial period. A fourth strand might be termed "English," that stemming from the six Lutheran churches of London and the Lutheran chaplains at the Hanoverian court. The first three require separate discussion.

The Lutherans of New Sweden

Sweden's colonial adventure on the Delaware, conceived under King Gustavus Adolphus, led to the founding of Fort Christina in 1638; it was brought to an abrupt and inglorious end by the soldiers of Peter Stuyvesant in 1655. The Swedish colony holds little interest for the colonial historian except that it provides a starting point for one of the thirteen colonies and marks the introduction of that venerated American institution, the log cabin. But New Sweden commands the closer attention of the church historian because of its relation to the Anglicanism of the area, because of Swedish support for the German churches, and because immigration would restore Swedish Lutheranism to the American scene long after New Sweden was a memory.

In its early days New Sweden was served by a continuous line of ministers, some good, some bad, and at least one of them extraordinary. This was the Reverend John Campanius, the saintly apostle to the Indians, whose translation of Luther's Catechism into the Delaware Indian tongue antedates John Eliot's Indian Bible by several years. In 1690, however, when Andrew Printz, nephew of a former governor of that name, visited the thousand or so Swedish and Finnish people on the Delaware, he found them without ministers. When this news reached King Charles XI, he aroused the interest of the energetic Jesper Svedberg (later bishop of Skara, 1702–35), whose efforts resulted in the dispatch of a large supply of books including a printing of the Campanius catechism, and three new and capable young pastors, who arrived in 1697. One became pastor of Holy Trinity at Tranhook (the "Old Swedes' Church" at Wilmington, where a new building was consecrated in 1699), another of Gloria Dei at Wicaco (the "Old Swedes' Church" of Philadelphia, where a new building was consecrated in 1700), and the third was to make a survey for the king. For seventy-five years these and several other churches were supplied with learned and devoted ministers from Sweden. One of them was always designated as a "provost," with powers similar to those of a suffragan bishop. The doctrine and beautiful liturgy of the Church of Sweden was maintained; matins and High Mass were celebrated on Sundays, and some of the ministers conducted both matins and vespers daily.

Concern for America lagged for a time due to Bishop Svedberg's declining vigor, but it was revived by Archbishop Jacob Benzelius. Provost John Sandin of the Swedish church helped to organize the Ministerium of Pennsylvania (1748) and two succeeding provosts, Israel Acrelius (1749–56) and Karl Magnus von Wrangel (1759–68), not only revitalized the parish life of the three thousand Swedish church members, but helped to further the work among the Germans. Acrelius is also remembered for his valuable history of these churches. Under Wrangel the Swedish ministers for a time virtually became a part of the Germans' Pennsylvania Ministerium.

The difficulties of maintaining Swedish tradition and culture in the midst of these complex circumstances became almost insuperable with the passing years. Because Swedish immigration, unlike the German, did not continue, the language problem became increasingly troublesome, and brought about an inevitable rapprochement between the Swedish and Anglican churches. For the same reasons, the forms, liturgy, vestments, theology, and constitution of the Church of Sweden were not projected into American Lutheranism at this time. Its chief contribution was a measure of stability and continuity during the critical years when support from Germany was very weak.

The Dutch Lutherans

The two oldest continuously existing Lutheran parishes in the United States (Saint Matthew's in New York City and First Lutheran in Albany) trace their origins to the small group of Lutheran laymen in New Netherland who organized a congregation in 1649 in order to call upon the Lutheran consistory in Amsterdam for a pastor. Even in the mother country, however, any church but the Reformed was allowed only by "connivance," so that a man could not be ordained for American service until 1657. When Pastor Johannes Gutwasser arrived, Governor Stuyvesant promptly had him arrested and shipped back to Holland. The struggling group of laymen had to await the more tolerant rule of the English. Even so, it was 1669 before the Amsterdam consistory had found a man who would or could accept a call to New York. The man who then came, Jacob Fabritius, was a quarrelsome eccentric who lasted only two years—though later he redeemed himself as pastor of the Swedish church at Wicaco. His successor, Bernardus Arensius, served until 1691—the years of Leisler's execution for rebellion, hence very troublous years for the colony—after which the New York–Albany congregation was pastorless for twelve years.

Justus Falckner (1672–1723) began his two decades of tireless activity in 1703. He had no more than begun when thousands of Palatines began to arrive in New York with only Joshua Kocherthal to minister to their spiritual needs. When Pastor Kocherthal died in 1719, Falckner was left with the care of fourteen congregations strung from Albany to New Jersey. This proved more than one man could handle, and it remained for William Christopher Berkenmeyer (1686–1751) to bring some regularity into the churches of this sprawling area. Arriving in 1725, Berkenmeyer divided the vast "parish," and before he died, he was able to see five pastors serving the twenty-three congregations in his area. He also established rules for assuring an orthodox and duly commissioned ministry. In 1735, in order to settle a parish controversy in New Jersey, he convoked what some have considered the first Lutheran "synod" in America. True synod it was not, but Berkenmeyer did lay the foundations upon which the New York Ministerium would rest when it was founded just after the Revolution.

By 1750 it was clear that a new order of things was on the horizon in New York: the immediate future would see a German Lutheranism in the vast area over which Berkenmeyer presided. Even in Albany, where the Dutch had yielded to the English, the German language was being demanded, while in New York City Germans now outnumbered the Dutch and were causing a good deal of contention. The bulk of this new migration would go to Pennsylvania, and its ministry would come from the pietist center at Halle rather than from Amsterdam and Hamburg. Berkenmeyer viewed this invasion by pietistic *Schwärmer* as tragic, and his bias had a longlasting influence on the New York churches—doubtless prolonged by his son-in-law, Peter Sommer, who took over his work in the upper Hudson area and served until his death in 1795. But by the time of the Revolution, Halle men were numerous in New York too.

The Dutch Lutherans at least had the satisfaction of knowing that in matters of church order, the experience of the Netherlands would stand American Lutherans in good stead as they began the enormous task of organizing the Lutheran church in the wilderness, without benefit of sympathetic kings and state-church traditions, and in an ethos which was predominantly Puritan insofar as it was religious at all. The combined pressures of American democracy, the inescapable importance of the laity in so scattered a church, and the preponderance of various Reformed churches would cause basically presbyterian forms of government to be utilized by the Dutch Lutherans as the safest constitutional model. Formally adopted in New York in 1786, this constitutional pattern would also be followed in 1792 by the Ministerium of Pennsylvania.

The German Lutherans

The great exodus from the Palatinate and the other Rhenish provinces began in earnest during the first decade of the eighteenth century. Pastor Kocherthal of Landau (Palatinate) had led one party to Newberg (now Newburgh), New York, in 1708; and in 1710 he brought a larger group, numbering some three thousand. Queen Anne's promise of land near the Schoharie River was betrayed by the governor's desire for a colony that would produce tar and other products for the British navy, however, and a large proportion of the émigrés drifted away to other parts. Gradually, the New York–New Jersey region witnessed the emergence of a major German community with several congregations of Lutherans.

After 1712 the main tide of Lutheran immigration flowed into the immense haven created by William Penn. The Lutherans arrived in general somewhat later than the other German Protestant groups, their chief influx coming during the decade or so after 1735, and by this time they, like their predecessors, also pressed southward and westward from Pennsylvania. During the first three decades after the colony's founding only very few congregations had been formed, though a few Lutherans seem to have been among even the earliest German immigrants. Gloria Dei, the Swedish church at Wicaco, was for a long time the only well-established church in the area; it included the congregation at Germantown until that church achieved independent status. At New Hanover a congregation could trace its origins back to 1703. There were also services held in Philadelphia very early; but before 1730 the congregation was loosely organized and without a regular pastor. Three or four ministers and a number of unordained men of varying personal dedication served the southeastern counties. The situation here became desperate as more people, almost always without pastors and usually without schoolteachers, continued to arrive.

A turning point came in 1733. Pastor John Christian Schultze led a lay delegation from Philadelphia, New Provi-

dence, and New Hanover to Dr. Frederick Michael Ziegenha-
gen, the court chaplain in London, who, with others, finally
aroused the authorities at Halle to the missionary needs of
America. In an open letter the chaplain quoted the report of
one of the laymen: "We live in a country that is full of heresy
and sects. As far as our religious interests are concerned, we
are in a state of greatest destitution; and our means are utterly insufficient to effect the necessary relief, unless God in
his mercy may send us help and means from abroad."[1] What
finally seems to have bestirred the men at Halle was not cries
such as these, nor the offer of a definite salary for ministers
(which they had been demanding), but the arrival in Pennsylvania of Count Zinzendorf and his representation of himself as a Lutheran pastor.

Henry Melchior Muhlenberg (1711–87), whose destiny it
was to be the chosen instrument of Halle's response to these
needs, proved to possess gifts as far beyond imagining as was
the difficulty of the tasks that lay ahead. He was born in Eim-
beck (Hanover) and educated nearby at the new university
in Göttingen. Guided chiefly by a theology professor there, he
became firmly committed to a pietistic understanding of the
faith. After helping to found an orphanage, he taught at the
famous orphan house at Halle; at the same time he continued
to develop his lifelong interest in music and languages. In
1739 he was ordained in Leipzig (Saxony) and began his
ministry in a parish of Upper Lusatia, a few miles from Zinzendorf's estate. Only two years later, while visiting Halle, he
was convinced by Johann Gotthilf Francke that he ought to
accept the call to America, and after a two-month visit in
London, he embarked for Charleston, South Carolina. On 23
September 1742 he went ashore, remarking in the first American entry of his journal on the tragic fact of Negro slavery:
"This is a horrible state of affairs, and it will entail a severe
judgment." He proceeded almost immediately to visit the
Salzburger Lutherans at Ebenezer near Savannah, then
began the journey north to his life's work.

Ecclesia plantanda (Let the Church be planted) was Muhlenberg's motto. He came with the highest credentials: as a
deputy of the younger Francke at Halle, with the approval of
the consistorium of Hanover (whose ruler was King George

[1] Quoted in Henry E. Jacobs, *A History of the Evangelical
Lutheran Church in the United States*, ACHS, vol. 4 (New York,
1893), p. 192.

II of England), and bearing letters from the royal chaplain in London. Almost from the first it was evident that his "errand into the wilderness" was not merely to answer the call of three destitute congregations, but to work toward the ideal of a united, independent, self-sustaining church. During a career contemporaneous with a half-century of America's most tumultuous history, Muhlenberg became a denominational "founder" in a fuller sense than anyone except Francis Asbury, the Methodist, and Bishop John Carroll, the Roman Catholic, who began their American careers about the time that he ended his. Jacobs remarks that "the history of the [Lutheran church in America] from his landing in 1742 to his death . . . is scarcely more than his biography."[2]

Muhlenberg arrived in Philadelphia on 25 November 1742. Unheralded, unreceived, and alone, he rode through the mud to New Hanover—to discover that all three of the congregations whose call he was answering were now shepherded by others, the most formidable of whom was Zinzendorf, installed in Philadelphia. Within a month he was master of the situation, and was legally preaching in the carpenter shop in Philadelphia, the barn at New Providence (Trappe), and the half-built log chapel at New Hanover. Over the years his tact, patient firmness, and spiritual power had an ever deepening impact. Both in Pennsylvania and in Europe long pent-up potentialities were released, conflicts were healed, pastors and catechists were brought to America, congregations were rallied, and church buildings were erected or enlarged at Tulpehocken (1743), Providence (1745), Germantown (1746), New Hanover (1747), and Philadelphia (1748). The three huge volumes of his translated journal are one of the finest records extant of the frontier missionary, pacificator, preacher, teacher, pastor, and priest. The saga of his indefatigable ministry is capsuled in many an entry:

June 10 [1747]. I set out from New Hanover with the schoolmaster, Jacob Loeser. Eight miles from New Hanover we stopped in at the home of an old man, one of the sect called Newborn, who had married Kasebier's widow some twenty years ago, and begotten with her five children, whom I had instructed and baptized at the mother's request without the father's consent. . . . In the afternoon we traveled four or five miles farther to the home of an

2 Ibid., p. 305.

aged God-fearing widow, who with her family and neighbors was anxiously awaiting us, desiring edification. The old widow had prepared herself with penitential prayer and exhibited a hunger and thirst for the Lord's Supper, which I administered to her after prayer and singing. . . . From there we rode nine miles farther and took lodgings with an old man of our congregation, who refreshed and edified himself with us in prayer and good conversation. . . .

June 11. We rode nine miles farther to a place where the Lutherans and the Reformed had built a church together and where they were in controversy with one another. The members of both faiths are so intermarried in this country [and] occasionally the two parties have made trial of building a common church. . . . Our people elect as pastors the schoolmasters who have come of their own accord. . . . In general, such preachers are not only ignorant, but unconverted besides.

June 13. Rode six miles farther up to the church [Stouchsberg, Berks Co.] and conducted preparatory and confessional service with the members of the congregation who desire to receive the Lord's Supper the next day.

June 14. Trinity Sunday. Preached on the Gospel to a numerous assembly, baptized several children, and administered the Lord's Supper to over two hundred communicants. . . . In the afternoon I rode nine miles in another direction to another congregation [Northkill, Lebanon Co.] and preached there to an attentive audience; also baptized several children, announced that Holy Communion would be celebrated there three weeks hence, and exhorted them to pray God for repentant hearts and hunger for grace and to devote the intervening time to true self-examination.

June 15–18. Instructed a number of young people who wanted to be confirmed and also visited various ones in the congregation with whom I spoke a word of edification.

June 19. We journeyed from Tulpehocken to the new city of Lancaster which is thirty miles away by road and arrived towards evening.

June 20. Visited several deacons and elders of the congregation and inquired concerning their spiritual and congregational condition.

June 21. First Sunday after Trinity. I preached in the congregation, catechized the young people, baptized children, and had the congregation elect a new deacon, one of the others having died. . . . In the afternoon had to ride twenty-two miles farther because I had promised to preach in Maryland on June 24. . . . [The trip was extremely difficult because of rainstorms and swollen rivers.]

June 24. The heavy rain continued. We went to the church where most of our people and also a few of those who were Zinzendorf-minded were present. Before we began divine services, I had them give me the church book and I wrote in it in English several brief articles to the effect that the subjects of His Majesty, George, in this country enjoy the free exercise of religion; that the Lutherans adhere to the Holy Word of the prophets and apostles, to the Unaltered Augsburg Confession and the rest of the symbolical books and have the Sacraments administered to them in a regular manner by regularly called and ordained preachers in accord with the Word and the Confessions; that they will not suffer open, gross, willful sinners against the holy Ten Commandments of God and the laws of the government to be considered among them as true members, and so on, etc., etc. I read this publicly to the congregation and explained it to them in the German language, and said that whoever desired to be such a Lutheran and member of the church and congregation, and to conduct himself in accord with these articles, should subscribe his name. The Lutherans who were present willingly signed their names, but when it came to the two or three Zinzendorfers, they refused to sign it and brought in their complaint. . . .

June 25. We rode several miles farther to a newly founded town [Frederick, Maryland] where lived a number of Lutherans who belonged to the congregation, but were unable to be present on the previous day on account of the heavy rain. Most of them signed their names to the articles in the church book and they also elected several from their midst as deacons and elders. . . .

June 26. We set out on the return journey. . . .[3]

[3] *The Journals of Henry Melchior Muhlenberg*, ed. Theodore G. Tappert and John W. Doberstein, 3 vols. (Philadelphia: Muhlenberg Press, 1942–58), 1:149–59.

The climax of Muhlenberg's early labors came in August 1748, when the need to ordain a minister and to consecrate Saint Michael's Church in Philadelphia brought together six Swedish and German pastors and twenty-four lay delegates. This meeting marks the beginning of the Pennsylvania Ministerium, the most important single event in American Lutheran history. It not only attended to the immediate business at hand, but outlined a synodical organization and prepared a book of common worship which drew upon the church's liturgical tradition.

At the second meeting of the ministerium the delegates showed a further sign of independence by electing an "overseer" for the united congregations; this office was filled briefly by Pastor Peter Brunnholtz of Philadelphia, then transferred to Muhlenberg, who occupied it for many years. The ministerium met annually through 1754, but obstacles were so great that the pastors grew discouraged and no meetings were held for five years. In 1760 it was revived under a new constitution, never to lapse again. This reorganization was due largely to the efforts of the newly arrived provost of the Swedish churches, Karl Magnus von Wrangel, who became during his years of American service (1759–68) Muhlenberg's closest friend and co-worker. During these years the German and Swedish churches were drawn into close cooperation, though they were not formally merged.

Almost as significant as the synodical organization was the written constitution adopted for Saint Michael's in 1762. Muhlenberg, in response to urgent appeals from the Lutherans of New York, had spent the summers of 1751 and 1752 ministering to the Dutch Lutheran church in New York City. This congregation was almost one hundred years old, and represented the church order of Amsterdam. The experience acquainted Muhlenberg much more fully with the details of church organization, and when he prepared (with Wrangel's help) the constitution for the Philadelphia church, he incorporated many of the provisions he had observed in New York. In this way the Amsterdam order was not only transferred to Pennsylvania, but became an important pattern for the organization of Lutheran congregations in America.

With these great formative actions in which Muhlenberg and the Swedish provost played so important a role, the main lines of Lutheran development were laid down in the area which would witness its greatest colonial growth. It was done none too soon, for the rate of immigration was increasing sharply. Twelve thousand Germans landed at Philadelphia in 1749 alone, and by 1771 there were eighty-one congregations in Pennsylvania and adjacent states, plus some thirty more in other parts of America. Lutheran churches, along with the Presbyterian and German Reformed, were being founded in the valley of Virginia and in North Carolina. Although in the face of the vast work to be done the resources were pitiably inadequate, not only had a start been made, but a decisive turn had been taken. Lutheran leaders were thinking in terms of an American church with an American ministry and an American future, not in terms of a transitory mission abroad on the part of representatives of the European churches. The actualization of this ideal, and solutions for many of the difficulties along the way, began to emerge early in the next century.

III

The Century of Awakening and Revolution

Under the execrable race of the Stuarts [James I and Charles I] the struggle between the people and the confederacy of temporal and spiritual tyranny became formidable, violent, and bloody. It was this great struggle that peopled America. It was not religion alone, as is commonly supposed; but it was a love of universal liberty, and a hatred, a dread, a horror, of the internal confederacy [of an ecclesiastical hierarchy and despotic rulers] that projected, conducted, and accomplished the settlement of America. After their arrival here, they began their settlement, and formed their plan, both of ecclesiastical and civil government, in direct opposition to the canon and feudal systems.

John Adams, *Dissertation on the Canon and the Feudal Law* (1765)

What do we mean by the American Revolution? Do we mean the American war? The Revolution was effected before the war commenced. The Revolution was in the minds and hearts of the people; a change in their religious sentiments of their duties and obligations. . . . The people of America had been educated in an habitual affection for England, as their mother country; and while they thought her a kind and tender parent (erroneously enough, however, for she never was such a mother), no affection could be more sincere. But when they found her a cruel beldam, willing like Lady Macbeth to "dash their brains out," it is no wonder if their filial affections ceased, and were changed into indignation and horror. This radical change in the principles, opinions, sentiments, and affections of the people was the real American Revolution.

John Adams, *Letter to Hezekiah Niles* (1818)

By 1700 the colonial commonwealths of North America were becoming a prosperous extension of British provincial society, in which the prevailing outlook on life and the world was unmistakably conditioned by a Reformed and Puritan ethos. Yet the modes of institutionalizing this system of nurture were very uneven. In most of New England a regulated ecclesiastical and educational system was duly established. As the decades rolled by, the "southern ethic" came to reflect many similar emphases, yet more decisively it bore the marks of the steady expansion of chattel slavery. The Middle Colonies were anticipating the American future by dealing with the actuality of ethnic and religious pluralism. Yet all of these colonies were pervaded by an ideology which, though increasingly secularized, was Puritan at the level of both personal and social ethics.

Fundamental to this entire process of church extension and cultural modification was a great international Protestant upheaval, manifested in pietism on the Continent, the Evangelical Revival in Great Britain, and the Great Awakening in America, where its intrinsic relation to Puritanism was most marked. In New England it was an apocalyptic outburst within the standing order, a challenge to established authority. Everywhere it extended the range of gospel preaching; in the South it brought personal religion to the slaves for the first time. Everywhere it brought rancor and division along with popular enthusiasm and new theological depth. Everywhere it rejuvenated the politically potent elements of the Puritan ideology. Most important for the future of American Protestantism, revivalism itself became an institution, and two denominations, Baptist and Methodist, were set on a course that was to make them the nation's largest. Vital for the political future of the colonies, the Awakening also made the people aware of their common spiritual heritage, and of their existence as an American nation.

After the revivals had waned (as such things must), the imperial situation was suddenly changed by the British conquest of New France in 1759. With this external danger removed, the long maturing "American Revolution" almost immediately took political form. A familiar course of events involving a famous cast of Patriot heroes from James Otis to Thomas Jefferson began to unfold. And this epoch of political and military turmoil did not end until Jefferson entered the White House four decades later.

Accompanying these religious and political events was a wide-sweeping intellectual revolution—the Enlightenment. The Age of Reason had begun to create theological problems for the Puritans even before 1700, leaving Jonathan Edwards no less than Benjamin Franklin to struggle with its religious implications. It also provided a philosophical basis for the work of the Founding Fathers. The long preoccupation of Americans with government and politics, not to mention with the war itself, raised immense problems for the churches, bringing on, among other things, a prolonged religious depression. Yet the first "new nation" never for a moment lost the Puritan's sense of America's special destiny, and as if to demonstrate that God had not despaired of his chosen nation, the very year of Jefferson's inauguration was marked by revivals of religion in both the East and the West. Part III charts the course of these events from the first signs of a "great and general revival" through the War for Independence to the settled operation of the new federal republic.

17

THE SHAPING OF COLONIAL PRESBYTERIANISM

Episcopalian, Presbyterian, Congregational—the very names of these great Protestant church communions indicate the intensity with which questions of church order rose to prominence in the age of the Reformation. In England, along with related questions of worship, they proved to be more divisive than elsewhere. In the Netherlands, certain parts of Germany, Switzerland, France, and Scotland, on the contrary, the prevailing mode of governing the Reformed churches had been from the first "presbyterian." Though terminology naturally varied, this meant in broad terms that a hierarchy of judicatories (or church courts) similar to those developed in Calvin's Geneva came to be regarded as the only true gospel order. Above the local or congregational "session" were ranged in ascending order the "presbytery," the "synod," and the "general assembly," each with certain fixed responsibilities and usually with definite geographical boundaries. At each of these levels both ordained and lay elders were represented, with the higher courts exercising functions and authority traditionally ascribed to bishops in an episcopal system. Such a system stressed universality, catholicity, and uniformity, while it discountenanced particularism and "independency."

In England the proponents of presbyterian order gradually declined after a show of considerable strength in the earlier part of Elizabeth's reign. Their place was taken on the left by various forms of Puritan congregationalism, and on the right by Calvinistic episcopalianism. But during the Civil War and the early Commonwealth, when Presbyterians again rose to power in England, Scotland played a powerful role, and America became involved in the consequences. A brief consideration of the Scottish development is therefore an essential part of United States religious history.

Scotland in 1500 had been a weak, poor, and strife-torn cultural backwater, its politics polarized by French and English factions. Patrick Hamilton was burned for his Lutheran preaching in 1528 and George Wishart met a similar fate in 1546, with several martyrdoms in between serving to indicate the suffering and ineffectual state of Protestantism during that period. One follower of Wishart named John Knox (1505–72) was captured and sent to the galleys by the French. Later released, he became a royal chaplain in England under Edward VI. With the accession of Queen Mary (Tudor) he fled to Frankfurt, then to Geneva where he worked on the Geneva Bible, preached to other English exiles, and became a devoted disciple of Calvin. In 1558, the year Elizabeth became queen of England, Mary Queen of Scots (a Roman Catholic who also claimed the English throne) married Francis II of France. These events made the situation ripe for a nationalistic revolt, and Knox returned in the following year to ensure that his native land should also become firmly Protestant. By 1560, with strong English support, both ends were accomplished: papal power was abrogated, the Scottish Parliament adopted Knox's Calvinistic confession of faith, and the first General Assembly of the new Scottish Kirk was convened. Its *Book of Discipline* and Knox's *Book of Common Order* set up a presbyterian system of church government and worship for the entire kingdom.

What uncertainties remained in the situation were largely removed when Mary of Scotland was forced to abdicate in 1567. Her execution in 1587 at Queen Elizabeth's order removed still another threat to Roman Catholic recovery in both kingdoms. When Mary's son, James VI of Scotland, became King James I of England in 1603, the importance of Scotland's church for America was immeasurably increased. Its integrated and firmly established system of doctrine and order became extremely influential in the English Reformation during the decade after 1640, especially at the Westminster Assembly, whose formularies of doctrine, worship, and polity were enforced in both kingdoms—temporarily in England, to the present day in Scotland. After the Restoration (1660) Presbyterianism lost its vitality in England, but through force of example and by immigration, the Scottish church in later years became a very powerful influence in America.

During the seventeenth century immigrants of presbyterian inclination were so few and so scattered that only the Dutch churches could be said to have upheld this tradition in America—although they did so very incompletely, since they remained under the classis (presbytery) of Amsterdam until 1754. This situation began to change after the turn of the century, however. The Saybrook Platform (1708) revealed a persistent inclination of many New England Puritans, and frankly transformed the congregational independency of Connecticut into a connectional order that greatly increased its rapport with emergent presbyterian interest in the Middle Colonies. More significant was the influx of Scotch-Irish peoples, which began to reach sizable proportions after 1714, swelling to a tide later in the century. In this context a genuinely American form of presbyterianism began to take shape, but the process was not smooth, peaceful, or easy. Serious problems existed on every side and deep-seated theological and ecclesiastical issues had to be resolved.

ORGANIZING THE PRESBYTERIAN CHURCH

Men with presbyterian ideals and hopes had since the earliest years been scattered the whole length of the colonies from Londonderry, New Hampshire, to Charleston, South Carolina, in certain areas in considerable potential strength. Only after 1700 did the accentuated official pressures for Anglican establishments lead a few leaders among these groups to think of founding an inclusive organization. To this end a group of Presbyterian ministers met in Philadelphia in 1706 and organized the first American presbytery. The leader of this effort was Francis Makemie (1658–1708), a tireless Scotch-Irishman who was educated at Glasgow and ordained in Northern Ireland as a missionary to America in 1681. He had preached or organized churches in Barbados, Maryland, Virginia, New York (including Long Island), and New England. On good terms with the Mathers of Boston and the Congregationalists and Presbyterians of London, who in 1691 had united under the "Heads of Agreement," Makemie was ideally suited for bringing together various disparate ele-

ments at that first meeting. Associated with him on this occasion were one Scottish, two Scotch-Irish, and three New
England ministers. Their congregations were even more diverse. The presbytery they organized was conceived more or
less on the Scottish model, but it remained independent of
any existing church. During its early years it drew most of its
accessions from the scattered Puritan churches of Long
Island, Delaware, and New Jersey, all of whom felt a need
for interchurch connections similar to that which was to mo-
tivate the Saybrook Synod in Connecticut. They had no practical way of achieving this end save by joining the new presbytery. Common ties to the doctrinal formulations of
Westminster facilitated their association. Thus a "New England" element gained an early preponderance in the nascent
church.

But the increased immigration of Scotch-Irish, particularly
to the Pennsylvania area, soon began to alter this ethnic balance, and by 1716 Presbyterian churches had become so
numerous that there were three presbyteries—Philadelphia,
New Castle, and Long Island—and a synod was formed.
Seventeen ministers had been gained, bringing the total to
twenty-five, eight of whom had come from New England,
three from Wales, eight from Scotland, and seven from
Ireland. The Presbyterian Church in America was now
clearly in being, with a membership of at least three thousand distributed in forty or more churches; but its adversities
were many. Only a few of its congregations were in com-
pactly settled areas. Poverty and poor communications sad-
dled them with difficulties on every hand. No American
ministerial training was available outside of New England,
and no adequate procedures for examining immigrant ministers or disciplining functioning ones were in force. There
was increasing tension over the proper method of bringing
some semblance of proper presbyterian order into this situation.

The questions which could not be postponed naturally
affected both polity and doctrine. Specifically, how should
disciplinary authority be vested in presbyteries and synods?
What standards for approving ministers and ministerial candidates should be adopted? Above all, should subscription to
the Westminster symbols be required, and if so, how?
Around these interrelated issues definite factions or parties
began to emerge, as they had already in the various British

Presbyterian churches. The alignment in America tended to follow ethnic lines, with the Scots and Scotch-Irish, strongest in the New Castle Presbytery, demanding doctrinal subscription and stricter presbyterial discipline. At least as early as 1724 this presbytery required subscription to the Westminster Confession. In 1722 it deposed a minister because he bathed himself in a creek on the Sabbath. The New Yorkers and New Englanders, on the other hand, argued that the Bible alone was a sufficient rule of faith and practice.

In 1722 a compromise was reached which allowed some authority to presbyteries and synods; but the controversy continued. John Thomson, spokesman for the Scotch-Irish party, asserted that the American synod was utterly independent of every other judicatory on earth and hence responsible for its own purity and duty-bound to make the Westminster formularies its official confession and to require its ministers to subscribe. Jonathan Dickinson (1688–1747), Yale graduate, pastor at Elizabethtown, and leader of the antisubscriptionists, voiced the immemorial alternative: the purity of the church would be better safeguarded by a close examination of every candidate's religious experiences and strict disciplining of scandalous ministers. He pointed out the "glorious contradiction" of subscribing to Chapter 20 of the Westminster Confession, which calls God alone "Lord of the conscience," and then submitting to the rigid authority of the other chapters.

As the intensity of these disagreements increased, it became necessary to adopt some more explicit compromise; this was done at the Synod of 1729. Its fateful "Adopting Act" affirmed the idea of subscription, but with two important qualifications. First, refusing to make literal subscription to the Westminster standards a condition of ordination, it drew a distinction between essential and nonessential articles and allowed the examining judicatory to decide if a given candidate's scruples violated the intent of the confession. Second, it made the synod an administrative and not a legislative body; and then merely recommended the Westminster Directory on church government as a guide. These qualifications left quite uncertain the limits of orthodoxy, as well as the respective authority of sessions, presbyteries, and synods in the calling, examination, ordination, and installation of ministers. In general, it marked a victory for the antisubscriptionist party of Jonathan Dickinson.

The peace resulting from the Adopting Act of 1729 was, to say the least, an uneasy one. The two factions with their characteristic nostrums for saving the church remained at heart unpacified. The stability of the denomination was soon imperiled from another quarter by the emergence of a new group among the Scotch-Irish led by William Tennent, Sr. (ca. 1673–1746), an Irish-born Scotsman, ordained in the Episcopal Church of Ireland. Emigrating to America in 1716, he married a Presbyterian minister's daughter and was accepted without reordination into the Presbyterian church in 1718. He served churches in Bedford, New York, and Neshaminy, Pennsylvania. He was an excellent teacher, and by 1733 had trained three of his sons (Gilbert, John, and William) and Samuel Blair for the ministry. Since the elder Tennent fostered a very "experimental" form of evangelical Puritanism, his students were potential allies of Jonathan Dickinson. Such an alliance became more imminent when Gilbert and John Tennent took congregations in New Brunswick and Freehold, New Jersey. At the former place Gilbert was profoundly influenced by the Dutch Reformed pastor four miles away in Raritan, Theodore Jacob Frelinghuysen (1691–1748). Frelinghuysen, who deserves to be known as an important herald, if not the father of the Great Awakening, had come from the Netherlands in 1720. He taught the necessity of personal conversion and subsequent holiness of life, and enforced strict standards for admission to the Lord's Supper. The revivals which he fostered at Raritan were forerunners of the Great Awakening in the Middle Colonies.

When Gilbert Tennent took up his ministry in New Brunswick he was both rebuked and inspired by Frelinghuysen's success as a preacher of experimental piety, a pastoral counselor, and above all a converter of souls. Tennent adopted no new or unusual doctrines except that staple insistence of the New England Puritans which was so dramatically exemplified in Frelinghuysen: that a definite experience of regeneration followed by assurance of salvation was the indispensable mark of a Christian. Rededicating himself to the task of preaching and counseling with individuals, he made the conversion of sinners the chief end of his ministry. By 1729, Tennent's scattered congregations between New Brunswick and Staten Island began to show new signs of life. The Great Awakening had begun in the Presbyterian churches. In the meantime, John Tennent's church at Freehold was blessed with a quiet revival which, after that pastor's untimely death, was stimulated still further by his brother William's ministry.

By natural gravitation this new revival party among the Scotch-Irish tended to coalesce with Jonathan Dickinson's group, whose affinities were also with New England Puritanism. The alliance was further cemented by the elder Tennent's "seminary" at Neshaminy, established in 1726 for the training of his sons and others in the gospel ministry. This "Log College," as its enemies termed it derisively, performed a significant service during these critical years by turning out nearly a score of pietistic revivalists for the Presbyterian churches. Many of them made important contributions to the church generally, and to the Awakening in particular. It should be added in this connection that their revivalism was by no means the tumultuous type scouted by their critics. "Stirrings" and seasons of excitement there may have been, weeping of sinners under conviction there certainly was; but permanently changed lives were the goal toward which the immense energy and pastoral care of these men were directed.

While these advances were being made by the revival party, immigration from northern Ireland was slowly augmenting the strength of the subscriptionist, antirevival faction. This was a mixed blessing, even to that group, because religious life in Ulster had been at a very low ebb. It was still lower on the American frontier where most of them settled, and where poverty and distance placed additional obstacles in the path of their few and not overly fervent ministers. The church was again heading for a confrontation, though it came by degrees. One large step was taken in 1738, when the synod demanded that ministers without degrees from major universities submit to examination by a synodical committee. This struck directly at the Log College men. Other measures were designed with similar intent to keep revivalists out of the church, while various incidents witnessed to the rapidly growing strength of the subscriptionist party in the higher church courts, and their determination to deprive the presbyteries (notably that of New Brunswick) of their authority.

In November 1739 the tide was turned quite dramatically by the appearance in Philadelphia of George Whitefield (1714–70), who was now beginning his second missionary journey in America. He preached first in the Anglican church there, and then from the courthouse steps to vast multitudes.

This spectacular beginning was followed by a series of meetings at many Presbyterian churches, which produced a strong resurgence of lay support for pietistic religion. This effect was widened and deepened after Whitefield returned from a visit to Georgia. During his wide itinerations, he also strengthened the relations between the Dickinson group of New Englanders and the Log College men, while these Presbyterians, in turn, gradually drew Whitefield away from Methodist-Moravian pietism toward a stricter Calvinism. The popular result of this activity was a great rejuvenation and numerical increase in the ranks of the revival party.

By the time the Synod of Philadelphia convened in May 1741, things had come to a hopeless pass. Gilbert Tennent's sermon at Nottingham, Pennsylvania, on "The Danger of an Unconverted Ministry," besides being an unauthorized intrusion on another presbytery, had touched the antirevival party at its sorest point. Whitefield's whirlwind campaigns had stirred other controversies. Both sides had hurled many unsubstantiated accusations at the other. It was too much to expect that any synod could long survive the rancor of such deeply divided factions. Gilbert Tennent was quite just in refusing arbitration by some British judiciary on the ground that nobody could agree on what the issue was. Even today there is disagreement on this point.

In retrospect, the historian can clarify matters, perhaps, by designating the question as to the place of the presbytery in the Presbyterian system as the *formal* issue. The Log College and New England men insisted that it had an unimpeachable authority in its own sphere and that the higher courts could not encroach legislatively upon it. The *material* issue concerned the place of revivalism in the Westminster tradition, or, put more broadly, the relation between doctrinal orthodoxy and experimental knowledge of Christ. The Tennent-Dickinson group was unanimous in its support of experimentalism, questioning the value of strict orthodoxy in the absence of personal religious experience. The issue of ministerial education which the Scotch-Irish party sought constantly to exploit was superficial, even irrelevant: as the past revealed even then, and as the future was to reveal more fully, both sides were determined to maintain an intellectual tradition and a learned ministry.

But issues were lost in the synod's turbulent proceedings. The Scotch-Irish group presented a protest against the

"Brunswick-Party" which concluded with the assertion that "these brethren [!] have no right to be acknowledged as members of this judicatory of Christ." In rushing to sign it they discovered that they had a majority, whereupon they declared themselves to be the synod. The Log College men, thus ejected, withdrew after the closing prayer. The proceedings were illegal, but there was no recourse.

The "New Side," as the revival party was popularly known, responded to the need for regrouping their forces by organizing their churches into the Conjunct Presbyteries of New Brunswick and Londonderry. This body faced many difficult problems, not least of which stemmed from constant abuse by the "Old Side," but in general it conducted its affairs with diligence and decorum. It evidenced commendable openness to reunion and great evangelical zeal for converting the people then moving in large numbers into the western parts of Pennsylvania and Virginia. Jonathan Dickinson and the ministers of the New York Presbytery sought to heal the schism; and when that proved impossible, they united with the conjunct Presbyteries to form the Synod of New York in 1745. The new synod took its stand essentially on the Adopting Act of 1729, made ordination a responsibility of the presbytery, and took no specific action prejudicial to the Log College men. They stressed the need for educational, doctrinal, and experiential qualifications for the ministry, affirmed revivals as a work of God, and indicated their desire to see the church reunited. The moderate course taken by the new synod is exemplified in Gilbert Tennent himself, who in 1743 had accepted a call to the Second Presbyterian Church in Philadelphia. In this church built by Whitefield's supporters so that the great evangelist might have a pulpit in the city, Tennent pursued a more temperate ministry—so much so that some of his more enthusiastic followers became disappointed and moved off to the Baptists or the Quakers.

ESTABLISHMENT OF THE COLLEGE

The New Side's sense of responsibility for the future of Presbyterianism (could they have known how much it lay in their hands?) was shown further in their move to found a college. Initial actions in this direction were taken by the group of New Englanders led by Jonathan Dickinson, and they succeeded in overcoming Anglican opposition to the institution and secured a charter in 1746, the very year of the elder Tennent's death. It was, to be sure, a shaky instrument gained shortly after Governor Lewis Morris's death while the president of the council was serving *ad interim;* this possibly explains their decision to enlarge the board of trustees to include the Log College men. In any event, it was a foregone conclusion that Dickinson would be the first president. He was duly elected, and began in May 1747 to conduct classes for eight to ten pupils in his parsonage at Elizabethtown. The Reverend Caleb Smith served as tutor.

But within five months the president was dead. He was succeeded by another New Englander, the Reverend Aaron Burr, who had just married a daughter of Jonathan Edwards. The students moved to his parsonage at Newark. At this time their cause was favored by the appointment as governor of Jonathan Belcher, an admirer and friend of Whitefield, under whose patronage a new, less tenuous charter was obtained and the board of trustees enlarged. They immediately invested Burr with the presidency, but he too was carried away by an untimely death in 1757, though not before becoming the veritable founder of the institution. He had broadened the base of its support, located it at Princeton, and erected the spacious and beautiful Nassau Hall—at that time the finest college building in America. Burr was succeeded by his father-in-law, Jonathan Edwards, who died of a smallpox inoculation in 1758 before he had properly assumed the duties of his office. The next president, Samuel Davies, also died after two years; and in 1766 Samuel Finley, one of the seasoned leaders of the Log College group, had his term cut short by an early death. In two decades the College of New Jersey had devoured the best leadership of both the New England party and the Log College men.

The next presidential election at Princeton marked the end of the formative period. By now the institution was secure; with 120 students in attendance, it had become an educational mainstay of the entire region. For the church the next election was even more significant, but explication of this fact requires a brief résumé of the way in which the schism of 1741 was healed in 1758.

The outstanding characteristic of the period of schism is the phenomenal growth of the New Side. It had about twenty-two ministers in 1741, but had increased to seventy-three in

1758. More important, it had won the respect and enthusiastic support of the laity. The Old Side, meanwhile, had not even held its own, and its educational efforts had been feeble. In view of these facts, the New York Synod's strong desire for reunion speaks eloquently of their magnanimous spirit and genuine concern for the church as a whole. Gilbert Tennent's *Irenicum Ecclesiasticum, or A Humble Impartial Essay Upon The Peace of Jerusalem, Wherein the Analogy between Jerusalem and the visible church is in some Instances, briefly hinted . . . Also a Prefatory address to the Synods of New York & Philadelphia* (1749) and other conciliatory gestures indicate that overtures for peace were initiated almost entirely from the New Side. Finally, after committees had combed out the main obstacles, the reunited church met in Philadelphia with Gilbert Tennent as moderator. The terms of union were essentially those for which the New Side had stood: the attitude toward subscription was that of the Adopting Act of 1729, with some verbal modifications; presbyteries were charged with the examination and licensure of ministerial candidates; learning, doctrinal fidelity, and an "experimental acquaintance with religion" were affirmed as equally needful to the minister; revivals were approved as a blessed work of the Holy Spirit.

A reunion—especially on one-sided terms—rarely erases all the malice of the past, and many sharp words remained to be spoken. In 1761 schism even threatened again, especially in areas where the two parties overlapped, for there was much disagreement on the importance and knowability of "holiness" in the ministry, and cognate disputes occurred over the problem of ministerial discipline. Several of the Old Side ministers went over to Anglicanism as a result of their position on these matters. This, plus the fact that vast numbers of nominally Presbyterian immigrants continued to stream into the Middle Colonies, made it evident that the training of an adequate ministry was urgent. The College of New Jersey, therefore, occupied a position of paramount importance, and this made the choice of its president extremely crucial. Although the first five presidents had all been men of New Side sympathies, by 1768, with the Scotch-Irish influx reaching record proportions, it became eminently desirable that the next incumbent be a man who could attract and hold the support of the entire church. After a long series of factional maneuvers, the trustees' choice finally fell on the Reverend John

Witherspoon (1723–94) of Scotland. After almost coercive supplications, long delays, and much vacillation, he finally agreed to come.

The choice was a fortunate one, and Witherspoon's acceptance a godsend. He was by any account an impressive man, and had already become a recognized leader of the evangelical cause in the Kirk of Scotland. He was also a man of considerable intellectual stature, conversant with the exciting philosophic developments of the "Scottish renaissance," and well prepared to take the burden of leadership in a church now stripped of many of its more capable men. As events were to prove, even his political ideals were admirably suited to a country that was hurrying toward its independence— and he would be the only clergyman to sign the Declaration of Independence. His temperament, moreover, made him an ideal instrument of reconciliation in a situation deeply in need of an irenic spirit. Finally, he was a Scot. This made him sensitive to the church's most pressing challenge, and enabled him to lead it to its greatest opportunity: ministering to the large and restless potentially Presbyterian tide of Scotch-Irish settlers who were altering the ethnic constituency of the Presbyterian churches.

In August 1768 the eminent Scotsman was joyfully received in Philadelphia, then escorted to Princeton to begin his duties, including that inevitable burden of American college presidents, fund raising. His successes were many and varied; and when he died a quarter of a century later, his college had assumed a prominent place in the new nation. It had also lost its grim reputation as a death trap for presidents. Within the Presbyterian church there had come significant changes traceable in large part to him, notably the passing of the New England tradition. Witherspoon's advocacy of the Scottish Philosophy, common sense realism, gradually eclipsed the Edwardsean New Divinity. At the same time the congregational emphasis of the Dickinsonian New Englanders lost its appeal, and Witherspoon made a large contribution to the constitution of 1788 and the formation of a General Assembly. The tendency to value religious experience more highly than doctrinal rectitude likewise abated. The acceptance of revivalism and insistence on the need for conversion remained, but in the days of the Enlightenment and the Revolution even these emphases began to fade until revived again in the new evangelical resurgence that would begin in the 1790s.

THE IMPACT OF IMMIGRATION

The Scotch-Irish

In the last analysis it was not a theologian or a college that changed the character of Presbyterianism in colonial America, but the arrival of wave upon wave of Scotch-Irish immigrants. For a half-century England had sought to attract Scotsmen to Ulster, and by the time of the Civil War it had succeeded in bringing in a hundred thousand or more. After 1660, however, the enactment of various repressive measures put the Scotch-Irish to flight. A few departed in the later years of the seventeenth century, but during the eighteenth century this trickle swelled to a tide. At certain periods the exodus was especially heavy: in 1717–18 because of a drastic increase in rents by Anglo-Irish landlords, in 1727–28 and 1740–41 because of poor harvests and the resultant famine, and in 1771–73 because of the decline of the Irish linen industry. The entire eighteenth century in Ireland is marked by unrest and rebellion due to English mismanagement, severe commercial restrictions on Irish industry lest it compete with English, and religious bigotry that deprived both the Roman Catholics of the south and the Presbyterians of the north from any part in government.

Resentment over these conditions combined with the tempting lure of opportunity in America to draw thousands of Scotch-Irish to the New World. Most of them came to Pennsylvania, which received in the later 1740s some twelve thousand immigrants each year. Some fifty thousand came during the 1770s, and perhaps five times that number during the whole colonial period, of which the large majority settled in the Quaker State. By 1776 Benjamin Franklin estimated their strength at three hundred fifty thousand, a third of the colony's population. Those who did not remain in Pennsylvania most often moved into adjacent areas: the Shenandoah Valley and the valley between the Alleghenies and the Blue Ridge in western Virginia, the back country of New Jersey, and western New York.

The Scotch-Irishman was, as historians keep saying, "the

typical frontiersman," bold, courageous, lawless, individualistic, resentful of constituted authority, a hard drinker, a
hater of Indians, and an inveterate "squatter" on land he had
not bought. Historians also speak of his "rigid Calvinism" as
if he were invariably a psalm-singing covenanter; but such
was not the case. He had been twice uprooted. Both the
migration to Ulster and that to America were made by people
who were more restless than pious. And to America, at least,
he brought with him little of his religious tradition and very
few ministers. Although doubtless he carried a residual loyalty to the Scottish Kirk and a violent antipathy to anything
Anglican, in America he and his companions constituted
chiefly a mission field. This was the enormous challenge to
the reunited Presbyterian church.

The challenge was accepted; and though the church was
restricted in its work by its constitution and ministerial
requirements, its accomplishment was immense. By 1788 the
church consisted of at least 220 congregations, organized in
sixteen presbyteries divided among four synods, with about
177 ministers serving this constituency. Bringing large
numbers of these Ulster Scots into the church, however,
resulted in a radical alteration of its character. "The future of
the church belonged to the descendants of the Scotch-Irish
. . . and before many years of the nineteenth century had
passed, a Scotch-Irish party arose within the Church in
whose eyes the New England group were interlopers, who
had somehow crept into a Church that had always been essentially Scotch-Irish."[1] In this subsequent struggle another
type of New England influence would be confronted and
another schism would be endured. But that is a nineteenth-
century story.

OTHER PRESBYTERIAN CHURCHES

Not all Presbyterians of the Scottish tradition were willing
to abandon the specific churches of which they had been a
part in the home country. Remarkably, the Kirk itself—the
established Church of Scotland—was not projected onto the
American scene as were the state churches of England,
Sweden, or Holland. This is explained in part by the fact that

[1] Leonard J. Trinterud, *The Forming of an American Tradition*,
p. 227.

the Stuart kings after 1603 were primarily rulers of England, secondarily of Scotland. This made their Anglican relationships preeminent, and often led them to try to impose episcopacy on Scotland. After the Act of Union (1707) Scotland ceased to be an independent political entity. During the seventeenth century, moreover, except for those who had spent one or more uprooted generations in Northern Ireland, the Scottish people did not leave their country in great numbers. Nor was the missionary spirit strong during the eighteenth-century heyday of Scottish rationalism. Yet those dissenting groups which seceded from the state church of Scotland did succeed in perpetuating their traditions in America.

The first dissenting group to withdraw from the main line of the Scottish Kirk were the scattered Covenanters who after 1660 refused to accept Charles II and the Restoration settlement in Scotland; some of these "Old Dissenters" maintained this role even after the Glorious Revolution, on the ground that the church must not be subservient to the state. The Reformed Presbytery which they organized in 1743 became the Reformed Presbyterian Church in 1811; with some accessions and losses, this group has maintained itself in Scotland to the present time. Lay members of this group came to America as early as 1720; and in 1750 their first minister arrived, though not until 1773 was this lone itinerant joined by two others so that the Reformed Presbytery of America could be organized. This was accomplished the following year at Paxtang, Pennsylvania, near Harrisburg.

In 1733 the same issue in a somewhat different form arose in Scotland when Ebenezer Erskine led a group of Seceders out of the Kirk in protest against "lay patronage," the prevalent policy of allowing patrons or landholders to bestow livings on ministers without congregational approval. Such a system tended naturally to prefer the more complacent, urbane, and even worldy men of the "moderate" party in the clergy. The Associated Synod of the Secession Church, as it was called, grew rapidly, and in Scotland it counted over two dozen settled charges by 1747, when it divided over the propriety of religious clauses in the oath tendered to city officials (burghers). The two synods which resulted, "Anti-Burgher" and "Burgher," perpetuated themselves in Northern Ireland, and by 1753 the Anti-Burghers had formed an associate presbytery in the Susquehanna Valley of Pennsylvania. Because the issue dividing them was unreal in America, a Burgher minister was admitted in 1764 and the schism in the Secession church was healed, though in spirit the American Seceders remained in the more strict Anti-Burgher tradition.[2]

Because of the difficulties created in America by widely scattered constituencies, and because they shared the very conservative Covenanter spirit, the Reformed and Associate churches were gradually drawn together. A plan of union broached during the Revolution was consummated in 1782 by the formation of the Associate Reformed Synod. This church suffered several divisions and secessions over the years, yet the main body persevered. A few of the Seceders who balked at the merger maintained a separate existence until 1858, showing in the meantime a most remarkable vitality despite great obstacles. In that year they united with the Associate Reformed Church to form the United Presbyterian Church, which continued for a century, merging with the Presbyterian Church, U.S.A., in 1958.

The relative ineffectiveness in evangelism of the Covenanters and Seceders as compared with the larger Presbyterian body highlights the importance of the English, Welsh, and New England influences which from the first directed American Presbyterians to deeper and broader theological currents than those of Scotland, and turned its attention to essentially American problems. This contrast also suggests that the Northern Ireland experience had the effect of uprooting men from specifically Scottish concerns. When the Scotch-Irish began to put their mark on American Presbyterianism after 1768, their spirit was far different from that of the Scottish Dissenters.[3]

[2] The Anti-Burgher strictness is indicated by the fact that when the Secession was reunited in Scotland in 1820, the American Synod condemned the act as a sacrifice of principles and in 1832 joined two small protesting groups who had constituted themselves as the Associate Synod of Original Seceders. (Probably the most famous Anti-Burghers to come to America were Thomas and Alexander Campbell, father and son, who founded one of the main branches of the Disciples of Christ. See pp. 541–48 below.)

[3] In 1821 the General Assembly of the Presbyterian Church, U.S.A. did make an overture for union with the Associate Reformed Church, whose General Synod was a delegated body that had lost its southern and western presbyteries. This merger proposal was railroaded through the General Synod against the prevailing sentiment of the constituency. Its ultimate result, there-

The issues that were seriously contended within the two groups—as well as the presuppositions of the controversy between them—betoken the same difference in spirit. While one argued about the continuing relevance of the Scottish covenants, closed communion, and fine points of doctrine, the other was debating the importance of subscription to the Westminster symbols and the necessity of personal religious experience. In 1801 the latter group was willing to make drastic departures from traditional Presbyterian church order as laid down in the Westminster Directory, in order to cooperate with Congregationalism in the West. Even when the same questions were discussed by both groups (e.g. temperance, slavery, Masonry, or psalmody), the spirit and presuppositions were different. In one case we find a dissenting tradition desperately seeking to justify the issues that had brought it into being; in the other, an eclectic tradition bent chiefly on making a maximum Presbyterian witness in a new and rapidly changing environment. In both traditions and both attitudes there were important sources of strength and weakness, but only the historian of the future can evaluate their interaction and reciprocal influence in the decades following the merger of 1958.

For the colonial period, the important fact is that "American," rather than Scottish, Presbyterianism became the chief bearer of the Reformed tradition in the Middle Colonies. Of almost equal significance is the parallel fact that the Great Awakening enabled an emphatically revivalistic party stemming from the Log College and from New England to put a characteristic and enduring mark on this influential church.

---

fore, was negligible, though a few large urban churches in New York, Philadelphia, Baltimore, and Washington were lost to the Associate Reformed Church.

18

THE GREAT AWAKENING IN NEW ENGLAND

Cotton Mather made his greatest bid for earthly immortality in 1702 with his *Magnalia Christi Americana,* a vast biographical and historical record of New England's founders which was also a call to his own generation to save themselves from the ruck of routinization. He did not perceive that his own Latin-larded writings were signs of the very trend he lamented. The ideal of a Holy Commonwealth standing in a national covenant with its Lord was fading. Mather's own defense of inoculations for smallpox was undermining the popular conception of pestilence as a sign of God's wrath. The Half-Way Covenant, though itself no proof of declension, documented the passing of churches composed solely of regenerate "saints." The Enlightenment, meanwhile, was eating away at the federal theology: the national covenant, once a mainstay of Puritan thought, was yielding to moralistic individualism. The first generation's fervently held convictions had become a formal doctrinal position upheld by an outmoded structure of Ramist *technologia,* to be passed from the notebooks of third and fourth generation preachers to those of the fourth and fifth, with few of any generation being able to invest it with relevance and ardor.

Having seen Samuel Willard's posthumous *Compleat Body of Divinity* (1726) drop stillborn from the press, a massive memorial to the previous century's achievement, Mather went to his grave in 1728 with small grounds for hope that a resurgence was on the horizon. Ironically, he never suspected that much promise was hidden in the Connecticut revivals of 1721 or in the periodic "harvests" of souls being reaped in the Northampton parish of his arch-antagonist, Solomon Stoddard. He was in communication with the pietists at Halle, but he could hardly foresee their potential impact on America. Nor was Cotton Mather the only disappointed man. The ministerial utterances of the period—from pulpit and press—were equally gloomy.

In retrospect, however, we can see what these prophets of declension could not see. There would be a resurgence of pietism among the Dutch and Germans, traceable in part to New England's own theological hero, William Ames. John Wesley would inaugurate a great evangelical revival in Great Britain which would spread to America. George Whitefield, meanwhile, would become a tremendous engine of transformation in all of the colonies.

Although Jonathan Edwards was surprised in 1734 when a revival of religion became manifest in Northampton, that event was neither accidental nor strange; the soil had in many ways been prepared. In the first place, Puritanism was itself, by expressed intention, a vast and extended revival movement. Few of its central spirits had ever wandered far from a primary concern for the heart's inward response, and its laity inwardly knew that true religion could never be equated with dutiful observance. Even in years of most lamented declension the churches were informed by a carefully reasoned theology and warmed by a deeper faith than the jeremiads acknowledge. Far out in the Berkshires, for example, the little community of Westfield was blessed for a half-century by the ministry of Edward Taylor (1642?–1729), without knowing that posterity would consider his meditative poems and intricately wrought sermons to be the work of a literary and theological master. Taylor's first Preparatory Meditation on the Lord's Supper (1682), like the two hundred that followed, displays this animating spirit. It is also a prayer for personal awakening that could serve as an epigraph to the life work of Jonathan Edwards.

> What Love is this of thine, that Cannot bee
> > In thine Infinity, O Lord, Confinde,
> Unless it in thy very Person see
> > Infinity and Finity Conjoyn'd?
> > What! hath thy Godhead, as not satisfi'de,
> > Marri'de our Manhood, making it its Bride?

Oh, Matchless Love! Filling Heaven to the brim!
　O'rerunning it: all running o're beside
This World! Nay, Overflowing Hell, wherein
　For thine Elect, there rose a mighty Tide!
　That there our Veans might through thy Person bleed,
　To quench those flames, that else would on us feed.

Oh! that thy love might overflow my Heart!
　To fire the same with Love: for Love I would.
But oh! my streight'ned Breast! my Lifeless Sparke!
　My Fireless Flame! What Chilly Love, and Cold?
　In measure small! In Manner Chilly! See!
　Lord, blow the Coal: Thy Love Enflame in mee.[1]

Cotton Mather was himself a preparatory voice. Despite his ostentatious vanity and contradictory moods, he made memorable contributions as an historian, thinker, and defender of the new science, and also as a sensitive interpreter of the times who developed a theology and a conception of piety keyed to the increasingly individualistic spirit of his age. For all of his nostalgia, he called for a new kind of theology, and in *The Christian Philosopher* (1721) he attempted in his old age what the young Edwards was even then striving toward. He also sought to set Christian ethics and eschatology in a new and more promising direction without sacrificing what he considered to be the old orthodoxy. Nor were Taylor and Mather isolated exceptions.

PRELIMINARY STIRRINGS

The Great Awakening of New England began, as has been suggested, in Northampton, Massachusetts. But Jonathan Edwards, to whose preaching the first stirrings are usually traced, did not bring it into being. Nor, in plain fact, did it come suddenly. For sixty years Northampton parishioners had heard the solid and powerful preaching of Solomon Stoddard (1643–1729), and they had experienced five separate seasons of revival. Since the great man's death, they had heard his grandson's carefully wrought sermons. At first Edwards found his people "very insensible of the things of

[1] *The Poetical Works of Edward Taylor,* ed. Thomas H. Johnson (New York: Rockland Editions, 1939), p. 123.

religion," but by 1733 he began to notice a change. Then late in 1734, while he was in the midst of a closely reasoned sermon series on justification by faith, the response began to accelerate. During the spring and summer it continued. "This town," he wrote in his original narrative letter to Benjamin Colman of Boston, "never was so full of Love, nor so full of Joy, nor so full of distress as it has lately been. . . . I never saw the Christian spirit in Love to Enemies so exemplified, in all my Life as I have seen it within this half-year." Edwards came to the only conclusion possible for him: it was a work of the Holy Spirit and a vindication of sound doctrine.

News of these remarkable providences of God quickly spread to the adjoining towns; and showers of blessing were soon felt in these localities as well, especially in Suffield, South Hadley, and Hatfield in Massachusetts, and in East Windsor (where Edwards was born and where he had experienced his first revival), Lebanon, and New Haven in Connecticut. Before long there were similar visitations in towns along the whole Connecticut River valley and spreading slightly eastward as that river approached Long Island Sound. A recent student of these events stresses the importance of word-of-mouth transmission in this new fervency. "From Northfield to Saybrook Point, the religious stirrings of Northampton were known many months before Edwards sat down to write this *Narrative*."[2] He also points out its brief duration, and distinguishes it from the Great Awakening proper by calling it a "frontier revival." It was clearly on the wane in 1737, when Edwards's *Faithful Narrative of the Surprising Work of God* appeared, and it was past history in 1738 when he published the *Discourses* which had occasioned the revival four years earlier.

Yet neither the churches nor the ministers fell back into their former lethargy, and hopes for a new revival were fed by news from the Presbyterian awakeners in the Middle Colonies. Far away in Boston, and farther still in England and Scotland, prominent theologians and ministers were thrilled by the news and convinced that a new day of the Lord was at hand. Edwards himself became convinced that America was the chosen place for the Kingdom's coming, and he invited the great Whitefield to preach in Northampton.

[2] Edwin Scott Gaustad, *The Great Awakening in New England*, p. 20.

"A GREAT AND GENERAL AWAKENING"

To have reckoned the revival as finished in 1738 would have been to reckon without George Whitefield—a gross miscalculation. The *Great* Awakening was still to come, ushered in by the Grand Itinerant. Whitefield had gradually widened his American circuit: in 1738 only Georgia had been favored, but in 1739, on his second visit to the colonies, he had made a triumphant campaign north from Philadelphia to New York and back to the South, ostensibly in behalf of his orphanage in Georgia. In the Middle Colonies his influence, then and later, extended beyond the British churches to the Dutch and Germans. Muhlenberg tells of a German woman who, after hearing Whitefield preach, asserted that she had never in all her life been so edified, though she understood not a word of English. And Muhlenberg himself was sometimes more drawn to "converted" ministers of other churches than to Lutherans who were not.

In 1740 Whitefield brought New England within his orbit, and at every place he visited, the consequences were large and tumultuous. Sailing from Charleston, South Carolina, to Newport, he landed on 14 September 1740, and on the following day (Monday) preached twice in the Anglican church. He recorded in his journal that there was "great Reason to believe the Word of the Lord had been sharper than a two-edged sword in some of the Hearers Souls." On Tuesday he preached again "with much Flame, Clearness and Power to still greater Auditories," before moving on to his greatest and most decisive triumph—a solid week of amazing activity at Boston. There were prayers at King's Chapel on Thursday morning; preaching to an overflow crowd at Brattle Street Church in the afternoon; preaching to a vast auditory in South Church on Friday morning, and to five thousand people on the Common in the afternoon. He preached on Sunday afternoon in the First (Old Brick) Church, and afterward outside to eight thousand who could not gain entrance. On Monday he preached to two large outdoor audiences; on Tuesday at Second Church, Wednesday at Harvard, and on the last day of this visit, he honored the "Great and Thursday Lecture" at First Church, where Edwards nine years previously had made his Boston debut.

Whitefield then extended his conquests up the coast as far as Portsmouth, and returned to bid farewell to thirty thousand Bostonians on the Common on 12 October. Leaving Boston, he journeyed out to Northampton, where he spent a few days with Edwards, preaching twice in the parish church while Edwards wept profusely. He then made his way to New Haven, where he found that at Yale, as at Harvard, "Light is become Darkness." After preaching on down the coast, he crossed over into New York on 29 October, thus concluding a whirlwind evangelistic tour of six weeks. Of the religious situation in New England he had a dim view: "I am verily persuaded, the Generality of Preachers talk of an unknown, unfelt Christ. And the Reason why Congregations have been so dead, is because dead Men preach to them." Concerning the effect of his own efforts he was more sanguine: "Dagon falls daily before the ark." Basically both estimates had a great deal of truth in them. Everywhere his preaching had had a sensational impact; and though he raised some suspicions at Cambridge and New Haven, he had at least effectively raised the Puritan churches from their "declension."

On meeting the Presbyterian Gilbert Tennent on Staten Island, Whitefield persuaded him to visit Boston in the near future "in order to blow up the divine fire lately kindled there." Tennent did as he was bidden, and in December continued the mission which Whitefield had left off in October, preaching in Boston with an outward success hardly less than Whitefield's. Although Timothy Cutler, the former rector of Yale, now an Anglican priest at Christ Church in Boston, reported that "people wallowed in snow, night and day, for the benefit of his beastly brayings," most of the Boston ministers acknowledged the enlivening effect of his visit, and conceded that he was not the barbarian that the antirevivalists had pictured. In other towns throughout southeastern Massachusetts, Rhode Island, and southern Connecticut, the response to his three-month tour was much the same —great crowds, considerable tumult, many conversions, a heightening of revivalistic fervor, and an aftermath of violent controversy. Thus Tennent succeeded both in extending the revival and in deepening the animosities which Whitefield had left behind.

What Whitefield had done in the fall of 1740 and Tennent in the winter, James Davenport (1716–57) attempted to do

in the following summer. If Whitefield and Tennent brought
to the New England pulpit an unprecedented degree of
explosive power, they seemed models of decorum in comparison with Davenport. Yet this young man was a New England
product: born at Stamford, Connecticut, great-grandson of
New Haven's founder John Davenport, graduate of Yale
(1732), theological student of the highly respected Elisha
Williams, and since 1738 minister of the old Puritan church
at Southold on Long Island. From his youth he had been im-
pressionable and imitative, and he had readily adopted
Whitefield and Tennent as his heroes. In the summer of 1741
he determined to follow in their footsteps as awakener of
New England. After a trial run at Easthampton, he began his
assault on the southern coast between Westerly, Rhode
Island, and New Haven. Everywhere he aroused resentment
and opposition by his fanatical harangues and his arrogant attacks on "unconverted" ministers. A year later, after a similar
foray, he was arrested at Stratford under Connecticut's new
law against itinerant preaching, tried by the General Assembly at Hartford, adjudged mentally disturbed, and deported
under guard to Long Island.

Now filled with the spirit of martyrdom, Davenport set out
immediately for Boston, where after some days of wild and
denunciatory preaching, he was again arraigned, declared
non compos mentis, and expelled. His ill-starred career
reached a height of fanaticism in March 1743, when he returned to New London to organize some of his followers into
a separatist church. After ordering that wigs, cloaks, rings,
and other vanities be burned, he then gave out a list of books
to be committed likewise to the flames—works of piety by
evangelical greats such as Flavel, Colman, Increase Mather,
and others. In a frenzied ceremony down at the wharf, the
books were burned, though someone spared the clothes.
These excesses were Davenport's last. Heeding the counsel of
two "New Light" ministers and apparently returning to a less
febrile state of health, he published in 1744 his *Confessions
and Retractions.* In 1748 he soberly took up parish duties
among the Presbyterians of New Jersey, where he spent the
few remaining years of his life. His return to favor among the
more moderate revivalists was acknowledged by the New
York Synod when they elected him moderator in 1754. He
seems to have seen in retrospect that he had done the revival
more harm than good by bringing discredit upon the more

constructive labors of Whitefield and Tennent and all who had enlisted in its cause.

The chief events of the awakening were of two sorts: first, the whirlwind campaigns of the "Grand Itinerants," Whitefield, Tennent, and the highly unstable Davenport, followed by a large number of lay itinerants and clerical interlopers; second, the intensified extension of the preaching and pastoral labors of the regular New England ministers, now awakened to the power of personal evangelism. Historians have stressed the first of these because of the immense controversy it stirred up, but the latter was by far the more lasting and significant. The chief work of reviving New England was carried forward by the regular ministry, though many conceded the effectiveness of Whitefield's witness and viewed their own labors as an extension of his. Sometimes the stimulus of a revival was simply regular preaching by the parish minister, many of whom had been hoping for years for such a harvest. At other times one of New England's own itinerants, respected and sought after by his clerical colleagues, was the instrument of reviving a church. At still other times, one of the customary exchanges of pulpits by two ministers would be the occasion. More often it was a combination of these circumstances, but in and through all there was the atmosphere of revival—the general air of expectancy and the increasingly avid public interest in the literature of religious experience. So widespread were these manifestations that a brief account could be reduced to a simple list of the 150 New England towns touched by the movement. The important fact is that New England did experience a "great and general Awakening" during the years 1740–43. Even in Boston, where opposition was most vocal, chiefly in the persons of the Congregationalist Charles Chauncy and the Anglican Timothy Cutler, the revival party held a three-to-one majority among the settled clergy. By an interesting irony, their leader was Benjamin Colman of the prestigious Brattle Steet Church, while Cotton Mather's son, Samuel, and his nephew, Mather Byles, took their stand with the Old Lights.

The Great Awakening in New England was not essentially different from the "frontier revival" of the preceding decade; but it nevertheless bore certain distinguishing marks. Flamboyant and highly emotional preaching made its first widespread appearance in the Puritan churches (though by no means in all), and under its impact there was a great increase in the number and intensity of bodily effects of conversion—fainting, weeping, shrieking, etc. But we capture the meaning of the revival only if we remember that many congregations in New England were stirred from a staid and routine formalism in which experiential faith had been a reality to only a scattered few. The ideal of a regenerate membership was renewed, while Stoddardeanism and the Half-Way Covenant were called into question. Preaching, praying, devotional reading, and individual "exhorting" took on new life. In spite of far more demanding requirements, the increase in church membership is estimated variously between twenty and fifty thousand.

Yet the other side of the phenomenon is equally important: the high pitch of religious excitement subsided. By the time of Davenport's New London debacle it was already past its apogee. The year 1743 was occupied with retrospective and highly polemical evaluations. Ministerial friends and foes of the revival held conventions in Boston to praise or blame, but their "testimonies" came after the fact. All things considered, however, there could have been no other result. The conversion experience as defined by the revivalists was a single soul-shaking experience; when assurance came, it brought release, and the emotion subsided. Without an infinitely large reservoir of susceptible sinners, the enthusiasm simply had to wane. In addition, there were widespread misgivings over the excesses of spirit. Davenport's recantation is perhaps an extreme but illustrative example. When further distractions were provided by the French and Indian War, and after 1763 by the declining state of Anglo-American relations, the revivals lost priority as a general concern in New England.

Equally certain is the fact that the Awakening had many far-reaching, even permanent, results. Consideration of the social and political legacy of the revivals must be deferred until the movement can be surveyed as a broad intercolonial phenomenon—indeed, the first such. But certain developments in New England provide a basis for this broader view.

CHANGE IN THE STANDING ORDER

In the long run the influence of Jonathan Edwards and the unfinished edifice of his thought is the most enduring result of the New England Awakening. For this reason it is the subject of the next chapter. Yet Edwards expounded a theological tradition that had deep popular roots; and its revival among the laity had important cultural results. A new and irrepressible expectancy entered the life of the churches. A national sense of intensified religious and moral resolution was born. Millennial hopes were kindled. The old spirit of the jeremiads was extinguished. Evangelicalism in a new key was abroad in the land, and its workings had a steady internal effect which was nowhere more apparent than in the Congregational churches.

It is difficult to see how Congregationalism could have survived the revolutionary epoch and emerged as a large New England denomination had it not benefited from the enlivenment which was a primary result of the Great Awakening. The most obvious sign of new life was an increase in membership, not vast (because owning the covenant became a more serious thing than ever) but considerable. Of equal importance was the increased seriousness among existing members and clergy. Edwards's powerful witness and his development of a distinct school of theology would help to nurture these results. For a century his influence would put its stamp on New England preaching, keeping the concerns of the Awakening alive in the pulpit even as the excitement ebbed away. Yet the price of concern was the perpetuation of extremely divisive controversies. Revival issues created antagonistic schools of Old Lights and New Lights, each claiming with obvious justice to be orthodox, and each insisting that it was the bearer of the authentic New England traditions. For a half-century and more "Old Calvinists" and Edwardseans would contend for control of local parishes, educational institutions, and other corporate enterprises of the churches. Such contention had serious negative consequences, in that it drove many peace-loving souls out of the churches and led many more to embrace milder forms of religion.

The Great Awakening thus became the single most important catalyst of that "Arminian" tradition which had been growing surreptitiously and half-consciously since the turn of the century. One can, in fact, regard Charles Chauncy's critique of the Awakening, *Seasonable Thoughts on the State of Religion in New England* (1743), as a primary document in the rise of Unitarianism. When this book appeared, both Harvard and Yale were considered seminaries of Puritan learning; but thereafter Harvard became increasingly a bastion of liberal thought, and its graduates became suspect wherever the Awakening had won acceptance. By the time of the Revolution, Harvard men generally were serving in the churches of the eastern seaboard, while Edwardseans predominated elsewhere in New England. In due course, the "broad and catholick" party against which Edwards had inveighed in 1734 was to be arrayed against the "New England Theology" which he fathered. The Anglican churches also benefited from the drift to liberalism, for they gladly offered refuge to those in flight from the doctrinal rigors of orthodoxy, the vigorous application of discipline, and the objectionable features of revivalism. As the nineteenth century dawned, however, the clear emergence of Unitarianism and a reconstituted Episcopal Church would lead orthodox Old Lights and New Lights to close ranks for the great task of evangelizing the new nation as well as the heathen beyond the seas. In this manner the Second Great Awakening grew out of the colonial revival.

The missionary spirit itself was a fruit of the Awakening—in America just as in Great Britain and Europe. Whitefield indeed was the very model of a missionary. In New England this spirit is especially apparent with respect to that foreign field which lay at home—the Indians. Jonathan Edwards figured in this campaign both personally at Stockbridge and through his celebration of the piety and missionary zeal of David Brainerd (1718–47), who had worked with Indians west of Stockbridge. Edwards preached Brainerd's funeral sermon and edited his autobiography. Dartmouth College grew out of another Indian enterprise; at the same time, its early years demonstrate the importance of the Awakening for the founding of colleges.

The rejuvenation of higher education was a field in which New England's efforts matched those of the New Light Presbyterians of the Middle Colonies. Eleazar Wheelock (1711–79), one of the most active promoters of the revival in eastern Connecticut, was one of the most ambitious of the educational pioneers. Wheelock was a graduate of Yale (1733) who served as minister of the north parish in Lebanon (now Columbia), Connecticut. He conceived a plan for educating Indian boys so that they could spread the gospel effectively to their own people. After gaining support for his project from Joshua Moor of Mansfield, he opened Moor's Indian Charity School in Lebanon in 1754 with two pupils. By 1762 he had some twenty students under his tutelage. Contributions were solicited in various parts of America and in

Scotland and England as well, eventuating in a trust fund managed by a board under the chairmanship of the earl of Dartmouth. When in 1769 the province of New Hampshire invited Wheelock to transfer his school to Dresden (now Hanover) and to establish a college there, he complied, opening it to whites as well as to Indians. Dartmouth College, as it became known, was most influential in supplying the new churches of that frontier territory with New Light ministers, sending out some forty before 1800.[3]

At the already established colleges, the impact of the Awakening was somewhat different. Most consequential for Yale College was the process by which the revival interests of students gradually overcame the official hostility which had greeted the efforts of Whitefield, Tennent, and Davenport. "It was the beginning of what is known today as the 'Student Movement,'" wrote the historian of religion of Yale in 1901.[4] The expulsion of David Brainerd and others for their pious excesses had if anything a stimulating effect. By 1753 President Thomas Clap had been converted to the cause; and in 1757 the professor of divinity whom he had installed as preacher to the newly founded Church of Christ at Yale was rewarded by a revival. When Whitefield returned to New Haven for his fourth visit in 1764, he was invited to preach in the college chapel. So moved were the students that they urged President Clap to call the great preacher from the coach in which he was departing and persuade him to give them another quarter-hour of exhortation. By this time Yale and its graduates were assuming a role in the American evangelical movement that they would not relinquish for over a century.

THE REVIVAL OF SEPARATISM

The New England churches had been troubled by problems of fellowship since the stormy 1630s, when Roger

[3] Brown University, established by Baptists as Rhode Island College in 1764, also furthered the emphasis on experimental piety and revivalistic fervor in New England; but its originating impulse stemmed from the Philadelphia Baptist Association and was less a direct institutional effect of the Great Awakening (see pp. 226, 389, 455–56).

[4] Cyrus Northrup, ed., *Two Centuries of Christian Activity at Yale* (New York: G. P. Putnam's Sons, 1901), p. 25.

Williams and Anne Hutchinson had raised the issue. The Half-Way Covenant had precipitated later divisions, while Baptists had never ceased to stir the waters. And now the Great Awakening again aroused these separatistic impulses. One of the earliest incidents was James Davenport's affair at New London, but others soon followed. The dissenters in these cases were "Strict Congregationalists," who objected to the semipresbyterian structure of Connecticut's Saybrook Platform and appealed to the old Cambridge Platform of 1648, which was more explicitly congregational. Above all, they insisted on evidence of regeneration as a condition of church membership. Because their withdrawal threatened to disrupt the uniformity of the ecclesiastical establishment, the Connecticut Assembly passed in 1743 a law which denied them the toleration granted to Baptists, Quakers, and Anglicans. Persecution followed, but failed to bring compliance; and "Separate" congregations were gathered in many towns. The statement of those who withdrew in Preston, Connecticut, delineates the most prominent issues:

> This Church is Caled the Seperate Church because [it] . . . Came out from the old Church in the Town. which caled its Self Partly Congregational and Partly Presbyterial: who submitted to the Laws of the Governments to settle articals of faith; to govern the gathering of the Church, the settlement and support of its Ministers, building of meeting houses, Preaching, Exhorting &c: as also the Church Refuses the members should Improve there Gifts of Preaching and Exhorting Publikly &c: as also were offended at the Powerful opperations of the Spirit of God: and Did Not Make Saving Conversion the necessary termes of Communion: but admitted unbelievers to Communion: also made half Members: Baptized there Children, &c:—
>
> We bore our testimony to them and Came out from them: to Carry on the worship of God according to our Knowledge of the will of God: and gathered into Church order: and the Lord has graciously owned us ever sence.[5]

Here opposition is expressed not only to the ecclesiastical constitution which subjected the churches to governmental

[5] From the handwritten entry of the minister, Paul Parke, in the church record book (1747); quoted in Clarence C. Goen, *Revivalism and Separatism in New England: Strict Congregationalists and Separate Baptists in the Great Awakening*, p. 82.

support and control, but also to the suppression of exhorting and testifying by awakened laymen, to Stoddardean views of the Lord's Supper and Half-Way Covenant terms for baptism, and to the denial of revivalistic doctrines of conversion and regenerate church membership.

Wherever there were Congregationalists there were likely to be persons of separatist inclination, and wherever the standing churches retained broad "halfway" standards of membership, movements for secession tended to accompany the revival. In Connecticut, where the standing order was rigorously upheld by law, about forty Separate churches were formed, most often in the less thickly settled eastern part of the commonwealth. In Massachusetts, where Congregationalism was also established, there were over thirty, most of them in the old Plymouth Colony area and around Boston and northward. In the outlying areas of Maine, New Hampshire, Vermont, and New York, Separate churches also appeared, though many of these had migrated from older regions. Even free Rhode Island witnessed some separations from its few Congregational churches. In all New England approximately one hundred Separatist congregations emerged from the revivalistic ferment. Due to inadequate leadership and strenuous official opposition, however, few of these separations achieved permanent status as Congregational churches. One notable exception is the United Church of New Haven, in which two separations from the First Church are merged, one of them having been occasioned in 1769 by a ministerial call to Jonathan Edwards's son. As this date indicates, separatistic agitation continued for decades.

THE BAPTIST REVIVAL

When the Great Awakening began, the Baptists were a weak and dispirited denomination, especially in New England. Even the famous old congregations in Boston, Providence, and Newport had become placid in manner and complacent in spirit. They bitterly resisted the ministry of the revivalists, denouncing Whitefield as "a second George Fox." They showed no awareness whatever that Baptists would be by far the greatest beneficiaries of the revivals in general and of the Separatist movement in particular. Yet many of the most zealous among the "awakened" came to regard Congregationalism—even in its classic Puritan form—as only a half-way house on the road to true and complete church reform. When conversion came to be viewed as the decisive Christian experience, infant baptism was an anomalous embarrassment. Among many revivalists, moreover, both baptism and the Lord's Supper ceased to be regarded as "means of grace" in the traditional sense of the term. When these tendencies were conjoined with doubts about established churches and tax-supported ministers, the road to a Baptist outlook was open. The ways in which Separate Baptist congregations came into existence were various. In some cases, a Separatist church accepted Baptist beliefs in a body; this happened at Sturbridge, Massachusetts, in 1749, and elsewhere in following years. In other cases, members of a Separatist church who had accepted believer's baptism withdrew and covenanted together as a Baptist congregation; this happened at North Middleborough, Massachusetts, in 1756. Perhaps most important, however, was the fact that for more than a half-century after the outbreak of the Great Awakening, there was a steady stream of individuals moving from New Light Congregational churches into organized Baptist churches where the fires of the revival remained alive much longer because no tradition of community inclusiveness tended to smother it. The shift to Baptist principles was also encouraged to some degree by laws which made it easier for Baptists to organize legally than for Strict Congregationalists; but the extent to which this was a real motive cannot be assessed.

Perhaps no single separatistic convert augured larger consequences for New England church history than Isaac Backus (1724–1806). Born into a devout Congregational family in Norwich, Connecticut, Backus was "brought to a saving knowledge of the truth" in 1741 at a local revival. The following year he united with the church of his fathers; but five years later he was among the group who formed a Separate church on Strict Congregational principles and refused, despite fines and jailings, to relinquish their convictions. In 1748 he accepted a call to minister to a Separate church at North Middleborough, where he became exceedingly disturbed over the question of baptism. After some vacillation he was baptized, but he refused to make believer's baptism a norm of communion. For five very troubled years during which one council of twenty-seven Separate churches (1753) and another representing forty churches (1754) met to adjudicate matters, Backus tried to conduct his church on the basis of mutual tolerance. Compromise produced nothing but strife and stricken consciences, however, and in 1756 he covenanted with five others to form a strict communion Baptist church. Thus began a half-century of distinguished service as pastor, evangelist, apologist, and historian in the cause of the Baptists and religious freedom.

Repeated experiences of this sort account for the remarkable Baptist growth in New England during the latter half of the eighteenth century. In 1740 Baptists had only eleven churches in Rhode Island, eleven in Massachusetts, and three in Connecticut. Thirty years later these states had twelve, thirty, and thirty-six respectively. In 1804 New England had 312 Baptist churches grouped in thirteen associations, besides the growing Freewill (or Arminian) connection and a number of unassociated churches. But these figures do not indicate the most portentous events, for they do not include the many Separate Baptist preachers who fanned out into the newer frontier areas, and those who began their amazingly productive missionary labors in the South.

TOWARD WIDER ASSOCIATIONS

The final factor to consider is the Great Awakening's unitive effects, which were felt in two distinct ways. Paramount was the way in whch the renewed emphasis on Christian experience and the religious affections led to the recovery of an old aspect of Puritanism: an inclination to regard conversion and regeneration as a bond of fellowship that transcended disagreements on fine points of doctrine and polity. Whitefield, Tennent, and Edwards—Anglican, Presbyterian, and Congregationalist—felt themselves to be of one mind in their great undertaking. Similarly, the revivals led other American evangelicals to discover each other. Here was recompense for the controversy and acrimony which they had experienced so often and which, in fact, they could never long avoid.

Almost equally important was the geographical corollary to this discovery. Fellowship became not only interdenominational but intercolonial. In this regard Whitefield was unparalleled as an influence, yet many others widened their horizons through similar activities. Jonathan Edwards's move to the presidency of Princeton symbolizes both kinds of rap-

prochement and points to a new era of Protestant cooperation. Based on a wide and durable consensus, evangelicalism
would become a powerful force in the future development of
American culture.

Given the immense social consequences of the Awakening,
it is unfortunate that historians have been almost totally unable to agree as to why it occurred. Few if any improvements
have been made on the conflicting explanations advanced by
Edwards and Chauncy in the mid-eighteenth century. It
came to pass that the message of sin and redemption spoke
with sudden and peculiar power to the condition of many
New Englanders—though these sons of the Puritans seemed
to be no more receptive during those years than other Protestants in Europe, Great Britain, and the more southerly parts
of America. Efforts to establish political, social, and economic
explanations have been conflicting and unconvincing. Revivals and conversions seem to have come to churches and persons in all areas and classes and walks of life. Given present
limitations of knowledge, it is enough to say that in New
England as elsewhere the revivals became a major means by
which people of many diverse types responded to changing
moral, religious, intellectual, and social conditions.

As for the social and political consequences of the Awakening, they are so important and so widely ramified that they
can be discussed only in the context of the country's ongoing
experience. Richard Bushman's observation summarizes the
overall effect: "A psychological earthquake had reshaped the
human landscape."[6] Many of the chapters which follow attempt to measure and describe the reverberations of that
earthquake.

[6] Richard L. Bushman, *From Puritan to Yankee: Character and
the Social Order in Connecticut, 1690–1765,* p. 187.

19

JONATHAN EDWARDS AND THE RENEWAL OF NEW ENGLAND THEOLOGY

During the critical first decade of the eighteenth century, higher learning in New England underwent an important transition. In Massachusetts the age of the Mathers drew to a close, and Harvard was virtually refounded when "the great John Leverett" was installed as president in 1707. The path he marked out for the college would lead naturally to the tradition of William Ellery Channing and Ralph Waldo Emerson. Six years earlier, the leading divines of Connecticut had obtained a charter for another collegiate institution, and installed Abraham Pierson to lead it. The path they and he marked out, and which was set even more firmly after the apostasy of 1722, would lead to the tradition of Jonathan Edwards, the Dwights, Nathaniel William Taylor, and the Beechers. It is this latter tradition that concerns us here.

Connecticut's college was chartered on somewhat broader principles than Harvard had been; it would fit its students for "Imployment both in Church and in Civil State." Theologically and doctrinally, however, it was committed to conserving the Puritan heritage; to this end its founding fathers donated to the nascent seminary of learning forty ponderous tomes, the great bulk of them works by Alsted, Wollebius, and other Dutch, Swiss, or Rhineland theologians. The regulations of the institution prescribed the Westminster Catechism and William Ames's *Marrow of Sacred Theology* as guides to scriptural truth. Divinity was to be taught and defended by the sixteenth-century logical methods of Petrus Ramus. But within a couple of decades, the adequacy of this curriculum began to be questioned, especially as new textbooks in science, logic, and ethics began to reflect the new world of thought created by Descartes, Newton, and Locke. Incongruities between the old learning and the new deprived the covenant theology of its power to inspire. Perry Miller's description of the situation is overdrawn but essentially accurate:

> The period becomes a complex of tensions and anxieties, in which, in sober fact, the die was cast. . . . This society had become a time-bomb, packed with dynamite, the fuse burning close. It was a parched land, crying for deliverance from the hold of ideas that had served their purpose and died.[1]

Two brilliant Yale students of those years, each of whom was to become a noted thinker and college president, exposed the fundamental nature of the problem. Both Samuel Johnson and Jonathan Edwards, moreover, each in his own way, were to mark out the main lines of a *via moderna*.

Samuel Johnson (1696–1772), born in Guilford of an old New Haven Colony family, was prepared for Yale by various of its earliest graduates. He was granted the B.A. degree in 1714, and during the next few years, as he studied the new English books which Jeremiah Dummer and other British benefactors had contributed to the college library, he broadened and modernized his thought. In retrospect he would refer to the old learning as "a curious cobweb of distributions and definitions," and his published *Works* include the youthful notebooks which demonstrate that this condescending judgment was not entirely unwarranted.

The initial instrument of deliverance in Johnson's case was Lord Bacon's *Advancement of Learning*, which he chanced upon shortly after graduation while keeping school in Guilford. After reading this old attack on scholasticism he found himself "like one at once emerging out of a glimmer of twilight into the full sunshine of open day." Thus illuminated, he turned with a still greater sense of discovery to other books in the library. In 1715, when student disaffection and disputes over the school's location led to a dispersal of the infant college, his opportunity to gain further light was increased. The students from upper Connecticut went to

[1] Perry Miller, *The New England Mind: From Colony to Province*, p. 484.

Wethersfield, a few others stayed at Saybrook, and some were under Johnson's care at Guilford. A year later, when New Haven was chosen as the future home of the college, he became a tutor along with his friend and classmate, Daniel Brown. By 1720, when Johnson accepted a call to the church in nearby West Haven, the trustees had pacified New Haven's rivals, put Elihu Yale's £500 gift to use, and installed the Reverend Timothy Cutler of Stratford as rector.

Institutional concord was soon followed by spiritual unrest. Johnson by now had not only been released from scholastic thralldom; his intellectual horizons had been widened by various English philosophers and cosmopolitan essayists. He also began to confront some of the newer Anglican divinity that was then being so reasonably and felicitously expounded. As old foundations crumbled, the problem of ecclesiastical authority began to bother him. Doubting the validity of his own ordination, he had to re-examine the question of episcopacy. Nor was he alone in the doubts created by his vicarious translation to the realm of English urbanity. A coterie of Anglican admirers had come into being in the New Haven area, with Rector Cutler at their head. Then in 1722 there occurred a great defection from Yale and the Congregational ministry, as the entire faculty (Cutler and Brown) and two ministers in the area, Johnson and James Wetmore of North Haven, announced their intention to seek Anglican orders in England.[2]

The incident is an important sign of the times. Johnson's dissatisfaction with the state of New England's theological and philosophical orientation illustrates the uneasiness of many thoughtful spirits who were feeling the impact of a new, scientifically ordered world view. In this connection Johnson is the most important of the Yale apostates, for he took his discovery seriously and became a comparatively effective disciple of Bishop Berkeley's unique idealistic system of philosophy. He also became a moderate Arminian in theology—which involved him in controversy with Jonathan Dickinson, Princeton's first president. In ethics Johnson took

[2] Other men in the immediate group were John Hart of East Guilford, Jared Eliot of Killingworth, and Samuel Whittelsey of Wallingford, who remained in the Congregational ministry. They exemplify the prevailing restiveness as well as those who found greater security in the older Establishment. Brown died of smallpox in England. See pp. 284–85.

a rationalistic stand, defended natural law, and held morality to be "the same thing as the religion of Nature," not discoverable without revelation, to be sure, yet "founded on the first principles of reason and nature." Moral goodness consisted in a man's being what he is essentially. Johnson's social philosophy was antidemocratic, and with the years he became an outspoken Tory, viewing the extension of the episcopate to the colonies as an essential preventive to independence.

Johnson's sympathetic and admiring biographer opens his work with the observation that it would not have been worthwhile to write his life "had it been as barren of incident and historic interest as the lives of most clergymen." The remark is just. Had Johnson not been a participant in a sensational apostasy at Yale and the first president of King's College, he would be remembered only as a moderately effective advocate of Berkeleyan philosophy. Of Jonathan Edwards, however, the reverse is true. Edwards would be remembered if he had lived out his days in a peaceful parish; in fact, his largest claim to remembrance stems from words on freedom, sin, virtue, and God's purposes which were put to paper in remote frontier villages. His chief contribution is an enduring intellectual and spiritual reality, a monumental reconstruction of strict Reformed orthodoxy which is remembered for its exegetical insight, its literary power, and its philosophical grandeur.

The remainder of this chapter, therefore, is devoted entirely to Edwards. Later chapters will consider the New Divinity men who carried on the Edwardsean tradition, and the ways in which the New England Theology affected the Second Great Awakening. For the present we deal with the source, in the conviction that Bancroft's judgment is correct: "He that would know the workings of the New England mind in the middle of the [eighteenth] century, and the throbbings of its heart, must give his days and nights to the study of Jonathan Edwards."

THE EARLY DEVELOPMENT OF EDWARDS'S THOUGHT

Jonathan Edwards was born in East Windsor, Connecticut, in 1703, the fifth child and only son among ten daughters of the Reverend Timothy Edwards and his wife, the daughter of

Solomon Stoddard. Both parents were persons of rare endowments, deeply concerned for the liberal education and spiritual nurture of their children. Jonathan entered Yale before he was thirteen, while the college was still fragmented. He received part of his education in Wethersfield and the other part in New Haven, where the unpopular Samuel Johnson was his tutor. By the time of his graduation in 1720, he may have discovered the new philosophy of John Locke, and the bent of his mind was becoming established. He stayed in New Haven two years to pursue theological studies. After he was licensed to preach in 1722, he served a Presbyterian church in New York for ten months, then returned to Yale as a tutor for two more years. By this time (1726) the immense fertility of his mind would have been apparent to anyone who could have read his private writings. In "Notes on the Mind" he had marked out, quite independently of Berkeley, the main lines of his lifelong commitment to an idealistic understanding of reality; in "Notes on Natural Science" and in other youthful writings such as his observation of spiders, he had shown his devoted concern for empirical data; and in his diary he had already revealed that passionate interest in religious experience which was never to leave him. In these early writings, indeed, one may find anticipations of nearly every theme he was to develop during his lifetime. Yet all of these interests were to remain utterly captive to the Reformed tradition as Edwards knew it through the Synod of Dort, the Westminster Assembly, and his Puritan forebears.

One of the remarkable facts of his intellectual history during this period is that, despite a very strong propensity to theological innovation, he seems almost completely untouched by the questions of ministerial authority that were perturbing Cutler, Brown, and Johnson. Perhaps this testifies to the fine example and nurture provided by his father, who had not sacrificed the affective dimension of the Christian faith to the aridities of dogma and polity. Nor can one discount the possibility that Edwards may have simply reacted negatively to tutor Johnson's personality (as most students seem to have done). Finally, one must consider at least the possible impact of his being called as a tutor in 1724 to help repair the shattered prestige of the college; because he now became an official defender of the college, was he not led to uphold the faith of his fathers?

Whatever the explanation, the fact is that Edwards's own

conversion experience, as he describes it later in his *Personal Narrative,* involved a genuinely new kind of vision of God's visible glory in every aspect of the natural world. For his sense of nature's beauty there is no precedent among his Puritan forefathers, with all their talk of the "howling wilderness." Indeed, he even seems to move beyond the Enlightenment's characteristic attitudes. In this frame of mind he began his appropriation of Locke. As he undertook the serious study of theology, he was thus involved in the creative process of conforming his inherited Puritanism to a larger manner of apprehending the world.[3]

According to the custom of the day, however, tutoring was only an apprenticeship to the ministry, and in 1727 Edwards was ordained in Northampton as the junior colleague of his grandfather, Solomon Stoddard. Two years later Stoddard's death left him the full ministerial responsibility in a town that was becoming the most influential in western Massachusetts, and in a church to which his grandfather had already brought notoriety and prominence. Young Jonathan was now more observed and listened to simply by virtue of his situation.

He formally stepped onto a wider stage in 1731, when he accepted the invitation to deliver the "Great and Thursday

[3] One may ask if passages like the following from his *Personal Narrative* should not be included in anthologies of preromanticism: "The first instance that I remember of that sort of inward, sweet delight in God and divine things that I have lived much in since, was on reading those words, 1 Tim. 1:17. *Now unto the King eternal, immortal, invisible, the only wise God, be honor and glory for ever and ever, Amen.* . . . Not long after I first began to experience these things. . . . I walked abroad alone, in a solitary place in my father's pasture, for contemplation. And as I was walking there, and looking up on the sky and clouds, there came into my mind so sweet a sense of the glorious majesty and grace of God, that I know not how to express. I seemed to see them both in a sweet conjunction; majesty and meekness joined together. . . . After this my sense of divine things gradually increased, and became more and more lively, and had more of that inward sweetness. The appearance of every thing was altered; there seemed to be, as it were, a calm, sweet cast, or appearance of divine glory, in almost every thing. God's excellency, his wisdom, his purity and love, seemed to appear in every thing; in the sun, moon, and stars; in the clouds, and blue sky; in the grass, flowers, trees; in the water, and all nature" (*The Works of President Edwards,* 4 vols. [New York, 1879], 1:16–17).

Lecture" in Boston, thus giving an august body of Harvard men the opportunity to hear Stoddard's successor and at the same time to witness the result of a Yale education (perchance to discover that Timothy Cutler, now rector of Boston's Christ Church, had left little influence on at least one of his students). The sermon delivered by the light-framed, soft-voiced, twenty-eight-year-old divine spoke not to old controversies that had racked New England, but to the condition of the times—and thus, as it were, to future controversies. He stood before his elders, well aware of the "enlightened" drift of things, and called them to the faith of their fathers, castigating "schemes of divinity" that in any way mitigated the doctrine announced in his title: "God Glorified in the Work of Redemption, by the Greatness of Man's Dependence upon Him, in the Whole of It." Youth called age to its heritage.

Yet the distinctiveness of his utterance lay not only in its assertion that "reasonable" moderations of doctrine were "repugnant to the design and tenor of the gospel," but in two other characteristics: the terms and concepts of the old Puritan covenant theology were notably absent, and (to the discerning) the thought was invaded by concepts of the new learning. Here is Edwards's first public hint of high Dortian doctrines being maintained from a new perspective, one that in a complex way combined philosophical idealism and Lockean psychology. It is not surprising that the audience was troubled by his message. Beneath the urbane congeniality that had graced the ministers' meetings since the passing of the choleric Mathers, there was a growing conflict between the "Old-Style Calvinism" and the incipient rationalism that marked the men of more "free and catholick" temper. Lines of cleavage that were eventually to divide New England more deeply and irreparably than ever before were already forming, and the more perceptive listeners surely knew that the young successor to the "pope" of the western regions had taken a firm doctrinal position.

For two or three years after the Boston lecture Edwards carried on the usual round of pastoral duties without abnormal interruption. In 1734, in compliance with his congregation's wish, he published another of those subtly inclusive sermons that reveal so much of his thought to the discerning reader: *A Divine and Supernatural Light, Immediately Imparted to the Soul by the Spirit of God, Shown to be Both a Scriptural, and Rational Doctrine.* This sermon, too, defends something very much like "Calvinism," but in a very new and rational way. Also in 1734 he began a more ambitious project with the same objective: a series of sermons directed against the increasingly popular tendency toward Arminianism which was observable even in his own Hampshire ministerial association. Published in 1738 as *Discourses on Various Important Subjects, Nearly Concerning the Great Affair of the Soul's Eternal Salvation,* the leading one of which was on the doctrine of justification by faith, these sermons seem to have precipitated the "surprising conversions" in Northampton during 1734–35. As the revival spread elsewhere, Edwards's renown increased, although his involvement in these events was limited primarily to his own parish.

This continued to be the case even in the more widespread awakening that began in 1740. To be sure, he made a few sallies out of Northampton; and on one such occasion at Enfield he delivered the sermon "Sinners in the Hands of an Angry God," which for many Americans has been the only thing he ever produced.[4] If Edwards did not become an itinerant, however, his influence was widened by the many ministers and evangelists who visited his Northampton parish. In addition, nearly all of his publications between 1737 and 1746 dealt with central issues of the Awakening, and through these carefully qualified writings he emerged as the chief New England spokesman for a somewhat restrained type of revivalism. He also became one of the most important interpreters of religious experience and experiential religion in post-Reformation history.

APOLOGIST FOR EXPERIENTIAL RELIGION

During the revival period proper, Edwards published two works of extensive influence. The first of them was *A Faithful*

---

[4] Actually there are fewer than a dozen imprecatory sermons among the more than a thousand for which manuscripts are extant. This sermon's popularity with anthologists indicates the journalistic level of interpretation by which Edwards has been victimized. Hell, of course, did have a place in Edwards's thought. Those who have internalized Auschwitz and Hiroshima may find the Enfield sermon less absurd than have many intervening commentators. But readers of even this chapter may discover that its precise place is a complex matter (see H. Richard Niebuhr, *The Kingdom of God in America,* p. 137).

Narrative of the Surprising Work of God in the Conversion of Many Hundred Souls in Northampton, and Neighboring Towns and Villages (1737), in which he combined minute detail and remarkable reserve in describing the marvelous and to him quite inexplicable (on the human level) works of the spirit that had constituted the frontier revival in 1734–35. He saw it, as he almost had to, as "an Extraordinary dispensation of Providence." He was grateful, too, that it was accompanied not by censorious behavior and emotional excesses, but by many signs of charity, moral reform, and a deep renewal of faith in those doctrines "that we account orthodox." A major aspect of the *Narrative's* influence stemmed from its masterly portrayal of the true Christian convert. Reading it today, we can easily understand how John Wesley, pondering its pages as he walked from London to Oxford, should have exclaimed, "Surely this is the Lord's doing, and it is marvelous in our eyes."

Many of the excesses for whose absence Edwards was grateful in 1737 did appear in the new outburst of revival fervor that accompanied Whitefield's visit in 1740. This fact gives special importance to Edwards's discourse delivered at Yale's commencement exercises in 1741: *The Distinguishing Marks of the Spirit of God, Applied to that uncommon Operation that has lately appeared on the Minds of many of the People in New-England: With a Particular Consideration of the extra-ordinary Circumstances with which this Work is attended* (1741). The heart of the matter is suggested in the subtitle, for Edwards defended those manifestations that were found so objectionable by most critics of the revivals (including the authorities at Yale who were still smarting from Whitefield's castigation of their coldness). After a discerning exegesis of his text (1 John 4) and a careful survey of the revival, he concluded that "we must throw by our Bibles, and give up revealed religion; if this be not in general the work of God." Yet he was not undiscriminating in his approval, and he granted both that persons might be saved without apparent bodily effects and that some of the physical manifestations might be demonic. Two years later, when Edwards reworked this subject into a full-length book, the opposition was stronger, and he altered his defense accordingly. In *Some Thoughts Concerning the Present Revival of Religion in New-England* (1742), he spoke not to a local situation but to all the world.

Charles Chauncy of Boston was not one to leave Edwards unchallenged, however. In his *Seasonable Thoughts on the State of Religion in New-England* (1743), Chauncy threw off his earlier reserve and in point by point refutation denounced the revival as a resurgence of the antinomian and enthusiastic heresies that had plagued the early Puritans. He provided at the same time a valuable mine of information on the screechings and agitations of persons overcome by powerful emotions, and poured special venom on Whitefield, Tennent, and Davenport for their role in arousing these horrendous passions. In conclusion, he laid bare the chief intellectual issue posed by the revival: "There is the Religion of the Understanding and Judgment, and Will, as well as of the Affections; and if little Account is made of the former, while great Stress is laid upon the latter, it can't be but People should run into Disorders."

Chauncy set the stage for the first of Edwards's great theological works, his "ultimate philosophy of the revival": *A Treatise Concerning Religious Affections* (1746). This book was ignored by Chauncy, who had written off Edwards as a "visionary enthusiast, and not to be minded in anything he says." It became, nevertheless, one of his most widely read treatises, and it remains one of America's profoundest inquiries into the nature of religious experience. It is a classic evangelical answer to the question, *What is true religion?* Edwards's thesis, directly stated, is that "true religion, in great part, consists in holy affections." The "affections" to Edwards are not simply the emotions, passions, or even the "will," but more fundamentally, that which moves a person from neutrality or mere assent and inclines his heart to possess or reject something. Love, therefore, "is not only one of the affections but it is the first and chief . . . and the fountain of all the affections."

Edwards's purpose in the book is to delineate the twelve signs of genuine piety and the rightly inclined heart. Under the First Sign he clarifies the basic point that holy affections are spiritual, supernatural, and divine. He even quotes John Smith, the Cambridge Platonist: "A true celestial warmth . . . is of an immortal nature; and being once seated vitally in the souls of man, it will regulate and order all the motions in a due manner; as the natural head, radicated [rooted] in the hearts of living creatures, hath the dominion and the economy of the whole body under it. . . . It is a new nature, informing the souls of men." This point is further developed under the Fourth Sign: "Holy affections are not heat without light; but evermore arise from some information of the understanding, some spiritual instruction that the mind receives, some light or actual knowledge." The argument culminates in the Twelfth and "principal" sign: "Gracious and holy affections have their exercise and fruit in Christian practice." In describing this practice, moreover, Edwards closes off the possibility of any kind of antinomianism by presenting it as that "which is universally conformed to, and directed by Christian rules," and persisted in to the end. On the other hand, he also closes the door to utilitarian legalism by insisting that "the first objective ground of gracious affections, is the transcendently excellent and amiable nature of divine things, as they are in themselves, and not any conceived relation they bear to self, or self-interest. . . . What makes men partial in religion is, that they seek themselves, and not God, in their religion."[5] Here was a defense of holy affections that could arouse true religion and at the same time present a stern rebuke to arrogant and censorious enthusiasts.

By the time the *Religious Affections* appeared, affairs in Northampton were moving toward a crisis. For one thing, Edwards was ill at ease under the lax standards for church membership sanctioned by the Half-Way Covenant, and even more disturbed by Stoddardean views on admission to the Lord's Supper—and he said so. He also ran into trouble with some respectable families when he proposed to discipline certain young people who had been circulating "bad books" (a manual for midwives). This antagonism was fully manifested in 1748, when Edwards's request to deliver a series of sermons on the qualifications for admission to communion was met not only by a firm refusal, but by a demand that he tender his resignation as minister. The tangled skein of events which culminated in a council that advised his dismission cannot be traced here, but on 1 July 1750, he preached his farewell sermon, an utterance whose quiet compacted strength still proclaims the man's greatness in a tragic hour. After dedicating twenty-three years of his life to Northampton, making it for a time a famous center of orthodoxy and

[5] Jonathan Edwards, *Religious Affections,* ed. John E. Smith (New Haven: Yale University Press, 1959), pp. 95, 188, 219, 266, 383, 393–94.

revived spirituality, he was set adrift with a wife and seven dependent children.

Edwards was lifted from the anxieties of his expulsion by a call to Stockbridge, Massachusetts, a frontier town where the Society for the Propagation of the Gospel in New England (the so-called New England Company) and the Bay Colony's Board of Commissioners for Indian Affairs maintained a mission. Though hardly a promotion, the new post was not an exile. During the first years he was diverted by the necessity to foil the plans of those who at this early date were building the great American tradition of Indian exploitation. Although he also had to carry on a double ministry, to the whites and to the Indians, he now was free from many time-stealing distractions, and his most brilliant and understanding disciple, Samuel Hopkins, was in nearby Great Barrington. The Stockbridge years actually became the most productive in his life.

His first task was to conclude his elaborate answer to the "communion question" which had been brought to such a disheartening issue in Northampton. On this matter he had stated his case massively in 1749 with *A Humble Inquiry into the Rules of the Word of God, Concerning the Qualifications Requisite to a Complete Standing and Full Communion in the Visible Church*. This work, to put it mildly, left Northampton unconvinced; more troubling still, his cousin Solomon Williams of Lebanon, Connecticut, had ventured a full-scale refutation which now required and received a rejoinder: *Misrepresentations Corrected, and Truth Vindicated* (1752). Edwards's writings on this entire controversy were once very influential, but they have been slighted by scholars. Consistent with the stand taken in the *Religious Affections*, they are not extreme. The membership pledge he asked for was no more rigorous than the Anglican confirmation vow. Yet he did make a decisive break with the accepted principles of Stoddardeanism, and he cast a shadow upon the Half-Way Covenant. He accepted what his Congregational colleagues were unwilling to admit—that the Holy Commonwealth and its "national covenant" were gone, utterly dead. The church was living in a new age; it stood in a new relation to the world. He rejected the older view that New England's total corporate errand was part of God's design. His grandfather's easy identification of town meeting and church meeting was found wanting. The church, he was convinced, must be gathered out of the world. On this general point Edwards's influence, exerted through his books, sermons, and example, was decisive; and he has been called in truth "the father of modern Congregationalism."[6] No works document this aspect of Edwards better than those on the problem of church communion.

When Edwards turned from ecclesiastical controversy to an immemorial philosophical problem, the result was his most celebrated treatise: *A Careful and Strict Enquiry into the modern prevailing Notions of that Freedom of Will, Which is supposed to be essential to Moral Agency, Vertue and Vice, Reward and Punishment, Praise and Blame* (1754). The second installment of the vast revision of current thought on the moral and religious life which Edwards began in the *Religious Affections,* this was one of the literary sensations of eighteenth-century America, and it has continued to be the most seriously analyzed of all of his works. What metaphysical situation could be more exciting: the chief critic of Arminianism forging a weapon out of the very Lockean materials which "enlightened" theologians and deists had claimed as their own. In a word, Edwards insisted that this was an orderly universe; in Ramsey's nice phrase, "either contingency and the liberty of self-determination must be run out of this world, or God will be shut out." Said Edwards:

> Yea, if once it should be allowed, that things may come to pass without a cause, we should not only have no proof of the being of God, but we should be without evidence of the existence of anything whatsoever, but our own immediately present ideas and consciousness. . . . If things may be without causes, all this necessary connection and dependence is dissolved, and so all means of our knowledge is gone.[7]

6 Alexander V. G. Allen, *Jonathan Edwards* (Boston, 1894), p. 270. Allen, of course, was writing in 1889, before liberal theology had transformed the denomination. We perhaps should now say "middle Congregationalism," which was primarily a nineteenth-century phenomenon, though its origins lay in the Great Awakening. After the Civil War it was progressively altered by influences best represented by Horace Bushnell.

7 *Freedom of the Will,* ed. Paul Ramsey (New Haven: Yale University Press, 1957), p. 183. For the quotation from Ramsey, p. 9.

Not only do we set science at nought, but we make an absurdity of the biblical teaching of an omnipotent, omniscient God. For once Edwards indulged his sense of humor:

> In such a situation [where the deeds of men are not caused] God must have little else to do, but to mend broken links as well as he can, and be rectifying his disjointed frame and disordered movements, in the best manner the case will allow. The supreme Lord of all things must needs be under great and miserable disadvantages, in governing the world which he has made, and has the care of, through his being utterly unable to find out things of chief importance, which hereafter shall befall his system; which if he did but know, he might make seasonable provision for.[8]

God Almighty would become the Great Tinkerer who could not even know if "the incarnation, life, death, resurrection and exaltation of his only begotten Son" had provided "any tolerable restoration" of the divine economy.

Edwards did not leave his case in so generalized a state, however, but in a closely reasoned argument distinguished between moral and physical causation, going on to show that the determinations of the will are no exception to the general principle. This he does by rooting human choice in the motives that dominate the will. Man chooses as he pleases, not in indifference; the will is determined by the strongest motive. This is the link between our deeds and our nature, without which our acts would be utterly capricious and irresponsible. But this linking of human choices with human nature involves an inescapable determinism, because human nature is corrupted and depraved by sin.

Here we move out of the area of primary concern in the *Freedom of the Will* and enter the domain of Edwards's next Stockbridge treatise, *The Great Christian Doctrine of Original Sin Defended* (1758), which was going through the press at the time of his death. This work should be read as one with its predecessor, for the question of human motive so central in the former is resolved only in the latter, where the empirical and biblical basis for the doctrine of man's sinful nature is expounded. Edwards begins this work by describing in great detail the matrix out of which human motives arise.

[8] *Ibid.*, p. 254.

Proceeding inductively, he shows the inadequacy of the optimistic anthropology of the Arminians in accounting for the facts. "He invited [the disbelievers in Original Sin] to a reading of history, a realistic report of village gossip, and a frank inspection of the police blotter. He left each to judge for himself . . . how far disinterested love . . . rules the world."[9] The undeniable truth is that sin and death are everywhere.

Edwards followed this rehearsal with a long survey of the biblical evidence (parts 2 and 3), a marvelous testimony to his command of scriptural materials and an impressive exhibition of Old and New Testament exegesis. Here he heavily reinforced the empirical data, underlining again and again that it was through Adam that sin came into the world, and that his fate was the fate of mankind. Throughout the book Edwards wages a vigorous polemic against the English Unitarian John Taylor of Norwich, whose critiques of this doctrine were the most formidable and influential of the time, largely because of the high seriousness with which Taylor had dealt with the evidence of the Scriptures. Finally (part 4) Edwards deals with objects to the doctrine and states his own views, insisting at the outset that one must not ignore the plain evidence already presented. "It signifies nothing to exclaim against a plain fact." He concedes difficulties, even mystery, but insists that "fact obliges us to *get over* the difficulty, either by finding out some solution, or by shutting our mouths, and acknowledging the weakness and scantiness of our understandings."

The argument that bears the chief burden in Edwards's defense of the doctrine of Original Sin is his insistence on the unity of mankind in Adam. What is exciting here is not the bare doctrine—it is traditional Augustinianism, articulated most recently to Edwards's satisfaction by Johann Friedrich Stapfer, the eminent Swiss dogmatician—but the *way* in which Edwards stated it. Here again he brought forward the grand conception adumbrated in his youthful notes "On Being" and reiterated in his Boston lecture on man's dependence. The creation, he insisted, does not possess the absolute independent identity of the First Being.

Nay, on the contrary, it may be demonstrated that even this oneness of created substance, existing at different

[9] Perry Miller, *Jonathan Edwards*, p. 269.

times, is a merely *dependent* identity, dependent on the
pleasure and sovereign constitution of Him who *worketh
all in all.* . . . God not only created all things, and gave
them being at first, but continually preserves them, and
upholds them in being. . . . It will certainly follow from
these things, that God's *preserving* created things in being
is perfectly equivalent to a *continued creation,* or to his
creating those things out of nothing at each moment of
their existence. . . . And I am persuaded, no solid reason
can be given, why God, who constitutes all other created
union or oneness, according to his pleasure . . . may not
establish a constitution whereby the natural posterity of
Adam, proceeding from him, much as the buds and
branches from the stock or root of a tree, should be treated
as *one* with him.[10]

This has been justly called the most profound moment of his
philosophy. Its power is increased by his daring explanation
of Adam's (and man's) fall as a fall from "original righteousness," wherein man was governed by a higher, supernatural principle, to a state of sin (or natural righteousness)
where even man's "good" behavior never breaks out of the
circle of self-interest. Since the Fall, man lives in darkness
because the candle has been withdrawn; now only a "divine
and supernatural light" can lead him to redemption and
righteousness. Weighty as this part of his theology may be,
however, it proved to be the most evanescent. Perhaps no
doctrine Edwards developed was so ignored by his disciples.
This development, in turn, is an aspect of the larger fact that
the metaphysical foundations of Edwards's theology were not
or could not be preserved by the New Divinity men who attempted to sustain the tradition. Amid the turbulent and
untheological preoccupations of the revolutionary epoch, they
turned to other forms of argument. It was not long, therefore,
before both orthodox and liberal theologians of New England
abandoned altogether the idea of the imputation of Adam's
sin.

Not even the opus on Original Sin fully revealed the "rational system" which informed Edwards's entire life work.
During his Stockbridge years, in fact, four years before

[10] Edwards, *The Doctrine of Original Sin Defended,* in *Works,*
2:487–91. See also pp. 579–80, 581–82, 590–91.

Original Sin appeared, he wrote two other "dissertations" which serve even better to link his lifework with his youthful projects. As he concluded the work on Original Sin, he mentioned the manuscript of *The Nature of True Virtue* "lying by me prepared for the press," though the public was not to see it until seven years after his death. One who consults it now can see clearly how Edwards's highest thought moved out of the realm of Lockean psychology and into the great tradition of Christian Platonism. Appropriately, this is one of the few works in which he does not take a polemical stance. He frees himself from eighteenth-century moralism and expounds a doctrine of Being as the basis for understanding the nature of sanctified living. At the same time clarifying the "Twelfth Sign" of holy affections, he puts his central proposition clearly in the first chapter:

> Virtue is the beauty of those qualities and acts of mind, that are of a *moral* nature. . . . And therefore when we are inquiring concerning the nature of true virtue, viz., wherein this true and general beauty of the heart does most essentially consist—this is my answer to the inquiry: True virtue most essentially consists in benevolence to Being in general. Or perhaps to speak more accurately, it is that consent, propensity and union of heart to Being in general, that is immediately exercised in a general good will.[11]

The argument that the cordial consent of being to being is the definition of beauty and that spiritual beauty is the essential quality of true virtue, together with criticism of more restricted notions, provides the chief content of this fine contribution to the perennial discussion of moral philosophy. At the same time, however, its exalted conception of true virtue forcibly underlines both the fact and the tragedy of man's sinfulness.

These notions are put in a still larger and more clearly Neoplatonic frame in the posthumously published *Dissertation Concerning the End for which God Created the World* (1765). Shining through these sometimes laborious pages is a genuine mysticism, though a mysticism kept within bounds by Edwards's commitment to the Reformed doctrines of human depravity and irresistible grace. A passage like that

[11] Edwards, *The Nature of True Virtue*, in *Works*, 2:261–62.

which follows also explains why William Ellery Channing would later classify Edwards as a pantheist:

> The great and last end of God's works . . . is indeed but *one:* and this *one* end is most properly and comprehensively called, THE GLORY OF GOD . . . and is fitly compared to an effulgence or emanation of light from a luminary. . . . Light is the external expression, exhibition and manifestation of the excellency of the luminary, of the sun for instance: it is the abundant, extensive emanation and communication of the fulness of the sun to innumerable beings that partake of it. . . . It is by this that all nature is quickened and receives life, comfort and joy. . . . The emanation or communication of the divine fulness, consisting in the knowledge of God, love to God, and joy in God, has relation indeed both to God, and the creature; but it has relation to God as its fountain; and as the communication itself, or thing communicated is something divine. . . . as the water in the stream is something of the fountain, and as the beams of the sun are something of the sun. . . . In the creature's knowing, esteeming, loving, rejoicing in, and praising God, the glory of God is both exhibited and acknowledged; his fulness is received and returned. Here is both an *emanation* and *remanation*. The refulgence shines upon and into the creature, and is reflected back to the luminary. The beams of glory come from God, and are something of God, and are refunded back again to their original. So that the whole is *of* God, and *in* God, and *to* God, and God is the beginning, middle and end in this affair.[12]

This is a long quotation for a book of this sort, but it ought to be longer, for here is the true center of Edwards's rational account of the Christian religion, around which his earliest thoughts revolved and around which all his sermons, polemics, and treatises must be grouped. It defines the lines of force according to which his other writings arrange themselves.

The great *summa* which Edwards was planning when he died was, to be sure, conceived on another plan. It was to be a vast "history of the work of redemption"—a sacred history. Using facts and interpretations gathered for many years, he

[12] Edwards, *Dissertation Concerning the End for which God Created the World,* in *Works,* 2:254–55.

planned to consider all the parts of God's grand design in their historical order, "with regard to all three worlds, heaven, earth, and hell; considering the connected, successive events and alterations in each" so as to show "in the most striking manner the admirable contexture and harmony of the whole."[13] Edwards was here proposing to enlarge upon ideas that he had presented in an unpublished sermon series of 1739, "The History of the Work of Redemption," and in his published work *Union in Prayer* (1747). This treatise would expound Christian doctrine in the context of an account of physical nature, all of whose motions "tend to the striking at the appointed time . . . as in a clock," and of all human history, in which "all the changes are brought to pass . . . to prepare the way for that glorious issue of things that shall be when truth and righteousness shall finally prevail." It would also interpret Scripture in the light of actual events—including the American revivals—so that men might know the hour when God "shall take the Kingdom." He would thus clarify the opinion broached in his *Thoughts* of 1744: "What is now seen in America, and especially in New England, may prove the dawn of that glorious day."[14] This work was never finished; but the sermon series, published in 1774, became Edwards's most popular book during the nineteenth century, especially among those with strong interests in biblical prophecies. Many scholars, therefore, have dismissed this work as little more than a "textbook for Fundamentalists." But it may yet be that Edwards will win a reversal of these judgments when it becomes possible to view his theology of nature and history as a whole. Regardless of that issue, the fact remains that he was speaking directly to that powerful millennial concern which the Awakening had accentuated and which in various forms became a prominent and distinctive feature of American thought on the nature, purpose, and destiny of the nation. Powerfully in the Great Awakening and repeatedly in later revivals, this old Puritan conception of the Redeemer Nation would be enlivened. It was on men's minds on the first Fourth of July, and in somewhat more secularized form it would become an enduring feature of American patriotic oratory.

[13] Edwards, Letter to the Trustees of the College of New Jersey at Princeton, 19 October 1757, *Works*, 1:48–49.

[14] Edwards, *Union in Prayer*, in *Works*, 3:450–51; *Thoughts on the Revival*, in *Works*, 3:316.

EDWARDS'S INFLUENCE: SOME REFLECTIONS

The workman must be judged by what he did rather than what he might have done, though that is not easy when one of the most prodigiously productive thinkers of the age is cut down in mid-career. When Edwards was called in 1757 to the presidency of Princeton, he hesitantly accepted; but shortly after his installation he died of an unsuccessful small-pox inoculation on 22 March 1758. He was followed in a few months by his wife, who was buried beside him in Princeton. His works, of course, did not die. In a general way his categories, his statement of the theological problem, and his reconstruction of Reformed orthodoxy had a profound impact on Congregational and Presbyterian theology in America for more than a century. Yet as will be seen in chapter 25, he did not have a single disciple who was true to his essential genius. His three most dedicated followers, Joseph Bellamy, Samuel Hopkins, and Jonathan Edwards, Jr., were all men of another type and temperament. Even when they were true to the letter, they proved themselves to be of another spirit, at once more congenial to their age and less able to transcend it than Edwards had been.[15] What is still more surprising, the Edwardsean spirit was really never infused into the life and thought of his church (as was that of Saint Augustine, for example, whom he resembles in so many respects). He remained a kind of perpetually misunderstood stranger.

The explanation of this strange circumstance rests on two closely related facts. One, the more simple, is that no generation (least of all his own) has ever been able to read and consider Edwards's complete works. Two of his most essential treatises were published posthumously, as were some of his most crucial sermon series. The main body of his sermons has never been published, and the vast collection of "miscellanies" and notebooks into which he poured much of his heaviest exegetical labor and profoundest speculations have been only very incompletely published. To make matters worse, Edwards was not the kind of thinker who reveals himself fully in any one work; nor did he, like Augustine, Rous-

[15] See chaps. 25, "The New England Theology," and 26, "The Second Great Awakening in New England: Revival, Evangelism, and Reform."

seau, or Wesley, lay bare his soul in a lengthy personal journal, autobiography, or "confessions."

Yet there is a second and deeper reason for the peculiar shape of Edwards's influence: his thought seems not to have achieved in its outward expression that inner unity which we know or suspect it had in his own consciousness. Hence his contemporaries (and much of his posterity) have confronted at least five distinct aspects of the man, and each of these aspects has been portrayed from time to time as the essential Edwards.

There is first of all Edwards the exegetical preacher, the man above all who has seemed to deserve the encomium: "the quintessence of Puritanism." His dedication to the minister's homiletical task has as its monument a thousand sermons in the rigorous tradition of his New England fathers, a body of exposition which in one arrangement could serve as a biblical commentary and in another as a system of divinity. A thoughtful Northampton parishioner might have beheld this Edwards. But in all but a few of these sermons only the scholar acquainted with Edwards's other works could discern the marks of a bold and original conception of the Christian faith.

Edwards the New England polemicist is bodied forth in a second cluster of writings on revivals and church order. These were occasional works, often on regional affairs and specific problems, and for this reason his larger views can be perceived only by the specialist who has an objective understanding of the events. Thirdly, we have Edwards the apologist for strict Reformed doctrine and "New Light" experientialism in a world that was making enlightened reasonableness the criterion of faith. What made Edwards such a conundrum to so many of his contemporaries was precisely his relation to the prevailing ethos—his positive evaluation of its leading ideas. Even his friends had no way of appreciating the audacity of a man who would champion John Locke (little better than a deist in many minds) and attack the blessed Isaac Watts (whom latter-day Puritans worshiped as the virtual successor to King David).

The fourth Edwards became fully public only after his death, when his dissertations on *True Virtue* and *God's End* were printed (1765). In them one beholds the Christian ontologist enraptured of Being in general. This Edwards, of course, was never completely hidden, yet most of his writing in this vein still lies unpublished in his notebooks. Even those fragments which have been published—like his remarkable speculations on the Trinity—remain simply potential elements of a full systematic statement. Yet these elements of his total vision of reality have, more than any others, placed Edwards in the lineage of Plotinus, Malebranche, and Spinoza, to name only a few. They have inspired most of the perennial interest in Edwards. Because he brought to this tradition a kind of Calvinistic unsentimentality, his religious philosophy maintains its power or even gains strength amid the rudest shocks of the twentieth-century experience.

Then finally we confront Edwards the sacred historian, dealing with God's disposition of the world through successive ages, from the Creation to his own times of millennial expectation. Aside from the Northampton people who heard his sermons, the public knew little more of this Edwards than appeared in his *Humble Attempt to Promote Union in Prayer* of 1747. The sermons of 1739 that make up the *History of Redemption* were posthumously published in 1774, while the lifelong development of his thought on scriptural exegesis, eschatology, and history was largely ignored until the critical edition undertaken in 1970. Only in our own time, therefore, can it be expected that a reasonably complete edition of Edwards's works will become available, and with it, the possibility for a fuller comprehension of his thought. The midtwentieth century has already seen a renaissance of Edwards scholarship,[16] and the signs of the times point to its continuance.

[16] In addition to the Yale edition of the *Works of Jonathan Edwards*, 4 vols. (New Haven: Yale University Press, 1957–72), see the studies of Edwards cited in Bibliography, sec. 18 (Volume 2).

20

EVANGELICAL EXPANSION IN THE SOUTH

Between the Great Awakening and the Revolution some of the most momentous developments in evangelical Protestantism were taking place in the less established areas of the southern colonies. Here as nowhere else new Christian congregations were being gathered. To say this is not to imply that religious affairs elsewhere were static. In New England the "New Divinity" was gathering strength which would enable it, in due course, to redeem the promise of the early revivals. In addition to separations, a dozen new Congregational churches were being founded each year as New England's population grew. The continuing separatistic ferment was also creating new centers of zeal. At the opposite pole liberalism and Anglican churches were also gaining strength. All through the Middle Colonies, meanwhile, churches were ordering their institutional life and numerically outdistancing the many sectarian movements that had bulked so large earlier in the century. Here the Baptists pursued their most free and normal course. Here too the Presbyterians, Dutch Reformed, German Reformed, and Lutheran churches, though faced with staggering tasks, had the main problems of synodical organization more or less solved.

In the tidewater sections of the South the Church of England was slowly disengaging itself from its Puritan past, adjusting its message to the spirit of the Enlightenment, and regularizing its parish life. The ubiquitous Whitefield, to be sure, had left his mark, though much less indelibly than among the more religiously prepared peoples of the Middle and New England colonies. On his first brief visit to Georgia in 1738, he spoke to "the most thronged congregation . . . ever seen" in the colony, and influenced many "loose

Livers"; but his efforts there were much restricted by the colony's very thin population. His second tour, which began in 1739 with sensational successes in Philadelphia, New York, and New Jersey, also involved a southern itinerary. Although he spoke as usual to some large groups, he found "no stirring among the dry bones" in the southern colonies. At Charleston he ran into especially strong resistance from his fellow Anglicans, and he found no other churches in which to promote a revival. In Georgia he was chiefly preoccupied with his ambitious orphanage project at Bethesda. Whitefield never failed to create some stir, but the chief work of evangelizing the South was to fall to those who used less grandiose methods and who were less dependent upon a large semicommitted constituency.

During these prerevolutionary decades a restless and expanding American population was rapidly creating new fields for missionary labor. The Piedmont, lying above the fall line of the rivers whose wide estuaries divided the tidewater tobacco country, was the first area to be occupied. Almost vacant during the seventeenth century, it began during the early decades of the eighteenth to be filled by former indentured servants, small landowners, and newcomers moving out from the coastal regions of Virginia and the Carolinas. After 1730 the valley between the Blue Ridge and the Alleghenies began to be settled by another stream of migrants, largely Germans and Scotch-Irish sifting down from Pennsylvania. By 1775 there were over two hundred Scotch-Irish communities strung all the way down to the Georgia uplands, and the way into Kentucky and Tennessee had been opened. Despite the fierce British and Indian wars on the frontier, the expansion of white settlements in the western border area was one of the phenomenal aspects of the revolutionary years, and with the coming of peace the westward migrations accelerated to both the Old Southwest and the Old Northwest.

The "Great Awakening in the South," as it has come to be called, was in fact not so much a revival as it was an immense missionary enterprise. Revivalism was the chief method of church extension, and its dynamic methods effected a radical transformation of the older religious groups in the area. Insofar as Old Side Presbyterians, Lutherans, Mennonites, or the earlier Baptist groups moved into these burgeoning frontier districts, they were not part of the "awakening"; in fact, they were often opposed to its emotional emphasis. The future, however, belonged to the revivalistic groups who soon took the back country by storm.

THE PRESBYTERIANS

The New Side Presbyterians who were cut from the vine by the Philadelphia Synod in 1741 were emphatically evangelistic. Direct evidence of this concern was the decision of the New Brunswick Presbytery to ordain William Robinson and send him as a missionary to "western" Virginia and Carolina. This was to ignore the Old Side propensities of the Scotch-Irish who dominated the region and to invade a territory where four Old Side ministers of the Donegal Presbytery had already begun a widespread work. Robinson's itinerant ministry in the Piedmont and Valley districts during 1742–43 marks a new epoch in Presbyterian activity in that area. The popular response to his preaching was great—so great, in fact, that he inspired a whole series of Log College men to undertake similar visitations. These included John Samuel Blair, John Roan, Samuel Finley, Gilbert and William Tennent, and others.

The expansion of Presbyterianism in the South was to depend on this constituency, but for a time Hanover County, farther to the east, proved to be a much more fruitful field. Here among people untouched by established Anglicanism and quite ignorant of Whitefield's first Virginia visit, a devout and determined layman, Samuel Morris, had for several years been leading an enthusiastic, undenominational revival movement based on a few devotional or sermonic works and Luther's *Commentary on Galatians*. "Reading houses" were built, and their leaders had even been summoned to appear before the Governor's Council in Williamsburg. Until the arrival of Robinson this movement had called itself Lutheran, but thereafter it began to take on a more Presbyterian hue. Its denominational organization was furthered by Samuel Davies of the New Castle Presbytery, who, until called to the presidency of Princeton eleven years later, conducted an immensely productive ministry at many widely scattered preaching points. One may legitimately speak of his pastorate as the "Hanover County Revival," though in later years the Baptists would bear off much of its fruit.

These events concluded the Presbyterian phase of the

Great Awakening in the back country. The extension of the church went on, though not swiftly. Physical obstacles were great, the number of qualified ministers few, and the people did not yearn for spiritual ministrations. Even the slumbering loyalty of the Scotch-Irish often proved unresponsive to the usual calls. By the time of the Revolution there were not a dozen settled Presbyterian ministers in the two Carolinas, and probably few more than that in Virginia. Their preaching, moreover, was limited in its appeal, and they did not try to reach the unchurched masses of Southern people. On the other hand, the Presbyterian church was strategically poised for responding to the home missionary challenge that would confront it in the trans-Appalachian migration after the Revolution. Its western presbyteries would open out into the "promised land" and make large contributions in spite of new and increasing difficulties.

THE BAPTISTS

If the Presbyterian phase of the southern awakening was a comparative failure, the Baptist phase was a remarkable evangelistic success as well as one of the most consequential religious developments in American history. In 1740 the Baptists were everywhere a relatively weak and scattered denomination; and in the South, where they are often thought to be as indigenous as the red clay itself, they were weakest and most scattered of all. But this picture began to change after the middle of the eighteenth century.

Early Baptist Life in the South

The most important center of Baptist activity in the American colonies was the Philadelphia area. The influences which decisively affected Baptist life in the eighteenth century radiated to the North and to the South from this central point. Two years after William Penn arrived in Pennsylvania, a Baptist church was gathered at Cold Spring in Bucks County. The church survived only a few years, but the men who were to lay the foundations for future growth were already in the field. One was Elias Keach, son of a leading Particular Baptist minister in England, who at the age of nine-

teen had come to seek his fortune in the New World. Though
not even a professing Christian, Keach represented himself as
a minister, and he was soon invited to preach. In the middle
of his attempted sermon he confessed his imposture and was
subsequently baptized and ordained.

By the end of 1688 Keach had organized at Pennepek a
church composed of Baptists from England, Wales, and Ireland. At about the same time Thomas Killingworth also arrived from England and gathered a church at Piscataway
(or Piscataqua) in New Jersey. By 1691 these two men had
formed two more churches in the area. Then in 1703 a
congregation organized in Wales occupied a large tract of
land in Delaware which became known as the Welsh Tract
Church, and these five churches united in 1707 to form the
Philadelphia Baptist Association. The provincial name of this
body should not be allowed to hide its national scope. It soon
attracted other newly organized Baptist churches to its fellowship, and by the middle of the century it embraced
churches from Connecticut to Virginia. Its doctrinal platform
was a slightly revised version of the Second London Confession of Particular Baptists (1677), which was in turn based
on the Westminster Confession.

Although the early Baptists in the Middle Colonies were
predominantly Particular (i.e. Calvinistic) with a strong
Welsh element, the first churches in the South were formed
by General (i.e. Arminian) Baptists from England. This
group began to settle in southeastern Virginia soon after
1700; by 1729 two churches had been formed, and possibly
others. There were also Baptists living in North Carolina
from earliest times, but there is no record of a Baptist church
before 1727, when one was gathered in Chowan County by
an emissary from the Welsh Tract Church. Although this
church was soon scattered, another formed two years later in
Camden County is still in existence. Its pastor after 1750 established a half-dozen other churches, including one in Virginia, and by 1755 there were sixteen churches in eastern
North Carolina, reaching as far south as the Great Cohara.
From these came a number of younger preachers zealous to
extend the work.

These were all General Baptist churches; but while their
evangelistic zeal surpassed that of any other group in the
region, these churches were often established on a somewhat

careless constitution, with loose discipline and no "conversion" requirement for baptism. There was, however, a "reformation" in the offing.

The response of the Philadelphia Association to two separate pleas for ministerial aid brought the first signs of rejuvenation. Two men were dispatched in 1752 to survey the field in Virginia, and in the next four years missionaries from the association effected reorganizations in nearly all of the old General Baptist churches in Virginia and North Carolina, while agents of the Charleston Association came northward for the same purpose. The result was that between 1752 and 1756 all but two or three churches were transformed into the Particular Baptist pattern. They dismissed many unconverted members (in some cases reducing the membership from over a hundred to fewer than a dozen), tightened discipline, adopted a Westminster-oriented confession, and fostered a spirit of unity. These reorganized churches in eastern North Carolina and Virginia joined to form the Kehukee Association in 1769. These Particular Philadelphia-oriented churches styled themselves "Regular" to distinguish themselves from the "irregular" Separate Baptists who began to flood the southern colonies after 1755.

The Coming of the Separate Baptists

The "missionary" work of the Philadelphia Association in the South consisted of little more than reorganizing the old General Baptist churches. But in the sixth decade the unchurched and rapidly filling back country of Virginia and the Carolinas received a new and much more dynamic influence: the Separate Baptists from New England, whose fervency and drive were destined to become determining factors in Baptist expansion throughout the South and the Old Southwest. The exuberant revivalism of the Great Awakening in New England was transplanted to the southern back country by Shubal Stearns (1706–71) and his brother-in-law Daniel Marshall (1706–84). Born and bred in Boston, Stearns was converted in 1745 during Whitefield's second visit. He became a Separate New Light. In 1751 he was baptized at Tolland, Connecticut, and ordained as a missionary preacher to New England. After three years of this work he made his way to Opekon (Now Winchester, Virginia), where he joined Marshall. His brother-in-law, a native of Windsor, Connecticut, had also been converted in 1745 and had withdrawn from the Congregational church. In 1752 he was a missionary among the Mohawk Indians on the upper Susquehanna River; but after eighteen months he made his way to Opekon, where he was baptized.

Stearns and Marshall now joined in the gigantic task of evangelizing the settlers who were streaming out to the southern frontier. After a brief period of only moderately successful labor, they received word that in the Piedmont section of North Carolina people were so hungry for preaching that they would ride forty miles on horseback to hear a sermon. This was tantamount to a divine summons. Late in 1755 Stearns led a company of fifteen (mostly his family and Marshall's) to Sandy Creek in Guilford (now Randolph) County, North Carolina, where they immediately constituted themselves into a church.

> Soon after the neighbourhood was alarmed and the Spirit of God listed to blow as a mighty rushing wind in so much that in three years time they had increased to three churches, consisting of upwards of 900 communicants, viz: Sandy Creek, Abot's Creek, Deep River. . . . [Sandy Creek] is a mother church, nay a grand mother, and a great grand mother. All the separate baptists sprang hence: not only eastward to wards the sea, but westward towards the great river Mississippi, but northward to Virginia and southward to South Carolina and Georgia. The word went forth from this sion, and great was the company of them who published it, in so much that her converts were as drops of morning dew.[1]

Under the leadership of the patriarchal Stearns, these three churches united in 1758 to form the Sandy Creek Association, which by 1760 included ten churches. John Gano of the Philadelphia Association attended their second meeting as an ambassador of the Regular Baptists and began an important process of rapprochement. He overcame the Separates' suspicions of "Regular" preaching by his own demonstration, while he himself went away convinced that the Separates "had the root of the matter at heart" even though they were

[1] Morgan Edwards, "Tour of . . . American Baptists in North Carolina," in George Washington Paschal, *History of North Carolina Baptists*, 2 vols. (Raleigh, N.C.: General Board of the North Carolina Baptist State Convention, 1930), 1:227.

"rather immethodical." Such mutual understanding had the future in it, though for many years there was much animosity and rivalry.

Stearns and Marshall were passionate evangelists, incredibly energetic, not a little eccentric, and rather extreme in their employment of emotional appeals. Both itinerated widely, and they inspired many converts to do likewise. Despite the antagonism of the Regulars their growth was little short of phenomenal. When fierce repressive measures by the government began in 1768, there were only five Separate churches; at the first meeting of the General Association of Separate Baptists in Virginia in 1771, there were twelve churches with 1,335 members. In 1773 there were thirty-four churches reporting 3,195 members, and the association divided again along the line of the James River. By the end of 1774 there were churches of the Separates in twenty-eight of the sixty counties of Virginia.

Political disturbances in North Carolina forced many dissenters to seek new homes in other states. Baptist work in the Piedmont also received a serious blow at the battle of Alamance (16 May 1771), not far from Sandy Creek, when Governor Tryon's militiamen crushed the Regulators for revolting against the eastern aristocracy.[2] But Separate Baptist expansion had already begun in South Carolina, though growth here was less rapid than in Virginia (seven churches in 1771, sixteen in 1789). In 1771 the far-ranging Marshall settled in Kiokee, Georgia, and gathered the first Baptist church in the colony. Shortly before his death in 1784, he presided over the initial meeting of the Georgia Baptist Association, formed with six constituent churches.

The Union of Separates and Regulars

The older Baptists and the newcomers naturally regarded each other with suspicion at first, the Separates objecting to the creedal rigor of the Regulars, the latter chary of the unrestrained enthusiasm of the Separates. The Regulars

[2] The Regulator movement of the Carolina back country (1765–71) was organized by small farmers to protect themselves, in the absence of duly constituted authorities, from lawless elements; but its supporters also had economic and political grievances not unlike those which led to Shays's Rebellion in Massachusetts (1786–87). It is perhaps not coincidental that Baptists were numerous in both of these discontented areas.

proved able to appreciate evangelistic success, however, while the Separates did tend to agree with the doctrinal substance of the Philadelphia Confession. Led by their common Baptist convictions, they broached merger in Virginia as early as 1767, although it was not consummated until two decades later, when both parties felt it urgent to unite in order to press for the removal of all barriers to complete religious liberty. With the proviso that the Confession of Faith be received only "as containing the great essential doctrines of the gospel, yet, not in so strict a sense, that *all* are obliged to believe *everything* therein contained," the Virginia Separates and Regulars agreed in 1787 that these party names should be "buried in oblivion; and that, from henceforth, we shall be known by the name of the *United Baptist Churches of Christ, in Virginia.*" In North Carolina the Kehukee Association had been receiving both Regular and Separate churches for several years, and by this means the two groups gradually coalesced without any formal action.

Although the name of the Separates was buried, their influence was not. They put their characteristic stamp on much of southern Baptist life and thought. Revivalism was encouraged and meetings were often tumultuous. Their preachers held forth with a characteristic "holy whine" and encouraged all the extremer forms of religious expression. Far from the staid surroundings of New England, the behavioral extravagance of the Great Awakening was if anything exceeded. Because most of the ministers as well as most of their converts came from backwoods areas, restraints were lacking; intellectual sophistication was considered unnecessary and even undesirable. Yet the significance of these "primitive traits" is not nearly so great as some have tried to make it. More worthy of remark is the moral and spiritual discipline which the Separate Baptists brought to these unchurched areas. It was for laxity in these matters that they most often criticized the older Baptist churches, and at first they adopted very strict requirements—even to prescribing plainness of dress and speech in the Quaker manner. They compensated for their lack of education by close and serious searching of the Scriptures; this led some to revive the "nine Christian rites," many of which remind one of the German Dunkers: baptism, Lord's Supper, love feast, laying on of hands, foot washing, anointing the sick, right hand of fellowship, kiss of charity, and devoting children. Doctrinal concerns imbibed from the Regular Baptists served to check the aberrations of an uneducated ministry and helped to prevent preoccupation with trivial details or fantastic interpretations.

The general doctrinal position of the resulting Baptist tradition was distinctly Reformed, a modified version of Westminster; yet the prevailing distrust of rigid creedal definitions allowed considerable latitude for doctrinal differences. An Arminian or "free will" party persisted, as did a strict predestinarian party, with various "hard-shell," antimission, and "primitive" Baptists stemming from the latter during the nineteenth century. Probably most of the preachers shared the feelings of John Leland, who came to Virginia from Massachusetts in 1776:

> I conclude that the *eternal purposes* of God, and the *freedom of the human will,* are both truths; and it is a matter of fact, that the preaching that has been most blessed of God, and most profitable to men, is *the doctrine of sovereign grace in the salvation of souls, mixed with a little of what is called Arminianism.* These two propositions can be tolerably well reconciled together, but the modern misfortune is, that men often spend too much time in explaining away one or the other, or in fixing the lock-link to join the others together; and by such means, have but little time in a sermon to insist on those two great things which God blesses.[3]

The net result was a blending of revivalistic and "orthodox" tendencies along the lines suggested by John Leland's compromise. Gradually the New Hampshire Confession (published in that state in 1833) came to express this majority view.

Finding a proper balance between local church autonomy and associational authority also exercised the Separates, and their love for local freedom counterbalanced the centralizing influences stemming from Philadelphia. That association seemed to regard itself competent to "determine the mind of the Holy Ghost" and enjoin upon its churches obedience to the commands of Scripture. It became a virtual denominational body, whose cohesiveness consisted in the willingness

[3] John Leland, "A Letter of Valediction on Leaving Virginia, 1791," in *The Writings of the Late Elder John Leland,* ed. Louise F. Green (New York, 1845), p. 172.

of like-minded churches to limit their independence. Something of the same advantage must have appealed to Stearns, whose background, it will be remembered, was in the semi-presbyterianized Congregationalism of Connecticut. Facing the multiplication of members and churches, the Sandy Creek Association greatly reduced the autonomy of particular churches.

Backwoods converts, however, were not ready for such strict ecclesiasticism; and their dissatisfaction was doubtless a primary cause for dividing the Sandy Creek Association in 1770. It is noteworthy that the new Virginia body declared at the outset that it had "no power or authority to impose anything upon the churches, but that it [should] act as an advisory council, provided that all matters brought before the Association for advice be determined by a majority voice." Yet the retreat to radical independency did not go unchallenged; and the need to assert the rights of Baptists against governmental discrimination gave rise to "connectional" sentiments, just as the union of Separates and Regulars was hastened by the necessity to make a common cause. The independent Separates readily saw the advantages of cooperative action in this instance and agreed to the formation of a General Committee to represent all the Virginia associations. After its ends were attained, the committee declined steadily, and in 1799 it was dissolved. Not until 1823 would a really representative body of Baptists in Virginia be formed.

This entire development points to the fact that the continuing concern for denominational order in the South was fostered mainly by the Regular Baptists through their connection with the Philadelphia Association. Early attempts by the New Englanders misfired; the pioneers who swarmed into the Separate Baptist churches via a highly emotionalized conversion experience were no more ready for a "presbytery" than for a pope. Nor would people who later overthrew a foreign despot and his church be anxious to thrust their necks into an ecclesiastical noose even of their own making. The influence of the Separates on Baptist ecclesiology, therefore, was *against* centralization—simply because of the character of their converts, who by sheer weight of numbers overwhelmed the older Baptist life in the South. The Philadelphia order eventually prevailed, but only because the more influential leaders in the East persistently pressed for its acceptance.

The surge of Baptist growth among the rural population in

the South is not to be accounted for without considering the farmer-preacher, a figure rightly celebrated as one of the most important institutions in the westward expansion of the American people. This immensely effective servant of God was usually of humble agrarian origin, from a family on the move, living in a region where schools were nonexistent and hopes for "higher education" unheard of. He had in all likelihood been shaken out of his dreary agricultural routine by one or more visits from some itinerant evangelist. Under the force of an "awakening" sermon or a new convert's testimony, he had been "born again" and baptized. Recognizing gifts of preaching in himself and feeling a "call" to exercise them in the locality where he lived (or one to which he might be led), he would then gather a congregation and be ordained as its minister. Since the preacher did not leave his farm, the question of support did not arise—indeed, paying a minister might even be frowned upon—and since a home, barn, or shaded clearing would suffice for a meeting place, the poverty of his people scarcely hindered the work of his church. Thus churches sprang up and grew wherever people were. The Presbyterian revival in Hanover County collapsed after Samuel Davies went off to become president of Princeton, leaving no educated and ordained minister to succeed him in that remote area. The Baptists, on the other hand, continued to grow there and elsewhere, except in communities where the people, due to their church traditions or social status, were repelled by unrestrained religious enthusiasm, or where —as came increasingly to be the case—they were reached first by Methodist evangelists.

THE EMERGENCE OF METHODISM

Although John and Charles Wesley had come to Georgia in 1736 and been repulsed as inflexible High Churchmen, within fifty years they returned to America with power—not in person, except for Charles's brief visit in 1757—but through the ministry of their words and their followers. Between these two "Methodistic" manifestations lay the Wesleys' decisive confrontation with German pietism, out of which was born one of the most dynamic and consequential religious movements in modern times, a movement whose import would nowhere be more forceful and enduring than in

America. To understand it, one must go back to the beginning in the rectory at Epworth, the rough country parish in Lincolnshire where Samuel and Susanna Wesley, but particularly Susanna, brought up their remarkable family. The Wesleys nurtured the eleven of their nineteen children who survived infancy in devout, thoroughly Anglican ways, even though both their fathers had been ejected from the church's ministry for Nonconformity in 1662. John was born in 1703, Charles in 1707. Both children were nearly lost in the burning of the rectory in 1709.

The two boys were well prepared for the university, and both distinguished themselves at Christ Church, Oxford. John was ordained in 1725 and made a fellow of Lincoln College in 1726. During the ensuing years both brothers were much preoccupied with their spiritual well-being, and they took prominent roles in a "Holy Club" at Oxford. Because of their emphasis on devotional reading, ascetic practice, and frequent communion, these rigoristic Anglo-Catholics (as we might term them now) were dubbed Methodists—and the name stuck even after their rigorism had become pronouncedly evangelical. George Whitefield (1714–70) also became a member of this club in 1735, only a year before he embarked on his sensational preaching career, and three years before he went to Georgia, where he succeeded to a degree on the scene of the Wesleys' resounding failure.

Upon returning to London from America in 1738, John Wesley pursued his search for peace with God, spending many hours with Peter Böhler, a Moravian missionary who continued the spiritual tutelage begun in Georgia. He even joined a pietistic society that Böhler had organized in London. Then at about a quarter to nine on the evening of 24 May 1738, while attending an Anglican society meeting in Aldersgate Chapel and listening to a reading of Luther's Preface to Romans, Wesley's heart, as he said, "was strangely warmed." By 4 June his peace had become joy: "all these days I scarce remember to have opened the New Testament, but upon some great precious promise. And I saw more than ever, that the gospel is in truth but one great promise." In time his thought deepened and stabilized, but this experience transformed his career and provided the central theme of his amazingly powerful preaching. It is the clue to the conception of the Christian life that shaped Methodism. Not long after the world's first Aldersgate Sunday, John went to Germany, consulted with Count Zinzendorf, and visited at Herrnhut. On returning he began a serious study of the early English Reformers.

Three days before John's "conversion" Charles had been similarly changed. Thereafter he pursued a parallel career, less noted as a preacher than as the author or translator of over four thousand hymns, the best of which rank him with Isaac Watts in the annals of English hymnody. He would always remain more conservative than his brother, dubious about field preaching at first, and vigorously opposed to separatistic tendencies. Although Charles was not so deeply schooled in patristic theology as his erudite brother, he was equally influenced by the mystical writings of William Law, the nonjuring mystic and perfectionist who in turn owed so much to the German mystic, Jacob Boehme. Traditional motifs tended to figure more strongly in Charles's faith and conduct, and at his death in 1788 he was deeply perturbed by Methodism's imminent rupture with the established church.

Within a year of their conversion, the Wesleys were preaching in the fields at Whitefield's request, having decided that this was God's will by casting lots in the Moravian manner. For John, the discovery of his power as a preacher was a decisive personal event. When the brothers died a half-century later within three years of each other, the "Evangelical Revival" was a momentous British actuality, and a Methodist Church of over seventy thousand members was only a few legal steps from independent status. In that span of time John Wesley's itinerations carried him more than two hundred thousand miles in the British Isles, mostly on horseback. He aroused similar dedication in countless converts, and made Methodism a marvel of organization, with all its property vested in him personally. Societies dotted the British Isles, and in each of them "classes" under separate leaders were organized to enforce discipline and to nurture the groups' religious life. The Puritan impulse, reshaped to answer eighteenth-century needs, was once again a transforming force in the land. Then in 1784 John Wesley took the decisive step of ordaining ministers for the orphaned Methodists of America, setting apart two superintendents to direct that work.

The basic theology of Wesleyan Methodism was expressed in the Forty-four Sermons, which John Wesley formally designated as normative. Further definition was provided by his *Notes on the New Testament* (a brief commentary clarifying his interpretation of key passages) and a condensed version of the Thirty-Nine Articles. The message was Reformed and Puritan in many of its major themes, above all in its moral emphases. Its stress on the sinner's penitential conflict was due in large part to the powerful influence of Moravian pietism.

Wesley's own theology, however, was profoundly wrought, thoroughly integrated, and, after 1740, remarkably stable. He took man's sinful state with entire seriousness and preached salvation through grace by faith; yet he was forcefully Arminian, stressing the universal efficacy of Christ's Atonement and assailing those who preached man's utter and helpless depravity. Denying the doctrines of irresistible grace and perseverance, he believed that men could both resist the Spirit and fall from grace. Wesley widened this breach with Calvinism still further with a doctrine of Christian perfection which is, nevertheless, his most original contribution to Protestant theology. In developing this distinctive phase of his theology, he drew upon many sources, including early Eastern Orthodoxy.[4] More important than such scholarly considerations, however, is the degree to which the life of every sincere Methodist became a quest for complete sanctification or holiness (i.e. sinlessness). Like Wesley, his followers believed that this "second blessing" of the Holy Spirit had been and could be attained. Justification of the sinner was absolutely essential to salvation, but sanctification was the "fullness of faith." Through a dynamic interaction of divine grace and human will the Christian could and should respond to the scriptural bidding, "Let us go on to perfection" (Heb. 6:1).

These "innovations" of Wesley led to his break with Whitefield, who took a strong predestinarian stand that led his pious patroness, Lady Selina, Countess of Huntington, to found a separate group of societies and encouraged the formation of a distinct Calvinistic Methodist church among the

---

4 For these assertions about Wesley's theology I am indebted to Albert C. Outler, ed., *John Wesley*, Library of Protestant Thought (New York: Oxford University Press, 1964), pp. 9, 10, 14, 251, 252. This volume of writings is an invaluable corrective, but it unduly minimizes Reformed, Puritan, Anglican, pietistic, and Roman Catholic influences that Cell, Schmidt, Piette, and other Wesley scholars have rightly stressed.

Welsh. Objections to Wesley's allegedly "papist" doctrines also arose among Calvinistic Anglicans who were loyal to the established church and even more vehemently among those, both in Britain and in the colonies, who were committed to the Westminster standards. Perhaps no anti-Wesleyan utterance became so well known and beloved—ironically, even by Methodists—as the hymn "Rock of Ages," written by the Anglican priest Augustus M. Toplady (1740–78):

> Should my tears for ever flow,
> Should my zeal no languor know,
> All for sin could not atone,
> Thou must save, and thou alone;
> In my hand no price I bring,
> Simply to thy cross I cling.

These doctrines became cardinal points of controversy whenever Methodists confronted the older Reformed theology, whether among Anglicans or among denominations of Westminster orientation in Great Britain and the colonies. Along with Methodism's highly organized and extremely centralized church polity, Arminianism and Perfectionism became the denomination's most distinctive features. Beneath all and through all, however, was the sustained Wesleyan demand for penitential conflict, conviction of sin, and the experience of regeneration. Among American Methodists especially there also developed a deep skepticism about the value of the more objective aspects of religion, whether doctrinal, liturgical, or sacramental. In many ways, nevertheless, Wesleyanism blended very easily with the other forms of evangelical revivalism that flourished in the eighteenth and nineteenth centuries. In England it also played a large role in stimulating a parallel resurgence of evangelicalism among the Anglicans.

EVANGELICAL ANGLICANISM IN AMERICA

In the colonial period Methodism per se was neither strong enough nor persuasive enough to have much effect anywhere except within the Anglican church, from which it had not yet separated when the Revolution came. Into this communion it infused a great deal of badly needed (though little appreciated) vitality. Between 1766, when the first American Methodist society was organized in New York, and the opening of hostilities with England a decade later, the movement had gained but 3,148 adherents. Twenty-five hundred of these were in the South, notably around Baltimore and in Brunswick County, Virginia, areas where Nonconformity had been prevalent from earliest colonial days. Francis Asbury, who as the first Methodist bishop in America would play a powerful formative role, was already active here in 1771. Certain permanent traditions of American Methodism began to develop from this time forward, but these trends will be discussed in connection with the formation of the independent Methodist church after the Revolution.

Of more immediate significance for the growth of organized church life in the southern back country was the work of a very small group of evangelical and revivalistic. Anglicans who carried on a "counter-awakening" in the established church before Methodism had gained momentum. Devereux Jarratt (1733–1801) was unquestionably the most important of these men. Born in New Kent County near Richmond, Virginia, he had taken up the profession of schoolmaster. Although he had received very little evangelical nurture in his youth, he was brought to a "full persuasion" that he was a "stranger to God and true religion" while hypocritically feigning to enjoy the sermons of John Flavel which the mother of his pupils was wont to read aloud. Other reading and the counsel of some Presbyterians finally led him to vital faith and a decision to enter the ministry. Since his spiritual education, both personal and literary, had up to this point been Presbyterian, he had no other thought than to make that way his own. Further study, however, convinced him that Anglican worship and doctrine did no violence to his strict Reformed principles; and because he also saw in the established church a vast field for one with his views, he undertook the harrowing wartime adventure of seeking ordination in London. Upon returning to Virginia in 1763, he went to the vestry of Bath in Dinwiddie County, where a vacancy existed, and preached with ready acceptance. At the age of thirty-one he began a remarkable ministry that ended only with his death.

Jarratt's efforts to end the "carnal repose" of the people soon sparked a revival that burst the boundaries of his parish and county. After 1776 he was itinerating in a dozen counties of Virginia and North Carolina with a circuit from five to six hundred miles long. He carried on this work almost alone against the nearly unanimous opposition of the Anglican clergy. Even the one rector whom he won to his cause defected to the Presbyterians. When the Methodist preachers began to arrive in 1772, Jarratt cooperated with them closely and let his revival blend with theirs, partly to counteract Baptist inroads on his farflung flocks, but also because he accepted their protestations of Anglican loyalty, not realizing, as he said later, that he "jumpt out of the frying pan into the fire."

For some years this cooperation with the Methodists produced rich fruits. Many "Christian societies" were formed within Jarratt's large circuit; he cooperated with the Wesleyan revivals in the nearby counties of Brunswick and Sussex, and 1776 this combination was blessed by the most extensive revival in Jarratt's career. By the same token, it was the high point from which a steady decline of his evangelical Anglicanism can be measured. Deism, the Revolution, and religious factionalism decimated the movement's gains. After the war, however, the Presbyterians and, to a far greater extent, the Baptists and Methodists extended their conquests in the back country by following the great migration into the trans-Appalachian regions. They would thus continue the Great Awakening—or at least keep revival fervor alive when it flickered low elsewhere. For this reason the story of the frontier awakenings in the South is not only an important chapter in itself, but a prologue to the "Great Revival in the West," which is, in turn, a vital link between the colonial Awakening and the tumultuous events which shaped American evangelical Protestantism during the early nineteenth century.

21

ROMAN CATHOLICISM IN THE AMERICAN COLONIES

During the period of American exploration Roman Catholics in one way or another made their appearance almost everywhere. Earliest of all were the Norsemen who came to "Vinland." There is also a tradition—probably false—that Bishop Eric of Greenland visited Rhode Island in the twelfth century. Cabot, Verrazano, Estavan Gómez, and several others in the employ of England, France, or Spain explored the coastline in the sixteenth century. New York's harbor and river had been named for Saint Christobel and Saint Antonio eighty years before Henry Hudson saw them. The southern colonies, too, had a Roman Catholic "prehistory" associated with the extension of Spanish missions out of Florida into Georgia, Carolina, and as far north as Chesapeake Bay. New France made approaches from the north and west. Intermittent individual contacts occurred, sometimes accidentally, as with the Dutch rescue of Father Isaac Jogues from the Mohawks in 1643, sometimes intentionally, as with the brief visit to Boston by the French Jesuit missionary, Jean Pierron, sometimes officially, as with Father Gabriel Druillette's negotiations with Massachusetts on the problems in Maine. There are also military advances, particularly by the French in the Great Lakes–Mississippi basin. The long French and Indian Wars from beginning to end involved a hostile Roman Catholic presence in various areas, and they left an enduring legacy of heightened anti-Catholic animosity among colonial Americans. Aside from these developments there is also a Roman Catholic "nonhistory" written during this period by people (innumerable because unknown) who for any number of reasons drifted into various colonies where they forgot their church allegiance or were too far removed from the ministrations of any priest.[1]

In Maryland, however, Roman Catholics contributed a highly significant chapter in American church history; in fact, they built foundations that made Baltimore a virtual primatial see during the nineteenth century. Pennsylvania also acquired a considerable Catholic population, and New York for a time enjoyed some favoring circumstances, but outside these three areas the colonial history of the Roman Catholic church is almost nonexistent.

RELIGIOUS FREEDOM AND POLITICAL TURMOIL IN MARYLAND

"Mary-land," wrote one of her early chroniclers, "may (without sin, I think) be called Singular." Nor did the writer sin—for this colony does exhibit many peculiarities. It was carved out of an existing crown colony (Virginia) and chartered anachronistically as a feudal barony in an age of entrepreneurial expansion. This generous grant was made, moreover, by the Protestant king of England to a Roman Catholic convert so that the founder's coreligionists might be free from the statutory disabilities they suffered in England. George Calvert, first Lord Baltimore, had become secretary of state in 1619, a post he was forced to resign upon espousing the Roman Catholic faith in 1625. He remained in royal favor, however, and shortly after his death in 1632 Charles I delivered the Maryland charter to his son, Cecilius Calvert. Governing through his brother Leonard Calvert, the second Lord Baltimore allowed freedom of religion to all Christians who settled in Maryland. Nothing in the charter itself can be interpreted as a guarantee of these rights, but the instructions prepared by the proprietor for the colony's governors are remarkably explicit. He asks them to see that "they suffer no scandal nor offense to be given to any of the Protestants, whereby any just complaint may hereafter be made." He also

[1] Thomas Pheland makes the most of these scattered facts. He also claims that Myles Standish of Plymouth came from "an ancient Catholic family" and made "annual visits to the Kennebec settlements where the Catholic missionaries were located, presumably to perform his Easter duty" (*Catholics in Colonial Days* [New York: P. J. Kenedy & Sons, 1935], p. 121).

bids Roman Catholics to worship "as privately as may be," and not to discuss religious matters in public.[2]

Aside from the extremely liberal grant of proprietary authority the unusualness of the colony was more apparent than real. The grant itself was part and parcel of Stuart foreign policy, which was aimed at conciliating the great Counter-Reformation powers. Neither James I nor Charles I gave wholehearted support to the Protestant forces in the Thirty Years War, not even to their kinsman in the Palatinate when his territory was invaded by the French. Charles I married the sister of Louis XIII of France, Henrietta Maria, for whom Maryland, by a fortunate *double entendre*, was named (Terra Mariae). Charles II and James II, of course, would go even further in this direction. The grant to Calvert, therefore, whatever else it may have been (a settlement of a debt or evidence of real sympathy for English Catholics), was a domestic corollary to the crown's international aims in this period.

The years from 1612 to the Civil War (1640) were for English Catholics generally the most satisfactory period between the reign of Mary Tudor and the Relief Act of 1778. Lord Baltimore's allowance of religious liberty was far ahead of its time, even if freedom for Catholics and a desire for profits were the motives. John Tracy Ellis rightly complains that many historians, including Charles M. Andrews, have been unduly niggardly in their recognition of the proprietor's openmindedness on religious matters. To what degree Lord Baltimore or Father White were influenced by the undeniably democratic implications of Cardinal Bellarmine's political philosophy is not clear.[3] Given the fact, however, that during these years the crown itself had shown, and was to show, amazing liberality in granting colonial charters to groups and individuals of the most radically Nonconformist stamp, the strategy of Lord Baltimore is not an idealistic breakthrough. Religious toleration in Maryland was the only conceivable basis upon which Roman Catholics could have obtained any rights at all. The Roman Catholic James II followed the same course both as ducal proprietor of New York and as king of England.

[2] John Tracy Ellis, ed., *Documents of American Catholic History*, pp. 100–01.

[3] John Tracy Ellis, *Catholics in Colonial America*, pp. 325–26.

No other policy, moreover, would have given an incentive to immigration and settlement. This practical consideration influenced many proprietors during the seventeenth century, as is evidenced by the liberality shown in the Carolinas, the Jerseys, and Pennsylvania, not to mention Newfoundland (Avalon) for which George Calvert received a charter before becoming a Roman Catholic. In all these instances, principle seems to have blended with expediency. Only in Rhode Island and Pennsylvania did religious freedom have profound theological undergirding. Thus the common tendency to bracket Maryland with these other two colonies as "experiments in religious liberty" confuses as much as it clarifies. Maryland's toleration is best remembered as one more instance of English liberality during a century when France and Spain ruled their empires without the slightest allowance for deviation from Counter-Reformation norms.

In the spring of 1634, when the *Ark* and the *Dove* had discharged their small company of sixteen to twenty gentlemen (all or nearly all Roman Catholic) and two or three hundred servants and laborers (predominantly Protestant), the town of Saint Mary's was founded on the Potomac. The settlement which gradually took shape was in a social and legal sense unique among English colonies: nowhere else was the manorial system with its attendant distinctions and privileges and with its aristocratic and seignorial life so fully established and realized. "At the beginning," wrote C. M. Andrews, "Maryland was no mere palatinate on paper; it was a land of actual manors, demesne lands, free-hold tenements, rent rolls, and quitrents. . . . Socially there was a great gulf fixed between the upper and lower classes."[4] The story of Maryland in the seventeenth century is that of the gradual but often violent breaking down of this system. Nevertheless, the colony prospered for many reasons: it was a healthful, pleasant site; its farm lands were lush and fertile; Leonard Calvert was farsighted and firm in his governing, and he avoided the terrible mistakes of Virginia. Diversified agriculture was practiced at first, but tobacco rapidly became the staple crop and the main base of the colony's economy. The resulting plantation system accorded well with the paternalism implicit in the Calverts' hopes for creating a medieval barony in America.

The extremely complex and tumultuous political develop-

4 *The Colonial Period in American History*, 2:297.

ment in Maryland during the seventeenth century can here be only briefly summarized. Her first difficulties arose over the territorial claims of neighboring Virginia. Quarrels over the possession of the Isle of Kent in the Potomac estuary near the Maryland shore led William Claiborne of Virginia to armed combat. This island had been an active parish of Virginia and had sent delegates to the House of Burgesses, but ultimately it was yielded to Maryland. Aside from these hostilities, Maryland's first decade was relatively peaceful; but its future was threatened both by the deterioration of royal authority in England and by the constant growth of Puritan strength in the colony itself. For two years after 1644—the "Plundering Time"—public order broke down almost completely while Richard Ingle and his men, incited by Claiborne, carried on their depredations, allegedly on behalf of Parliament. To preserve his province in this darkening situation the proprietor in 1648 appointed a Protestant, William Stone, to replace the lately deceased Leonard Calvert as governor. More firmly to establish the principle of religious liberty, he bound the new governor by a very specific oath not to "trouble, molest, or discountenance any person . . . professing to believe in Jesus Christ, and in particular no Roman Catholick, for or in respect of his or her religion, nor in his or her free exercise thereof . . . and to relieve and protect any person so molested or troubled."[5]

To the same end the Maryland Assembly on 21 April 1649 passed its celebrated Act Concerning Religion, putting the long-practiced policy of toleration in precise terms. Roman Catholics, though a minority in the colony, probably dominated the assembly by a small margin; and certainly proprietary pressure hastened the act's passage. Its concluding article contained the following stipulations:

And whereas the inforceing of the conscience in matters of Religion hath frequently fallen out to be of dangerous Consequence in those commonwealths where it hath been practised . . . Be it Therefore . . . enacted . . . that noe person or persons whatsoever within this Province . . . professing to believe in Jesus Christ, shall from henceforth bee any waies troubled, Molested or discountenanced for or in respect of his or her religion nor in the free exercise

[5] Maryland Archives, *Proceedings of the Council, 1636–67*, 2:210.

thereof . . . nor any way compelled to the beliefe or exercise of any other Religion against his or her consent.[6]

These idealistic provisions were preceded by narrower and harsher articles: (1) that deniers of the Trinity receive the death penalty; (2) that the Virgin, Apostles, and Evangelists be not spoken of reproachfully; (3) that reproachful names for religious groups (papist, heretick, puritan, etc.) be not used; and (4) that the "Sabbath" or Lord's day called "Sunday" be not profaned.

This law in no way advanced the position taken by the Calverts from the beginning: it simply documented the assembly's support of past policy. Almost certainly the Roman Catholic deputies in the assembly supported it, and probably the more moderate Protestants did too, valuing the peace that such toleration promised to secure for the colony. The more fervent Puritans, wishing to impose their own principles, opposed it altogether and insisted on including the first article, which is an adaptation of a parliamentary statute then in force in England. Opportunity for Puritan revolt increased when Stone left the colony in 1651 and designated Thomas Greene, a Roman Catholic and a Royalist, as his deputy. Parliament, now firmly in Puritan hands, dispatched an investigative commission which temporarily deposed Stone and asserted its own authority. Baltimore retrieved the situation but soon faced new difficulties. Fired by social and economic grievances against Catholic magnates and manorial lords, the Puritans called an assembly in 1654 which repudiated the proprietor's authority and abrogated the Toleration Act. Aided by Roundheads from Virginia, they captured Stone and routed his forces at a battle on the Severn in 1655. The victorious Puritans then outlawed Roman Catholicism, plundered the estates of the Jesuits, forced all priests into exile, and executed at least four Roman Catholics. Lord Baltimore regained his proprietary privileges in 1657 only on condition that Josias Fendall, a Protestant, serve as governor in Stone's place.

After the Stuart Restoration, Maryland's political and religious affairs were hardly less troubled. In 1660 an antiproprietary party gained temporary control; other revolts occurred in 1676 and 1681, with deep-seated economic griev-

[6] Maryland Archives, *Proceedings and Acts of the General Assembly*, 1:244–47.

ances and religious animosity figuring centrally in each. Finally in 1689, as the Maryland concomitant to the Glorious Revolution, an insurgent "Protestant Association" led by John Goode took control of the government and held power until 1691, when King William III vacated the Baltimore charter and made Maryland a royal province with Sir Lionel Copley as governor, the Calverts being allowed to retain their property rights. In 1692 the Church of England was formally established, though an approved law was not passed until 1702, and in 1695 the capital was moved to the Protestant town of Annapolis.

Maryland continued as a royal colony until 1715, when the Calvert heir was reinvested with a proprietary charter—two years after his father had led the family back into the Anglican communion. (The "Anglican phase" of the colony's church history has been considered in chap. 12 above.) Dissenters probably constituted the great majority of seventeenth-century settlers, but because of the diversity of these groups and their lack of solidarity except in times of civil conflict, they are treated in connection with various denominational narratives in subsequent chapters.

THE ROMAN CATHOLIC CHURCH IN ENGLAND AND IN MARYLAND

The church history of Maryland during the entire colonial period is closely related to the conflicts and difficulties of the Roman Catholic church in the mother country. In England its constituency was a persecuted and highly suspect minority, prospering slightly when royal favor or a turn in foreign affairs so conduced, suffering severely when events led to a resurgence of overt hostility, and inhibited always by the paucity of clergy, the absence of a regular hierarchy, and many social or political seductions to apostasy.

England might be said to have been constituted as a Roman Catholic mission field in 1570 when Pope Pius V excommunicated Queen Elizabeth and released Roman Catholics from allegiance to her. The massacre of Saint Bartholomew's Eve in France (1572) heightened animosity even more, and severe penal legislation was enacted in 1580 and 1585 against the practice of Roman Catholic religion by either laity or priests. Yet missionary work had already begun.

A seminary in exile to train an English priesthood had been founded at Douai (Flanders) in 1568, and missionary priests had been entering England at least since 1574. In 1580 Edmund Campion and Robert Persons left the Jesuit residence at Saint Omer across the channel, and thus began the long, fruitful, but conflict-ridden English missionary campaign of the Society of Jesus. A year later (1581) Cardinal William Allen was made "prefect of the mission," and from time to time thereafter a cardinal was designated as "protector" of English interests. In 1622 Pope Gregory XV established the Congregation de Propaganda Fide to oversee the work of missions everywhere.

Although there were perhaps fifty priests in the English mission by 1610, it remained without episcopal supervision until 1623, when William Bishop was appointed vicar apostolic. Bishop died in less than a year, but set up subvicariates and archdeaconries whose heads formed the core of a "chapter" which exercised a measure of regulation in his absence. Bishop Richard Smith, who succeeded him, strengthened the chapter further. It needed what strength it had, for after 1631 English Catholics were again without resident supervision until James II allowed the consecration of a vicar apostolic who then consecrated three others. The realm was then divided into four districts, the American colonies being informally considered part of the London district until officially so designated in 1757. Since these men often led a harried existence, and since their clergy were often virtually the employees of various "recusant" families, a great deal of effective direction came from the English provincial of the Society of Jesus. This division of authority, when imposed on ancient rivalries of the regular and secular clergies, continued to disrupt Roman Catholic work in England for nearly two centuries. Pope Benedict XIV finally resolved the issue in 1753, though not even the pope could quiet the resentments building up against the Jesuits.

During the first decade in Maryland, the conduct of church affairs was entirely in the hands of Jesuit priests and a few lay brothers associated with them. They were, of course, responsible to the English provincial of their order. Andrew White and John Altham, who quietly joined the initial company as it passed the Isle of Wight, were thus able to renew the Jesuit mission in the Chesapeake area which had been attempted under Spanish auspices in 1570–72. From the start they were involved both in a parochial ministry to Roman Catholic colonists and in missionary activities among the Indians. Joined later by other Jesuit priests, these two carried on a very successful work in both directions, even converting a considerable number of the Protestant settlers. A church building was erected at Saint Mary's almost immediately, and by 1639 parish life had been established in at least four other centers. Work with the Indians also produced tangible results; and many converts were made among the Patuxents and the Piscataways, from whom the Jesuits also received large grants of land. Indian missions in Maryland, however, soon began to suffer from precisely the same difficulty that beset those in New England—the encroachment of settlers. The result was also very similar, except that in Maryland the vast land grants which the Jesuits received from the proprietor in return for settling lay brothers upon them provided material support for their church work elsewhere in the colony.

The leading spirit among these pioneer Jesuit missionaries was Father Andrew White (1579–1656), their superior until 1638 and justifiably called the Apostle to Maryland. Father White's career illustrates the life pattern of Roman Catholic priests of the English mission during these years. Born near London in Queen Elizabeth's reign, he was educated at Saint Albans College, which had been organized in Spain at Valladolid, and at the English College in Seville. He continued his studies at Douai and was ordained there in about 1605. He left for work in England, but after a year he was apprehended and banished. Father White entered the Society of Jesus, and after another season in England he took up a career as professor of scriptural studies and theology in Louvain and Liège, only journeying to England from time to time. By 1629 he had been contacted by Lord Baltimore with regard to an American colony, and he helped to advertise Maryland by writing a glowing declaration of the proprietor's intentions.

Within a month after the *Ark* and the *Dove* arrived in Maryland, Father White wrote a report to his superior general which has become the classic account of the journey and first days of the colony. His activities were diverse, encompassing regular pastoral duties at first, but also including increasing amounts of missionary work among the Piscataways. He was probably the first Englishman to reduce an

American Indian language to writing, and after preparing a grammar and dictionary he also translated a catechism. For the English settlers, he sought to establish a college at Saint Mary's. But this enterprise was shattered by Ingle's invasion of the colony in late 1644. In this anarchic period the Indian mission was laid waste, Father White and Father Thomas Copley were seized and sent back to England in chains, and the other three priests fled to Virginia. White was acquitted when tried, but he defied the rule of banishment and spent the remainder of his days in a quiet, semisecret ministry in England.

The energy and success of the Jesuits, however, had the same result in Maryland that it seemed to have in most other parts of the world. It antagonized the more numerous Protestants, very few of whom belonged to the dominant landed class, and who in any event objected to the evangelistic advances of Roman Catholicism. It also aroused the apprehensions of the proprietor, who shared (or was led to share) the somewhat Erastian attitudes of many leading Catholic families in England. Concerned about the growing discontent and fearful of a powerful ecclesiastical threat to the proprietary authority, the Calverts themselves began after 1641 to limit the activities and landholding privileges of the Jesuits. The first Lord Baltimore, while arranging for his colony, had sided with the Jesuits against the vicar apostolic, Bishop Richard Smith, who advocated expulsion of the order from England. Now a decade later the second Lord Baltimore also became involved in the church's jurisdictional conflicts. He sought to have the Jesuits replaced by secular priests or Franciscans, and even carried the matter to the Congregation de Propaganda Fide in Rome. It was finally adjudicated to his satisfaction by the general of the Society of Jesus in 1643.

Lord Baltimore's measures so severely curtailed the whole work of the church that by 1669 there were only two priests in residence, and only two thousand of the colony's twenty thousand inhabitants were regarded as faithful. In response to urgent requests from the proprietor in that year, several Jesuits and Franciscans were sent during the next decade, and the resulting Franciscan mission continued from 1672 to 1720. After 1650 the Jesuits were also active in neighboring provinces. In New York the administration of the duke of York and his Roman Catholic governor, Thomas Dongan (1682–89), provided a promising field of labor both among

Roman Catholic Europeans and among the Iroquois. Maryland missionaries also carried on some early missionary work in Pennsylvania after its openness to all faiths became known.

The Glorious Revolution, as a name for the change of monarchs and the Parliamentary settlement of 1688–89, is an epitome of the Whig interpretation of England's history. From a Roman Catholic standpoint it was misnamed, because the accession of William and Mary ended many of the advantageous circumstances for Catholic missions in England and her colonies. Maryland did remain virtually the only stronghold of the Roman Catholic church, but even here the establishment of the Church of England and the enforcement of English law put Roman Catholics under serious disabilities. The period from 1692 to the American Revolution justifiably became known as the Penal Period, during which the church subsisted on a private, almost clandestine basis, while individual Catholics constantly were threatened or visited with legal actions. Since there were probably not more than three thousand Maryland Catholics in 1708, survival was a serious question. This small core nevertheless proved sufficient to guarantee the continuity of the Roman church in America, because its laity was a landed and moderately wealthy group which could sustain the church's work and was possessed of sufficient social prestige to withstand the seductions to apostasy that eighteenth-century circumstances would offer.

During this long and difficult period seventy Jesuit priests and at least seven Franciscans served in Maryland and adjacent areas, though often no more than two or three were in active service at one time. At Bohemia Manor, a vast tract of land in their possession near the Pennsylvania border which they cultivated with slave labor, the Jesuits maintained a rectory and chapel. In 1745 or 1746 they even founded a more substantial and long-lived secondary school than those at Saint Mary's (1650) and Newtown (1670), which had been established in more favorable times. At this institution several of the colony's most distinguished leaders, including John and Charles Carroll, received part of their education. In Maryland, at least, the Society of Jesus was spared the expulsion and confiscations it suffered in Portugal, Spain, Naples, and France. The Jesuits managed to survive partly through their successful resistance to the appointment of a vicar apostolic for the colonies, an appointment which, if made, would not only have aroused anti-Jacobite feelings among American Protestants and English officials, but would have brought the secular hierarchy's anti-Jesuit politics into play.[7] In Maryland, furthermore, they were able to stay on as secular priests; and in 1773, when Pope Clement XIV abolished their order, they made property arrangements for the future.[8] In any event, the American Revolution was soon to bring a new day of religious freedom, when Roman Catholic church life could be conducted above ground.

NEW YORK

The Roman Catholic history of New York properly begins only with the assumption of authority by James, duke of York, who in 1674, with Edmund Andros as governor, established a policy of religious toleration.[9] When Andros was recalled a few years later, his place was taken by the Roman Catholic deputy governor, Anthony Brockholles. From 1683 to 1685 Thomas Dongan, another Catholic governor, proved unusually successful both in maintaining domestic tranquillity and in countering the work of the French among the Iroquois in the West. At times he used English Jesuits to counteract the work of French Jesuits. Dongan also contributed to the work of his church by bringing a Jesuit as his chaplain to minister to scattered Catholics, and by inviting two others (Fathers Henry Harrison and Charles Gage) to extend such work in the colony. After the accession of James II, Andros returned to America with a commission to head a united government of New York and New England; but this plan met

[7] Papal policy at this time still supported the deposed Stuarts as England's legitimate monarchs; the grandson of James II was a cardinal, moreover, and actively working for the suppression of the Society of Jesus. The vicars apostolic in London, including Richard Challoner, shared this disposition. American Catholics justly feared "anti-Jacobite" feeling, especially when Bonnie Prince Charlie led a rebellion against George II in 1745.

[8] In 1801 the Society of Jesus was authorized in Russia, where the papal ban was not effective, and in 1805 American Jesuits affiliated with the order there. The society was restored worldwide by Pope Pius VII in 1814.

[9] The duke of York first gained the surrender of New Netherland in 1664, but the colony was reoccupied by the Dutch in 1673–74.

with determined resistance, especially in New England. When news of the king's flight was received, it collapsed completely. In New York Leisler's Rebellion and brief regime followed, and with it the violence of a bitter antipopery campaign that brought Dongan's earlier efforts to nought. The former governor, who since his retirement had taken up residence on Long Island, was forced to flee, as were the three priests whom he had admitted.

After the arrival of Governor Henry Sloughter in 1691, Leisler was duly tried and put to death, order was reestablished, and New York, like Maryland, was governed as a crown colony. Roman Catholic liberties were now categorically denied; and during the administrations of the more than thirty governors who served New York before 1776, the situation of Roman Catholics did not improve. In 1701 they were deprived of the franchise and rights of office; the Church of England was established in the lower counties; the Penal Laws were put in effect; and under Governor Bellemont "Jesuits and Popish Priests" were prohibited from entry. During a season of especially virulent anti-Catholic feeling in 1741, even a nonjuring Anglican priest was hanged. For seventy-five years Roman Catholics had no public place of worship in the colony, though occasionally the Mass was surreptitiously celebrated, as when the Jesuit priest Ferdinand Steinmayer (alias Farmer) of Pennsylvania would arrive incognito and convene a little congregation in the house of a devout German living on Wall Street. After the Revolution, this priest organized a congregation in New York City which became an important nucleus for further church activity when Roman Catholic immigrants began to flow into the growing city.

PENNSYLVANIA

In the proprietary domain of William Penn, including Delaware, Roman Catholics were less persecuted than elsewhere in the colonies, and quite naturally Catholics were from the earliest days among the diverse multitudes who immigrated. Father John Harvey, Governor Dongan's chaplain, visited the colony in these early years, and others followed. By 1700, in order to embarrass Penn in England, reports of the public celebration of the Mass were circulated. These threats seem not to have deflected the proprietor from his principles, but under Queen Anne the colony was finally required to enforce laws that prevented Roman Catholics from voting or holding office (1705). These laws prevailed in Pennsylvania as elsewhere until the end of the colonial period.

In 1729 Father Joseph Greaton of Maryland, after several years of mission work in Pennsylvania, took up residence in Philadelphia in order to minister to its Roman Catholics. In 1733 he was instrumental in having Saint Joseph's Church erected, the first completely public Catholic church in the English colonies. It sufficed for its English, Irish, and German constituency until 1763, when Saint Mary's was built. Meanwhile two German Jesuits arrived in 1741. One of them, Theodore Schneider, who had formerly been on the faculty at the University of Heidelberg, opened a school in Goshenhoppen outside the city; the other erected a stone chapel at Lancaster in 1742. Except for occasional outbreaks of hostility, public worship in these places was able to continue without molestation, as was the operation of a few other short-lived schools. In 1757 there were 1,365 persons, about two-thirds of them German, under the care of three Jesuit priests. The two colonial church buildings in Philadelphia, having survived the nativist riots of the nineteenth century and the ravages of urban change, still remain.

Outside of Maryland and Pennsylvania, where small islands of Roman Catholicism managed to survive either in public view or half in secret, Roman Catholic church history in the later colonial period is little more than a matter of rumor, unsubstantiated "tradition," and cautious inference. Only occasionally is there significant information about a fairly prominent individual, such as John Tatham (alias John Gray) of New Jersey, who gained some political prominence and whose house provided a refuge and convening place for occasional visiting priests. Even in Maryland Roman Catholics constituted not more than an eighth, probably only a twelfth, of the population. Richard Challoner, who was coadjutor to the vicar apostolic of the London district from 1741 to 1758, and vicar apostolic from 1758 to his death in 1781, gave this report in 1756 in connection with his continuing efforts to have a bishop or vicar apostolic sent to the colonies:

There are no missions in any of our colonies upon the continent, excepting Mariland and Pennsylvania; in which the exercise of the Catholic religion is in some measure tolerated. I have had different accounts as to their numbers in Mariland, where they are the most numerous. By one account they were about four thousand communicants; another makes them amount to seven thousand, but perhaps the latter might design to include those in Pennsylvania, where I believe there may be two thousand. There are about twelve missionaries in Mariland, and four in Pennsilvania, all of them of the Society [of Jesus]. These also assist some few Catholics in Virginia upon the borders of Mariland, and in New Jersey bordering on Pennsilvania. As to the rest of the provinces on the continent, New England, New York, etc. if there be any straggling Catholics, they can have no exercise of religion, as no priests ever come near them; nor to judge by what appears to be the present disposition of the inhabitants, are ever likely to be admitted amongst them.[10]

A decade later Father George Hunter reported 10,000 adult communicants, and in 1785 John Carroll, who was then Superior of the American Mission, put the figures at 15,800 for Maryland, including 6,000 children and slaves. George Bancroft's estimate of 32,500 for the thirteen colonies and 12,000 for the formerly French population beyond the mountains follows the church's official estimate and represents the outside maximum. Committed adults would probably not have numbered more than a fourth or a third of this total—adequate justification for Bancroft's emphasis on the overwhelming Protestant character of colonial civilization. But however slender, these foundations proved to be a sufficient basis for renewing Roman Catholic church life when the Revolution brought substantial religious freedom to the new nation.

[10] Edwin H. Burton, *The Life and Times of Bishop Challoner, 1691–1781* (New York: Longmans, Green and Co., 1909), 2:125–27.

22

PROVINCIAL AMERICA AND THE COMING OF THE ENLIGHTENMENT

George Fox's journal of his travels through the colonies from North Carolina to Rhode Island in 1671–73 leaves no doubt that its author and his hardy followers were making their way through essential wilderness. "A tedious journey we had through bogs, rivers and creeks, and wild woods where it was said never man was known to ride"—so he wrote of a day's trip beyond the Delaware. His traverse of New Jersey offered almost as little comfort:

> And we did pass with a second guide about 200 miles from New Castle, through many Indian towns and they helped us over a great river in a canoe and swam our horses over. And so we passed through the woods and bogs, and had lain many nights in the woods, and came to Middletown, a place in New Jersey, and were very glad when we got to a highway.[1]

Glad he had a right to be, for the impression left by his account is that the chief elements of American civilization were bogs, mud, and overflowing streams. What the "highway" was like we can only imagine. Such amenities as travelers found were as often given by Indian sachems as by the traditional refuges for wayfarers. Things were better on Long Island and in Rhode Island, to be sure; and if he had dared venture into the Boston area he could have seen a situation in which Puritan divines were already lamenting an excess of worldly comforts in Zion.

[1] *The Journal of George Fox*, p. 619.

In another half-century, the picture everywhere would be remarkably altered. The roads were still bad—and getting mired to the hubs was to remain a basic American experience until well into the twentieth century—but in other respects the ways of English life were being impressed upon the wilderness by a half-million industrious people.

THE SHAPING OF A COLONIAL AMERICAN CULTURE

The most fundamental change, of course, was the remarkable rise in population from an estimated 360,000 in 1713 to 1,600,000 in 1760, and to nearly three million by 1776. This sensational growth resulted mostly from natural increase, for the predominance of farming together with the availability of land encouraged large families, and the colonists responded with gusto. Marriages were made early—an unmarried girl of twenty-one was "an antique virgin"—while families with a dozen children were common, and those with a score not rare. The other great factor in population growth was immigration. From England, Wales, Northern Ireland, Scotland, Germany, and many other areas the influx continued, making America even then the great melting pot of Western peoples and civilizations. Slavery accounted for 502,000 black Americans, 89.7 percent of them south of New Jersey, and they, too, were showing a natural increase not equaled elsewhere. As the foregoing chapters on religious history have made clear, moreover, this rapidly growing population included many elements of diversity besides that of nationality.

The mere fact of the colonies' growth in area and population involved still another diversifying process, in that the general subsistence economy of the early years soon yielded to many types of specialization. Agriculture itself was diversified. A few staples became predominant in the South: rice in South Carolina, tobacco in Virginia and Maryland. Baltimore and Philadelphia became great exporters of wheat and flour from their hinterlands. Accentuated by these adaptations to land and climate, but inevitable even without them, were other complicating developments. Most obvious were the growth of towns and cities with all their multifarious trades and activities, the emergence of much more clearly demarcated social classes, and the rise of clashing interest groups. The spirit of this burgeoning society was not feudal or traditional but fervently capitalistic and individualistic. The colonies were populated by individuals and groups, immigrants all, who were always beginning anew, even if they had left Europe in tears and with a determination to perpetuate its ways. America always destroyed preconceived designs, whether for Bible commonwealths or medieval baronies, and usually it assuaged the sorrow. Men and women, as in no other country, were on their own with their niches to carve.

From one end of the country to the other a Puritan emphasis on work and frugality gave impetus to the changes wrought by rising farm production and commercial growth. During the period of "salutary neglect" (1713–60), rising prices on the world market gave further inducement to international trade, while the very European wars that caused this price rise prevented England from implementing the prevailing theories of mercantilism. American produce found a wide market; American ships and traders were actively engaged in prosperous seaports from Salem to Charleston. A powerful gentry of merchants and landholders rose to social eminence and economic power in most of the colonies. In the South, where slavery fostered this trend, a closely knit but distinguished planter aristocracy had arisen; and it was already producing the kind of leadership later to flower as the "Virginia dynasty." In the coastal cities, on the other hand, a merchant class greatly increased its political and cultural importance, and set the tone of a middleclass society.

These transformations did not happen without tensions and turbulence. Both North and South, there was a strong tendency for economic factors to sharpen the cleavage between coastal areas, which often if not invariably retained preponderant influence in the colonial governments, and the so-called Old West, the long, uneven, and constantly enlarging region of backcountry farmers. England's persistent refusal to solve the currency problems of the colonies heightened the tension, arousing especially sharp animosities over the issues of paper money and land banks. Indeed even aside from the conflicts which the expansion of slavery was preparing, there existed by 1760 a considerable basis for civil strife within the colonies, and these problems would remain during the succeeding decades even as the spirit of independence waxed stronger.

Beneath the discontent, however, the colonies as a whole

were moving steadily toward a state of political and social self-sufficiency. In the middle of the eighteenth century real democratic freedom was still severely restricted by ecclesiastical establishments, aristocratic power blocs, restrictions on the franchise, and above all, by the extraordinary prevalence of chattel slavery; yet its advances were marked because land was easily obtained and class lines were fluid. A kind of middle-class democracy such as the world had never seen was developing. Increasing numbers of men were taking an active part in the legislative process. Except for the Anglicans, the English-speaking clergy of the churches was largely American-educated; the legal profession and a colonial judiciary were assuming form. An experienced class of leaders was emerging.

Signs of cultural self-sufficiency were becoming equally apparent by 1760. Homes of governors, planters, and successful merchants began to display the grace of distinctive architectural modes. Carpenters and cabinetmakers, freed from primitive limitations, began to study English books of design and to manifest a corresponding concern for aesthetic embellishment. Painted surfaces, fanlights, brass fixtures, gambrel roofs, and classical balustrades appeared. Meeting houses, too, lost their primitive severity and functional simplicity as Georgian towers and pilastered portals in the manner of Christopher Wren set off the newer church exteriors, and well-finished pews, chandeliers, and finely joined woodwork graced the interiors. In portraiture, the sturdy primitivism of itinerant limners gave way to the grander manner of Benjamin West, Gilbert Stuart, and John Singleton Copley. Even religious painting of traditional scope made its appearance in the work of Gustavus Hesselius.

By 1763 secondary schools had made Americans residing in the older, more settled regions the most literate people in the world, while New England possessed an educational system that was probably excelled nowhere. Six colleges from Hanover, New Hampshire, to Williamsburg, Virginia, provided an unusually broad range of possibilities for higher education, and three more would be added before the Revolution,[2] although some people still sought advanced training in

[2] The following colleges were founded before the Revolution: Harvard (1636), William and Mary (1693), Yale (1701), the College of New Jersey at Princeton (1746), Philadelphia Academy (1751, later the University of Pennsylvania), King's College

England or Scotland. Ambitious publishing efforts had been undertaken in New England almost from the first. *The Bay Psalm Book* came from the press in 1641; and Samuel Willard's 914-page tome *A Compleat Body of Divinity, in Two Hundred and Fifty Expository Lectures on the Assembly's Shorter Catechism* set a North American record for size in 1726. For thirty-eight years after 1739 the press of Christopher Sauer and his son at Germantown issued a steady stream of German publications, including the famous Luther Bible of 1743. Johann Arndt's 1,388-page *Vom Wahren Christenthum* appeared in 1751. By the end of the colonial period there were over forty newspapers and over fifty public or semipublic libraries in existence.

Gradually taking shape beneath these signs of cultural maturity was a growing but unrebellious sense of common destiny. External factors contributed to this growth, notably the existence of an utterly alien and hostile Indian "civilization" beyond the frontier, resisting white encroachment and making frequent incursions on the westward-pushing white settlements. Ever since the New England Confederation of 1643, this peril had led the colonies to make common cause against mutual dangers. The menace of New France and New Spain accentuated that impulse. Because of these dangers and constantly improving economic interrelationships, the common history of these commonwealths, as well as their similar constitutional arrangements, became all the more important. Already one might speak of an English provincial culture that was characteristically American. The "American" himself would not become clearly aware of this fact until after 1763, when English rule was asserted over the former domain of the French, and when the king, the English Parliament, and the Board of Trade began to tighten their economic and political reins on a colonial empire which they had governed previously by such loose and haphazard methods.

The resentment and hardship resulting from these changed circumstances would lead, of course, to the War for Independence. Yet the "American Revolution" began when the first English settlers came to stay, and the complex process of colonial growth which went on for the next century and a half was just as decisive as the dramatic sequence of events

(1754, later Columbia), Brown (1764), Queen's College (1766, later Rutgers), Dartmouth (1769), and Hampden-Sydney (founded 1775, incorporated 1783).

that ensued between 1760 and 1776. Bernard Bailyn quite properly insists that "the Revolutionary ideology could be found intact—completely formed—as far back as the 1730s; in partial form it could be found even farther back, at the turn of the seventeenth century."[3]

No factor in the "Revolution of 1607–1760" was more significant to the ideals and thought of colonial Americans than the Reformed and Puritan character of their Protestantism; and no institution played a more prominent role in the molding of colonial culture than the church. Just as Protestant convictions were vitally related to the process of colonialization and a spur to economic growth, so the churches laid the foundations of the educational system, and stimulated most of the creative intellectual endeavors, by nurturing the authors of most of the books and the faculties of most of the schools. The churches offered the best opportunities for architectural expression and inspired the most creative productions in poetry, philosophy, music, and history.

A more specific element in the religious background was Puritanism itself, which even under Queen Elizabeth began to be a powerful factor in the transformation of English society and government. In this context the long-term American revolution should be seen as a great extension of the Cromwellian and Glorious revolutions. These relationships would be more readily perceptible to present-day Americans if by some accident of history the original colonies had peacefully matured as independent republics, and if generation after generation of Americans had studied the Mayflower Compact as assiduously as they now study the Declaration of Independence. With Jamestown or Plymouth Rock rather than Independence Hall as our point of focus, we would see first of all the way in which the Reformation heritage strengthened the colonist's conception of his "calling," or vocation, making him more serious, purposeful, and responsible in both his civic and economic roles. We would note in the second place the crucial susceptibility of Puritanism to transmute its power into secular impulses. This was due above all to the immense place of law (divine, natural, moral, and statutory) in its overall view. Law restrained man's sin, law humbled the sinner, law guided the saint and sinner alike in the quest for

[3] Bernard Bailyn, *The Ideological Origins of the American Revolution*, p. xi.

both personal holiness and an orderly society. The good man was a law-abiding man; that insistence remained even after the rapture of regeneration dropped from view. Puritanism, in a word, virtually sacrificed itself on the altar of civic responsibility. It helped to create a nation of individualists who were also fervent "moral athletes," with a strong sense of transcendent values which must receive ordered and corporate expression in the commonwealth. In this context a completely secularized son of the Puritans like Benjamin Franklin is quite as potent a symbol of the movement's lasting influence as his more orthodox contemporaries, such as Samuel Adams, Roger Sherman, and Patrick Henry.

The congregational method of governing churches, whether it stemmed from theological convictions (as in Massachusetts) or from New World necessities (as in Virginia) also strengthened the average American's desire for a voice in government, and gave him experience and competence in making his will known in an orderly and effective way. Put less abstractly, ecclesiastical localism prepared men to regard the social compact as the proper basis of government.

When joined with a pervasive antipathy to medievalism, ceremonial pomp, moral profligacy, ostentatious indolence, and aristocractic privilege, Puritanism became an even stronger factor in the formation of Whiggish attitudes. "No bishop, no king," James I had told the Hampton Court Conference in 1604. Samuel Johnson, the American Tory and Anglican convert, agreed: the colonies need a bishop, he said, if they are to remain loyal to England. In New England the people's memory of English kings was especially jaundiced, and the potency of Puritan teaching was unusually strong. It was no accident, therefore, that Boston became the chief thorn in the side of English authority. Attacks on the Stuart kings could be dusted off for service against the threat to liberty presented by Hanoverian kings and their corrupt court. Thus America, too, developed its radical opposition. Old Whig became New Whig. When seen in this large sense, Ralph Barton Perry's estimate of Puritanism's significance for the American tradition is eminently justified: "It is safe to assume that the influence of puritanism, in the broad Calvinistic sense, was a major force in the late colonial period, and that it contributed uniquely and profoundly to the making of the American mind when the American mind was in the making." And Edmund S. Morgan underlines the same point.

"The Puritan Ethic as it existed among the Revolutionary generation had in fact lost for most men the endorsement of an omnipresent angry God. . . . The values and precepts derived from it, however, remained intact and were reinforced by a reading of history that attributed the rise and fall of empires to the acquisition and loss of the same virtues God had demanded of the founders of New England."[4]

"Declension" and secularization had put Puritanism's potential influence in jeopardy, to be sure, but this fact merely heightens the significance of the Great Awakening, which lifted the evangelical cause from its doldrums, revitalized the "dissenting" churches, threatened the established churches, aroused widespread suspicion of the SPG, focused attention on the threat posed by the possibility of an American bishop, and stirred up precisely those elements of the colonial population most unlikely to be fervent Loyalists on political grounds.

The Great Awakening wrote a crucial prologue to the political and ideological transformation that characterized the dramatic years between 1763 and 1775. This is not to say, however, that it was chiefly a response to social and economic pressures. Though young people may have been especially numerous among the new converts, it attracted or repelled people of every class and station, rural and urban, young and old, and in every region. And it did make forceful contributions to American self-consciousness. The leaders of the revival were the first to plan their activities in explicitly intercolonial terms. George Whitefield was perhaps the first "American" public figure to be known from New Hampshire to Georgia. He was heard by hundreds of thousands and left nobody noncommittal on his merits; his death, which ended his seventh tour in 1770, was commented upon by the entire colonial press. Gilbert Tennent and Jonathan Edwards also achieved a large measure of intercolonial fame.

In his detailed study of the Awakening in Virginia, Professor Gewehr has emphasized the social and political implications of religious rejuvenation. It heightened back-country opposition to the religious restrictions of the royal government and conduced to a more thorough democratization of

[4] Ralph Barton Perry, *Puritanism and Democracy*, pp. 18, 81. Edmund S. Morgan, "The Puritan Ethic and the American Revolution," *William and Mary Quarterly*, 3d ser. 24 (January 1967): 6.

society. In a similar manner everywhere, the Awakening probably increased the willingness of people in all walks of life to open controversies, to criticize complacent dignitaries, to protest infringements of religious freedom, and to question accepted truths of constituted authorities. It also intensified the general tendency of the Reformed tradition—the religious heritage of three-fourths of the American people in 1776—to set bounds on the will of kings and the arbitrary exercise of governmental power. Above all, it awakened millennial hopes that a covenanted nation, repenting its sins and trusting in God, could become an instrument of Providence in realizing the Kingdom.[5] Taken as a whole, therefore, the religious foundations of colonial life were a powerful factor in American development. Few cultures are so intractable to purely secular categories of historical interpretation.

THE EMERGENCE OF ENLIGHTENED RELIGION

To speak of cultural maturation and growing evangelical self-consciousness is not, from the standpoint of religious history, to touch upon the only crucial developments taking place in provincial America. One of the greatest revolutions was going on quietly, even imperceptibly, in men's minds as they confronted the momentous issues of the Enlightenment. We have already mentioned how later Puritanism wrestled with this crisis of the European mind in its early stages. As

[5] See the final chapter of Wesley M. Gewehr, *The Great Awakening in Virginia, 1740–1790*. That the Great Awakening played a vital role in the American tradition there can be no doubt; but one must avoid exaggerated claims. Alan Heimert, in his *Religion and the American Mind from the Great Awakening to the Revolution*, attributes undue political influence to the predestinarian Awakeners and unduly deprecates the Arminian and liberal tradition that runs from Mayhew and Chauncy to John Adams as elitist and ineffectual. He ignores the liberal-Arminian party's influence upon the "power elite" of that day. Bailyn's work, cited in n. 3 above, provides a remarkably balanced and insightful account of Puritan and dissenting elements in the American revolutionary ideology.

The significant work of awakened Separates and Baptists in the cause of church disestablishment and religious liberty is thoroughly covered in Clarence C. Goen, *Revivalism and Separatism in New England, 1740–1800;* and in William G. McLoughlin's massive *New England Dissent, 1630–1833*.

early as 1710 John Wise opposed the Saybrook Platform and the centralizing proposals of the Mathers with a natural law philosophy derived from Pufendorf. So clearly did he anticipate later revolutionary attitudes that his tracts were republished in the 1770s to bolster the Patriot cause. Samuel Johnson revealed another dimension of the new spirit in his well-reasoned break with the old Puritan order in New England. Most impressive, however, was the life work of Jonathan Edwards.

While still a very young man, Edwards read John Locke's *Essay Concerning Human Understanding* with more pleasure "than the most greedy miser finds when gathering up handfuls of silver and gold from some newly discovered treasure." A few years later he was dwelling with equal enthusiasm on the works of "the incomparable Mr. Newton." Then in his mature years, despite a career at the center of the Awakening —with all of its anti-intellectual tendencies—he infused the spirit of the Age of Reason into the faith of his fathers with a transforming sublimity equaled by no Reformed thinker of the century. He thus participated actively in the great spiritual transition that marks the end of a period when American culture was still recognizably medieval in its outlook and inner spirit, and the emergence of distinctly "modern" religious ideas. During the revolutionary era the American Enlightenment and its characteristic religious forms would flower even more luxuriantly—and with major political as well as eccelesiastical consequences.

The Rise of Rationalism

As with all large intellectual movements, the search for the origins of the Enlightenment leads into an infinite regress. The rise of the rationalistic spirit must be seen as an enlargement or continuation of scientific and naturalistic impulses which gained special boldness of expression during late medieval and Renaissance times as the intellectual heritage of antiquity was being rediscovered. There followed a long and involved series of theoretical, mathematical, and experimental efforts to explain the world of nature in a reasoned, orderly, and verifiable way. Modern science came into existence with epoch-making discoveries succeeding each other in several fields. But most earthshaking and provocative in the theological and philosophical sense was the transformation in cosmology demanded by the discoveries of Copernicus (1543),

Galileo (1610), and Newton (1687), to name only the three most famous. Paralleling these scientific contributions was a series of equally disturbing philosophical statements such as those of Nicholas of Cusa (1440), Giordano Bruno (1584), and Descartes (1644). Most basically, Western man was now required to come to terms with an infinite universe in which the motions of known inanimate entities could be explained in terms of mathematically demonstrable laws. Alfred North Whitehead, his focus chiefly on the culminating work of Newton, has made a famous summation of the scientific achievements involved in this collective enterprise:

> The subject of the formation of the three laws of motion and of the law of gravitation deserves critical attention. The whole development of thought occupied exactly two generations. It commenced with Galileo and ended with Newton's *Principia;* and Newton was born in the year that Galileo died. Also the lives of Descartes and Huygens fall within the period occupied by these great terminal figures. The issue of the combined labours of these four men has some right to be considered as the greatest single intellectual success which mankind has achieved.[6]

Newton, the great terminal figure in Whitehead's sequence, was hardly a "man of the Enlightenment." He regarded his work as a defense of the Christian faith, and in later years he busied himself with elaborate exegesis of biblical prophecies. Yet the fundamental Newtonian ideas were soon reverberating through almost every corridor of Western thought. Reformulation became a necessity, with many social and political factors piling need on need; and "Enlightenment" is the name given to the vast and multifarious process of reconstruction that took place. Enlightenment thought, therefore, is not a well-defined systematic structure of consistent ideas. Its "productive significance," says Ernst Cassirer, its greatest analyst,

> is revealed not so much in any particular thought content as in the use the Enlightenment makes of philosophic thought, and the position and task it assigns to such thought. . . . Philosophy is no longer limited to the realm

[6] Alfred North Whitehead, *Science and the Modern World* (New York: New American Library, 1948), pp. 46–47.

of mere thought; it demands and finds access to that deeper order of things whence all intellectual activity, like thought itself, springs.[7]

Philosophy becomes "the all-comprehensive medium" in which the principles of natural science, law, government, and religion are formulated, developed, and founded. The Enlightenment is thus not a doctrine, but a campaign for world renovation based on certain broad presuppositions which are informed above all by the achievements of the new science.

In this enormous task no one thinker was more important or more revealing than the man so often designated as America's philosopher, John Locke (1632–1704). No one thinker so well exemplifies the Enlightened desire to take the thrust of scientific method, so central in Newton, and to apply it to all the agitated problems of the day: the operations of human understanding, the need for toleration, the nature and basis of civil government, and—most germane to the present study—the genius of the Christian religion.[8] In terms of subsequent thought, Locke is not so much a milestone as the designer of a large section of highway. He more nearly personifies the reigning spirit of the eighteenth century than any other thinker. His thought is guided by three great optimistic principles: that the chief end of man is felicity in this world and probably in the next; that man's rational powers, if rightly disciplined and employed, provide a means for solving the problems of life and attaining this felicity; and that the essential truths of such a view are so self-evident, and man himself so responsive to such evidence, that progress in human felicity is inevitable.

Still another reason for Locke's representative significance is that he was a champion of common sense, with unique gifts for gathering the presuppositions and implications of his age into an eminently reasonable system. He was also a moderate; and especially as a religious thinker does he exhibit

[7] Ernst Cassirer, *The Philosophy of the Enlightenment*, p. vii.

[8] Locke's treatises indicate this full gamut of concern: *Essay Concerning Human Understanding* (London, 1690; five editions by 1706), *Letters on Toleration* (1689–90), *Two Treatises of Government* (1690), *Some Thoughts Concerning Education* (1693), *The Reasonableness of Christianity* (1695), and *Paraphrase of Romans, First and Second Corinthians, Galatians, Ephesians* (1705–07).

these gifts, being opposed to antichristian or atheistic views and active in the controversy against the deists. He was in truth a *defensor fidei*, exuding intellectual confidence as he faced the perennial paradoxes of existence and the ancient mysteries of Christianity. No thinker better exemplified that confidence in man's mental powers which gives the Age of Reason its name. In the eighteenth century's "Deistic Controversy," in the debate over the nature of Christian morality, and in the ongoing contest with skeptics, there gradually came to prevail among the educated classes a climate of opinion in which moderate common-sense views prevailed. High-ranking churchmen as well as poets, essayists, and statesmen expressed this outlook. The effect on the Enlightenment on Christian thought thus became deep and pervasive. The central—indeed, almost the solitary—thesis of its religious message is expressed in the title of Locke's great work, *The Reasonableness of Christianity* (1695).

BUTLER, PALEY, AND THE SCOTTISH PHILOSOPHY

The history of British philosophy in the century after Locke can in no sense be reviewed here, not even the crucial developments linked with Locke, Berkeley, and Hume, except to say that churchmen all over the world trembled when they faced what they regarded as the "skeptical" implications of David Hume (1711–76), particularly his critique of natural theology, the age's great stock in trade. (Hume saw fit to have his *Dialogues* on this subject published posthumously.) Churchmen were equally disturbed by the mechanistic psychology expounded by David Hartley in his *Observations on Man* (1749). Utilitarianism, materialism, and atheism seemed to be building great empires in European thought with weapons drawn from Locke.[9] Against these enemies Berkeley's theistic idealism was too subtle and too contrary to

[9] These radical tendencies were an intrinsic element of the Enlightenment, and they became increasingly important with the passing years, especially in France, where Condillac did much to advance Lockean ideas. This may, indeed, be the movement's most essential phase. In provincial America, however, radical views had very few advocates. Peter Gay describes the "Era of Pagan Christianity" in *The Enlightenment: The Rise of Modern Paganism*.

common sense to be an effective defense. At the other extreme were the champions of strictest orthodoxy who would brook no accommodation of modern ideas and the revivalists who often denied the compatibility of true religion and philosophical discourse altogether. There was thus great need for men who could provide intellectual defenses for a middle empire of reasonableness and a moderate sort of orthodoxy. From three sources came notable reponses to this need: Bishop Joseph Butler (1692–1752), Archdeacon William Paley (1743–1805), and the "Common Sense" school of Scottish philosophy, led chiefly by Thomas Reid (1710–96) and Dugald Stewart (1753–1828).

Butler's celebrated work was his *Analogy of Religion, Natural and Revealed, To the Constitution of Nature* (1736), a closely reasoned attack on the deists in which he argued that the objections against the Christian faith apply equally to natural religion, and that given their common assumptions and the limitations of human reason, a prudent man will not abandon the church. Though far less impressive than his essays on ethics, Butler's *Analogy*, despite its skeptical tendencies and lack of positive argument or edifying content, was for a full century regarded as a major defense against infidel attack.

Paley's great contribution came toward the century's end. He provided a new and even more popular synthesis of empirical science and reasonable religion. Unlike Butler he wrote with marvelous clarity and with much greater confidence in the power of rational argument. Paley, too, wrote on ethics and political economy, taking what was often regarded as a dangerously utilitarian position; but he was most widely celebrated for two other efforts. One was in the extreme popular field of "Christian evidences," where his book of that title (1794), supported by a companion work on Saint Paul (1790), became a classic. In these works Paley sought to demonstrate the reliability of the New Testament, drawing chiefly on the proof from miracles, but also marshaling other arguments to prove that the biblical writers were trustworthy witnesses. In his *Natural Theology* (1802) he supplied the English-speaking world with its best compendium of arguments for the existence and benevolence of Deity on the grounds of the design in nature. In this work he offered his famous (though unoriginal) argument that, just as we infer a watchmaker on discovering a watch, so we can infer an Almighty Designer when we study the marvelous designs of the human eye, a bird's beak, or a snake's mouth. His book, indeed, became a kind of rationalistic introduction to natural history. Paley summarizes the religious implications of the *saeculum rationalisticum* with unrivaled lucidity and comprehensiveness. He was widely imitated, and his message, directly or indirectly, reached millions of students, ministers, and churchgoers before he passed out of vogue.

Common Sense Realism (as it was often called) was a characteristic flowering of the Enlightenment and of the Scottish renaissance of the eighteenth century. It was developed by the Presbyterian Moderates who successfully controlled the established Kirk of Scotland and the four Scottish universities, which were then at the height of their influence and vitality, while the two great English universities were at the bottom of theirs. The founder and most creative contributor to this school of philosophy was Thomas Reid of Aberdeen and (later) Glasgow University; and his more systematic disciple, Dugald Steward of Edinburgh University. The first great exponent in America was John Witherspoon, who left Scotland in 1768 to become president of Princeton.

The Scottish Philosophy, as it came to be called, sought to create first of all a position free from absurdity or unreasonable subtlety (faults that were laid to Berkeley and Hume despite the deep respect shown them). In other words, they tried to give solid metaphysical content to common-sense acceptances. In accord with their age they rang the changes on the greatness of Bacon and Newton, and they insisted on being scientific and empirical. They denounced the reduction of man's mental and moral powers to physical terms, however, and turned their empiricism inward with a view to clarifying the nature of man's faculties. In this enterprise they "discovered" the agency or genuine powers of man: first, a rational freedom that made man a genuine cause (not a complex reactor mechanism); and second, an ability to make self-evident moral intuitions (not simply pain and pleasure judgments). In addition, they discovered principles which were anterior to experience (thus in a way anticipating Immanuel Kant), and argued further that man experienced the objective world without the mediation of "ideas." They thus respected the ancient dualisms: mind and matter, subject-object, and Creator-Creation, by the same token escaping materialism, idealism, subjectivism, hedonism, utilitarianism, pantheism, and skepticism. Because they did accord with the "common sense" of things, the Scottish philosophers produced, in short, precisely the kind of apologetic philosophy that Christians in the Age of Reason needed. Above all they provided a wonderful philosophical corollary to the one thinker who vies with Hume as Scotland's greatest philosopher of the century, and who outdistanced all of them in concrete influence: Adam Smith (1723–90), Reid's predecessor in moral philosophy at Glasgow and the author of a treatise on the "Moral Sentiments," whose *Wealth of Nations* (1776) became the classic exposition of laissez faire capitalism.

That the Scottish Philosophy reached as large an audience as Butler or Paley is unlikely, since its best expositors wrote in accordance with the technical demands of their calling; but as digested and retailed by others, the Scottish Philosophy achieved a wider influence by far than any other school. It also broke down denominational barriers with amazing facility, becoming very popular in Great Britain, almost the official philosophy of France under the Restoration and July Monarchy, and a strong influence at the Roman Catholic University of Louvain. In America it would rise to dominance for longer or shorter periods among Unitarians, Congregationalists, Presbyterians, "American" Lutherans, and Episcopalians, as well as among many others whose church ties were tenuous. During the first two-thirds of the nineteenth century, at least, it was to become among American Protestants the chief philosophical support to theological and apologetical enterprises.

REFORMULATIONS IN THEOLOGY

Not many Christians, obviously, would or could go all the way with deists and the more extreme *philosophes*. Genuine radicalism did exist, but it was a small subcurrent in Britain and almost unheard of in the colonies. Various sorts of orthodox traditionalism, on the other hand, had strong popular support. But among many thoughtful liberals and moderates a distinct form of Enlightenment theology arose, though men differed as to which doctrines deserved attack or defense. The English Unitarian John Taylor of Norwich thought that the issue lay with the doctrine of Original Sin, and he directed a scriptural and rational barrage in its direction. The liberal Bostonian Congregationalist Charles Chauncy delivered his most vigorous salvo against the "limited atonement" and eventually went all the way to Universalism. The Anglican latitudinarian Daniel Whitby (1638–1726) considered the doctrine of predestination most in need of reformulation. Samuel Clarke (1675–1729) directed his attention to *The Scripture-Doctrine of the Trinity* (1712) and made recommendations for revising the Book of Common Prayer on this subject. Archbishop John Tillotson had anticipated Locke (who took much comfort in so prestigious a forerunner) by arguing for a redefinition of faith as intellectual assent. Yet many of these men, even to the radical Unitarian Joseph Priestly, were conservative in their views of scriptural authority and the centrality of miracles. Despite this diversity, there emerged a recognizable type of "enlightened" Christianity, several chief characteristics of which can be enumerated:

1. It was Arminian in its desire to emphasize or augment the human role in redemption. Man's freedom and goodness accordingly were posited, the possibility of falling from grace admitted, and the particular application of God's predestinating decrees denied.

2. It emphasized the simplicity of Christian faith and ridiculed the complexity of both medieval and post-Reformation dogmatics. Locke in a famous reduction noted only two "rules": believe in Jesus as Lord, and lead a virtuous life.

3. Ethics was the chief end of its advocacy. Archdeacon Paley argued that damnation in hell betokened God's goodness in that it roused men to lives of virtue. More profoundly, this interest turned most of the best minds of the time to the philosophical analysis of morality.

4. Due to its emphasis on simplicity and morality, "reasonable Christianity" tended to view any credence in the objective nature of the sacraments as superstitious, and to deprecate the ministry except insofar as it concerned itself with moral instruction.

5. Enlightened theology was usually exceedingly unhistorical, in that it mistrusted tradition and ignored the ways in which thought and belief are conditioned by the historical situation. It rather viewed reason as freeing man from history and its oppressive relativities. This, however, is not to deny that certain great thinkers of the Enlightenment really began what Ernst Cassirer called "the conquest of the historical

world," a conquest which the nineteenth century would complete.

6. The idea of progress was given a prominent place in both secular and religious thinking. The typical thinker of the Enlightenment was optimistic about man and confident that his destiny on earth would involve a continual conquest of nature and ever greater human felicity. In Christian terms, this would lead to a postmillennial eschatology; that is, the kingdom of God would be realized in history, whereupon Christ or his Spirit would in some sense return.

7. Man's relation to God, in the enlightened scheme of things, was increasingly understood in impersonal terms. "Deity" (a favorite word) was conceived as the Architect and Governor of the universe, who ruled from long ago and far away through immutable law, a *Dieu fainéant*. The enlightened man might say, "The earth is the Lord's and He made it," but he had trouble with "The Lord is my shepherd." He knew God as Power and Principle, not as a person capable of love and wrath. Enlightened piety, therefore, was rational, reserved, and law centered. Its preachers were the surrogates of a Judge; their sermons, like a winter day, were short and cold.

Needless to say, not every person (or even every intellectual) of the age was "Enlightened" in precisely the manner just described. Each country also had its dissident voices: pietists, Methodists, and New Lights on the one hand; secular rebels, skeptics, pessimists, and precursors of romanticism on the other. The basic intellectual trend of the century, however, is unmistakable, and in the perspective of history the Enlightenment's overall accomplishment clearly constitutes a decisive modern rupture with the medieval tradition even though many continuities remained.

The influence of these new currents of thought in America was very strong. Yet the ultimate popularity of Locke, Butler, Paley, Reid, and Smith should not veil the hindrances to their advance in a country where Puritanism was still so lively a reality, and where the Great Awakening aroused such widespread concern for evangelical Christianity. Even in the "broad and catholick" party of Boston, whence came much of the opposition to the revivals, the wines of the Enlightenment were sipped with cautious moderation. As late as 1782 Charles Chauncy thought it wise to publish his defense of Universalism in London—anonymously. Yet the wines were sipped, and the inevitable result was an extension of rationalism. Under ambitious and forward-looking spirits like Cotton Mather the rational principle in the older Puritanism was given wider berth. It also became an integral part of the witness of the Old Calvinist, or Moderate, party in the years after the Great Awakening. The coming of John Witherspoon from Scotland to Princeton in 1768 initiated a similar tradition among the Presbyterians. In the Anglican clergy of the South the new theology also won numerous adherents. When Devereux Jarratt went to conventions of the Virginia ministers, he heard "some of the most sacred doctrines of Christianity treated with ridicule and profane burlesque."

Against this total background of theological and philosophical change, most of the men who were to become the new nation's founding fathers were led into essentially enlightened modes of understanding history, government, law, God, man, and destiny. This is as true for Ethan Allen of Vermont's Green Mountains as it is for George Washington of Virginia's tidewater. And from each of the three main sections of the country would come one man who by international standards represented the classical Enlightenment at its typical best: John Adams, Benjamin Franklin, and Thomas Jefferson. Each of these men sought to express the new rationalism with complete integrity. Each of them tried in a serious way, through a long and active career, to deal coherently with the separate but interrelated problems of man, God, nature, and society. Each of them exemplified in a unique way how the Puritan heritage, an emerging pattern of middle-class democracy, and the fresh influences of the Enlightenment were preparing the American colonies for a common and united destiny.

23

THE REVOLUTIONARY ERA

Seventeen sixty-three was a memorable year for Great Britain and her American colonies: the Treaty of Paris ended a half-century of conflict—at least for the present. Quebec and Florida were in English hands, the power of France on the North American continent was broken, and Spain was relegated to remote expanses beyond the Mississippi. The situation seemed to promise a new day for Anglo-American ambitions in the New World. Further enhancing this possibility, the Conspiracy of Pontiac in the West had been shattered. Yet neither in Europe nor in America did an Era of Good Feelings ensue. Quite to the contrary, the new situation entailed difficulties that in a dozen years resulted in open conflict, followed by eight years of declared war. With independence won, the new nation then entered upon another fifteen years or more of domestic uncertainty, conflict, and experimentation before the basic political forms of a democratic country had been established. It is this period as a whole—from 1763 to 1800—that the term "revolutionary era" is here meant to designate.

In political terms, the four decades between the end of the "Old French War" and the election of Thomas Jefferson as president of the United States divide with a minimum of confusion into four fairly definite eventful periods, each of them very familiar to most Americans:

1760–1775   A time of deteriorating relations with England and of growing sentiment for independence

1775–1783   A time of war, reorganization, and state-forming

1783–1789   The so-called Critical Period during which the

problems of federalism were exposed, fiercely
contended, and officially resolved

1789–1800   The Federalist Period in United States history, a period of crucial self-definition during
which the problems of federal union under the
Constitution and foreign relations of the new
state were settled

In the events of these four periods the churches, their ministers, and their membership were, of course, actively involved.

RELIGION AND THE REVOLUTIONARY MOVEMENT

The years of mounting crisis found the churches implicated
on both sides of every issue under debate, but in general they
became increasingly identified with the Patriot tide of opinion and contributed powerfully to its rise. In terms of church
affiliation, the chief strength of Loyalism lay in the Anglican
clergy everywhere and in the Anglican laity of the middle
and northern colonies. There was also considerable Tory sentiment among the wealthier Quakers, the older Lutheran
clergy, and the leaders of the pacifistic German sects. In the
South, however, the Anglican laity joined the Patriot cause
and furnished much of its leadership. All in all, the Protestant
disposition of the American people, regardless of how secularized their Puritanism had become, involved their viewing
the king and English rule with suspicion. Their tribal memories of early persecution strengthened this hostility, while
proposals for sending a bishop to America constantly reinforced it. In fact, the drift of American opinion during these
years can hardly be explained unless one takes into account
the deeply ingrained "antiprelatical" bias of all but a small
percentage of the population. The Scotch-Irish, Scots, and
Irish, as well as the fervent evangelical "dissenters" still
suffering discrimination in Virginia and some other colonies,
had more positive grounds for similar views. Parliament's solicitude for Canadian Roman Catholicism, shown in the Quebec Act (1774), provided additional provocation, while
American Roman Catholics, on the other hand, had good
reasons for wanting freedom from English disabilities. That
the "Black Regiment" of colonial clergy addressing large, reg-

ular audiences from positions of great prestige was a major force in arousing the spirit of independence after 1761, was asserted at the time by both Tory and Patriot interpreters. Professor Bridenbaugh in his masterful history of the subject has heavily underlined the revolutionary potency of the "Great Fear of Episcopacy":

> For us of the twentieth century, it is very, very difficult to recover imaginatively a real understanding of the enormous effect of this controversy on the opinions and feelings of a pious, dissenting people grown accustomed to ecclesiastical self-government and currently engaged in a struggle to protect their liberties in the civil sphere. The bad news or threats they read in every week's newspaper produced a cumulative effect like the rising crescendo of a bolero. The agitation over an American episcopate reached its peak by 1770, and the public had grown almost frenzied in the course of it.[1]

Far more important than the overt activities of ministers and church assemblies or the resentment of specific minorities were the factors stressed in the foregoing chapter on the longterm American Revolution, 1607–1776. This was the revolution in men's hearts, to which, in John Adams's view, the Declaration of 1776 gave only belated expression. And the source of its strength lay in the religious substratum, which was always Nonconformist, Dissenting, and Puritan in its basic disposition. For this reason the heroes and leaders of the radical opposition in eighteenth-century politics—John Milton, Algernon Sidney, John Locke, John Trenchard, Thomas Gordon, James Burgh—gained a vastly stronger following in America than in England. But much more than a simple dislike for the existing form of government and a desire for political independence developed in the minds of these people. A new conception of freedom and equality took shape, involving conceptions of God, man, human rights, the state, and history, which became inseparable from the Enlightenment's outlook on reality. On 4 July 1776, these conceptions became a cornerstone of the American political tradition; during this period they were given further embodiment in state constitutions (and in due course in the federal

[1] Carl Bridenbaugh, *Mitre and Sceptre: Transatlantic Faiths, Ideas, Personalties, and Politics, 1689–1775,* p. 313.

Constitution). In the words of the nation's Patriot heroes and Founding Fathers these ideas were woven into the very texture of American thinking. The American nation was born in the full illumination of the Enlightenment, and this fact would permanently distinguish it from every other major power in the world.[2]

The influence of the Enlightenment and its leading themes upon many thinkers and religious movements of the eighteenth century is evident, but after 1760 its political uses and implications came to be drawn upon with special fervor, and in this connection John Locke again became a much valued resource. His reasoned justification of the Glorious Revolution now became peculiarly relevant for the colonies as they strove to define their liberties and to limit the authority of Parliament and King George III. Government, Locke had affirmed, is not absolute, but rather the result of a "social compact" made by free, equal, and independent men. It is instituted with the consent of the governed and should be reformed or replaced if it fails to fulfill its purpose. Permeating Locke's thought, of course, was an abiding confidence in natural law, which, though eternal and transcendent, was yet accessible to human reason whenever the mind was freed from bondage, superstition, and the passions. Such law controlled the relations of mankind as well as the natural order of things. Since man was a cosmopolitan constant in this scheme, Americans often saw themselves as sharing a common cause with the champions of republican principles in ancient Greece and Rome; and the Declaration of Independence would be addressed to a "candid world."

In one very important respect, however, Americans were participating in a fairly revolutionary departure from the traditional precepts of natural law. Reflecting a typical Puritan emphasis on inward experience, they shifted the emphasis from the *order* of nature and government to the reality of natural *rights*. In other words, they "interiorized" the significance of natural law and rendered it more man-cen-

[2] Only France would have a vaguely similar experience; but in that case the French Revolution merely engrafted the Enlightenment experience on a tradition that already included centuries of national glory. After 1800, moreover, a succession of kings, emperors, and republics would break and diffuse the influence of the Revolution. The rallying to General de Gaulle was hardly an evocation of 1789.

tered, stressing human rights rather than cosmic order, the individual rather than the state, liberty rather than obedience. To a remarkable degree these solemnly proclaimed "rights" were the end product of centuries of English legal and constitutional history, clarified by the momentous revolutions of the seventeenth century and deepened by the Puritan's persistent emphasis on covenantal responsibility. In America, a generation of remarkable men thought through the implications of this political philosophy and invested it with new urgency and relevance.

After the military phase of the Revolution was accomplished, political issues again moved into the foreground, and problems of self-government rather than relations with king and Parliament now provided the occasion for controversy and creative thought. Enlightened motifs continued to prevail—perhaps above all a vast faith in written constitutions—but more than ever these motifs were modified by a realistic hardheadedness and an absence of illusion about the sinfulness of men. The *Federalist Papers,* published in 1787–88, as well as John Adams's defenses of the American constitutions, can be read as Puritan contributions to Enlightenment political theory.

In all the heated controversies of this period the churches were almost as much divided as the country. Liberalism in theology was by no means a concomitant of liberalism in social, economic, or political advocacy; nor was the orthodox host any more solidly conservative in policy. The theologically conservative Patriot heroes, Patrick Henry and Samuel Adams, showed more than average political radicalism. Daniel Shays's rebels of 1786 were probably more orthodox than their opposition. In Massachusetts generally, the more orthodox west stood opposed to the emerging Unitarianism of the Boston area where the ultra-Federalists would later make their last stand. The clergy, no doubt, held more conservative political views than their constituencies as a general rule, and after 1795 they became increasingly alarmed over the rise of the outspoken infidelity exemplified by Thomas Paine. By this time they were also disturbed by the declining state of the churches and the threat, in the person of Thomas Jefferson, of a president who was an articulate critic of "sectarianism" in religion and an eloquent defender of deism. Yet even in Connecticut, where President Timothy Dwight of Yale was exposing the errors of Jeffersonian infidelity, evangelical Baptists and Methodists together with High Church Anglicans were moving toward the Democratic Republican party in order to oppose the Congregational standing order. Theological-political correlations, in other words, are not easily established.

THE CHURCHES DURING THE REVOLUTIONARY ERA

The church-historical significance of this turbulent epoch is many-sided. First and most obviously, the churches experienced a period of distraction, disruption, and decline, for reasons that any political and military history of the period makes obvious. Second, the protracted political crisis extending from the Stamp Act furor to the election of Jefferson accelerated the advance of Enlightenment philosophy, natural theology, and secularized thought. It also gave priority to political issues, and hence to governmental or legalistic ways of conceiving traditional theological questions. In short, the age introduced modes of thought which in subtle ways contributed to theological transformation. Third, the churches were to varying degrees required to respond to the new political circumstances created by the War for Independence and the Treaty of Paris (1738). Some needed literally to reconstitute themselves, and nearly all experienced significant changes. Fourth, all religious groups were provided with new opportunities for increased vitality and growth by important adjustments of church and state relationships, adjustments which they, in turn, had helped to bring about. Established churches lingered in New England, to be sure, while social arrangements and Protestant pressure maintained "quasi-establishments" in most other regions; yet a new epoch in the history of religious freedom had unquestionably opened.

The Religious Depression

The revolutionary era was a period of decline for American Christianity as a whole. The churches reached a lower ebb of vitality during the two decades after the end of hostilities than at any other time in the country's religious history. In many ways the war itself began the process of decline: occasioning the flight of partisan ministers when opposing armies approached (Samuel Hopkins from British-occupied

Newport, the rector of King's Chapel from encircled Boston); drawing many ministers into the chaplaincy (Timothy Dwight with the Continental army, Samuel Seabury with the British); or leading some into actual combat (the Reverend General Muhlenberg leading his brigade against Cornwallis at Brandywine; the aged Naphtali Daggett, professor of divinity at Yale, dashing off with his old fowling piece against the invaders of New Haven). In addition to these instances and hundreds like them, the more generalized disruption and occasional devastation wrought by the war left the churches disorganized and their members preoccupied by burning questions of a military or political nature.

As for the years after 1783 under the Articles of Confederation, historians have largely reinterpreted the state of the nation, finding its health considerably better than later Federalists would have had us believe. John Fiske's conception of a "critical period" is under a fair-sized cloud. But nobody has arisen to deny that it was indeed a "critical period" for the churches. Their difficulties were the product of distraction, attack, and apathy; and the greatest of these was apathy. A colonial people almost congenitally exercised with religious questions of all sorts—and possibly exhausted by or in reaction against the Great Awakening—became preoccupied for forty years chiefly with the problems of politics. When independence was achieved, social unrest flared up again, as in western Massachusetts, where outraged farmers under Daniel Shays resorted to armed force in 1786. After the federal Constitution had been ratified, unrest was translated into bitter partisan political struggle. When revolution in France and a new European war complicated the issues and aroused even fiercer passions, the churches had little opportunity for recuperation; and even if they had, the intellectual climate was too debilitating. By the end of the period, church membership had dropped both relatively and absolutely, so that not more than one person in twenty or possibly one in ten seems to have been affiliated; in many churches membership itself became increasingly nominal. Tory ministers fled; patriot ministers often had their labors interrupted. Most of the college faculties were scattered and their facilities appropriated for military use, disastrously affecting the recruitment and training of a clergy. "Enthusiasm" was widely spurned, and revivalism came to a temporary halt everywhere except in the remoter parts of the South.

The Spread of Religious Rationalism

One religious movement which enjoyed a season of popularity and great prestige during this era, in America as in France, was the cult of reason. Rational religion, or deism, is of course ancient, and even its modern renewal began early, often being dated from the appearance of Lord Herbert of Cherbury's *De Veritate* (1624). As the Enlightenment progressed, more and more thinkers came to accept its primary assertion that reason and scientific knowledge could supply all the necessary elements of religion and ethics, though many might concede that revelation was still needed by the masses. In America, to be sure, frank professions of pure deism were rare in the prerevolutionary period. Even the Arminians' cautious enlargement of the scope of man's reason and moral faculties was considered radical. Yet the growing enthusiasm for Newtonian cosmology and Lockean philosophy had broad effects, and "natural religion" flourished in alliance with "revealed religion" in the theology of many Christian rationalists. The trend is noticeable in the sermons of Anglicans like Timothy Cutler or Congregationalists like Charles Chauncy—not to mention those of Edwards.

In 1755 John Adams was deflected from a ministerial career by the forthright rationalism of a Worcester lawyer, and the religious views which he gradually formulated reflect this impact:

> One great Advantage of the Christian Religion is that it brings the great Principle of the Law of Nature and Nations, Love your Neighbor as yourself, and do to others as you would that others should do to you,—to the Knowledge, Belief and Veneration of the whole People. Children, Servants, Women and Men are all Professors in the science of public as well as private Morality. No other Institution for Education, no kind of political Discipline, could diffuse this kind of necessary Information, so universally among all Ranks and Descriptions of Citizens. The Duties and Rights of The Man and the Citizen are thus taught from early Infancy to every Creature.[3]

[3] Diary of John Adams, 14 August 1796, quoted in a very valuable context by Daniel Boorstin, *The Lost World of Thomas Jefferson*, p. 156.

More outspoken and less respectful of "Christian principles" was Ethan Allen (1738–89), a self-educated rebel from the Great Awakening, hero of Ticonderoga, and controversial figure in Vermont politics. His long-gestated work *The Only Oracle of Man* (1784) not only defended "natural religion" but attacked the Bible and "priestcraft" with sufficient boldness to earn Timothy Dwight's observation that it was "the first formal publication, in the United States, openly directed against the Christian religion." As Allen's life indicates, the war released many inhibitions, opening American minds not only to French liberalism and anticlerical thought, but to the larger and far more easily comprehended tradition of English rationalism. And of the English, none equaled the impassioned eloquence of Thomas Paine, the great pamphleteer of the war, whose *Age of Reason* (1794–96) became one of the period's most famous (or infamous) expositions of deism.

An American counterpart of Paine was Joel Barlow (1754–1812), a Yale graduate, sometime Revolutionary War chaplain, "Connecticut Wit," and patriotic epic poet, who later in his life went to France and became actively involved in the French Revolution. In his *Advice to the Privileged Orders* (1792), Barlow took forceful exception to Edmund Burke's negative *Reflections on the French Revolution*, and before he died he had become a thoroughgoing *philosophe*. Elihu Palmer (1764–1806), however, is most often remembered as the leader of those few Americans who thought deism or "Republican Religion" could be institutionalized in a more or less traditional way. After a brief career as a Congregational, Baptist, and then Universalist preacher, he became a devotee of the *philosophes*, and later, a friend of Paine. In 1794 he organized a "Deistical Society" in New York among a group of enthusiasts for the French Revolution, and after Jefferson's election in 1800 sought to enlarge its influence with a weekly paper, the *Temple of Reason*. These efforts won scant support and fierce opposition, perishing altogether in the surge of revivalism which was then beginning. But they dramatized for a while an unorganized impulse that had considerable popular rootage and distinguished intellectual leadership.

Thomas Jefferson (1743–1826) was unquestionably the most significant of the American rationalists, and his place in the history of American religion is exceedingly important because he was, as Saul Padover has said, "the St. Paul of American democracy,"[4] and because his philosophy of religion and his political theory form such a thoughtfully unified whole. Jefferson was also so important an architect of the United States' solution of the church and state problem that some have seen this "solution" as the virtual establishment of his own theology. In content his theology was similar to that of Adams, Barlow, Palmer, and Paine, though Jefferson was more doctrinaire in his materialism than most of his American confreres and hence had more difficulty in stating his views of human freedom and moral responsibility. Because of the ferocious attacks against him by Federalist clergymen, he also became more bluntly anticlerical. Generally speaking, however, only an extensive essay could clarify the religious differences of the major Founding Fathers. They were all inhabitants of that "lost world" which Daniel Boorstin has delineated—a brief and beautiful flowering of confidence in man, education, and political institutions which Americans for over a century fervently and uncritically appropriated, and which all still honor even after seeing how far the country fell short of its founding principles.

Independence and Church Reorganization

If "Republican Religion" or deism gained ground for a while during the revolutionary era, the Church of England in America suffered a devastating blow. When hostilities ceased, "its fragments lay scattered from Portsmouth to Savannah." Outside of Virginia and Maryland and a few coastal cities in other states, the Society for the Propagation of the Gospel had provided the main body of clergy; and with the open rupture of relations with the mother country, most of its missionaries (who were Tories almost to a man) withdrew to areas held by British armies. Even in self-supporting parishes

4 Saul K. Padover, ed., *Thomas Jefferson on Democracy* (New York: New American Library, 1967), p. 1. It is of interest in this connection to consider Jefferson's view of Saint Paul. In a letter of 1820 he contrasts the "lovely benevolence" of Jesus with the "charlatanism" which followed. "I separate, therefore, the gold from the dross; restore to him [Jesus] the former, and leave the latter to the stupidity of some, and roguery of others of his disciples. Of this band of dupes and imposters, Paul was the great Coryphaeus, and first corruptor of the doctrines of Jesus" (ibid., p. 121).

the incidence of Loyalism among the clergy was high. Two-thirds of Virginia's rectors left their parishes during the war. William White, the future bishop, was for a time the only Anglican priest in the whole state of Pennsylvania. Even Jacob Duché, who gave a moving invocation at the First Continental Congress, later joined the Tory exodus. At the war's end, there were but five priests in New Jersey, four in Massachusetts, one in New Hampshire, and none in Rhode Island or Maine. Nor was it only the clergy who remained loyal to the king. Among the Anglicans of New York, New Jersey, and Georgia, Loyalists were probably in the majority; and they were strong in Virginia, Massachusetts, and Maryland as well. Over seventy thousand of them left the country during the war or immediately after. A large part of those who were able to leave were merchants, wealthy landowners, or former royal officials, and since these classes were predominantly Anglican many very prominent parishes were depleted.

This was not the end of woe for the Church of England. Kings (Columbia) College and the University of Pennsylvania were all but severed from their Anglican origins. In every state where it had been established, church and state were separated—usually with surprising promptness, though in Virginia the basic disestablishment of 1785 was not fully achieved until 1799. By this legislation the Anglican churches lost much of their customary public or landed support. Finally and most seriously, in the very areas where its parish structure was strongest, Anglicanism was probably more pervaded by the extreme latitudinarianism of the Enlightenment than any other church body. This penetration began long before 1760, though it was considerably deepened during the revolutionary era, with the result that neither the large Patriot majorities in Maryland and Virginia, nor the fact that two-thirds of the signers of the Declaration of Independence were nominally Anglican, contributed much to the future restoration of the Episcopal church in America.

As a matter of fact the reverse is true. When the time came to rehabilitate the church, the most constructive leadership was provided by men from states where the Church of England had not been established. Connecticut, where Anglicans had been a suspect minority and often Tories, furnished the chief spiritual impulse. Fourteen of the twenty ministers who were still in the state when the war ended stood in a close relationship to the famous Yale "apostasy" of 1722; they had held their ground in an intensely theological environment, and they knew more clearly than the Anglican clergy of any other state what they wanted. Shortly after the peace treaty was signed, ten of these men held a secret conclave in rural Woodbury and made provisions for one of their number to seek consecration as a bishop. The man finally chosen was Samuel Seabury (1729–96), a strong-minded High Churchman, outspoken Loyalist, and sometime chaplain to British troops. Failing after almost a year's wait to obtain consecration in England, Seabury went to Scotland, and in November 1784 he was consecrated in Aberdeen by three nonjuring bishops.[5] On his return, America had its first Anglican bishop.

Elsewhere other plans were maturing. In Maryland certain actions had been taken during the war to preserve Anglican properties. On these foundations, Dr. William Smith, former provost of the College of Philadelphia, convened the clergy of the state at Annapolis in 1783. At this meeting the Protestant Episcopal Church was declared to exist, and Dr. Smith was chosen to seek consecration as bishop. In Philadelphia, William White, the Patriot rector of Christ Church, was also taking steps toward reorganization; and perhaps because he breathed the atmosphere of that politically conscious city, his ideas were dominated by the desire for a national church. Theologically he was vastly more latitudinarian than Seabury. In 1782 he published his proposal for organizing the church on a federal basis and for resorting to presbyterial ordination until an episcopate could be established. White also approached the Lutherans and Methodists, and in 1784 a Pennsylvania committee under his leadership, together with a more broadly based group from New Jersey, pressed for implementation of these plans. In due course a larger meeting, with delegates from the middle and northeastern states, proposed a general convention.

The convention met in 1785; and shortly afterward three states (New York, Pennsylvania, and Virginia) elected bishops, while White and Smith pressed ahead with their proposed revision of the prayer book. In the meantime Parliament had passed laws allowing the English bishops to

---

[5] The "nonjuring" bishops stood in the succession of "Jacobite" clergy who had remained loyal to James II and his heirs. They refused to swear allegiance to William and Mary after the Parliamentary settlement of 1689.

consecrate an American. This they did in February 1787, Dr. William White of Philadelphia and Samuel Provoost, rector of Trinity Church in New York City, being the two candidates. As a result the United States had two episcopates: one Scottish, High Church, and Tory; the other English, latitudinarian, and Patriot. Nor was it obvious that the twain would meet, for Provoost considered Seabury a traitor to his country, while the Connecticut men as a group were suspicious of the other's doctrinal aberrations and concessions to the laity. What finally brought the two parties together was a request from Massachusetts that its candidate for the episcopate be consecrated by the three American bishops. With this issue before them, the convention of 1789 worked out the compromises that made union possible: Seabury acquiesced to lay representation in the convention and the omission of the Athanasian Creed but won approval for a separate House of Bishops; and though he thwarted the more radical proposals for revising the prayer book, he made good his promise to the Scottish bishops to incorporate elements of their communion liturgy. With agreement on these matters, the Protestant Episcopal Church in the United States came into existence. Perhaps the relatively desperate situation of the church accounts for the success of these negotiations, but this fact does not lessen the magnitude of the event. A quiet revolution had been wrought in the tradition of Anglican episcopacy, as monarchical institutions gave way to those of a democracy: lay representation, elected bishops, and strong vestries at the local level.

The Methodist predicament was entwined with the Anglican because it originated as a revival movement within the Church of England. Methodist Patriots in America were profoundly perturbed when in 1775 John Wesley published *A Calm Address to Our Own American Colonies,* in which he restated much of Dr. Samuel Johnson's *Taxation No Tyranny,* urging Americans to be grateful for England's beneficent rule. Public notice of this pronouncement did little to enhance Methodist popularity in the now openly rebellious colonies; and matters became still worse after the Declaration and the widespread imposition of loyalty oaths. Every one of Wesley's English preachers in the colonies returned to England except Francis Asbury (1745–1816), who since 1772 had superintended the American clergy. Even Asbury was greatly restricted in his activities, and for over two years he lived in virtual exile. Despite these adversities, the revivals in Virginia offset other losses, so that the four thousand members of 1775 had trebled by 1780. At the annual conference of 1778, for example, five old circuits were discontinued in Pennsylvania, Maryland, and New York, while six new ones were added in Virginia and two in North Carolina. By 1784, four-fifths of the country's fifteen thousand Methodists were located south of the Mason-Dixon line. Yet the status of the movement had before that year become increasingly uncertain: was it an independent denomination or not?

When the Revolution began, the answer to this question was unhesitatingly negative; and in England it remained so until 1791, the year of John Wesley's death. As the Anglican clergy began their exodus, however, and after widespread disruption of parish life in the South, pressure grew to make Methodism an autonomous church with a clergy authorized to administer the sacraments. The "Virginia brethren" were especially "warm for the ordinances." Proposals for American ordination were made in 1777 and 1778; and when in 1779 the Southern Conference appointed a committee with ordaining powers, it began to exercise them immediately in spite of remonstrances from Asbury and the societies of the North.

Methodism's year of decision in both England and America was 1784. In February Wesley executed for England the "Deed of Declaration," which vested the 359 Methodist chapels in a self-perpetuating Annual Conference of one hundred preachers. Then on 1 September he recorded in his diary the fateful decision concerning a ministry for America. "Being now clear in my own mind, I took a step which I had long weighed in my mind, and appointed Mr. [Richard] Whatcoat and Mr. [Thomas] Vasey to go and serve the desolate sheep in America." A few days later, Wesley, Thomas Coke, and James Creighton, all priests of the Church of England, ordained Whatcoat and Vasey. Thereafter Wesley, "assisted by other ordained ministers," also ordained Coke to be a superintendent in the United States. The three were then dispatched with this authorization: "Know all men, that I, *John Wesley*, think myself to be providentially called at this time, to set apart some persons for the work of the ministry in America." He acknowledged a departure from Anglican church order, but in an accompanying letter justified his decision on the basis of apostolic praxis and America's need, above all stressing concern for "feeding and guiding these poor sheep in the wilderness." His realization that "for some hundreds of miles together there is none either to baptize or to administer the Lord's Supper" put his scruples at an end. "I conceive myself at full liberty . . . and invade no man's right by appointing and sending laborers into the harvest."[6]

In September 1784 the three emissaries set sail, arriving after a stormy passage in November. The next month at Baltimore they convened the famous "Christmas Conference" for the great work of organizing the American church. Sixty preachers were present, thanks to Asbury's untiring efforts to notify the farflung circuits. "It was agreed," says Asbury, "to form ourselves into an Episcopal Church, and to have superintendents, elders, and deacons." Asbury and Coke were elected unanimously as superintendents, and Asbury was ordained successively as deacon, elder, and superintendent by the three English ministers, assisted by Philip William Otterbein of the German Reformed church in the last rite. With a few obvious adaptations to the American situation, including complete independence from Anglicanism, the discipline of English Methodism was adopted, as were the liturgy, prayer book, hymns, and Twenty-four Articles of Religion which Wesley prepared for his American brethren. The new church acknowledged themselves to be Wesley's "sons in the gospel, ready in matters belonging to church government to his commands." They also seemed to welcome his pruning away of "Calvinism, Romanism, and ritualism" from the Thirty-nine Articles.

An institution of great significance for America came into existence at this Christmas Conference. With Francis Asbury positively at its head, American Methodism would begin its great forward surge, just when the English movement was lapsing into formalism and stagnancy. Throughout the next century it would be the chief engine of evangelical Arminianism in this country. Expanding almost exclusively by domestic evangelism, it would exceed in its rate of growth all other large Protestant churches. By direct impact and negative reaction it would work large effects on nearly every other denomination, until by degrees it imparted its energy and spirit to American Protestantism as a whole. So complex and

[6] Diary of John Wesley (while in Leeds), quoted in J. M. Buckley, *A History of Methodists in the United States*, ACHS, vol. 5 (New York, 1895), p. 232.

involved were these religious currents, however, that it is possible to evaluate the Methodist legacy only from a vantage point at the end of the nineteenth century. At the present time it is more important to note two fundamental aspects of the new church: its message and its structure.

The chief characteristics of the American Methodist message were its emphasis on personal religious experience, its legalistic views on Christian behavior, and its doctrinal simplicity. Each of these was an authentic Wesleyan tendency which came to be accentuated on the frontiers where Methodism flourished. The experience of regeneration and its penitential accompaniments were a requirement for church membership. The specific behavioral and moral demands laid upon the regenerate Christian were basically those of Puritanism, but they included prohibitions on alcohol and slaveholding. The doctrinal message rested on three primary points: (1) God's grace is free to all; (2) man is ever free to accept or reject it; and (3) the justified sinner, with the aid of the Holy Spirit, must seek the goal of "perfection" (i.e. freedom from willful sin). What made Methodism so dynamic an element in American Protestantism, however, was the remarkable institutions by which this message was spread and enforced.

Methodism from the first had been very strictly governed. Until 1784 every chapel in the connection (359 in the United Kingdom alone) was vested in Wesley himself, and even after that date (in America no less than in England) his will had almost the force of canon law. In the independent American church, the superintendent (or bishop, as he came to be called)[7] wielded more actual authority than any other Protestant official. Once elected, he could define the circuits which the traveling preachers were to cover and assign men to these circuits or to local charges as he saw fit. He appointed the presiding elders who in turn supervised the several districts into which the circuits were arranged. Thus he could marshal his men and resources in such a way as to make maximum gains in domestic missions. At the lowest level, meanwhile, was another crucial institution, the class

---

[7] Asbury's use of the term "bishop" was contrary to the views of Wesley, who wrote Asbury, "For my sake, for God's sake, for Christ's sake put a full end to this!" Wesley to Asbury, 20 September 1788, *The Letters of the Reverend John Wesley, A.M.*, ed. John Telford (London: Epworth Press, 1931), 8:91.

meeting, or local unit of Christians who gathered weekly to strengthen each other by testimony, admonition, prayer, and joint study. They could also seek the licensing of a local lay exhorter when one with appropriate gifts was discovered. So long as it prospered, the class meeting was the institution which did most to guarantee that church membership was not merely a nominal affiliation.

With this message and this structure Methodism clearly met the requirements suggested by a recent historian of the frontier:

> A church with real hopes for success in the West should have been optimistic in its faith, with stress on the importance of the individual. It should have provided social and emotional content. It should have had an organization adapted to the widely scattered [and one should add, constantly moving] western population. Further, it needed a clergy which could speak the language of the crude and hardworking West.[8]

The Congregational churches were not nearly so directly or drastically affected by the events of the revolutionary era as the Anglicans and Methodists. Outwardly their position was improved. The Anglican challenge was reduced by the taint of Toryism and by great physical losses. Congregationalism could ride the crest of patriotism, taking credit for having done much to foment the revolutionary spirit and having provided much institutional and theoretical groundwork for America's self-government. This was true, moreover, of both wings of the church. Jonathan Mayhew of Boston might be a spokesman for Arminianism, and Samuel Hopkins of Newport for "Consistent Calvinism," but they stood together as fervent Whigs, and neither had many Loyalists among his colleagues.

Such signs of prestige and prosperity, however, betray the internal facts of the matter. In actuality the Puritan ideal of which these churches were the custodians was being corroded by the Enlightenment's demand for simplicity and reasonableness. The "orthodox" churches were almost as thoroughly permeated by the tendency to rationalism and

[8] R. E. Riegel, *America Moves West* (New York: Henry Holt & Co., 1947), p. 107; quoted by John L. Peters, *Christian Perfection and American Methodism*, p. 91.

formalism as those which were professedly Arminian. Church membership became increasingly nominal. Revivals were sporadic and localized, and most of what "enthusiasm" there was, was channeled into the Baptist and Methodist churches.[9] Most ominous of all was the widening rift between liberals and conservatives, and hardly less serious, a division of the conservatives themselves into New Divinity men of Edwardsean stamp and the so-called Old Calvinists. Open schism in the Massachusetts churches would not occur until the next century, but the reorganization of King's Chapel and its antitrinitarian revision of the prayer book (1787) were signs of things to come.

For the Presbyterian church the revolutionary era involved a gradual severance of the bonds with Congregationalism that the Great Awakening had forged. In the years just before the war, they had united in a General Convention to resist the possible imposition of an Anglican episcopate on the colonies; but in theology, polity, and internal spirit they subsequently drew apart. The growth of Princeton, the coming of Witherspoon, and, above all, the very large migration of Scotch-Irish peoples during the 1770s hastened the process. At the end of the century, however, revivalism and the western missionary challenge would again draw the two churches together.

The single most positive response of the Presbyterian church to the needs of the time was constitutional. As the church grew in size, attendance at synod relatively decreased, indicating the inadequacy of the old structure. Finally in 1785 the church attacked the problem by appointing a committee to draw up a manual of discipline. There were also motions to reorganize the church and to prepare a new book of psalmody. Though badly attended as usual, the synod of 1786 continued these deliberations and appointed a new committee with Dr. Witherspoon as chairman. In 1787 a fierce debate raged over the committee's printed *Draught of a Plan of Government and Discipline,* and the perennial tension between the Scottish and New England factions was clearly visible. There was, nevertheless, some progress, and

---

[9] After a few earlier visits by itinerant evangelists, Methodism was introduced into New England by Jesse Lee, who began a circuit at Norwalk, Connecticut, in June 1789. He preached at Fairfield, Danbury, and New Haven, and shortly afterward established a circuit in Rhode Island.

the synod of 1788 was able to approve a Plan of Government and Discipline, a Directory of Public Worship, and a slightly revised version of the Westminster Confession of Faith. The new constitution provided for a General Assembly, four synods (New York and New Jersey, Philadelphia, Virginia, and the Carolinas), and sixteen presbyteries. The presbyteries retained full powers of ordination. The church then had 420 congregations, 214 of which had pastors, 177 ministers, and 11 licentiates. Under its new constitution the church settled down to orderly democratic procedures, and the overall result was distinctly American. Scottish forms and precedents naturally predominated, but it was basically a compromise of the diverse traditions and influences that had flowed into the American Presbyterian church from many sources.

In the revolutionary period Baptists continued to profit from the revivalistic fervor infused into their ranks by the Separates. In New England they joined forces with the Calvinistic Baptists and almost completely overwhelmed the older Arminian Baptists of the area. In 1740 there had been only twenty-five Baptist churches in all New England: eleven each in Rhode Island and Massachusetts, and three in Connecticut. By 1790, in spite of the distractions of the times, these had multiplied to thirty-eight in Rhode Island, ninety-two in Massachusetts, fifty-five in Connecticut, fifteen in Maine, thirty-two in New Hampshire, and thirty-four in Vermont—a total of 266. Whereas only a half-dozen of the churches in 1740 had been Calvinistic, the vast majority in 1790 adhered to this theology.

In 1763 James Manning (1738–91), having graduated from the College of New Jersey (Princeton) the previous year, led the movement to establish a Baptist collegiate institution in Rhode Island. The Philadelphia Association had conceived this project and chose Rhode Island because they felt that a more liberal charter could be obtained there. Actually the charter as passed by the colonial assembly in 1764 was "liberal" in more ways than one. While it specified that a majority of the trustees and fellows were to be "forever Baptists," it admitted approximately one-third from other denominations. The college president was required to be a Baptist, but other officers and teachers, as well as students, were subjected to no religious tests. Manning began immediately with a group of young men in Warren, and graduated his first class of seven in 1769. The next year the college moved to Providence, secured additional instructors, and acquired the beginning of an endowment. During the war its faculty and student body were scattered and its buildings used for barracks, but it recovered speedily after the cessation of hostilities. In 1804 it assumed the name of Brown University in honor of its chief benefactors.

In the South, where revivalism continued even more vigorously, Baptists made larger and more important advances. Virginia alone had in 1790 almost as many churches (218) as all of New England, while the union of Separates and Regulars in 1787 left them poised to capitalize on the westward movement into Kentucky and Tennessee. In this entire process the Separate Baptists continued their aggressive advance, not only through personal and mass evangelism, but because of their ultimately successful fight against all forms of religious favoritism in Virginia. As this campaign gained momentum they were joined by the Presbyterians and Regular Baptists (who previously were content with toleration), and by many of the Old Dominion's greatest statesmen, most importantly Thomas Jefferson and James Madison—both nominal Anglicans.

With the coming of war, the rising tide of sentiment against the established church finally prevailed, and a series of enactments by the assembly eventually removed every vestige of religious inequality. In 1776 compulsory taxation for the support of the clergy was set aside, in 1785 the basic guarantee of religious freedom was enacted, and in 1799 the old glebe lands were returned to the public domain. In this long struggle, which in its later stages became a battle to enforce the First Amendment to the federal Constitution, the Baptist cause was ably led by John Leland and Reuben Ford.

America's many other denominations responded to the issues of the revolutionary era in ways so similar to those already described that details are scarcely necessary. The Dutch Reformed church, experiencing the inevitable difficulties, formed its own Coetus in 1748; then under the leadership of Theodore Frelinghuysen it declared its freedom from Dutch control in 1755. (A small group of ministers wishing to remain under the aegis of the Classis of Amsterdam withdrew and formed the Conferentie.) The chartering of Queens' College (now Rutgers) at New Brunswick, New Jersey, in 1770 represented a further step in the direction of self-sufficiency. The next year the denomination was reunited, mainly through the efforts of John H. Livingston (1746–1825), a graduate of Yale (1762) and the last American to go to Holland for theological training and ordination. In 1810 Livingston became president and professor of theology at Rutgers, offices which he held until his death. His work in bringing together the Coetus and the Conferentie in a fully independent organization, as well as his decisive influence in shaping the constitution and preparing the hymn-book, earned for him the appellation "father of the Reformed Dutch Church in America." A fully autonomous Reformed Dutch Church in America did not come into being until 1792–94, however, when it organized itself along the presbyterial lines laid down by the Synod of Dort.

Lacking formal ties with a parent European body, the Lutheran church adjusted to the problems of the times with a minimum of trouble. Although Lutherans as a group were overwhelmingly behind the Patriot cause,[10] Muhlenberg, the patriarch, was a devoted subject of the house of Hanover, and he was therefore disinclined to involve the church in revolutionary or military activity. He found the singing of a *Te Deum* for a military victory not unlike celebrating an act of adultery which had evaded the law. His sons, however, took an intensely active part in the war and in the new republic. One left his pulpit to become a general in the Continental army, and another, who was prominent in politics, became the first Speaker of the House of Representatives.

Since the church itself had no organizational ties to sever, its structural adjustments were of minor importance, and the provisions of the constitution which had gradually evolved since the first synodical meeting in 1748 were formally entered in the minutes for 1781. This constitution was used also by the Synod of New York until its revision in 1792. There was no doubt a response to the American democratic spirit involved in the revision, which provided for lay voting. The most important influences were the subtle changes of attitude reflected in the liturgy published in 1786, which revealed the extent to which American evangelicalism and the Enlightenment had weakened the commitment of Lutherans to traditional liturgies.

[10] The two chief German-language newspapers, the *Geschict-Schreiber* of Christopher Sauer and the *Pennsylvanische Staatsbote* of John Henry Miller, were both critical of British rule.

Another sign of these broad cultural influences were the close ties established between Lutheran and German Reformed churches. As old confessional differences lost their force, the only differences perceived by the average layman were minor externals such as a preference for *Vater unser* (Lutheran) or *Unser Vater* (Reformed) in the Lord's Prayer, and variant ways of numbering the Ten Commandments. Hence many union congregations were formed, and in 1787 the two denominations joined forces in opening Franklin College in Lancaster, Pennsylvania, with one of Muhlenberg's sons as president. In 1818 these joint efforts were enlarged by plans for a joint evangelical seminary with no other doctrinal basis than that it should shield students from error and lead them to truth. This institution never did materialize; but in the previous year a joint Lutheran-Reformed *Gemeinschaftliches Gesangbuch* was published as a substitute for Muhlenberg's hymnbook of 1787.

But perhaps no single event illustrates the decay of historic Lutheran doctrinal standards so forcefully as the decision of the New York Ministerium in 1814 to replace Luther's catechism with a new one written by the synod president, Frederick Henry Quitman (1760–1858). Quitman (D.D., Harvard, 1814) was graduated from Halle after it had become a stronghold of rationalism, and his catechism is a monument to the enlightened theology of that age, "a skillful effort to Americanize German rationalism." He was a member of the New York Ministerium from 1796 until his death in 1832, its president for twenty-one years, and a learned student of later eighteenth-century German theology and biblical criticism.

For the Quakers the last half of the eighteenth century was doubly difficult. As pacifists they were subject to attack first for their principled inaction against the French and Indian menace, a dilemma which led them, after 1756, to abandon civil officeholding in Pennsylvania. As the revolutionary spirit grew, they were criticized both for the Loyalism they sometimes evinced and for their failure to aid the Patriot cause in any direct way. More seriously, their religious life, like that of the German "peace sects," proved highly vulnerable to the age's pervasive rationalism. The Quakers became a community withdrawn, but the withdrawal was chiefly social and political. Commerce became an even greater preoccupation than before (as it had for Dissenters in England ever since the Restoration), and gradually the intense evangelical fervor of George Fox was lost from view. Even the period's two greatest Quaker saints demonstrate this tendency. John Woolman (1720–72) exemplifies the movement of Quaker spirituality toward a generic form of mysticism and thus away from the christocentric piety of the seventeenth-century Friends, while the great humanitarian reformer, Anthony Benezet (1714–84), exemplifies a transition from piety to moralism very similar to that taking place in New England Puritanism during these same years.

CHURCH-STATE RELATIONS AND RELIGIOUS FREEDOM

It is ironic that a time of religious desuetude should also provide the circumstances for a resurgence of churchly activity in America, but such is the case—made doubly ironic by the fact that religious apathy contributed directly to the result. The "great tradition of the American churches," as it developed in the nineteenth century, depended upon—almost consisted of—(1) the reality of religious freedom, (2) the relatively distinct separation of church and state, (3) the growing acceptance of the idea of "denominationalism," (4) the rapid growth in favor of the "voluntary principle" in matters pertaining to church membership and support, and (5) the steady advance of patriotic piety, with its belief in the divinely appointed mission of the American nation. In the revolutionary era each of these aspects of the great tradition took on new importance.

Religious Freedom

The principle of religious freedom was formally recognized in at least two American colonies (Rhode Island and Maryland) at the time of their founding in the 1630s, though it survived only in the former. Later in the century it came to be recognized as well in the Carolinas, Georgia, New York, New Jersey, Delaware, and Pennsylvania, though Anglicanism was to receive some measure of public support in all but the latter two. Yet even where churches were established and undergirded by a parish system, as in Virginia, Maryland, Connecticut, and Massachusetts, the English Bill of Rights and toleration laws, coupled with the inescapable pluralism of the colonial peoples, brought about during the eighteenth century a continuous series of legal concessions. Baptists and Anglicans both made significant gains in Massachusetts; Baptists and many other groups were advancing in the South. By 1775 toleration verging on freedom had become a fundamental part of the long-term American revolution being enacted in the colonies.

Yet these libertarian trends accelerated during the revolutionary era, with the Virginia Declaration of Rights and the Declaration of Independence setting the pace. In every commonwealth a new spirit of liberty was evident—even Rhode Island's famous freedom was extended after Roger Williams's death by the removal of disabilities imposed on Roman Catholics. Toleration was granted to at least all Protestants in every colony. Most sensational of all, however, was the enactment of complete religious liberty in Virginia, where up to 1775 restrictions had been more strictly enforced than anywhere else. With the ratification of the federal Constitution (1787) and its first ten amendments (1791), the full range of Protestantism possessed liberties enjoyed nowhere else in the world. Roman Catholics suffered legal disabilities of various sorts, but in no other thoroughly Protestant land were they so free. At the same time humanists, deists, rational Unitarians, and persons with no professed religious beliefs were also at liberty to propagate their views and to aspire to (even to gain) the highest office in the land.

Separation of Church and State

Closely but not strictly coordinate with these new extensions of religious freedom was the disestablishment of churches. Most fundamental to this process was the federal Constitution itself, which in Article Six prohibited religious tests "as a qualification to any office or public trust under the United States," and the First Amendment, which stated that "Congress shall make no law respecting an establishment of religion or prohibiting the free exercise thereof." The ideals articulated in these provisions and the popular attitudes they reflected had already had effective results in the states where Anglicanism was established, though South Carolina experimented briefly with a constitution (1778) that established all forms of orthodox Protestantism. The most decisive acts of disestablishment were passed in Virginia, though here as in every other state but Rhode Island religious tests of one kind or another were required for state offices. Only in Massachusetts, Connecticut, and New Hampshire were the old colonial establishments continued. Even in the old Puritan strongholds, however, the era brought marked liberalization of old forms and great pressure for their complete elimination. New Hampshire disestablished the church in 1819. In 1817 Connecticut Baptists, Methodists, and Episcopalians joined other more political Jeffersonians to elect Oliver Wolcott of the Democratic Republican party to the governorship on an antiestablishmentarian platform. In 1818 the old charter was replaced by a new constitution providing that "no preference shall be given by law to any Christian sect or mode of worship." Two years later Maine came into the union, leaving behind its Massachusetts church-state heritage; and finally in 1833 Massachusetts abrogated what was left of its establishment by amending the constitutional provision which gave special privileges to the old congregational parishes, whether Orthodox or Unitarian. Beyond the original thirteen, no new state except Vermont allowed for any sort of an establishment.

Denominationalism

In one sense "denominationalism" is the most available term for the religious situation created in a land of many Christian churches and sects when none of them occupies a privileged situation and each has an equal claim to status as a Christian communion in the eyes of the law. In the United States, however, the term designates something more. It has theological dimensions, and especially among the mainstream churches of British origin, it very soon came to constitute a virtual ecclesiology (i.e. a theology of the Church). Denominational doctrine first of all repudiates the insistences of the Roman Catholic church, the churches of the "magisterial" Reformation, and of most sects that they alone are the true Church. This naturally leads to a repudiation of the idea that all Christians under any government must be comprehended in a single church. More positively, the theory affirmed an inclusive conception of the church, whereby each communion was respected, and, within limits, none was denied the right to the Christian name.

This form of ecumenicity was anticipated by the non-separating Puritans; but it was first clearly formulated for a single country of diverse religious views by the small group of Congregational "Dissenting Brethren" who objected to the presbyterian inflexibility of the Westminster Assembly. The Evangelical Revival of the eighteenth century gave this view wide currency in England, and John Wesley stated it forthrightly:

> I . . . refuse to be distinguished from other men by any but the common principles of Christianity. . . . I renounce and detest all other marks of distinction. But from real Christians, of whatever *denomination*, I earnestly desire not to be distinguished at all. . . . Dost thou love and fear God? It is enough! I give thee the right hand of fellowship.[11]

What the Evangelical Revival did for England the Great Awakening did for America, with the antidoctrinal animus of the Enlightenment and the cohesifying force of patriotism furthering the process. In the 1780s Wesley's statement might seem somewhat extreme to most church leaders, but the resurgence after 1800 would lead to even more exaggerated versions of the theory.

Beneath American denominationalism lay a large Protestant consensus, Reformed and Puritan in spirit, which further prepared American Christians to have done with establishments. This consensus also accounts for the also complete absence of anticlericalism that differentiates the American from the French Revolution and helps to explain why innumerable ties between church and state were left unsundered. Each of the major Protestant denominations contributed to the total effort and each of them in some situations felt the advantages of the result. Baptists like John Leland, leading the assault on Anglican privilege in Virginia, could almost assume the language of Thomas Paine on this subject or see eye to eye with a deist like Jefferson. In Connecticut Baptists and Anglicans would become allies in such a cause. For these reasons, the victories for religious freedom and separation of church and state were by no means won by "left wing sects" battling against magisterial churchmen. Statesmen and *denominational* leaders solved the problems of American pluralism

11 John Wesley, "The Character of a Methodist," *Works* (1841), 8:332–33; quoted in an important chapter on the subject by Winthrop S. Hudson, *American Protestantism*, p. 33.

in the only way that was consonant with the ideas and necessities of the American Revolution.

Voluntaryism

The form of church life that resulted from these revolutionary developments depended on the voluntary support of a committed laity. This typically American arrangement was accompanied by certain other developments, even in the Roman Catholic church: a tendency to foster the democratically governed local church and to discount or oppose hierarchies and higher judicatories of the church, a concern for practical achievements rather than doctrinal purity, and a pervasive and growing disinclination for formalism in worship, intellectualism in theology, and otherworldly conceptions of piety and morality. Because the religious situation became more competitive, ministers were obliged to please their constituencies—and hence lost authority and status. Naturally there were many who viewed the future of religion and the churches with foreboding. Lyman Beecher gloomily confronting the election defeat of the standing order in Connecticut is the best known example.

Yet Beecher lived to rejoice in the revived evangelicalism which freedom seemed to inspire; he came to see the Church of God as the gainer in the transaction. Everywhere his enthusiasm was echoed; and this great chorus of approval arose, above all, because the revivals of the early nineteenth century brought to the churches a greatly increased measure of influence. Evangelical attitudes and assumptions very nearly became constituent elements of Americanism. Because many of the customary ties between religion and government had not been severed, moreover, evangelical Protestants were able to create a new sort of "quasi-establishment," or what Elwyn Smith has termed a "voluntary establishment."[12] In this system Jews and Catholics would feel the brunt of Protestant condescension and discrimination as well as the fierceness of nativist campaigns; yet opportunities would by no means be foreclosed to them. Roman Catholics would experience such continuous expansion of their church that "Americanism," as an enthusiastic Catholic movement applauding democracy and "voluntaryism," would finally engage the most serious attention of European Catholics and the pope himself.

[12] Elwyn A. Smith, ed., *The Religion of the Republic*, p. 155.

Patriotism

Overarching all of the foregoing circumstances of the
churches was the patriotic spirit which soon pervaded every
aspect of the country's thought and feeling. When the Founding Fathers designed the new republic's Great Seal, they exposed their acceptance of an old Puritan idea that Providence had assigned a world mission to the American nation.
In effect they reaffirmed the words Governor John Winthrop
had uttered in 1630: "The God of Israel is among us. . . .
We shall be as a city upon a hill." E PLURIBUS UNUM—
ANNUIT CŒPTIS—MDCCLXXVI—NOVUS ORDO SECLORUM. With
this sublimely confident and optimistic principle the Federal
Union entered upon its destiny—a beacon to all peoples and
a refuge for the oppressed. With the passing years a new
kind of national feeling came into existence. The Union became a transcendent object of reverence, a stern author of
civic obligations as well as a source of faith and hope. Americans became stewards of a sacred trust, while the country's
statesmen, orators, and poets gradually brought a veritable
mystical theology of the Union into being:

> Sail on, O Union, strong and great!
> Humanity with all its fears,
> With all its hopes of future years,
> Is hanging breathless on thy fate!

So would Longfellow hymn the national majesty. "The Union
exists in absolute integrity," William H. Seward would declare; even if crucified, it must rise again, triumphant.[13]
From the start both national reverence and Christian piety
came to be seen as intrinsic elements in the religion of Americans. It thus became the duty of the churches to uphold the
sacred trust and yet avoid the temptations of idolatry; to remind men of the country's ideals and yet preach that the God

[13] Paul C. Nagle, *One Nation Indivisible: The Union in American Thought, 1776–1861*, pp. 107, 216–17; see also by the same
author *This Sacred Trust: American Nationality, 1798–1898*; and
compare the statement by Alexis de Tocqueville in the epigraph
to Part IV, p. 468. The Latin in the Great Seal may be translated: ONE OUT OF MANY—[GOD] HAS SMILED ON OUR UNDER-
TAKINGS—1776—A NEW ORDER OF [OR FOR] THE AGES.

of Israel is a Judge of all nations. But in decade after decade the supreme difficulty of that task would be exhibited. Patriotism would protect and enliven the churches, yet threaten their integrity.

So it was that the unique institutional and ideological heritage of colonial America passed through the turmoil of revolution—transformed but yet intact. Many long-hidden implications became explicit affirmations, while old informal working arrangements were enacted into law. The pragmatic compromises and undefined aspirations of the past became guiding principles of the first new nation.

IV

The Golden Day of Democratic Evangelicalism

Upon my arrival in the United States, the religious aspect of the country was the first thing that struck my attention; and the longer I stayed there the more did I perceive the great political consequences resulting from this state of things, to which I was unaccustomed. In France I had almost always seen the spirit of religion and the spirit of freedom pursuing courses diametrically opposed to each other; but in America I found that they were intimately united, and that they reigned in common over the same country.

Religion in America takes no direct part in the government of society, but nevertheless it must be regarded as the foremost of the political institutions of that country; for if it does not impart a taste for freedom, it facilitates the use of free institutions. Indeed, it is in this same point of view that the inhabitants of the United States themselves look upon religious belief. I do not know whether all the Americans have a sincere faith in their religion, for who can search the human heart? But I am certain that they hold it to be indispensable to the maintenance of republican institutions. This opinion is not peculiar to a class of citizen or to a party, but it belongs to the whole nation, and to every rank of society.

Alexis de Tocqueville, *Democracy in America* (1835)

The Second Great Awakening began during the 1790s in New England with scattered renewals of piety in various towns. It then gathered momentum in the early decades of the new century. In the southern back country Baptists and Methodists kept the First Wakening alive and carried it over the mountains to the new settlements in the Old Southwest. But the most cataclysmic outbreaks of religious enthusiasm occurred in Kentucky at the great camp meetings of 1800 and 1801—most memorably at Cane Ridge. Thereafter revivalism became a steady feature of advancing Protestantism throughout the nineteenth century and into the early twentieth. But the antebellum period was the great time of evangelical triumph. These were the days above all when the "Evangelical United Front" took up the manifold causes of moral renewal, missionary advance, and humanitarian reform —with revival preaching almost always leading the way. Its aim was to bring the gospel to all America and to heathen lands abroad, but primarily it hoped to make America the world's great example of a truly Protestant republic. The institution by which this vast program was carried out was the interdenominational voluntary association, one society for each cause: missions, antidueling, Sunday schools, temperance, Sabbath-keeping, and any number of other worthy objectives. Less worthy were the attacks on Masonry, Mormonism, and Catholicism. Most decisive for the nation was the great crusade against slavery and the "Slavocracy," which is treated in Part VI.

Another sign of the reforming spirit was the rise of utopian socialism and the founding of communitarian ventures, some native, some originating in Europe, some fervently religious, others explicitly secular. In this experimental atmosphere, moreover, unconventional prophets and radical church reformers seemed always to find a following, and three memorable American contributions to world religion had their origin: Christian restorationism, led by Alexander Campbell; Seventh-Day Adventism, which grew out of the millennial furor aroused by William Miller; and above all, Mormonism.

But there were many other sectarian movements which stayed within or only slightly transgressed the limits of evangelicalism. Despite controversies and schisms—or perhaps because of them—evangelical Protestant churches, with their message and methods tuned to the patriotic aspirations of a young nation, reached their high point of cultural influence.

24

THE EMERGENCE OF AMERICAN UNITARIANISM

Early in the spring of 1776, British officials in Boston recognized the hopelessness of their military situation, and on 17 March they withdrew their troops, little realizing that they were providing future Irish-Americans with a perpetual occasion for the joint celebration of Saint Patrick's Day and the British Evacuation. The army, about eight thousand in number, and more than eleven hundred refugees began their embarkation at four in the morning; in less than six hours, all were aboard, and before ten o'clock, they were under way. The flower of Massachusetts Anglicanism sailed with them, including Henry Caner, the aged rector of King's Chapel. When Caner's assistant departed in the following November, this church had perhaps the largest measure of religious freedom in the town; it was beholden to neither the Church of England nor that of New England. In 1777 the chapel building was "loaned" to the Old South congregation, whose meetinghouse had been made into a riding school by the British army; but after 1782 the remaining members decided to reactivate the church. As a lay reader they called James Freeman, a Harvard graduate of strong liberal tendencies, who in 1785 introduced substantial revisions in the Book of Common Prayer. When both Bishop Seabury of Connecticut and Bishop Provoost of New York refused to recognize the church as Anglican, Freeman was ordained by the senior warden on 18 November 1787, and "the first Episcopal church in New England, became the first Unitarian church in America."[1]

[1] Francis William Pitt Greenwood, *History of King's Chapel in Boston* (Boston, 1863), p. 139. The open avowal of liberal sentiments was greatly encouraged by a visitor from England, William

The liberal "revolution" at King's Chapel between 1776 and 1787 was outwardly an isolated phenomenon. Yet it was symptomatic of spiritual changes in the Boston conscience that ran far deeper than men realized, and it proved a portent of other disruptions to follow. King's Chapel is especially valuable as a symbol because it points to the immense significance of Anglican latitudinarianism as the means by which the century's harsher forms of religious radicalism were transmuted into a benign, optimistic, and utterly respectable Christian rationalism. This Anglican response had an immense effect on the dissenting traditions in England, and both of these in turn continued to have a compelling effect on New England thought, an effect which the Revolution actually made more acceptable. In other words, the King's Chapel incident signalized the gradual maturation of a long continuing New England trend.

The "broad and catholick" party had emerged in 1699 with the formation of the Brattle Street Church (which would eventually keep Unitarian company with King's Chapel) and the election of John Leverett to the presidency of Harvard College. As this "catholicity" had assumed the lineaments of Arminianism, it had aroused the fears and defined the life task of Jonathan Edwards. As it waxed in strength, it had involved the New Divinity men in incessant debate which grew in intensity as the years passed. By the end of the war a self-conscious group of liberals proud of their role in the revolutionary cause had emerged; and by the end of the century more than fifty ministers announced their membership in it by forthright publication. Even at the time of James Freeman's ordination there were many Congregational ministers who half-consciously envied the freedom of that church's pulpit.

Arminianism flourished best in the "maritime province" of New England, those towns along the Atlantic coast from Longfellow's birthplace in Portland to Channing's in Newport. Indeed, such tendencies were becoming apparent even while the Mathers yet lived. During the early years of the

Hazlitt, father of the famous essayist and an active Unitarian. James Freeman (1759–1835) was a follower of Joseph Priestley and more radical than most Boston Unitarians of his time, a determinist ("Necessitarian") in metaphysics and a "humanitarian" in Christology.

republic this area was to be the stronghold of Federalism, implacable in its suspicion of France and Thomas Jefferson, warm in its regard for England and the settled order of things. The focus of its intellectual life was Harvard; but because of its orientation toward the sea and its commercial ties with England, a certain cosmopolitanism characterized its outlook. With an economic life constantly strengthened by a world at war, it had brought forth an impressive merchant aristocracy that preferred a religious stance looking out on wide contemporary horizons rather than back to old Puritan ideals. After the Tory-Anglican exodus, these aspirations affected the Congregational churches more than ever before.

At the same time, one must recognize that the churches of eastern Massachusetts were peculiarly open to these influences. As did all Puritan churches, they had a venerable tradition of respect for the light of reason. To the enlightened mind of John Adams it might seem that the first founders were "enthusiasts," but the more patient scholarship of a later day has shown how persistently the Puritans tended to make revelation rational. They did not understand God's truth as bare, dogmatic fiat.

> New England had never been of that mind; it had always assimilated doctrine within the nexus of a logical system. . . . Because man is still benighted, the defects of his reason are supplied by the Bible, in which he must believe, not because the content is reasonable but because the testimonies are convincing. Thus he becomes rationally persuaded of irrational mysteries, such as the Trinity, because, in a phrase originated long before the Reformation, the truths of revelation may be above reason but are not contrary to it.[2]

The church covenants of the early Puritans, moreover, were so simple as to allow of almost any interpretation. At Salem, where in later days the liberal faith was to flourish so verdantly, the saints of 1629 had said:

> We Covenant with the Lord and one with another, and doe bynd ourselves in the presence of God, to walke together in

[2] Perry Miller, *The New England Mind: From Colony to Province*, p. 422.

all his waies, according as he is pleased to reveale himself
unto us in his Blessed word of truth.

Where New Divinity men had not moved in and revised
these covenants, people could "walke together" into a theological world wholly removed from the covenantal faith of
their fathers—and so they gradually did. In Massachusetts,
where the Mather "Proposals" of 1705 had been defeated,
there was no synodical or consociational means of hindering
either the progress of liberal views or the ordination of liberal
ministers. In the Bay area even the ministerial associations
were weak, and that of Boston did not take measures for
licensing candidates for the ministry until 1792. In such a
context it is hardly surprising that the "self-evident truths" of
liberalism would finally lead more than three-fourths of the
hundred oldest churches of eastern Massachusetts away from
their orthodox allegiance.

THE SHAPING OF A LIBERAL FAITH

In view of many foregoing observations on the Enlightenment, no detailed examination of New England's emerging
liberalism is necessary; but a brief survey of its central tenets
may serve to make this movement less of an abstraction—
especially since each of these tenets continually involved its
adherents in serious biblical exegesis, strenuous theological
endeavor, and much acrimonious argument.

A firm opposition to revivalism and the whole pietistic emphasis on a religion of the heart was a settled conviction with
the liberals. As this opposition came into the open during the
Great Awakening, it created a deep and longlasting rift in
New England church life. Its leader during his long pastorate
at the First Church in Boston was Charles Chauncy (1705–
87), whose *Seasonable Thoughts* of 1743 still stands as the
classic expression of this attitude. He and his colleagues also
reshaped the old preaching tradition. The sermon became a
well-styled lecture, in which the truths of religion and the
moral duties of man were expounded in as reasonable a
manner as possible. Sermons thus became a species of polite
literature, to whose perfection the prose tradition of Addison
and Steele was more important than the homiletical corpus
of Puritanism. Reviews of published sermons frequently were

critiques of syntax and style rather than of content. Social stratification began to emerge as a side effect, as unlettered people with little or no appreciation for Augustan periods drifted away from the liberal churches and found their way into the more popular societies of Baptists, Methodists, Universalists, and revivalistic Congregationalists.

Closely related to antirevivalism and almost inseparable from it was a deep-seated disinclination to regard a specific experience of conversion as essential to the Christian life. The liberals did not deny the possibility of conversions (even Channing traced his mature views to two decisive experiences), but only their necessity. In terms of old Puritan concepts these men also favored the Half-Way Covenant and the still larger concessions of the Brattle Street Church's manifesto, yet their aim was not (as it had been for the early advocates of halfway membership) to strengthen the baptismal covenant. They affirmed rather that the Christian life was a continuous rational process of self-dedication. A radical distinction between communicant and noncommunicant members was seen as undemocratic, illiberal, and anachronistic, especially since the Lord's Supper was regarded more and more as neither a sacramental "means of grace" nor a "converting ordinance," but as simple memorial.

The central doctrinal characteristic of the liberal movement was that which gave its early adherents the name "Arminian." They assaulted the Reformed or Westminster conceptions of God, man, and the divine-human relationship, stressing God's role as the Architect and Governor of the universe, though also placing an unmistakably Christian emphasis on his fatherhood. Yet this was a fatherhood bereft of awfulness and wrath, defined chiefly in terms of "benevolence," one of the chief marks of which was that men were not consigned to heaven or hell irrespective of their actual belief and willful deeds. Man was a free agent—John Locke, democratic statesmen, and later and less ambiguously, the Scottish philosophers had given assurance of that. Man worked out his own salvation and suffered his just deserts. God's grace and mercy were needed, to be sure; yet with regard to the nature of man and human ability, these liberal ministers showed perhaps a greater measure of confidence than any significant group of churchmen in the Reformed tradition. And what buoyed their confidence above all was the exhilaration of national independence, the economic and social advances of the American people, and the great destiny (already manifest) of this New World democracy. The idea prevailed widely that "this new man, this American" was a new Adam, sinless, innocent—mankind's great second chance. Nowhere was it given so well-rooted a Christian interpretation as among these New England liberals, whose ideas on man were far more determinative than the ideas about the Godhead which later won them the name "Unitarian."

Departures from traditional views on the Trinity were rare, cautious, and long-delayed. Conrad Wright is no doubt correct in saying that "Anti-Trinitarianism in New England before the Revolution was in a stage comparable to Arminianism before the Great Awakening."[3] Yet there were immensely influential English thinkers who led this way, above all, the Anglican Samuel Clarke, with his *Scripture-Doctrine of the Trinity* (1712), and the pro-American Unitarian Richard Price. These men, like their American followers, took what was then called the Arian position that Christ, though less than God, was more than man—a preexistent divine being. Only James Freeman of King's Chapel and a very few others went on to the Socinian, or "humanitarian" view that Jesus was a man with a special divine mission. In general, however, these liberal Congregationalists were probably not far in spirit from those leaders of the Protestant Episcopal church who quietly dropped the Athanasian Creed from the prayer book. Had the issue not been seized upon by their enemies, it might have lain dormant.

Liberal ideas concerning man's relation to God were to lead eventually to belief in universal salvation, or at least future probation,[4] but the early liberals were similarly cautious on this issue. That redemption is for all men is clearly implied in their ideas on the benevolence of the diety, but universalism was seldom advocated. Chauncy seems to have begun his full-length exposition of the doctrine as early as 1750, but his manuscript was not published until 1784, and then anonymously in London. His fellow ministers never made universalism a prominent part of their preaching except insofar as they tended to ignore the doctrine of eternal dam-

[3] Conrad Wright, *The Beginnings of Unitarianism,* p. 202.
[4] Belief in future probation involves the idea that man's life on earth is not the sole basis for his eternal destiny, but that after this life God carries man from strength to strength until (it was sometimes argued) all men shall behold the beatific vision.

nation. It was left for the Universalists to take the initiative on these matters; but they were a movement utterly different in origin and in social background, so that even in the twentieth century, when all doctrinal distinctions have faded from view, these two New England movements of religious liberalism have only slowly begun to coalesce.

A final issue on which the liberals took a firm stand was that of religious freedom and complete congregational independency. While New Divinity men were busy devising new and more detailed church covenants, the liberals defended the old simple ones. When anyone proposed tests of orthodoxy, or—worse yet—insisted that closer organization of the churches was necessary, they were at the forefront of the opposition. They revived and applauded the early arguments of John Wise, who in 1710 and 1717 had brought natural law theories to the defense of true congregationalism, but abhorred Nathanael Emmons's thesis that "unity of sentiment among Christians [was] necessary to unity of affections." They felt that "harmony in the spirit" could be maintained without coercion, and that the idea of "heresy" was a relic of less enlightened ages. On the other hand, they rarely questioned the privilege of legal establishment which their churches enjoyed. Like their orthodox brethren, the liberals regarded a tax-supported church as essential to the preservation of morality and the regulation of society.

THE OUTBREAK OF CONTROVERSY

For two decades King's Chapel stood alone in its "Unitarianism," and ecclesiastical peace was maintained among Massachusetts Congregationalists despite the growing strength of Arminianism in the Boston area. Then just after the turn of the century, while camp-meeting religion was expanding in Kentucky and signs of a "Second Awakening" were stirring orthodox hopes in Connecticut, death jogged the wheel of fortune by removing two key divines in the Boston community. David Tappan, Hollis Professor of Divinity at Harvard, died in 1803, and in 1804, before Tappan could be replaced, so did President Joseph Willard. Both men were moderate Calvinists, much respected and widely mourned, whom it would not have been easy to replace under any circumstances. It became impossible to do so without controversy when Jedidiah Morse (1761–1826), minister in Charlestown and an overseer of the college, forthrightly and publicly opened the doctrinal dispute by demanding that both appointments go to sound and orthodox men. Inflamed feelings erupted in many quarters. The governing boards of Harvard were seriously divided, and a long delay ensued; but Morse lost. Henry Ware (1764–1845), the minister in Hingham and a well-known liberal, became Hollis Professor in 1805. In 1806 Samuel Webber, another liberal, was elected president, to be followed in 1810 by John Thornton Kirkland (1770–1840), not only a liberal but a much more dynamic and far-seeing leader than Harvard had had since Leverett a century earlier. After Kirkland's election, three more liberals were appointed to the faculty, young John Quincy Adams among them, and the die was cast. Harvard was firmly in liberal hands.

But to have considered the issue closed would have been to reckon without Morse. A native of Connecticut and admirer of its church way, a graduate of Yale now ministering at Harvard's back door, he was not a man to ignore. A national reputation as America's leading geographer and an extremely large network of friends among both New Divinity men and the moderate Calvinists of his own persuasion made him even more formidable. Morse had come to the conclusion that the two orthodox parties must draw together in the present danger, and to that end he opened the long-drawn-out "Unitarian Controversy." His first decisive act was a published blast, *True Reasons on Which the Election of a Hollis Professor of Divinity in Harvard College was Opposed at the Board of Overseers* (1805); and he soon after founded the *Panoplist*, a periodical which was used as a sounding board for orthodox viewpoints. He then began engineering the coalition which in 1808 was to found a new and rigorously orthodox theological seminary at Andover, Massachusetts. Although there were many active participants in this ambitious undertaking, the seminary is undoubtedly Morse's most enduring ecclesiastical memorial. Andover almost immediately became a major rallying point for orthodoxy. Its faculty was brilliant and aggressive, its student body large and enthusiastic. In a few years its influence was being felt all across the country and in farflung mission fields abroad.

Yet not even the founding of this "West Point of Orthodoxy" satisfied the relentless Morse. In 1815 he aimed a blow at the standing order itself by publishing a chapter from Thomas Belsham's *Life of Theophilus Lindsey,* in which the bellicose English Unitarian recounts the progress of Unitarianism in America and quotes selected statements of the Boston liberals. Morse accompanied his reprint of some one hundred pages with a quotation of Belsham's radical creed, and strongly implied (as did a simultaneous review article in the *Panoplist*) that this creed was accepted by many respected Boston ministers. He concluded with a strident call to break off communion with the crypto-Unitarians. It was a charge which the accused could not ignore in silence.

Nor did they. Almost immediately the quiet and dignified young minister of the Federal Street Church, William Ellery Channing, made reply. In a manner befitting his nature and position he published an open letter to one of his ministerial colleagues, Samuel Thatcher of the Brattle Street Church, lamenting the rudeness and injustice of the attack. Samuel Worcester of Salem, "an inflexible Hopkinsian," hastened to reply, thus beginning a notable exchange of controversial tracts in which he published three and Channing two open letters during 1815. Channing was much more sensitive to the semantic problem than some of his opponents, and well aware of the emotional images conjured up by party labels. He pleaded that "earnestly desiring Christians" seriously try to gain "accurate ideas of the most important point in the present controversy."

Let them learn the distinction between Trinitarianism and Unitarianism. Many use these words without meaning, and are very zealous about sounds. Some suppose that Trinitarianism consists in believing in the Father, the Son and the Holy Spirit. But we all believe in these; we all believe that the *Father* sent the *Son,* and gives, to those that ask, the *Holy Spirit.* We are all Trinitarians, if this is belief in Trinitarianism. But it is not. The Trinitarian believes that the one God is *three distinct persons,* called Father, Son, and Holy Ghost; and he believes that each is the only true God, and yet that the three are only one God. This is Trinitarianism. The Unitarian believes that there is but one person possessing supreme Divinity, even the Father. This is the great distinction; let it be kept steadily in view. . . . I am persuaded, that under these classes of high Unitarians many Christians ought to be ranked who call themselves orthodox and are Trinitarians. In fact, as the word Trinity is sometimes used, we all believe it. Christians ought not to be separated by a sound.[5]

Channing's definitive word, however, was delayed until 1819, when he used the occasion of Jared Sparks's ordination at an explicitly Unitarian church in Baltimore to deliver what became the manifesto of a new liberal faith, "Unitarian Christianity." The Baltimore sermon was recognized immediately for what it was intended to be: a comprehensive and forthright proclamation of principles. Its publication quickly drew replies from the two most powerful defenders of orthodoxy at Andover Seminary.

The strongest formulation of the biblical argument from the orthodox camp was published by Moses Stuart (1780–1852), a disciple of Timothy Dwight and a former minister of the First Church in New Haven, who since 1812 had been revolutionizing American biblical studies as a professor at Andover. By 1819 Stuart had become a learned scholar of Hebrew with probably a larger command of German critical literature than any other American. President Kirkland had not allowed Andover to preempt the theological field, however, and by 1811 he had begun to gather the nucleus of a divinity school around Henry Ware. Andrews Norton (1786–1853) had become Dexter Professor of Sacred Literature in 1819, and in the same year he answered Stuart with *A Statement of Reasons for Not Believing the Doctrines of the Trinitarians*. This production grew with the passing years from an essay to a large book, reaching final form in 1833. Seen in its entirety, this long controversy documents a momentous transition in American Christianity. After Stuart and Norton had made their mark, it would be almost impossible for men to debate biblical matters without taking full account of historico-critical questions. Advancing scholarship in both camps would soon make Channing's manifesto of 1819 a somewhat archaic monument to enlightened rationalism.

In the meantime, however, the view of human nature set forth in Channing's Baltimore sermon had been challenged by Leonard Woods (1774–1854), whose *Letters to Unitarians* (1820) opened another famous debate. Henry Ware

[5] William Ellery Channing, *Remarks on the Rev. Dr. Worcester's Letter to Mr. Channing on the "Review of American Unitarianism" in a Late Panoplist* (Boston, 1815), pp. 38–39.

picked up his challenge, and the so-called Wood 'n Ware Controversy was under way. Woods was a graduate of Harvard (1796), who had studied theology with Charles Backus of Somers, Connecticut. Upon joining the Andover faculty in 1808, he had become the chief mediator between the Hopkinsians and the moderate Calvinists. Woods was also a forceful if somewhat uninventive champion of orthodoxy. Ware, on the other hand, displayed great acuity in his replies, thus fully justifying the confidence the liberals had placed in him. The debate extended for four years and ran to five good-sized volumes, two by Woods (besides the *Letters*) and three by Ware. Ware's central claim was that man was essentially good, and that "even in the worst men good feelings and principles are predominant." Despite admitted metaphysical difficulties in his own position he insisted that Andoverian theology was "immoral." Wood countered with biblical, empirical, and philosophical arguments drawn from the arsenal of the New Divinity men, especially Nathanael Emmons, of whose distinctive views Woods was a major champion. Taken together the volumes of this debate constitute one of the best theological discussions of human nature in American church history.

EMERGENCE OF A UNITARIAN DENOMINATION

While these theologians (and many others) were taking the issues to the court of public opinion, other institutional problems were being settled. Individual churches were coming down on one side or the other of the matter or, as frequently happened, on both sides—in which case a division would occur. Jedidiah Morse's church in Charlestown suffered a secession of liberal sympathizers in 1816. The First Church in Cambridge was also divided, with Abiel Holmes (father of the "Autocrat of the Breakfast Table") leading out the conservatives. In the Bay area many churches, Boston's First Church, for example, simply became Unitarian by gradual acceptance, without conflict, schism or change of covenants, and often without even a change of name. Park Street Church in the center of Boston—memorable for Peter Banner's fine architectural design—was organized in 1809 as a separately incorporated and gathered church, and it has remained a bastion of orthodoxy to this day. But the determining event of this sort was the 1820 "Dedham decision" of the Massachusetts Supreme Court. Written by Chief Justice Isaac Parker, a Unitarian, it held that the larger parish or religious society had the legal power to call a minister and retain control of the property, even if a majority of the communicant members of the church were opposed. With this precedent on record, a great many of the old territorial parishes of eastern Massachusetts moved into the Unitarian fold.

Unitarians meanwhile were not organizationally idle. The Boston Ministerial Association became a veritable Unitarian agency, and in 1820 Channing organized the Berry Street Conference as an informal advisory body for the Unitarian ministers of Massachusetts. There was considerable disagreement as to how much denominational form the movement should take; Channing favored a minimum, while Andrews Norton advocated a more definite and responsible organization. The American Unitarian Association, founded in 1825, was something of a compromise; it did assume certain denominational functions, yet its support from both churches and individuals was meager. Although at the time of its organization there were 125 churches under the Unitarian banner, most of them venerable, socially prominent, and conveniently grouped for collective action, the association was able to carry on little more than a modest propaganda campaign. The series of tracts which it published prior to the Civil War, however, is one of the most distinguished collections of denominational literature that any American church has produced.

Unitarians also expressed themselves in other less popular ways, however. One means was the learned journal, and in this field they were particularly successful. At the beginning of the century the *Monthly Anthology* (1803–11), published in Boston, pioneered in the field of literary journalism. It soon died, but in due time two other outstanding and long-lived journals emerged from its remains: the *North American Review* in 1815 and the *Christian Examiner* in 1824. The first of these was somewhat less religiously oriented, but both were outstanding for the wide range and high quality of writing they carried. The editors of these two journals alone constitute something of a hall of fame of the New England flowering: Edward Everett, William Emerson (father of the poet), George Ticknor, Jared Sparks, Richard Henry Dana,

Henry Adams, James Russell Lowell, and Edward Everett Hale.

Harvard College also became essentially and conscientiously Unitarian. The divinity school which gradually took shape between 1811 and 1819 professed to be simply Christian; but its faculty and students were Unitarian and remained so with few exceptions during almost the entire nineteenth century. Although its faculty rarely numbered more than three full-time teachers, it naturally had a great deal to do with forming the mind of the Unitarian ministry. Until after the Civil War, moreover, the entire university was pervaded by the spirit of the movement. Most of its presidents and faculty were Unitarians, whether ministers or devout laymen, while the curriculum in almost all of its parts reflected the outlook and presuppositions of Unitarianism. Professors of rhetoric John Quincy Adams and Edward Tyrell Channing (William Ellery's brother), philosopher Francis Bowen, professors of modern languages George Ticknor, Longfellow, and Lowell, and even the distinguished professor of medicine, Oliver Wendell Holmes, were all consciously Unitarian and served to make Harvard a major force in the entire Unitarian movement. Add to this the immense literary output of two or three generations of early Unitarians, and it becomes clear that the "flowering of New England" which Van Wyck Brooks made a household word in America was chiefly a flowering of Unitarianism—though some of its representatives (as we shall see) were rebellious and unappreciative of their fathers' piety.

The "representative man" of Unitarian Christianity during the period when it provided the religious background for the American renaissance was unquestionably William Ellery Channing (1780–1842). Both for his contemporaries and for subsequent historians he was the Luther of the Boston reformation; and during his single forty-year ministry the Federal Street Church became, after Harvard, the central institution of Unitarianism. Though he was to reject the New Divinity, Channing was grateful to his youthful nurture under the ministry of Samuel Hopkins in the Second Church of Newport, Rhode Island. He came to Harvard College at a time of religious desuetude, but nevertheless he looked back fondly to a conversion experience there which he traced to the Scottish thinkers and to Richard Price—who saved him, he said, from the materialistic implications of Locke. While employed as a private tutor in Virginia his religious commitment deepened further. He entered upon theological studies and in 1803 he was ordained.

From that time until his death, Channing's influence constantly increased, while his theological stance shifted from a softened form of Hopkinsianism to the "liberal faith" whose champion he became. Except for a few reviews, his large corpus of published works consists entirely of sermons, lectures, and addresses; and he died with a larger, more systematic presentation of his views still unwritten. Had he carried out this plan he would, no doubt, have set forth the broadminded consensus of his ministerial colleagues as to the Bible and its interpretation, miracles, God, Christ, and the mission of the Church. Channing perpetuated an essentially eighteenth-century outlook, yet he did so with a generosity of spirit, a disinclination for combat, and an openness to modern nuances that quite rightly led Emerson in his old age to look back upon him as the "bishop" of early Transcendentalism. In his Federal Street ministry he brought "convincement" and moral rededication to a wide range of socially prominent and intellectually distinguished men and women.

It seems to me of singular importance [he proclaimed in 1830], that Christianity should be recognized and presented in its true character, as I have aimed to place it before you this day. The low views of our religion, which have prevailed too long, should give place to this highest one. They suited perhaps darker ages. But they have done their work, and should pass away. Christianity should now be disencumbered and set free. . . . It should come forth from the darkness and corruption of the past in its own celestial splendour, and in its divine simplicity. It should be comprehended as having but one purpose, the perfection of human nature, the elevation of men into nobler beings.[6]

His "perfectibilitarian" message brought self-confidence to those who heard him, but making them dissatisfied with the contemporary situation, it sent them into the world to reform society and renovate man's spiritual condition.

[6] "The Essence of the Christian Religion," from *The Perfect Life* (1873), in Sydney E. Ahlstrom, ed., *Theology in America: The Major Protestant Voices from Puritanism to Neo-orthodoxy,* p. 208.

THE ANTEBELLUM UNITARIAN ETHOS

As a Christian denomination Unitarianism during its flower-ing time was inseparable from its cultural context. It be-longed not only to a region, but in large degree to the upper social classes of that region. Unlike orthodox Congregation-alism it seemed bound to the town and city streets that the early Puritans had marked out and settled. Its missionary efforts in the West were generally unfruitful. Meadville Semi-nary, founded in western Pennsylvania in 1844 jointly with the Christian Connection, never developed a constituency. Unitarian churches that prospered outside the Boston region were usually organized by migrating Yankees, and they re-tained the character of isolated colonies. Outside of maritime New England liberalism was more effectively spread by Alex-ander Campbell or the Universalists, or by impious free-thinkers.[7] On the other hand, when Lyman Beecher left Litchfield, Connecticut, for a church in Boston, he felt like an alien. His revivalistic efforts gained no support or response from the people of status and learning, whom he himself identified as overwhelmingly Unitarian.

In New England's maritime province, however, Uni-tarianism did put its mark on a rich and distinctive culture; or, to put it another way, it articulated the moral and religious dimensions of that culture. But this was not a small or subservient role. No group of ministers so clearly earned the respect which Puritan tradition assigned to the clergy as did the Unitarians of this period. They were genuine moral and spiritual leaders, and the laity whom they influenced became a moving force in the social order in ways that were theologically congruent with the liberal faith. Unitarian preaching in an age of intellectual transition brought peace of

[7] Among the several "Christian" movements that coalesce with Campbell's to make up the Disciples of Christ was one which had New England origins as well as a following in the West. This "Christian Connection" was founded chiefly by Abner Jones (1772–1841) and Elias Smith, two Vermont laymen who objected to the tenets of "Calvinism." Unitarians cooperated with the Con-nection in maintaining Antioch College in Ohio, and they later took it over entirely. Horace Mann played a vital role in saving the institution. See chaps. 27 and 29 on the Disciples and the Universalists respectively.

mind to its hearers (too much peace, too little contrition, Lyman Beecher would have said); but it also encouraged philanthropy, humanitarianism, love of education and learning, and a strong sense of civic concern. Unitarianism thus gave meaning to certain fundamental aspects of the Puritan heritage which orthodoxy had had to abandon when it took up the banner of revivalism, perhaps because both revivalistic and rationalistic tendencies were latent in the original Puritan impulse. In any case, the guiding spirits of the movement, both lay and clerical, despite the handicap of many elitist assumptions, were a beneficent and enduring influence in a dozen realms. No adequate history of the later Social Gospel can ignore them; and they must also be credited with providing the circumstances that prospered a large part of the American renaissance. The old remark that Unitarian preaching was limited to "the fatherhood of God, the brotherhood of man, and the neighborhood of Boston," has more rhyme than reason in it. Only the geographical reference is approximately true. Yet when Unitarianism's aspiring spirit was conveyed to the nation in the literary forms of Bryant, Longfellow, Lowell, and Holmes, it was accepted, loved, and learned by heart. It undoubtedly changed the minds of many without their knowing it. Emerson's words about "corpse-cold Unitarianism" and its "pale negations" are equally unsatisfactory. The Christian Unitarianism that flourished in the Boston area in the first half of the nineteenth century was a distinctive, cogently reasoned religious movement that conceived of itself with some justice as the modern cutting edge of Protestantism. Yet its originality should not be exaggerated; it owed much to its closest neighbor in spirit, the rationalistic theology of eighteenth-century Anglicanism, and to the liberal movements in English Dissent which took the same hue. It also drew heavily upon the philosophic resources of the Scottish renaissance; indeed, the Scottish Philosophy nowhere found a task so fitted to its genius as when it provided rational undergirding for this liberal urbane culture. Obviously it was imbued with the optimism of the Enlightenment and of American democracy; but just as obviously, it had inherited the church ways and moral fervor of Puritanism, as well as something of the corporate concern of the Holy Commonwealths. It was thus a unique blending of seventeenth- and eighteenth-century traditions, American and British.

In doctrine the Unitarian movement continued along lines drawn by the early Arminians. It remained fervently biblical. The standard Unitarian commentaries wrestled with every verse of Saint Paul; the "extremes" of German scholarship and philosophy were no more acceptable to Unitarians than to Andoverians; the new geology and Darwinism would be received with equal or even greater alarm. Trinitarian formulations faded from their sermons and treatises, to be sure; but the Holy Spirit was regarded as a divine influence, while Jesus Christ if not God was indeed Teacher and Redeemer. There were sharp disagreements among them as to Christ's precise nature and the meaning of his atoning work; tendencies to Universalism were strong. Natural theology assumed a more important place in their thought than it did among their orthodox assailants, and the idea of progress decisively controlled their idea of human history and Last Things. Beneath all was their conviction as to the perfectibility of man —or as Channing put it, man's "likeness to God."

The rationalistic and liberal bent of their thinking did not mean that they ceased to be evangelical. Andrews Norton nearly deserved the appellation he won as the "Pope of Unitarianism," and no American labored more zealously to ward off attacks on "the genuineness of the Gospels" (the title of his major work), the miracles, and the finality of Christianity. Historical relativism, forms of "pantheism," and subjective notions of revelation became the chief objects of his polemic. This theological disposition was widely shared, and it was clearly expressed by the American Unitarian Association in 1853, when it was seeking to dissociate itself from the ideas of Emerson, Theodore Parker, and the Transcendentalists. After reaffirming its profound belief in the supernatural element of Christianity, the Association made a declaration that was often criticized for its overwrought prose:

We desire openly to declare our belief as a denomination, so far as it can be officially represented by the American Unitarian Association, that God, moved by his own love, did raise up Jesus to aid in our redemption from sin, did by him pour a fresh flood of purifying life through the withered veins of humanity and along the corrupted channels of the world, and is, by his religion, forever sweeping the nations with regenerating gales from heaven, and visiting

the hearts of men with celestial solicitations. We receive
the teachings of Christ, separated from all foreign admix-
tures and later accretions, as infallible truth from God.[8]

What particularly troubled the men who framed this effusive
statement was that the emergence of transcendentalism
seemed to fulfill a prophecy made by Moses Stuart in 1819,
that Unitarianism was a halfway house on the road to
infidelity. This embarrassing accusation was to loom large in
the so-called Second Unitarian Controversy, which Emerson
would help to precipitate. Before taking up that episode in
American intellectual history, however, it is necessary to survey other immensely influential church developments, which,
while contemporaneous with the emergence of Unitarianism,
were of another spirit entirely.

[8] *The Twenty-eighth Report of the American Unitarian Society*
(Boston, 1853), pp. 22, 23.

25

THE NEW ENGLAND THEOLOGY IN DEMOCRATIC AMERICA

When Jonathan Edwards died in 1758, the Great Awakening in New England was a thing of the past. But short-lived flames continued to shoot up in various localities from time to time, especially during Whitefield's later tours. In 1763–64 a more general awakening took place. Contention over revival issues, moreover, was almost continual, with church separations an ever recurring result. As a consequence, the Puritan body ecclesiastic as a whole became seriously divided. Over the decades three quite distinct parties emerged.

Most numerous at the outset were the Old Calvinists, or Moderates, who cherished the traditional doctrine and polity of New England as it had gradually adjusted to changing American circumstances. They accounted themselves orthodox and resented the excesses of revivalism which had brought so much unrest to the established order. By no means, however, did they repudiate the Puritan conviction that a circumcision of the heart—regeneration—was essential to the Christian life, nor did they cease to hope that the Holy Spirit would descend with special favor on whole communities and nations. Until the turn of the century men of this stamp were predominant at Yale, as were others of a somewhat more liberal tendency at Harvard. Although for some years after the Awakening Moderates held the largest number of pulpits in western Massachusetts and Connecticut, they were by nature rather undistinguished in strictly theological enterprises, and they won few new recruits to succeed them in the ministry. Yet many of them were undeniably accomplished men who revealed their gifts in diverse ways.

Among them were such distinguished leaders, for example, as Jedidiah Morse, minister in Charlestown, Massachusetts; David Tappan, professor of divinity at Harvard (1792–1803); Joseph Willard, president of Harvard (1781–1804); Thomas Clap, president of Yale (1740–66), who obtained a new charter for the college and moved to a middle position on revivals; Isaac Stiles (1697–1760) Clap's supporter in nearby North Haven, whose election sermon of 1742 has been called "the first public attack on the Great Awakening in New England"; and Isaac's son, Ezra Stiles (1727–95), an urbane and learned Congregational minister, after 1778 president of Yale, and possibly New England's most articulate and appealing Moderate. In 1761 he would look back on the "late enthusiasm" as a time when "multitudes were seriously, soberly, and solemnly out of their wits."

More liberal than the Moderates was a slowly growing party of "Arminians," as they were often called with no little inaccuracy.[1] Chiefly products of the "broad and catholick" culture championed at Harvard since Leverett's day, they usually went on to occupy pulpits in eastern Massachusetts. Charles Chauncy at Boston's First Church and the more radical Jonathan Mayhew at the West Church were most prominent. These serious and rationalistic ministers came only gradually to full consciousness of their divergence from the Reformed tradition. Social and intellectual ties kept them from a definitive break with the Old Calvinists until the disruptive events of the Unitarian controversy shattered the standing order in Massachusetts between 1805 and 1820.

The "New Divinity" men constituted a much more clearly delineated party. They acknowledged Edwards as their hero, and despite the distractions of Indian unrest, colonial wars,

[1] Named after the Dutch theologian Jacobus Arminius (1560–1609), whose views were condemned by the Synod of Dort (1618–19), Arminianism was a term used to designate almost any form of Reformed theology that modified the traditional doctrines of total depravity, limited atonement, or unconditional election and accentuated man's role in salvation. By the eighteenth century there were two major but not always clearly defined types of Arminianism, evangelical (with John Wesley as its greatest proponent) and rationalistic (with Daniel Whitby and John Taylor as representative advocates). The Arminians here referred to tended toward the latter type but often not decisively. Some may not technically have been Arminians at all. In America the term often was a synonym for "liberal" or "broad and catholic."

revolution, political upheaval, and religious dissension, they sought to establish their churches on strict principles of regenerate membership and on sharply defined (albeit new) standards of doctrinal orthodoxy. Almost all were graduates of Yale, and most of them were settled over churches in Connecticut and the Connecticut River valley. They were closely tied by teacher-student relationships, kinship, and marriage. Although they defended revivals and sought (with little success) to fan the fires of religious fervor anew, their concern with doctrine and metaphysics, their fondness for controversy, and their harsh and acrimonious ways tended to hinder those efforts; and their churches were often beset by declining membership, factional troubles, or open schism. Moderates and liberals often dismissed them as a "metaphysical school," yet they persisted, and at the end of the century they were rewarded by a Second Great Awakening, just when eastern Massachusetts was being swept into the ranks of Unitarianism.

The contribution of the New Divinity men to this result was almost entirely in the realm of ideas. Building on the older Puritan divinity as it had been enlivened in the Awakening and set on a new course by Edwards, they maintained and extended the New England Theology. They thus contributed creatively to the single most brilliant and most continuous indigenous theological tradition that America has produced. The course of its development through a century and a half belongs in part to later chapters, but here we shall treat its growth in the difficult half-century after Edwards's dismissal from Northampton. Even in this formative period there were almost a dozen men who would deserve consideration in a general account, but four in particular merit special attention. Two of these, Samuel Hopkins and Joseph Bellamy, are in a special sense "Edwardseans" in that they studied with Edwards, became his personal friends, and dedicated themselves to developing and defending his doctrines. Closely associated with them is Jonathan Edwards, Jr., only thirteen years old when his father died, who studied under both Hopkins and Bellamy and who belongs to the inner circle. Nathanael Emmons belongs in a class by himself as a highly distinctive, almost eccentric theological genius, who in spite of personal idiosyncrasies belongs to the Edwardsean tradition. In the works of these men one may find many grounds for the complaint that they degraded Puritan theology by turning it into a lifeless system of apologetics. But it is equally important to perceive in these intricate theological reasonings a series of transmutations that form a bridge between the still recognizably Puritan outlook of Edwards and nineteenth-century American Protestantism.

Not the least of their achievements is the degree to which the New Divinity men kept alive a tradition of theological concern in the laity. Horace Bushnell described the services of his home church in rural Connecticut during "the Age of Homespun."

> There is no affectation of seriousness in the assembly, no mannerism of worship; some would say, too little of the manner of worship. They think of nothing, in fact, save what meets their intelligence and enters into them by that method. They appear like men who have digestion for strong meat, and have no conception that trifles more delicate can be of any account to feed the system. Nothing is dull that has the matter in it, nothing long that has not exhausted the matter. . . . Under their hard and . . . stolid faces, great thoughts are brewing, and these keep them warm. Free-will, fixed fate, foreknowledge absolute, Trinity, redemption, special grace, eternity—give them anything high enough, and the tough muscle of their inward man will be climbing sturdily into it; and if they go away having something to think of, they have had a good day.[2]

Evidence of such theological maturity abounds, even in the writings of a statesman like Roger Sherman. Governor John Treadwell of Connecticut (1745–1823) also published his views on various controverted points and earned serious responses from the divines.

ARCHITECTS OF THE NEW DIVINITY

Joseph Bellamy (1719–90)

Of the early life of this first and most undeviating of Jonathan Edwards's disciples, little is known except that he

[2] Horace Bushnell, "The Age of Homespun," in *Work and Play* (New York, 1864), pp. 387 ff.

was born in Cheshire, Connecticut, educated at Yale (B.A. 1735), and trained for a time in the Edwards household. He was ordained to the ministry at Bethlehem, Connecticut, in 1738, where he remained throughout his career. Here a revival began while he was still a candidate-preacher. He was, as Ezra Stiles put it, "highly carried away with New Lightism in 1741," and during the Great Awakening his talents were widely demanded. In later years, however, his attitudes were much moderated "by the friendly counsels of President Edwards, to whom he was greatly attached." Though called to the First Presbyterian Church of New York City in 1754, Bellamy chose to devote a full half-century to his Bethlehem parish founding there what was possibly the country's first Sabbath school. He was much beloved for his pastoral care, and his home became a favorite resort of theological students, with more than fifty future ministers being trained there.

What Bellamy's parishioners, students, and readers received from his lips and pen was an ordered foundation in the polemical and dogmatic theology of the emerging New Divinity tradition. Edwards himself indicated his approval in a laudatory preface to Bellamy's *True Religion delineated; or experimental Religion, as distinguished from formalism on the one Hand, and Enthusiasm on the other, set in a scriptural and rational Light* (1750), a long treatise in which questions of law and gospel were extended into many other areas of systematic theology. In subsequent writings Bellamy took up problems of theodicy, the most notable of which was his discussion of God's wisdom in permitting sin. He also wrote several essays of varying scope on the question of "experimental religion," attacking "antinomians" on one side and advocates of an "external graceless [Half-Way] Covenant" on the other. In all of these works Bellamy was motivated by regret that in a land where in 1740 there had been "so general an outpouring of the Spirit" there were now "so many fallen away to carnal security, and so many turned enthusiasts and heretics."

Edwards probably would have been pleased with Bellamy's labors on behalf of orthodoxy and experimental piety, yet the changing times brought some very important shifts of emphasis. The most conspicuous of Bellamy's theological innovations was his concept of God as Moral Governor. This was, to be sure, an eighteenth-century commonplace, but in his hands it was prefatory to the most salient revisions of the

Reformed tradition to be proposed by the New Divinity men. One of these revisions, and possibly the fundamental one, was the exoneration of God as the cause of sin through an emphasis on the divine *permission* of sin as the necessary means of achieving the greatest good in this best of all possible worlds. This was followed quite naturally by a muting of Edwards's argument for mankind's unity with Adam, which in turn opened the way for excising the idea of the imputation of Adam's sin. For Bellamy, man was sinful because he sinned. Another corollary was a redefinition of reprobation, according to which God's punishment of sin was not seen as an expression of holy wrath, but rather as an essential means of maintaining the authority of God's Law. Perhaps most famous (or notorious) of all was Bellamy's reinterpretation of the Atonement, whereby God was no longer considered an "offended party" receiving Christ's death as a "satisfaction" for man's infinitely evil ways and limited in its effect only to the elect. Bellamy rather took Christ's sacrifice as an outworking of God's love accomplished for the well-being of the universe.

In the last analysis, Bellamy carried his rationalism a long stride farther than Edwards; and his most characteristic doctrines sprang from his efforts to justify the ways of God to the enlightened conscience of his day. In a not too controversial sense he was the founder of the more popular and apologetic branch of the New England Theology, which would later include Jonathan Edwards, Jr., Timothy Dwight, and Nathaniel William Taylor.

Samuel Hopkins (1721–1803)

The founder of the stricter and more aggressive branch of the Edwardsean school nearly made his name synonymous with the New Divinity. The author of "Hopkinsianism" (or "Hopkintonianism") was born in Waterbury, Connecticut, and graduated from Yale in 1741. He was profoundly affected by Edwards's commencement sermon of that year (*Distinguishing Marks of a Work of the Spirit of God*), and spent eight months as a student in the Northhampton parsonage. From 1743 to 1769 he served as minister of a struggling frontier parish in what is now Great Barrington, Massachusetts. When his former teacher moved to nearby Stockbridge, Hopkins took full advantage of every opportunity for further conversation and fellowship. Forced from his charge when Tories and the well-to-do opposed his strict views of church membership and his Whig politics, he responded to a call from the First Church in Newport, Rhode Island. Here, where he served until his death, his native abilities were permitted to flower in a much larger and more influential ministry, despite an exile caused by the British occupation of Newport during the Revolution. American temperance, antislavery, and missionary movements owe a great debt to Hopkins's pathbreaking efforts. His chief influence and largest claim to remembrance, however, issued from his theological work, above all, from his two-volume *System of Doctrines* (1793). This was the first systematic theology to reflect the Edwardsean impulse, and his contemporaries had good grounds for placing Hopkins among the Reformed tradition's greatest divines. The least that can be said is that he did for the theology of the eighteenth century in New England what Samuel Willard had done for the seventeenth.

Hopkins's first work (in 1759) was an amplification of Bellamy's sensational proposal that "God's greatest and most glorious work is . . . to make sin in general, which is [the] greatest evil, the means of the *greatest* good." Others of Bellamy's new emphases were similarly carried over into Hopkins's system, and some of these were accentuated further—most importantly his virtual elimination of any idea of *original*, as distinct from *actual* sin. Yet in certain significant respects Hopkins put his own mark on the New England theology. Most memorable are his identification of sin and self-love, and his very forceful exposition of its Edwardsean corollary that true virtue consists in "disinterested benevolence," even unto complete willingness to be damned if it be for the greater glory of God. The metaphysical heart of Edwards's thought—his doctrine of Being—had no more prominent place in Hopkins's thought than it had in Bellamy's.

Probably larger in its effect on future church practice was the way in which Hopkins made the doctrines of total depravity and absolute divine sovereignty consistent with his entire moral and evangelistic enterprise. To do this in the face of growing Arminian criticism, Hopkins called "regeneration" an entirely imperceptible work of the Holy Spirit in which man is completely passive. "Conversion" was then made to rest wholly upon the active exercise of the human will, which leads to growth in positive holiness. In this dualistic view, regeneration lays a foundation "in the mind for holy exercises, for hungering and thirsting after righteousness"; while conversion consists in the volitional "exercises of the regenerate, in which they turn from sin to God, or embrace the Gospel." Against this background one can easily understand how Hopkins could work so large a moral and reformatory effect in the church, and yet be a champion of both revivalism and intellectualism. He combined strict views of covenanted church membership with a certain reasonableness about the criteria for regeneration. His most serious weakness —and it was well-nigh fatal to his tradition—was that he allowed himself to be dominated by the moral emphasis of his age and was overly concerned with detailed and acrimonious theological controversy. "In Hopkins, Calvinism was suffering from focusing attention on its enemies instead of on its God."[3]

Jonathan Edwards, Jr. (1745–1801)

The younger Edwards made only a small theological contribution beyond what was accomplished by Bellamy and Hopkins, but he did play a vital role in defending his father and his teachers. He is also remembered for developing the first full modern statement of the "governmental theory" of the Atonement in the New England Theology, though he must share these honors with Bellamy and with Stephen West, who had succeeded the elder Edwards at Stockbridge.[4]

[3] Joseph Haroutunian, *Piety versus Moralism: The Passing of the New England Theology*, p. 62. As if to counterbalance his polemics, Hopkins wrote and edited a moving life of Edwards that drew on Edwards's own personal writings (1765), reprinted in David Levin, ed., *Jonathan Edwards: A Profile*.

[4] The "governmental" or New England theory was also indebted to the thought of Grotius, the great Dutch theorist on international law. It interpreted Christ's infinite sacrifice as a demonstration of God's concern for legal government. Man's infinitely evil sin had to be expiated in the interests of moral order. This made sense to the revolutionary generation, which was deep in controversy over natural law, natural rights, and the nature of government. Stephen West (1735–1819) was a formidable thinker and a worthy successor of Edwards. Connecticut-born and Yale-educated (B.A. 1755), West studied under Timothy Woodbridge of Hatfield, Massachusetts, before taking up his lifetime pastorate

Edwards's *Three Sermons on the Necessity of the Atonement, and Its Consistency with Free Grace in Forgiveness* was published in 1785.

Actually the younger Edwards's career as a whole reveals more about the nature of the New Divinity tradition than anything he wrote. He was graduated from Princeton in 1765, and remained there as a tutor until John Witherspoon began to expunge Edwardsean "idealism" after he had assumed the presidency in 1768. In 1769 Edwards was called to the White Haven Church, formed in 1742 out of a New Light secession from New Haven's First Church. This church, however, had reverted to the practice of the Half-Way Covenant in 1760. Edwards immediately demanded its abrogation, and his insistence on this point (as well as his unpopular metaphysical discourses) caused a portion of the church to withdraw from his ministry. This group organized itself as the Fair Haven Church in 1771, and maintained a separate existence until after Edwards left New Haven in 1795.

Edwards compensated for his rigor with neither great powers as a preacher nor a winning personality, so that his congregation finally dwindled to the point where his resignation was demanded. Had he not been one of New Haven's foremost supporters of the Patriot cause, and had not the famous Roger Sherman been one of his most devoted parishioners, the end would have come sooner. As it was, he followed in the footsteps of his father, moving first to a small frontier village (North Colebrook, Connecticut), then to a college presidency (Union College, Schenectady, New York), and very shortly thereafter to his final resting place. Perhaps his most significant labors were those in behalf of a closer alliance between the Middle States Presbyterians, among whom his father had died, and the consociated Congregationalists of Connecticut.[5] His fierce loyalty to the New

---

at Stockbridge. In addition to his *Scripture Doctrine of the Atonement* (1785), he wrote treatises on *Moral Agency* (1772), and *Evidence of the Divinity of our Lord Jesus Christ* (1816). He also wrote a controversial work on the meaning of baptism (1794) and edited an autobiography of Samuel Hopkins (1805).

[5] The Plan of Union between these two groups was formally adopted in 1801, the year of Edwards's death. Union College itself was a cooperative venture on the part of Dutch Reformed, Presbyterians, and Congregationalists. See pp. 552–55.

England Theology, his strict churchmanship, his dry, doctrinal preaching, his profound incompatibility with the drift of popular religion in the revolutionary epoch—all of these make Jonathan Edwards, Jr., a fit representative of the Edwardsean epigone.

Nathanael Emmons (1745–1840)

The longest-lived of the New Divinity men was also the most intellectually independent and creative. Nathanael Emmons was a colorful personality, given to aphoristic expression and unusual opinions. He referred to his birth date in the Old Style of the Julian calendar, and died in Jacksonian America still wearing the knee breeches and buckled shoes of colonial times. As a student at Yale, he was deeply affected by his reading of Edwards's *Freedom of the Will*. After receiving his baccalaureate in 1767, he took postgraduate theological training first with Nathan Strong of North Coventry, for whom he mastered Willard's *Compleat Body of Divinity*, followed by a far more influential stint with John Smalley of New Britain, Connecticut. Smalley was a disciple of Edwards, a student of Bellamy, and an ardent New Divinity man whose "scheme of sentiments" the young Emmons received "with great avidity." At his examination for licensure as a minister, this "novel scheme" of Smalley's was bitterly resisted by a minority, so that Emmons emerged, as he said, "in some measure a speckled bird."[6]

These speckles may have had something to do with the fact that Emmons was not called to a church until 1773. On the other hand, he was a hard man to please, for he had to be sure that the congregation would accept his didactic doctrinal preaching. "As soon as I entered into the ministry," he said (and his determination was fairly characteristic of his school), "I resolved to devote my whole time to the sacred

[6] The written protest of the Reverend Edward Eells objects to the New Divinity man's contention that man's rational faculties were unaffected by either sin (the Fall) or salvation. Emmons taught that the *imago Dei* was not upon Adam's understanding any more than on his fingers and toes, but upon his heart and will (Edwards Amasa Park, *Memoir of Nathanael Emmons: with Sketches of His Friends and Pupils* [Boston, 1861], pp. 39 f.). "Emmons was, by common consent, the boldest thinker and writer in the entire school," says George N. Boardman (*A History of the New England Theology*, p. 14).

work, without encumbering myself with the cares and concerns of the world." He once refused to replace a fallen bar on his fence, lest it start him down the road to worldly preoccupations. The way to keep church members in peace, he felt, "is to keep them interested in the great truths of the Bible." The necessary conditions were finally found in the completely rural parish at Franklin, Massachusetts, where for fifty-four years Emmons conducted a ministry according to his desires. Five very thick octavo volumes of his collected *Works* attest to the vigor with which he lived out his axioms. These tomes also help to account for the fact that eighty-seven students studied for the ministry under his care—and repaired his fences.

The theology which these students learned was forged in many controversies—against Arminians, Antinomians, Universalists, Unitarians, and the whole diverse band of eighteenth-century infidels. Nevertheless, it was steadfastly systematic, sermonic in form, and rational in structure, though neither intensely exegetical nor rigorously philosophical. Emmons professed to hold ontology in horror, and never expressed himself clearly on many very relevant metaphysical issues. His views were basically and professedly Hopkinsian, and his students did more to perpetuate that outlook than Hopkins's own. Yet Emmons's thought had a definite tendency, which he himself described as not "Calvinisticalish, Calvinistical, nor Calvinistic—but Calvinist." Emmonsism as a term arose later in reference to the extreme view of "the sole causality of God" which became a key doctrine of his system. Holiness and sin consist in actions, or "exercises," of which God is the immediate agent; yet as introspection reveals, these exercises are willed, voluntary, and free. Sin is in the sinning; it springs neither from a prior disposition nor from a sinful nature.

Emmons was a highly original theologian who shaped every doctrine to his systematic needs. Yet it is not misleading to accept his own insistence that he chiefly extended and clarified the New England Theology. The future significance of these labors was, of course, increased by the great number of his disciples who entered New England pulpits; Leonard Woods, later on the faculty of Andover Seminary, was perhaps the most influential. Almost all of the New Divinity men, on the other hand, persistently exerted a kind of involuntary reverse influence. A famous example is the eminent educational reformer, Horace Mann, who grew up in Franklin under the stern preaching and imperious "rule" of Emmons. Mann looked back on his Christian nurture as a blight on his life; he consciously rebelled at an early age, and became a pronounced liberal in theology.

AN EVALUATION OF THE EDWARDSEAN SCHOOL

The New Divinity tradition has not been treated kindly by historians and theologians. Herbert W. Schneider found it "one of the most intricate and pathetic exhibitions of theological reasonings which the history of Western thought affords. The dialectic involved is so replete with apparently meaningless technical distinctions, and the literature of the movement is so controversial in spirit, that the few theologians who have taken the pains to pick their way through this desert have merely succeeded in convincing others that there are no signs of life in it." In a chapter entitled "The Decline and Fall," Schneider associates himself with "modern Protestants [who] are so thankful to be rid of the Puritan incubus that they point to these post-Edwardseans as the death agony of a monstrious theology which should never have been born."[7]

Joseph Haroutunian, a theologian of Reformed background, is almost as harsh, though his judgments are unusually penetrating:

The profound tragedy of Edwards' theology was transformed into a farce by his would-be disciples, who used his language and ignored his piety. . . . Edwards' "true virtue" was buried under a mass of distinctions invented in order to make the church acceptable to men of secondary virtue. . . . Holy love faded into conformity to the moral law, and such conformity was not the measure and substance of "true virtue." Such bleak and cruel Calvinism was doomed in New England, when, with the opening of the new century, a humanized liberalism won the day, and introduced a new and softer note into the religious life of New England. . . . The difference between "Christians" and "moralists" [according to Emmons] is that the former believe a body of doctrinal truths, while the latter do not. Calvinism thus degenerated into a scheme of theology *plus*

[7] Herbert W. Schneider, *The Puritan Mind,* p. 208.

an independent set of "duties." Its holy fire was quenched, and its theological ashes lay exposed to the four winds. . . . The logic of Calvinistic piety was being transformed into a vast, complicated, and colorless theological structure, bewildering to its friends and ridiculous to its enemies. It was like a proud and beggared king, hiding his shame with scarlet rags and yellow trinkets.[8]

Jonathan Edwards himself is usually exempted from the more sweeping denunciations, but not always. Vernon Louis Parrington is typical of the once large but now diminishing group of undiscriminating interpreters, though few have misunderstood Edwards so utterly:

Edwards was at the dividing of the ways; he must abandon transcendentalism or the dogma of total depravity. Instead he sought refuge in compromise, endeavoring to reconcile what was incompatible. Herein lay the tragedy of [his] intellectual life; the theologian triumphed over the philosopher, circumscribing his powers to ignoble ends. . . . The greatest mind of New England had become an anachronism in a world that bred Benjamin Franklin. . . . The intellectual powers were his, but the inspiration was lacking; like Cotton Mather before him, he was the unconscious victim of a decadent ideal and a petty environment.[9]

Having thus disposed of the founder of the New England Theology, Parrington simply dismisses the ensuing tradition without comment. Still other scholars, most notably Frank Hugh Foster, veer to the other extreme, not only lavishing superlatives on Edwards, but describing the work of his successors as a continuous ascent, with Nathaniel William Taylor and Edwards Amasa Park ensconced on the nineteenth-century summit. George N. Boardman regarded the best of these men as possessed of original power as thinkers, and he thought the power of the tradition itself "really a matter of wonder."[10]

[8] Joseph Haroutunian, *Piety versus Moralism: The Passing of the New England Theology*, pp. 96, 130, 176, 127, 71.

[9] Vernon L. Parrington, *Main Currents in American Thought*, 1:158, 162–63.

[10] Frank H. Foster, *A Genetic History of the New England Theology*; Boardman, *History of the New England Theology*, p. 14.

In view of such radically conflicting judgments some concluding observations are necessary. The first is simply that Edwards no longer stands in need of merely qualitative defense. His reputation as America's greatest speculative theologian is fairly secure. It is not at all apparent that the Reformed tradition anywhere in the world has produced his equal between John Calvin and Karl Barth, or that America had a metaphysician of his stature until late in the nineteenth century. As the quotations from Schneider and Haroutunian indicate, Edwards can easily be disjoined from "Edwardseanism." Yet the successors of Edwards discussed in this chapter are his legitimate offspring, and the father, regardless of his greatness, must bear part of the burden of abuse. The historian of ideas may still consider the New Divinity of the eighteenth century as a single tradition.

The chief extenuating circumstance for the post-Edwardsean tradition as a whole is that it was a victim of the Enlightenment and the country's political concerns, whereas Edwards alone benefited from his proximity to the Puritans and from the religious support provided by the Great Awakening. He could more easily continue the perennial dialogue of philosophic Christians that reaches back to Saint Augustine and the early Fathers. But his disciples faced the difficult task of carrying on their labors when other ideas and aspirations had become dominant. After 1760 Americans were increasingly preoccupied by issues of government, law, trade, war, and nation-building—not theology. The New Divinity men, therefore, had to take up huge apologetical questions while performing their ministry in hostile parishes on the farflung edge of Anglo-European civilization. Nevertheless, they succeeded in doing what almost no one else in the Reformed tradition was then doing creatively: they maintained a dogmatic tradition and steadily developed it in the face of both revivalistic and rationalistic challenges to theological rigor. Never have theologians struggled against greater odds. Yet no one who reads their productions patiently can deny that they executed their task with brilliance. For the churches their works served as a highly effective sheet anchor during the period's political storms, enabling the New England religious tradition to move ahead again under the fair winds of the new century. Yet the metaphor may be too static—for these thinkers were, in a sense, at the helm, and in their way they charted a route through difficult seas.

At the dawn of the nineteenth century, the churches which they influenced were no longer restricted to the intellectual categories of the sixteenth century. These men were by no means a provincial aberration: the Second Great Awakening in New England would not be their doing, but it did vindicate their steadfastness and should allow posterity to forgive them their contentiousness.

26

THE SECOND GREAT AWAKENING IN NEW ENGLAND:
REVIVAL, EVANGELISM, AND REFORM

While Jedidiah Morse was mounting his first campaign against the Boston-Harvard liberals and working to form the orthodox coalition that would found Andover Seminary, he was in correspondence with fellow Yale alumni who were rejoicing in a spiritual renewal of their churches. As the new seminary became an actuality, its students and faculty knew that it was a strategic outpost of these resurgent churches. When Moses Stuart and Leonard Woods took up the cudgels against William Ellery Channing and Henry Ware, they also knew that they were no longer merely spokesmen for a disappointed New Divinity underground. Every one of these men, in fact, was already participating in the Second Great Awakening. "God, in a remarkable manner, was pouring out his Spirit on the churches of New England," said one of the revival's leaders and earliest historians. "Within the period of five or six years . . . not less than one hundred and fifty churches in New England, were visited with times of refreshing from the presence of the Lord."[1]

The years since the great ingathering of the first Awakening had been hard to understand. God seemed almost to have withdrawn his blessing from New England, and above all from those who most cherished "true" doctrine. There had been occasional local revivals since those great wonder-working days, especially in the years 1763–64. But at the end of

[1] Bennet Tyler, *The New England Revivals . . . from Narratives First Published in the Connecticut Evangelical Magazine* (Boston, 1846), p. v.

the century, though the number of New Divinity men had grown from a small band to over a hundred, the main signs of refreshing seemed to come to Baptists and the invading Methodists, not to the churches of the standing order. It was then that the new revivals occurred, almost uniformly under the strictest preaching of the New Divinity, and the orthodox took new heart.

Just where they began or which came first will probably never be settled. Edward Dorr Griffin, so far as his "personal observation" was concerned, traced them to 1792, when he had come home from Yale as a theology student and seen his family and many kinspeople become "professors of religion." But the first phase of the Second Awakening proper took place between 1797 and 1801, when many towns from Connecticut to New Hampshire felt refreshing showers. "I saw a continued succession of heavenly sprinklings," wrote Griffin, "at New Salem, Farmington, Middlebury, and New Hartford . . . until, in 1799, I could stand at my door in New Hartford, Litchfield County, and number fifty or sixty contiguous congregations laid down in one field of divine wonders."[2] In 1800 the *Connecticut Evangelical Magazine* was founded to report and encourage the revival spirit. Then in 1801, just as it began to flag in the towns, it came to Yale to reward the earnest preaching of President Timothy Dwight. A third of the students (many of them destined for the ministry) were converted. Membership in the student "Moral Society" rose to unprecedented numbers in 1802; and Benjamin Silliman, the future "father of American science," wrote home that "Yale College is a little temple; prayer and praise seem to be the delight of the greater part of the students, while those who are still unfeeling are awed with respectful silence."[3]

This tardy but highly influential college revival won Dwight the undeserved credit for having begun the Second Awakening, though the religious interest in the college soon flagged, not to return with power until 1812–13 and 1815. But in 1807–08 it was felt in New Haven, after one of Dwight's protégés, young Moses Stuart, succeeded a stern and aging Moderate as minister of the First Church. In due course these revivals too became statewide, and soon they

[2] Quoted in Charles Roy Keller, *The Second Great Awakening in Connecticut*, pp. 37–38.

[3] George Park Fisher, *Life of Benjamin Silliman*, 2 vols. (New York, 1866), 1:83.

became almost continuous on a local basis, though more intense manifestations of the Spirit were felt in 1815–16 and in 1820–21. This last was especially powerful in New Haven, where Nathaniel William Taylor, another of Dwight's students, was Stuart's illustrious successor. In 1825–26 and in 1831 still other "displays of divine grace" occurred; but by this time a basic pattern had been set, and influences from great western revivals were flowing back into New England. For two or three generations the revival remained a characteristic feature of Congregational life.

Until western and Methodistic practices and a revised "New School" theology began to take hold in this later period, the Second Awakening was remarkably uniform in almost all of its appearances. In the first place, revivals came to the parishes of New Divinity men with a consistency that they could interpret only as a sign of divine favor. In the words of the Edwardseans, it was the preaching of "plain gospel truths, with which the people had long been acquainted, and had heard with indifference." These "plain gospel truths" were God's absolute sovereignty, man's total depravity, and Christ's atoning love.

It has been no uncommon thing for the subjects of the work, whose chief distress and anxiety antecedently arose from a sense of their being in the hands of God, unexpectedly to find themselves rejoicing in that very consideration. . . . They have . . . apparently rejoiced in God's supremacy, and in being at his disposal, calmly leaving their case to his wise and holy decision.[4]

One feature of such preaching which certainly conduced to the awesomeness of the phenomena and to the calmness of the results was that the revivals were seen as in very fact God's work, not man's. The God who had spoken to Abraham was speaking in New England. The main street of any village led into Jerusalem the Golden. This was an exciting fact; yet the revivals were without the hysteria and commotion that had brought the Great Awakening into disrepute in many quarters, and which would soon be arousing similar opposition to the tumultuous camp meetings in the West.

That people were calm was indeed the second important feature of these revivals, and one for which the ministers

[4] Tyler, *New England Revivals,* p. 59.

unanimously thanked God. They were not marked by "outcries, distortions of the body, or any symptoms of intemperate zeal. . . . You might often see a congregation sit with deep solemnity depicted in their countenances, without observing a tear or sob during the service." The fruits of conversion, moreover, were incontestably shown in renewed spiritual seriousness and reformation of morals. This helps most to account for the sustained character of the Second Awakening, and shows that the clergy were not being simply prudish in their gratitude for the prevailing sobriety. Over and over again the effects on individual behavior were attested as permanent, while undue excess and the reaction it would have caused were rare. Very different from the first Great Awakening, the unbelievers (as young Silliman reported from Yale) were awed into "respectful silence" rather than provoked to antagonism and ridicule.

LEADERS OF THE PERIOD

For the most part these revivals were conducted not by sensational itinerants like Tennent, Whitefield, and Davenport, but by settled ministers within their own parishes. But this did not prevent the assertion of leadership by certain naturally dominant personalities whose memory enhances the history of more than revivalism. The more outstanding of these may be singled out for brief attention.

Timothy Dwight (1752–1817)

First by virtue of his unquestioned ability, by the prestige accruing from his presidency of Yale (1795–1817), and by his own personal assertiveness, was the grandson of Jonathan Edwards, Timothy Dwight. Born in Northampton, graduated from Yale (1769), and remaining there as a tutor, Dwight was sorely disappointed at not being made president of the college in 1777. He entered the army chaplaincy instead; following this, by laborious efforts he sought to establish himself as an epic poet of the new nation. Serving a pastorate at Greenfield Hill, Connecticut, Dwight also began to make his mark as a philosophical defender of the faith and as a hymn writer, extending the revolution begun by Isaac Watts with his departure from metrical paraphrases of the Psalms. ("I Love Thy Kingdom, Lord" is perhaps Dwight's most famous hymn.) Elected president of Yale in 1795, he set about making his administration memorable as a time of educational broadening and deepening, just as John Thornton Kirkland, his contemporary at Harvard, was to do. Also like the Unitarian leaders of Boston, Dwight was an ardent Federalist; politically he (and even more forcibly, his brother Theodore) would continue to ally with the Unitarian and Episcopalian Federalists of Boston and Essex County, even at the Hartford Convention of 1815.

But Timothy Dwight was not chiefly a political leader; his primary crusade was against infidelity and in behalf of true doctrine and experimental religion. This led him to undertake at Yale his four-year cycle of discourses on the Christian religion, expounding its nature, defending it against detractors, and pointing out at great length its moral implications. After six years of declaiming this "system" to unenthusiastic students through warm weather and cold, in greatcoat and mittens when necessary, his first collegiate revival finally happened. The lectures, first published in 1818 and often reprinted, became a major theological guide for a generation.[5]

Whether Dwight was an Old Calvinist or a New Divinity man has often been debated, but the question cannot be settled in those terms. He was neither. As the founder of the New Haven Theology, he begins a new trend that was carried to completion by Nathaniel William Taylor. In preferring the Scottish Philosophy to Locke and Berkeley, and in enlarging upon man's moral and intellectual agency, he was certainly not a strict Edwardsean. The first emphasis made him practical and commonsensical; the latter pointed him in the direction of a "system of duties" based on a utilitarian notion of happiness which was far removed from Edwards's conception of true virtue as love for Being as such. At no other point did the New England Theology move so decisively toward that unloved moral legalism which later Americans were to condemn and abandon.[6] Dwight represents, even if he did

[5] *Theology Explained and Defended in a Series of Sermons,* 5 vols. (Middletown, Connecticut, 1818–19). Reprinted in 5 vols. (London, 1819), in 2 vols. (Glasgow, 1822–24), in 4 vols. (New Haven, 1825; New York, 1829), et al.

[6] If any one group can be credited with identifying Puritanism and moral legalism, it is Dwight and his immediate disciples. All Reformed theologies tend to be legalistic, but Dwight and his influential followers almost extinguished the idea of free Christian decision in a given situation or moral context.

not shape, the tradition that would later be so roundly condemned by liberals as "Puritan."

Nathaniel William Taylor (1786–1858)

But such forward glances must not divert us from the immense evangelical energy that was loosed on New England and America by Dwight's devoted students, of whom none is more important than the real architect of the New Haven Theology, Nathaniel William Taylor.[7] After beginning his career as a reader and amanuensis for Dwight (whose eyesight was very poor), Taylor proceeded to an outstanding ministry at New Haven's First Church (1811–22). His most important services, however, were rendered as professor of theology at the Yale Divinity School, established in 1822 mainly to supply the swiftly increasing demand for ministers, but also to provide Taylor with a platform on a par with Andover. He presaged things to come by remarking that Leonard Woods's arguments against Henry Ware had set back the orthodox cause fifty years. In 1828 Taylor shocked some of the stricter Edwardseans with his *Concio ad Clerum,* an address before the General Association of Connecticut. But even then, and long before his death in 1858, "Taylorism" was a definite and recognizable point of view. In spirit the New Haven Theology, as it became known, remained distinctly Reformed, for Taylor would never concede that he had departed from the Westminster Confession; he professed his deep indebtedness to Dwight and his respect for Edwards. But more importantly, he gathered together the innovations of the intervening New Divinity, especially as set forth by Bellamy, based them firmly and knowledgeably on the Scottish Philosophy, and propounded a plausibly rationalistic "revival theology" for mid-nineteenth-century America.

Taylor's fundamental insistence was that no man becomes depraved but by his own act, for the sinfulness of the human race does not pertain to human nature as such. "Sin is in the sinning," and hence "original" only in the sense that it is universal. Though inevitable, it is not—as with Edwards—causally necessary. Man always had, in Taylor's famous

[7] Chronologically, Asahel Nettleton, the Second Awakening's most important itinerant evangelist, and Lyman Beecher, who did almost everything, were on the scene before Taylor; but Taylor's position as the chief successor to Dwight makes it logical to consider him first.

phrase, "power to the contrary." As a free, rational, moral, creative cause, man is not part of the system of nature, at least not a passive or determined part. Preachers must confront sinners with this fact, and address them in the knowledge of it.[8] Unlike Leonard Woods, Taylor was consciously formulating a reasonable revival theology that could prosper in the democratic ethos of Jacksonian America. As these ideas gained acceptance with the passing years, revivals came to be understood less as the "mighty acts of God" than as the achievement of preachers who won the consent of sinners.

Bennet Tyler (1783–1858)

Not surprisingly, Taylor's views attracted opposition from many quarters. Leonard Woods, at whom they were to some extent aimed, turned from his battles with the Unitarians to a new controversy on this front. When Woods was joined by Bennet Tyler, the "Tyler-Taylor Controversy" became a New England conversation piece. Tyler was Connecticut-born and Yale-trained (1804), a former president of Dartmouth College (1822–28), and after 1828 minister in Portland, Maine. While on a visit to Connecticut in 1829, he opened a correspondence with Taylor in protest against the latter's *Concio ad Clerum.* The dispute became public, and the objections to Taylorism multiplied. In 1833 dissatisfaction with Yale had grown so strong that the conservatives founded the Theological Institute of Connecticut (later Hartford Theological Seminary) in East Windsor as a counterseminary, with Tyler as president and professor of theology. Here until his death he sought to build a bastion of what he thought was unrevised and uncompromised Edwardseanism.[9]

Asahel Nettleton (1783–1844)

Unsuccessfully sought for the first faculty of the new seminary in East Windsor was the evangelist Asahel Nettleton, a

[8] Worth noting in this connection is the fact that Taylor's alleged "Arminianism" is far more liberal than John Wesley's. He argues from the nature of man, not, as did Wesley, from the scope of Christ's atoning work and the generality of God's grace.

[9] Perhaps the seminary drew strength from the fact that it was located in the very precincts where Jonathan Edwards had received his first intuitions of God's great glory. More material was the longstanding rivalry between the New Haven and the Hartford areas.

figure far more representative of the Second Awakening. Stirred during the early years of that revival, Nettleton was converted in 1801 and determined to spend his life in the foreign mission field. His health prevented that, but his peculiar abilities as a revivalist were discovered almost by accident when he was asked to interrupt his postgraduate theological studies at Yale to take an interim preaching assignment in eastern Connecticut. Aware that the first Great Awakening had produced its most enthusiastic and disorderly responses in this region, Nettleton adopted very sane and sober methods. His effectiveness was a minor sensation, however, and he was ordained as an evangelist by the Consociation of Litchfield County in 1811.

His next assignment was among the churches of western Connecticut, which were being decimated by the great "Yankee Exodus" to the West. So fruitful was his preaching, so self-effacing and cooperative was he, and so decorous and unsensational were his methods, that he was soon in great demand not only in Connecticut but in New York and elsewhere in New England. Yet his invariable success in calling sinners to repentance undermined the idea that a revival was the work of God, despite the fact that Nettleton himself insisted on understanding conversion in a thoroughly Edwardsean sense. He thus became another in the long succession of professional revivalists, adding to his powerful appeals from the pulpit a systematic approach to home visitation, personal conference, inquiry meetings, and follow-up instruction. After his health broke in 1820, his activities were much curtailed. He traveled abroad for a time, and from 1834 until his death he resided at East Windsor, lecturing occasionally at the new theological institute which he had helped to found.

Lyman Beecher (1775–1863)

If Nettleton was a self-effacing apostle who gravitated toward Tyler's camp, Lyman Beecher was a self-asserting apostle of Taylorism, who even in death lies side by side with his friend and theological hero in the old Grove Street Cemetery in New Haven. No other figure sums up in his own life the many facets of the Second Awakening and its enormous consequences for American history.

Beecher was graduated from Yale in 1797, having spent two years under Ezra Stiles and two under Timothy

Dwight. He then remained another year to study theology. It was Dwight who converted him, turned him to the ministry, formed his mind, and won his undying admiration and perhaps exorbitant praise. When in 1798 he accepted his first charge, a Presbyterian church in East Hampton, Long Island, Beecher had already been "baptized into the revival spirit"— and no baptism ever had more persistent effect. In East Hampton he won a reputation both as a moral reformer (for a crusade against dueling) and as a revivalist. He was called in 1810 to the First Church in Litchfield, Connecticut, where he weathered "Mr. Madison's War" and the successful assault of Jeffersonians, Baptists, Methodists, and Episcopalians on Connecticut's ecclesiastical establishment.

Pursuing his career as a revivalist during these years at Litchfield, Beecher brought to fullness the conception that most distinguishes the evangelical resurgence of the next half-century: the intimate association of evangelism in its broadest sense with moral reform and social benevolence. As a reformer, he was especially active in the temperance movement. When he was called in 1826 to the Hanover Street Congregational Church in Boston, he brought the tactics of revivalism to the service of conservatism against the liberals and Unitarians. Thereafter he returned to the Presbyterian fold, and in 1832 he moved out west to become president of Lane Theological Seminary. The controversies and campaigns in which he and his numerous family later became involved will be treated in subsequent chapters. His autobiography, compiled with the aid of his children shortly before his death, provides an extraordinary picture of evangelical Protestantism in antebellum America.

THE FORMATION OF VOLUNTARY ASSOCIATIONS

One of the startling features of Professor Kenneth Scott Latourette's labors as an historian of the expansion of Christianity is his designation of the nineteenth century, despite all its distractions and temptations, as "the Great Century." The things which, to his mind, make it great in America take their rise with remarkable consistency from the evangelical enthusiasm aroused by the Second Awakening in New England. Most basic perhaps was a new kind of religious institution, the voluntary association of private individuals for missionary, reformatory, or benevolent purposes.[10] Usually these societies were chartered and governed independently, even when they had a nominal relation to some church body. Their membership grew wherever interest could be created, often on an interdenominational basis. Their activities were carried on without church or state control, and in most cases they were focused fairly sharply on one specific purpose. To give even a brief account of all the many cooperative agencies would require a large volume; but certain representative ones must be considered if the significance of the Second Awakening is to be grasped.

Missionary Societies

Both logically and chronologically prior was the Connecticut Missionary Society, formed in 1798 when the General Association of Connecticut (following a resolution of the previous year and the example of the Hartford North Association) voted to become the core of an agency "to christianize the Heathen in North America, and to support and promote Christian knowledge in the new settlements, within the United States." In 1800 the *Connecticut Evangelical Magazine* was founded to further the society's work and to promote financial support. A similar society and magazine were founded in Massachusetts, with Nathanael Emmons playing a leading role in the conduct of both. After the Congregational-Presbyterian Plan of Union in 1801, this kind of work was accelerated. In 1812–13 the two societies sent Samuel J. Mills, Jr., and John Schermerhorn on a remarkable tour to estimate the religious needs of the West, which led to the setting of still more ambitious goals. Finally, as the western populations grew and as the home mission movement expanded, the consolidated American Home Missionary Society was formed in New York in 1826. For two generations its missionaries were a major force in the development of the West,

[10] There were several precedents for this type of organization, such as the Society for the Propagation of the Gospel in New England, formed in 1649, which under the name of the New England Company still supports the education of Indians in Canada with the revenues from its ancient government grant. The SPG was a different type of organization, being more nearly an arm of the Church of England. Later in the eighteenth century the Evangelical Revival generated many voluntary associations in Great Britain.

not only as apostles and revivalists, but as educators, civic leaders, and exponents of eastern culture. The reports of its missionaries, its fund-raising activities, and its publications, on the other hand, had a constant invigorating influence on the supporting individuals and churchs in the East.

The foreign missions story is very similar, though it has somewhat more dramatic origins in the famous "Haystack Prayer Meeting." While seeking shelter from a summer shower one day in 1806, Samuel J. Mills, Jr., and a few fellow students at Williams College dedicated themselves to missionary service in the foreign fields. Later at Andover Seminary they and other interested students organized themselves more formally, and in 1810 they were able to enlist the official support of the newly constituted General Association of Massachusetts. Before the year was out a group of Connecticut and Massachusetts ministers had incorporated the famous and long-lived American Board of Commissioners for Foreign Missions.

Mills's poor health forced him into home mission work, but in 1812 a group of foreign missionaries did set sail for India under the auspices of the board. Two of the young missionaries, however, were unexpectedly converted to Baptist views, Adoniram Judson on board ship and Luther Rice shortly after arriving. Judson and his wife remained to begin a mission which led eventually to memorable achievements in Burma.[11] Rice meanwhile returned to America to sever their connection with the American Board, and to enlist American Baptists in organized support of foreign missions. Rice discovered or aroused considerable missionary interest, which was harnessed in 1814 with the formation of the General Convention of the Baptist Denomination in the United States of America for Foreign Missions—a name long enough to kill many an organization, but not this one, for it not only survived but became a major coordinating force among American Baptists until divided by the slavery issue.

No general history can chart the remarkable expansion of the work of these and other missionary societies in every part

[11] Judson's lifelong work in Burma, which included pathbreaking language studies, translation of the entire Bible from Hebrew and Greek into Burmese, and the preparation of a massive two-way lexicon, illustrates the way in which the piety and the scholarship of Andover Seminary reached around the world (see the excellent biography by Courtney Anderson, *To the Golden Shore*).

of the world, or trace the manifold ways in which the missionaries almost created the nineteenth-century American's image of "heathendom" and heavily influenced American foreign policy. But in countless ways the Haystack Prayer Meeting continued to have repercussions throughout the world. Perhaps more germane to our story is the way in which the work of these societies strengthened the home churches themselves. When one society representative was seeking a new charter from the Massachusetts legislature, he observed that "religion is a commodity of which the more we exported the more we had remaining." Certainly no evangelical labor undertaken by the churches had a larger rejuvenating effect than the foreign mission enterprise.

Publication and Education Societies

Closely allied to the missionary societies were a group of similarly organized associations for the promotion of Christian knowledge and education. Earliest of these were the Bible societies modeled on the English organization of 1804, the first of which appeared in Philadelphia in 1808. But in 1809 others were formed in Connecticut, Massachusetts, Maine, and New York. Then in 1816, after the idea of a national organization had been advanced in many quarters, the American Bible Society was organized. In less than four years it had distributed nearly a hundred thousand Bibles. For the work of distributing tracts a similar pattern developed: a highly successful English model, a series of well-functioning state associations in America, then an enlargement of scope and the emergence of a national society. In 1814 the New England Tract Society came into being, and nine years later it was transmuted into the American Tract Society. By that time it had already printed 777,000 tracts and was publishing a bimonthly magazine, a Christian almanac, and a series of children's books. In 1825 it became a truly national organization by merging with another New York society which had the same name and a similar history.

Education was as much an object of associative effort as the publishing of Christian literature. The foundation of seminaries signified the immense new demand for ministers resulting from the revivals and from America's westward expansion. These needs led also to corollary efforts in behalf of some kind of scholarship program. In that age, a pressing need was all it took to spark the creation of a new society. This one began at New Haven in 1814–15, when a charitable society for aiding indigent theological students was founded, along with a "female auxiliary." In 1826 this movement too achieved national form as the American Education Society. Its reports are a vital chapter in the history of American higher education.

Finally, and to some extent parallel to these other societies, came the Sunday school movement and its cluster of ascending organizations. Its English precedents included the famous work begun by Robert Raikes as early as 1781. In America, Philadelphia moved first, while in New England the Second Awakening soon stimulated a like response. The schools, of course, were organized locally, but the need for an adequate supply of literature and educational materials required a larger organization, and in 1824 the American Sunday School Union was organized. Because of its primary concern as a publisher, it acted from the first as something like a non-denominational tract society, though the predominantly Reformed cast of American Protestantism at that time kept it from being so ecumenical an endeavor as it might sound. In New England especially, the state organizations were for all practical purposes Congregational agencies.

Moral Reform

Antinomianism and moral license were always special horrors to Puritan piety, and Reformed preaching never neglected to stress radical amendment of behavior as a necessary concomitant and sign of true conversion. If one recalls the intense moralism in the theology of latter-day Puritans like Dwight, it goes without saying that the revivals led also to associations for moral reform. At Yale a Moral Society existed secretly among the students as early as 1797; but before long such societies were statewide, then nationwide—and anything but secret.

The first of the great moral crusades to emerge was that directed against intemperance, which was then very widespread. Puritans had never been abstemious: rum was a vital factor in the economy of early New England, and distilled spirits had long been a popular feature of marriages, funerals, ordinations, and meetinghouse raisings, not to mention private hospitality. Most of the early attacks on drinking (John Adams's assault on the taverns in his native town of

Braintree, for example) rested on a civic or hygienic rationale. In 1811, when Lyman Beecher was awakening gradually to the need for a moral crusade on Sabbath-breaking, profanity, and intemperance, there was still considerable political reasoning involved. The "ruff-scruff" among whom the abuses were worst seemed to be infidels and Jeffersonians as well as reprobates. "Our vices are digging the grave of our liberties," Beecher cried, "and preparing to entomb our glory." Due largely to his labors the Connecticut Society for the Reformation of Morals was organized in 1813, and men like Beecher soon infused the movement with an evangelical spirit that transcended political party labels. In Massachusetts a parallel movement was launched by Jeremiah Evarts, a lawyer associated with Jedidiah Morse and intimately connected with the foreign mission cause. The Massachusetts Society for the Suppression of Intemperance resulted. Both societies encouraged the formation of local auxiliaries. The War of 1812 slowed these efforts but inspired plans for wider campaigns lest infidels, slaveholders, and backwoodsmen provoke still other wars. But when peace came Dwight took the lead in making drinking, not intemperance, the sin—and in demanding total abstinence. Beecher took the same stand in his *Six Sermons* on the subject. First published in 1826, this volume made a strong and persuasive case for temperance. It was many times reprinted and constantly quoted by other temperance leaders.

To further the cause, the American Society for the Promotion of Temperance was formed in Boston in 1826 by men active in the missionary movement. In 1829 Connecticut followed suit, and its temperance society within a year reported 172 branch societies with twenty-two thousand members. In 1836 the American Temperance Union was formed on a total abstinence platform. The extraordinary success of the temperance movement during the next two decades forms a familiar chapter in American social history. The Maine Law, passed under the leadership of Neal Dow in 1846, was the first statewide prohibition law, and as revised in 1851 it became the model for numerous other states.[12] But the relation of this success to the evangelical counterreformation springing from the Second Awakening is less often noted.

[12] Similar laws were passed in 1852 in Vermont, Rhode Island, and Minnesota Territory; in 1853 in Michigan; in 1854 in Connecticut; and in eight other states by 1855.

As moral rigor increased in this field, so did it in others. The Sabbath was protected by an organization which became national in 1826. Dancing and theatergoing became increasingly suspect. Lotteries, which once had financed buildings for both Harvard and Yale and for innumerable churches, also fell under the ban. Obscenity and profanity came to be defined in far more rigorous terms, and in due course these evils aroused the crusading impulse of other moral reformers. Gradually Americans would come to identify Puritanism and blue-nosed Victorianism.

Humanitarian Interests

The first half of the nineteenth century was also the age of the humanitarian reformer, a time for assailing the status quo with a wide variety of campaigns and benevolences. Taken together, these many causes constitute a movement deeply rooted in the Puritan's compulsion to transform the world, the democratic American's conviction that men ought to be free, and the new Adams's soaring faith in human progress. Some sprang unmistakably from the enlightened ideals which were expressed in the Declaration of Independence and reinforced in the age of Jackson. Others were brought into being by the liberal Unitarians and Transcendentalists of eastern Massachusetts. Another important and characteristic pattern of humanitarian philosophy, however, was linked intimately with the Second Awakening; and it would produce as its ultimate classic Harriet Beecher Stowe's *Uncle Tom's Cabin*. But long before that work burst upon a nation already riven by sectional strife, the leaven of revivalism was doing its benevolent work. The service of the poor and unfortunate (*diakonia*, whence the word "deacon") is an immemorial obligation of the church, and the Puritans had taken it seriously from the beginning. At the end of the eighteenth and the beginning of the nineteenth century this work became increasingly the concern of voluntary associations of one sort or another. Characteristically (and fatefully) these societies brought women into the work of organized philanthropy, thereby setting off the woman's rights movement on a history of its own.

The physically handicapped provided another important incentive to action, and among the most famous resultant enterprises was Hartford Asylum for the Education and Instruction of the Deaf and Dumb. The initial impulse came from Dr. Mason F. Cogswell of Hartford, whose daughter was so afflicted. Cogswell turned to the Congregational General Association, and was encouraged to further action by Timothy Dwight, Benjamin Silliman, and Professor Jeremiah Day of Yale. The institution really came into existence when the Reverend Thomas Gallaudet of Hartford, a graduate of Yale and Andover, devoted himself to its cause. Gallaudet went to England and France in search of technical knowledge and returned in 1816 not only adept himself, but bringing with him an accomplished protégé of the Abbé Sicard of Paris. Thereafter the Hartford Asylum became an important center for this special sort of education. Other kinds of sympathy led to other institutions: the Hartford Retreat for the Insane founded between 1822 and 1824, the General Hospital Society of Connecticut, and the movement for the new and reformed prison at Wethersfield. Unquestionably the most important issue of all was slavery, which already by 1817 had led to the founding of the Colonization Society. Indeed, the entire impulse for humanitarian and moral reform was inexorably converging on this nation-shaking question; but these are matters for later chapters.

The "American as Reformer" was by no means exclusively the child of revivalistic Protestantism. Men and woman of every possible intellectual and religious persuasion undertook countless campaigns for various causes, and often joined forces. Unitarians, Transcendentalists, and belligerently secular reformers helped to advance this half-century's reforming impulse. The extent to which a vague and secularized Puritan transformationism underlies all of these characteristically American movements is difficult to say, but it would be hard to imagine the American's persistent "interferiority complex"[13] without the substructure of Puritan concern for amending the ways of this world and his "theocratic" insistence that God's moral government applies to societies as well as to individuals. During the early nineteenth century the Puritan began to gain his reputation as a meddlesome legalist, narrow-minded, joyless, and small-bored. But this stereotype needs correction. Even in an age when Puritanism was undergoing profound inner changes, it remained a cre-

13 The term, for better or worse, was used by the elder Arthur M. Schlesinger, who by himself and through his many students made an immense contribution to the study of American reform impulses.

ative and energy-releasing power. And that power was generated not only in New England, but ever westward as Americans restlessly pressed the frontier farther and farther from the Atlantic. In this vast inland empire the Puritan impulse would join with others, changing them and being changed, but always making its mark on American evangelical Protestantism as well as on the nation's life and institutions.

27

THE GREAT REVIVAL IN THE WEST AND THE
GROWTH OF THE POPULAR DENOMINATIONS

After victory in the last French and Indian War, the English government, without much thought for enforcement problems, prohibited settlement beyond the Appalachian Mountains. Long before that, however, fur traders had penetrated those areas, and there was no way to prevent settlers from flowing into a land which Christopher Gist described in 1751 as "Watered with a great number of little streams and Rivulets, and full of beautiful natural Meadows, covered with wild Rye, blue grass, and Clover." By 1772 there were four settlements in the upper Holston Valley, in 1776 Kentucky County was erected, and during the Revolution George Rogers Clark led a contingent of western Virginians on his famous conquest of the British forts at Vincennes and Kaskaskia. By 1783, when the Treaty of Paris established the Mississippi River as the western boundary of the United States, the population of these settlements in Kentucky and Tennessee was approaching fifty thousand, with the chief areas of settlement in the valleys of eastern Tennessee, the Nashville basin, the limestone areas of Kentucky, and the Ohio River lowlands. A year later the people in the Wautauga area organized themselves, elected John Sevier as governor, and applied to Congress for recognition as a state. Though they were unsuccessful then, after eight years and nine conventions Kentucky achieved statehood, and four years later (1796) Tennessee was admitted to the Union, both with constitutions and bills of rights similar to those in other states. At the time of their admission, the two states had respectively 73,000 and 77,000 inhabitants. The settlers, most of whom were from Maryland, Virginia, and the Carolinas, were thinly scattered. Lexington, Kentucky, was the largest town, with 1,795 people in 1800, while Louisville, Frankfort, Nashville, and Knoxville all had fewer than 500. Even in 1810, when Kentucky boasted 406,501 people and Tennessee 261,727, the two areas had only 10 and 6.2 persons per square mile respectively.

It was a rude civilization dominated by the desire for land.

The Indian understood when the "tall men came/Whose words were bullets" that he had to reckon with a people quite different from the pleasure-loving *coureurs de bois*, the peaceful Quakers, and the English traders. These grim backwoodsmen were not concerned, as the Jesuit fathers, with his salvation, or, as the traders, with his beaver, but came to kill his deer and occupy his land permanently. Under the circumstances, it is not surprising that the Indian fought the settler in buckskin.[1]

Between the rough tasks of expelling the Indians and subduing the wilderness, the frontiersman acquired a reputation for wild and lawless living. His barbarity never failed to shock the occasional easterner who ventured a visit.

It may not be improper to mention, that the backwoodsmen, as the first emigrants from the eastward of the Allegheny mountains are called, are very similar in their habits and manners to the aborigines, only perhaps more prodigal and more careless of life. They depend more on hunting than on agriculture, and of course are exposed to all the varieties of climate in the open air. Their cabins are not better than Indian wigwams. They have frequent meetings for the purposes of gambling, fighting and drinking. They make bets to the amount of all they possess. They fight for the most trifling provocations, or even sometimes without any, but merely to try each others prowess, which they are fond of vaunting of. Their hands, teeth, knees, head and feet are their weapons, not only boxing with their fists, . . . but also tearing, kicking, scratching, biting, gouging each others eyes out by a dexterous use of a thumb

[1] Arthur K. Moore, *The Frontier Mind: A Cultural Analysis of the Kentucky Frontiersman* (Lexington, Ky.: University of Kentucky Press, 1957), p. 50.

and finger, and doing their utmost to kill each other, even when rolling over one another on the ground.[2]

Whether or not this traveler "reported rather more than he observed" and contributed to the romantic haze which soon enveloped the frontiersman, the western settlers did speedily acquire an unequaled reputation for violence and heedless ways. The society to which circuit riders, farmer-preachers, and evangelizers of all kinds were to make their gospel appeals offered a challenge equal to any in the church's long history.

The religious life of the vast area did not simply remain dormant until one fine day in August, 1801, when the fires of revival suddenly sprang up at Cane Ridge in Bourbon County, Kentucky. The settlers did, to be sure, outrun the organized churches, but many were earnest and some were zealous in religious matters. It was said of the Scotch-Irish farmers that when crops failed and food was short, they could live off the Shorter Catechism, and this exaggeration could also be applied to many Baptists and Methodists. The most important single factor in the westward movement of popular piety was the extended "Great Awakening" in the southern back country. Because of the revivals (Presbyterian, Baptist, and Methodist in turn) there were among the migrants a significant number of strongly committed laymen who became missionaries without formal commissioning.

Each of these three denominations, furthermore, had certain important assets for the immense new work before it. The Presbyterians were strategically poised in western Pennsylvania, where the Redstone Presbytery had been formed in 1781. It soon gave birth to others in the Ohio Valley. Presbyterians had also penetrated the southern back country. The first Presbyterian preacher in Kentucky was David Rice, who in 1784 moved from Hanover County, Virginia, and organized at Danville the first church of his denomination in the state. Largely as a result of his labors, twelve other churches were organized by the next year, and the Transylvania Presbytery was formed. By 1802 two more presbyteries had been organized, making it possible to constitute the Synod of Kentucky. Their secure footing in the old Middle Colonies ensured the Presbyterians resources of money and

[2] Moore quotes the English traveler, Fortescue Cuming, ibid., p. 54.

personnel, while their hierarchical polity facilitated an organized missions program. Not least, they could appeal to the Westminster birthright slumbering in the consciousness of so many of the pioneers.

The Methodists were less solidly based in the East, but they had formed a highly efficient organization which was closely superintended by a man of amazing energy and foresight, Bishop Francis Asbury. They sent the first regularly appointed circuit rider over the mountains in 1782, and within nine years there were ten Methodist circuits in the new West: four in Tennessee, three in Kentucky, and three along the upper Ohio. By 1800 there were more than two thousand Methodists in Kentucky and Tennessee. Bishop Asbury himself took a personal interest in the growth of Methodism in the "Western Conference," as the tramontane area was called, crossing the mountains several times to confer with the preachers and minister to the churches.

The Baptists, on the other hand, were much more flexible than either of these two bodies; they opposed the idea of settled, educated, and paid ministers, relying instead on preachers who could move along with their migrating flocks. They were also well situated on the trails that led through the mountains. Daniel Boone himself was of Baptist background, and there were at least two Baptist preachers at Harrodsburg by 1776. Several others followed, and in 1781 the first church was organized at Severn's Valley. Within four years there were a dozen churches grouped in three associations, two of which were Regular (Elkhorn and Salem) and one Separate (South Kentucky). Efforts to unite these two groups were begun in 1793 and finally consummated in 1801. Though the 1790s were deemed "a period of spiritual dearth," a constant influx of settlers added to the number and size of Baptist congregations.

THE WESTERN REVIVALS

As providence would have it, the Presbyterian work in this new mission field was to have the most dramatic historical consequences. The first well-remembered actor in the drama was the Reverend James McGready (1758?–1817), a bold and uncompromising Scotch-Irishman whose family had moved from Pennsylvania to western North Carolina when

he was a child. Showing great religious interest as a youth, he
was sent back to Pennsylvania for theological studies under
John McMillan, a Princeton graduate, and he was later
licensed by the Redstone Presbytery. McGready ministered
in Carolina until 1796, when he took charge of three parishes
in southwestern Kentucky. At the Gasper River Church in
July 1800, he and his associates gave decisive impetus to that
great institution of western evangelism, the camp meeting,
which may be defined as "a religious service of several days'
length, held outdoors, for a group that was obliged to take
shelter on the spot because of the distance from home."

Another Presbyterian who attended this Logan County revival was Barton Warren Stone (1772–1844). Born in Port
Tobacco, Maryland, Stone had moved into western Carolina,
where he was converted under McGready. In 1800 he was
serving the small Cane Ridge and Concord churches in Bourbon County, Kentucky. Greatly impressed by what he saw at
Gasper River, the more so because of his concern over the
prevailing apathy in his own area, Stone adopted McGready's
methods. After some preliminary revivals, he announced a
great meeting to be held at Cane Ridge on 6 August 1801.
When the day arrived, so did a great many ministers, including some Baptists and Methodists, and an unbelievably large
concourse of people. The crowd was estimated at from ten to
twenty-five thousand—and this at a time when nearby Lexington, the state's largest city, barely exceeded two thousand.
This "sacramental occasion" continued for six or seven days
and nights, and would have gone on longer except for the
failure of provisions for such a crowd. When it was over,
Cane Ridge was referred to as the greatest outpouring of the
Spirit since Pentecost. It marks a watershed in American
church history, and the little log meetinghouse around which
multitudes thronged and writhed has become a shrine for all
who invoke "the frontier spirit" in American Christianity.

The Cane Ridge meeting has challenged the descriptive
powers of many historians, yet none has risen fully to the occasion. Critics and sensationalists then and since have dwelt
almost exclusively on the rampant emotionalism and bodily
agitations. Most of those who were caught up in the enthusiasm were never able to report it objectively. Barton Stone
himself stated the basic fact: "Many things transpired there,
which were so much like miracles, that if they were not, they
had the same effects as miracles on infidels and unbelievers;

for many of them by these were convinced that Jesus was the Christ, and bowed in submission to him."[3] One must first try to re-create the scene: the milling crowds of hardened frontier farmers, tobacco-chewing, tough-spoken, notoriously profane, famous for their alcoholic thirst; their scarcely demure wives and large broods of children; the rough clearing, the rows of wagons and crude improvised tents with horses staked out behind; the gesticulating speaker on a rude platform, or perhaps simply a preacher holding forth from a fallen tree. At night, when the forest's edge was limned by the flickering light of many campfires, the effect of apparent miracles would be heightened. For men and women accustomed to retiring and rising with the birds, these turbulent nights must have been especially awe-inspiring. And underlying every other conditioning circumstance was the immense loneliness of the frontier farmer's normal life and the exhilaration of participating in so large a social occasion.[4]

The physical effects of so drastic a conjunction of apathy and fervor, loneliness and sociality, monotony and miracle, could not have been mild. Critics thought they noted a greater increase of fleshly lust than of spirituality, and charged that "more souls were begot than saved"; while even the most sympathetic observers conceded that camp-meeting conversions were not decorous religious transactions. Barton Stone devoted a whole chapter of his memoirs to a description of the outward manifestations of strong religious emotions; and this account by the meeting's leader merits extensive quotation, for it reveals his serious estimate of the very excesses that made Cane Ridge not only a landmark in the history of revivalism, but a cause of controversy and schism.

The bodily agitations or exercises, attending the excitement in the beginning of this century, were various, and called by various names. . . . The falling exercise was very common among all classes, the saints and sinners of every age and of every grade, from the philosopher to the clown. The subject of this exercise would, generally, with a pierc-

[3] "A Short History of the Life of Barton W. Stone Written by Himself," in *Voices from Cane Ridge,* ed. Rhodes Thompson, facsimile ed. (Saint Louis: Bethany Press, 1954), p. 68.

[4] Nowhere in the world were farmers so scattered on their isolated homesteads as in America, and until the advent of the automobile, churches would continue to be their chief social bond.

ing scream, fall like a log on the floor, earth, or mud, and appear as dead. . . .

The jerks cannot be so easily described. Sometimes the subject of the jerks would be affected in some one member of the body, and sometimes the whole system. When the head alone was affected, it would be jerked backward and forward, or from side to side, so quickly that the features of the face could not be distinguished. When the whole system was affected, I have seen the person stand in one place, and jerk backward and forward in quick succession, their head nearly touching the floor behind and before. All classes, saints and sinners, the strong as well as the weak, were thus affected. . . .

The dancing exercise. This generally began with the jerks, and was peculiar to the professors of religion. The subject, after jerking awhile, began to dance, and then the jerks would cease. Such dancing was indeed heavenly to the spectators; there was nothing in it like levity, nor calculated to excite levity in the beholders. The smile of heaven shone on the countenance of the subject, and assimilated to angels appeared the whole person. Sometimes the motion was quick and sometimes slow. Thus they continued to move forward and backward in the same track or alley till nature seemed exhausted, and they would fall prostrate on the floor or earth, unless caught by those standing by. While thus exercised, I have heard their solemn praises and prayers ascending to God.

The barking exercise, (as opposers contemptuously called it,) was nothing but the jerks. A person affected with the jerks, especially in his head, would often make a grunt, or bark, if you please, from the suddenness of the jerk. . . .

The laughing exercise was frequent, confined solely with the religious. It was a loud, hearty laughter, but one *sui generis;* it excited laughter in none else. The subject appeared rapturously solemn, and his laughter excited solemnity in saints and sinners. It is truly indescribable.

The running exercise was nothing more than, that persons feeling something of these bodily agitations, through fear, attempted to run away, and thus escape from them; but it commonly happened that they ran not far, before they fell, or became so greatly agitated that they could proceed no farther. . . .

> I shall close this chapter with the singing exercise. This is
> more unaccountable than any thing else I ever saw. The
> subject in a very happy state of mind would sing most
> melodiously, not from the mouth or nose, but entirely in
> the breast, the sounds issuing from thence. Such music
> silenced every thing, and attracted the attention of all. It
> was most heavenly. None could ever be tired of hearing it.

Stone concludes by admitting that "there were many eccentricities, and much fanaticism in this excitement," but insists
that "the good effects were seen and acknowledged in every
neighborhood."[5]

GROWTH OF THE POPULAR DENOMINATIONS

The most important fact about Cane Ridge is that it was an
unforgettable revival of revivalism, at a strategic time and a
place where it could become both symbol and impetus for
the century-long process by which the greater part of American evangelical Protestantism became "revivalized." The organized revival became a major mode of church expansion—
in some denominations the major mode. The words evangelist
and evangelism took on this connotation. A second consequence of this historic camp meeting and the great revival
which swept across Kentucky, Tennessee, and southern Ohio
during the next three years was the vitality which it poured
into the participating churches. The future of the country's
denominational expansion was in large part determined by
the foundations laid during this period. Denominational
growth began to reach a new order of magnitude, not only in
the West, but in the East as well due to the stimulating effect
of enthusiastic reports that soon drifted back to the older and
more settled parts of the country. In the positive sense this
development was primarily Baptist and Methodist, for Presbyterian leaders were repelled by the reports and began to
take disciplinary action. From this time forward Presbyterian
growth would lag far behind. A third consequence of the revivals was the rise of conflict and schism, from which the
Presbyterians suffered most severely, though the Baptists sustained considerable losses as well. Finally, a new Christian

[5] "Life of Stone," pp. 69–72.

movement, destined to become a large American denomination, came into being during these enlivening years.

The Methodists

No group prospered more in the West or seemed more providentially designed to capitalize on the conditions of the advancing American frontier than the Methodists. A small and highly suspect adjunct to Anglicanism before the Revolution, this church had begun its independent American history only in 1784. Since then its web of preaching circuits had come to cover almost the entire country. In 1789 even New England had been invaded. Yet the 1790s had generally been unencouraging, with almost as many years showing a net decline in membership as those which showed a gain. The hierarchical structure of the church was seriously challenged in 1792, when James O'Kelly of Virginia led out the "Republican Methodists" to become a separate movement. Cokesbury College, the first Methodist experiment in higher education, had burned to the ground in 1795. At the turn of the century there were probably not sixty-five thousand Methodists in the country, and Asbury's health was in serious decline. The General Conference at Baltimore in 1800, however, was the scene of a great revival among those in attendance—strangely synchronous with more tumultuous developments beyond the mountains—and as the preachers returned to their circuits the whole church began to feel and respond to the new impulses.

John Magee, one of James McGready's most vigorous aides in Logan County, was a Methodist. At Cane Ridge another Methodist, William Burke, seems to have preached with as powerful an effect as anybody else. After 1800 other men continued their tradition, and "because early Methodists did not turn their backs on groans and jerks," writes Bernard Weisberger, "they could slay their thousands while the other denominations counted their hundreds." Circuits were laid out both to create and to tap the religious potential of the Old Southwest; the circuit became an institution of the region, and the Methodist Episcopal church itself experienced a virtual second birth.

When the century began there were 2,622 white Methodists and 179 colored in the whole western country; in 1812 there were 29,093 white and 1,648 colored, while the circuits had increased from 9 to 69. In 1830, instead of 1 conference west of the Alleghanies, there were 8, while the membership had grown from 30,000 to more than 175,000, and among these were nearly 2,000 Indians and more than 15,000 negroes.[6]

By 1844, when the church divided north and south, the Methodists had become the most numerous religious body in America, with 1,068,525 members, 3,988 itinerant preachers, 7,730 local preachers, and an incalculable number of regular hearers. Even in New England, where its progress was slowest, it had become the second largest denomination.

The most important factor in this amazing expansion was the system of circuits and preaching stations, and the disciplined, basically autocratic way in which they were laid out, staffed, and supervised. The country was subdivided into districts in 1796, each overseen by a presiding elder, and after 1808, with the enormously active, knowledgeable, and far-sighted William McKendree as bishop of the Western Conference, Methodists were in a position to evangelize a moving population. They had been in such a position from the beginning, as a matter of fact; but they became even more effective by virtue of a second factor—their appropriation of the camp meeting, which they made an instrument for satisfying both the social and the religious impulses of a scattered, though naturally gregarious, people. When other denominations abandoned it as leading to excess and division, the Methodists became its sponsors. Bishop Asbury was one of its most enthusiastic champions, and it became fully subject to the famous Methodist penchant for meticulous planning. Nothing was left to chance, from the scheduling of the meetings and their advertisement to the sharing of duties among the camp leaders and management of the camp services. From one end of the country to the other there were great Methodist conclaves, sometimes organized within a single circuit, sometimes for a whole conference, often serving as the annual conference itself. Due both to overuse and overorganization, however, they slowly lost their spontaneity and became decorous and formal. Cabins and two-storied residence houses replaced the tents, and by the 1840s the original impulse was dying. In later years the

[6] William W. Sweet, *Religion in the Development of American Culture, 1765–1840*, p. 119.

camp meeting became a resort, a place for an edifying vacation—an outcome shown in the multiplication of summer assemblies and Bible conferences, both denominational and interdenominational.[7] But during the early nineteenth century "harvest time," the camp meeting was a great engine of Methodist expansion and a very important part of the church's system.

A third factor which had been operative from the first was this church's recruitment of its ministry from among the common people, and its continuing interest in the masses. Ordination was conferred only on well-proved preachers, with the result that ordained men were something of an elite within the system. But they were by no means a social elite. With little formal training to divorce them from the common idiom, they reduced the Christian message and its implications for life to the simplest possible terms, and preached it simply, directly, and forcefully. Peter Cartwright (1785–1872), most famed of the circuit riders and a great presiding elder of the West, scorned theological education, which he considered often even a hindrance in preaching the Gospel: "I have seen so many educated preachers who forcibly reminded me of lettuce growing under the shade of a peach-tree, or like a gosling that had got the straddles by wading in the dew, that I turn away sick and faint." The Methodists also made maximum use of informality, as Cartwright likewise made clear:

> The Presbyterians, and other Calvinistic branches of the Protestant Church, used to contend for an educated ministry, for pews, for instrumental music, for a congregational or stated salaried ministry. The Methodists universally opposed these ideas; and the illiterate Methodist preachers actually set the world on fire, (the American world at least,) while they [the others] were lighting their matches![8]

The fourth factor, implied in Cartwright's statement, was the preaching of Wesleyan theology, sometimes described as

[7] By the middle of the twentieth century at least one of these has become a "place not to miss" for those who followed Duncan Hines's advice to gourmets.

[8] *Autobiography of Peter Cartwright,* ed. Charles L. Wallis, p. 64.

"Arminianism set on fire." There is no justification for the conclusion of many historians (including the most fervent Methodists) that the Methodist message was a "democratic theology" or a "frontier faith." In the earlier part of the nineteenth century, at least, its theology was derived not from American democracy or the frontier but from John Wesley—a very different source indeed. The conference courses of study instituted in 1816 for prospective ministers in lieu of divinity schools were thoroughly Wesleyan in spirit. And the starting point of this theology (as of all Reformed theologies, whether "Arminian" or not) was the sovereignty of God and the depravity of man. No one spoke more forcefully of man's abject need for divine grace than Wesley, and the true Methodist demand for repentance—or, more often, penitential conflict—stems from the heart of the Puritan movement. Arminianism in this context meant not an optimistic view of human nature (as with the Boston liberals), but a reinterpretation of the strict Calvinistic understanding of atonement, grace, and the sanctifying work of the Holy Spirit. Had this not been the case, Methodism would never have been the moral force that it was on the frontier. Decades of vulgar, simplistic theological polemic between Wesleyans and Calvinists ultimately forced both sides to exaggerate their distinctive tenets and banish subtlety from theological discussion. Revivalistic preaching thus in time worked its effect on Methodist theology, shifting the emphasis from "grace for all" to "human freedom," but there is no evidence that the new patterns of thought which emerged brought any increased effectiveness in preaching. In fact, one must insist that the force of primitive Wesleyan theology constituted a major factor in the Methodist explosion on the frontier.

German Evangelicals and United Brethren

The contagiousness of the Wesleyan appeal is further indicated by two other Methodistic movements that emerged at the same time among the German-speaking peoples, and which flourished under very similar circumstances. These served even more effectively to perpetuate the traditions of pietism and even to revive the earlier Anabaptist vision of an *ecclesia restituta*. The outstanding leader of this revival was Philip William Otterbein (1726–1813), a native of the Reformed duchy of Nassau in Germany, who in 1752 answered the call of Michael Schlatter for American missionaries. Already well known for his efforts to restore experiential religion, Otterbein extended his reputation during a series of five pastorates in America, the last, longest, and most eventful one in an evangelical German church in Baltimore. While in Lancaster, Pennsylvania, he also felt a notable deepening of his own experience of God's grace. His new perspective on the church gained significance in subsequent years, especially after his meeting with the Mennonite preacher Martin Boehm (1725–1812), and the Methodist Francis Asbury. In 1784 the attraction of these new contacts finally overcame his allegiance to the German Reformed church. During the famous Christmas Conference of the Methodist church in that year, he participated in the ordination of Asbury as general superintendent. The following year Otterbein set up rules for the government and devotional life of his own congregation, which in due course defined the character of a new pietistic, semi-Methodist German denomination in which "inward spiritual experience" became a requirement of membership.

This group progressed toward separation in 1789, when fourteen like-minded pastors (nine German Reformed and five Mennonite) met in Otterbein's parsonage and adopted regulations and a confession of faith adapted from the Apostles' and Nicene creeds. They stressed especially "the fall in Adam" and affirmed the importance of both the human will and the sanctifying work of the Holy Spirit in salvation. Particularly interesting are the passages which compromise the conflicting Reformed and Mennonite views on baptism, communion, and foot washing. What was emerging here was a new version of the same sort of religious impulse that a century before had created the Church of the Brethren in Schwarzenau, and which a century and a half before that had brought the Mennonite movement into being.

The final moves toward denominational independence came in 1800, when Otterbein and Boehm were elected bishops, and in 1815, when the first general conference of the United Brethren in Christ was convened, and a more complete discipline adopted. In the permissive American milieu, such an organization could develop rapidly; and by this time its preachers had made their way to wherever Germans were settling. Like the Methodist church, which continued to absorb many of its English-speaking younger people, it moved west. In 1810 the Miami (Ohio) Conference was formed, and there were congregations in Kentucky and Indiana as well.

While the leaven of pietistic and Wesleyan influence was bringing the United Brethren into existence, still another revivalistic movement was emerging among the Germans of eastern Pennsylvania. Its founder was Jacob Albright (1759–1808), who had been born and reared in the spiritual desolation of the revolutionary era. Stirred from his lethargy by a funeral sermon in 1790, he was converted some years later, and joined the Methodists. Gradually Albright became disturbed over the religious welfare of his German-speaking neighbors, for whom the church showed little concern, and in 1796 he embarked on a preaching career. Eventually he organized his scattered converts into locally led "classes," which were soon brought together in an essentially Methodistic "Evangelical Association." When a formal council in November 1803 officially declared its denominational integrity and acknowledged the leadership of Albright, a new religious body was on the American scene. At the first regular annual conference in 1807, though the movement was still very small (consisting of only three local preachers, five itinerants, and twenty lay leaders), they elected Albright as bishop and adopted as their official—though temporary—name "The Newly Formed Methodist Conference."

In structure, doctrine, and discipline, this movement was decidedly Wesleyan, and it would doubtless have integrated with the Methodist church had not that body repulsed it.[9] During the early decades of its existence, its "large meetings," protracted revivals, and enthusiastic employment of emotionalism won the allegiance of numbers of America's westward-moving German population, until this very migration shifted the center of gravity of the group to the Old Northwest. In 1815 they began publication work at New Berlin, Pennsylvania, and their *Christliche Botschafter* (1836) became an outstanding German religious periodical. In 1853, however, they deemed it advisable to move the publishing house to Cleveland, Ohio. The Eastern Confer-

[9] In 1810 (two years after Albright's death) Bishop Asbury declined proposals of merger from "the Albright People." Pursuing thereafter an independent course, the group was greatly divided in the latter half of the century over Wesley's doctrine of complete sanctification.

ence organized in 1838 the first "German Evangelical Missionary Society of North America," which was transmuted the next year into a general denominational organ for missionary endeavor. Although they had no schools before the Civil War due to a strong prejudice against education, they moved to establish several in the latter part of the century. In 1946 they effected a merger with the United Brethren, forming the Evangelical United Brethren Church, and finally, in 1968, this united church returned to the Methodist church, which now added the word "United" at the head of its corporate name.

The Baptists

Baptist growth in the West in the decades after Cane Ridge was almost as sensational as that of the Methodists, a resurgence that lifted the Baptists into a prominent position in American religious life from that time forward. As with other churches, the effects of this western revival also flowed back into the older churches of the East. The Baptist expansion also underlines again the fact that successful evangelism did not require a congenial "frontier theology," for Baptist preaching continued to be strictly Reformed in spirit. Adherence to the Philadelphia Confession was not so strict as the Regular Baptists had hoped, but the creedal basis on which Regulars and Separates of Kentucky united in 1801 was at least as Reformed in temper as, say, the Thirty-nine Articles of the Church of England. Since this historic compromise of Arminian and Calvinistic views set a pattern, it deserves to be quoted in full:

We, the committees of the Elkhorn and South Kentucky Associations, do agree to unite on the following plan. 1st. That the Scriptures of the Old and New Testaments are the infallible word of God, and the only rule of faith and practice. 2nd. That there is only one true Godhead or divine essence, there are Father, Son and Holy Ghost. 3d. That by nature we are fallen and depraved creatures. 4th. That salvation, regeneration, sanctification, and justification, are by the life, death, resurrection, and ascension of Jesus Christ. 5th. That the saints will finally persevere through grace to glory. 6th. That believers' baptism by immersion is necessary to receiving the Lord's supper. 7th.

That the salvation of the righteous, and punishment of the wicked will be eternal. 8th. That it is our duty to be tender and affectionate to each other, and study the happiness of the children of God in general; to be engaged singly to promote the honour of God. 9th. And that the preaching [that] Christ tasted death for every man shall be no bar to communion [that is, deviation from strict Reformed teaching on "limited atonement" is allowed]. 10th. And that each may keep up their associational and church government as to them may seem best. 11th. That a free correspondence and communion be kept up between the churches thus united.[10]

Again it must be stressed that such a confession proclaimed not the "religion of democracy" or a "frontier faith" but a basically Calvinistic theology, with concessions made only to those whose interpretation of Christ's work was in the tradition of Jacobus Arminius—who was, after all, a Reformed theologian. The basic doctrinal differences between Baptists and Methodists, therefore, should not be exaggerated. But frontier preachers did precisely that in their constant efforts to evangelize or "proselytize" the people[11]; and in the highly competitive situation that ensued, they debated the issues of election, grace, and human freedom almost as frequently as the doctrine of baptism. In the early part of the century the effect of all this popular controversy was to widen the rifts that separated the denominations, as well as to work significant changes within them.

Like the Methodists, the Baptists had a long history of minority status everywhere except in Rhode Island. With the Great Awakening this began to change throughout the country, and the flourishing Baptist revival in the southern back country even gave Baptists political power, especially in Virginia. Of special strategic importance was the location of several very zealous congregations along the fringe of the old frontier, where they could reach the migrants streaming past their doors. In 1790 only 3,105 of Kentucky's 73,677 people were Baptists, and these were scattered in 42 churches with

[10] William W. Sweet, *Religion on the American Frontier: The Baptists, 1783–1830*, pp. 23–24.

[11] "Proselytizing" was (and is) the term for the widely discountenanced but nevertheless very widely practiced policy of trying to win members from another denomination.

some forty preachers, of whom only nineteen were ordained. By 1800 these had increased to 5,110 members in 106 churches, which were organized into one Separate and two Regular associations. Then came the great revival, in which "all were visited and refreshed by the copious and abundant rain of righteousness which was poured over the land," and by 1803 Kentucky numbered 10,380 Baptists; by 1820, when Kentucky's population had climbed to 564,000, they had 491 churches with 31,689 members. In other parts of the Old Southwest, in the lower parts of the Old Northwest, and in the seaboard states, there was a corresponding development as the revival became a general national phenomenon.[12]

The proliferation of Baptist churches depended above all upon their spiritual vitality and their individualistic emphasis on conversion.[13] Yet they also were remarkably well adapted to the social structures (or lack of them) on the frontier. Baptists did not exceed Presbyterians in zeal, but they were unhindered by the bottlenecks to evangelistic work created by strict educational requirements and a rigid presbyterial polity. The genius of Baptist evangelism was also at the opposite pole from the Methodist insistence on order and authority. Its frontier hero was not the circuit rider but the farmer-preacher, who moved with the people into new areas. Unpaid, self-supporting, and hence financially independent, the farmer-preacher was usually a man who had heard the "call" to the ministry and got himself licensed to preach. In due course he would be ordained by a church, sometimes one which he had gathered himself. From such churches sprang other candidates for the ministry, and by this process the Baptists advanced into the wilderness, or moved back in among the unchurched multitudes of the older areas, without direction from bishops or synods, and without financial support from denominational agencies or special societies. On many occasions an entire church would move on to a new location, just as Lewis Craig's congregation moved from Virginia to become Gilbert's Creek Church in Kentucky in 1783. Baptist work was not as disorganized as all this may imply,

[12] In 1812 the entire denomination registered 172,972 members in 2,164 churches with 1,605 ministers, having doubled in the previous decade.

[13] On this individualistic emphasis on conversion and its later consequences, see Samuel S. Hill, Jr., *Southern Churches in Crisis*, chap. 5.

however, for their regional associations fostered a spirit of unity, as well as a concern for discipline and doctrinal harmony.

Like the Methodists, the Baptists grew because they sprang from the most numerous class of Americans—the common people of the country and small towns—and they spoke to these people with simplicity and power, without pretense or condescension. Peter Cartwright tells of stopping on his circuit at Stockton Valley during his early years to make a preaching appointment in an old crumbling Baptist church:

> When I came there was a very large congregation. While I was preaching, the power of God fell on the assembly, and there was an awful shaking among the dry bones. Several fell to the floor and cried for mercy. . . . I believe if I had opened the doors of the Church then, all of them would have joined the Methodist Church.[14]

But Cartwright moved on, and the Baptists, having heard of his twenty-three conquests, sent three preachers to the place. The few scattered Methodists in the neighborhood then took alarm, he said, "for fear these preachers would run my converts into the water before I could come round." They persuaded Cartwright to return, and he was able to save his spiritual children only at the very brink of the creek, by a most desperate stratagem. Cartwright presented himself for Baptist membership, recounted his own Christian experience, and was received gleefully by the Baptist preacher. At the last moment, however, in the hearing of all, he declared that he still believed in infant sprinkling, thus forcing the Baptist to reject him publicly. At the sight of his rejection, his twenty-three converts returned to the Methodist fold. This story indicates the depths to which theological controversy descended, but it also illustrates the enthusiasm with which both Methodists and Baptists sought to bring wandering frontiersmen of every rank and station within the influence and discipline of their churches.

The Presbyterians

The Baptists and Methodists were the two great popular churches of the frontier; but this is not to deny the popular

[14] *Autobiography of Peter Cartwright*, pp. 55–56.

aims of the Presbyterians, who were among the first to work beyond the mountains, and in whose churches the revivals of 1800 and 1801 took place. Since the days of Whitefield and the Tennents they had been aggressive in their evangelism, but on the frontier they were beset with obstacles which they were unable to overcome. As legatees of a monumental dogmatic tradition, Presbyterians were committed to a concept of education and instruction. The doctrinal system of the Westminster formularies was ill-adapted to the simplifications of frontier preaching; it demanded a genuinely "teaching church," a catechetical system, sustained preaching, and a well-educated ministry. Faced with these realities, Presbyterians responded, with varying degrees of intensity, in one of two ways. In some cases, they modified their message, as the Separate Baptists had done, or adopted the New Haven Theology and even explicit forms of Arminianism. The other recourse was to break away completely from the doctrinal and educational restrictions of Presbyterianism. Because many chose the latter alternative, conflict and schism became characteristic features of Presbyterian history in this period and region. The new churches thus formed became rivals of the Baptists and the Methodists due to their message, popular approach, and appeal.

The first division within the newly formed Synod of Kentucky was a direct aftermath of James McGready's revivals in Logan County. The men who had led this renewing work soon gained control of the Cumberland Presbytery (organized in 1802), which in 1806 was exscinded from the Synod of Kentucky on account of its revivalism, its waiving of traditional educational requirements for the ministry in order to meet more quickly the region's religious needs, and its growing tendency to depart from the Westminster standards (especially in regard to divine sovereignty and human ability). After the General Assembly unanimously supported the synod's action in 1809, the outcasts organized an independent Cumberland Presbytery, which in 1813 in Sumner County, Tennessee, divided in three and formed a synod. They adopted a revised, Arminian version of the Westminster Confession, and set in motion the Cumberland Presbyterian Church. During these early years the new group made extensive use of the camp meeting as an evangelistic instrument. By the time their own General Assembly was formed in 1829, they had presbyteries in Kentucky, Tennessee, Alabama,

Mississippi, Arkansas, Indiana, Illinois, and Missouri—and missionaries from Pennsylvania to Texas. In 1906 most of the Cumberlands would be reunited with the Presbyterian church more or less on their own terms; but during the intervening century their growth was impressive, with their membership composed almost entirely of "converts won from Satan's dominions, and not of proselytes won from other churches."[15]

RISE OF THE DISCIPLES MOVEMENT

The Stonites

While these events were moving toward their final issue, Barton Stone and other New Light leaders of the Cane Ridge revival were coming under suspicion not only for indecorous churchmanship and low educational standards, but for heresy as well. Rather than stand trial, they withdrew and in 1803 organized the Springfield Presbytery. The degree to which these men had removed themselves from Reformed doctrine and Presbyterian polity was revealed in their *Apology for Renouncing the Jurisdiction of the Synod of Kentucky*. This document was so explicitly and violently critical of historic Presbyterianism that it was only a matter of time before the New Lights realized the incongruity of their being in a "presbytery" even of their own making. In June 1804 they published the "Last Will and Testament of the Presbytery of Springfield," abandoned the "traditions of men," took the Bible as their only creed and law, and adopted for themselves the name "Christians." What they derived from the Scriptures was a decisively Arminian theology, a radically congregational polity, and a contractual conception of the ministry which all but dissolved the idea of ordination. The common charge that the Stonites were deists, Unitarians, and infidels in revivalistic guise is perhaps unjustified; but their doctrinal outlook was a compromise "somewhere between Unitarianism and orthodox popular Calvinism."[16] Of the six men who started the movement, two went on to the further excesses of

[15] The reunion was facilitated by the larger body's revision of its doctrinal standards in 1903.

[16] William Garrett West, *Barton Warren Stone: Early American Advocate for Christian Unity* (Nashville, Tenn.: Disciples of Christ Historical Society, 1954), p. 82.

the Shakers, and two returned to the Presbyterian fold, leaving only Stone and David Purviance in the role of "founders." Yet they had many followers, and the "Christians" grew rapidly in Kentucky. In southeastern Ohio they swept every Presbyterian church but two into their movement. Until 1832, when they coalesced with the followers of Alexander Campbell, they were a broad, extremely congregational, never precisely defined current in the moving stream of frontier revivalism.

Other Currents of "Reform"

Two or three much smaller currents were also flowing beside the "Christians," sharing their concern for return to the "primitive gospel." One of these was the so-called Christian Connection, a minority revivalistic movement among people of lowly station on the New England frontier. Strongly anti-Calvinistic in sentiment, it grew contemporaneously with the similar body of Freewill Baptists who were also strongest in Vermont, New Hampshire, and Maine; and many of its ministers had been ordained by Freewill congregations. At the beginning of the nineteenth century, the two groups contemplated merging, since both held similar doctrines, inclined toward primitivism, and practiced open communion. But as they expanded westward across New York State, the "Christians" began more and more to show Unitarian tendencies, which alienated them from the Baptists and turned them toward the Stonites—and occasionally toward the Unitarians.

Out of Virginia and North Carolina flowed still another "Christian" movement, this one of Methodist background. It arose from the revolt of "Republican Methodists" against the authoritarianism of the Methodistic system, especially as it was embodied so strenuously in Bishop Asbury. Led by James O'Kelly and Rice Haggard, by the end of the eighteenth century it had assumed the shape of a separate movement. After 1804 Haggard wielded considerable influence upon Stone, convincing him that "Christian" was the only proper biblical way to designate the true believer.

The Campbellites

The "Christians" and other closely related movements were soon to be overshadowed by still another offshoot of frontier

Presbyterianism led by Thomas Campbell (1763–1854), a Scotch-Irish minister of the Anti-Burgher faction of the Secession church. On coming to America from northern Ireland in 1807, Campbell continued his ministry in western Pennsylvania; but after being censured by the Associate Synod of North America for laxity in admitting people to the Lord's Supper, he withdrew from it and began a private ministry to any who would hear and follow him. In 1809 this group organized itself as a nondenominational "Christian Association of Washington" (Pennsylvania). Taking Campbell's *Declaration and Address* as their statement of purpose, they also approved the now well-known maxim, "Where the Scriptures speak, we speak; where the Scriptures are silent, we are silent." For a time it seemed that Campbell, like Zinzendorf and Wesley before him, had no plans to organize a new denomination. His announced purpose was to promote Christian unity by preaching a simple gospel which would rise above denominationalism. But the arrival that same year (1809) of Campbell's aggressive and disputatious son Alexander (1788–1866) caused this irenic intention to be put aside. Before the year was out, the "Christian Association" had compiled a complete catechism and initiated a periodical to point out the "errors" of the existing churches. As was perhaps inevitable, only two years elapsed before a new denomination was virtually in existence, though at that time it consisted of only one country church of thirty members at Brush Run, Pennsylvania, with Alexander Campbell as its leader and pastor. In 1813 this independent denomination seemed to disappear for a time as it entered the Redstone Baptist Association; but this uneasy affiliation was to last only until 1827.

From the very beginning, it was perfectly clear to anyone with an attentive ear that the message of Brush Run was unique on the American frontier—in fact, on the American scene. It was equally obvious that the source of its uniqueness was the younger Campbell. What the disturbed Baptists were confronting was a complex of doctrines, usages, and historical interpretations which this young man had heard and adopted while a student in Scotland. Even in Glasgow Campell was so far estranged from his traditional church allegiance as to walk out of a Presbyterian communion service. The ideas which were churning within him then, matured by further thought and study in America, became the largest single formative influence on the whole group of "Christian Reformers" in the Ohio River valley. Several widely publicized debates and the circulation of his periodical the *Christian Baptist* (1823–29) made Alexander Campbell a man to reckon with. By any standard he is an important figure in American church history, a curious compound of the rationalistic theologian on one hand and the eccentric and legalistic sectary on the other. To deepen the paradox, Campbell's campaign for undoing denominationalism was the chief factor in the origination of a new denomination.

An effort to place Alexander Campbell must begin with the fact that his early nurture was in the Presbyterian Church of Scotland, where he learned the Reformed distrust of historical tradition and accretions in every aspect of church life. Like so many other "reformers," Campbell sought to reestablish the patterns of primitive Christianity as he conceived them. Although he also shared the Reformed emphasis on divine law, he broke decisively with Reformed-Puritan views by insisting on a far more drastic disjunction between the Old Covenant and the New than early covenant theologians had dreamed of. Discarding the typically Puritan adulation of the Old Testament, Campbell put his whole emphasis on the New Dispensation, finding the "law" for Christian life and worship in the New Testament. In its interpretation, moreover, he took silence to be as eloquent as specific injunction. Since musical instruments were not mentioned specifically as contributing to Christian worship, they must be banned; since there was no command to form missionary societies, they were not to be organized. On such grounds the Campbellite "reformers" developed a rigorous church order. Baptism was by immersion, for believers only, and necessary for the remission of sins; the ministry was in no sense above the laity, and not to be set apart by the title "reverend"; communion was to be celebrated on each Lord's Day (the word "Sabbath" was avoided as belonging to the Old Testament dispensation); the autonomy and self-sufficiency of the local congregation was primary, and all higher levels of ecclesiastical organization (if allowed at all) were regarded as purely informal and without authority. Worship was conducted in the free-church tradition of simplicity and informality.[17]

[17] Alexander Campbell's ideas were drawn from the reform impulse stemming from John Glas (1695–1773) of Perth and his son-

But Campbell was not only a restorationist and a legalist; he was also a fervent exponent of eighteen-century rationalism, a disciple of John Locke and the Scottish philosophers. Natural law concepts figured prominently in his ethical thought. An intellectualist bent determined his understanding of faith as the mind's assent to credible testimony, an emphasis which served powerfully to divorce his movement from the prevailing currents of emotional revivalism. This rationalistic note stands out in his views on baptism, which occasioned his ruptures first with the Presbyterians, then with the Baptists. For Campbell baptism was neither a gift of grace—a "sacrament"—as with the Roman Catholics or Lutherans, nor merely a symbol signifying God's redemptive act, as with the Baptists. It was the decisive, formal compliance of the believer with the command of Jesus, a washing away of sins, not a "mysterious" supernatural transaction.

Formation of the Disciples Denomination

The emergence of the "Christians," "Reformers," or "Disciples" as a distinct denomination, disengaged from both Presbyterians and Baptists, was not the work of the Campbells alone. Very influential was another Scotsman, Walter Scott

---

in-law Robert Sandeman (1718–71), who in 1730 led a number of "Old Scotch Independents" out of the established Kirk and into several separatist congregations. Glas was a fervent restorationist who advocated (in addition to congregational independency and the separation of church and state) a return to the early church's practice of weekly communion, believer's baptism by immersion, and a charismatic ministry. Sandeman came in 1764 to New England, where his doctrines excited several controversies with the Baptists and Congregationalists. After organizing several churches, he died at Danbury, Connecticut. In Scotland the "Glasites" or "Sandemanians" might have remained inconspicuous if their movement had not been invested with a new vitality at the end of the century by the work of the Haldane brothers, Robert (1764–1842) and James Alexander (1768–1851), of Edinburgh. Depressed by the cold "moderatism" of the established Kirk, these two wealthy laymen began a movement of evangelism which soon after 1794 (the date of their conversion) began to produce independent congregations bent on restoring the worship and ordinances of the early Christians. In their group the doctrines of Glas and Sandeman found fertile soil, and this is the circle of influence in which Alexander Campbell had moved when he was in Edinburgh.

(1796–1861). Upon graduating from the University of Edinburgh in 1818, Scott came to America as a school teacher. The next year he secured a position at Pittsburgh in the academy of George Forrester, the pastor of an independent Haldanean church which met in the courthouse. Forrester soon convinced Scott of the importance of restoring the pattern of the New Testament Church in every detail. The young teacher gradually became aware of other restorationist movements in America, such as that of Elias Hicks and Abner Jones in New England, James O'Kelly in North Carolina, and Barton Stone in Kentucky; and between 1821 and 1827 he drew close to that of the Campbells. In 1827 Scott was teaching school in Steubenville, Ohio, where he attended the meeting of the Mahoning Baptist Association, largely Campbellite even then, and soon to become expressly so. The vitality of the association was at such a low ebb that Scott was persuaded to become its traveling evangelist. This was a fateful appointment, for he was then on the verge of his great "discovery" that the "restored gospel" he had long sought was an *objective* plan of salvation, in contrast to the subjective plan preached by the revivalistic groups. Scott's "restoration" can be dated quite exactly in 18 November 1827, when he preached at New Lisbon, Ohio, using the new plan of salvation for the first time.

> In this sermon he gave the invitation according to what he conceived to be the original pattern of the ancient gospel, and received his first convert, William Amend, whom he baptized immediately without asking for an experience, without having a church vote, at the end of the meeting that very evening. This was the exciting beginning of a new program of expansion for the Disciples of Christ.[18]

The objective plan which Scott preached with such effectiveness from that time forth was nothing more than Campbell's popular theology shaped to peculiarly practical, simple, and matter-of-fact conceptions. It had six points: faith, repentance, baptism, remission of sins, gift of the Holy Spirit, and life eternal. To make them even simpler, the last two were combined, and the whole scheme reduced to a "five-finger ex-

[18] Dwight E. Stevenson, "Walter Scott and Evangelism," in *Voices from Cane Ridge*, p. 171. See also Stevenson's *Walter Scott: Voice of the Golden Oracle*.

ercise" which could be comprehended even by children. This became a popular key to "the ancient gospel," at once simple, rationalistic, and authoritarian. In summary it was:

1. Faith consists in accepting the proposition (which Scott called "the golden oracle") that "Jesus is the Christ."
2. If faith is genuine, repentance follows logically (one may almost say, automatically), motivated by Christ's authoritative promises.
3. Baptism for the remission of sins is obedient response to the Lord's command, making one's commitment complete. These are the three things for a man to do.
4. The remission of sins is the fulfillment of God's promise, as are
5. The gift of the Holy Spirit and eternal life. These are the three things God does.

It was all as simple as that. And western folk liked its directness. Within a year the Mahoning Association, which in 1827 had received only thirty-four members while losing thirty-one by death, exclusion, and dismissal, increased from six hundred to sixteen hundred. And for the next thirty years Scott alone continued to "convert" a thousand people a year. In 1830, as an almost inevitable climax to this development, prompted by the agitation of Scott, the Mahoning Association dissolved itself as an unscriptural and unwarranted organization. The alliance with the Baptists was over after seventeen years of uneasiness. The "Campbellites" as a separate wing of Christian restorationism were an acknowledged reality.

Campbell meanwhile was making a name for himself and his movement through the pages of the *Christian Baptist*, as well as in his public debates, where he argued for believer's baptism against the Presbyterians, for baptismal regeneration against the Baptists, for Protestantism against Archbishop John Baptist Purcell of Cincinnati, and for Christianity against the agnostic Robert Owen of New Harmony. He also scourged the Mormons in a controversial volume that in part balanced the loss of Sidney Rigdon, the most outstanding restorationist evangelist in northern Ohio, to Joseph Smith's Church of the Latter-Day Saints. With men like Walter Scott playing similar roles in other associations, Campbellism speedily became anathema to the Baptists, especially in Ohio and Kentucky. Since the Baptists' specific condemnations expose the innovations of the restoration movement, they too deserve summary here.

1. They distinguish sharply between the Old and New Covenants and hence abolish the Law of Moses.
2. They hold conversion to be wrought through the Word alone without any direct operation of the Holy Spirit. Thus "faith" and "repentance" in their sense constitute regeneration.
3. They believe baptism should be administered on profession of belief that Jesus is the Christ, without examination of experience or consent of the church.
4. They believe that baptism procures the remission of sins and the gift of the Spirit. It is thus man's obedience which alone can bring him within the purview of God's "electing" grace.
5. They believe that none have a special call to the ministry and that all baptized persons have a right to administer the ordinance of baptism [and the Lord's Supper].
6. They believe that the Christianity of the New Testament is simple and clear, with no element of mystery or mysticism. Creeds and enthusiasm, which obscure this fact, are therefore not to be tolerated.[19]

What Presbyterians, Baptists, and Methodists apparently faced during these decades of Disciple expansion was a remarkable projection into the American frontier scene of a popular, down-to-earth form of eighteenth-century Christian rationalism, a movement all the more striking because it was successfully propagated in the ethos of revivalism and by an adaptation of its methods. Its unusual prescriptions regarding the ban on musical instruments, its demand for weekly observance of communion, and its rejection of "unscriptural" interchurch organizations and agencies served only to set it farther apart.

[19] This list of Disciples "errors" is drawn from the widely adopted "anathema" of the Beaver Association (Baptist) of Pennsylvania in 1829, and from a similar pronouncement by the Tate's Creek Association (Kentucky) in 1830 (see Errett Gates, *The Early Relation and Separation of Baptists and Disciples* [Chicago: Christian Century Co., 1904], chaps. 9 and 10, especially pp. 92-93).

Then in 1832 an event occurred which strengthened considerably the "Christian" movement in the West: the gradually realized similarity of the Stonite and Campbellite movements became the occasion for a merger, as far as their loose organizations allowed. There were some differences between the two. Campbell was suspicious of Stone's antitrinitarianism, while Stone was more lenient toward divergent doctrinal views, and feared that Campbell vaunted himself too much. These suspicions were little by little overcome, and representatives of the two groups who met at Lexington, Kentucky, in January 1832 agreed that they should become one.[20] During the months and years which followed, an increasing number of congregations implemented their agreement. Due especially to the dynamic leadership of Campbell and the evangelistic success of Scott, the Disciples entered a period of dramatic growth. Literally dozens of little periodicals spread their message and coordinated their activities. Zealous preachers brought lucid and simple sermons to hundreds of frontier communities, and by 1850 they could claim perhaps 118,000 adherents. After the Civil War the denomination would enjoy a still more dramatic growth, until by 1890 it counted 7,246 churches with 641,051 members. Then, as in the beginning, its chief strength lay in the border states and the Ohio River basin; but many new and seriously divisive issues were to arise during the intervening period.

RETROSPECT

Despite the temptation to be retrospective about frontier religion, any major effort of the sort must be postponed. The "frontier" in America is not a region, but a process, and the

[20] Stone represented about eight thousand "Christians," while some five thousand Campbellites were represented by Raccoon John Smith. Though Stone had taken the initiative in these proceedings, the practical result was the absorbing of his followers into the more precisely defined and aggressively led Disciples movement. Some of the "Christians" refused to follow their leader, and gradually tended to identify themselves with the Hicks-Smith and O'Kelly movements as a "Christian Connection." This Connection entered an informal entente with Unitarians in the founding of Meadville (Pennsylvania) Seminary in 1844, but further merger never materialized. In 1929 what was left of it merged with the Congregationalists.

process began, as Frederick Jackson Turner insisted, with the arrival of the *Susan Constant* and the *Mayflower*. Contrary to his observations, the process did not halt even in 1893, but still continues in Alaska and elsewhere. Insofar as that great historian and his church-historical disciples provided a clue to the understanding of modern America, the events discussed in this chapter are but a part of a vast whole. Yet certain things are clear. The creativeness of the frontier, or rather, the power of the frontier to alter or refashion whatever came into it, must not be exaggerated. Gothic cathedrals, to be sure, were delayed for a while and even Georgian meetinghouses had to bide their time. Churchly decorum was not easily found, although all of these marks of civilization were exhibited as soon as time, effort, and money would allow. Borderland and semi-wilderness, in other words, remained just that; and religion inescapably bore the impress of this actuality.

Far more remarkable than the primitive and rudimentary aspects of frontier religion was the persistence with which the thought, institutions, and practice of Europe and the settled East crossed the mountains and penetrated the life of the newly settled areas. At this point, therefore, one can and must contradict the assertions of Turner, Sweet, and the other frontier enthusiasts. Turner minced no words in his assertion about democracy and the frontier:

> American democracy was born of no theorist's dream; it was not carried in the *Susan Constant* to Virginia, nor in the *Mayflower* to Plymouth. It came stark and strong and full of life out of the American forest, and it gained new strength each time it touched a new frontier.[21]

Church historians are always tempted to see a religious corollary, and speak of "democratic churches" and "democratic theology." Yet it would seem that here in the classic frontier experience, not to speak of Virginia and Plymouth, the opposite phenomenon is more striking. The continuing force of the Westminster Assembly behind all of these movements

[21] Frederick Jackson Turner, "The West and American Ideals," *Washington Historical Quarterly* 5 (October 1914): 245. Quoted in an important context by Henry Nash Smith, *Virgin Land: The American West as Myth and Symbol* (New York: Vintage Books, 1957), p. 295.

defies calculation. Equally remarkable is the way in which the deliberations of the London Baptists in 1677, or of the Philadelphia Association a half-century later, would shape Baptist articles of association in frontier Kentucky. Even more forcefully did the message and methods of John Wesley mold a movement continuing long after his death in an environment he could scarcely have imagined. Similarly, the restorationist proposals of the Haldane brothers of Glasgow altered the church life and religious experience of thousands of American frontier farmers.

Slowly and inexorably the total American experience did put its mark on all of these impulses. And the frontier is, of course, an important part of that experience. The most crucial change in American religion to be linked to the great western revivals is the shift in America's denominational equilibrium which the revivals portend in part and bring about in part: most notably the growth of the Methodists and Baptists, the emergence of the Disciples, and the relatively slow expansion of the three denominations which were dominant in the colonial period—Congregational, Presbyterian, and Episcopal. In the Old Northwest, which was settled somewhat later than Kentucky and Tennessee, different eastern influences would come to bear, shaping quite a different frontier experience. The nation as a whole, meanwhile, was maturing in significant ways as a New World frontier of Western civilization.

28

PRESBYTERIANS AND CONGREGATIONALISTS IN THE
OLD NORTHWEST: ADVANCE AND CONFLICT

In 1788 the founders of Marietta, Ohio, floated down the Ohio River in a flatboat named the *Mayflower* and on landing reenacted the arrival of the Pilgrim Fathers at Plymouth. The persisting influence of the British and the extremely unsettled state of Indian affairs, however, kept these hopeful beginnings from rapid fruition. The famous Northwest Ordinances of 1785 and 1787 had made excellent provisions for surveying the land and organizing local governments, but full-scale settlement could not proceed until after General Anthony Wayne's victory at Fallen Timbers in 1794. When settlers began to stream in, a large proportion of them were from Kentucky, Tennessee, and the western parts of the Old South, which meant that from very early times the southern parts of Ohio, Indiana, and Illinois would share many viewpoints with the Old Southwest, with the Hoosier State being most thoroughly affected by this influx.

From the beginning, however, historical as well as geographical circumstances set the Old Northwest, including upstate New York, markedly apart from the region south of the Ohio. The chief factor was the prominence of northerners, especially of New Englanders, among the settlers. Very early they had formed land companies to develop the tracts along the Ohio. Massachusetts made the most of its original sea-to-sea charter by obtaining land titles in western New York, while Connecticut was even more successful in staking out its "Western Reserve" in northern Ohio. This was the natural line of advance for migrants from New England's rock-strewn fields, and consequently the society and institutions of the

Old Northwest took on a strong Yankee tincture. Timothy Dwight sensed this kinship with his homeland during his travels in New York; and the Methodist preacher Peter Cartwright quickly realized that when he left Kentucky for a northern circuit he was facing a new kind of challenge. Ohio became a state in 1803, with a population of about fifty thousand, and Indiana followed in 1816, after the War of 1812 had removed the harassments of the British and Indians. Although large numbers of settlers continued to come from below the river to these areas, as well as to Illinois (statehood 1818), the region retained its New England flavor. Even today, a traveler to towns like Oberlin or Beloit can observe the transplantation of New England that resulted from the great Yankee exodus.

CONGREGATIONAL AND PRESBYTERIAN EXPANSION

For the churches as well as for the nation generally, central and western New York was the proving ground for further westward expansion in the more northerly areas, providing a base of operations not dissimilar to that which the southern back country had provided for the Old Southwest. This New York challenge hastened the rapprochement of Presbyterians and the consociated Congregationalists of Connecticut. Schenectady Academy, started by the Dutch Reformed pastor Dirck Romeyn in 1785 and chartered as a college in 1795, provided the point of convergence when it became Union College and called Dr. Jonathan Edwards, Jr.—a Connecticut Congregationalist educated at Princeton—as its president in 1799. Though he met an untimely death in 1801, Edwards helped to institute the famous Plan of Union of 1801, whereby Presbyterians and Congregationalists agreed to combine their efforts for the winning of the western missionary field. In this "presbygational" arrangement, each group agreed to recognize the other's ministry and polity.[1]

The Plan was a large scale comity arrangement to allow Congregational and Presbyterian settlers in a given community to combine or to found a single congregation and to have a minister of either denomination. If the majority were Presbyterians who preferred their discipline, the church could be

[1] George M. Marsden, *The Evangelical Mind and the New School Presbyterian Experience*, p. 11.

so organized even if the minister were a Congregationalist, and vice versa. Similar rules allowed congregations to affiliate with either a presbytery or a Congregational association. If a disagreement arose between pastor and church the matter could be referred to the presbytery or association of which the pastor was a member or, if this was not agreeable, to a committee consisting of equal representatives of each group. Arrangements for appealing cases were also made. As Williston Walker says, "it was a wholly honorable arrangement, and was designed to be entirely fair to both sides." But in its long-range institutional effect, the Plan of Union operated in favor of Presbyterianism, which because of its intrinsic connectionalism tended to absorb the more independent Congregational churches. Walker suggests still other reasons for Presbyterian strength:

> They were nearer the scene of missionary labor: their denominational spirit was more assertive than that of the Congregationalism of the day; their Presbyteries were rapidly spread over the missionary districts, and the natural desire for fellowship where the points of separation seemed so few led Congregational ministers to accept the welcome offered therein. Moreover, the doctrinal discussions of New England and the development of Connecticut consociationism had created a widespread feeling in the older Congregational churches that Congregationalism could not thrive in unformed communities.[2]

In doctrinal matters a reverse tide of influence was observable. Advocates of New England Theology were more fervent in evangelism because of their participation in the Second Awakening, and this led to their dominance among the Congregationalists participating in the Plan of Union. The rise of the great voluntary associations, above all the American Home Missionary Society (1826), further extended the New England influence in the West as graduates of Andover and Yale took up the missionary challenge in large numbers. By an ironic turn of fate, the Presbyterian church's absorption of Congregationalist missionaries vastly extended the influence of the New Haven Theology of Nathaniel William Taylor and the revised Hopkinsianism of Andover. It created

[2] Williston Walker, *A History of the Congregational Churches in the United States*, ACHS, vol. 3 (New York, 1894), p. 318.

a situation that was pregnant with controversy and schism despite the prevailing enthusiasm for a campaign to transform an uncouth frontier and bring it into a pious and well-behaved Christian republic.

In addition to their joint efforts, both churches continued to be independently concerned with evangelizing the West. The actual westward extension of the Puritan heritage proceeded most directly in centers where New England people simply gathered churches, called ministers, and organized associations in the time-honored way. Because of the high regard these people had for each other's company, this became a fairly familiar pattern of advance, reaching far across the land to places like Beloit, Wisconsin (whose church was organized in 1838), and Minneapolis, Minnesota (whose church was organized in 1851 at Saint Anthony). The emergence of such "little New Englands" had a striking effect not only on the religious nature of the western communities, but also on their political, economic, and cultural life; for this reason, it constitutes a highly significant factor in any estimate of Puritan influence on American life.

The voluntary associations and the Plan of Union account for the largest extension of evangelical influences, however. Through these channels a steady stream of devoted missionaries, church founders, and educators moved westward. Sometimes, as in the case of Julian Monson Sturtevant (1805–86), they came from New England families who had moved west but who nevertheless sent their children "home" to Yale College for a liberal education. They then went to Yale Divinity School and the lecture room of Professor Taylor before returning to their western labors. But whether from the West or from New England, whether products of Yale Divinity or Andover, they became enthusiastic emissaries of eastern culture, education, and above all, the Christian gospel as it was understood in New England's Second Awakening. The record of their ministry is written in the multiplication of Congregational churches across the northern West. Estimates differ as to the number of churches of Congregational origin which became Presbyterian. Older estimates ran to more than two thousand, while a more recent study concludes that not more than six hundred ever placed themselves under the care of the General Assembly. Between 1807 and 1834 Presbyterian communicant membership as a whole grew from 18,000 to 248,000, and at the later date an "allied population" of two million was reliably reported. Modes of definition and computation vary, but nearly all accounts affirm the large degree to which missionary concern outweighed the denominational spirit in the early evangelizing of the Old Northwest.

BEECHER AND FINNEY

No single person better illustrates the methods and spirit of the great campaign mounted by the "evangelical united front" than Lyman Beecher. Already nationally famous for his great revival preaching, his campaign against Boston Unitarianism, and his work as a temperance reformer, Beecher was called in 1832 to become president of Lane Theological Seminary in Cincinnati, a Presbyterian school owing much to the philanthropy of Ebenezer Lane (a Baptist), the Kemper family, and Arthur Tappan (a wealthy layman of New York City who pledged $60,000 on condition that Beecher accept the presidency). Beecher did accept—mainly because he was convinced of the West's great significance in the future growth of the new nation. His *Plea for the West* (1835) is a classic statement of that widely held conviction; and though the need for "saving the West from the Pope" figured prominently in this manifesto, he also showed more liberal and far-sighted views:

> The West is a young empire of mind, and power, and wealth, and free institutions, rushing up to a giant manhood with a rapidity and a power never witnessed below the sun. And if she carries with her the elements of her preservation, the experiment will be glorious.

In this sense Beecher anticipates Frederick Jackson Turner's belief in the force of the West in determining the future cast of the emerging nation. Yet no man was more sure than he that the civilizing influence of New England was required to rescue the region from barbarism and license.

In Cincinnati, Beecher also became pastor of the Second Presbyterian Church, where his known affinities for the New England modifications of strict Calvinism immediately aroused the suspicions of the conservative Presbyterians. In 1835 Dr. Joshua L. Wilson placed three formal charges against Beecher: heresy, on the ground that he differed from the Westminster standards; slander, on the ground that he claimed to represent true evangelical Christianity; and hypocrisy, on the ground that he claimed to agree substantially with the Scriptures and the Westminster Confession. Despite the fact that the Presbyterian organizations of the region were controlled by conservatives, Beecher was acquitted by a large majority in both presbytery and synod. But these proceedings indicated that a long-standing source of tension in the Presbyterian church was beginning to erupt. It would be occasioned, as the Old Side protest had been of a century before, by an excess of New England influence.

Beecher represents the New England establishment responding with vigor to the new empire beyond the Hudson. But there was another, more tempestuous son of Connecticut who found his vocation in the West—Charles Grandison Finney (1792–1875), "the father of modern revivalism." Finney was born in Warren, Connecticut, but two years later his parents joined the westward trek, so that he grew up in small towns of Oneida and Jefferson counties in central New York. Returning to Warren for secondary schooling, Finney then kept school for a while. But in 1818 he began to practice law in Adams, New York, where he came under the influence of a young Presbyterian minister, George W. Gale (later to be founder of Knox College in Galesburg, Illinois). Finney admired Gale personally, but disagreed violently with his theological views. Led by a personal reading of the Scriptures, the skeptical lawyer finally experienced a soul-shaking conversion in 1821, which he said brought him "a retainer from the Lord Jesus Christ to plead his cause." His career as a highly successful converter of souls began that very week on the streets of Adams. Refusing formal theological training but already evincing great power as a preacher, Finney was licensed—somewhat reluctantly—by the local Saint Lawrence Presbytery. Soon he was making news in the local papers, and before long he gained national attention by a series of spectacular evangelistic meetings in Rome, Utica, Troy, and other cities along the Erie Canal.

This is where the "new measures" with which Finney's name was to be linked took form. His speech was tough, direct, forceful—and inescapably popular. Like God, he was no respecter of persons: sinners were sinners. He prayed for them by name; and when occasion required he included in his prayers any persons, lay or clerical, who were notable by their absence or their opposition to his efforts. Finney also departed from the regular stated times for religious services and made extensive use of the "protracted meeting," which continued nightly for a week or more. He introduced the "anxious bench" to cull from the multitudes the almost-saved, so that they might be made objects of special exhortation and prayer, and encouraged women to testify in public meetings, despite Saint Paul's admonition of female silence in the churches (I Cor. 14:34). He also discovered the advantages of publicity, and as his followers became sufficiently numerous, he was able to make a "team approach" to prospective Sodoms. Nor did Finney mince words on his efficacy; in his *Lectures on Revivalism* (1835) he declared that a "revival is not a miracle, or dependent on a miracle in any sense. It is a purely philosophical [i.e. scientific] result of the right use of the constituted means."

Finny's emphasis on the human production of conversions was not the only point on which he strayed from strict Westminster standards. And far from concealing the fact, he proclaimed it. From the first he demanded that some kind of relevant social action follow the sinner's conversion, and in time this led to an even more disturbing emphasis on "entire sanctification." In Finney's theology sin was a voluntary act and theoretically avoidable, hence holiness was a human possibility. Even from the liberated ground of Taylorism, the Finneyite departures seemed bold and extreme.

So alarmed and critical were Lyman Beecher, Asahel Nettleton, and a number of others, that a conference of eight representatives of each party met 18–27 July 1827, in New Lebanon, New York, to discuss their differences. This meeting only heightened the rancor and perhaps signalized a renewal of the rupture in the American Reformed tradition which had been agitated periodically ever since the Great Awakening.

I know your plan [declared Beecher] and you know I do. You mean to come into Connecticut, and carry a streak of fire to Boston. But if you attempt it, as the Lord liveth, I'll meet you at the State line, and call out all the artillery-men, and fight every inch of the way to Boston, and I'll fight you there.[3]

Finney, needless to say, was not intimidated; he went on to new successes at Wilmington, Delaware, and Reading and Lancaster, Pennsylvania, before moving on to New York City, where he held forth for over a year under the pa-tronage of Anson G. Phelps. By this time Finney was essen-tially a free-lance revivalist. After another year of touring which included Boston, he returned in 1832 to New York to preach for a year in the Chatham Street Theater which Lewis Tappan and others rented for him. They called it the Second Free Presbyterian Church, for it had grown out of Finney's earlier ministry in New York; but even its "free-ness" was in-sufficient, and Finney soon withdrew to become an independ-ent Congregationalist and minister of the Broadway Taber-nacle which had been built for him. His tenure here was brief, however, since ill health and an intricate series of events connected with the antislavery movement led him in 1835 to accept an appointment as professor of theology in the newly founded Oberlin College. He also served as president of Oberlin from 1851 to 1866, and his dynamic presence made Oberlin a center of influence for revival theology, the "new measures," and a growing emphasis on perfectionism—all combined with an urgent sense of Christian activism.

Finney is an immensely important man in American history by any standard of measure. His revivals were a powerful force in the rising antislavery impulse and in the rise of urban evangelism. He was an influential revisionist in the Reformed theological tradition, an enormously successful practitioner, almost the inventor, of the modern high-pressure revivalism which, as it spread, would have important conse-quences for the religious ethos of the nation as a whole. Yet Finney was also an extremely divisive figure, and in the Pres-byterian church the tensions created by his kind of ministry contributed to a recurrence of schism.

[3] Forty years after the New Lebanon conference Beecher attrib-uted these ringing words to himself, but Finney had no memory of them. Whether spoken then or not, they nevertheless reveal a common Eastern estimate of Finney's worth to the cause of religion. In any event Beecher later had to eat crow and invite Finney to Boston (see Beecher's *Autobiography*, ed. Barbara Cross, 1:75).

PROBLEMS OF PRESBYTERIANISM

Despite the gains resulting from the Plan of Union, the Presbyterian Church during this period was beset with a number of problems, chief among which were a shortage of ministers for the western churches and sharp differences of opinion over theology, polity, and missionary methods. Pursuing an independent course for evangelizing the West, the General Assembly established in 1802 a Standing Committee of Missions. Before it was replaced by a Board of Missions in 1816, this body had sent out 311 itinerant ministers, usually for a two-month tour each. Follow-up efforts were poorly managed, however, and the results were disappointing. Competition from Methodists, Baptists, and Disciples was strong, especially among the southerners who were moving into the Old Northwest. The church's official membership reports, on the other hand, did show substantial Presbyterian growth in the country as a whole. At the beginning of the century there were an estimated 13,470 communicants in about 500 churches; in 1820, 72,096 members in 1,299 churches; and in 1837, 226,557 members in 2,865 churches. The most impressive growth took place in western New York and in Ohio, where the Plan of Union was functioning best. During the same period the percentage of churches with ordained ministers rose from fifty to seventy-five.

In the long run, the most important consequences of this period may have been the growing awareness of an acute ministerial shortage in the Presbyterian Church and the realization that Princeton College was in no position to meet the urgent need. With Andover as an example of what a theological seminary could do, various individuals and synods began to consider the problem. The man who finally emerged as the catalyst of this growing interest was Archibald Alexander (1772–1851). Grandson of a Scotch-Irish immigrant who had been deeply touched by the Great Awakening, Alexander had grown up in the Great Valley of Virginia, where he slowly came of a mind to enter the ministry. With only an "academy" education and informal theological training under the Reverend William Graham of Lexington, Virginia, he had become president of the struggling little Hampden-Sydney College in 1796. Ten years later he was a prominent Philadelphia minister, from which position he led the movement to found a seminary at Princeton. When in 1812 his efforts succeeded, the General Assembly asked him to be its first professor. He set the new center of conservative divinity on its course, and through his sons and pupils and their sons, the direction he gave the Princeton Theology prevailed for a century.

The theological history of Presbyterianism owes much to the fact that this powerful Scotch-Irishman sought and found the intellectual and doctrinal guidance he needed not in the Edwardsean tradition of New England (though the writings of Edwards had helped bring about his own conversion), nor in the New Divinity of the later Puritans, nor yet in the Scottish philosophical traditions of Witherspoon (though this element remained prominent as a conditioning factor in the Princeton Theology), but in the seventeenth-century scholasticism of François Turretin (1623–87), a stalwart defender of orthodoxy at Geneva, who above all attacked efforts to modify a strict doctrine of predestination and a literalistic view of scriptural inspiration. Until replaced in 1873 by the *Systematic Theology* of Alexander's admiring protégé Charles Hodge, Turretin's *Institutio Theologiae Elencticae* (Geneva, 1679–85; reissued in 4 vols. at Edinburgh, 1847–48) stood side by side with the Swiss Confessions and the Westminster formularies to provide both structure and content for the message which hundreds of the seminary's graduates carried across the land and into many foreign mission fields.

Especially as developed and defended by Charles Hodge, the Princeton Theology became the criterion of Reformed orthodoxy in America. When judged by these standards, Taylor's New Haven Theology was found utterly wanting, Andover's Edwards Amasa Park was attacked almost as violently, Hopkinsianism was viewed with suspicion or disdained altogether, Moses Stuart's biblical studies were held suspect, and even Jonathan Edwards was considered unduly venturesome. Yet despite its negative features, the Princeton Theology was a great positive force, affording theological substance wherever revivalism threatened to vaunt experience only, fostering education and the learned tradition, and striving desperately to provide a Christian message that was not simply an amalgam of folk religion and Americanism. In the West, however, it would ultimately precipitate an immense crisis.

The founding of other Presbyterian seminaries sharpened the approaching crisis. Responding to the same demand for ministers, the Synod of Virginia established Union Seminary at Hampden-Sydney in 1812 and won the support of the North Carolina synod in 1828. Later moving to Richmond, it became a virtual Princeton of the South. During the twenties still other seminaries were established in Tennessee, South Carolina, and western Pennsylvania. But the most consequential was Auburn Seminary, founded in 1821 by the Geneva Synod in western New York. Well supported and powerfully led, catering to Plan of Union churches and drawing many students from New England, Auburn soon became a strong theological counterweight to Princeton—serving, in fact, to magnify Princeton's role as the preserver of orthodoxy.

The schism between Old and New Sides which had rent the Presbyterian Church in the period of the Great Awakening had been healed in 1758, largely to the advantage of the revivalistic party of New Englanders and Log College men. The college at Princeton during its early years was molded to their ideals. With the great Scotch-Irish migrations which reached their peak just before the American Revolution, however, the balance of sentiment shifted away from the New Side. John Witherspoon's election to the presidency of Princeton in 1768 was one sign of this transformation, and Archibald Alexander's appointment to Princeton Seminary another. Yet theological views were not merely ethnic manifestations, and as an indigenous intellectual and theological tradition developed, Presbyterians gravitated to one pole or the other on various grounds.

One of these groups, known then and since as the "Old School," increasingly came to admire the church's traditional polity and took very seriously the Reformed tenet that matters of church order were within the divine law (*jus divinum*). To them the constitution of the church was not a structural convenience which could be altered to suit the circumstances; it was an article of faith. The hastily contrived arrangements of the Plan of Union were regarded as almost blasphemous; and the motley congeries of Congregational churches, elders, messengers, associations, and presbyteries which had resulted seemed a monstrous deformation of God's plan for his Church. Further incongruities were provided by the extra-ecclesiastical voluntary associations which were assuming the missionary and even the teaching role of the church. To many, the situation seemed so chaotic that within the church justice could no longer be done nor wise action taken.

By a natural grouping of tendencies, these Old School men also had grave suspicions about the new kind of revivalism that seemed to be breaking out everywhere in the years after 1800. Many, indeed, were suspicious of all revivalism, fearful of the growing emphasis on conversion and religious experience, and disturbed over the corresponding laxity with regard to doctrine and the sacraments. The Great Awakening in America and the Evangelical Revival in Great Britain, of course, had put an indelible mark on Presbyterian thought and practice. Even Old School thinkers like Alexander and Hodge reveal at every turn that they are part of the Great Awakening's progeny. But this was a matter of degree: some men put more emphasis on the baptismal covenant, or cherished decorum in church affairs, or found greater consolation in the doctrinal heritage of Reformed churches, or clung more fondly to tradition itself. To the extent that they leaned in this general direction, they resisted the movements that brought "new measures," new thoughts, and new constitutional arrangements into Presbyterianism.

What aroused Old School men most was the growth within the church of what they could only regard as heretical departures from the Westminster standards. The source of these departures was traced usually to New England theologians, especially to Samuel Hopkins and Nathaniel William Taylor, with Taylor being regarded as the more dangerous by far. Since the American Board of Commissioners for Foreign Missions and the American Home Missionary Society were both associated intimately with these New England trends, the Old School men interpreted the church's official support of these missionary agencies as outright propagation of error. The Plan of Union was to them an open gate through which alien ideas and practices entered the Presbyterian church. The only corrective was to establish definitively Presbyterian agencies and to make missions a responsibility of the church as a whole.

The conservative set of mind here described was common throughout the church at the opening of the century; it was observable even in Kentucky during the great revivals there. At the time of the frontier schisms, neither the Synod of Kentucky nor the General Assembly was inclined to compromise, and the Cumberland and Springfield presbyteries were allowed simply to go their way. But this pervasive immobility faded with the growth of the revival spirit, as Presbyterians beheld not only the sensational increase of Methodists, Baptists, and Disciples, but also the alarming inroads these groups were making on "good Presbyterian stock." Even more serious was the defection of whole congregations.

After 1800 the influence of Congregationalism began to create within Presbyterianism itself a "New School." It was at first a rather unorganized movement of those who valued the united work of the interdenominational societies, who worked harmoniously with the New Englanders and regarded them as fellow champions of evangelical Christianity, and who welcomed the additional strength that such an alliance provided on a thinly settled frontier where aggressive and vulgar rivals were advancing everywhere.[4] They by no means forsook Presbyterian principles as Barton Stone and Alexander Campbell had done; but they did feel that the urgency of the situation made stronger claims than the traditional forms of ecclesiastical government. They regarded the voluntary societies, even though interdenominational, as mighty evangelistic instruments; and like Taylor, Beecher, and Finney, they felt that "improvements" could be made in the traditional doctrinal system.

These improvements were first of all in the direction of simplicity: on the American frontier they were understandably embarrassed to confront their untutored hearers with the baroque intricacies of Westminster. Secondly, they wanted—like most other Americans east and west—a religious faith more obviously consonant with the Enlightenment ideals that had been woven into the nation's democratic faith. In its later eighteenth- and early nineteenth-century form, strict Calvinism, especially double predestination, seemed inadequate to this need, especially as interpreted by Turretin. Finally, perhaps most importantly, the obvious effectiveness of revivalism in winning people to the gospel seemed to demand theological revision. Both east and west, the Scottish Philosophy and the Enlightened principles of American democracy

---

[4] I am, of course, using the word "vulgar" as it might then have been used. The degree to which Congregationalists and Presbyterians considered themselves the chosen means for bringing learning, culture, and religious sophistication to the frontier is difficult to exaggerate.

had obliterated so completely the meaning of the great Christian paradoxes that something had to give. Among New School men, Taylorism or Arminianism of some sort seemed the only recourse. Resistance to Finney's doctrinal revisions was so strong that he left the Presbyterian church. Even Taylor seemed too daring for many. But the general tendency of New School theology was undeniable and steady.[5]

SCHISM IN THE PRESBYTERIAN CHURCH

In a thoroughly connectional system like the Presbyterian, where any controversy could come to the highest court (the General Assembly) for ultimate adjudication, it was impossible that such inner tensions could be suppressed, especially when conservatism was rooted so deeply. Indeed, portents of future struggle had been evident ever since the Plan of Union was approved. They became more obvious after 1812, when the American Board of Commissioners for Foreign Missions was given official support, and especially so after 1826, when the American Home Missionary Society was formed as the chief instrument for furthering the Plan of Union. The heavily Scotch-Irish, rigorously orthodox Pittsburgh Synod in 1802 had converted itself into an every-member missionary society. Out on the marches Edward Beecher, Julian M. Sturtevant, and Theron Baldwin, all former Congregationalists and former members of Yale's "Illinois Band" who had led in the founding of Illinois College, were accused of heresy in 1833, only to be exonerated by synod. In 1835 Lyman Beecher, who by then had made peace with Finney, was similarly accused and acquitted, though he was asked to publish for the record the arguments that had freed him from suspicion. The church was obviously moving toward a showdown.

What finally drew the issue to a head, ironically, was not a

[5] By 1906, when the main body of Cumberland Presbyterians was reunited with its parent body, the Northern Presbyterian church in effect committed itself to Arminianism, though, of course, many individuals dissented from this action. From among these dissenters came those who led another schism between 1929 and 1936. The Baptists meanwhile exhibited the same trend. By 1911, when the Freewill Baptists returned to the main body of Northern Baptists, the old Philadelphia Confession had become almost a dead letter. Indeed, the so-called New Hampshire Confession of 1833 won widespread approval for this very reason. So the tide was with the New School.

frontier revivalist at all, but an immensely respected pastor, biblical commentator, and theologian from the urban East, Albert Barnes (1798–1870). Having come fresh from Princeton Seminary to his first pastorate at Morristown, New Jersey, in 1824, Barnes five years later preached (and soon thereafter published) a sermon, "The Way of Salvation." Though Edwardsean in much of its argument, the sermon was critical of Westminster and clearly Taylorite in tendency, especially with regard to the doctrine of Original Sin. When Barnes was called the next year to the distinguished First Church of Philadelphia, therefore, the conservatives seized the occasion to raise all the troublesome issues that had been seething for so long. They charged him with heresy and ultimately brought the case before the General Assembly of 1831, where a New School majority sustained his call.

In 1835 Barnes reiterated his views in a new commentary on Romans.[6] Renewing its attack, the Old School carried their charges from presbytery to synod to assembly, and this time they succeeded in having him silenced. In a reversal of sentiment the next year, however, the Assembly restored Barnes to his pulpit. The General Assembly of 1836 then proceeded to approve the American Board in preference to the purely Presbyterian Western Foreign Missionary Society (an agency of the Pittsburgh Synod), and almost succeeded in blending the church's education and home mission boards with the interdenominational associations. More than that, it extended the policy of "elective affinity," which permitted separate liberal and conservative presbyteries (and even synods) within the same geographical territory. To make the issue even sharper, in 1836 the liberals joined with Congregationalists to establish Union Theological Seminary in New York City as an institution independent of all official church control. The strength of the New School party at this point is indicated partly by the fact that additional presbyteries dominated by their men had just been created in New York and Philadelphia, with the latter joined to the newly formed Synod of Delaware.

[6] This was the first volume of Barnes's *Notes, Explanatory and Practical, on the Scriptures*, which became an immensely popular semischolarly series of expositions widely read by the laity and of special usefulness to Sunday school teachers. Hodge of Princeton and Stuart of Andover also joined this controversy with commentaries and articles on Romans.

Such drastic New School advances had the effect of consolidating conservatives, moderates, and neutrals of the Old School, to which Princeton Seminary now also gravitated. The southern Presbyteries, who were beginning to sense a growing antislavery spirit in the New School, were also predominantly of this party. As a result, the Assembly of 1837 was decisively in conservative hands. It acted with dispatch. First it abrogated the Plan of Union. Then in a sweeping unconstitutional act it made this abrogation retroactive, and without providing recourse or appeal to the judicatories concerned, proceeded to exscind from the church four western synods which had grown out of the union plan. In one blow 553 churches, 509 ministers and between sixty and a hundred thousand members were lopped from the rolls. In other actions, the General Assembly made the Western Missionary Society (an official board) its sole missionary agency, and warned the American Board of Commissioners and the Home Missionary Society not to encroach on Presbyterian work.

Immediately New School men rallied their forces, published a denial of heresy charges in the "Auburn Declaration," and made plans to press their case at the Assembly in 1838. When that body convened, however, a resolute and high-handed Old School moderator kept the New School forces at bay. Finally, the Reverend Nathaniel Beman, an old champion of Finney from the unexscinded Troy Synod, took charge of the New School elements present and led them to organize separately on the ground that they were the legal continuation of the General Assembly. During the years which followed, litigation both ecclesiastical and civil failed to heal the division, and ultimately two churches came into existence, the New School engrossing about four-ninths of the total membership.

RESURGENCE OF DENOMINATIONAL CONSCIOUSNESS

The years following the schism in the Presbyterian church saw a resurgence of denominational consciousness among all the groups that had figured in the events leading up to that development. In the South the secession crisis would soon bring Old and New Schools together in a separate Southern Presbyterian church. The Civil War and the continuing southern racial situation would give it a self-consciousness and corporate spirit that would show few signs of disappearance even in the mid-twentieth century.

In the North, where the New School was much larger, the two bodies prolonged their parallel labors for twenty-two years until their reunion in 1869. During the interim, the Old School showed slightly greater growth, largely because it faced fewer problems of reorganization, and because it was unaffected by the contemporary revival of Congregational self-consciousness in the areas where the Plan of Union had prevailed. During the period of separation, however, many Old School leaders came to regret the inflexibility which had occasioned the schism and to work for reunion.

The New School meanwhile experienced a Presbyterian awakening, perhaps chiefly out of the need to demonstrate the injustice of the exscinding action and to legitimate their claim to be a legal continuation of the old church. They were further prodded by dissatisfaction with the policies of the American Board of Commissioners for Foreign Missions, which despite large Presbyterian support had prevented a single Presbyterian mission field from developing. Professor Henry B. Smith of Union Seminary (New York) gave theological strength to the Presbyterian cause by transcending the older dependence on the New England Theology and the issues it aroused, and turning attention to broader and deeper resources, both contemporary and traditional. Domestic "Presbygationalism" also lost favor, and local churches increasingly declared themselves for one side or the other. During the period of separation (1837–69), the New School grew much more slowly than before, because whatever gains were registered in local congregations were often offset after 1837 by energetic Congregational evangelism. This meant that the steady westward flow of New Englanders no longer augmented New School Presbyterian churches.

The corollary to this development was the revival of Congregational interest in its own traditions and characteristic institutions. From 1830 on, Congregationalists were planting their own churches in Illinois, Iowa, Wisconsin, and Minnesota. In 1846 a Congregational convention in Michigan questioned the wisdom of the Plan of Union; and in 1852 a national convention of Congregational churches at Albany, New York, renounced it altogether, declaring it to be deleterious to the interests of their heritage in both theology and government. Two years later a Congregational seminary was founded in Chicago, with the encouragement of two of the denomination's most renowned historical scholars, Leonard Bacon and Henry Martyn Dexter. By the time the National Council was convened in 1865 for its historic deliberations, Congregationalism had become continental in scope, with about six hundred churches in a score of states and territories, strongest in New England but also to be found wherever migrating New Englanders had paused to work and prosper.

THE EVANGELICAL MAINSTREAM

The Old Northwest, needless to say, did not become a Presbyterian or Congregational preserve despite the civic and cultural leadership these two communions provided for the region. If one were guided by statistics alone, a discussion of the Northwest would concentrate upon the popular denominations treated in the previous chapter. In 1840, for example, when the Old and New School Presbyterians together numbered less than 250,000, the Methodists counted over 850,000 members and the Baptists over 570,000. These two churches were making their chief advances elsewhere, but they soon far outnumbered Presbyterians and Congregationalists even in Ohio, Indiana, and Illinois.

Such quantitative canons, however, obscure a fundamental phenomenon: the way in which these several denominations, all of them profoundly affected by the evangelical resurgence dating from the century's first decade, were forging a mainstream tradition of American Evangelical Protestantism. Theologically it was Reformed in its foundations, Puritan in its outlook, fervently experiential in its faith, and tending, despite strong countervailing pressures, toward Arminianism, perfectionism, and activism. Equally basic, and almost equally religious, was its belief in the millennial potential of the United States as the bearer and protector of these values. This mainstream would play a vast sustaining and defining role in the life of the nation during the entire nineteenth century. It would not gain unified institutional embodiment in anything more substantial than the World Evangelical Alliance, founded in 1846 and provided with an organized American branch in 1867. But many voluntary associations, including some which had helped to forge the evangelical united front, continued to advance important causes even after denominational self-consciousness reduced their power. Denominational rivalry, on the other hand, tended both to stimulate evangelism and to expose the existence of a common tradition. Despite the legal separation of church and state this American Protestant mainstream would enjoy the influence and self-confidence of a formal establishment.

These general observations, however, should not usurp the place of a summary observation on the overall contribution or impact of the evangelical advance in the trans-Appalachian West which has been described in this and the preceding chapters. The basic fact is that generalizations about the impact on frontier society of these churches—or of others yet to be discussed—cannot easily be made. Churches were not independent forces but complex cultural institutions which contained judges, doctors, educators, politicians, social reformers, and much else in their membership. Yet the churches functioned with enormous and unrivaled effect as organizing centers. To lonely, scattered people they brought vital fellowship and an intimate personal concern which shored up both individualistic and social aims of the people. In Scott Miyakawa's words, they functioned as informal institutions of adult education, giving practice, counsel, and direction in a society where very few other institutions were available.[7] Out of these impulses, moreover, came many of the collective efforts which led to the founding of other institutions, above all the myriad schools and colleges that soon were organized (they did not "spring up" as is so often said).

The church members also constituted reference groups for an unformed social order; with many admitted limitations, they thus provided standards of personal behavior, vocational stability, family responsibility, and civic concern which contributed significantly to the establishment of social peace, order, and the mutual acceptance of differing values. Had the missionary impulse been lacking, life on the frontier would have remained violent, lawless, disorganized, culturally barren, and out of touch with the subtler and profounder aspects of Western civilization much longer than was the case. Even in the area of race relations—with regard to Indians and Negroes—the most effective humanitarian impulses would be

[7] T. Scott Miyakawa, *Protestants and Pioneers: Individualism and Conformity on the American Frontier*, p. 215.

church-related though they would long be weak and half-hearted. There was much narrowness, bigotry, censoriousness, and petty factionalism in these evangelical churches. Some groups in the American population could only regard their very existence as a misfortune, and one can bring forward strong critiques of their sense of priorities. They were by no means exclusively beneficent in their works or their effects. Yet just as in the preceding century, when the East had been a frontier, they did answer to fundamental human needs, facilitating the efforts of men and women to make their life together more humane.

Our final conclusion regarding all of these social results—good, bad, and questionable—is that in one sense they are only side effects of efforts that were ineffable and beyond mundane measuring, for the missionaries and church founders came above all to minister the consolations of religion—to bring word of amazing grace to wretched souls. In what measure they succeeded in that primary task God only knows.

29

SECTARIAN HEYDAY

Revivalism has always provoked both praise and blame, but the concurrent waves of enthusiastic religion and sectarian strife which swept the nation in the early decades of the nineteenth century made judgments of its worth more extreme than ever. Robert Baird, an American Presbyterian who served as a missionary to Roman Catholics in Europe, held aloft the American ideals of freedom and "voluntaryism" as a banner for Europeans, and lauded revivalism for making Christian experience a bond of unity between churches that had been drawing farther apart ever since the Reformation:

> When viewed in relation to the great doctrines which are universally conceded by Protestants to be fundamental and necessary to salvation, then they all form but one body, recognising Christ as their common Head. They then resemble the different parts of a great temple, all constituting but one whole; or the various corps of an army, which, though ranged in various divisions, and each division having an organization perfect in itself, yet form but one great host, and are under the command of one chief.[1]

Almost simultaneously John Williamson Nevin was designating the "sect-spirit" as the Antichrist and condemning revivalism as the single most scandalous feature of American Christianity.

> We have reason [wrote Nevin] to stand upon our guard against the inroads of an unchurchly spirit. . . . It

[1] Robert Baird, *Religion in America*, p. 220. Still a valuable account, as well as a near classic document of the epoch.

magnifies the inward and spiritual, and affects to call the soul away from a religion of forms and outward show. . . . It will know nothing of a real revelation of Christ in the flesh. This is emphatically Antichrist. . . . The old Gnosticism has been long since shorn of its glory. But what is it but a more subtle phase of the same error to deny the existence of a real, historical *Church* in the world? Without a real Church we can have no real Christ. Let us beware of the Gnostic, unchurchly, Nestorian spirit. . . . Let us have no fellowship here with Antichrist.[2]

Later scholars show equally wide disagreement. Do we face a paradox, or simply confusion? The situation calls for interpretation.

First of all let us get the record straight. The most fundamental divisions in America's religious life are a direct inheritance from the Old World, whose Christian subgroups have simply been projected across the seas by immigration. Many American religious bodies, moreover, are simply regional variants or else parallel churches of different national origin, but within a single confessional communion. Still others have resulted for various reasons from the process of denominational division, not through sect formation. Yet America is undeniably the home of many sects, and evangelical ferment frequently did stimulate their formation. It is imperative, therefore, to establish a working definition of terms and to consider the role of revivalism.

As used here the term "sect" refers to a movement, almost necessarily small at the outset, which secedes from or forms the periphery of a more stable, socially adjusted, and often culturally dominant religious group.[3] Sect formation is thus usually an expression of alienation; it is a movement of people who are spiritually, socially, economically, educationally, or in other ways "disinherited." If not disinherited in this sense, the sect's following is at least in search of values, fulfillment, or fellowship that a dominant, socially acceptable church by its nature cannot ordinarily satisfy. It is usually "joined" by adult believers; and as soon as it begins to face

[2] John Williamson Nevin, "Sermon on Ephesians 1:23" (15 October 1846), in *The Mercersburg Theology*, ed. James H. Nichols, pp. 75–76. See also the statement by Philip Schaff on p. 616.

[3] On early sectarianism, see chap. 15 above.

the problems of nurturing children in its faith, it is threatened by extinction or stagnation, or it is gradually transformed into a movement or institution for which the term "church" or "denomination" is more appropriate, with sectarian withdrawal now becoming a potentially disruptive factor in its own organizational life. Sociologically speaking, Christianity was at first a Judaic and Roman sect; it became a "church," however, and thereafter was constantly confronted with the threat of secession by those who demanded a purer, more rigorous membership. Montanism, Novatianism, and Donatism are classic examples of such movements. American church history is replete with sects, some now extinct, others alive but stagnant, some dynamic, and others now become "churches."

Characteristically, sects take shape with some charismatic leader at their head; they have this leader's personality or some single, sometimes unusual, tenet (or cluster of tenets) as their reason for being. Personalities and heroes loom large in the origin of all kinds of movements, of course, but they are usually of crucial importance in sect formation. Finally, a sect is recognizably related to the movement whence it emerged; usually it accentuates a traditional tenet which it regards as in danger of being lost. Protestant sects, for example, almost invariably justify themselves with their own "correct" interpretation of the Bible; they frequently insist that the parent movement is apostate, and that they alone now confess the true faith. Because the Christian Church had persistently defined itself as a sect vis-à-vis the "world," it was inevitably haunted and challenged by sectarianism and other manifestations of spiritual discontent. For the same reason the study of sects and similar groups reveals much about the broader course of history.

When a movement's origins and structure have all the sociological or institutional characteristics of a sect except that its doctrinal stance represents a fundamental departure or that it seeks essentially different objectives, the term "sect" is probably inappropriate. But no alternative term has so far won acceptance, though the term "cult" is often so used. If a movement invokes new scriptures or another principle of authority, it is perhaps more appropriate to recognize the emergence of a new religion.[4] These distinctions, of course, are

4 Cultic phenomena and related "religions," including Christian Science, are discussed in chap. 60 (of Volume 2); Mormonism in

famously easier to make than to apply. But they do serve, nevertheless, to give some direction to historical investigations. This and the succeeding chapter are concerned with a wide variety of the "sect-like" movements which abound in American religious history.

REVIVALISM AND SECTARIANISM

By any standard of measurement, the United States during the first half of the nineteenth century provided a good setting for the emergence of many disruptive and revolutionary religious movements. It was a time of rapidly shifting social standards and institutional life. After the War of 1812 nationalism had a new birth, and with it came a unique blending of jingoism and Christian eschatology. Colonial traditions of rank and station fell to pieces in an "age of the common man." American political conservatives, even the "God-like Daniel Webster," were forced down on their hands and knees in the rough and tumble of the Log Cabin and Hard Cider campaign of 1840. Tumultuous population growth and the westward movement transformed the map and makeup of the country. Social and geographical mobility took on new meaning. Canals, railroads, textile mills, and the cotton gin led to or symbolized other transformations. Voluntaryism, freedom, and personal initiative brought the individual and collective aspirations of Americans to a new order of magnitude. The nation was on the make.

Yet there were frustrations of equal magnitude for those who were displaced by the new egalitarian order, and more drastically for those left behind in the race. Immigration, exploitation, dislocation, loneliness—and, very significantly, the financial panic of 1837—darkened the dream. Modern thought and the newer science, meanwhile, seemed to controvert one traditional belief after another. All these factors served to ripen the sectarian harvest.

Into and across this turbulent scene moved the great surge

---

chap. 30. No accepted term exists for those divergent movements which encompass the population and political leadership of entire national, ethnic, or regional units (e.g. Arianism, Albigensianism, American Unitarianism, etc.). It is, in fact, well to realize that historical reality does not lend itself to neat classification.

of evangelical revivalism. It was by far the dominant religious movement of the period, and it served in many ways to open channels for diverse kinds of innovation and disruption. Put most simply, the "new measures" weakened the old measures; traditional church ways were directly challenged. This wrenching occurred among old "magisterial denominations" like the Presbyterians as well as among the Baptists who in many areas (notably in Rhode Island and around Philadelphia) had lived down their sectarian past. On the intellectual level, revivalism also served mightily to undermine doctrinal moorings, emphasizing personal experience instead. It opened opportunities for exploiting a new kind of freedom. The cry went up against hierarchies, seminary professors, dry learning, "hireling ministers," unconverted congregations, and "cold" formalism. Geographic localities, congregations, ministers, and individual laymen assumed new prerogatives. Farmers became theologians, offbeat village youths became bishops, odd girls became prophets.

Beyond these general tendencies, America's kind of revivalism served to arouse other long-dormant but always latent forms of enthusiasm. Leland Jamison in an important essay has pointed to some of the more prominent ones:

> The real impact of revivalism is not to be measured in membership statistics or the number of new religious groups which it has historically brought into being. Rather, its significance lies in . . . the ideas, attitudes, feelings, dreams and hopes which revivalism helped to disseminate and to be expressed among the American people. . . . Here [in America], as probably nowhere else or ever in Christendom, people had the opportunity of implementing and institutionalizing various particular religious emphases, most of which were as ancient as the Bible itself.[5]

[5] A. Leland Jamison, "Religions on the American Perimeter," in *The Shaping of American Religion*, ed. A. Leland Jamison and James Ward Smith, pp. 197–98. Peter Berger makes an exceedingly valuable classification of three leading sectarian motifs: (1) Enthusiastic (an experience to be lived), (2) Prophetic (a message to be proclaimed), and (3) Gnostic (a secret to be divulged), ("The Sociological Study of Sectarianism," *Social Research* 21, no. 4 [Winter 1954]: 467–85).

He singles out four of these emphases as especially prominent, stressing the close connection between revivalism and
the first two, but pointing out that each of the four could and
did arise quite aside from a revivalistic context:

1. *Perfectionism,* the doctrine that "perfect sanctification"
   or complete holiness and the "second blessing" were at-
   tainable or even necessary to the salvation of the converted Christian.
2. *Millennialism,* a doctrine of "last things," often based on
   precise and extremely individualistic interpretations of
   the apocalyptic books of the Bible, urging Christians to
   ready themselves and the world for the imminent coming of the Kingdom or Christ's second advent.
3. *Universalism,* the doctrine, diversely stated, that in
   Christ's sacrifice the ultimate salvation of all mankind
   had been accomplished or revealed.
4. *Illuminism,* the claim that "new light" or further revelation of God's purpose and nature had been given to men
   in these latter times and that such new teachings,
   whether simply modifications of received doctrine or
   revolutionary conceptions of religion, should be heeded.
   [The possibilities in this realm were obviously almost
   infinitely various.]

These dominant emphases, which appeared as often in combination as singly, were given still greater intensity by the
willingness of converts to regard anyone who opposed or
doubted them as perdition-bound, or to believe that the entire Church was now apostate and lost or, indeed, that it had
been for centuries. These themes sometimes became so unanimously the preoccupation of whole denominations that little
or no sectarian activity resulted; but when resistance developed, secessions and self-conscious new movements often
followed.

Ancient Christian concerns were by no means the only
ideas to come to the fore, however, nor was revivalism the
only stimulant. Religious excitement, for one thing, had a
way of producing its opposite: disappointment, disgust, remorse, ennui, and even a sense of betrayal. An old associate
of Finney put it eloquently in reporting on an earlier harvest
of souls in western New York: "I have visited and revisited

many of these fields, and groaned in spirit to see the sad, frigid, carnal and contentious state into which they had fallen . . . within three months after we left them."[6] Chronic ill health, disease, and accidents, as always, cried out for healing and assuagement. Socialistic and communitarian theories reinforced literalistic concern for the early Christian communism described in the New Testament (Acts 2:41–47). Mysticism and various forms of pantheism provided links to important philosophic trends of the time. Other interests, often with only remote Christian rootage or none at all, kept appearing and reappearing in different contexts. The discovery and popularization of "animal magnetism" (hypnotism) added a new dimension to popular conceptions of human consciousness. Lurking under America's puritanic Victorianism was a persistent and not sufficiently appreciated restiveness about sex and the monogamous family, a restiveness that the antinomian preaching of the revivals often heightened.

Certain of the new movements, especially among the communitarian experiments discussed in the succeeding chapter, found a place for almost every emphasis and minor theme we have just been considering. Not all of these can be illustrated in a survey history; but certain representative and influential movements require attention, not as an odd assortment of eccentricities introduced to provide comic relief, but as an essential part of the age and a genuine symptom of tensions latent in American life and religion.

PERFECTIONISM AND HOLINESS

John Wesley is unquestionably the greatest modern Protestant preacher of Christian perfection, the church he founded was its dynamic bearer, and the first half of the nineteenth century was American Methodism's greatest hour. Emerging as a semisectarian secession from Anglicanism during the later eighteenth century, Methodism had become by the

6 Finney himself lamented "the awful declension" in Oneida County that had followed his successes there (see Whitney R. Cross, *The Burned-Over District*, pp. 257–58). Wave after wave of diverse religious excitements made New York State notoriously "burned-over."

dawn of the twentieth the largest Protestant denomination in America. The place of perfectionist preaching in this great success story was, however, anything but secure. During the 1820s and early 1830s its popularity definitely waned, after which a great perfectionist revival occurred, not only within Methodism, but after 1835, in the preaching of the country's greatest revivalist, Charles G. Finney, as well. In 1837 Phoebe Palmer of New York began her extraordinary career as the greatest among countless other Methodist propagandists for the doctrine. In the atmosphere of the antebellum years, therefore, advocates of the "second blessing" felt little need to secede from the Methodist churches. In 1860, however, when the Genesee Conference excommunicated one minister for his strident criticism of Methodism's laxity in these matters, the nucleus for a perfectionist sect was provided. And before the year was out, B. T. Roberts with fourteen other ministers and eighty laymen had brought the Free Methodist Church into existence. The event was premonitory of larger disruptions if and when the church's commitment to perfectionist preaching should decline, but only late in the century would the great Holiness-Pentecostal chapter in the history of American sectarianism be written.

Long before those far-off events, however, perfectionism found its place in many radically untraditional contexts, often in strange combination with other tenets. The most celebrated instance of organized perfectionism was John Humphrey Noyes's Oneida Community, but this "scientific" and closely regulated socialistic experiment had its origins in the radical evangelical perfectionism which flourished among the more enthusiastic preachers of the great revival sweeping the country in the early 1830s. Noyes belonged to a group of seceders from a "free church" which radical "new measures" men had founded in New Haven. With them were affiliated various other groups in New England. These "New Haven Perfectionists" were ostracized at Yale and by the leading churches, but they were moderate in comparison with other movements in New York City and Albany. Everywhere their extreme doctrines were disruptive; and when their assurance of being "beyond the Law" led them to take "spiritual wives," county sheriffs sometimes enforced the law of the land if not that of Moses. During the 1830s perfectionist emphases were becoming pervasive among the revivalists. As Timothy Smith has stressed, moreover, "Eastern and urban evangelism played the dominant role," whereas Western and rural revivalism was lagging.[7]

ADVENTISM

The teaching that the Kingdom of God is at hand is inescapably biblical, and although apocalyptic or chiliastic prophecy has put its mark on many chapters of church history, a distinctly new kind of concern for Christ's Second Coming arose amid the anxieties and evangelical enthusiasm of antebellum America, as the ancient doctrine became first an urgent popular expectation, and then a "great disappointment" which the Seventh Day Adventists slowly shaped into a stable sectarian witness. Later in the century, when millennialism had again become a widespread concern, Jehovah's Witnesses would begin their sensational ascent from obscurity to national and international prominence. In the meantime, millennial hopes and fears won a prominent place even in many of the large old denominations. All across the country Protestants were singing:

> Stand up, stand up for Jesus,
> The strife will not be long;
> This day the noise of battle;
> The next, the victor's song.[8]

William Miller (1782–1849) grew up on the frontier of upper Vermont. He was a radical Jeffersonian and a deist with something of the stamp of Ethan Allen upon him until conversion in a local revival made him a devout member of a "Calvinist" Baptist church. He tended a large farm and studied the Bible intently in a King James Version bearing Archbishop Ussher's chronology in the margins. Deeply concerned as to when Christ would come again, Miller pondered the Book of Daniel. Counting the days referred to in certain passages of this highly symbolic apocalypse (especially 9:24–27 and 8:14), making each "day" a year, and accepting Ussher's

[7] Timothy L. Smith, *Revivalism and Social Reform in Mid-Nineteenth-Century America*, p. 59.

[8] The hymn's author, George Duffield (1818–88), with his father a leader among the "New School" Presbyterians, was noted for his strenuous millennial preaching.

date for these events as 457 B.C. (see Neh. 2:1), he discovered that "seventy weeks" added up to the date of Christ's death (A.D. 33, according to Ussher) while "two thousand three hundred days" added up to A.D. 1843. He described his findings with fine New England bluntness: "I was thus brought, . . . at the close of my two-year study of the Scriptures, to the solemn conclusion that in about twenty-five years from that time [1818] all the affairs of our present state would be wound up." Confessing great diffidence, Miller feared to "go before the world" with his awesome news. In time he overcame his hesitations, however, and won wide acceptance as a revival preacher in Vermont, New Hampshire, and New York.

Miller was ordained as a Baptist minister in 1833 and published his lectures on the Second Coming in 1835; but he was not catapulted into national prominence until two years later when he was heard by Joshua V. Himes (1805–95), a minister of the Christian Connection whose Chardon Street Chapel in Boston was a favored meeting place for reformers and prophets of all sorts (including early abolitionists). Himes was a born publicist and a lover of crowds and camp meetings. After 1839 he became Miller's promoter, a great organizer of millennial fear and fervor, the editor of two millennialist papers, and the compiler of a hymnbook, *The Millennial Harp*. Between 1840 and 1843 meetings were organized all across the country, with Miller himself lecturing over three hundred times during one half-year period. Despite warnings and condemnation from many quarters, thousands, no doubt hundreds of thousands, began to prepare for the Lord's coming. As in Reformation times, there was even a comet to heighten popular apprehension. Yet March 1843 and March 1844 passed by, and time still continued. Finally 22 October 1844 went by, the last definite date to be set by the movement's leadership. The mass movement collapsed amid a general feeling of betrayal, widely circulating charges of profiteering, and harsh disciplining in the Baptist, Methodist, and other revivalistic churches from which the millennial throngs had been chiefly drawn. Sick, discouraged, and cast out by the Baptists, Miller, who had never been as specific in his predictions as Himes, formed a little Adventist church in Vermont. He died without seeing any tangible result from his labors. But the leaven was now abroad in the land as never before. To the hard core of true believers who survived, the "Great Disappointment" was only a challenge.[9]

In 1845 a group of these convinced Adventists, including Miller himself, had convened in Albany and adopted a rudimentary organization along congregational lines. But they were by no means united. Some opposed evangelism, believing that the door was now shut, the Foolish Virgins were forever outside. Others were convinced that the millennial Great Sabbath had in fact arrived, and with it the time for jubilee and alms but not for work. In 1844, however, on the very morrow of the Great Disappointment, Hiram Edson, a New York farmer and staunch Millerite, had beheld a vision as he walked through a cornfield: the "cleansing of the temple" *had* actually been accomplished on the date forecast—but in heaven! Meanwhile, fraternization with the Seventh Day Baptists and further scriptural study led another group to accept the cruciality of observing the Seventh Day rather than the popish Sunday. New advocacy followed, and fierce disagreements on the state of the dead, the fate of the damned, the role of Satan, the nature of the Millennium, the Judgment, and the Atonement. Within a decade the once grand movement was reduced to a disorganized welter of Adventist controversy.

Yet out of this chaos emerged an agent of reorganization in the person of a slight teen-aged girl of Portland, Maine, the "Adventist Prophetess," Ellen G. Harmon (1827–1915). Converted to the movement in 1842 and soon extruded from the Methodist Church, she (like Edson) had her first vision shortly after the Great Disappointment, and therewith began her life's mission. After marrying James White, an Adventist elder, in 1846, the range of her activities increased. Given as she was to visions and transports—an estimated two thousand before she died—she poured out her version of the Adventist message in an endless stream of publications. Gradually she more or less absorbed the Edsonites and the Sabbatarians, gathering a reasonably united following that

[9] Leon Festinger et al., *When Prophecy Fails* (Minneapolis: University of Minnesota Press, 1956) is an important and fascinating study of group responses to apocalyptic disconfirmation, though he treats "Millerism" only in passing, pp. 12–23. See also Festinger's more general work *A Theory of Cognitive Dissonance* (Stanford, Calif.: Stanford University Press, 1962).

not only accepted her claims to be the "Spirit of Prophecy," but also her doctrinal teaching and her special views on health and diet.

In 1855 Battle Creek, Michigan, became the movement's headquarters when the Whites took up residence there. Five years later, a representative group took the name "Seventh-Day Adventists," incorporated the publishing house, and projected a general conference, which was duly organized in 1868. Soon Mrs. White's vegetarian protégé, Dr. John H. Kellogg, would begin his career—and eventually make Battle Creek the nation's breakfast cereal center. With fidelity to Mrs. White's nine-volume *Testimonies* as its chief unifying factor, the church continued to expand. In 1903, not long after returning from a ten-year mission in Australia, Mrs. White moved the central offices to Takoma Park, near Washington, D.C. Since her death in 1915 the church has continued its worldwide growth, using new communications media as they became available, displaying the largest measure of lay dedication of any church in America, and organizing extensive works of mercy, notably in the realm of health and medical care. At the same time, they have remained in almost complete isolation from all other churches. With the passing years their doctrinal stand has moved somewhat closer to that of general American fundamentalism, but any significant cooperation with these groups is prevented by the Adventists' extreme legalism, Sabbatarianism, and unusual doctrines on the Atonement, Satan, and the damned, as well as their strongly held views on health, medicine, and diet. Most distinctive of all is the special authority that they continue to show for the writings of Mrs. White.

UNIVERSALISM

Though not usually discussed in the context of American sectarianism, the Universalists are an important reminder of how an ancient "heresy" could be revitalized as a divisive force through the interplay of revivalism and the American social situation. The central Universalist contention, that "it is the purpose of God, through the grace revealed in our Lord Jesus Christ, to save every member of the human race from sin," has a long lineage. Richard Eddy's history of the denomination, in fact, devoted more pages to the documentation of its antiquity than to its American history.

The Universalist church in the United States was founded by John Murray (1741–1815), an Englishman of "high Calvinist" background, who had been brought into the Methodist movement by the preaching of John Wesley and George Whitefield. He was converted to Universalist teaching by James Relly (1720–ca. 1780), another British Methodist who, while remaining a Trinitarian of Calvinist tendency, had extended the logic of Wesley's proclamation of "grace to all" to mean that Christ's sacrifice had purchased salvation not only for the Elect but for the entire human race. Excommunicated in England, Murray reached American shores in 1770, preached in several states, and finally went to live in Gloucester, Massachusetts, where he had found a small group of Relly's converts. These he organized into the first American Universalist church in 1779. Murray was also present at the convention held six years later when an association was formed to gain Universalist liberties in Massachusetts, a right that was won in the courts in 1786. In 1793 a New England "Convention" began to meet. In the meantime spokesmen for similar but not identical views had organized groups in Boston, Philadelphia, New Jersey, and New Hampshire.

The definitive prophet of this movement was to be Hosea Ballou (1771–1852). Like several other early Universalist ministers, Ballou was of Baptist background, but was also influenced by the liberal sentiments of Boston Congregationalism, many of whose leaders (most notably Charles Chauncy) were arriving at Universalist views through an emphasis on the goodness of man and the benevolence of Deity. In 1804 Ballou published his *Treatise on the Atonement*, which displays a very strong biblical interest, deep evangelical conviction, and strong Rellyan influence. It departs from Murray in its shift toward Unitarianism and away from a substitutionary view of Christ's sacrifice. Ballou defended a "moral theory" of the Atonement, holding that Christ suffered for men but not instead of them. This revision had great effect on organized Universalism, which increasingly moved toward Boston Unitarianism in theology even while remaining socially and spiritually an entirely different sort of movement. The Universalists grew steadily in strength, established a weekly paper in 1819, and in 1831–41 (when it suffered a minor schism on the issue of future punishment) claimed over five hundred ministers. By the Civil War there were state conventions throughout most of the North, with district associations at a lower level and a very weak General Convention above. Tufts College (1852) and Divinity School (1869) in Medford, Massachusetts, became its major educational institutions, though there were several colleges and a seminary elsewhere.

The sect became a small denomination which throughout the nineteenth century was far more evangelical than is generally realized. Its leaders had the further satisfaction of seeing its chief tenet win acceptance not only in liberal constituencies but in revivalistic movements ordinarily considered conservative. On the frontier their views frequently found favor. Throughout this period it bore the marks of its sectarian origins, especially in New England, where it began as a revolt from the standing order by humble, unlettered people rather than by the intellectual and social leaders. Although in 1961 the Universalists would merge with the Unitarians in a new Association of Liberal Religion, their beginnings contrast sharply with the process by which the culturally dominant elements of Eastern Massachusetts gradually drifted away from their ancient moorings and became a separate denomination.

THE SWEDENBORGIAN IMPULSE

Of all the unconventional currents streaming through the many levels of American religion during the antebellum half-century, none proved attractive to more diverse types of dissenters from established denominations than those which stemmed from Emanuel Swedenborg. His influence was seen everywhere: in Transcendentalism and at Brook Farm, in spiritualism and the free love movement, in the craze for communitarian experiments, in faith healing, mesmerism, and a half-dozen medical cults; among great intellectuals, crude charlatans, and innumerable frontier quacks. When Emerson's *Nature* appeared anonymously in 1836, many thought that it was a manifesto from the Swedenborgian church; and in *Representative Men* Emerson not only paid homage to Swedenborg as the "last Father in the church," but also revealed essential aspects of his own world view. Bronson Alcott put Swedenborg in his hall of fame along with Plato, Plotinus, and Boehme. William James was linked with Swedenborgianism by birth (his father had been so attracted) and many interpreters have remarked on the continuities from father to son.

There are many clues to Swedenborg's amazing capacity to satisfy such varied yearnings, but first among them was his self-assured optimism and his sweeping comprehensiveness. He made the whole universe religiously intelligible, giving satisfaction to those who were surfeited with revivalism and narrow-mindedness. Swedenborg dealt with nearly every historic doctrinal issue, yet he pleased those who desired freedom from all ancient dogmas. Powerfully asserting the freedom of man and the promise of the times, he gratified those who would flee Calvinistic doctrines of sin, reprobation, and hell. And in all this he not only made the Bible his constant point of departure but gave a thrilling new impulse to biblical exegesis. Thus each of the major sectarian themes of the day—perfectionism, millennialism, universalism, and illuminism—had their place in his message. Its popularity, in short, is an essential guide to much that was new in America's great period of religious innovation.

Behind this immense ramification of influence, naturally enough, is the thought of an incredibly versatile religious genius, Emanuel Swedenborg (1688–1771). He was the son of Jesper Swedberg, an eminent Swedish theologian and bishop. After his university studies Swedenborg dabbled in poetry, turned to natural science, traveled widely in Europe, and then served brilliantly on the Council of Mines. In various capacities and through many publications he made memorable contributions in geology, anatomy, neurology, paleontology, physics, and astronomy. Then in his fifty-seventh year he announced his concern for religion in his book *The Worship and Love of God*. The vital turning point had been a vision in which God had directed him "to explain to men the spiritual sense of the Scripture." His first response was the *Arcana Coelestia*, an enormous eight-volume commentary on Genesis and Exodus in which nearly his entire system is expounded or foreshadowed. Before his death thirty more volumes had given scope and specificity to the "Heavenly Doctrines."

The central claim of Swedenborg is that the Lord had come again in accordance with John's vision in the Apocalypse: "And I John saw the holy city, New Jerusalem, coming down from God out of heaven" (Rev. 21:2). The Second Coming of Jesus Christ is made in the inspired Word of God through Swedenborg's disclosure of its spiritual meaning; it is thus a way of reading the Bible revealed in God's good time by most extraordinary means. "I enjoy perfect inspiration," said the Swedish seer in his strange, matter-of-fact way. "The inner sense of the Word of God has been dictated to me out of heaven." Swedenborg was himself an eschatological event.

Swedenborg's formal principle, his method of disclosing the Bible's spiritual meaning—as against the literal, historical sense of the letter—was a corollary of his doctrine of correspondences, which may be said to be his material principle. Emerson described this doctrine as "the fine secret that little explains large, and large, little. . . . Nature iterates her means perpetually on successive planes." In Swedenborg's system there are three distinct orders of being: the natural world of mineral, vegetable, or animal "ultimates," the spiritual, and the celestial. He described the Bible in terms of these same three degrees: "The Word in its bosom is spiritual because it descended from Jehovah the Lord, and passed through the angelic heavens; and . . . was in its descent adapted to the perception of angels, and at last to the perception of men." When interpreted through Swedenborg's special visions, the Bible clarified the correspondences that linked together the one system of God. Hence he could assert that "all heaven in the aggregate reflects the single man." On the other hand, such are the correspondences of the cosmos that every "ultimate," including man in all of his parts, corresponds to some higher reality. The Divine and the Natural are consubstantial in God and Man. All of this, moreover, has historical implications, for it means that the historic church and its old controversies are done and gone. In this new era of rational clarity there is hope for the heavenly conquest of hell. "The object of creation was an angelic heaven from the human race; in other words, mankind, in whom God might be able to dwell as in His residence." Swedenborg's ethic, naturally enough, was neither ascetic nor extreme. One need not renounce all to be saved; one must rather keep his loves —to God, neighbor, world, and flesh—in the proper order.

Taken as a whole the Heavenly Doctrines were gauged to attract persons of liberal and thoughtful tendency. Yet the more esoteric features of his writings also attracted more eccentric followers. Swedenborg's visions and his communications with famous men long dead encouraged emulation, while his unusual views on sex and conjugal love provided a rationale for defying laws and social conventions on marriage. His spiritual interpretations encouraged new views on health, healing, and sickness, and his disdain for tradition encouraged radicalism in every direction: in social and religious matters, and particularly in biblical interpretation. Swedenborg, in sum, meant many things to many minds.

Since he believed that his appeal was limited only to intellectuals, and that the New Church would manifest itself gradually, Swedenborg would not have been surprised at its slow growth. Whether he in fact intended to found a visible church organization is uncertain, even doubtful. But in England an institute for the extension of his reformation was organized soon after his death, and it spread from there to other countries. After bitter controversy among Anglicans between separatists and nonseparatists, the first New Church society in the world was founded in London in 1787. Its first apostle to America was James Glen, a rich planter from British Guiana who had been converted by a chance reading of Swedenborg's *Heaven and Hell*. Slowly small groups of intense and sometimes distinguished adherents were formed in Philadelphia, Baltimore, Boston, New York, and a few other places. The first General Convention, held in Philadelphia in 1817, reported seventeen societies, with a total of 360 members living in nine states. During the next few years the New Church seemed to be declining; but even when this trend was reversed, growth was very slow. It never has numbered even 10,000 members in the United States; but through articulate spokesmen, an active publication program, and the phenomenal appeal of its "founder," it has wielded an influence very disproportionate to its size. Swedenborgianism, moreover, has spread far beyond the institutional New Church. Indeed, the way in which Swedenborg stimulated or became associated with other deviations from mainstream Protestant impulses is the major aspect of his American influence.

SWEDENBORGIAN VARIATIONS

The first of the eccentric religious impulses with which Swedenborgianism became closely allied sprang from mesmerism or "animal magnetism" (i.e. hypnotism, somnambulism, and related phenomena). Friedrich Mesmer (1734?–1815) was an Austrian physician and astrologer who identified the force of the stars with electricity and magnetism; he was also a mystic and a born showman who during a long "practice" in Paris accomplished healings and many strange psychic phenomena. Due to this early association of "mesmerism" with magic and the black arts, and later with spiritualism, it was denounced and ignored by the medical profession, but for precisely this reason it flourished in the religious underground. Nowhere was it possible to find a more attractive basis for a Christian understanding (even a biblical theology) of these phenomena than in Swedenborg's writings. This fact had the double effect of attracting many doctors and pharmacists into the New Church, and of making Swedenborg a favorite resource of innumerable itinerant healers and quacks. Homeopathy or homeopathic medicine provides an important case in point. Both Swedenborg and S.C.F. Hahnemann (1755–1843), the originator of this medical theory, were intensive students of Paracelsus and held that disease was, essentially, a "dynamic aberration of the spirit." Hahnemann's accent on natural forces and spiritual healing explains why homeopathy spread through the New Church like wild-fire. Dr. Hans B. Gram, a Dane who had studied with Hahnemann in Germany, introduced the practice in America and soon became a New Churchman, and many others in the church also became very prominent in the "profession."

Homeopathy also was taken up in diverse ways by many other healers, including those who had animal magnetism in their quiver. Phineas P. Quimby of Portland, Maine, who tried in his way to evolve a scientific view of mental healing, did not stress these affinities, but Warren F. Evans, a former Methodist minister in that city, became an ardent Swedenborgian after being healed by Quimby. Evans published his views on healing well before Mary Baker published *Science and Health*, and with other disciples of Quimby he founded the New Thought movement. Such linkages to Swedenborg continue throughout the century, and as we shall see in a later connection, Christian Science itself may be usefully understood as a precisely formulated, highly organized, and authoritatively led instance.

Mesmerism and spiritualism were so intimately related that

for several generations they were deemed to be virtually inseparable. It is by no coincidence, therefore, that Swedenborg, too, became implicated. In fact, there is some ground for seeing Swedenborg as the greatest medium in modern times and the New Church as the first spiritualist church. In 1818, when a spiritualistic phenomenon was described to William Schlatter (one of the early New Church leaders in Philadelphia), he was not at all incredulous and urged that the person be won for the New Church with a copy of Swedenborg's *Heaven and Hell.* Many similar but isolated instances followed. Then in 1845 a series of articles on the subject appeared in the *New Jerusalem Magazine.* The major outcropping of interest in intercourse with the other world, which came in 1848 with the Fox sisters' rappings, was not directly traceable either to Swedenborg or to the New Church; but it did conduce to so rapid a growth of spiritualism among Swedenborgian "liberals" that the New Church was threatened by schism in the 1850s and after.

The most widely read philosopher-theologian of spiritualism was Andrew Jackson Davis, the "Poughkeepsie Seer." Davis was an apprentice cobbler when an itinerant mesmerist found him an exceptionally apt subject. For a time thereafter he was a professional medium and exhibition piece of hypnotic marvels. Later, while under hypnosis and professedly in contact with Swedenborg and others, he gave lectures published with the aid of scribes as *The Harmonial Philosophy* (1852), which went through twenty-four editions in thirty years. Professor George Bush of New York University in his book *Mesmer and Swedenborg* (1847) did much to dignify these efforts by publishing an enthusiastic appendix on "The Revelations of Andrew Jackson Davis." A member of the New Church and convinced that Davis could not possibly have absorbed such wisdom by any other means than spirit-contact, Bush was doubly rejoiced. Actually Davis's works exhibit nothing that an intelligent person of his background and absorptive propensities could not have produced under hypnosis; and they serve admirably to illustrate the way in which Swedenborg's unitive thinking could be combined in the popular mind with both animal magnetism and many of the popular reform panaceas of the day, including socialism. This complex syndrome was even better illustrated by Thomas Lake Harris (1823–1906), a Universalist minister of New York who was much impressed by Davis, and also by the

Utopian theorists Charles Fourier and Robert Owen. In 1850 Harris and an associate founded a short-lived cooperative community of spiritualists in Mountain Cove, Virginia, before returning to New York to found an independent Christian spiritualist church and a periodical to propagate Swedenborgian views. Yet he honored Swedenborg chiefly as a "forerunner" and in 1857 scandalized orthodox New Churchmen by publishing *The Arcana of Christianity,* wherein it was announced that to Harris had been revealed not merely the spiritual but the *celestial* meaning of Scripture. From this point he went on from excess to excess, even to the hour of his death.

SPIRITUALISM

Spiritualism both as an organized movement and as a vast congeries of commercialized disorganization stems from exciting events in the "burned-over district." In 1847 a Methodist farmer, John D. Fox, his wife, and six children moved into an old house in Hydesville, New York. True to rumors about the house, their peace was soon interrupted by strange rappings. During the following year the two youngest children, Katherine (age twelve) and Margaret (age thirteen), established contact with the rapper with the command, "Hear, Mr. Splitfoot, do as I do." A simple code communication was set up; the neighbors, sometimes in fear and trembling, flocked to see the marvels. Some time later an older married sister living in Rochester became a kind of manager of the sensation; and on 14 November 1849, Margaret Fox appeared for the first time in public with admission charged. Later in the year the Fox sisters were signed up by P. T. Barnum, and they soon became celebrities. The news spread rapidly, not least because Horace Greeley of the *New York Tribune,* long since a devoted follower of Fourier, became a fervent believer.

Soon countless other mediums began to make contact with the spirit world. Scoffers probably outnumbered believers, but investigations made by various persons of dignity and authority sometimes led to affirmative reports and enthusiastic discipleship on the part of the investigators. Séances and spiritualist societies became a common phenomenon all across the country. Various groups combined spiritualism and free love. Mesmerists, magicians, and fortune-tellers also discovered an important opportunity, with the result that a whole new era in American roadshow entertainment was opened. As was inevitable, the first simple feats of the Fox girls gave way to other marvels: table turnings, slate writings, mysterious appearances, and great feats of clairvoyance. Margaret Fox, meanwhile, had won the affections of Elisha Kent Kane, the arctic explorer and socially prominent Philadelphian. He even proposed marriage, and for a time, as his prospective wife, she left "the tables" behind to pursue a polite education. Before his death in 1857 they had been married in an informal "Quaker" ceremony, and Margaret subsequently claimed his name and received a small legacy.

Spiritualism was not merely commercialized entertainment, however. It was a religious force—for some it was a religion —and this was true long before the Hydesville rappings. There were always the bereaved and the remorseful who desperately needed and wanted to make contact with the departed—a fact that stimulated interest in spiritualism after each of the country's major wars. Mrs. Lincoln herself showed such an interest after her husband's assassination. Still others, having drifted away from the churches, now sought and found confirmation of their religious yearnings in an objective and "scientific" way. In the pre-Civil War period the actual denominational possibilities of the movement went unrealized, even though an increasing number of clergymen became interested. Because the mediums almost invariably stressed the general immortality of man, Universalists were especially attracted. For reasons already indicated Swedenborgianism added other incitements.

Because of its extra-ecclesiastical auspices and lack of doctrinal complications, spiritualism also appealed to liberals and anticlericals, and it often became affiliated with communitarian and reformist movements. The best-known example in this category was Robert Dale Owen (1801–77). Owen had been a freethinker and a proponent of his father's communitarian socialism, but in 1856, while serving as an American diplomat in Naples, he experienced occult phenomena in a decisive way. The year after his father died in 1858, Owen began writing the book that betokened his conversion. *Footfalls on the Boundary of Another World* (1860) became the most famous American defense of the movement's central conviction. Owen's fame even won him an invitation to read a paper in the White House, which led to Lincoln's classic remark: "Well, for those who like that sort of thing, I should think it is just about the sort of thing they would like."[10]

Since 1863 there have been several attempts to organize spiritualism as a national denomination. The first effort collapsed within a decade, but a more permanent National Spiritualist Association was organized in 1893 (the year Margaret Fox died) on a loose congregational basis with a very liberal statement of principles. At this time it had about fifty thousand members and over three hundred affiliated organizations. In some cities, as in Boston, the Spiritualists achieved a fairly stable and respected denominational status, with an enlightened and liberal membership, a fine edifice in the Back Bay, and a well-edited paper, the *Boston Banner of Light*. Generally, however, the chief constituency has been a vast unorganized multitude which has ebbed and flowed with changing times and circumstances, but which reached its floodtide around 1870, when the movement claimed eleven million adherents. Spiritualism was not a "sect" in the usual sense of the term, yet it became a component in many kinds of sectarian revolt from the more traditional churches. It sometimes merged with various forms of occultism—as had astrology in ages past—to form an undercurrent of esoteric religion from which new movements would continuously arise. Its growth in America and elsewhere reveals a fundamental kind of religious uneasiness. In its popularity one may observe both the threat of modern science to traditional faith and the appeal to empirical confirmation of cherished hopes. It is thus a form of theological liberalism in which such eminent thinkers as Alfred Russel Wallace, Victor Hugo, and William James were seriously interested.

[10] Quoted in Earl Wesley Fornell, *The Unhappy Medium: Spiritualism and the Life of Margaret Fox*, p. 118. See also Richard W. Leopold, *Robert Dale Owen*, pp. 321–39.

30

THE COMMUNITARIAN IMPULSE

"We are all a little wild here with numberless projects of social reform. Not a reading man but has a draft of a new community in his waistcoat pocket." The words of Emerson's, one of his most quoted observations, from a letter to Carlyle written in 1840.[1] As was so often the case, he spoke the truth. The United States was the Promised Land for both American and European communitarian planners, and the antebellum half-century was their great seedtime. Most of the new communities, of course, remained simply the ideas of "reading men," yet six score of them were actually founded, a few dozen of them became celebrated though transient successes, and, if we include Mormonism, one became a major American cultural force. Like sectarianism, however, this communitarian impulse is difficult to characterize, because these experiments were so often but the lengthened shadow of some charismatic leader; and as Max Weber observed, "Charisma knows only inner determination and inner restraint." Almost by definition, the innovators rejected codes and statutes, traditions and customs—and this they did with more than usual abandon in the open society of the young American republic. In many cases they not only founded new sects, but called them out of the world. Thus they challenged the individualism and conformity of the nation as well as the conventional views of the churches. Rare were the times, nevertheless, when these efforts were not motivated by a belief in Christian perfection and the conviction (as old as

[1] Carlyle in turn revealed his estimate of such efforts by referring to the founder of Brook Farm as a "Socinian minister who left the pulpit to reform the world by growing onions" (quoted in Charles Crowe, *George Ripley*, p. 69).

cenobitic monasticism) that a dedicated community provided the ideal conditions for attaining it.

Socialistic communities of one kind or another have had a long history in America. Even Jamestown before the advent of John Smith had its "communitarian" phase. Necessity pushed our beloved "Pilgrim Fathers" to the same resort for a time. The Mennonites and other German sects often verged on such a social system, and some openly adopted it. The early nineteenth century brought another resurgence of this communitarian impulse, manifesting itself in the most diverse ways among both anticlerical freethinkers and Christian enthusiasts. In the events of the preceding chapter there were intimations of such an impulse, but in this chapter the communitarian movements themselves are considered, particularly those which are significant episodes in religious history. We begin with the Shakers, one of the earliest and most radical communitarian sects to organize, yet one which America took peculiarly to its heart—though only after it had become virtually extinct.

THE SHAKERS

The United Society of Believers in Christ's Second Coming (the Millennial Church) was brought to this country from England. Its founding spirit was Ann Lee Stanley (1736–84), who immigrated with eight followers (including her brother and her husband) in 1774. Mother Ann Lee's early life was one of almost unmitigated tribulation, culminating in the most remarkable exaltation. The daughter of one Manchester blacksmith and while very young the wife of another, she was unschooled and illiterate when she was converted by Jane and James Wardley, leaders of the so-called Shaking Quakers. (This sect, resembling the Camisards, may have been brought to England by refugees from the France of Louis XIV, and reinvigorated by the millennialist fervor of the Wardleys, who were also committed to various Quaker ideas.) Ann Lee seems to have outdone all others in the intensity of her piety; and after some years during which she suffered much distress and gave birth to four very short-lived children, her trances and visions convinced others and then herself that Christ's Second Coming would be in the form of a woman, and that she was that woman. She had also become convinced that sexual relations, ever since Adam and Eve, had been the root of all sin. Yet few people in England were persuaded by the little group of noisy worshipers and irrepressible preachers of which she was now the recognized head. Mistreatment, mob action, and imprisonment seemed to be their lot and only expectation—and so, they departed for America.

Even upon arrival in the promised land, poverty compelled a two-year dispersal of the little group. In 1776, however, they reconvened near Albany at what is now Watervliet, where economic difficulties led them to organize themselves in a socialistic Christian community, although communitarianism had heretofore had no part in their message. Mother Ann, now deserted by her husband, joined the company at its forlorn gathering place, but until 1779 they made no evangelistic advances. Then came an incident that would become the pattern for Shaker growth during the entire period of their greatest significance. In the aftermath of a revival in nearby New Lebanon, certain "New Light" Baptists who had been spiritually moved but left dissatisfied visited the Shakers and were further converted. As other people began seeking them out in ever greater numbers, the little community began a more concerted mission into communities where revivals had occurred. To those who wondered what to do with their reborn lives, the Shakers offered a meaningful answer. You have not left the world and the flesh, they would say, bidding the seeker to confess his sins to Mother Ann Lee and enter the true millennial church.

The Shakers made important gains during the Revolution despite their pacifism and British origins, and when Mother Ann died in 1784, capable leaders took her place. In the Harvard-Shirley area of Massachusetts they capitalized on the groundwork of a prophet who had recently preached very similar doctrines. Among Baptists they were especially successful. They made deep inroads on the newly formed Freewill Baptists, especially in New Hampshire, where one such congregation became the nucleus of a new Shaker community, and where many others were decimated by Shaker influence. Among the early Baptist converts was the Reverend Joseph Meacham, who in 1787 became the church's first American leader, an excellent organizer, and a powerful factor in the sect's expansion. By 1794 there were twelve communities: two in New York, four in Massachusetts, two in

New Hampshire, one in Connecticut, and three in Maine.
The community at New Lebanon remained the center of authority.

But the great harvest would be gathered when the Second
Awakening created ideal conditions both in New England
and in the West. The Shakers' most sensational coup was in
Kentucky, when they carried off three former Presbyterians
who had led the Cane Ridge revival. One of these, Richard
McNemar, became the Shakers' outstanding western leader.
Between 1805 and 1809 four new communities were founded
beyond the mountains: two in Kentucky and two in Ohio.
Two more in Ohio and one in Indiana were added later, and
once founded these communities grew both in numbers and
in extent. Union Village in Ohio came to embrace 4,500
acres. During its period of greatest size and vitality, between
1830 and 1850, the church as a whole numbered about six
thousand persons living in nineteen communities.

The Shaker communities became one of the American marvels, visited by almost every systematic foreign observer. In a
simple Yankee way these Shaker villages were, in fact, idyllic: the wants of life were fully, even abundantly supplied;
the clean-lined functional buildings, spotless interiors, grace-
fully practical furniture, wonderful cattle herds, fine herb
gardens, and perfectly tended fields all witnessed to organizational, social, and economic success. Within the community
a straightforward, strait-laced, and peaceable but minutely
regulated life went on, with duties clearly assigned, authority
clearly demarcated, and the sexes separated so far as practicality would permit.

Shaker communities, however, were not conceived primarily as secular utopias, and it was only after the Civil War
that economic and worldly considerations gradually became
predominant—a trend which, with other factors, hastened
their decline. By the century's end they had become a mere
remnant. But during their great period the Shakers were an
intense biblically oriented sect, millennialist in primary doctrinal concern and revivalistic in spirit. For them the Second
Coming was a past fact, consummated in and through Ann
Lee, who was a feminine incarnation as Jesus had been the
masculine. Mother Lee was the "Second pillar of the Church
of God," and the Shakers were the advance guard or the in-
tercessory remnant whose example and prayers would ultimately lead all men into blessedness. They were thus univer-

salists in their total view. In the moral demands they placed upon this remnant they were legalistic perfectionists: twelve classic virtues and four moral principles would bring men from the animal to the spiritual plane. Because the Kingdom was literally at hand, procreation was unnecessary, which accounts for their rule of celibacy, the only moral precept which they did not share with standard Protestant statements of Christian virtue.

In addition to this theology, which owed much to the revelations of Ann Lee, the Shakers were from the first spiritualists. They communicated with the departed, and for a decade or so after 1837 public séances were a very important part of their corporate religious life. At all times their worship was extremely important, regularly scheduled, and intensely communal, though Pentecostal gifts of speaking in tongues and personal testimonies had their place. The most distinctive feature of Shaker worship was the group dance, a legacy from the Camisards which, when accompanied by lively singing, could at times become quite frenzied. With due allowance for its special doctrines and practices, Shakerism was at once both an extraordinary embodiment of basic monastic motifs and a remarkable example of the special Christian emphases generated by revivalism. The Shakers were perhaps the single most influential source for the country's widespread interest in communitarian experiments during the early nineteenth century.

THE SOCIETY OF THE PUBLIC UNIVERSAL FRIEND

The earliest indigenous American communitarian experiment so closely resembled the Shakers in its origins and leading tenets that contemporaries spoke of deliberate imitation. At the outset, nevertheless, the two movements were quite independent. Jemima Wilkinson (1752–1819) was the daughter of a prosperous Quaker farmer in Cumberland, Rhode Island, who in 1776 was expelled from the local meeting because of her affiliation with the revivalistic "New Light" Baptists. Very soon thereafter, she emerged from a period of illness and visions as a Publisher of Truth in her own right, announcing that she had died to self and had been reborn as the Public Universal Friend, with a Christlike mission to preach repentance, other-worldliness, and preparation for death. A sense of millennial expectancy pervaded her pronouncements, but except for a strong emphasis on the virtues of celibacy, her message was a fairly conventional form of New School evangelicalism, as modified by her Quaker nurture and her reading of Fox, Penn, Barclay, and Penington. Far more sensational in that day was her itinerant preaching and the "personality cult" which she fostered. Mounted sidesaddle at the head of a small cavalcade of followers, she moved in ever-widening circles, first in Rhode Island, then in Massachusetts and Connecticut, and finally to eastern Pennsylvania.

By 1789 Jemima Wilkinson's "Universal Friends" were a recognized denomination of about two hundred members, many of them former Quakers, some of surprisingly high social station. Several local groups were meeting in Rhode Island, with others in New Milford, Connecticut, and Worcester, Pennsylvania. On this basis she projected an isolated community in western New York, which at that time was still an unsurveyed wilderness. In 1788 a settlement was begun on Lake Seneca, and within two years, by which time the Universal Friend was on the scene herself, her 260 followers were the largest community in the region. In 1794, due to land title problems and the encroachment of outsiders, they founded a new "Jerusalem" twelve miles farther west on Crooked (Keuka) Lake. Here as before freehold farms were laid out, and the Universal Friend, with her entourage of a dozen or more celibate women, was provided with a fine frame house, later replaced by still another, more ambitious one.

Evangelism ceased in this frontier outpost, but until her death in 1819 the Friend continued to minister to her society, preaching with particular effectiveness at services for the deceased. Despite growing internal dissension and continued land problems, meetings were held in Jerusalem more or less in the Quaker manner even after her death. A semblance of organization remained until 1863, and the last of her converts did not die until 1874. By that time the publicity of her community's pioneering had done its part to spur the region's rapid population growth. Out in the "burned-over district" as back in the East, however, the society suffered from the indistinctiveness of its leader's message and from the absence of strict communitarian organization. It gradually coalesced with the surrounding culture, leaving a great frame house on the hill overlooking the lake as a monument to Jemima Wilkinson's forceful personality.

GERMAN PIETISTIC COMMUNITIES

From the early eighteenth-century Ephrata Community in Pennsylvania to the controversial expansion of the Hutterites in the twentieth century, German Anabaptism or radical pietism has made a continuous contribution to the history of American communitarianism. The six hundred followers of George Rapp (1757–1847) who organized Harmony, Pennsylvania, in 1804 were in this tradition. They were extreme pietists who had separated from the established church of Württemberg. Their doctrine was characteristically strong in its anticipation of the millennium, universalistic, uninterested in evangelism, and after 1807 opposed to procreation and marriage. Like the Shakers the Rappites practiced auricular confession and set themselves on the road to perfection by close personal discipline in order that a pure remnant could be presented to God on the Great Day. In the social and physical sense Harmony became a famous success, a garden in the wilderness. And this was equally true of the new Harmony in Indiana to which they removed in 1815, or of Economy (in Ohio, near Pittsburgh) which became the "permanent" location of the Rappites ten years later.

In addition to the Rappites there were several other German sects who during the lifetime of their leaders maintained highly successful communities. Wilhelm Keil, a Prussian immigrant converted by the German Methodists and for a time a preacher in that connection, made a group of disaffected Rappites the nucleus of two flourishing communities: Bethel (in Missouri), which flourished as a supply post for the Oregon Trail, and Aurora (in Oregon), which was reached by a famous trek in which the coffin of Keil's son was borne across the plains. Though it perpetuated an extreme form of antisacramental pietism, Keil's group was characterized by much less doctrinal eccentricity than most.

Somewhat similar was the group of three hundred Quaker-like pietists led from harassment in Bavaria, Württemberg, and Baden to Zoar (Ohio) by Joseph Michael Bäumler (Bimeler) in 1817. Like the Bethelites (and later the Mormons), they were greatly aided in the economic sense by the American westward movement, in this case by the Ohio Canal. Although the community continued for some time after Bimeler's death in 1853, it finally was dissolved in 1898.

Still another group of this type was the Amana Society, or Community of True Inspiration. As lowly in its origins as the other German pietistic movements but more charismatic in its leadership, this group had been gathered in various places in the German Rhineland before the decision to migrate. In 1843 they founded Ebenezer near Buffalo, New York; then in the 1850s to gain more land and to escape urban seductions, they gradually removed to east-central Iowa, where they maintained a plain but thriving cluster of villages. In the late twentieth century they continue to prosper on their 25,000-acre holdings, though since 1932 as an incorporated cooperative.

UTOPIAN COMMUNITARIANISM

In addition to a wide variety of experiments in Christian communitarianism, the early decades of the nineteenth century witnessed the formation (and usually the early dissolution) of dozens of utopias which lacked sectarian or churchly aspirations, or were even antireligious. The most famous of these experiments was New Harmony, founded by Robert Owen (1771–1858), a Welshman, who had distinguished himself in Scotland as an industrialist with a passionate concern for the well-being of his labor force. Owen was also an amateur philosopher of deterministic persuasions who considered the social environment the decisive factor in personal development. He made New Lanark a model factory town; then discovering in 1824 that the Rappite property in Indiana was for sale, he acted on a long-considered plan to establish a true model of socialism in America.

On arrival in the United States, Owen continued to publicize his views, even lecturing once in the national capital to a large and distinguished audience that included President John Quincy Adams. He became more confident that America was socialism's promised land. A great many distinguished scientists, educators, and social dreamers (but far too few competent craftsmen) answered the call; and early in 1826 *New* Harmony was occupied. Owen was often dictatorial; his odd assortment of followers showed little capacity for maintaining peace and order in his absence; his sons (William and Robert Dale) were ineffective as his lieutenants. By 1827 Robert Owen was ready to confess that he had invested four-fifths of his fortune for naught. The community was dissolved. By 1830 nearly two dozen other Owenite groups had also come and gone. All of these communities rested their hopes on education, freethinking, and human idealism. They had only theory as an integrative force, and in the midst of American opportunity, freedom, and individualism, this proved, over and over again, to be an insufficient basis for communitarian success.

At least in theory a religious ingredient was present in the ideas of the French Utopian Charles Fourier (1772–1837). In Arthur Brisbane, Horace Greeley, William Henry Channing, and Parke Godwin, Fourier gained persuasive American propagandists; and within two decades about fifty ephemeral communities had testified to both the popularity and the impracticality of his proposals. All of these secular communities demonstrated what many a foreign observer had declared: that a community's failure was almost certain when its participants lacked the intense religious commitment which could repress individual inclinations and render paternalism agreeable. One might add that charismatic leadership was equally necessary—and this Owen and the American disciples of Fourier invariably lacked. Never were such observations borne out more strikingly than by the contrast between the Harmony of the Rappites and the New Harmony of the Owenites. Yet there was an intermediate type of community that occupies an important, almost legendary niche in American memory. These experiments were informed by fundamentally religious aspirations at least in their origins, though they were distinctly liberal, even radical, in their revisions of orthodox doctrine. Among many others, three that originated in the early 1840s are best remembered: the Oneida Community, the Universalist experiment at Hopedale, and Brook Farm.

The Oneida Community

The most successful, most widely publicized, and most ably defended example of evangelically inspired communitarianism in the United States was the Oneida Community founded by John Humphrey Noyes (1811–86). Although his background and training were not the usual ones for such a career, his story reveals with remarkable clarity how the evangelical fervor generated by a great revival could create a Christian radical. Noyes was the son of a well-to-do merchant, a first cousin of Rutherford B. Hayes, a graduate of Dartmouth, a convert in the great revival of 1831, and soon after that a divinity student at Andover and Yale. At Yale he was a troubler of the waters from the start. He was active in Garrison's abolitionism and in a separatistic revivalist church in New Haven. Most troubling of all, he declared that the Second Coming of Jesus *had* ended the Jewish dispensation in A.D. 70. For Noyes "salvation from sin" (perfectionism) was the only gospel for the present age. Barred from ordination on account of these views, he continued nevertheless as an unlicensed itinerant preacher, propagating his views by tracts and forging contacts with other perfectionist groups in New York City, Albany, Connecticut, and Massachusetts.

Noyes's social theory, ethics, and theology meanwhile took on more permanent structure. He came to view socialism as the means by which Christian love would bring in the Kingdom of Heaven on earth. Both personal experience and antilegalistic doctrines served to make him doubt the morality of exclusiveness in wedlock, and soon after his own "marriage" in 1838, he gathered various members of his family into a small perfectionist colony in Putney, Vermont, where he began to publish his views in a periodical that soon won new converts. When "complex marriage" was instituted in 1846, the surrounding community was scandalized, and in 1848 the group was obliged to flee, only to be reconstituted at Oneida in western New York. Here a large communal dwelling was built, and by 1851 the community had grown to 205, with farming and logging providing its economic support. Three years later they began what became an immensely successful manufacture of steel traps, and still later, after an allied community had been organized in Wallingford, Connecticut, they moved with equal success into the production of sewing silk and silver-plated flatware.

The community was increasingly rationalized in all that it did, becoming almost a model of efficient organization. This applied, of course, even to matters of love, sex, and marriage. Wives and husbands in the possessive sense were forbidden, as was "special love." Each adult was a spouse to every other adult; male continence was required and eugenics (or "stir-piculture") was systematically practiced; procreation (as distinguished from sexual "transactions") was made a matter of overt communal decision. Life was not ascetic or unduly arduous, cultural activities were encouraged, and the communal children were reared and educated in a progressive spirit. Descriptions of Oneida remind one of Brook Farm, though the philosophy was less elevated and practical affairs more under control. In a logical sense as well as in terms of its own tendency, moreover, it moved steadily toward secular communitarianism. Its concern for God's final judgment faded, and its perfectionism drifted from that of Finney to that of Channing. The Oneida Community, however, crashed head on into the most sacred institution in Victorian America: the monogamous family; and in the long run the cumulative effect of external criticism was more than it could withstand. In 1879 Noyes recommended the abandonment of complex marriage, and two years later he proposed that a joint-stock company be formed with shares distributed to members. The community became in due course a prosperous Canadian corporation.

Hopedale

Contemporary with Noyes's community and even less concerned with evangelical enthusiasms was the Hopedale Community set up by Adin Ballou, a Universalist minister. Ballou was an inveterate champion of reform causes, sympathetic to the views of Channing, Parker, and Garrison, as well as to those of the kinsman who had founded his denomination. He was also committed to actualizing God's kingdom on earth and convinced that a successful communitarian embodiment of "practical Christianity" would trigger a world movement. To this end he founded a periodical, devised a utopian constitution, sold stock in a company, and bought a farm near Milford, Massachusetts. In 1841 the experiment began, and for over a decade it flourished, adding acreage and buildings, promoting many reform causes, and winning fame as a "Christian republic." But its end occurred suddenly in 1856, when two members who had bought up three-fourths of the stock decided to liquidate the company. Like so many other communities, it yielded to the seductions of freedom and the lure of private enterprise.

Brook Farm

The forces that converge in Brook Farm are many and diverse. Without Immanuel Kant and post-Kantian philosophers, says one of the experiment's historians, the experiment would "very likely have never existed." But Transcendentalism and the small group of its leaders constituting the Hedge Club provided the major context. The immediate occasion was George Ripley's dissatisfaction with his Unitarian ministry at the Purchase Street Church in Boston, and his belief "that some practical application should be made of the fresh views of philosophy and life" which were turning the quiet club into a reformist cell. In deciding on this "practical application" the founders also drew inspiration and ideas from early experiments, notably Zoar, the Shakers, and the Rappites.

As at Hopedale, a joint-stock company was formed, and many shares were bought by philanthropic friends of the experiment. A pleasant but unfertile farm was bought in West Roxbury, and in April 1841 the Ripleys and fifteen others moved in, with Articles of Association to govern their common life. Nathaniel Hawthorne was on the committee for the Direction of Agriculture. In due course a printing press and means for woodworking and the manufacture of Britannia ware were added, and for three or four years these activities combined with a variety of progressive and excellently staffed schools kept the community economically viable. Conversation abounded, distinguished visitors came and went, and the community managed to maintain its morale. The *Dial* provided an invaluable platform for expounding the transcendental good news, though it was not published by or at Brook Farm.

The fateful turning point was in 1844, when the trustees following the lead of Ripley yielded to the cult of Fourier, which was then at its American apogee. In 1845 the Articles of Association were redrawn so as to convert Brook Farm into a Fourierist "phalanx." An ambitious program of industrialism was projected and construction of a large "phalanstery" begun. A new socialist paper, the *Harbinger*, began its brief four-year existence. When in 1846 the nearly completed phalanstery burned, bankruptcy threatened, membership declined, and in 1847 the entire property was transferred to a board of trustees for disposal.

Brook Farm's life was brief, but waves of the splash it made rippled to shore for a long time and often far away. Bronson Alcott undertook a still more ideal but even briefer experiment at Fruitlands in Harvard, Massachusetts (1843–44); Isaac Hecker and several others were led to the Roman Catholic Church for a peace that utopias could not give; and many who studied in its schools gratefully remembered Brook Farm as an enduring inspiration. Nobody seemed the poorer for having participated in its common tasks and partaken of its fervent, hopeful spirit.

THE MORMONS

During the summer of 1844, while the energies of Brook Farm were being redirected by the visions of Fourier, another more ambitious venture was in travail far away on the Mississippi. In Carthage, Illinois, Joseph Smith, Mormon prophet, Lieutenant-General of Nauvoo, and "King of the Kingdom of God," was murdered; and his followers were contemplating the horrors of still another "Mormon War." Two celebrated communitarian ventures were in crisis: for one it was the beginning of the end, for the other it was the real beginning.

This Joseph Smith, Jr., who came to the end of his tether in 1844, had lacked all of the advantages that led people to Brook Farm. His great adventure had begun less than two decades before in western New York. Yet he, too, was a New Englander with a measure of "come-outerism" in his family inheritance; he would in due course exhibit an almost uncanny sensitivity to the yearning and frustrations that underlay the religious turmoil of his age. While still in his twenties Smith would found a church which has outlasted or outdistanced every other sect and communitarian movement brought into being in America. While other movements floundered or slid into oblivion or stagnated, his shaped a regional culture-area of the United States, and in 1970 counts a membership of about three million people. Moreover, as Fawn Brodie has correctly insisted, "Joseph's was no mere dissenting sect. It was a real religious creation, one intended to be to Christianity what Christianity was to Judaism: that is, a reform and a consummation."[2] For the drama in its story no

---

[2] Fawn Brodie, *No Man Knows My History*, p. viii.

less than for its revelations of the American religious character, Mormonism deserves far more extensive and intensive consideration than any of its contemporary parallels.

Joseph Smith was born in 1805 under unpromising circumstances. His father was one of the many farmers who were finding the difficulties of farming in Vermont unsurmountable. In 1816 after several failures he moved his family to Palmyra, New York, in the Erie Canal boom country. But the boom passed them by. They continued to be failures at farming, and Joseph was no more successful in his treasure hunting and money digging. While engaged in this "work," in fact, young Joseph was once found guilty in a local court of being "a disorderly person and an imposter" for his use of a certain "seer stone." Between 1826 and 1830, however, this unschooled farmer's son with a disinclination for the plough changed roles. No longer was he simply the village necromancer who saw more wonder on Mulberry Street than anybody else: he became the "author and proprietor" of a new bible and the founder of a new religion.

The highly problematic order of events by which the book and the movement came into existence can no longer be precisely reconstituted, but it is known that within a year after his marriage in January 1827, Smith was rumored to have found some long lost treasure which would unlock the mysteries of the area's Indian history. Before long, he let it be known that the angel Moroni had appeared to him in a vision and had led him to a cache of golden plates inscribed in "reformed Egyptian" hieroglyphics, as well as a set of seer stones (Urim and Thumim) wherewith to read them. (Except within essentially ecstatic experiences no person beside Smith ever saw these plates; and soon after the translation was completed they were swept away by an angel.) Late in 1827 Joseph began translating with his wife as copyist—he on one side of a curtain, she on the other. In 1829, after three other copyists had filled in for Emma Smith, the task was completed; a printer was found and paid, and in March 1830 the Book of Mormon was put on sale.

Like the Old Testament Hexateuch, this book is primarily historical in form. It is a five-hundred-page account of the wanderings, vicissitudes, and battles of America's pre-Columbian inhabitants: first, the Jaredites, who left the Tower of Babel and crossed to America in remarkable windowed, reversible barges only to extinguish their race in continuous intestine wars; second, the evil sons of Laman (Lamanites), who were the American Indians; and third, the good sons of Nephi, who after many battles were all but extinguished by the Lamanites. Finally, only Mormon and his son Moroni were left, and they buried their chronicles in A.D. 384 so that in God's good time their spiritual descendants could establish the Nephite stake in Zion before the Last Day.

Also like the Old Testament, the history is interspersed with sundry exhortations and many pronouncements on topics of doctrinal or social contention. Yet taken as a whole, the Book of Mormon, like the Mormon church itself, shows cohesiveness, structure, and purpose to such a degree that a certain kind of learning and a considerable measure of imagination (or inspiration) must be attributed to its author. The language resembles that of the King James Version of the Bible, and not a line of it requires one to posit either wholesale plagiarism or supernatural powers. The theories which attribute authorship to the Reverend Solomon Spaulding or to Sidney Rigdon are farfetched in the same way and for the same reasons as the Baconian views on Shakespeare are farfetched. As with Shakespeare, sources and influences can, of course, be traced; but the most remarkable fact is the entirely natural way in which the book is related to Smith's nature, to his purposes, and to the total social and spiritual situation of the "burned-over district" of western New York. The author apparently possessed absorptive powers far beyond the ordinary, a roving curiosity, boundless imagination, a facile, easygoing, uncommitted set of mind, and a keen sense of the religious needs of those who had been seared but not consumed, both by revivalism and by the various forms of dark and irrational eccentricity which swept over the land.

This familiarity with the religious situation is as important a factor as any other, though non-Mormon writers have minimized it. Joseph Smith may or may not have had a decisive religious crisis in which his agony over the multiplicity of sects led to the vision that made him a seer and prophet (his description of the event was written many years later). But he and other members of the Smith family certainly had experienced revival preaching, and he was familiar with a wide gamut of doctrinal contention. Universalism, Methodism, and skepticism had made their mark on his father; his mother was a seeker after cultic certainties; and in 1824 Joseph himself had heard a local preacher consign his dead brother to hell. He was also thoroughly at home with the King James Version of the Bible. About 27,000 words of the Book of Mormon were borrowed from that source, while the book as a whole as well as subsequent "revelations" would reflect not only its English style, but its heterogeneous structure.

Beyond these general and personal factors, there were other important regional concerns that Smith could not ignore: the increase of anti-Catholicism, the intense anti-Masonic movement which arose in western New York, and the question of Indian origins, provoked with special force around Palmyra by nearby Indian mounds and old palisaded forts atop certain hills.

Fawn Brodie, whose sympathetic and insightful account of Joseph's life and work is unequaled, has put the matter eloquently:

> Its matter is drawn directly from the American frontier, from the impassioned revivalist sermons, the popular fallacies about Indian origin, and the current political crusades.
>
> Any theory of the origin of the Book of Mormon that spotlights the prophet and blacks out the stage on which he performed is certain to be a distortion. For the book can best be explained, not by Joseph's ignorance nor by his delusion, but by his responsiveness to the provincial opinions of his time. He had neither the diligence nor the constancy to master reality, but his mind was open to all intellectual influences, from whatever province they might blow. If his book is monotonous today, it is because the frontier fires are long since dead and the burning questions that the book answered are ashes.[3]

A few isolated, atypical individuals can still read it as a religious testimony; a few dedicated historians can study it profitably as a help to understanding a bygone day. But not even loyal Mormons can be nourished by it as they were a century ago. At that time, before anthropology and archaeology had developed plausible alternatives to Joseph's mythic rendering of America's ancient past, the Book of Mormon brought a satisfying answer to many needs: it undercut sectarian pluralism and emotionalism with objectivity, moral legalism, a liberal answer to many old issues, a positive this-

[3] Ibid., p. 69.

worldliness, and even a kind of rationalism that had grown, perhaps, out of Joseph's own disdain for frontier sermonizing. Fable or not, the Book of Mormon provided the kind of stability immemorially brought to Christianity by the Old Testament. Yet the book did not make Mormonism: Joseph did that from day to day as circumstances demanded; and after the mob at Carthage did him in, Brigham Young carried on, more soberly and with more concern for this world than the next, but not with less determination.

Within a month of the book's publication, six members of Joseph's unorganized following were baptized by immersion and formed into a church; within another month there were forty persons who acknowledged Joseph as "Seer, a Translator, a Prophet, an Apostle of Jesus Christ, and Elder of the Church through the will of God the Father, and the grace of your Lord Jesus Christ" (his official title). Thereafter a steady flow of revelations began to define the shape and goals of Mormonism. Sensationally administered healings of the familiar sort won some converts then as later; and a further crescendo of warnings about the impending Millennium added others. Five months after the church's founding, the Prophet announced that the New Jerusalem would be found out "on the borders by the Lamanites," and he sent a three-man party to look for land.

On their way, this group won over the most impressive convert so far received, Sidney Rigdon (1793–1876), an ex-Baptist who had become a major disciple of Alexander Campbell in Ohio. With true Restorationist rigor Rigdon had gathered a small following into a communistic colony near Kirtland, Ohio. The prospecting party soon baptized him and nearly his entire colony into the Mormon church; and sometime later (after Smith and Rigdon had met) the Prophet issued a revelation in the form of a Book of Enoch which commanded the gathering of an earthly "City of Holiness." Then came a momentous decision to move the church to Kirtland, which was said to be on the eastern boundary of the Stake in Zion. In January 1831, therefore, Mormonism's first westward movement began.

In Kirtland the "United Order of Enoch" took positive form, while many revelations brought the Rigdon-Smith constituencies under common authority. As in New York there was hostility from surrounding people, and on one occasion Joseph was torn from his home and tarred and feathered. But converts poured in, the economy was organized, surprisingly large loans were floated, and a stately temple was built and dedicated with festivities pervaded by pentecostal fervor. Though the panic of 1837 was on the horizon, a bank was organized and notes were issued with abandon. Then the bubble burst and the creditors swarmed in. Schism, rioting, fires, and other woes followed. Joseph, with those who would, fled to Missouri, choosing that remote land because since 1831 the most numerous colony of Mormons had been gathered there at the "crossroads of the West," where the indefatigable and ingenious Edward Partridge was chiefly responsible for receiving and allotting land to the steady stream of converts and seeing that the United Order functioned according to revealed regulation.

Unfortunately the western woes had been of far greater magnitude than those in Ohio. First the Mormons had been mobbed and harried out of Jackson County, near Independence. Finding less hostility in the counties north of the Missouri River, they settled there, and again began to prosper and multiply, yet only to arouse new hostilities. When Joseph went west in 1838, their situation was becoming precarious, and it must be said that he soon made it hopeless. On 4 July 1838 at a great celebration, Joseph delivered an oration which ended with a spine-chilling promise to wreak vengeance on his oppressors. Election day brought further violence, followed by the Prophet's infamous cry "I will be a Second Mohammed." In the bitter Mormon War the Stake in Zion was again desolated; and with Joseph in jail, the Latter-Day Saints were forced to move again, this time across the Mississippi into Illinois, where Nauvoo was founded on the river in Hancock County.

It was a most propitious time, for with the elections of 1840 in the offing, Whigs and Democrats outdid each other to win the fifteen thousand Mormon votes. Nauvoo was given a charter that made it almost an autonomous theocratic principality. Here Joseph forgot the woes and ignominy of New York, Ohio, and Missouri; he did great things and dreamed far greater dreams. Nauvoo became the largest and fastest growing city in Illinois as redoubled evangelistic efforts brought results especially among the urban poor of England, who began immigrating by the thousands. Under Illinois militia laws the Nauvoo Legion became a disciplined military force with Joseph in command; he was declared King of the

Kingdom of God and became increasingly despotic. In a series of revelations in 1841–43, Smith introduced many new teachings which made Mormonism much more clearly a new religion and much less obviously Christian than it had been in 1830. More than ever Mormons were defined as a people apart.

His megalomania constantly growing, Smith announced his candidacy for president of the United States in the election of 1844. Yet again the horizon darkened; popular fear and jealousy mounted as Mormon apostates and dissidents published horrendous tales of polygamy, corruption, and lawlessness. At last the Prophet overreached himself by destroying the opposition press in Nauvoo without due process. The case aroused widespread agitation and when the Illinois militia threatened, Joseph and Hyrum Smith yielded themselves to the authorities. Finally, on 27 June 1844, the militia became a mob, moved upon the Carthage jail where the two leaders were awaiting trial, and lynched them in cold blood.

After this awful sacrifice Nauvoo was spared the worst kind of atrocities, but the Saints prepared to leave. Joseph had long been conceiving plans for a western empire, and now these plans were taken up by the main body of Mormons, who recognized Brigham Young as Joseph's successor. This fierce and sturdy disciple was a former Vermont Methodist who had been converted and made one of the twelve Apostles during the Kirtland period. Young had organized the exodus from Missouri, and now, after a brief period of preparation in Iowa, he led the Mormons in their famous trek to the place he chose in the Great Salt Lake basin. In July 1847 the first wagon train ended its hundred-days crossing. After a constitutional convention in 1849, the autonomous state of Deseret took shape on the outer rim of the Mexican republic as a church-regulated community. Within a decade ninety communities had been founded, most of them in the Salt Lake area, yet some three hundred miles north of the lake, and some as far south as San Bernardino, California. In most of these communities, the need for irrigation gave a functional base both to communitarian ideals and to the power of the church's leaders.

But the Stars and Stripes were borne to Utah in 1850, and the old conflicts were renewed, especially after 1852 when Young published Joseph's heretofore "secret" (but much discussed) revelation on "the order of Jacob," i.e. plural marriage. When in 1857 President Buchanan replaced Young with a non-Mormon as territorial governor, another "Mormon War" broke out, the most sensational incident of which was the Mormon massacre of a peaceful group of California-bound settlers. In 1879 the Supreme Court finally rendered its verdict against polygamy in the United States, ruling that religious freedom did not involve the right to subvert an institution upon which "society may be said to be built," and hence that the 1862 Act of Congress against bigamy was constitutional. The Edmunds Act of 1882 brought still more stringent political pressures to bear, to which an act of 1884 added economic penalties. Only in 1890, after long delays and various legal maneuvers, did the church revise its teaching on polygamy, thus opening the way to statehood, which was granted in 1896. By that time a straitlaced kind of prosperity and stability had replaced enthusiasm and millennial expectation as the leitmotiv of Mormon life. Creeping capitalism had taken over the communitarianism of the old Order of Enoch. Yet Mormon missionaries were abroad throughout the world, and in 1970 about three million people with greatly varying degrees of intensity accounted themselves Latter-Day Saints.[4] The church was growing and its people prospering.

As the dominant group in Utah, with much strength in surrounding states, and with Salt Lake City as their mecca, the Mormons constitute an important American subculture. Their movement has changed, in Thomas O'Dea's words, "from 'near-sect' to 'near-nation.'" They had not merely avoided becoming a small isolated sect, he continues, but "had developed so far away from that possibility that they almost became a separate nationality."[5] It was a remarkable monument to the visions of Joseph Smith, if not precisely to his vision. Even Young's achievements in the West rested on the Prophet's culminating accomplishment: "Utah had its

[4] Between 1840 and 1900 close to ninety thousand immigrants from abroad entered the church, most of them from England, but many from Scandinavia as well. At a much slower pace immigration has continued into the twentieth century. By this time, however, the accent has been placed on gathering converts wherever they live. In 1970 about twelve thousand missionaries were at work to this end in more than sixty-five countries all over the world.

[5] Thomas O'Dea, *The Mormons*, p. 115.

roots in Nauvoo; without that seven years' experience in Illinois the development of the Great Basin . . . would not have been the same."[6]

Almost no one denies that the entire saga of Joseph Smith and Mormonism is a vital episode in American history. A vast literature, both hagiographic and critical, covers each phase of the movement's development. Yet the exact significance of this great story persistently escapes definition. It is certainly the culminating instance of early nineteenth-century sect formation, and at the same time that period's most powerful example of communitarian aspiration. On the other hand, the transformation brought about by numerical growth, economic adaptation, internal divisions, external hostility, and heroic exploits renders almost useless the usual categories of explanation. One cannot even be sure if the object of our consideration is a sect, a mystery cult, a new religion, a church, a people, a nation, or an American subculture; indeed, at different times and places it is all of these.

With attractive edifices on Brattle Street in Cambridge, Massachusetts, and in many other cities and suburbs, and with a reputation for conservatism in both personal ethics and social policy, Mormons sometimes appear to have become another white middle-class denomination with obvious Yankee origins. Yet they remain a people apart, bound to a very distinctive tradition that was brought into the world by a most unusual man. Their inner intellectual and spiritual problems cannot easily be shared with others. The problem of history—in the Book of Mormon itself and as it pertains to the people of that book since 1830—has been especially acute; and the fact of contradictory interpretations is inescapably felt by every historian. In retrospect, nevertheless, the Mormons can be likened to a fast-growing hardwood towering above the sectarian underbrush of the burnt-over dis-

6 Robert Bruce Flanders, *Nauvoo: Kingdom on the Mississippi*, p. v. Nauvoo also inspired at least three other branches of Mormonism. One remnant survived in Texas until the Civil War; another maintained itself on an island in Lake Michigan until its leader, James Strang, was murdered in 1856. The Reorganized Church dating from 1852 won the allegiance of the Smith Family and under the presidency of Joseph's son and grandson established itself in southern Iowa. As the lawful legatee it also holds property in Nauvoo and Kirtland. Its headquarters since 1921 has been in Independence, Missouri. Its membership in 1970 stood at about 170,000.

trict: a witness to the possible social potency of prophetic religious ideas. Interpreted in detail, the movement yields innumerable clues to the religious and social consciousness of the American people.

V

Countervailing Religion

Puritan Protestantism forms properly the main basis of our North American Church. . . . We may never ungratefully forget that it was this generation of godly Pilgrims which once for all stamped upon our country that character of deep moral earnestness, that spirit of strong intrepid determination, that peculiar zeal for the Sabbath and the Bible, which have raised it to so high a place in the history of the Christian Church. . . . But while we thankfully and joyfully acknowledge this, we have no right still to overlook the fact that an unhistorical and unchurchly character has inserted itself into the inmost joints of our religious life. . . . Thus we have come gradually to have a host of sects, which it is no longer easy to number, and that still continues to swell from year to year. Where the process of separation is destined to end, no human calculation can foretell. . . .

The most dangerous foe with which we are called to contend, is not the Church of Rome but the sect plague in our own midst; not the single pope of the city of seven hills, but the numberless popes—German, English, and American— who would fain enslave Protestants once more to human authority. . . .

Let our watchword be: One spirit and one body! One Shepherd and one flock! All conventicles and chapels must perish, that from their ashes may rise the One Church of God, phoenixlike and resplendent with glory, as a bride adorned for her bridegroom.

Philip Schaff, *The Principle of Protestantism* (1845)

The prevailing spirit of the American nation during the antebellum decades was informed by a popular and patriotic version of the Puritan hope for the Kingdom of God on earth, as that notion had been freed of its medieval and aristocratic components. But this individualistic and evangelical outlook was not accepted by all America, and not everyone living in the United States was admitted to the elect company of true Americans. The most obvious outsiders were the black slaves and the red Indians—the latter being regarded until 1871 as a foreign power against whom one waged wars and made treaties of peace. In addition to these drastic cases, there were many subtle shades and degrees of exclusion. There was the South, which in a sense regarded the Constitution itself as a kind of treaty guaranteeing the perpetuity of the peculiar institution in its midst. There were Old School Presbyterians, Hard Shell Baptists, and other mainline Protestant conservatives who challenged prevailing concessions regarding man's free will and perfectibility. Lutherans, whose numbers were being rapidly swelled by immigration, were becoming increasingly dissatisfied with the theological and moral stance of the Protestant mainstream—especially when its actions were overtly nativistic. Equally unenthusiastic were various smaller groups whose often unusual tenets aroused the evangelicals to countersubversionary tactics: the Mormons, especially, but also for a time the Masons and various communitarian movements that challenged American taboos. The Jews were potentially in this category, but until after the Civil War they were too few in number to attract significant notice.

Most numerous and most easily isolated of all were the Roman Catholics, who by 1850 had become the largest denomination in America, and who continued to immigrate at an increasing rate. Because they resisted religious assimilation and were suspected of subservience to a "foreign potentate," they became the object of the most powerfully organized opposition, first by voluntary associations, and finally by a very strong, semisecret political party. The conversion of several well-known Protestant thinkers intensified the polemical spirit. Also viewed with suspicion were various Protestant groups—and not only Lutheran and German Reformed—who during these very years were becoming disenchanted with revivalistic evangelicalism and finding spiritual solace or aesthetic satisfaction in various aspects of the Catholic tradition. Least criticized were those romantics who were merely attracted to Catholic externals such as Gothic architecture and the celebration of Christmas. More controversial were those Episcopalians who took England's Oxford Movement seriously, for they impugned the entire Reformation heritage.

The rising interest in things Catholic, however, was sometimes expressed in the context of pronounced theological liberalism; indeed, Boston Unitarians were a common source of it. And this fact points to another truly major countervailing force in American religion—the emergence of new forms of religious modernism that were far more seductive than the rationalistic "infidelism" of Tom Paine. Emerson and the Transcendentalists stand out as proponents of the new spirit, but other equally radical groups existed outside of New England. Even in the orthodox churches themselves liberal theology and scholarship were being articulated and defended by men like James Marsh and Horace Bushnell. The chapters of Part V deal with the religious communions and new currents of thought which intruded upon the evangelical consensus, and with the Protestant opposition to these tendencies.

31

THE ATLANTIC MIGRATION AND LUTHERAN CRISIS

"Once I thought to write a history of the immigrants in America," wrote Oscar Handlin in 1951. "Then I discovered that the immigrants *were* American history." This widely shared discovery has given rise to basic reinterpretations of American culture in every period. Many of the ensuing revisions arose from a new awareness of the experience of immigration as a shaping influence on the spirit of this nation of movers. Anyone who has left behind the familiar surroundings and comforting associations of one community and begun to adjust to another has had at least a sample of the myriad migratory traumas that have formed the life style of this "nation of immigrants." It is the accumulated pain and sadness of more drastic departures from native lands and the tribulations of beginning again in an alien, often hostile, environment that makes the immigration residuum so important to the American character and to the religious institutions which served so many purposes in the process of adjustment. From John Winthrop's sad farewell to England in 1630 to the anguish of the latest refugee, the "uprooted" have been shaping the national life.

Immigration is also the source of this country's fabled diversity. In 1790 when the first federal census reported a population of 3,929,214,[1] 22.3 percent of the white population stemmed from non-British lands, while 700,000 slaves

[1] Richard B. Morris. ed., *Encyclopedia of American History* (New York: Harper & Brothers, 1953), p. 445 (taken from the census of 1790 as analyzed by the American Historical Association, *Annual Report,* vol. 1 [1931]). At this time the slave population was about 700,000 (17 percent) and the free Negro about 20,000 (0.5 percent).

added a huge component of African origin. During the next
three decades, when Europe was embroiled by the French
Revolution and the Napoleonic wars, only 250,000 immigrants arrived on American shores; but then the tempo
began to accelerate, and during the hundred years between
1832 and 1932 the influx would reach an altogether different
order of magnitude.[2] Irish troubles occasioned the first wave;
a great movement of Germans and Scandinavians dominated
the next phase, and the "Great Atlantic Migration" would
culminate after 1890 in a vast exodus of eastern European
Jews, southern Italians, and Balkan peoples. Before the gates
were closed over 40 million immigrants had cast their lot
with the United States. Seen as a totality, this movement of
European peoples is probably the greatest *Völkerwanderung*
in human history. And it is scarcely surprising that in 1920,
when the Bureau of the Census made its somewhat arbitrary
breakdown of the population on the basis of "national origins," only 41 percent of the white population was of British
or North Irish origin.

Underlying this extended upheaval was an industrial and
agricultural revolution which all but destroyed the ancient
peasant economy of Europe.

> The immigrant movement started in the peasant heart of
> Europe [writes Oscar Handlin]. Ponderously balanced in
> a solid equilibrium for centuries, the old structure of an old
> society began to crumble at the opening of the modern era.
> One by one, rude shocks weakened the aged foundations
> until some climactic blow suddenly tumbled the whole into
> ruins. The mighty collapse left without homes millions of
> helpless, bewildered people. These were the army of emi-
> grants.[3]

In a brilliant chapter Handlin goes on to describe the process
by which Europe as a whole, from Ireland to the Ukraine,

[2] The dates are not arbitrary. In 1832 the influx almost trebled
that of any previous year, and not until 1932 did the figure ever
fall below the 60,482 of 1832. Between 1845 and 1931 it never
fell below 90,000. During six different years between 1905 and
1914 immigration went over the million mark. Between 1820 and
1950, 39,325,482 people migrated to the United States (ibid.,
pp. 446–47).

[3] Oscar Handlin, *The Uprooted*, p. 7.

from Norway to Sicily, was involved in a large insoluble agricultural crisis. It was worse in some lands than in others: Scandinavians, for example, never fled a famine-stricken land as did the Irish, while Germans and Italians never faced persecutions and pogroms as did the Russian Jews. As immigrants in America, therefore, these different peoples looked to the "old country" and conceived of the past with varied sentiments. They also faced the future with sharply contrasting attitudes, and the dynamics of Americanization varied correspondingly.

Supporting this great influx on the American side was the continuous expansion of industry, beginning with the growth of textile manufacturing and the canal and railroad building booms, and the opening of agricultural opportunities in the West. These developments naturally had as many consequences for the country's native stock as for the immigrants. Both alike suffered from industrial exploitation and unplanned urban growth. Both alike experienced the loneliness and isolation of life in a land of scattered farms and miserable roads. Everyone in America lived in the uncertainty caused by boom periods, financial panics, and depressions. Yet a major fact remains: the newcomers—whether they ended up in a city tenement or in a farmhouse—came in overwhelming proportion from the little agricultural villages of Europe. They were joined by a few political exiles, idealistic intellectuals, entrepreneurs, musicians, teachers, and priests; but in general they were not bearers of civilization. They came in many cases from countries rich in learned and artistic traditions, from lands and churches famous for their universities; but these they left behind. On the other hand, the home countries for a variety of reasons—resentment, indifference, or poverty—did little or nothing to assist the outwanderers. In America the immigrants had to begin anew, individually and in groups, to achieve their aspirations for culture and well-being. Religious institutions, therefore, often became a more vital factor than they had ever been before.

IMMIGRATION AND THE CHURCHES

Immigration has had from the first a decisive effect on the religious affiliation of Americans and the relative size of the various churches. The statistics of church membership, to be sure, are a notorious quagmire.[4] But even when full allowance is made for the known inadequacy of existing figures, certain drastic changes are manifest when one compares the ecclesiastical situation before and after the Great Migration.

At the end of the colonial period (1775) three large ecclesiastical blocs, all of British background, accounted for at least 80 percent of the Americans who could be regarded as affiliated with any church. They were distributed about evenly among the Congregationalists of New England, the Anglicans of the South, and the Presbyterians whose chief strength lay in the Middle Colonies. Small but influential Quaker, Baptist, and Methodist groups added two or three percentage points to the British Protestant total, while Dutch Reformed churches, strongest in New York and New Jersey, had over the years become very closely affiliated with the English-speaking population. Roman Catholics and Jews constituted at most 0.1 percent of the population. Because evangelism among the slaves had been widely neglected, the largest non-British religious minority in the colonies may have been African, but investigations of its nature and strength have only belatedly begun.[5]

The Great Migration of the nineteenth century, as everyone knows, drastically altered the religious composition of the American people. Steady acculturation was naturally a major feature of the passing decades, yet by the twentieth century the United States had become far more than before a nation of religious minorities whose self-consciousness was by no means rapidly disappearing.[6] In 1926, by which time 40 percent of the population claimed a religious relationship, Roman Catholics were the largest single group (18,605,000), while the next three largest denominations—Baptist (8,011,000), Methodist (7,764,000), and Lutheran (3,226,000)—accounted for 59 percent of the Protestants. At that time

[4] The statistics developed and used by historians show wild variations; yet they tend to agree on the proportional relationships of various groups, which in turn tally with the census figures of 1790. Percentage figures are only estimates. On this problem see Winthrop S. Hudson, *Religion in America*, pp. 129–30.

[5] Melville J. Herskovitz, *The Myth of the Negro Past* (Boston: Beacon Press, 1958) reveals the paucity of evidence. See pp. 149–58 in Volume 2.

[6] See Michael Parenti, "Ethnic Politics and the Persistence of Ethnic Identification," *Political Science Review* 61 (September 1967): 717–26.

Jews constituted 3.2 percent of the total population. Immigration, of course, was not the only reason for these radical changes in the American religious balance, but it alone had ended the possibility of speaking of the American churches solely in terms of a common British background. Other traditions had not only introduced new ranges of variety and color to the situation, but had also put serious pressures on the American tradition of equality and toleration. In successive chapters, therefore, the antebellum history of immigration and religion will be considered: first the Lutheran because of its contiguity with the foregoing accounts of Protestant resurgence, then the growth of Roman Catholicism and the hostile response of "native" Americans to this seeming threat, and finally the arrival and early development of Judaism.

THE LUTHERAN CHURCH

During the half-century after the Declaration of Independence, the Lutheran church in America experienced many remarkable changes and reversals. Having entered the new nation as an independent church, it encountered few organizational difficulties. In churchly matters the leadership and continuing influence of the elder Muhlenberg and his sons was a powerful stabilizing force. Furthermore, the process of Americanization was moving rapidly ahead. In 1807 the Ministerium of New York (Presided over by Muhlenberg's son-in-law, a professor at Columbia) changed its official language from German to English. Yet with acculturation and the passage of time, the influence of the American Enlightenment (strengthened by patriotic fervor) made deep inroads on the faith of the founders, modifying the firm but practical concern for the historic Lutheran confessions which Muhlenberg and Berkenmeyer had established in Pennsylvania and New York. This decline in vigor led to a gradual rapprochement with the Episcopalians. In 1797 the New York Ministerium made it an official policy not to recognize English-language churches in localities served by the Episcopal church, and in North Carolina there was sporadically a similar integration of activities. Mutual proposals for consolidation of the churches were heard from time to time.

Countering these accommodations, however, were strong

undercurrents of sentiment and conviction that portended difficulty and conflict. In rural areas, and among those church leaders who tended to regard true piety and German culture as inseparable, a strong opposition to Americanization developed. The Pennsylvania Ministerium especially took strong measures to insure the perpetuation of the German language. Since men who held these views were also opposed to rationalism and imbued with the revival spirit, they drew closer to similarly minded leaders in the German Reformed church, with whom they were often closely tied by intermarriage, village associations, and joint worship in "union churches." Sharing the antidoctrinal temper of early nineteenth-century evangelicalism and insensitive to ancient confessional cleavages, they saw the separation of Lutheran and Reformed as a perpetuation of mere trivialities. Meanwhile, these men could observe the progress of unionism in Prussia, where Napoleon's invasions had aroused German longings for unity.

When the Ohio Conference of the Pennsylvania Ministerium was formed in 1812, this pan-German tendency was already apparent. In 1818 it took more definite form in the proposal of the two communions to found an "Evangelical Seminary" in conjunction with Franklin College, which they were already operating jointly. Though this seminary never got beyond the planning stage, it was chiefly intended to shield students from rationalistic error without an emphasis on creedal allegiances. The declining Lutheran consciousness is also visible in the Pennsylvania Ministerium's liturgy of 1818, in which most of the responsive, corporate, and ritual characteristics of Muhlenberg's liturgy were sacrificed. Even more illustrative of nonconfessional evangelicalism, both Lutheran and Reformed, is the *Gemeinschaftliches Gesangbuch* (Congregational Hymnbook) of 1817, from which much of the classical hymnody of both communions was eliminated.

Reaction

As a kind of intrusion on this nondenominational spirit came the tercentenary of Luther's Ninety-five Theses in 1817. This observance did not create harsh confrontations, since all the non-Roman churches accepted the Reformer as a great religious hero; and Bishop William White responded warmly to the invitation given him to join the celebration in Philadelphia. As in Prussia, however, the occasion did underline the contrast of confessional and unionistic tendencies.

These incipient difficulties became evident in 1818 when the Pennsylvania Ministerium proposed that a general synod be organized in order to provide a central advisory agency for the existing synods and such new ones as the westward expansion and immigration would bring into being. Yet indecision and divided opinion were to hinder these bold designs.

In 1817 three loosely organized territorial synods were in existence (Pennsylvania, New York, and North Carolina), and in 1818 Ohio was organized, followed in 1820 by Maryland-Virginia and Tennessee. In 1820 the delegates of these (Ohio and Tennessee not participating) drafted a constitution for the General Synod to accomplish the desired unification, but they could agree on no more than the Lutheran name to show their confessional consciousness, and they made no mention whatever of the historic standards of faith. Because New York declined to join until 1837, while Pennsylvania separated itself between 1823 and 1853, even this witness lacked sustained support from the two largest American synods. Thus in 1834 the General Synod only encompassed 20,249 Lutherans—which was 6,000 less than the Pennsylvania Ministerium alone.

During these dark years of the General Synod, however, Samuel Simon Schmucker (1799–1873), a brilliant young pastor in Maryland, determined to save it. And save it he did—first by persuading the newly formed West Pennsylvania Synod (1823) to join, and then by leading the movement to found a seminary at Gettysburg, which opened in 1826 with Schmucker as professor of theology. In all these endeavors he was spurred on by a desire to save his church from the corrosions of rationalism and indifference. To this end he wrote a professor's oath for the new seminary, demanding loyalty to the Augsburg Confession and to Luther's Catechisms. The ordination oath which he later drafted compelled "substantial" agreement with these standards.

Even in these early measures, however, and throughout the four decades of his career as a theologian and church leader, Schmucker was torn between a desire to hurl traditional Lutheran symbols against infidelity, and an equally strong or somewhat stronger desire to avoid doctrinal commitments which ran counter to his own pietistic background, the Reformed substratum of American Protestantism which he had studied at Princeton Seminary, or the interdenominational voluntary movements for evangelism and reform in which he

vigorously participated. With the passing years he made
more explicit his dissent from both the emphasis and the substance of the traditional Lutheran teaching on the sacraments
and on many other matters. In a Reformation Day address in
1837, he defended the Lord's Supper as a "mnemonic ordinance" and "a pledge of his [the Savior's] spiritual presence
and blessing on all worthy participants."[7]

The doctrinal basis thus laid down was probably the only
kind of compromise on which anything could have been accomplished at that time, and upon it the General Synod grew
and prospered. By 1839 it included 316 congregations organized into seven regional synods, varying in viewpoint
from the extremely free attitudes of New York to a fairly rigorous confessionalism in parts of Pennsylvania. The General
Synod had also established fraternal relations with many
other denominations and voluntary associations, and was
beginning to evince an anti-Catholicism that would spill over
into nativism. Schmucker had also gained national attention
in 1838 with his *Fraternal Appeal* for an "apostolic Protestant
union." This ecumenical interest would lead him to take an
active role eight years later in the founding of the World
Evangelical Alliance.

It should not be concluded, however, that all was peace
and concord. From the very first the General Synod had been
roundly condemned by the Reverend Paul Henkel on strict
confessional principles, and the Tennessee Synod which Henkel had helped to found embodied his protest in an ecclesiastical structure of considerable strength. The influence of
Henkel's energetic sons and other associates also helped to
keep the Ohio Synod from joining. There were other men in
the Pennsylvania Ministerium who on similar grounds defended that synod's isolation. But ultimately of far greater
significance than any of these factors were three new developments: the powerful Lutheran awakening in the churches
and universities of Germany, the growth of indigenous dissatisfaction with American evangelicalism, and the immensely
increased flow of non-English-speaking immigrants from Germany and later from Scandinavia.[8]

[7] Quoted in Vergilius Ferm, *The Crisis in Lutheran Theology*,
p. 111.

[8] In references to the Lutheran Confessions and "confessionalism"
the Augsburg (*Augustana*) Confession of 1530 is aways primary.
But in 1580, after fifty years of controversy, the Lutheran churches

The first of these phenomena is too complex to be taken up here, except to note that important roles were played by tercentenary observances of the Reformation, a surfeit of rationalism, the rise of new spiritual and historical interests, and the emergence of many talented theological and ecclesiastical leaders. This "Lutheran awakening" began a process of theological recovery which was sustained during the entire century, until it finally joined with the so-called Neo-Orthodox impulse of the early twentieth century. Among the German Reformed, Philip Schaff became a brilliant but characteristic participant in a similar movement of recovery; and John W. Nevin drew much inspiration from it through private reading even before Schaff joined him on the faculty at Mercersburg Seminary. The "Mercersburg Theology," in fact, was a corollary to Lutheran developments. A similar spirit took hold at the same time in Scandinavia and other Lutheran lands, where parish life was often revitalized by movements which reasserted old pietistic ideals, or by other movements calling for a churchly renewal similar to that of the Oxford Movement in England. At all events, a marked shift in temper was very soon communicated to America, giving added impetus to an indigenous movement of Lutheran recovery. In the period after 1830 one notes almost everywhere an increasing denominational consciousness and a concurrent rise in church-historical interest.

Probably more important than these purely intellectual influences was the actual migration of Germans in the pre-Civil War period, and an equally large influx of Scandinavians beginning more or less at midcentury. The crescendo of German immigration was dramatic, as the following statistics reveal. In the period from 1821–30, 6,761 German immigrants arrived; in 1831–40, 152,454; in 1841–50, 434,626; and in 1851–60, 951,667. Not all of these people were Lutherans, to be sure; many were Roman Catholic, Reformed, "Unionists," adherents of various sects, completely unaffiliated, or (as with some exiles from the abortive revolution of 1848) bitterly anticlerical. But the impact on the Lutheran church in America was heavy, especially since many of the laity and pastors who came were deeply touched

---

of Germany agreed to a "Formula of Concord" which together with other accepted "symbolic" documents was published in the *Book of Concord*. The first complete English edition of this book was published by David Henkel and others in 1851.

by the revival in Germany. They settled almost everywhere,
but with a noticeable preference for northern states and
border areas where slavery was not a prominent feature.
When settlers came to places where the Lutheran church was
already planted, they usually joined existing congregations,
often drastically changing their character. In 1837 the New
York Ministerium reversed its decision of 1807 and again
made German an official language—and in this as in most
other cases of the time, doctrinal concern tended to follow
language. As the immigrants moved into the Old Northwest,
thinly scattered bodies like the Joint Synod of Ohio were
greatly augmented in numbers. Still farther west, many new
synods, organized with the aid of the General Synod, soon
became members of the larger body. Completely new and independent synods were also formed, some of them holding
fraternal relations with the older synods, some not. Almost all
of them took definite confessional stands, however; and their
influence flowed back to the East.[9]

Lutheran Crisis

With the passing years two parties or tendencies became
increasingly visible, one deeply affected by American evangelical ideas and practices, the other much more intran-
sigently rooted in Continental ways and Reformation
thought. After 1833, when Benjamin Kurtz (1795–1865)
made the *Lutheran Observer* an outspoken defender of the
"new measures" in revivalism, of Sabbatarianism, and of
Schmucker's point of view generally, the tensions increased.
The founding of Wittenberg College and Seminary in 1845
provided an important anchorage in Ohio for this "American"
party, and Samuel Sprecher (1810–1906), during a long career as its president followed by a further term as a professor
of systematic theology, did for the western flank what Kurtz
did for the eastern. The conservatives, however, were also
gathering strength and developing greater intellectual depth;
and by 1849 three journals were upholding its cause, including the scholarly *Evangelical Review* published by Professor
Charles Philip Krauth and others at Gettysburg Seminary. At
the General Synod convention of 1850 Krauth stated the con-

[9] The founding of these new synods will be taken up in a later
chapter, since they gained their significance only during the post-
Civil War decades.

servative position clearly; and in July of that year he published his manifesto in the *Evangelical Review:*

> Too ignorant have we been of our own doctrines, and our own history . . . and we have taken pride in times past in claiming a paternity in every reputable form of Christianity, and have denied our proper parentage, in our mendicancy for foreign favors. Shame that it has been so! . . . Let us go back to our father's house.

After 1840, on the other hand, Professor Schmucker became much more explicit and vigorous in his exposition of "American Lutheranism." Yet the contrary tide grew stronger after 1853, when the now increasingly confessional Pennsylvania Ministerium returned to the General Synod. The "American Lutheran" leaders seem to have decided at this point that the conservative strategy of slowly absorbing its opposition must be halted in some decisive way. The means chosen were almost melodramatic. An anonymous forty-two-page pamphlet entitled *Definite Synodical Platform* was sent out to the ministers of the General Synod in the autumn of 1855. It contained an "American Recension of the Augsburg Confession," a highly polemical statement defending the deletion of "errors" from this historic symbol as well as from other confessional documents, and a proposal that in this revised form it be made a standard of faith for the synod. Nine traditional doctrines were condemned as remnants of Catholicism. Three of these (private confessions, ceremonies of the mass, and exorcism of evil spirits) were regarded as so serious that retention of them would be a bar to fellowship. Six others were roundly condemned, including baptismal regeneration, the Real Presence in the Eucharist, the remission of sins through the Eucharist, and denial of the divine obligation of Sabbath observance. The last issue carried with it the whole question of the force of Jewish law under the New Covenant and the problems of Law and Gospel. By any standard, the Platform was a bold stroke. It made manifest what critics had been saying all along, that Schmucker's "American Lutheranism" was little more than another name for "modern American Puritanism." There was almost no chance that any peaceful settlement would result—and none did.

The decade following the issuance of the Platform brought

a showdown. The General Synod now comprised over a score of regional synods, and each one had to face the issue or explicitly evade it before the convention of 1857. By that time, however, no action by the General Synod was necessary, because the "American Lutheran" plan had already been killed by the express disapproval of eight of the synods, including the influential Pennsylvania Ministerium and Professor Schmucker's own synod of West Pennsylvania. Yet the prevalence of "American Lutheranism" was clearly demonstrated by the fact that three synods in Ohio and Indiana unanimously adopted the Platform as their own, while six others indicated basic concurrence with its most outspoken claims. Six were noncommittal, equivocal, or silent. Most of those who opposed it did so less on theological principle than because they wanted ecclesiastical peace or less dogmatism. In not more than three synods could the resurgence of traditional doctrine be held clearly accountable for disapproval.

Peace, naturally, did not follow. In 1857 Dr. Kurtz led a small group of his sympathizers in the Maryland Synod into a new Melanchthon Synod which specifically rejected the "errors" condemned in the Platform. Its admission to the General Synod in 1859 brought a storm of protest. A year later, as part of the secession crisis and Civil War, the entire group of Southern synods formed their own general body on a fairly conservative basis, though their basic tendency and sympathy, like the views of their most distinguished leader, John Bachman of Charleston, were broadly evangelical rather than emphatically Lutheran. In the North a kind of "civil war" in the General Synod went on even during the national crisis. The break finally came in 1864 when the General Synod admitted the Franckean Synod, which had been formed in western New York in 1837 under the influence of Charles G. Finney's preaching. Since it professed no Lutheran ties at all, the Pennsylvania Ministerium withdrew, founded another seminary in Philadelphia, and issued a call to all explicitly confessional Lutheran synods in America to affiliate themselves with a new General Council. This organization became a reality in 1867. The Lutheranism of "Muhlenberg descent" was thereafter to move into separate channels.

Certain things were clear even in 1867. "American Lutheranism" as a dominating tendency was a thing of the past. Schmucker's chair at Gettysburg was filled in 1864 by one of his bitterest critics. In that same year the General Synod took a definite stand not for the Platform, but far more explicitly than ever before for the Augsburg Confession—and this despite the fact that it no longer included the conservative delegates from Pennsylvania and the South. The age of Schmucker's dominance was over.

In 1860 the General Synod's 864 ministers and 164,000 communicants comprised two-thirds of the Lutherans in America. Ten years later two competing organizations had replaced the unified church for which Muhlenberg had hoped. Yet in light of the total situation, the rupture seems as inevitable as the Civil War. In 1820 it would have been folly to propose a general synod on strict Lutheran principles. By 1860 it was no more possible for a church to be half Lutheran and half Puritan than for the nation to be half slave and half free. In both cases it was the end of an era.

The new era found its spokesman in Charles Porterfield Krauth (1823–83), the first professor of theology in the new seminary at Philadelphia and also a professor of philosophy at the University of Pennsylvania. Krauth, who was the son of professor Charles Philip Krauth of Gettysburg, became the chief defender of the General Council. In his early years he had tended toward "American Lutheran" views, but between 1841 and 1864, while serving as a pastor, he became imbued with the newer German theology. As he was drawn into the controversies of the day, he increasingly emphasized that Luther had led a *conservative* Reformation which was essentially at odds with the radicalism not only of the sectaries but of the Reformed tradition as well. Entering into the exciting historical research of the time, he came to regard the Eucharistic question as central in the Reformation. The doctrine of the Real Presence which Schmucker had dismissed Krauth defended as crucial. As only a few followers of the Oxford and Mercersburg movements had ever done in America, Krauth challenged the basic presuppositions of the prevailing Reformed and Puritan theology from the conservative side. In his magnum opus, *The Conservative Reformation and Its Theology* (1872), he synthesized a vast amount of German scholarship and consolidated his writings as a controversialist, producing one of the most influential books in American Lutheran history. The work also places him among this country's pioneers of Neo-Reformation thinking.

In time the scholarship and advocacy of men like Krauth

would merge with similar influences flowing into American Lutheran life and thought through newer synods of more direct immigrant background, but these groups had barely begun their organized existence in the pre-Civil War years. Largely because of the way in which the Lutheran crisis was resolved, the older eastern synods and the newer German and Scandinavian synods would remain in contact. The General Council which sprang from a division in the church would in later years become a powerful agency of unification.

32

THE FORMING OF THE ROMAN CATHOLIC CHURCH

The Roman Catholic church has a longer history in America —even in the United States—than any other Christian denomination, and each of its several American beginnings has at least a tenuous connection with the present day. These ancient traditions notwithstanding, no major church in America experienced a more decisive break between its colonial phase and its development after the Revolutionary War. Unlike the Congregational, Presbyterian, Baptist, and Lutheran churches, whose patterns of development were established long before 1776, the Roman Catholic church began almost a second history in the national period. So incredibly large was the flow of immigrants that by 1850 Roman Catholics, once a tiny and ignored minority, had become the country's largest religious communion. The Revolution transformed the church's legal and psychological situation to such an extent that Roman Catholics could participate with few legal restrictions in a free democratic society such as the world had never seen, and for which neither Roman Catholic theology, canon law, nor ancient precedent provided much guidance. Indeed, the American cultural ethos in its totality constituted so drastic a break with tradition that even after decades of explaining by American bishops, it still remained an enigma to popes and curial officials in Rome. And at the end of the nineteenth century "Americanism" would become a serious doctrinal issue both in Europe and America.

THE ROAD TO INDEPENDENCE

For Roman Catholics as for all other American colonials the Treaty of Paris in 1763 marked the end of an epoch. Great Britain's resounding triumphs swept away the entire continental empire of the French and brought the Spanish Floridas under British rule. The perennial threat on the frontier was pushed beyond the Mississippi; Roman Catholics were no longer suspected as potential collaborationists, and tensions were eased. With regard to the ecclesiastical rule of Roman Catholics in British America, however, a new problem was created. Was a resident bishop to be sent, or could the diocese of Quebec be enlarged, or should regular visitations from Florida and Quebec be arranged, or should the old arrangements continue? Richard Challoner, after 1758 vicar apostolic of the London district with jurisdiction over the American colonies, persistently pressed the Vatican to provide closer regulation than he himself could exercise from afar. The Jesuits in the colonies, on the other hand, were deeply suspicious of anti-Jesuit sentiments among the bishops and cardinals in Rome and in other Catholic countries. Also aware of the uproar aroused by Anglican proposals for an American bishop, they warned against a move that would revive Protestant hostility. Challoner, in turn, interpreted these warnings as a Jesuitic maneuver, and dwelt on the tragedy of American Catholics being deprived of the sacrament of confirmation. In fact nothing was done to alter the old arrangements except that after the suppression of their society in 1773 the Jesuits were placed directly under Challoner's authority as secular priests.

In the meantime, relations between England and America were steadily deteriorating, and most Catholics apparently shared the outrage of their countrymen at Parliament's new taxes and tightened colonial administration. Charles Carroll of Maryland even entered into journalistic combat for the Patriot cause in 1773. Into this era of good feelings for Catholics, however, Parliament cast a bomb in 1774—the Quebec Act, which not only freed Quebec Catholics of the traditional oath of loyalty to the king and granted them full freedom of religion, but attached the entire trans-Appalachian territory north of the Ohio to Quebec. This provided new incitement to the rise of revolutionary sentiment, at the same time that it goaded colonists to another round of anti-Catholicism. So violent were the formal protests of the First Continental Congress, indeed, that future possibilities for Canadian participation in armed resistance were rendered out of the question. Had not the War for Independence begun, another season of domestic intolerance would undoubtedly have followed.

During the war, Roman Catholics seem to have participated in a way that justified Charles Carroll's signature on the Declaration of Independence. Few of his coreligionists could rejoice over their stakes in the British Empire. If they were Irish, as were many, they were not likely to have forgotten the treatment that England had meted out in the past. They had every reason to expect much improvement of their situation in an independent America where no one church could expect to dominate the others. Their participation in the war effort, therefore, was wholehearted. Tories among them were very few; and though a Loyalist regiment was raised during General Howe's occupation of Philadelphia, it was more than balanced by two Patriot regiments and an unknown number of volunteers in the Continental armies. The American alliance with Roman Catholic France and Spain provided additional motivation, as did the work of foreign volunteers like Count Pulaski.

ORGANIZING AN AMERICAN CHURCH

Neither freedom and independence nor the grant of civil rights in Maryland and Pennsylvania (where most Roman Catholics lived) solved the serious ecclesiastical problems that lay before the twenty to twenty-five ex-Jesuit priests who were serving in America in 1783. In 1784, therefore, they organized themselves into a "Select Body of Clergy," adopted a constitution regulating their affairs, and formed a corporation to administer the properties which the Society of Jesus had owned at the time of its suppression. This group also realized the importance of reestablishing their authority now that English jurisdiction was terminated, but here they faced a perplexing situation. Because they were aware of the strong hostility against the Society of Jesus still entertained at the Vatican, and because they worried about Protestant antipathies, they feared the appointment of an ordinary bishop and objected strenuously to the erection of a vicariate apostolic which would be in the jurisdiction of Propaganda in Rome.

A complicated series of maneuvers followed in which even Benjamin Franklin had a hand, since he desired to link American Catholics more closely to France, perhaps under a French bishop. But the United States government stated an explicit policy of noninvolvement in the affair. Finally in Rome on 9 June 1784, without the consultation of the American priests, the Reverend John Carroll was appointed superior of the mission in the United States. Carroll considered this arrangement unsatisfactory, for it placed severe limits on his authority, and he hesitated four months before accepting. Yet he and his colleagues were gratified that a French bishop had not been given the jurisdiction, and at least some of his fellow priests hoped that Rome would soon recognize the need for a regular diocesan arrangement. In any event, the man chosen for this arduous task was well fitted for the role.

John Carroll (1735–1815) was born into an old Maryland family disguished for its material prosperity, its widely manifested civic responsibility, and its allegiance to the Church of Rome. As befitted his station, Carroll's father, a merchant in upper Marlborough, sent his son first to a Jesuit school at Bohemia Manor near the Pennsylvania border, and then in 1748 to the famous school conducted by the English Jesuits at Saint Omer in French Flanders. In the discipline and austerity of this academic and clerical world the boy found his vocation, and five years later he began his novitiate as a Jesuit. Upon completion of further studies he became a teacher in the school of his order at Liège. During the years which followed, however, an exceedingly disruptive series of events reached their climax, and the Society of Jesus was officially dissolved. In 1744 the long-smoldering opposition to the order had led to the condemnation of its missionary practices in China; then in 1759 it was expelled from Portugal. France, after various preparatory restrictions, proscribed it entirely in 1764, Spain followed suit in 1768, and finally, in 1773, Pope Clement XIV, a Franciscan, ordered its dissolution. After a tour of the Continent, Carroll returned to America in 1774, just as it was girding itself for armed conflict with England. He sympathized with this cause and even participated in an unsuccessful attempt to bring Canada

The Forming of the Roman Catholic Church

into the Patriot camp. Thus doubly separated from traditional sources of authority, Father Carroll spent the war years as a priest in his home district, helping to secure the ex-Jesuit properties for the future work of his church in the new nation.

Like his distant cousin who had signed the Declaration of Independence, John Carroll was a convinced Patriot. As early as 1779 he assured an English correspondent that "the fullest and largest system of toleration is adopted in almost all of the American states; public protection and encouragement are extended alike to all denominations, and Roman Catholics are members of congress, assemblies, and hold civil and military posts as well as others."[1] Though firm in his attachment to the Holy See and orthodox in doctrine, he was remarkably progressive in practical matters, favoring a vernacular liturgy and expressing fierce dissatisfaction with both the political and the ecclesiastical attitudes prevailing in Rome. Before receiving word of his own appointment he expressed the hope that if America were to have a bishop, it would be "an ordinary national bishop in whose appointment Rome shall have no share."[2]

Carroll's new status as superior of the mission was far from that of "an ordinary national bishop." In fact, his very limited powers barely augmented those he had been exercising. Quite clearly his authority was insufficient to assert and retain control of an undisciplined situation where congregations of Roman Catholics, north and south, were organizing and calling priests at their own pleasure. But four years later the pope responded to requests from the American priests and allowed them to elect a bishop. In 1790 Carroll went to England to be consecrated bishop of Baltimore and to obtain much-needed assistance for work in his vast, half-explored diocese. As he indicated in his first report, there were then about twenty-five thousand Roman Catholics in the United States, sixteen thousand of them in Maryland, seven thousand in Pennsylvania, fifteen hundred in New York, and two hundred in Virginia.[3] What remnants of Catholicity there were beyond the mountains Carroll had no way of knowing.

[1] Carroll to Charles Plowden, 28 February 1779, in Annabelle M. Melville, *John Carroll of Baltimore*, p. 55.

[2] John Tracy Ellis, *Catholics in Colonial America*, p. 426.

[3] Carroll's Report to Cardinal Antonelli, in John Tracy Ellis, *Documents of American Catholic History*, p. 152.

After his consecration Bishop Carroll began in earnest to order and to pacify the "Church Turbulent" which was in his charge. The first major event in the diocese's short history was the convocation of a synod in 1791, where his four vicars-general and sixteen other priests (of seven nationalities) gathered for the hard legal work of providing decrees to govern the church's affairs. They did their work impressively well, and the result "served as a happy model for all its successors." Aside from regulatory measures, however, Bishop Carroll had to make decisions—and to set precedents —with regard to one special problem which was to bring more consternation and tumult to the church during the ensuing sixty years than any other, namely, trusteeism. The American Roman Catholic equivalent of congregationalism, trusteeism was further evidence of the characteristic localism that in a practical way was to alter, at least temporarily, the traditional polity of almost every communion that moved onto the American scene. In many varying patterns and for a variety of reasons, nearly every early Roman Catholic diocese had to deal with the question. One case involving two fractious Irish Capuchins and a privately incorporated parish in New York City had already resulted in disgraceful public disturbances before Carroll became a bishop. In 1791, due to similar disruptions in Boston, he had to suspend two French-born secular priests. In Philadelphia he faced still another disturbing situation which stemmed from the founding in 1789 of Holy Trinity Church by a privately incorporated "German Religious Society of Roman Catholics," the first such expressly national congregation formed in the United States.

The reasons for the emergence of these "congregational" churches are obvious. Distances were great; priests were few; genuine piety searched for parish expression. Protestant examples were everywhere to be seen. The revolutionary spirit and American ideals encouraged ecclesiastical democracy. Moreover it became known that the American priests had been authorized to elect their first bishop. In a time when funds were lacking and when episcopal authority was weak or nonexistent, trusteeism was a way of providing a church for people who wanted one; in a time of ethnic tensions, it would get them a priest who spoke the right language. For such good reasons, and because he was a mild-mannered person, Bishop Carroll at first permitted or accepted these practices; but he did not live to deal with the many extreme cases where unworthy priests or trustees violated canon law, creating situations where bishops had no alternative but to use every legal sanction to eliminate the practice. Later bishops would reap the whirlwind.

More impressive and positive, though also fraught with present and future difficulties, was Bishop Carroll's chief stratagem for obtaining the priests he so desperately needed and for training the new American-born clergy that would ultimately have to be relied upon. To attain these ends he accepted the support of the Society of Saint Sulpice in France. Carroll's French contacts had been established during prerevolutionary days and had deepened during the war, but it was the outbreak of the French Revolution, with its attendant anticlericalism, that made available an invaluable reservoir of missionary zeal, educational talent, and administrative ability. During his visit to England and France in 1790, Carroll accepted the offer of Jacques André Émery, superior general of the Society of Saint Sulpice in Paris, to furnish not only priests, teachers, and some students, but important financial aid. In 1791 Charles François Nagot and three colleagues arrived in Baltimore and with little delay transformed the "One Mile Tavern" just beyond the town into Saint Mary's Seminary. The institution nearly collapsed at times, yet for nearly two decades it remained the primary seminary of the American Catholic church as its graduates assumed many positions of usefulness and prominence. The Sulpicians also opened Mount Saint Mary's College at Emmitsburg, Maryland, in 1808.

Before 1815 these teachers were joined by nearly a hundred other émigré priests from France. In 1817 Ambrose Maréchal, the rector of Saint Mary's College who had shortly before declined the see of Philadelphia, was made archbishop of Baltimore. When in 1808 another émigré, Benedict Flaget, became bishop of Bardstown, Kentucky, he took with him Jean-Baptiste David, who founded a seminary in the West and later succeeded Flaget as bishop. In the meantime Jean Dubois left the presidency of Mount Saint Mary's to become the second bishop of New York. Father François Matignon was sent to pacify the disrupted church in Boston, where he was later joined by Jean-Louis Lefebvre de Cheverus, who served as bishop there until translated to the see of Montauban in France. Cheverus was later made archbishop of

Bordeaux and a cardinal. In Bordeaux he was as fondly remembered for his gentle saintliness as he had been in Boston. Even Georgetown College, one of the favorite educational projects of Bishop Carroll, owed its reputation and almost its existence in these early years to the French priests who served as it teachers and administrators.

Few of these émigré priests played a more varied role than William Dubourg (1766–1833). After theological studies at Paris, Dubourg was ordained and entered the Order of Saint Sulpice in 1788. Fleeing the Revolution, he arrived in the United States in 1794, serving for a time as president of Georgetown College and later as the first superior of Saint Mary's College. In 1812 he was appointed apostolic administrator of Louisiana and the Floridas, and three years later he was consecrated bishop. Because the cathedral at New Orleans was in the hands of those who refused submission to the American hierarchy, he was forced to reside at Saint Louis, where he founded a college and a theological seminary as well as an academy which later became Saint Louis University. During his visit to Europe in 1815—when he was consecrated bishop of New Orleans—Dubourg also visited Lyons in France, and inspired a small group of laywomen with the need for missionary aid. Out of that seed grew the Society for the Propagation of the Faith, founded in 1822, which made a large and continuous financial contribution to church work in America. In 1826 Dubourg was transferred to the see of Montauban, in France, and in 1833 he became archbishop of Besançon.

Perhaps most eminent of all was the career of Ambrose Maréchal (1764–1828). Maréchal had entered the Sulpician Seminary in Orléans, but he sailed for Maryland immediately after his ordination in 1792. Here he served as a priest until 1799, when he became a teacher of theology first at Saint Mary's College of Baltimore, later at Georgetown, then again at Saint Mary's. Under Napoleon he returned to France for a time, but in 1812 he came back to his post in Baltimore, where he served until made archbishop. His years in that office—1817 to 1828—were stormy. There were disagreements with the Jesuits over ownership of the Whitemarsh plantation. Conflicts broke out continually over Irish and German resistance to priests of other nationalities. The issue of trusteeism erupted in several places. The Irish clergy were restive because of the obvious French dominance of the hierarchy. By exceeding his authority, Maréchal did take some measures to pacify the church, but he steadfastly refused to call a provincial council, preferring to keep his bishops isolated from each other.[4] On the other hand, he did succeed in reducing European intervention in American church affairs. And in 1821, he dedicated the fine cathedral of Baltimore which Benjamin Latrobe had designed and which Archbishop Carroll had begun.

The nature of the theological and spiritual influence of the Sulpicians on the Roman Catholic church in America is difficult to estimate. But the society was always known for its firm discipline and for its strict conception of orthodoxy rather than for its venturesomeness, and it is perhaps just to say that it propagated a similar spirit in America, where in any event the intensely practical necessities of an expanding church hindered the growth of theological profundity, a great tradition of learning, or even the ardent piety associated with Jean-Jacques Olier, the society's great founder. Here again a step taken by Bishop Carroll had a decisive impact on the church—in the immediate sense providing a source of priests and bishops when they were badly needed, but in the long run creating a very serious source of ethnic tension and jealousies that often sharpened trusteeship conflicts. Probably the most enduring legacy of the Sulpicians to the American church was their very conservative theological tradition.

The prominence of the Society of Jesus is another feature of American Catholicism which the church's first prelate, a Jesuit himself, tended to accentuate, though in no unusually overt manner. In America the former members of the Society of Jesus, who in fact constituted the main body of clergy in 1783, maintained their identity despite their official nonexistence. After 1805, capitalizing on the pope's recognition of the Society of Jesus in Russia, they reprofessed their vows and went ahead openly with their work, though there was no American province before 1833. During these early decades the college at Georgetown, opened in 1791, was the main center of their labor, but they made contributions as priests and bishops in every sector. It has been justly said that American Catholicism was "in its inception, wholly a Jesuit

[4] See Thomas F. Casey, *The Sacred Congregation de Propaganda Fide and the Revision of the First Provincial Council of Baltimore, 1829–1830* (Rome: Gregorian University, 1957), pp. 12–16; and the several works of Peter Guilday therein cited.

affair and [has] largely remained so."[5] What truth there is to this exaggeration is largely due to the success of the Jesuits of Carroll's generation in maintaining themselves and then in regaining a prominent place in the church's life.

It must be added, however, that Sulpicians and Jesuits were not the only orders at work in these early years. In 1806–07 Father Edward D. Fenwick and other Dominicans built the Church of Saint Rose of Lima in Washington County, Kentucky, and opened a novitiate that marks the origin of that order in the United States. The Dominicans also worked extensively as missionaries in the area; and in 1821 Father Fenwick was made the first bishop of Cincinnati. Women's orders, too, were at work. The Ursulines had been in New Orleans since 1727, and early in the nineteenth century they were carrying on their teaching work in New York and Boston. Outside of New Orleans the oldest convent in the United States is that settled by the Carmelites in Maryland in 1790; but the old established orders were not alone in advancing the course of education.

Notable in her own way was Elizabeth Seton (1774–1821). Widow of a well-to-do New York merchant and an Episcopalian, she became a Catholic soon after her husband's death in 1803. After a brief teaching experience in New York City, she went in 1808 to Baltimore, where, encouraged by Carroll and Dubourg, she opened an academy in a house adjoining Saint Mary's College. Moving to Emmitsburg a year later, she established Saint Joseph's Academy, and in order to staff it, founded the Sisters of Charity as a teaching order. In decades to come the American Sisters of Charity would make a major contribution as teachers and administrators of schools throughout the country. Mother Seton was beatified by the pope in 1963, and she may well become the first American-born canonized saint.

EXPANSION OF THE CHURCH

The trends established and the problems faced or created during the early years of a fully constituted Roman Catholic church in the United States have been the focus of our attention up to this point. This has perhaps obscured the major

[5] Thomas O'Gorman, *History of the Roman Catholic Church in the United States*, ACHS, vol. 9 (New York, 1895), p. 208.

fact that the church actively ministered to the widely scattered faithful in the new country, as well as to the ever increasing numbers arriving through immigration. The most obvious index of this activity is the expansion of the hierarchy and the increase in the priesthood and membership. In 1790 Bishop Carroll had been alone with little more than an ex-Jesuit remnant. In 1799, however, he received a coadjutor bishop, Leonard Neale, a Marylander and Jesuit; then, more momentously, in 1808 Pope Pius VII erected Baltimore as a metropolitan see. Archbishop Carroll now was given four suffragan see. Boston, Bardstown, New York, and Philadelphia. As nearly as the archbishop and his suffragans could determine, there were then eighty Roman Catholic churches, seventy priests and perhaps seventy thousand faithful in the United States, exclusive of Louisiana.

At Boston John Cheverus became the ordinary of a diocese that included all of New England but consisted of only three widely scattered congregations, one of which was the recently conflict-ridden Boston congregation of about seven hundred members. Cheverus was one of the few French émigrés who was deeply beloved by parishioners and non-Catholics alike; and the whole city mourned his departure when he returned to France in 1823. His successor, Benedict J. Fenwick, a Jesuit, took charge of a diocese that had grown only slightly to include eight churches served by three priests. Although his Boston membership was by then largely Irish, the great deluge still lay ahead.

The first bishop of Bardstown was Benedict Joseph Flaget, the Sulpician who since 1792 had been ministering in the West, at Vincennes and many other places. With a responsibility that at first included the entire trans-Appalachian region except the Louisiana Purchase lands, Flaget faced staggering problems. Yet aided by the Kentucky Dominicans and a small group of itinerant missionary priests (most of them French), he did much to organize the church life of old settlers and newcomers alike. The growth of his diocese was steady. In 1817 Flaget received a coadjutor, and the Dominican Father Fenwick was appointed to the newly erected see of Cincinnati with the Old Northwest as his charge.

The first bishop of New York was appointed in Rome and died at Naples in 1810 without ever seeing his diocese. His successor was another stranger to America, John Connolly, who did not occupy his unruly see until 1815. Until his death a decade later, Connolly's efforts to cope with the rising tide of Irish immigration were inhibited by bitter struggles with trustees and an acute shortage of clergy. In 1825 he had but ten priests for an estimated 150,000 Roman Catholic people. His successor, the Sulpician Jean Dubois, a former schoolmate of Robespierre, showed greater competence. Dubois founded a diocesan seminary, but because of his nationality he was doomed to even fiercer opposition from the trustees. It was not until 1837, when John Hughes, a former seminary student of Dubois's, was consecrated as coadjutor in New York, that the diocese gained a bishop fully able to deal with the rapidly growing Catholic population, serious trusteeship problems, and most ominous of all, the rising tide of anti-Catholicism. Orator, theologian, strenuous controversialist, and effective administrator, Hughes demonstrated the advantages and possibilities of a prelate who had been trained in the United States.

Philadelphia, the fourth suffragan see erected in 1808, had at that time and for some time continued to have the most substantial Catholic population in the country. Trusteeism raised greater problems here than elsewhere, and Michael Egan, a Franciscan who in 1810 became the city's first bishop, was unable even to assert his authority over the cathedral priests. The man appointed in Europe to deal with the Philadelphia diocese after Egan's death was Henry Conwell, the aged vicar general of Armagh in Ireland. Around him for a decade swirled the events of the Hogan affair, the *cause célèbre* of trusteeism, which finally did him in. William Hogan was a handsome priest who came from Ireland in 1819, the year of Conwell's consecration as bishop. He had been granted faculties as a priest in Saint Mary's Church by the interim administrator of the diocese, but these faculties were withdrawn after Hogan publicly ridiculed the new bishop. The trustees of the cathedral church supported the priest, who in turn intensified his attack, accusing the bishop of exceeding the canonical limits of his authority (as, indeed, several bishops had done). Hogan also urged Archbishop Maréchal to call a provincial council to rule on these matters; but he then outdid himself and forged a pastoral letter ascribed to Bishop Conwell. Conwell retaliated, admonishing the congregation and threatening Hogan with excommunication if he should exercise his faculties. Since Hogan, at the trustees' urging, did not desist, he was excommunicated in May 1822. The trustees then went still farther and published an "Address of the Committee of Saint Mary's Church of Philadelphia to their Brethren of the Roman Catholic Faith throughout the United States of America, on the Subject of a Reform of Certain Abuses in the Administration of our Church Discipline." They alleged intervention by "foreigners" sent among them by "the Junta or Commission directing the Fide Propaganda of Rome," and called for procedures allowing the "nomination and selection of our pastors from our own citizens." From among these pastors, moreover, bishops should be chosen. They went on to accuse the existing bishops of being "a disgrace to our religion," victims of "superstition and ignorance." Hogan and the trustees were, in effect, calling for an independent Catholic church of some sort.

In due course these events prompted a condemnatory brief, *Non sine magno*, from Pope Pius VII. Though it did not rule out benign trusteeship arrangements, it did declare Father Hogan's pastoral acts to be null and void. But even this did not end the affair. Hogan, after showing some reluctance, continued the struggle for a while, but he later resigned, became a lawyer, and was married in 1824. He died without the offices of the church in 1848. The trustees continued the conflict, however, by gaining the services of two other priests (Angelo Inglesi and then Thaddeus O'Meally) for another year. Thereupon the lay committee and the bishop worked out a compromise proposal for selecting pastors for Saint Mary's, which, together with a confusing counterdeclaration by the lay committee, found its way to Rome. A decree of the Propaganda approved by the pope reprobated this agreement. Bishop Conwell was called to Rome and ordered not to return to his diocese. He did return, however, and was pardoned, but he was not allowed to exercise his episcopal functions. In his place Francis Patrick Kenrick (1796–1863) was appointed in 1831. Irish-born, educated in Rome, only thirty-four years old, and by nature a theologian rather than an administrator or man of action, Kenrick now faced the problem that had broken two bishops and left a vast diocese in undeveloped disarray. In addition to these problems, and in part because of them, he also would have to deal in future years with the infamous Know-Nothing riots of 1844, the most violent ever to occur in the United States. More suited to his nature was the direction of the seminary which he founded in

1835. Bishop Kenrick was transferred to the metropolitan see of Baltimore in 1851, where he served till his death. When he died he left to the church a large corpus of writing on dogmatic and moral theology, an English version of the Bible, and numerous treatises and controversial works on baptism, justification, the primacy of Peter, and other subjects.

THE FIRST PROVINCIAL COUNCIL OF BALTIMORE

Even prior to some of these events in the first four suffragan dioceses, other sees had been erected and other bishops appointed, and in these areas many of the same circumstances had been encountered. Some unaccountable decisions were made in Rome, such as the erection of a see in Virginia where there were scarcely enough church members to support a single priest. Good and bad appointments were likewise made: Bishop John England of Charleston being one of the greatest prelates ever to grace the church in America and Patrick Kelly of Richmond one of the least effective. Both came from Ireland, both faced trusteeism in one form or another.

In 1815 Archbishop Carroll died. His coadjutor, Leonard Neale, served as archbishop for two years until succeeded by Maréchal. While this French prelate was metropolitan (1817–28) the need for uniform regulations and procedures and the consequent pressure for a council of bishops most forcefully arose. But Maréchal refused to call one, and it was his successor, James Whitfield, who upon authorization from Pius VIII convoked the First Provincial Council for 4 October 1829.[6]

[6] James Whitfield (1770–1834), fourth archbishop of Baltimore, was born at Liverpool, England, lived for a time in Italy, and when detained in France by the Napoleonic wars, was educated at Saint Irenaeus Seminary. Ordained in 1809, he continued on to England where he became for a time a Jesuit novice. In 1817 he departed for Baltimore to join his close friend and former rector of Saint Irenaeus, Ambrose Maréchal, then coadjutor to Archbishop Neale of Baltimore. Under Maréchal, who was soon made archbishop, Whitfield was appointed first rector of the Cathedral of the Assumption in 1821, and as coadjutor and titular bishop of Apollonia on 8 January 1828. Maréchal died three weeks later, and on 25 May, Whitfield was consecrated as archbishop.

It was an auspicious conclave in a critical period of American history. Its proportions were modest, but the actions taken as well as the trends observable in the country portended much. The canonical members of the council were the bishops, including coadjutors, of the sees in the province of Baltimore: Baltimore, Boston, New York, Philadelphia, Charleston, and Cincinnati (Richmond, which was vacant, was under the administration of the archdiocese of Baltimore). Also invited to be present were those bishops serving outside the province, and depending directly on the Congregation de Propaganda Fide in Rome: New Orleans, Saint Louis, and the vicariate of Alabama and Florida. In its collective letter to the Holy See, the council could rightly express thanks and something approaching amazement at the changes wrought in the state of the church during the past four decades. They could point to six "ecclesiastical seminaries," nine colleges, three of which were chartered universities, houses of Dominicans, Jesuits, Sulpicians, and of the Congregation of the Mission, thirty-three monasteries and houses of religious women of several congregations and orders, and, of course, a rapidly growing body of faithful laity which even then numbered over two hundred thousand. The Roman Catholic church had become a major force in American life.

33

THE EXPANSION OF THE ROMAN CATHOLIC CHURCH

The first Provincial Council of Baltimore, held in October 1829, was an epoch-marking event in American Catholic history in the United States. In the first place, it was a considerable achievement in the realm of ecclesiastical administration, for its influence would be wide and long-lasting. It also revealed to non-Catholic Americans in no uncertain terms that the Roman church was a substantial, growing, and well organized reality. With Andrew Jackson enjoying his first year in the White House, the council occurred at an important time of transition in the nation's history; what historians have called the "early national period" was over. The "era of good feelings" and the day of presidential knee britches was yielding to the "age of the common man." Amid sharpening sectional conflict, a notable increase in the rate of immigration was also heightening ethnic tensions.

The Roman Catholic church was especially implicated in immigration, and in two ways. First, because very many of the immigrants were Roman Catholic, the challenge of reaching them with the offices and sacraments of the church was to make all of its earlier efforts seem like pioneering sorties. Second, because the American people, in any event defensive, self-conscious, nationalistic, and somewhat xenophobic, were ill prepared to receive so large a component of "strangers" into their midst, the church was also required to adapt itself to a new atmosphere of suspicion and overt attack. The present chapter is concerned chiefly with the first challenge; that which follows will take up the matter of antebellum nativism.

THE COMING OF THE IRISH

Even in the late colonial period the Irish had constituted a large (possibly the largest) proportion of the church's laity. Michael J. O'Brien has argued that his compatriots of the revolutionary era virtually won the war. But the uncertain estimates of colonial times yielded to firm statistical fact after the turn of the century, when increasingly large numbers of Roman Catholics from Ireland began their historic migration to the New World.

Why four and one-half million Irish came to America in the century after 1820 is no mystery. If there were ever any doubts, Cecil Woodham-Smith has removed them with her recent research and unforgettable historical account of "the great hunger." Life on the Emerald Isle had become unendurable as population pressure increased. Food was scarce, agricultural methods backward, prices and wages disastrously low, taxation heavy, and government by absentee English landlords unbelievably ruthless and intolerant. After the close of the Napoleonic wars emigration increased, especially among the class of more substantial farmers. As economic conditions grew worse, and as American factories and construction projects beckoned, still poorer people began to leave; and to accommodate their needs, the "immigrant traffic" grew as a means of providing mass transportation at minimum cost. During the 1830s, 200,000 Irish arrived in the United States. After 1845 a succession of cold, damp summers and a mysterious blight ruined the potato crop on which life itself depended, and as a result about 1.5 million died. What this meant for the villages of Ireland is suggested by the parish record in Donoughmore, County Cork, where the future American bishop, Dennis O'Connell, was born.

December, 1847: This was the Famine Year. There died of famine and fever from November 1846 to September 1847 over fourteen hundred of the people and one Priest, Revd. Dan. Horgan. Requiescat in Pace. Numbers remained unburied for a fortnight, many were buried in ditches near their houses, many without coffins, tho' ther wer four men employed to bury the dead and make graves and [two], and sometimes four carpenters to make coffins. On this year also we were visited by the Cholera Mortis. 5 only died of it in this parish. [signed Michael Kane, Pastor][1]

The exodus from Ireland became a desperate, frantic flight, involving about 780,000 people in all. By 1850 the census reported 961,719 Irish in the United States, and over 200,000 came in that year alone. In another decade the total figure had risen to 1,611,304.

Yet statistics can never capture the meaning of this terrible exodus and its painful sequel in the shantytowns of America's too rapidly growing cities, or the hardships and disrupted family life wherever there were backbreaking jobs at low pay on canal projects, railroad and dam construction, or anywhere else at the mudsill of the American labor market. Nor were the obstacles only hard work, poverty, and miserable living conditions, for the Irish had to face the contumely, prejudice, and insulting condescension of Protestant and Anglo-Saxon America. In this context the work of extending the Roman Catholic church proceeded.

Within the Roman Catholic church, tension between the Irish and Germans persisted during the entire nineteenth century. It underlay early trusteeship conflicts in New York, Buffalo, and Philadelphia, then reached its most critical stage in the latter half of the century, when the issues had involved the highest levels of the American hierarchy and become entangled in the internal and external politics of the Vatican. Ethnic hostility was thus vented within the church as well as against it. Yet the primary fact of Roman Catholic history in antebellum America, aside from its basic task of reaching the immigrants, is the vigorous entry of the Irish into the life of the nation and the church.

The first and most obvious effect of Irish immigration was an immense multiplication of the church's missionary problems. As it met and overcame these obstacles, the church experienced a phenomenal growth in numbers, reaching 1.75 million by 1850, and doubling this figure in another decade. In the process, a church originally largely Gallic in its leadership became and remained dominantly Gaelic. But

---

[1] Quoted by Gerald Fogarty, "The Life of Dennis O'Connell" (unpublished manuscript, Yale University, 1968). On the Irish catastrophe as a whole, see Cecil Woodham-Smith, *The Great Hunger: Ireland, 1845–1849* (New York: Harper & Row, 1962).

such transformations do not usually come peacefully or without stress, and they did not in this case. Parishes revealed the conflict first, either through disagreements between Irish and French parishioners (as in Boston) or through the resistance of local trustees to a French bishop (as in New York).

In addition to disorderly manifestations by the laity, there were deep dissatisfactions among the lower clergy who, if Irish, resented the tendency of the hierarchy to award all the ecclesiastical plums to "foreigners." This is not to say that the French appointments were unwarranted or unjust. These men were, as Maynard has said, almost too good. "Men so learned, so able, so pious as Cheverus and Dubourg and Dubois and Flaget and Bruté and Maréchal simply *had* to be made bishops."[2] Such dispassionate judgments, however, could not come easily to those who had suffered real adversities in Ireland or America, who had come from humble circumstances, and who had received only such education as a raw young nation and a too rapidly expanding church could provide. And there were other grievances. Members of the higher clergy were known to speak in private (as did Maréchal) of "*la canaille irlandaise.*" And Archbishop James Whitfield, a French-educated Englishman, revealed the same kind of prejudice in a letter to his friend Joseph Rosati, then bishop of Saint Louis. Speaking in 1832 of the empty see in Cincinnati, he urged that "an American born be recommended" and then added that "(between us in strict confidence) I do really think we should guard against having more Irish bishops."[3] In the midst of such attitudes peace and good will could hardly flourish.

Gradually the situation changed, however, in part because the Irish in the church exploited the same aptitudes that were making their political leaders a force to reckon with, and in part because of the sheer force of numbers. Not only was the overall increase due to immigration in their favor, but Irish-Americans were entering the priesthood and the religious orders in numbers far exceeding those of other nationalities. Furthermore, these men simply demonstrated their abilities. Outstanding among these was John Hughes, who in 1837 became the coadjutor of Bishop Dubois in New York, soon

[2] Theodore Maynard, *The Catholic Church and the American Idea*, p. 184.

[3] John Tracy Ellis, *American Catholicism*, p. 49.

showed his superior talents for leading an harassed and growing church during turbulent times. Under these circumstances the Irish-American clergy gradually won their place in the church, and once they had attained a dominant position, they retained it successfully from that time forward except in sees which were tacitly reserved for Germans and a few other special cases. In the American church, unlike the ancient churches of Europe, these leaders would have to proceed without government aid or favor. Majority opinion in the nation would be hostile. Immigrant tides would roll in, and most of their constituency would be low on the social and economic scale. Yet the historic institutions of the church would rise—cathedrals, seminaries, colleges, monasteries, hospitals, and hundreds of parish churches—a tremendous testimony to the advantages of a free church in a free country and to their own ecclesiastical leadership.

GEOGRAPHICAL EXPANSION

If the Roman church's response to the challenge of immigration and the integration of wave upon wave of new Irish-Americans was one major fact of its growth during its first half-century in America, the geographical expansion of its jurisdiction was hardly less exciting. Frontier church history is usually considered a predominantly Protestant phenomenon. But the Roman Catholic church from the first carried on an active work in the West. The small remnants of French Catholicism in the upper Mississippi Valley provided the first incentive to western plans, and the work preceding and following the appointment of Bishop Flaget was a critical beginning. This organizational activity was extended into the Midwest and into the vast territory purchased from France in 1803. In New Orleans both the laity and the old clergy offered stout resistance to incorporation in the United States hierarchy, even preventing Bishop Dubourg from occupying the cathedral, but after 1818 peace and order were established. In 1821 Ohio was erected into a diocese; in 1826 upper and lower Louisiana were separated into two dioceses; and in 1837 Mathias Loras was consecrated bishop of Dubuque with jurisdiction over Iowa, Minnesota, and part of Dakota. In 1843 Minnesota and Wisconsin became dioceses. And so the process continued as each of the successive provincial councils meeting at Baltimore (1833, 1837, 1840, 1843, and 1846) recommended new sees and the men to occupy them.

The 1840s, however, were a decade in which the territorial extent of the United States itself was heatedly contested—and then vastly increased—by the annexation of Texas, the Mexican War, and the Oregon settlement. With regard to the war in which the "enemy" was a Roman Catholic country, the hierarchy was silent, though it approved some overt efforts to convince Mexican church leaders that the United States did not threaten them. Patriotism tended to tranquilize rather than exacerbate anti-Catholicism, however, and after the war Congress approved President Polk's recommendation that diplomatic relations be established with the sovereign of the Papal States. From 1848 until after the Civil War this representation was continued. More important for the church were the problems incident to a vast territorial gain in the Southwest.

In 1846, at a time when the Oregon question was still unsettled, a new stage in American hierarchical history was reached. A second metropolitan see was erected with the French-Canadian Francis N. Blanchet as archbishop, his brother as suffragan in Walla Walla, and another French-Canadian as bishop of Vancouver. In both fact and theory this province was at first an extension of the Canadian church. The first organized work in Oregon by the United States hierarchy was initiated in 1840, when Bishop Rosati of Saint Louis, having turned to the Jesuits, gave the assignment to Pierre Jean DeSmet (1801–73), a Belgian-born priest who had entered the Society of Jesus in Maryland in 1821. For thirty years DeSmet labored to extend and support the Northwest missions, making eight trips to Europe in search of aid, traveling over 250,000 miles, and even becoming a leading publicist of Indian missions. Led by DeSmet, the Jesuits conducted an extensive mission among the region's Indians. Their exploits, indeed, recall the history of their society in New France—both in its eventfulness and in its lack of enduring success. In 1852 the Jesuit mission in Oregon was abandoned. The Oregon province, nevertheless, became part of the American church after the territorial controversy with Great Britain was resolved.

Saint Louis was given similar status in 1847, with Nashville, Chicago, Milwaukee, Dubuque, and Saint Paul in-

cluded in the province. The country now had three archbishops, yet Americans and immigrants steadily moved west,
and before the century ended each of these cities except
Nashville had itself become a metropolitan see. Saint Louis
was by then a great ecclesiastical center, and one of the
dedicated pioneers who had helped to make it so was Mother
Philippine Duchesne (1769–1852).

Born in Grenoble, France, Philippine Duchesne had entered the Society of the Sacred Heart, a teaching order organized by Saint Madeleine Sophie Barat. Responding to the
missionary needs that Bishop Dubourg had described, she
won permission to go out to Saint Louis, where after 1818, in
close collaboration with the Jesuits, she and her sisters
founded several schools. She was over seventy years old
when she took up work in Indian territory. Philippine
Duchesne's career stands as a saintly example of the enormous
educational work her order would perform in America.[4]

In the meantime, a vast area of former Mexican territory
was added to the Union, a region with a storied Spanish past
but, by the mid-nineteenth century, very little organized
church life. In Texas, where nominal Catholics may have
numbered ten thousand, Vicar Apostolic Odin, a Frenchman,
was made bishop of Galveston in 1847. New Mexico, where
possibly twenty-five thousand Catholics were being served by
only nine priests under the bishop of Durango, was made a
vicariate apostolic under the American hierarchy in 1850.
Three years later the see of Santa Fe was erected and Jean-
Baptiste Lamy (1814–88) was named to lead this picturesque desert diocese where Indian, Spanish, Mexican, and
American traditions now crossed. The life of this remarkable
French churchman is the subject of Willa Cather's *Death
Comes for the Archbishop* (1926). California remained
under the bishop of Monterey until 1853, when the arch-
diocese of San Francisco was constituted—and with this ad-

[4] The Society of the Sacred Heart had been formed in the
restorationist underground of Napoleonic France in collaboration
with men who were working for the reorganization of the Jesuits.
Philippine Duchesne was virtually a cofounder. First authorized
in 1807 as *Dames de l'Instruction Chrétienne,* the society has
always made education its primary mission. By 1935 the work
begun in the United States by Mother Duchesne was an impressive
subsystem of Catholic education that included seventy-two elementary and secondary schools and ninety institutions of higher learning (see Louise Callan, *Philippine Duchesne*).

ministrative act the continent was spanned. Considered as a whole, this ecclesiastical conquest was a stupendous achievement, though not because dioceses were drawn on a map, but because countless men and women yielded themselves to a task and to a command.

One era was concluded and another opened, a fact which was fittingly documented when the archbishop of Baltimore, Francis Patrick Kenrick, received papal authorization to convoke the first plenary council in America. On Sunday, 9 May 1852, the council was convened with the solemn procession into the Baltimore cathedral of the incumbents or proxies of six metropolitan and twenty-seven suffragan sees, an abbot, and the superiors of many religious orders and congregations. The Catholic population stood at an estimated 1.6 million, served by 1,800 priests in about 1,600 churches and mission stations. A fine Roman Catholic historian who himself at Sioux Falls, South Dakota, in 1896 became the bishop of a western diocese is entitled to a measure of pride in summarizing the accomplishments of the six decades since John Carroll had become the country's first bishop: "The world beheld the objective lesson of a growth and extension within half a century for the like of which we must go back to the earliest days of Christianity, when in the freshness of youth and vigor of apostolic zeal the church laid hold of the Roman Empire. . . . The era of plenary councils begins."[5]

THE CHURCH AND AMERICAN CULTURE

The first half-century of American Catholic history is not simply a story of geographic expansion and external organization. There is another remarkable dimension to the story, involving a different kind of pioneering—the adaptation of this rapidly expanding, multinational immigrant church to an individualistic democratic society. For this undertaking, guidance or example could scarcely be found in the church's experience since the age of the Emperor Constantine. Father O'Gorman's fervent reference to the "earliest days" of the church was warranted. As for the Curia in Rome, it seems not to have understood the distinctive character of American developments until well into the twentieth century, if

[5] Thomas O'Gorman, *History of the Roman Catholic Church in the United States*, ACHS, vol. 9 (New York, 1895), p. 425.

then. Shaping an American Catholic church was an exciting venture, carried out on a grand scale by men who were often so involved in the multifarious details of their work that they did not know that they were ecclesiastical revolutionaries. Yet that something like an "American revolution" was accomplished in the Roman Catholic church as well as in society at large could not be hidden or suppressed. In the decrees of the First Plenary Council (1852) there are more than intimations of that fact, as the bishops dealt with the crosscurrents of language and national tradition which flowed through the American church. In their pastoral letter the bishops exhorted their vast flock: "Obey the public authorities, not only for wrath but for conscience sake. Show your attachment to the institutions of our beloved country."

The First Plenary Council was closely followed by the Civil War, during which the American sense of nationhood gained a new kind of profundity. Almost immediately after that appalling sacrifice of life and wealth, a Second Plenary Council was convoked in Baltimore by Archbishop Martin John Spalding on 7 October 1866. At the time, this was the largest formal conciliary assembly in the Roman Catholic church since the Council of Trent; seven archbishops, twenty-eight bishops, three mitred abbots, and over one hundred twenty theologians were in attendance. They spoke in behalf of a church of over three million members which had almost doubled in size since 1852. Behind them lay not only the war and Lincoln's assassination but the encyclical of Pope Pius IX (*Quanta Cura*, 1864) and the sensational "Syllabus of Errors" which accompanied it. This comprehensive attack on modern thought and political liberalism had long since been "explained" in public by several American Catholics, yet it undeniably created difficulties for the council because the clear meaning of its reactionary denunciations could not be avoided. Despite this dilemma, the council fathers wished to express their democratic faith and their thankfulness for American institutions. The decrees of the council and the pastoral letter of the bishops were, therefore, "the nearest to a definition of Catholic Americanism that any official body of Catholics ever reached in the nineteenth century."[6] The only serious complaint about the American situation voiced by the council pertained to the laws by which some of the

[6] T. T. McAvoy, *The Great Crisis in American Catholic History, 1895–1900*, p. 14.

states, most pointedly Missouri, denied the right of the church to possess property.

The process of adjusting the structures and attitudes of a European church which had relatively little experience in conducting itself as a minority in a large democratic society resulted in an important two-way flow of ideas. Catholicism, on the one hand, commended itself to a surprisingly large number of American Protestants despite nativism and an old tradition of antipopery. Democracy, on the other hand, was interpreted to the church both by general experience and by theologians and church leaders, of whom the two most significant were, as it happened, converts.

CONVERSIONS TO ROMAN CATHOLICISM

The Roman Catholic church had successfully sought converts to its faith and discipline during the whole course of American colonial history. In fact, one source of the hostility directed against the early Jesuits in Maryland was their success in this regard. Toward the end of the seventeenth century the example of the later Stuart royal family gave rise to a considerable number of "Jacobite" converts, though the age of the Enlightenment coupled with many legal harassments had a contrary effect. Around 1800, a surfeit of "reasonable religion" and reaction from the French Revolution led to a widespread "romantic" reassessment of the religious heritage. In its wake came a new wave of Catholic interest. This impulse was often only aesthetic or sentimental, but it sometimes resulted in movements of Catholic renewal in the Reformation churches; and it also stimulated a great increase of conversions to the Roman church. The romantic revolution in religion is considered in a later chapter, but certain aspects of it loom large in antebellum Catholic history. In the words of one Catholic, it was "a time when great throngs of Americans began to flock to the Roman Catholic church despite bitterly intense propaganda and overt opposition." Between 1813 and 1893 the number of converts may have reached 700,000.[7]

Even if greatly exaggerated or almost balanced by an equally large defection from the church, such figures reveal

[7] George K. Malone, *The True Church: A Study in the Apologetics of Orestes Brownson* (Mundelein, Ill.: Saint Mary of the Lake Seminary, 1957), p. 2.

an important fact of American religious life. They also point
to a significant factor in the shaping of American Catholicism. Mixed marriages probably account for most of the
losses and gains of the Roman church, but among the converts who attained some degree of public notice, the largest
number came from the ranks of High Church Anglicans who
were dissatisfied by the evangelicalism of the Protestant Episcopal church and who were carried forward by the implications of their own arguments on apostolic succession and
"valid" ordination. After the Oxford Movement's *Tracts for
the Times* began to appear, and especially after John Henry
Newman's sensational conversion to Rome in 1845, there was
considerable movement of Episcopalians toward Catholicism,
about fifty of whom were priests or seminary graduates. The
most publicized case was the conversion of a bishop, Levi S.
Ives of North Carolina, in 1852.

Some of these converts attained considerable eminence as
Roman Catholics, notably Edgar P. Wadhams, who in 1872
became bishop of Ogdensburg, New York, after twenty-two
years in the priesthood, and Augustine F. Hewit, one of the
first Paulists and the successor of Father Hecker as su-
perior-general of the congregation. Achieving the highest eminence of all was James Roosevelt Bayley, a relative of
Mother Seton, who, like so many of his fellow Episcopal
priests, turned to Rome during the 1840s. After serving in
several positions in the appointment of Archbishop Hughes
Bayley became bishop of Newark in 1853. His great ability
as diocesan leader finally led in 1872 to his translation to the
archepiscopal see of Baltimore.[8]

Among all the converts of the period, however, there
were two men who best expressed the thoughts and feelings
that lay behind this renewal of Catholic interest: Orestes
Brownson and Isaac Hecker. By an interesting irony, both
emerged from the Transcendentalist movement on the left
wing of Unitarianism, and perhaps because of this fact, both
men were especially eloquent interpreters of the reciprocal
benefits of democratic ideals and Catholic faith.

Orestes Brownson

Orestes Brownson (1803–76) was a self-educated spiritual
wanderer from rural Vermont whose pilgrimage brought him

[8] The Oxford Movement and American Anglo-Catholicism are
considered in more detail in their Episcopal context in Volume 2,
chap. 38.

to the Church of Rome at the age of forty-two—but by a notoriously winding route. In 1822 he ended a youthful period of haphazard religious drift by entering the Presbyterian church; but within three years he had recoiled from its doctrinal rigor, and from 1824 to 1829 he was active as a Universalist preacher and editor. Enticed from that tie by the earnest arguments of Fanny Wright, the British-born freethinker and humanitarian reformer, Brownson entered a period of atheism during which the Workingman's party was his chief preoccupation. In 1831, deeply moved by William Ellery Channing's writings, he became a Unitarian; and after ministries in various places he burst onto the Boston scene in 1836, editing a reform journal and preaching to a Society for Christian Union and Progress which he organized in order to reach laboring people untouched by the regular churches. In the same year he published his *New Views of Christianity, Society, and the Church,* which together with his lectures and articles soon made him one of the most influential leaders of the emerging Transcendental movement. Deeply imbued with the romantic religious philosophies of France, Brownson became the leading American expositor of Benjamin Constant, Victor Cousin, and a group of Saint-Simonian thinkers.

His radical Jacksonianism gave a sharp critical edge to his social prophecy, but the disgusting character and disappointing result of the 1840 presidential campaign diminished his political optimism and gradually religious perspectives again dominated his thought. In this context the French Saint-Simonian Pierre Leroux (1797–1871) became to him so sure a guide that Brownson would always regard him as, after Malebranche, "the ablest and most original philosopher France has produced." Leroux convinced him that human life and thought is a "joint product of subject and object," and that man's well-being and progress depend, therefore, on "communion"—with nature, mankind, and with God. For Leroux humanity was the means to communion with God; for Brownson the means slowly came to be understood as "the mediatorial life of Christ" (the "Providential man"), then more precisely the corporate church, and finally—despite the lifelong prejudices of a New Englander—the Roman Catholic church. On 20 October 1844, after a period of instruction under John Bernard Fitzpatrick, coadjutor-bishop of Boston, Brownson did as he had always done: he took the step to which his convictions had led.

Under the tutelage of Bishop Fitzpatrick he continued to publish *Brownson's Quarterly Review*, which he had founded in 1843 as successor to his *Boston Quarterly Review*, but he abandoned the line of thought that had led him to Rome, adopted the bishop's strictly traditional apologetics, and consigned all of his former friends and all other victims of Protestant "no-churchism" to the nether regions of hell. They, in turn, wrote off his last turn of mind as another example of his "vicissitudinary petulance" and struck him from their lists of Transcendental heroes. Brownson the Roman Catholic was still Brownson, however, as sure as ever that his convictions were based on unerring deductions from indubitable premises. In the midst of vigorous activity as America's foremost convert, he gradually reasserted his characteristic modes of thought, and for these reasons as well as for his impolitic criticism of parochial schools and of the Irish "rabble," he had soon aroused a Roman Catholic opposition which for the rest of his life would undermine his prestige and assault nearly every position he occupied.

In 1855 Brownson moved out of the Boston diocese to New York, but in this supposedly freer atmosphere his outspoken "Americanism" awakened the hostility of Archbishop John Hughes and many others, while his criticism of despotic rule in the Papal States and of even the idea of the pope's wielding temporal power aroused suspicions in Rome. Moving to New Jersey in 1857, he published *The Convert, or Leaves from My Experience*, which was, in effect, a declaration of intellectual independence.

Although to the end of his days this independence was limited by harassment and attack from all quarters, Brownson did nevertheless return to the lines of thought which led him to Catholicism, augmenting themes derived from Leroux with an equally great responsiveness to the writings of the Piedmontese philosopher-theologian Vicenzo Gioberti (1801–52). Gioberti was a fervent champion of Catholic truth and Italian unity whom Brownson declared to be "certainly one of the profoundest philosophical writers of this century." A critic of modern romantic pantheism, he convinced Brownson that ontology, not psychology, is the proper starting point of human thought, and that Malebranche, not Cousin, was the greatest of French religious philosophers. Since Gioberti's works were put on the Index, largely because of his alleged "ontologism," Brownson was also tarred with that brush despite his efforts to "correct" Gioberti's errors.[9]

Combing these various emphases in his own way, Brownson became again a bold and distinctive thinker. He continued to believe that religion and politics were virtually inseparable and that Catholicism was a fulfillment of American ideals, though his dual commitment to Calhoun's constitutional thought and to the antirevolutionary school of Catholic thinkers (notably Joseph de Maistre) gave a very conservative organicistic tincture to his advocacy. In the country's great sectional controversy he held a strong "Southern" position even through the Dred Scott affair. Only in the campaign of 1860 did he become an antislavery Unionist—and remain so throughout the war, to the great irritation of Archbishop Hughes and many powerful members of the hierarchy. During these years Brownson also became more liberal on theological issues, a fact which he documented in his one systematic work *The American Republic: Its Constitution, Tendencies, and Destiny* (1866). This work shows the continuing hold of Leroux, Gioberti, and Maistre on his thought, but it is also a ringing affirmation of democratic ideals. Yet Pius IX's sweeping condemnation of liberalism in *Quanta Cura* and its accompanying Syllabus of Errors created difficulties for Brownson. It seemed to sustain the view of his Catholic critics and hence reduced the influence of his best political thinking.

Brownson's lifetime literary production was enormous, running to twenty large volumes in the collected *Works;* and almost to the end of his life, his powers of analysis and expression remained impressive. But his influence was small, especially after 1844, and especially among Catholics. His "Americanism," his hostility to the Jesuits, and his condescending attitudes toward immigrant culture offended Roman Catholics at every level. His harshly stated defenses of papal infallibility and the church's authority struck Catholics as impolitic and Protestants as outrageous. The acerbity of his attacks offended everyone. Perhaps a realization of these

[9] Ontologism was a heresy which consisted of carrying the ontological argument to undue lengths, so as to assert that the primary or fundamental operation of intellect is the direct intuition of Being, identified as God. It was a view which nineteenth-century currents of philosophical idealism often encouraged.

shortcomings had something to do with his discontinuance of his *Review* for a decade. After 1873 he did reassert the ultra-orthodoxy of his early Catholic period, but at his death disappointment and bitterness loomed large in his thought. Ten years later, in a fitting tribute to an immensely creative but unappreciated thinker, his remains were reinterred in the Chapel of the Sacred Heart at the University of Notre Dame.

Isaac Hecker

Isaac Hecker (1819–88) was a convert of Brownson's before either of them encountered Catholicism, and despite many differences, their later lives ran in parallel channels as interpreters and defenders of the Roman Catholic church in democratic America. Both of them were just as interested in changing the attitudes of their adopted church as the Protestantism they left behind.

Born in New York to a modestly situated family of German immigrants, Hecker was first a Methodist. Very early his concern for the plight of working men had led him to be active in the antimonopoly faction of the Locofoco Democrats. He attended a lecture by Brownson in 1841, and from this meeting grew other associations that took Hecker to Boston, Concord, and finally, to both Brook Farm and Bronson Alcott's utopian fiasco at Fruitlands. Intensely contemplative and religious by nature, Hecker was drawn to Catholicism for quite different reasons than was Brownson, though it was the latter's advocacy that triggered his own. He entered the Roman church on 2 August 1844, more than two months before his mentor, and in the following summer, along with two recent converts from the Episcopal church, he sailed for Saint Trond in the Netherlands for his novitiate as a Redemptorist. A year later he took his vows, and in October 1849 he was ordained.

Hecker had chosen to enter the austere and ascetic Congregation of the Most Holy Redeemer (Congregatio SS. Redemptoris), founded in 1732 by Saint Alphonsus Liguori "to preach the gospel to the poor." During the succeeding century the Redemptorists had spread rapidly into most European countries, and in the United States they were performing valuable services among German immigrants. Almost immediately upon his return to the United States in 1851, Hecker became an active member of a Redemptorist team of parish revival missioners that achieved outstanding success in almost every part of the country. Hecker was even one of the three nominees for the vacant see of Natchez.

The appointment of a new Redemptorist provincial in 1854, however, brought these activities to an end; and in the midst of the ensuing difficulties, a small group of young American members of the order (all of them converts) informally delegated Hecker to present their case to the order's rector major in Rome. This group desired to found a distinctly American house where the English language (rather than German) would be used, and which would have as its primary missionary concern American Protestants rather than immigrants. But the rector major of the order was of another mind. For having made the visit to Rome Hecker was charged with disobedience, and dismissal would have shortly followed had he not won powerful support in the papal Curia. At last, after seven anxious months of working and waiting, he and his four associates received from Pope Pius IX a dispensation from their Redemptorist vows and permission to organize a new congregation with a specific mission to non-Catholic America.

After his Roman triumph Hecker sailed for America in April 1858, and by July he had won Archbishop Hughes's approval of the "Program of Rule" for the Congregation of Missionary Priests of Saint Paul the Apostle (CSP). Except for the substitution of a voluntary agreement in place of vows, the rule provided for a religious life very similar to that of other orders, notably the Redemptorists. At first their work consisted largely of preaching missions to Catholic parishes; but in 1859, having been assigned a parish in (then) suburban 59th Street, they occupied their own convent and church in New York. In 1865 they founded the *Catholic World* (the church's first general monthly magazine) and soon afterward they began a tract society to distribute far and wide the appealing and highly intelligent apologetic literature for which the Paulist Fathers were rapidly becoming famous. In all of their work they sought to confront Protestant America not with the traditional type of polemic, but with the sort of positive and comforting message that characterized Father Hecker's two most widely read books: *Questions of the Soul* (1855) and *Aspirations of Nature* (1857). Through these books and countless other articles Hecker accomplished what Brownson with his fiery, dogmatic temperament never could:

a genuinely persuasive portrayal of Catholicism as an answer to man's spiritual dilemmas and as a fulfillment and guarantee of democracy's highest ideals.

Even while commending his church to non-Catholics, Hecker and his Paulists became an extremely significant force within the Roman church as champions of a revised estimate of America, with its freedom, voluntary churches, and church-state separation, as an environment for Roman Catholicism. "Heckerism," to use a term that later gained controversial currency, became a recognizable point of view. Its foundation, of course, was a firm commitment to the dogmatic tradition; Hecker was not a "Minimalist" in doctrinal matters as was sometimes charged, and certainly not a Modernist. The closest he came to doctrinal revision was in the field of ethics, where he accented the "active" virtues rather than the "passive" emphasis of classic monasticism; and with regard to the Holy Spirit, where he stated his views so fervently that some suspected a depreciation of the instituted church. Like many American bishops, Hecker thought that the constitutions on papal infallibility of the Vatican Council of 1869–70 were inopportune and unnecessary. His greatest influence undoubtedly resulted from the Paulists' central campaign, which was at once reformatory and apologetic: to increase the rapport of the Roman Catholic church with democratic institutions and with modern modes of thought. Probably no nineteenth-century Roman Catholic in America so clearly foreshadowed the *aggiornamento* which Pope John XXIII would begin to call for when he became pope—on the centenary of the Paulists' founding.

When Hecker died in 1888 the Paulists were occupying their new church in New York, then the city's largest after Saint Patrick's Cathedral. The congregation continued to show modest but steady growth. At the turn of the century they numbered over 70 priests (in addition to novices and seminarians), and by 1965 this number had risen to 265. From the start, however, Paulist influence had never been a function of the order's size. During most of its first century it was a leading force in the "Americanist" movement in the church. Contributing much to Paulist effectiveness was the Apostolic Mission House founded in 1902 at Catholic University in Washington, D.C., to train priests for the apostolate to non-Catholic America. Its founder and rector was Father Walter Elliott (1842–1928), a Roman Catholic lawyer and

Civil War veteran whom Hecker had won for the Paulist priesthood in 1867. Few did more than he to continue the congregation's spirit and aims after Hecker's death. Elliott also did much to extend Hecker's personal influence beyond the grave, with his *Life of Father Hecker* in 1891. The translation of this book into French made "Heckerism" the focus of international controversy. The dramatic series of events that constitute the great Americanism crisis, however, is the concern of a later chapter in this history.

34

ANTI-CATHOLICISM AND THE NATIVIST MOVEMENT

During the first half of the nineteenth century the Roman Catholic church in the United States ceased to be a persecuted, numerically insignificant body and became the largest church in the country. Due to this unexpected shift in the nation's denominational equilibrium, America experienced the most violent period of religious discord in its history. Local, state, and national politics became involved, and in a culminating phase of the struggle, a bitter and secretive form of anti-Catholic nativism reached the very threshold of national power. Never before or since have religion and American politics been more explicitly interrelated, nor has ethnic conflict reached such ugly dimensions.

The basic reasons for such eruptions are not altogether mysterious. The inner security of individuals rests upon a sense of group identity. Groups define themselves against other groups. People are also disturbed by rapid social change. When one of the transitional factors is a rapidly accelerating immigration rate which disrupts established group relationships, a strong response is likely to ensue. Xenophobia is thus latent in almost every self-conscious people, and especially near the surface in a country which has only recently achieved full national status and which is vigorously engaged on many fronts in asserting its special character and destiny.

Within the Roman Catholic church itself, ethnic tensions played an exceedingly active role. Even distinguished prelates heightened the unrest; and during the heyday of trusteeism these fears and jealousies flared up in a continual series of power struggles. From New York to Charleston, and as far west as Saint Louis and New Orleans, Americans beheld a bitter struggle between French, Irish, and German elements in the Roman Catholic church. When conflicts of such intensity could break out *within* Catholicism, it is scarcely surprising that more violent conflicts and fiercer disagreements should arise between this increasingly assertive church and the great body of non-Catholic Americans.

A full explanation of American nativism and anti-Catholicism, however, requires consideration of peculiarly American factors. The subfoundation of nativism was the militant religious tradition which had been a basic element of Anglo-American thinking since the days when Queen Elizabeth led the Protestant cause against Philip of Spain and all the allies of popery. This sentiment became still more explicit and fervent among the Puritans, who carried it in one form or another to all the American colonies. Here it was kept alive by the imperial threat of France and Spain. These attitudes nourished the view that the United States had a special responsibility to realize its destiny as a Protestant nation. Emotional revivalism intensified such views even as it emptied them of doctrinal content. Finally, to many Protestants who were distressed by intersectarian conflict, anti-Catholicism offered a motive for Protestant solidarity and reunion.

To this aggressive Puritanic impulse was added the characteristic bias of the Enlightenment, which was, if anything, more negative. To a *philosophe* like Thomas Jefferson, the Roman Catholic church was simply the most powerful—and therefore the most dangerous—institutionalization of medieval superstition, sectarian narrowness, and monarchical despotism in religion. This "enlightened" form of anti-Catholicism figured prominently in the denunciation of the Quebec Act by the First Continental Congress, and it persisted long after the revolutionary era.

Resting on these foundations was the somewhat rambling structure of the American Protestant "quasi-establishment," which was enjoying its heyday of public influence between 1815 and 1860. Its moral attitudes and basic teachings were honored by lawmakers, and dominated newspapers and textbooks. The faculties and curriculum of the public schools and even state universities were molded according to its specifications. Any threat to this establishment, needless to say, would be strenuously resisted. There were also social, political, and economic factors which intensified group conflict.

The social factor was probably foremost: urban concentrations of working people were an obvious intrusion on the traditional patterns of American life. America's middle and upper classes would have reacted with consternation even if this new segment of society had been drawn entirely from older American stock (as indeed it was in some areas). The disruption of America's agrarian dream could not but disturb even the most thoughtful and humane. Protestant reformers had for years been castigating the strong thirst for gin and the disorderliness of the "lower orders," but now immigration and the growth of cities added an identifiable brogue and a new religious dimension to the old problem.

Political fears enlarged and stimulated this intolerance. The Federalist-National Republican-Whig tradition of American conservatism was put under severe strain by the widening popular base of politics. Every immigrant ship at the wharf made the older political elites more apprehensive about the country's future. With the politically adept, ideologically united Irish strengthening the Democratic hosts of Jackson and Van Buren, it seemed that decency, order, justice, and sound social principles (i.e. a conservatively structured society) were doomed. Since the Democratic party was far better geared (both ideologically and organizationally) to mobilize the immigrant population, a strong temptation to exploit popular fears was placed before opposition aspirants, and many political leaders, as well as voters, quickly yielded.

It may be stated parenthetically that the political needs and the fears of a conspiracy against democratic institutions which brought nativism into the anti-Jacksonian camp also fostered the anti-Masonic movement. The Christian opposition to Masonry was of long standing; and in 1798, when Jeffersonianism and the "French mania" were undermining the Federalist order, Jedidiah Morse of anti-Unitarian fame had raised the specter of subversion by the Bavarian Illuminati. In 1827 the old antipathy for the Masonic Lodge broke out again when William Morgan of Batavia, New York, was abducted and apparently murdered for exposing lodge secrets. Even the Book of Mormon reflects this uproar.[1] With

[1] For references to secret societies in the Book of Mormon, see Helaman 6:18, 19–26; Ether 8:15–26, and many other passages. During the Nauvoo period, on the other hand, Joseph Smith

much aid from evangelical ministers, William Henry Seward of New York, Thaddeus Stevens of Pennsylvania, John Quincy Adams of Massachusetts, and many opponents of Jackson in other states harnessed the resultant anti-Masonism into an effective political movement. It proved powerless on the national level, and by 1831 its independent life was almost over; but its great popularity in several states provided considerable voting strength to the Whig party. Soon Mormonism itself became the object of sustained attack because it, too, seemed to subvert American democratic aspirations and to violate prevailing views of religious orthodoxy. In the North a very similar countersubversionary campaign was directed against the "Slavocracy" on the grounds that it was the slaveholder's conspiracy with designs on ultimate governmental power. Anti-Masonry proved to be the most ephemeral of these crusades, yet the gravitation of all four toward the Republican party when it was formed points to the existence of a certain ground beneath them.

Finally, there were economic pressures. The influx of cheap labor brought an outcry, and often outright violence, from those who suffered from it—or thought they did. Later in the nineteenth century, neither the pope nor the American hierarchy of the Roman church could force German-American laborers to welcome Polish or Italian Catholic immigrants to their society or to their churches. In the twentieth century some of the harshest behavior toward Negroes and Puerto Ricans has come from the whites and blacks who were most imperiled by competition in the labor market. In the Jacksonian period, native American labor reacted to the Irish immigrants in a similar manner, making them objects of derision and aggression. To make matters worse, the immigrants were often jobless, and thus they began to fill the almshouses of coastal cities and to require a large proportion of the funds available for charity. By 1837 there were 105,000 paupers in

---

showed a positive interest in the secrecy and ceremonial aspects of Masonry. In this respect he reflected a propensity of vast numbers of Americans who before long would be flocking not only to Masonic lodges, but to many other national lodge organizations and (in the colleges) to various secret fraternities. Lodges as such soon ceased to be an object of concerted criticism except from the Catholic and Lutheran churches. For many they seemed to satisfy social needs and a yearning for rites and ceremonies that Protestantism lacked. For many others they seem to have provided a religious alternative to the churches.

the country, of whom perhaps half had immigrated recently. New York City alone in that year devoted $280,000 to their care.

In summary, it may be said that the lot of the immigrant has rarely been made easy by the receiving population, and that there were many factors in the American situation during the first half of the nineteenth century which conduced to make his plight harder than usual. Given the swiftly increasing immigration rate, these factors provided the materials for a sordid chapter in the nation's history. Yet it is equally important to bear in mind that most Americans favored immigration until the twentieth century, despite many campaigns to close the gates. One of the most remarkable facts about America's nativism was its inability to obtain significant supporting legislation. When successive showdowns came, the force of the movement proved illusory. Too many Americans, it seemed, always loved—or needed—the "foreigners."

ANTI-CATHOLIC AGITATION

Colonial history is full of overt and explicit anti-Catholicism. In the seventeenth century, as the Protestant obverse of Louis XIV's fierce dragonnades against the Huguenots, American Catholics faced disabilities in every colony, even Maryland. In some cases this legislation was supported by the very Huguenots who had fled France for their lives. After 1688 the principle of toleration emerging from the Anglo-American experience of religious pluralism gradually began to find practical expression, and the development of the idea of equality during the American Revolution produced further moderating effects. Even so, seven of the original thirteen colonies carried some kind of anti-Catholic legislation into the national period, the Bill of Rights notwithstanding.

Late in the 1820s, however, a new kind of anti-Catholic mood began to flow in American life, gradually changing its form and becoming increasingly political both in action and in ideology. Religious and political adventurers, profit seekers, publicity hounds, fanatics, opportunists, "joiners" of all kinds, and some men who in retrospect seem almost mad played their unseemly roles. Yet respectable church leaders did not avoid the fray, abetted by the great interdenominational voluntary associations and puritanical movements for temperance and Sabbath reform. Even the founding of the Evangelical Alliance in 1846 must be understood in this context. Horace Bushnell worked for its formation chiefly on anti-Catholic grounds, and he expressed his disgust when it adopted more positively evangelical aims. The Lutheran proponent of the alliance, Samuel S. Schmucker, also combined nativism with his desires for a "fraternal union" of Protestant churches, though in actuality the alliance took a very elevated stand on this issue. The essential unity of the "Protestant Crusade," however, and the peculiar ways in which it differs from colonial anti-Catholicism can be perceived only in a survey of its history down to the eclipse of the movement by the slavery issue, secession, and war.

As the immigrants kept coming and the Roman church kept growing, grave doubts about the future of American democracy began to displace the earlier optimism. During the 1820s, when the battle began to reach new heights of intensity and new depths of vulgarity, other catalysts besides immigration statistics began to have their effect. In 1827 Pope Leo XII announced a papal jubilee. In 1829 the First Provincial Council not only made the growth of American Catholicism manifest, but also castigated the King James Version of the Bible and encouraged the founding of parochial schools. In the same year the English Catholic Emancipation Bill provoked a tremendous outpouring of "No Popery" literature which quickly made its way into the United States and Canada.

As a result of such provocations, churches joined individuals in protest. In their pastoral letter of 1829 the Episcopal bishops warned of papist perils. The many evangelical periodicals founded to advance the Second Awakening gave increasingly more space to anti-Catholic writings. The very influential *New York Observer* (founded 1823) was particularly active in this cause, and it was joined in the next decade by a considerable brood of specifically nativist magazines. The *Protestant*, founded in 1830 by George Bourne, has the dubious distinction of chronological priority, though it soon gave place to the *Protestant Vindicator*, founded in 1834 by the Reverend William Craig Brownlee. This Dutch Reformed minister, who for several years had been the leading light in New York anti-Catholic circles, further augmented his influence in 1836 by helping to found the American Society to Promote the Principles of the Protestant Reformation. Organized along the interdenominational lines which had become standard for almost all evangelical and reformatory causes of the period, this was a voluntary association with a national agency and local auxiliary societies. The *Protestant Vindicator* became its official organ.

Roman Catholic publications naturally took up the gauntlet. The *United States Catholic Miscellany*, founded in 1822 by Bishop John England of South Carolina, was among the earliest—and most elevated. It was soon joined by vigorous papers in Boston, Philadelphia, and New York, and in 1827 the Catholic Tract Society was formed. Through these and many other channels the controversy was prosecuted in very strenuous terms, with the individual papers often reporting or featuring special debates between well-known figures. As the years went by, formal debates and recognizably theological discussion came to play an increasingly large role, but in the 1830s unprincipled exaggerations tended to preoccupy the Protestant forces, while desperate efforts at correction and contradiction were prominent in the Catholic papers. Bishops and priests had to take time off from the overwhelming problems of an immigrant church to deny (and somehow try to prove) that subterranean dungeons for the murder and burial of illegitimate babies were not standard furnishings in a Roman Catholic convent. So extreme was the tenor of this journalism that the highly inflammatory *Protestant* readily accepted as authentic and published a whole series of articles signed "Cranmer"—which turned out later to have been written as parodies of nativist writings by none other than John Hughes, later bishop of New York.

The horror literature, which often had a strong salacious appeal, found an even more popular outlet in book form. The first sensation in this category was published in Boston, where no Puritan raised a cry to have it banned. *Six Months in a Convent* (1835) purported to be the confessions of one Rebecca Theresa Reed, a well-known figure in Boston because of her uncertain connections with the Ursuline convent there. Despite a detailed answer by the mother superior, the book was widely praised in the Protestant press and became a best seller. Lurid though Rebecca Reed's account may have been, it seemed pale and innocuous when compared with Maria Monk's *Awful Disclosures of the Hotel Dieu Nunnery of Montreal* (1836), which was published (and in large part written) by a group of New York anti-Catholics, lay and clerical. Actually her popularity, as well as the public's credulity, had been seriously undermined by 1837 when her *Further Disclosures* appeared; and no small part of this undermining was accomplished by the even more transparent fraudulency of a companion piece, *The Escape of Sainte Frances Patrick, Another Nun from the Hotel Dieu Nunnery of Montreal,* published by an anti-Catholic competitor of the Maria Monk clique. Miss Monk (if we may call her that) had been quite forgotten by her former sponsors in 1849, when she died in prison after having been arrested for picking the pockets of her "companion" in a house of ill-fame. But her books continued to sell, reaching the 300,000 mark by 1860 and appearing in new editions after the Civil War (and in still another in 1960). It earned, as Professor Billington says, "the questionable distinction of being the 'Uncle Tom's Cabin of Know-Nothingism.' "[2]

But the conflict did not begin and end with mere words. In Boston, several years of mounting tension, punctuated by frequent outbreaks between Yankee and Irish workingmen and a great many anti-Catholic sermons, finally culminated on the night of 11 August 1834. A well-organized group burned the Ursuline convent in Charlestown which until then had been conducting a successful girls' school. The whole nation was shocked by this incident, and a flood of laments and disclaimers followed. Yet the remorse seemed to have been brief and limited. Men of prominence soon made plans for publishing Rebecca Reed's confessions, while the "meaner sort" made municipal heroes out of the men who were tried for arson and acquitted.

Lyman Beecher, whose sermons were at least indirectly related to the Ursuline tragedy, responded by publishing his *Plea for the West* (1834). It contains the substance of his fund-raising messages for Lane Theological Seminary in Cincinnati, of which he had been president since 1832. In this masterpiece of propaganda Beecher opens with a paean to the nation's destiny, an exposition of Jonathan Edwards's belief that the millennium would commence in America. But this exordium is followed by a 140-page tirade which depicts the pope and Europe's reactionary kings, with the Austrian

2 Ray A. Billington, *The Protestant Crusade, 1800–1860*, p. 108.

emperor at their head and Catholic immigrants for agents, as engaged in an organized conspiracy to take over the Mississippi Valley.

> "The spirit of the age," which Bonaparte says dethroned him, is moving on to put an end in Europe to Catholic domination, creating the necessity of making reprisals abroad for what liberty conquers at home. . . . Clouds like the locusts of Egypt are rising from the hills and plains of Europe, and on the wings of every wind, are coming over to settle down upon our fair fields; while millions, moved by the noise of their rising and cheered by the news of their safe arrival and green pastures, are preparing for flight in an endless succession. . . .
> No design! How does it happen that their duty, and the analogy of their past policy, and their profession in Europe, and their predictions and exultation in this country, and their deeds, should come together accidentally with such admirable indications of design?[3]

Taking a cue from Samuel F. B. Morse, Beecher put nativism and anti-Catholicism on a common ideological footing; and as this mode of thinking grew more prevalent, the popular strength of the Protestant crusade increased, especially since "native American" organizations and papers were springing up in almost all of the eastern cities due to growing economic pressures, certain honest fears for the functioning of democratic institutions, and an irrational repugnance for aliens.

These years also mark the emergence of nativistic anti-Catholicism as an intensely relevant political force, with Samuel F. B. Morse playing a prominent role. A son of the anti-Unitarian controversialist Jedidiah Morse, but best remembered for his invention of the telegraph and very worthy of remembrance for his contributions to American painting, Morse is said to have been incited to enter the nativist campaign by a soldier in Rome who knocked off his hat as a religious procession passed by. The anonymous letters which he began writing to the *New York Observer* were republished quickly in a volume entitled *Foreign Conspiracy against the Liberties of the United States* (1834). Through many editions it purveyed the theory which Beecher found so

[3] Lyman Beecher, *Plea for the West*, 2d ed. (Cincinnati, 1835), pp. 72, 117, 129.

convincing—that the Holy Alliance, through the pope, the Jesuits, and the hierarchy, was conspiring to subvert democracy by promoting Catholic immigration to America.

> What then shall be done? [Morse asked.] Shall Protestants organize themselves into a political union after the manner of the Papists, and the various classes of industry and even of *foreigners* in the country? Shall they form an Anti Popery Union, and take their places among this strange medley of conflicting interests? And why should they not?[4]

Morse became a nativist candidate for mayor of New York City in 1836, but he was defeated because his Democratic background gave him no hold on the Whig vote. A year later, when Whiggery was placated, nativists carried the election.

More significant still was the widening of the political rift between 1840 and 1842 as a result of the school issue. In this crisis Bishop John Hughes took the initiative, demanding a share of public funds for Catholic schools and roundly condemning the Protestant character of existing instruction, particularly their practice of reading the King James Version of the Bible. Thwarted at every turn and ignored by the major parties, Hughes finally entered a Catholic party in the contest of 1841, and taught New York City Democrats a lesson by whittling away their margin of victory. Under Governor William H. Seward, state legislation such as Bishop Hughes had desired was finally passed, but in the city itself nativist political strength prevented Hughes from reaping much more than a reputation for crafty political manipulation and jesuitical argument. This bishop thus did much to bring New York City's "American Republican" party into existence, to guarantee its successes there, and to provide the basis for its expansion as a national movement.

In May 1844 violence erupted in connection with meetings called by the American Republican party in Kensington, a suburb of Philadelphia, and one nativist, George Shiffler, lost his life. This disturbance led to the wildest and bloodiest riot-

[4] "Can the right with any propriety be refused to American Christians?" he asked in a footnote—and answered affirmatively (Brutus [Samuel F. B. Morse], *Foreign Conspiracy against the Liberties of the United States*, rev. ed. [New York, 1835], pp. 125–26).

ing of the entire crusade. Two Roman Catholic churches and dozens of Irish homes were burned, militia fired point-blank upon advancing crowds, a cannon was turned against the soldiers guarding Saint Philip Neri Church, and for three days mob rule prevailed in the city and its environs. The final toll was thirteen dead and over fifty wounded. Bishop Kenrick felt obliged "to suspend the exercises of public worship in the Catholic churches which still remain, until it can be resumed with safety."

When the same sort of hostilities under the same auspices threatened New York City a few days later, Bishop Hughes acted with his customary decisiveness. He stationed large numbers of fully armed men around every Catholic church, and by such a show of strength (which neither police nor militia had done in Philadelphia or would have done in New York), he prevented ominous nativist mass meetings from turning into anti-Catholic mobs. Thus again, ten years after the burning of the Ursuline convent in Boston, bigotry had resulted in violence.

THE RISE AND FALL OF KNOW-NOTHINGISM

Before the memory of these tense days had faded, America had a new diversion which also had indirect anti-Catholic implications. On 25 April 1846, shots were exchanged on the disputed Texas border, and soon the nation was embroiled in the Mexican War. Nativistic anti-Catholicism declined in the period from 1845 to 1850 as Americans were swept up in the momentous issues of war and territorial expansion and as economic conditions improved. Despite an enormous rise in the flow of immigration, tempers cooled. Many northern evangelicals turned to attacking the war as a slaveholder's conspiracy. A number of fanatics including William Craig Brownlee retired or lost their prominence, to be replaced by the more respectable type of controversialist exemplified by Nicholas Murray, a Presbyterian minister in Elizabeth, New Jersey. The specifically Protestant element in the movement turned to more positive approaches, especially through existing missionary and educational agencies. Brownlee's intemperate society and journal were replaced by the far more constructive American Protestant Society and its *American Protestant Magazine*. In 1849 the American and Foreign Christian

Union was organized with a program for diffusing "the principles of Religious Liberty, and a pure and Evangelical Christianity, both at home and abroad, wherever a corrupted Christianity exists." Its instruments were to be "light and love." Robert Baird's famous book *Religion in America* (1844) is a memorial of its relatively benign spirit. By far the most constructive of such organizational efforts was the Evangelical Alliance formed in London in 1846 by some fifty denominations of Great Britain and America.

While these religious developments unfolded, anti-Catholic sentiment broadened out through the middle and upper classes of "American" ancestry, becoming diluted but not disappearing as it blended with vague feelings of Anglo-Saxon pride and class consciousness. In the process, it helped to palliate Whig frustrations by providing something that looked like an "issue" to a party that had always had difficulty in finding anything more substantial than Clay's compromises, Webster's rhetoric, Tippecanoe, log cabins, and an intense distaste for Jackson. The almost incredible increase in immigration during the late forties and early fifties served meanwhile to give some basis to nativistic concern. It should be recalled that whereas the total immigration in the twenties was 128,452 and in the thirties 538,381, in the fifties it reached 2,811,554. Between 1850 and 1860, indeed, almost a third of the nation's population growth—from 23,191,000 to 31,443,000—was accounted for by immigration. Pauperism, labor-class rowdyism, and crime statistics showed that the country was facing a new kind of social problem, although immigration was merely the most easily exploited factor.

The impulse for nativism's sensational surge came from a secret "patriotic" society, the Order of the Star-Spangled Banner, founded by Charles B. Allen of New York in 1849 and reorganized by James W. Barker, a merchant, also of New York, in 1852. By 1854 internal difficulties and organizational kinks had been straightened out, and the entire "lodge" was set up on a federal basis with local, district, state, and national councils, each responsible for political decisions within its own jurisdiction. Only American-born Protestants without Catholic wives or parents were eligible; upon joining they swore to oppose the election of foreigners and Roman Catholics and to renounce other political ties. If a member advanced to the exalted second degree of the order, he was eligible for office in the order and for nomination by the order to public office. At this rank he had to swear that he would not appoint foreigners or Roman Catholics to public office and that he would remove them wherever it was legally possible. Upon initiation the member was introduced to all the glories of a secret lodge: grand titles, special handclasps, passwords, distress signals, and other types of mumbo-jumbo. George Washington's order, "put only Americans on guard tonight," was a favorite slogan. As a political entity, the body was called officially the American party; but because of their secretiveness and their frequent reliance on "I don't know," they were known popularly as the Know-Nothings.

As early as 1852 they exerted a real, though mysterious, influence in New York City politics. But the national Democratic victory which brought Franklin Pierce to the White House, allegedly on the strength of the "foreign" vote, spurred the Know-Nothings to greater activity during 1853 and 1854. In local and state elections in the spring and summer of 1854, they began to win sensational victories, sometimes snatching offices from unopposed candidates with write-in votes. By fall they were the rage of the day, and sent seventy-five men to Congress. In Massachusetts they won every state contest except in the House of Representatives, where one Whig and one Free Soiler won the right to sit with 376 Know-Nothings. In 1855 they also did very well in Rhode Island, New Hampshire, Connecticut, Maryland, and Kentucky; not much worse in Tennessee, New York, and Pennsylvania; and they very nearly carried Virginia, Georgia, Alabama, Mississippi, and Louisiana. A presidential victory and control of the national Congress appeared to be in sight for 1856.

The true sensation of 1856, however, was not a Know-Nothing sweep but the phenomenal strength of an even younger party, the Republican, which had come into existence in 1854. Ever more serious threats to national unity had been felt ever since the Mexican War and the Compromise of 1850 with its fugitive slave law. Then came the Kansas-Nebraska Act, which repealed the Missouri Compromise and provided for popular sovereignty in the new territories. Senator Charles Sumner said at the time that it was "at once the worst and best Bill on which Congress ever acted; the worst because it was a victory for the Slave Power, the best because it annuls all past compromises with slavery, and makes all future compromises impossible." Since the Know-Nothing party was at best a compromise on the slavery issue, its position did become impossible. At its national council of 1855 Senator Henry Wilson of Massachusetts, an abolitionist who had bored from within, led the party's northern delegates to repudiate the proslavery platform.

By 1856 Know-Nothing strength lay almost wholly in the South, where the party's unionism made it an expression of moderation. In searching for a standard bearer, they could find none better than the innocuous incumbent, Millard Fillmore, whom the Whigs also nominated. Fillmore had joined the Know-Nothing party for what political good it might do him, but he was little interested in nativism and went down to defeat essentially as a Whig. The Know-Nothing party survived only in Maryland and in a few other localities. As a political power it was dead, except for its continuing effect on the Republican party which absorbed—and held—most of the northern nativists as well as the main anti-Masonic remnant.

What explains the rise and fall of the political Know-Nothingism? Taking most obvious things first, it rose because two centuries of antipopery made a large part of the American population suspicious of Roman Catholics, and because immigration as well as many other social, economic, and political specters aroused fears of the foreigner. David Brion Davis isolates another important factor by noting how the Catholic stereotype, like that of Mormon and Mason, embodied "those traits that were precise antitheses of American ideals . . . an inverted image of Jacksonian democracy."[5] One may suggest a corollary to this insight: that the anti-Catholic attitudes of most participants in the antislavery movement were steadily heightened because the Roman Catholic hierarchy remained noncommittal on slavery and almost completely unrepresented in the abolitionist crusade. One subversive power seemed to be abetting the other.

Roman Catholic developments also conspired to aggravate American suspicions during these years. From Europe came persistent reports of the church's opposition to the revolutions of 1848, including its successful suppression of the Hungar-

[5] "Some Themes of Counter-Subversion: An Analysis of Anti-Masonic, Anti-Catholic, and Anti-Mormon Literature," *Mississippi Valley Historical Review* 47 (September 1960): 208; see also Davis's *Fear of Conspiracy: Images of UnAmerican Subversion.*

ian independence movement which had endeared itself to American hearts. This was brought forcefully to public attention in 1852 by the nationwide tour of Louis Kossuth, who had led that abortive revolt, and by many other anticlerical lecturers, sensationalists, and intellectuals, some of them in exile. These conflicts did not remain remote European questions, however, for the old trusteeship question flared up again in so virulent a way that Bishop Timon of Buffalo, New York, had to place a German church (Saint Louis) in that city under interdict in 1851. When John Hughes, now an archbishop, began agitation for legislation vesting all church properties in the hierarchy, the New York legislature reacted by passing in 1855 a bill requiring lay trusteeship. Then, as if to magnify both European reaction and the trustee problem in American eyes, Pius IX (who had just crushed a republican revolution in Rome itself) sent Monsignor Gaetano Bedini to the United States as a papal representative empowered to deal with the recalcitrant trustees. As an administrator of the Papal States, Bedini had helped to quell the upsurge of Italian liberalism in 1848. This role was exaggerated enormously by all the forces of anti-Catholicism in this country; but even if he had played no role at all in that affair, his coming would have been denounced as foreign intervention. His tour of the country in 1853–54 was a riot-ridden disaster which heads the list of Roman Catholic blunders during this period. Bedini probably stimulated as many Know-Nothing votes as any other single factor.

Despite all these very good reasons for the success of Know-Nothingism, one must not lose sight of the transitoriness of its triumph. It fell so swiftly and so resoundingly because, in the last analysis, the American people were more seriously divided by the slavery issue than by ethnic or religious issues. The latter issues were susceptible to a pluralistic settlement, the former was not; the country could be half "foreign," but not half slave. Had Senator Douglas decided one or two years earlier to run the Kansas-Nebraska Act through the gauntlet of the American conscience, political Know-Nothingism might be remembered as only a minor localized phenomenon. Yet at least two other factors also hastened its downfall: the continual eruptions of violence that accompanied campaigns in which nativists were active, and the inescapable contradiction between Know-Nothing methods—the sinister aspect of a large political party conducting its affairs in secrecy—and the anticonspiratorial ideals which most Americans honored.

The fall of Know Nothingism was as abrupt as its rise. However deep Protestant convictions about the errors of Rome may have been (and they were held at least as firmly as Roman Catholic views of Protestant error), however thoroughly anti-Catholic attitudes were inculcated (and they were disseminated with a thoroughness that rivaled the indoctrination of Roman Catholics), Americans in general were not ready to deny both their moral heritage and their national ideals.[6] Know-Nothingism failed most completely in the Old Northwest, where immigrants and Roman Catholics were more familiar to native Protestant Americans because they mingled on equal terms and in about equal numbers.

Yet antagonism and conflict continued. Just as anti-Catholic nativism was a blight on the reformist movements of antebellum America, so it would be after the Civil War. Against a background of rapid social change, both nativism and anti-Catholicism (joined in due course by anti-Semitism) would again become ugly realities. Race relations would also deteriorate steadily. A nation of immigrants dedicated to the proposition that all men are created equal would again postpone the new birth of freedom. Americans were discovering that Crèvecoeur's "melting pot" was easier to conceive than to realize. Not everyone wanted to be melted.[7]

[6] The parenthetical references in this sentence merely point to the stand-off in Catholic-Protestant relations that had prevailed since the excommunication of Luther (1520) and of Queen Elizabeth (1570). It would be another century before the "revolution" of Pope John XXIII would bring the Counter-Reformation to an end.

[7] See the quotation from *Letters from an American Farmer,* p. 34 above.

35

THE EARLY GROWTH OF JUDAISM

In proportion to its numbers, the Jewish community in America was more profoundly revolutionized by nineteenth-century immigration than any other. A tiny group that numbered scarcely a half-dozen active congregations when the century opened grew eight-fold in as many years, largely due to the immigration of German Jews. By 1880 this group had not only achieved a most remarkable accommodation to the American scene, but had institutionalized a new and distinct stage in the history of Judaism.

Jews had been involved in American history from the start. At least two Jews were aboard the ships of Columbus, and one scholar has argued that the admiral himself was a wandering Jew. During succeeding decades other Jews undoubtedly found their way into the American empires of Spain and Portugal. Yet the year 1492 is remembered for other events —events that explain why "Spanish Jews" were rare in New Spain, and why the first American synagogue was founded in New Amsterdam. In 1492 the Moors were forced from their last foothold on the Iberian Peninsula, and in the same year the systematic persecution of Jews within Spanish domains began. The full significance of these events cannot be appreciated, however, without a brief digression on the dispersion of Israel.

THE LONG, LONG HISTORY OF ISRAEL

The dispersion of Israel might be said to begin in 722 B.C.E. (Before the Common Era), when the Assyrian hosts of Sargon entered Samaria, the capital city of the Northern

Kingdom (Israel), and carried off thirty thousand of its people, leaving others to be taken captive in later years. When in 586 the Southern Kingdom (Judah) fell, Jerusalem was taken by Babylonians who during the preceding decades had overpowered both Assyria and Egypt. The famous Babylonian Captivity followed, while other Jews established refugee communities in Egypt and still others maintained a disorganized existence in Palestine. Babylonian dominance yielded to Persian rule in 538, when Cyrus the Great took Babylon, and Jews were allowed to return to their land.

Around the year 400 a great work of reconstruction was begun by these earliest of Zionists under Ezra and Nehemiah. They rebuilt Jerusalem and the Temple, and undertook as well a decisive reshaping of tradition, in which Jewish religion inevitably took on a less political and more priestly aspect. The Scriptures were given more definite form and status, and the Chosen People became a religious and cultic entity, a people of the Book more than an autonomous national state. The conquest of Palestine by Alexander the Great in 332 inaugurated an era of limited Jewish autonomy and religious freedom under Greek suzerainty, though this later had to be fought for again and wrested from the Selucid emperors who ruled in the Middle East after Alexander's death. The period of independence won by the Maccabees in 167 was cut short by the Roman conquest in 63 B.C.E., an event which marked the beginning of still another period of heavily qualified autonomy lasting until the destruction of the Temple by Titus and his Roman army in 70 C.E. (of the Common Era).

The historical period between the desecration of the Temple by the post-Alexandrian ruler Antiochus Epiphanes in 169 B.C.E. and its destruction by Titus was marked by outrage, factionalism, and bloodshed; yet in one governmental arrangement or another—as even the Christian New Testament reveals—the historic faith and worship of Israel was maintained. The impact of Hellenistic culture and religion was kept to a minimum, and Jerusalem held its place in Jewish aspirations and religious life. Not even disorganized vestiges remained after 135 C.E., however, for in that year the Emperor Hadrian put down a last desperate rebellion, renamed the city, and forbade Jews on pain of death to come within sight of Jerusalem.

With this ultimate disaster the *diaspora* (dispersion) became the fundamental circumstance of Judaism's continued existence. Yet because the dispersion of Israel had actually begun centuries before, notably during the Babylonian exile, by the opening of the Christian era Jews were gathered in various parts of the Middle East and in most of the cities of the Mediterranean world. In these scattered communities the synagogue, under the leadership of a rabbi (teacher), was the center of Jewish religious life; and in Hellenized areas the Scriptures were often read in the Septuagint version, a Greek translation made by Jewish scholars in Alexandria about 250 B.C.E. It was in Alexandria during the time of Christ that the philosopher-theologian Philo (ca. 20 B.C.E. to 42 C.E.) conceived his great accommodation of scriptural teaching and Greek (primarily late Platonic) philosophy.

The normative force that was to mold the Judaism of the coming centuries did not come from these Hellenized sources, however, nor even from the rabbinic tradition of Palestine, but primarily from those Jews who had found refuge in the Tigris and Euphrates region, the Babylonia of the ancient exile. Here under the lenient rule of the Persians they developed a way of life which produced the Talmudic commentaries on the Law. By 500 C.E. the huge Babylonian Talmud had taken definitive shape; the nature and rationale of Jewish isolationism and continuity were defined. "The law of the government is the law," they recognized; but with due allowances for alien rule, the possibilities for life under the Law of Moses were clarified and explicated. Judaism became more than ever a way of life according to the meticulously interpreted and rigorously applied provisions of the Torah. After 70 C.E. sacrifice and praise in the Temple at Jerusalem were a memory and a hope, as congregational worship in the synagogue, religious instruction by the rabbis, and above all the historic observance of Sabbath and holy days became the fundamental modes of Hebrew religion.

In the Roman Empire Jews were by no means accorded a secure place in society. Indeed, Roman laws governing their status, keeping them off the land, and limiting their occupations were to condition Jewish life in Europe for over a millennium. Yet life went on, and in every province of the empire Jews found a useful though precarious place. Those who found the restrictions unendurable drifted into regions beyond.

Then in the seventh century Islam exploded into the Levantine and Mediterranean world, expanding with dynamic, almost irresistible force. With Persia and the Byzantine Empire weakened, its sweeping conquests began under Omar (634–44). In a few decades the Ommiad Caliphate extended across the Persian Empire to the Indus River in India; and before the new century was very old, Arabia, Syria, Egypt, North Africa, and Spain were ruled from Damascus. Only at Tours in southern France in 732, the centennial of Mahomet's death, was the Moslem advance halted. In the vast realm of the Moslems the official laws against Jews were harsh, but they were so widely ignored that Jews on the whole lived a fuller and freer life under the Crescent than under the Cross.

In time a rich Jewish culture flourished at many points. Saadia ben Joseph (892–942), who as Gaon of Sura was in a sense the religious leader of Islamic Judaism, translated most of the Hebrew Scriptures into Arabic. His monumental treatise on philosophy and faith shows the remarkable degree to which Hellenic influences in Islamic thinkers were transmitted to the Jews. Spain gave rise to a particularly rich tradition. The philosopher and poet Solomon ibn-Gabirol (ca. 1021–58), whose great work *The Fountain of Life* was long thought to be the work of a Christian named Avicebron, carried Neoplatonic thought to exalted religious heights. Judah Halevi (ca. 1085–1140), born in Toledo, was one of its greatest and most versatile Jewish poets. Moses ben Maimon (Maimonides, 1135–1204), a native of Cordova who moved to Cairo, took his place with the Spanish Moslem Averroës (1126–98) and the Christian friar Thomas Aquinas (1225–74) in a great tradition of medieval philosophical theology that did much to extend the influence of Aristotle and Hellenistic rationalism.

Following the Spanish defeat of the Moors in 1492 the Jews were expelled from Spain by royal decree. They were expelled from Portugal in 1496, and the age of the Inquisition and the European ghetto began. Many Jews remained as real or apparent converts to Christianity, though they often persisted in private fidelity to the rites and faith of Judaism. But many of them—nobody knows how many—fled from Spain and Portugal to what refuge they could find in France, England, Germany, or even in eastern Mediterranean countries. In England these exiled *Sephardim* (as Jews of Iberian descent are called, see Obadiah 20) laid the foundations of the country's Jewish community. Holland, however, provided the best refuge, for Jews as for daring thinkers like Descartes and exiled English Puritans. During the seventeenth century, therefore, Jews participated in the great commercial conquests of the Dutch. They were investors in the trading companies which founded New Netherland in America; and in 1630, when the Dutch took Recife in eastern Brazil from the Portuguese, a number of Jews established residence there. When Portugal recaptured Recife in 1654, these Jews had to flee; and some of them came to New Amsterdam. With their arrival Jewish religious history in the United States begins.

JEWS IN THE BRITISH COLONIES

There were no rabbis or theologians among the early refugees from Recife; but since the only requirement for establishing a synagogue is the presence of ten adult males, this presented no problem. As soon as they could secure the right of public worship (the date is uncertain but 1685–95 seems probable) this Portuguese-speaking group formed the Congregation Shearith Israel (Remnant of Israel). By 1729 it had grown sufficiently to build a house of worship. With the passing years other Jews came to America, especially after 1740, when Parliament granted them naturalization rights in the colonies. Fifteen Jewish families came to Newport from Holland in 1658. Though this community may have died out, it later revived, and dedicated in 1763 the distinctive Touro synagogue designed by Peter Harrison of New Haven. Similar communities, largely Sephardic, grew up in other cities, including Charleston, Savannah, Richmond, and Philadelphia. But all of these groups were small: in 1773 the five hundred Jews in Charleston composed the largest such community in America. At that time there were only thirty Jewish families in New York, while other towns probably had even fewer. On the eve of the Revolution there was not a single rabbi in the American colonies. As late as 1800 all of American Jewry probably did not exceed two or three thousand.

Though small, and in some degree because it was small, the Sephardic community in the colonies was distinguished by a high sense of culture and a great competence in the ways of the world. Not all of these migrants were well-to-do;

in fact, many were poor. But as a group with greater freedom than Jews anywhere in the world, they soon took a prominent place in colonial life. In manner and dress they blended in with the rest of the people. Although when the Revolution came, like colonials generally they were of divided opinion, yet they tended toward the Patriot cause, and one of their number, Haym Salomon, participated actively. Despite its adaptation to the American life style, this Jewish community retained a devoted concern for its religious tradition of "dignified orthodoxy." (Only two years after the first arrival in America, their brethren in Amsterdam had excommunicated the great philosopher Baruch Spinoza for his daring rationalism, his critical attitude toward the Scriptures, and his nonobservant conduct.) Though no rabbis were among them during the colonial period, the chanters took on the role of ministers and a highly literate laity preserved the teachings of their tradition.

JEWS IN THE NATIONAL PERIOD

The basic homogeneity of the American Jewish community did not long outlast the colonial period. The end of the eighteenth century saw a shift in the predicament of the Jews in northern Europe. A new kind of Jewish immigration began to flow into the United States as a result of these changing circumstances, and it had three quite decisive effects: it destroyed the unity and religious consensus of the existing congregations; it served to turn the Sephardic traditionalists in upon themselves and to enliven their attachment to ancient orthodoxy; and finally, it greatly augmented the number of Jews in the nation. An understanding of these factors and their interaction requires another brief historical digression on the *Ashkenazim*.

The name for Ashkenazic Judaism stems from the reference in Jeremiah 51:27 to the kingdom of Ashkenaz, which was probably in the neighborhood of Armenia, but in medieval rabbinical literature was interpreted to mean Germany. The designation was broadened by usage to include all of those Jews whose centuries-long heritage involved habitation in north European Christendom. These people had enjoyed something of a golden age of toleration under Louis the Pious

(816–40), successor to Charlemagne; but after that, as the feudalization of Europe proceeded, society became "Jew-proof" and the ghetto with all of its concomitants became a characteristic institution. Regulations concerning these Jewish communities varied widely from one principality to another and from time to time, but isolation, persecution, and the communal existence which the laws required and which the ghetto made possible deepened the loyalty of Ashkenazic Jewry to the rabbinic tradition. As a result, its Judaism was at once deeper, narrower, and less cosmopolitan than that of the Sephardim; above all, its community life and its commitment to the Law was more intense.

With the rise of national states in the centuries after the Reformation, the Ashkenazic community itself came to be divided, though it was still unified by a strong commitment to Yiddish, Torah, and Talmudic study. Jews who moved or were forced eastward into Poland and later into Russia and the Slavic lands of the Holy Roman Empire experienced a fate very different from that of their brethren in the West. In these vast agricultural areas urban ghettos were rare, restrictions on Jewish movement and occupation were less confining, and the transformations wrought by modern commerce and industry were long retarded. The fervent piety and Orthodox ways of this eastern branch of the Ashkenazim did not enter into American history until the great migrations of the late nineteenth century. It is thus the western Ashkenazim in the more advanced German-speaking cultures that requires our prior consideration.

The Germany of 1800 was by no means the unified, heavily industrialized state that it was to become a century later. Social structures and economic life were relatively static. Antiquated taxation systems and inefficient modes of land division prevailed. After the crushing of revolutionary movements in 1830 and 1848, discontent was rife and emigration steadily increased. And since Jews continued to be harassed by many legal restrictions, they joined the exodus in increasing numbers. By 1840 the American Jewish community numbered 15,000; by 1850, 50,000; by 1860, 160,000; and by 1880, 250,000. Another estimate puts the nineteenth-century German immigration total at 5 million and the Jews among them at 200,000, with the largest number coming from Bavaria, where the anti-Semitic laws were strictest.

In the early years these Jewish immigrants were generally

poor and very limited in education and social experience. Since they were for the most part unaffected by the newer movements of "emancipation," they were relatively orthodox in belief and observance. Mayer Klein remembered his early days in New York:

> The greater part of the Jewish young men went peddling. There were two or three Jewish merchants who supplied peddlers with "Yankee notions," which they called *Kuttle Muttle*. . . . There was a synagogue in New York called the "India Rubber *shul*" because it was principally upheld by peddlers whose stock in trade was mostly suspenders. . . . All those absent from home hurried to the city on a holiday, in order to be there for the service.[1]

As the quotation suggests, they usually took up the peddling and small merchandising for which their experience (or inexperience) fitted them. For the first time in fifteen centuries, life on the land was legally open to them; but naturally enough, few took the opportunity. Because various types of retail business became their most common occupation, they tended to gather in America's cities and growing towns. Taking advantage of a rapidly expanding country, they established themselves in all parts of the nation, perhaps even more frequently in the South, for example, than in New England. In San Francisco the first *minyan* of ten men was assembled as early as 1849.

Everywhere they adapted themselves with singular success, and the federal survey of 1890 revealed the remarkable fact that by then less than 2 percent were laborers or peddlers, almost half were in business, 30 percent were in clerical or sales positions, and 5 percent in the professions; 40 percent were employing at least one servant; 20 percent, two servants and 10 percent, three or more. Increasingly in later decades as those of higher income levels also immigrated, they tended to identify themselves as Germans, and often participated in literary and musical organizations. As they made the transition to American ways, this group made an invaluable cultural contribution to the country. Religiously considered, however, emigration from Germany to America involved traumatic changes, and traditional forms of observance came

[1] Quoted in Louis Wirth, *The Ghetto* (Chicago: University of Chicago Press, 1928), p. 154.

under tremendous pressures. Because this trend bore many
similarities to European movements for emancipation, American Jews often sought guidance from the intellectual leadership developing in the cities of Germany. The leaders of
Reform Judaism thus came to have a powerful influence on
the generation or two of rabbis who provided spiritual leadership to synagogues formed by German Jewish immigrants.

What is known as the Enlightenment was chiefly a philosophical movement among the intelligentsia, though of course
the economic, social, and popular roots of this intellectual impulse were exceedingly important. As European rulers and
governments became uneasy about the presence of compulsory ghettos and irrational restrictions on Jewish activity and
dress, the laws were liberalized. Opportunities opened, and
in ever-growing numbers the Jews themselves began to yield
to the blandishments of reason and to the lure of political and
cultural—though not necessarily religious—assimilation. German Jewry began to follow in the way of the Sephardim,
even, at times, in the way of Spinoza. The real modern hero
of the *maskilim* (the enlightened) was Moses Mendelssohn
(1729–86). Born in the ghetto of Dessau, he very early made
his way to the liberal Berlin of Frederick the Great, where he
became a friend of the great poet and critic Lessing and won
early fame as the "Jewish Plato." Mendelssohn published a
German translation of the Pentateuch and became an ardent
advocate of a philosophic approach to religion and a thoroughgoing acceptance of modern scholarship and German
culture. Achieving prominence as he did just on the eve of
the French Revolution and the Napoleonic liberations of
Jewry, he made an enormous impact.

Mendelssohn remained—with whatever strain or inconsis-
tency—an observant Jew; but many of the liberated Jews,
especially young men of talent, found this very difficult. As
they became involved in the liberal political movements
aroused by the French Revolution and the revolutions of
1830 and 1848, the amount of nonobservance increased.
Some men, like Karl Marx, moved far to the left. Others, like
Heinrich Heine, Felix Mendelssohn (grandson of the philosopher), Augustus Neander (the great church historian and associate of Schleiermacher), C. P. Caspari (a strict Lutheran
confessional theologian who went to Norway), and Julius
Stahl (who became one of the great theologians and apol-
ogists for the old order in church and state) carried assimi-

lation all the way to an enthusiastic adoption of the Christian faith.

These trends and difficulties gave rise to the movement for reforming orthodox rabbinic Judaism. Moses Mendelssohn's combination of emancipation and observance seemed impossibly contradictory. Many regarded the subjection of modern men to an utterly outmoded way of life as intellectually impossible or even morally wrong, yet the complete cutting of traditional ties was worse. Facing these alternatives, the Reform movement in Judaism as a broad scholarly, philosophical, and theological impulse gradually began to take shape in the synagogues of urban Germany. At first its concerns were external: demands to the governments of various principalities for a larger measure of freedom, and revisions in the modes of worship carried on in the synagogue.

The ceremonial revisions, which involved the introduction of vernacular worship, sermons, and congregational hymns as well as the elimination of messianic prayers, naturally impinged on old commitments and brought intense conflicts to the Jewish community. This in turn drove the leaders of the movement deeper into historical investigation of the Jewish past. A Society for the Scientific Study of Judaism (*jüdische Wissenschaft*) was formed, and a brilliant tradition of historical scholarship arose. Others turned to the philosophical and theological movements most prominent in the universities, showing great intellectual distinction in deploying the dialectical thought of Hegel and Schelling in a Judaic context. David Einhorn (1809–79), an important leader first in Europe then in the United States, clearly expressed the rationale for reform:

Judaism has reached a turning-point when all . . . customs and usages as are lifeless must be abolished, partly with the object of retaining its own followers, partly to protect from moral degeneracy. In consequence of the insuperable conditions of life there has set in a violent antagonism between practice and religious conviction which will eventually cease to distress the conscience. The continuance of such a state of affairs would be the greatest misfortune that could befall Israel. On the one hand, the most important ceremonial laws are violated daily, laws which are still considered incumbent upon the Israelite; on the other hand, religious wishes and hopes are expressed in prayer which do not awaken the least response in the heart, and stand in absolute contradiction to the true spirit of Sinaitic doctrine. This must necessarily lead to one of two things, either that the religious sentiment will become completely dulled or take refuge in the bosom of some other faith. Experience has shown the futility of all attempts to breathe life into the obsolete and dead. . . . The evil which threatens to corrode gradually all the healthy bone and marrow must be completely eradicated. . . . Thus we may achieve the liberation of Judaism for ourselves and for our children, so as to prevent the estrangement from Judaism.[2]

Einhorn had been the chief rabbi of Mecklenberg-Schwerin and a leader of the movement in Germany; he had then gone to Pesth in Hungary until his congregation there was closed down after Kossuth's abortive revolution. The words quoted above were spoken at his inaugural sermon at Baltimore in 1855. In the United States it was the conjunction of leaders of his caliber with large numbers of upward mobile German Jewish immigrants gathered in hundreds of recently founded synagogues which would provide the dynamics for a major episode in American religious history. Perhaps no feature of this German Jewish wrestling with the problems of modernity and tradition was more remarkable than the fact that an almost complete transformation of historic Judaism was accomplished in little more than a single generation.

THE RISE OF REFORM JUDAISM IN THE UNITED STATES

Social distance, linguistic and cultural differences, and conflicting ritual traditions made Sephardic-Ashkenazic rela-

[2] Quoted in David Philipson, *The Reform Movement in Modern Judaism*, p. 347. Einhorn's commitment to German modes of thought was not easily exceeded; but other Jewish philosophers of religion such as Solomon Formstecher (1808–89), Samuel Hirsch (1815–89), and Solomon L. Steinheim (1789–1866) were more responsive to the ideas of Hegel, Schelling, and German romantic idealists, including the accompanying revival of Spinoza's thought. They also participated in the great movement of Jewish historical scholarship which Abraham Geiger (1810–74) had led in Germany. Geiger showed great originality in dealing with historical problems of the co-existence of Christianity and Israel.

tions difficult from the first. As early as 1802 the Congregation Mikveh Israel in Philadelphia had divided along these lines. In New York, where no separate Ashkenazic synagogue was established until 1825, long after German Jews had come to be a majority, leadership had remained in the hands of the Sephardim. But after 1840 rabbis who inclined to the Reform spirit began to arrive. By this time, too, the tide of German Jewish immigration began to reach its height, bringing to America increasing numbers of fully "emancipated" Jews and many liberal intellectuals. Except for a separation from the old Sephardic congregation in Charleston, the first explicitly Reform congregation in America was Temple Har Sinai, organized in Baltimore in 1842. It was followed by Emanuel in New York (1845), Sinai in Chicago (1858), and a whole wave of others. The changes that were initially effected in such congregations had usually to do with external reforms in the order of worship: the installation of organs, the use of mixed choirs, reductions in the proportion of Hebrew used in services, and seating by family groups. Yet in America as in Germany it was clear that even these alterations did such violence to the Law that ultimately a thoroughgoing revision in attitudes toward the Scriptures, the Talmud, and theology as a whole would have to follow. And the most important advocate and organizer of the American Reform movement in this crucial period was Isaac Mayer Wise (1819–1900).

The son of a poor school teacher, Wise was born in a small Orthodox Jewish community in Bohemia where life still followed its medieval patterns. He studied for certification as a rabbi both in traditional rabbinic schools and at the universities of Prague and Vienna. After two years as a rabbi in Bohemia, he came to the United States in 1846 and accepted the spiritual leadership of the Orthodox Congregation Beth-El in Albany, though his own ideas by this time were already markedly progressive. Wise began almost immediately to institute reforms which in 1850 led to a division of the congregation. A major cause of this schism was a controversy with a Presbyterian in which Wise won the approval of Theodore Parker, the Transcendentalist, but not of his own congregation. In fact, like Parker, Wise was becoming a free religionist, interested chiefly in the "permanent" elements of religion, not in its "transient" historical forms. A few years later he would publish a book on the origins of Christianity which showed how deeply he had been changed by modern

modes of thought. Eight days spent in the national capital in
1850 completed his conversion, and, as his biographer observes, Washington became his Jerusalem.

In 1853 Wise became rabbi of Congregation Bene Yesherun in Cincinnati, where he immediately founded English
and German weekly papers, *The American Israelite* and *Die
Deborah.* Three years later, having led his congregation
almost entirely away from traditional practices, he published
his revolutionary *Minhag America* (American Ritual). In
1873 he achieved another goal by founding the Union of
American Hebrew Congregations, a body which by 1880
"was closer to being the dominant organization in American
Jewish life than any other organization has ever been."[3] Wise
was also the animating spirit behind the founding in 1875 of
Hebrew Union College in Cincinnati, and he served as its
president until his death, thus fulfilling a longstanding ambition to provide modern American training for rabbis.

Wise was a voluminous writer and a learned man. He ventured widely in biblical criticism and the history of religions
—and in *The Cosmic God* (1876), he exposed his deep commitment to a pantheistic theology rooted in German romantic
idealism. Yet because his primary interests were practical and
organizational, he did not try to produce a broad systematic
work in theology. Indeed, his efforts often seemed chiefly
designed to increase the social mobility of American Jews.

The more serious theological task was carried out with considerable distinction by Wise's son-in-law, Kaufmann Kohler,
who also served as a professsor at Hebrew Union College and
later became its president. Kohler himself refers to David
Einhorn as "the Reform theologian, par excellence." This liberal scholar, whose European career has already been mentioned, was the rabbi at Temple Har Sinai in Baltimore until
his strong antislavery sentiments forced his departure at the
outbreak of the Civil War. He made his chief contribution to
American Judaism as leader of the more intellectual and radical group of Reform proponents, always avoiding ambiguity
on even the most sensitive problems and following out the
implications of his logic relentlessly. He abandoned the idea
of a personal Messiah and the hope for Israel's political restoration, speaking instead of the Jewish people as the suffering
servant whose hope was for a messianic *age* of charity and
truth. This belief was accompanied by an almost complete

[3] Nathan Glazer, *American Judaism,* p. 39.

rejection of the ceremonial law, the Talmud, and the whole tradition of rabbinic interpretation.

Judaism, Einhorn claimed, must be unfrozen and reinterpreted anew in such a way that the Jews might consider themselves no longer a "nation" alien until restored, but as citizens of various countries bound together only by the message of God and his will for all men. He called men to the "imperishable spirit" of the divine Law "whose spirit the Ten Commandments set forth exclusively." Einhorn's austere ethical monotheism seems to have been more deeply colored by the Enlightenment and less infused with romantic motifs than the prevailing thought of his colleagues in the Reform movement. Yet even he would probably have subscribed to the fervent testimony of Rabbi Bernard Felsenthal of Chicago:

> Racially I am Jew, for I have been born among the Jewish nation. Politically I am an American as patriotic, as enthusiastic, as devoted an American citizen as it is possible to be. But spiritually I am a German, for my inner life has been profoundly influenced by Schiller, Goethe, Kant, and other intellectual giants of Germany.[4]

Einhorn did not live to face the concrete issue of secular Zionism, but he probably would have opposed it, as Wise did. At the same time, he was ambivalent in his rejection of Israel's special peoplehood, and for all his radicalism he believed that Jews should retain their collective identity and not marry outside the faith.

The mature position of the Reform on the full range of issues in question was given clear and almost authoritative expression in an eight-point platform adopted at a conference of Reform rabbis meeting in Pittsburgh in 1885. Wise, who presided, called it a "Jewish Declaration of Independence," and David Philipson, the historian of the Reform movement, considered it "the most succinct expression of the theology of the reform movement that had ever been published to the world."[5] The document stated tersely that Judaism was "a progressive religion, ever striving to be in accord with the postulates of reason" and capable of adapting itself to the ad-

[4] Eric E. Hirshler, ed., *Jews from Germany in the United States*, p. 51. Bernard Felsenthal (1822–1908) was in 1854 in Lawrence, Massachusetts, but after 1858 in Chicago.

[5] Philipson, *The Reform Movement*, p. 355.

vances of modern knowledge. In addition to disclaiming all national aims of Judaism, it disowned the parts of Mosaic Law which "are not adapted to the views and habits of modern civilization." Taking their place in the pluralistic society of America, the conference recognized "in every religion an attempt to grasp the Infinite One." Then in an important reflection of newer forms of thought, they spoke of "Christianity and Islam as daughter religions of Judaism with a mission to aid in the spreading of monotheistic and moral truth." "We consider ourselves no longer a nation, but a religious community," they announced, "and therefore expect neither a return to Palestine, nor sacrificial worship under the sons of Aaron, nor the restoration of any of the laws concerning the Jewish state." Their hope was for a "Kingdom of truth, justice, and peace among all men." The "mosaic legislation" was interpreted as "a system of training for the Jewish people for its mission during its national life in Palestine"; only its moral laws are binding in the present. Rabbinic regulations were dismissed even more summarily. Asserting the doctrine "that the soul of man is immortal," but rejecting ideas of bodily resurrection, heaven and hell, and everlasting punishment or reward, they concluded with a call for participation "in the great task of modern times, to solve, on the basis of justice and righteousness, the problems presented by the contrasts and evils of the present organization of society."[6]

By the time this declaration was published Reform Judaism had almost come to *be* American Judaism. In only three decades, in fact, Rabbi Wise had been able to witness an authentic "second tradition" grow up in his adopted homeland. By 1880, when the Jewish community numbered about 250,000, the Reform body was more lively and vigorous in the United States than anywhere else in the world, boasting a heavy preponderance of the country's 270 congregations and possessing "temples" of great prestige led by rabbis of impressive intellectual power and civic influence in New York, Charleston, Philadelphia, Cincinnati, and Chicago. The movement was bound together nationally not only by a conference of rabbis and an association of congregations, but by a host of other social, religious, and philanthropic organizations. In place after place the little burial and mutual aid societies that had usually marked the existence of a Jewish community had long since yielded to benevolent organi-

6 Glazer, *American Judaism,* pp. 151–52.

zations and charitable institutions. Moreover, an optimistic esprit, a great feeling of confidence in human reason and good will, and a profound commitment to American freedom pervaded the movement. Understandably, there was also a measure of pride and a sense of achievement; but it led to an equally generous spirit of philanthropy and civic duty.

Yet into this world of Reform Judaism broke two disturbing manifestations in the century's last decades; "the contrasts and evils" dimly foreseen in the Pittsburgh Declaration became increasingly apparent. The first of these events was the vast migration to America of Eastern Jewry. Projected from Eastern Europe by persecution and the disruption of long established ways of life, knowing little of either Spinoza or Moses Mendelssohn, speaking various dialects of Yiddish, and committed to Orthodox observance, these new immigrants would bring a deep and protracted *crise de conscience* to the existing Jewish community. Almost simultaneously, anti-Semitism, new forms of nativism, and the rise of crowded urban ghettos would reveal the dangers of regarding the United States as the Kingdom come.

OTHER IMAGE BOOKS

These prices subject to change without notice

OTHER IMAGE BOOKS

These prices subject to change without notice

OTHER IMAGE BOOKS

These prices subject to change without notice

OTHER IMAGE BOOKS